[illegible]t[illegible] [illegible]rke[illegible]g

5[illegible] [illegible]on

Now in a fully revised and updated 5th edition, *Sports Marketing: A Strategic Perspective* is the most authoritative, comprehensive and engaging introduction to sports marketing currently available. It is the only introductory textbook to adopt a strategic approach, explaining clearly how every element of the marketing process should be designed and managed, from goal-setting and planning to implementation and control.

Covering all the key topics in the sports marketing curriculum, including consumer behavior, market research, promotions, products, pricing, sponsorship, business ethics, technology and e-marketing, the book introduces core theory and concepts, explains best practice, and surveys the rapidly-changing, international sports business environment. Every chapter contains extensive real-world case studies and biographies of key industry figures and challenging review exercises which encourage the reader to reflect critically on their own knowledge and professional practice. The book's companion website offers additional resources for instructors and students, including an instructors' guide, test bank, presentation slides and useful weblinks.

Sports Marketing: A Strategic Perspective is an essential foundation for any sports marketing or sports business course, and an invaluable reference for any sports marketing practitioner looking to improve their professional practice.

Ancillary materials are available online at www.routledge.com/cw/shank.

Matthew D. Shank is a Professor of Marketing and took office in July 2011 as the President of Marymount University in Arlington, Virginia, USA. Prior to Marymount, he served as Dean of the University of Dayton School of Business Administration. He came to UD from the College of Business at Northern Kentucky University, where he spent seventeen years as a faculty member and chair of the Department of Management and Marketing. Prior to his tenure at NKU, Shank spent a year as a visiting professor at the University of Mississippi and two years as a marketing research manager with Maritz Inc. In 2003–04, he was an American Council for Education (ACE) Fellow at Vanderbilt University. Shank's teaching and research interests include consumer behavior, marketing research and sports marketing. He recently served as editor of Sport Marketing Quarterly and has published in numerous journals and conference proceedings.

Mark R. Lyberger is an Associate Professor at Kent State University in the United States, where he serves as the undergraduate coordinator of Sport Administration and graduate coordinator of Sport & Recreation Management. His research interests have focused on consumer consumption behavior, sponsorship, marketing, marketing analytics, and leadership. He currently serves as the Editor of *The Journal of Sport*, has published and reviewed in numerous journals, and presented his works both nationally and internationally. In addition, Lyberger resides on the board of a number of non-profit and for profit organizations and currently serves as the Director for the Center of Sport, Recreation, & Tourism Development. He has worked collaboratively with a variety of community, educational and business organizations to enhance market and leadership development and to conduct market, market analytics, consumer behavior and facility usage [illegible] feasibility studies.

First published 2015
by Routledge
2 Park Square, Milton Park, Abingdon, Oxon OX14 4RN

and by Routledge
711 Third Avenue, New York, NY 10017

Routledge is an imprint of the Taylor & Francis Group, an informa business

British Library Cataloguing-in-Publication Data
A catalogue record for this book is available from the British Library

Library of Congress Cataloging-in-Publication Data
Shank, Matthew D.
Sports marketing : a strategic perspective / Matthew D. Shank, Mark R. Lyberger. – Fifth edition. pages cm
Includes bibliographical references and index.

1. Sports--United States--Marketing. 2. Sports--Economic aspects--United States. I. Lyberger, Mark R. II. Title.
GV716.S42 2014
796.068'8--dc23
2014020521

ISBN: 978-1-138-01595-1 (hbk)
ISBN: 978-1-138-01596-8 (pbk)
ISBN: 978-1-315-79408-2 (ebk)

Typeset in Univers LT by
Servis Filmsetting Ltd, Stockport, Cheshire

Sports Marketing

A Strategic Perspective

5th edition

Matthew D. Shank and Mark R. Lyberger

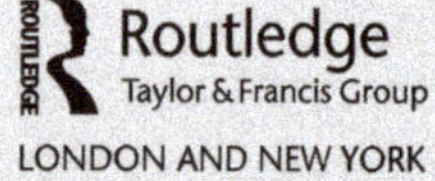

LONDON AND NEW YORK

Shank: *To Robert Ilseman and Donald Welling, for their dedication to youth sports*

Lyberger: *To all those who have supported my sporting endeavors, foremost, my father, wife, son and daughter*

Brief Contents

Contents

Preface

Overview

One of the greatest challenges for sports marketers is trying to keep pace with the ever-changing, fast-paced environment of the sports world. For example, since the first edition of this text was published in 1999, amazing changes have taken place and challenges to sports marketers emerge daily. First, costs and valuations have been rising quickly. For example, Merrill Lynch estimated Qatar will spend over $65 billion to prepare for the 2022 world soccer competition while Brazil's projected budget for hosting the World Cup is $13.3 billion and $18 billion for the Olympics, not counting projected public and private expenditures needed before the competitions. Furthermore, valuations of sport franchises have skyrocketed, Steve Ballmer's recent $2 billion offer for the Los Angeles Clippers, a bid nearly four times that of the last record sale, underscores the logical tendency and nonchalance in which sports brands are valued.

Athletes' salaries continue to escalate; for example, even though the Philadelphia Phillies have accumulated player salaries that encompass three of the top ten highest paid players in MLB, $25 million for Ryan Howard and Cliff Lee and $23.5 million for Cole Hamels, they rank third behind the N.Y. Yankees and L.A. Dodgers in total team expenditures. For the first time since 1998, the Yankees no longer can claim baseball's spending crown, that honor goes to the Dodgers in a runaway – with an estimated payroll of more than $235 million while the Yankees estimated payroll was just shy of $204 million.

To offset these costs leagues and teams alike are procuring lucrative television and media contracts and continue to expand and amend facilities. For example, the NFL recently secured extension deals with ESPN, CBS and FOX. ESPN recently agreed to expend $1.9 billion per year for the rights to broadcast Monday Night Football. CBS, which has aired NFL broadcast since 1956, recently agreed to pay $1 billion per year for the rights to broadcast the AFC Conference games while Fox Sports agreed to a $1.1 billion per year expenditure for NFC Conference broadcast starting in 2014. These expenditures top the SkySport's agreement, which amounted to €760 million ($1.22 billion) per year for broadcasting the Premier League.

To remain attuned to market demand sport teams are constantly on the lookout for ways to improve the sporting landscape, often through the use of public subsidies. Stadium new builds and/or retrofits continue to occur at a rapid pace with escalated costs. The Sochi Winter Olympics recently became the most expensive Olympics in history, with an estimated expenditure of $51 billion. The newest US pro stadiums have cost estimates of $975 million (Minnesota Viking Stadium), $1.15 billion (Cowboys Stadium) and $1.6 billion (Metlife Stadium). Furthermore, on the collegiate landscape, college sports organizations continue to build bigger, nicer, state of the art facilities to compete in the "competitive" arms race. Industry experts estimate that more than $17 billion have been spent on stadium upgrades in the last decade.

Each ticketholder will also pay more to attend the games in these plush new facilities. Ticket prices continue to increase and to drive the common fan out of the sport arena. For instance, the average seat price at an NBA game more than doubled from $22.52 in 1991 to $51 in 2014. But this may not be the largest problem in sports, as scandals emerge daily. For example, Donald Sterling's racial transgressions, the Penn State child sexual abuse scandal, Tiger Woods and his marital woes, Rick Pitino's extortion trial, the Ohio State football team tattoos-for-memorabilia, and the list goes on and on.

The one constant in this sea of change is the incredible appetite of consumers for sports. We get sports information on the Webwatch, sports in high definition on network and cable TV, read about sports in the newspaper and sports magazines, talk to friends about sports, purchase sports merchandise, participate in sports (both fantasy and real), and attend sporting events in record numbers. The sports industry has experienced tremendous growth and is estimated by AT Kearney to be a $480-$620 billion industry worldwide. Moreover, the sports industry is flourishing around the globe. The expansion of the sports industry has triggered a number of important outcomes: more sports-related jobs being created, and more students interested in careers in the sports industry. As student interest grows, demand for programs in sports administration and classes in sports marketing have also heightened.

In this book, we will discover the complex and diverse nature of sports marketing. Moreover, a framework will be presented to help explain and organize the strategic sports marketing process. Even if you are not a sports enthusiast, you should become excited about the unique application of marketing principles and processes that pertain to the sports industry.

Why this book?

Programs and courses in sports marketing have emerged at many universities across the country. Surprisingly, few sports marketing textbooks exist and not one is written from a strategic marketing perspective. In the first edition of this book, Dr. Shank sought to fill this void. The second edition represented an effort to improve the first edition and capitalize on its strengths. The third edition attempted to continuously improve the content and focus on the current relevant issues in sports marketing. The fourth edition provided more focus on the important issues in sports marketing theory and practice. Our goals for the fifth edition are to provide:

- *A framework or conceptual model of the strategic marketing process that can be applied to the sports industry.* The contingency framework is presented as a tool for organizing the many elements that influence the strategic sports marketing process and recognizes the unpredictable nature of the sports industry. In addition, the contingency framework allows us to explore complex relationships between the elements of sports marketing.
- *A more concise and focused approach describing the internet and social media and their relationship to understanding strategic sports marketing.* Advances in internet and social networking platforms, though constantly changing and often considered evolutionary, continue to have an impact on organizational strategy. They have had a dramatic impact on the delivery and use of market strategies. The continued emergence of social media as a viable platform has generated new and innovative ways to create dialog and receive feedback, as well as further enhance methods of engaging the consumer.

- *An appreciation for the growing emphasis on the globalization of sport.* As such, international sport topics are integrated throughout the text, and are also highlighted in chapters in the "Spotlight on International Sports Marketing."
- *An examination of current research in the area of sports marketing.* The study of sports marketing is still in its relative infancy and academic research of interest to sports marketers (e.g., sports sponsorships, using athletes as endorsers, and segmenting the sports market) has grown exponentially since the first edition of this text. It is important that students learn how academic research is applied to the "real world" of sports marketing.
- *An awareness of the many job opportunities available in the sports industry.* The one common denominator for all sports business students is the desire to secure their first job after graduation and start their careers. In this edition, we focus on several successful sports marketers who provide perspective about how and why they got started in the industry. Also, this edition retains an appendix devoted to careers in sports marketing.
- *A balanced treatment of all aspects of sports marketing at all levels.* This book attempts to capture the diverse and rich nature of sports marketing by covering the marketing of athletes, teams, leagues, and special events. Although it is tempting to discuss only "major league" sports because of their intense media coverage, the book explores different sports (e.g., cricket and women's football) and various levels of competition (e.g., collegiate and recreational). Moreover, the book discusses the activities involved in marketing to participants of sports – another area of interest to sports marketers.
- *An introduction of the concepts and theories unique to sports marketing and a review of the basic principles of marketing in the context of sports.* Even though many of the terms and core concepts are repetitive, they often take on different meanings in the context of sports marketing. Consider the term *sports involvement*. Although you probably recognize the term *product involvement* from your principles of marketing and/or consumer behavior class, what is sports involvement? Is involvement with sports based on participation or watching sports? Is involvement with sports deeper and more enduring than it is for other products that we consume? How can sports marketers apply sports involvement to develop a strategic marketing plan? As you can see, the core marketing concept of involvement in the context of sports presents a whole new set of interesting questions and a more comprehensive understanding of sports marketing.
- *Comprehensive coverage of the functions of sports marketing.* While some texts focus on specialized activities in sports marketing, such as sports media, this book seeks to cover all the relevant issues in designing an integrated marketing strategy. Extensive treatment is given to understanding consumers as spectators and participants. In addition to planning the sports marketing mix (product, price, promotion, and place), we will examine the execution and evaluation of the planning process.

Ground rules

This text is organized into four distinct but interrelated parts. Each part represents an important component in the strategic sports marketing process.

Part I: Contingency Framework for Strategic Sports Marketing

In Chapter 1, we introduce sports marketing and illustrate the breadth of the field. In addition, we will take a look at the unique nature of sports products and the sports marketing mix. Chapter 2 presents the contingency framework for strategic sports marketing. This chapter also highlights the impact of the internal and external contingencies on the strategic sports marketing process. Internal contingencies such as the sports organization's mission and organizational culture are considered, as are external contingencies like competition, the economy, and technology.

Part II: Planning for Market Selection Decisions

Chapter 3 presents an overview of the tools used to understand sports consumers – both participants and spectators. Each step in the marketing research process is discussed, illustrating how information can be gathered to aid in strategic decision-making. In Chapters 4 and 5, respectively, participants and consumers of sport are studied. Chapter 4 examines the psychological and sociological factors that influence our participation in sport, while Chapter 5 looks at spectator issues such as fan motivation. In addition, we will discuss the relationship between the participant and spectator markets. Chapter 6 explores the market selection decisions of segmentation, targeting, and positioning in the context of sport.

Part III: Planning the Sports Marketing Mix

Chapters 7 through 12 explain the sports marketing mix, the core of the strategic marketing process. Chapters 7 and 8 cover sports product issues such as brand loyalty, licensing, and the new product development process. Chapter 9 introduces the basic promotion concepts, and Chapter 10 gives a detailed description of the promotion mix elements of advertising, public relations, personal selling, and sales promotions. Chapter 11, the final chapter on promotion, is devoted to designing a sports sponsorship program. Chapter 12 tackles the basic concepts of pricing.

Part IV: Implementing and Controlling the Strategic Sports Marketing Process

While the previous sections have focused on the planning efforts of the strategic marketing process, Part IV focuses on the implementation and control phases of the strategic marketing process. Chapter 13 begins with a discussion of how sports organizations implement their marketing plans. In this chapter, we see how factors such as communication, motivation, and budgeting all play a role in executing the strategic plan. We also examine how sports marketers monitor and evaluate the strategic plans after they have been implemented. Specifically, three forms of control (process, planning assumption, and contingency) are considered.

Pedagogical advantages of sports marketing

To help students learn about sports marketing and make this book more enjoyable to read, the following features have been retained from previous editions of *Sports Marketing: A Strategic Perspective*.

- Text organized and written around the contingency framework for strategic sports marketing
- Chapters incorporating global issues in sport and how they affect sports marketing
- Sports Marketing Hall of Fame boxes featuring pioneers in the field integrated throughout the text
- Text incorporating up-to-date research in the field of sports marketing
- Internet exercises at the end of each chapter
- Experiential exercises at the end of each chapter that ask you to apply the basic sports marketing concepts and perform mini-research projects
- Vignettes throughout the text to illustrate core concepts and make the material come to life
- Detailed glossary of sports marketing terms
- Use of ads, internet screen captures, and photos to illustrate core concepts of sports marketing
- Appendix describing careers in sports marketing
- Appendix presenting Internet addresses of interest to sports marketers

Enhancements to the fifth edition

While we have attempted to retain the strengths of the previous editions of *Sports Marketing: A Strategic Perspective*, we also hoped to improve the fifth edition based on the comments of reviewers, faculty who adopted the text, and most importantly, students who have used the book. This edition includes the following features:

- Up-to-date examples illustrate the core sports marketing concepts in the text. As mentioned previously, the sports industry is rapidly changing and nearly 80 percent of the examples introduced in the previous editions are now obsolete. It was our goal to find new, relevant examples to illustrate key points in every chapter of the text. These new examples are meant to keep the book fresh and keep students engaged.
- New advertisements, web captures and illustrations have been incorporated into each chapter to highlight key sports marketing concepts and make the material more relevant for students. These ads and photos are examples of sports marketing principles that have been put into practice and bring the material in the text "to life."
- New spotlights on careers in sports marketing introduce students to successful sports marketers and their jobs.
- The spotlights on international sports marketing have been revised and updated for the fifth edition to highlight this key area of growth in the sports industry.
- New screen captures of relevant web sites illustrate key concepts. Because social media is now playing such a large role in sports marketing, screen captures from various web sites have been incorporated throughout the text to bring the material to life for students. In addition, social media/internet exercises appear at the end of each chapter, and discussions of these items as an emerging tool for sports marketers appear throughout.
- New exercises have been created that afford instructors the opportunity to further integrate real life up-to-date information utilizing auxiliary materials such as *Sport Business Journal*, *Sport Business Daily*, *Sport Business* and *Bleacher Report*.
- New spotlights on ethical issues are integrated throughout the text. Hopefully, this

will generate lively discussion in the classroom and make students more aware of the ethical issues that they will confront in the workplace.

Instructional support

Various teaching supplements are available to accompany this textbook. They consist of an Instructor's Manual, Test Item File, and PowerPoint presentation. These items may be found online only at www.routledge.com/cw/shank.

Acknowledgments

The new edition of any textbook is a challenge. In fact, much more of a challenge than people think. Typically colleagues joke that a new edition just means changing dates and examples. Nothing could be farther from the truth, and the fifth edition posed significant professional hurdles and opportunities. On the professional side, the fifth edition of *Sports Marketing: A Strategic Perspective* is the most significant revision of the text since its inception. Most importantly, I have added a co-author, Dr. Mark Lyberger, who adds a wealth of expertise and brings a fresh new perspective to the text. We also welcome our new publisher, Routledge. In addition, during the fifth edition, I moved from my position as Dean of the Business School at the University of Dayton to President of Marymount University. Obviously, a significant professional commitment. Before going any further, I have to thank my wife Lynne for her patience and support. The project could never have been completed without the expertise and encouragement of many others. Although there are countless people to thank, I was greatly assisted by the thoughtful reviews that undoubtedly improved all the editions of this text. These reviewers include:

Ketra Armstrong, *The Ohio State University*

Robert E. Baker, *Ashland University*

Ronald Borrieci, *University of Central Florida*

Chris Cakebread, *Boston University*

James Cannon, *University of South Alabama*

Joseph Cronin, *Florida State University*

Kathleen Davis, *Florida Atlantic University*

Eddie Easley, *Wake Forest University*

Renee Florsheim, *Loyola Marymount University*

Pat Gavin, *New Mexico State University*

Lynn Kahle, *University of Oregon*

Patricia Kennedy, *University of Nebraska, Lincoln*

Jerry Lee Goen, *Oklahoma Baptist University*

Deborah Lester, *Kennesaw State University*

Mark Lyberger, *Kent State University*

Ann Mayo, *Seton Hall University*

Mark McDonald, *University of Massachusetts, Amherst*

Stephen McKelvey, J.D., *University of Massachusetts, Amherst*

David Moore, *University of Michigan*

Susan Logan Nelson, *University of North Dakota*

Gregory Pickett, *Clemson University*

Michael Smucker, *Texas Tech University*

Joseph Terrian, *Marquette University*

Lou Turley, *Western Kentucky University*

In addition to the formal reviews, we are especially grateful to the graduate students and staff who have contributed their time and efforts to enhance the delivery and completion of the fifth edition, in particular Tami Gingerich, Katie Goldring, Kelly Leacoma, Danielle Novotny, Nick Pangio, Taryn Schmidt, Jennifer Schultz, and Josh Selden. We received informal comments from many of you who adopted the first four editions; we thank you for your feedback. We have tried to incorporate all of your suggestions and comments. We are very grateful to our colleagues both old and new at the University of Dayton, Kent State University, Marymount University, and Northern Kentucky University (NKU) who have supported us throughout this process. Additionally, thanks go out to all of our students who have helped fuel our interest in sports marketing. We would like to thank all of those sports business and management students who have used the book (and other universities) and pointed out their likes and dislikes.

One of the greatest challenges facing authors and publishers is the procurement and protection of intellectual work. Special thanks to Emma Davis for her assistance with securing copyright permissions for the text. In a world where technology and dissemination continue to precede copyright law this undertaking is no easy task, therefore, for her perseverance, we are forever grateful. Furthermore, a number of organizations have been very helpful in providing permission to use ads and articles throughout the text. Special thanks to all the individuals within these organizations who have made this book more meaningful and readable for students.

We would also like to thank Alison Jones for without her meticulous reading, due diligence, and expedient editing this edition would not have become a reality. We are grateful for her helpful suggestions, advice and constructive comments which ultimately enhanced the final presentation of materials within the fifth edition. Finally, we are indebted to the entire Routledge team for their encouragement and making the fifth edition a reality. Special thanks go to William Bailey, and Hannah Champney. Last, but certainly not least, thank you to Simon Whitmore for his superb project management.

Acronyms

Sports-related acronym list for *Sports Marketing*

ABA	American Basketball Association
ACC	Atlantic Coast Conference
ATP	Association of Tennis Professionals
BCS	Bowl Championship Series
CAPS	Coalition to Advance the Protection of Sports Logos
CSTV	College Sports TV
FBS	Football Bowl Subdivision
FCI	Fan Cost Index
FIFA	Fédération Internationale de Football Association
IBF	International Boxing Federation
IOC	International Olympic Committee
IPO	Initial Player Offerings
LPGA	Ladies Professional Golf Association
MAC	Mid-American Conference
MLB	Major Baseball League
MLBAM	MLB Advanced Media
MLS	Major League Soccer
MWC	Mountain West Conference
NAIA	National Association of Intercollegiate Athletics
NASCAR	National Association for Stock Car Auto Racing
NBA	National Basketball Association
NBDL	National Basketball Development League
NCAA	National Collegiate Athletic Association
NFL	National Football League
NFLP	NFL Properties
NFLPA	National Football League Players Association
NHL	National Hockey League
NHL-ICE	NHL-Interactive Cyber Enterprises
NJCAA	National Junior Collegiate Athletic Association
NLL	National Lacrosse League
NSGA	National Sporting Goods Association
PCT	Psychological Commitment to the Team
PGA	Professional Golf Association
PRCA	Pro Rodeo Cowboys Association
PSL	Personal Seat Licenses
SEC	South Eastern Conference
SFIA	Sports & Fitness Industry Association
SGMA	Sporting Goods Manufacturers Association

SMRI	Sports Marketing Research Institute
UFC	Ultimate Fighting Championship
USBA	U.S. Bungee Association
USOC	United States Olympic Committee
WAC	Western Athletic Conference
WBA	World Boxing Association
WBC	World Boxing Council
WBO	World Boxing Organization
WHA	World Hockey Association
WNBA	Women's National Basketball Association
WWE	World Wrestling Entertainment
YFF	Youth Football Fund

General acronym list

AARP	American Association of Retired People
AIO	Activities, Interests, and Opinions
BIRGing	Basking In Reflected Glory
BLS	Bureau of Labor Statistics
CIM	Chartered Institute of Marketing
CORFing	Cutting Off Reflective Failure
CORSing	Cutting Off Reflected Success
FIU	Florida International University
FSI	Free Standing Insert
GNP	Gross National Product
IMG	International Management Group
IPR	Institute for Public Relations
JND	Just Noticeable Difference
PLC	Product Life Cycle
POP	Point of Purchase
PPV	Pay-Per-View
PRIZM	Geodemographic segment set for the USA (62 segments)
PRIZM NE	New Evolution – updated version of PRIZM (66 segments)
ROI	Return on Investment
SMART	Specific, Measurable, Attainable, Reachable, Timely
SMSA	Standard Metropolitan Statistical Area
SMU	Southern Methodist University
STP	Segmenting, Targeting, Positioning
SRS	Sponsorship Research and Strategy
SWOT	Strengths, Weaknesses, Opportunities, Threats
TQM	Total Quality Marketing
UAB	University of Alabama at Birmingham
UCF	University of California – Florida
UTEP	University of Texas at El Paso
UTSA	University of Texas at San Antonio
VALS	Values and Lifestyles

List of illustrations

Figures

Tables

Photos

Web captures

Ads

PART 1

Contingency Framework for Strategic Sports Marketing

CHAPTER 1

Emergence of sports marketing

After completing this chapter, you should be able to:

- Define sports marketing and discuss how the sports industry is related to the entertainment industry.
- Describe a marketing orientation and how the sports industry can use a marketing orientation.
- Examine the growth of the sports industry.
- Discuss the simplified model of the consumer–supplier relationship in the sports industry.
- Explain the different types of sports consumers.
- Identify historical trends and significant impacts of sport marketing practices.
- Define sports products and discuss the various types of sports products.
- Understand the different producers and intermediaries in the simplified model of the consumer–supplier relationship in the sports industry.
- Discuss the elements in the sports marketing mix.
- Explain the exchange process and why it is important to sports marketers.
- Outline the elements of the strategic sports marketing process.

Mary is a typical "soccer mom." At the moment, she is trying to determine how to persuade the local dry cleaner to provide uniforms for her daughter's Catholic Youth Organization soccer team.

George is the president of the local Chamber of Commerce. The 10-year plan for the metropolitan area calls for developing four new sporting events that will draw local support while providing national visibility for this growing metropolitan area.

Sam is an events coordinator for the local 10k road race, which is an annual fund raiser for fighting lung disease. He is faced with the difficult task of trying to determine how much to charge for the event to maximize participation and proceeds for charity.

Ramiz is the Athletic Director for State University. In recent years, the men's basketball team has done well in postseason play; therefore, ESPN has offered to broadcast several games this season. Unfortunately, three of the games will have to be played at 10 P.M. local time to accommodate the broadcaster's schedule. Ramiz is concerned about the effect this will have on season ticket holders because two of the games are on weeknights. He knows that the last athletic director was fired because the local fans and boosters believed that he was not sensitive to their concerns.

"My fan focus groups indicate that I should show more of my legs."

Ad 1.1 Concept of sports marketing

Source: Reprinted with permission. www.cartoonstock.com

Susie works for a sports marketing agency that is representing a professional sport franchise. The franchise is planning to expand its international market presence. She is challenged with establishing relationships in a foreign environment which hosts a unique set of cultural values and customs.

What is sports marketing?

The American Marketing Association defines marketing as the activity, set of institutions, and processes for creating, communicating, delivering, and exchanging offerings that have value for customers, clients, partners, and society at large.[1] Sport and entertainment have been defined in a variety of ways, nonetheless, most definitions inclusively included terms such as: indulgement, divergence, and/or engagement; for valued outcomes of enjoyment, pleasure or amusement. Although sport may often consist of a more competitve nature, both are inclusive of retaining diverse exchange platforms. These diverse platforms provide a variety of engagement opportunities and yet, uniquely, are comprised of an array of outcomes that are distinctly similar.

Sports marketing is "the specific application of marketing principles and processes to sport products and to the marketing of non-sports products through association with sport." The sports industry is experiencing tremendous growth and sports marketing plays an important role in this dynamic industry. Many people mistakenly think of sports marketing as promotions or sports agents saying, "Show me the money." As the previous examples illustrate, sports marketing is more complex and dynamic. The study and practice of sports marketing is complex, yet interesting because of the unique nature of the sports industry.

Mary, the soccer mom, is trying to secure a sponsorship; that is, she needs to convince the local dry cleaner that they will enjoy a benefit by associating their service (dry cleaning) with a kids' soccer team.

As president of the Chamber of Commerce, George needs to determine which sports products will best satisfy his local customers' needs for sports entertainment while marketing the city to a larger and remote audience.

In marketing terms, Sam is trying to decide on the best pricing strategy for his sporting event; Ramiz is faced with the challenge of balancing the needs of two market segments for his team's products; and Susie, the sport marketer, is seeking to persuade international populations of the relevance of diversifying their sport culture. As you can see, each marketing challenge is complex and requires careful planning.

To succeed in sports marketing one needs to understand both the sports industry and the specific application of marketing principles and processes to sports contexts. In the next section, we introduce you to the sports industry. Throughout this book, we continue to elaborate on ways in which the unique characteristics of this industry complicate strategic marketing decisions. After discussing the sports industry, we review basic marketing principles and processes with an emphasis on how these principles and processes must be adapted to the sports context.

Understanding the sports industry

Historical development of sports marketing in (North) America

The evolution of sports marketing strategies to meet the needs and wants of the consumer continues to be a priority of practitioners worldwide. Today's realm of sports marketing and sponsorship, though a more dramatically effective and a much more diverse platform, is vaguely similar to what many identify as its origin, 776 BC, when the Olympic Games began. Marketers for the Ancient Olympic Games were no amateurs; these perceptive businessmen realized early on that an affiliation with a popular athlete could produce a potentially lucrative relationship.[2] Throughout its history, sport in some form has existed and, though the common-day term of sports marketing had not yet emerged, the process of utilizing marketing and promotion strategies to enhance delivery and production has been evident.

The roots of sports marketing in North America can be traced back to the 1850s and 1860s when many businesses, recognizing the popularity of sport, attempted to create linkages to enhance commercial opportunities by marketing through sport. Two events of this era in particular, one collegiate and one professional, illustrate the use of marketing through sport and helped lay a foundation for utilization of sport as a service medium in North America.

In 1852, a railroad official together with a group of local businessmen believed that they could garner enough interest in the marketing and staging of the event to produce economic and commercial profits. The end result was the first inter-collegiate match between Harvard University and Yale University – a two-mile rowing contest. This event took place at a quiet summer resort called Center Harbor on Lake Winnipesaukee, New Hampshire. The result demonstrated that the entrepreneurs were able to create a positive economic impact on the region, enhancing rail traffic, hotels occupancy, and revenue for the host city.

The second event is tied to the late 1850s and early 1860s and the commercialization of the new sport of baseball. Tobacco companies partnered with professional baseball leagues and began using photographs of the teams to help sell their products and services. These companies made baseball cards with pictures of the teams and players and then inserted them in cigarette packets to boost and enhance brand loyalties. Though the strategies of distribution have been altered over the years – that is, transition from the use of cigarettes, to bubblegum, to today's independent packages – these strategies laid the foundation for a new industry; the memorabilia and card collecting/trading market that exists today.

North American sport experienced a variety of popularity struggles in the late 1800s and early 1900s. A demand for reform arose and threatened sport at a variety of levels. In 1906, with the assistance of President Theodore Roosevelt, efforts were made to transform the image of sport. Strategies and regulations were implemented to enhance the safety and appeal of the game. Rules, regulations, and the control of lurking controversies, such as the controversy distinguishing the amateur and professional status of athletes, became a primary emphasis of sport organizations.

Although the early 1920s were a period of relative calm in American society, the country was intrigued by the newest technology of the day, the radio. Marketers, sports administrators, and broadcasters alike sought to integrate sports utilizing this medium; a medium at the time that many believed symbolized a coming age of enlightenment. For, as Beville noted, no other medium has changed the everyday lives of Americans as quickly and irrevocably as radio.[3] In 1921, the first American baseball broadcast occurred from Forbes Field. Though this broadcast was deemed a success, marketers of the era struggled to transcend executive opinions for some believed that the broadcast would have a negative impact upon attendance and demand.

In the 1930s and 1940s sports organizations utilized radio to enhance team revenue streams. Innovative marketers began relying on the radio to get their message across to the common man. In 1936, this same forum was used as a marketing and public relations campaign to pronounce the success of Jessie Owens and his Olympic debut.

Radio provided the impetus to solidify the era of patronage; however, the invention that soon followed remains to this day the most significant communication medium that has influenced and aided the development of sports. Who knew what sportscaster Bill Stern questioned and introduced in 1939 would enhance the growth and development of sports marketing practices for decades? The display platform, the television, though airing two mediocre baseball teams battling for fourth place, provided an incredibly formidable and profitable union between sport and the American public. The television provided a means for sports organizations to expand their market presence and a unique opportunity for marketers to engage their publics. The notion of a "picture being worth a thousand words" became a reality with the invention and its intervention and presentation of sports.

In 1946, radio and television broadcasting revenues together contributed only 3.0 percent of MLB revenues, but that rose to 16.8 percent by 1956. Executives such as Bill Veeck became innovators of sports marketing, utilizing radio and in-game promotional strategies to further market their teams. Owners, players, broadcasters, and fans recognized the variety of impacts television would have on the presentation of sports. In fact, television giant CBS dropped its Sunday afternoon public service emphasis to provide for a 12-week professional football broadcast.

An American consumer in the 1950s loved and demanded sports. Participation trends and fan demand steadily increased. Sports became a symbol of changing times in the United States. On April 15, 1947, Jackie Robinson broke the color barrier in baseball. The importance of this event in helping the Civil Rights Movement in the United States is evident, but it also proved the social power of sports in American culture and the impact that could be made utilizing sports as a communication medium. By including minorities in sports, the market grew. Cultural acceptance, along with media presence, provided the American public with a means to link personalities and audiences.

This prominence led to the identity era of the 1960s. Chuck Taylor/Converse, Muhammad Ali/Adidas/Champion, Jim Brown/NFL, Mickey Mantle/Major League Baseball, Arnold Palmer/PGA and Arnie's Army, to name a few, all became marketable entities. Marketers began to utilize sport to establish linkages with consumer publics. Endorsements and sponsorships evolved. Representation through agents became the norm for those who had prominence. For example, sport marketing giant International Management Group (IMG) founder Mark McCormack and golf great Arnold Palmer instituted a legendary handshake deal which lasted more than 40 years.

The 1970s included several evolutionary events in sports marketing. Consumer demand for sport continued to rise, while existing and emerging commercial entities such as Nike, Adidas, Puma, and others fought to snatch up endorsement opportunities. Sponsorships of products by athletes continued to emerge as a trend of the decade. In fact, the first corporate sponsorship of a stadium venue occurred in Buffalo in 1973 – Rich Stadium. Buffalo-based Rich Products agreed to pay $37.5 million, $1.5 million per year over 25 years.[4]

In the 1970s athletes too began to make a presence. Athletes such as Joe Nammath became sex symbols while advertisers began to realize that athletes could add a unique element to any product in the context of an endorsement campaign; e.g., Jack Nicolas, Muhammad Ali, Mario Andretti to name a few. This was further demonstrated at the end of the decade when Coke utilized Pittsburgh Steelers tackle, "Mean Joe Green," to star in one of the most acclaimed Coke advertisements ever.

Throughout the 1970s mergers, acquisitions, and governmental ramifications were prominent. Title IX entitled rights for women to have further access to participate in sports. Advertising laws, that forced the tobacco industry off the TV airways, freed funding for alternative marketing and advertising strategies. These tobacco companies could avert the law by developing sponsorship arrangements, thus affording the growth of events such as Virginia Slims Tennis and NASCAR Winston Cup.

Television markets were further expanded due to cable offerings and afforded network growth. Television began bringing teams from across the country into the spotlight. A health craze swept the nation further complementing commercial and consumer ties to sport. Entrepreneurs like Ted Turner, in 1976, were afforded an opportunity to develop and market a superstation, while ESPN's founder Bill Rasmussen, in 1979, was able to introduce the first true 24-hour sports broadcasting network.

In the 1980s salaries skyrocketed and leagues saw a need to remain competitive. Increased competition created a variety of economic and financial issues. Emphasis on television revenues became a priority. The money from media contracts became important to the team's bottom line and its ability to recruit and pay top players. Miracle workers such as NFL Commissioner, Pete Rozelle, and Olympics marketing and television guru, Richard Pound, continued to develop and enhance sponsorship and media contracts as they related to sport. Professionals such as Rozelle of the NFL, Peter Ueberroth of NBC, and Pound of the IOC had a significant impact on the explosion of so-called strategic alliances as a result of external competitive pressures such as globalism of economies and constantly advancing technologies.[5]

The 1980s represented the "me" decade in sports. Sporting goods were tailored to be aligned with specific sports. With the likes of Larry Bird, Magic Johnson, Joe Montana, and the introduction to Michael Jordan, fans continued through the turnstiles, disregarding the negative influences and impacts of the sky rocketing salaries, agents, greed among teams and players, drug use by athletes, and free agency. Despite or because of the greed, sports grew in popularity and became a more desirable marketing platform.

Sport sponsorship began to see double-digit growth. Sponsor dollars were abundant and even mediocre athletes began signing contracts to endorse or wear their products.[6] The expansion of sponsorship as a communication medium was greatly influenced by the emergence of sports leagues and corporate involvement during the 1970s and 1980s. However, this growth did not come without resistance. Resistance by broadcasters, event managers, and consumers alike focused on the intrusion of corporate America into this restricted arena.

Many corporate CEOs became involved with sponsorship for unsubstantiated reasons; i.e., they favored a sports activity or they chose to intermingle with famous sports celebrities. Exposure through affiliation was achieved, but without justification of the return on investment. Marketing strategies varied considerably due to the limited channels of exposure, but objectives were to align corporate endorsers to enhance the linkages and exposure of the events. This growth created a corporate reliance that would create many future marketing implications.

During the Michael Jordan era of the 1990s, television had become the driving force behind almost every league, including the NFL, NBA, NHL, MLB, NCAA, and NASCAR. In fact, the majority of teams and sport organizations became reliant upon these television revenues. Increased revenue streams offered opportunities for expansion. Organizations, such as the NHL, expanded to regions of the south while others such as the NBA began to focus beyond the Americas. Sponsorship continued to enhance the dollar pool and rose at a double-digit pace. Salaries continued to skyrocket, and leagues expanded to take advantage of untapped markets. Most fans wanted to be loyal; however, struggles such as the 1993 baseball strike had a severe impact on its popularity and adversely impacted consumer loyalty. Strategies became more focused and began to emphasize the transfer of unique connotations inherent in the property and brand image.

Although the modern world of mega-million dollar sponsorships had begun, marketers questioned the cluttered environment. The driving force behind the game and its growth had become clouded. Prior to the 1990s, management's use of sponsorship was often criticized for the cavalier and often frivolous approaches undertaken.[7] During this era sponsorship became entrenched as a legitimate corporate marketing tool. It saw an unprecedented double-digit growth and that had a significant impact on image, value, recognition, and method of delivery.

In recent years, sport marketing has continued to grow, but at a more moderate pace and not without restriction or limitations. In this era of social media, listening, networking, and enhancing relationships has become a priority, whereas selling is secondary. The continued advent of technology has created a much more audience-centered universe, thus, creating a paradigm that continues to evolve and innately requires sport marketers to develop a more audience-dictated framework to overcome a host of cybermarketing issues.

Demand through technology has created an international platform, a platform encompassing numerous cultural variances. Today's athletes are a global commodity. In today's sports marketing environment much more is at stake than free agency and escalated player salaries. Today, organizations seek to provision resources directly to an individual, authority, or body to enable the latter to pursue some activity in return for benefits contemplated in terms of the sports market strategy, and which can be expressed in terms of corporate, marketing, or media objectives.[8]

Organizations such as NFL, MLB, NASCAR, and the NBA have expanded scheduled exhibitions and displays. However, the unprecedented growth of these organizations and their popularity at the international level is not without increased marketing challenges. Technology has had a significant impact on the delivery of the product. The versatility and opportunities surrounding the use of technology enables organizations the opportunity to exploit a variety of platform delivery mediums to fulfill many of the basic functions of the marketing communications mix. In this era, the demand and usage of second screen platforms prevail. Therefore, interactive positioning of a product is a key to its marketing success.

For every Winston Cup or Jordan success there are at least as many ineffective sports marketing campaigns. Many athletes today capitalize on their image more than their athletic prowess. From athletes in their primes to athletes who have made lasting impressions, endorsement deals do not necessarily end when a professional career is over. Professional athletes are aware of the effect their image has on endorsement dollars, and most are not willing, nor ready, to give up a share of endorsements. If today's players had Babe Ruth's devil-may-care attitude, they would likely never see the kinds of endorsement dollars the more polished, public images today are garnering.[9]

Today's sport marketer recognizes that image influences the bottom line. The most prolific athletes are not always the most celebrated, and the most celebrated are often not the most gifted. However, in today's environment all are under the microscope of media attention. Because of today's growing media and social network influences, it is crucial for sports marketers to recognize need and define the 'why' as it relates to sports marketing applications. Defining the 'why' is crucial to its successful interpretation.

In today's sports marketing environment there is a threshold for clutter; however, scrutiny and integrity are the demanding forces that will impact its future. Consumers will continue to demand variety in the presentation of the sports product, but they will not overlook the overcommercialized tactics often employed by sports marketers that impact the integrity and presentation of its environment.

Sport as entertainment

Webster's defines **sport** as "a source of diversion or a physical activity engaged in for pleasure."[10] Sport takes us away from our daily routine and gives us pleasure. Interestingly, "entertainment" is also defined as something diverting or engaging. Regardless of whether we are watching a new movie, listening to a concert, or attending an equally stirring performance by Dwayne Wade, we are being entertained.

Most consumers view movies, plays, theater, opera, or concerts as closely related forms of entertainment. Yet, for many of us, sport is different. One important way in which sport differs from other common entertainment forms is that sport is spontaneous. A play has a script and a concert has a program, but the action that entertains us in sport is spontaneous and uncontrolled by those who participate in the event. When we go to a comedic movie, we expect to laugh, and when we go to a horror movie, we expect nail biting entertainment. But the emotions we may feel when watching a sporting event are hard to determine. If it is a close contest and our team wins, we may feel excitement and joy. But if it is a boring event and our team loses, the entertainment *benefit* we receive is quite different. Because of its spontaneous nature, sport producers face a host of challenges that are different than those faced by most entertainment providers.

Nonetheless, successful sports organizations realize the threat of competition from other forms of entertainment. They have broadened the scope of their businesses, seeing themselves as providing "entertainment." The emphasis on promotional events and stadium attractions that surround athletic events is evidence of this emerging entertainment orientation. Consider the NBA All-Star Game. What used to be a simple competition between the best players of the Western Conference and the best players of the Eastern Conference has turned into an entertainment extravaganza. The event (not just a game anymore) lasts for days and includes slam-dunk contests, a celebrity and rookie game, concerts, 3-point shooting competition and plenty of other events designed to promote the NBA.[11] In 1982, the league created a separate division, NBA Entertainment, to focus on NBA-centered TV and movie programming. NBA TV has created original programming featuring shows like *All-Access, Basketball International, Fantasy Hoops, NBA Roundtable* . . . and *Hardwood Classics*. As Alan Brew, a principal at RiechesBaird (now BrandingBusiness), a brand strategy firm states, "The line between sport and entertainment has become nearly nonexistent."[12]

Of course, one of the most highly visible examples of "sporttainment" is the WWE or World Wrestling Entertainment. For the past few decades, the WWE has managed to build a billion dollar empire and according to WWE.com the WWE posted revenue of $508 million in the fiscal year 2013. Live and televized entertainment accounted for 75 percent of those sales, followed by consumer products (15 percent), digital media (8 percent), and a new brand extension called WWE Studios at 2 percent.[13] Vince McMahon, the founder and chairman, has been called the P. T. Barnum of our time.

The sports entertainment phenomenon is also sweeping the globe as the following Forbes Inc. narrative and video link suggests: www.forbes.com/sites/mikeozanian/2012/02/26/nfl-expansion-could-include-London/. As organizations begin to recognize the value of sport as emtertainment in this global environment it is important for sports marketers to understand why consumers are attracted. Defining what consumer needs are and how those needs relate to the global environment will further complement the marketing exchange process.

Organizations that have not recognized how sport and entertainment relate are said to suffer from marketing myopia. Coined by Theodore Levitt, **marketing myopia** is described as the practice of defining a business in terms of goods and services rather than in terms of the benefits sought by customers. Sports organizations can eliminate marketing myopia by focusing on meeting the needs of consumers rather than on producing and selling sports products.

A marketing orientation

The emphasis on satisfying consumers' wants and needs is everywhere in today's marketplace. Most successful organizations concentrate on understanding the consumer and providing a sports product that meets consumers' needs while achieving the organization's objectives. This way of doing business is called a **marketing orientation**.

Marketing-oriented organizations practice the marketing concept that organizational goals and objectives will be reached if customer needs are satisfied. Organizations employing a marketing orientation focus on understanding customer preferences and meeting these preferences through the coordinated use of marketing. An organization is marketing oriented when it engages in the following activities.[14]

- ***Intelligence generation*** – analyzing and anticipating consumer demand, monitoring the external environment, and coordinating the data collected;
- ***Intelligence dissemination*** – sharing the information gathered in the intelligence stage;
- ***Responsiveness*** – acting on the information gathered to make market decisions such as designing new products and services and developing promotions that appeal to consumers.

Using the previous criteria (intelligence gathering, intelligence dissemination, and responsiveness), one study examined the marketing orientation of minor league baseball franchises.[15] Results of the study indicate that minor league baseball franchises do not have a marketing orientation and that they need to become more consumer focused. Although the study suggests that minor league baseball franchises

Table 1.1 The power ranking – 25 coolest minor league stadiums

Power ranking	Stadium	Team
1	Richmond Country Bank Ballpark	Staten Island Yankees
2	Metro Bank Ballpark	Harrisburg Senators
3	AT&T Field	Chattanooga Lookouts
4	Canal Park	Akron Aeros
5	Whitaker Bank Ballpark	Lexington Legends
6	Fieldcrest Cannon Stadium	Kannapolis Intimidators
7	Whataburger Field	Corpus Christi Hooks
8	Isotopes Park	Albuquerque Isotopes
9	Victory Field	Indianapolis Indians
10	Bright House Field	Clearwater Phillies
11	NewBridge Bank Park	Greensboro Grasshoppers
12	Dr. Pepper Ballpark	Frisco RoughRiders
13	First Energy Stadium	Reading Phillies
14	RedHawks Field at Bricktown	Oklahoma City RedHawks
15	Louisville Slugger Field	Louisville Bats
16	Coca-Cola Field	Buffalo Bisons
17	Modern Woodmen Park	Quad Cities River Bandits
18	MCU Park	Brooklyn Cyclones
19	AutoZone Park	Memphis Redbirds
20	Raley Field	Sacramento River Cats
21	Fifth Third Field	Dayton Dragons
22	Dell Diamond	Round Rock Express
23	Ripken Stadium	Aberdeen IronBirds
24	LeLacheur Park	Lowell Spinners
25	McCoy Stadium	Pawtucket Red Sox

Source: http://bleacherreport.com/articles/842135-power-ranking-the-25-coolest-minor-league-stadiums.

have not moved toward a marketing orientation, more and more organizations are seeing the virtue of this philosophy.

Growth of the sports industry

Sport has become one of the most important and universal institutions in our society. It is estimated that the sports industry generates between $480–620 billion each year, according to a recent A. T. Kearney study of sports teams, leagues, and federations.[16] This includes infrastructure construction, licensed products, and live sporting events. According to Plunkett Research,[17] the sports industry is twice the size of the U.S. auto industry and seven times the size of the movie industry. The industry is becoming increasingly global with respect to conventional and new media distribution fronts. This total is based on a number of diverse areas within the industry including gambling, advertising, sponsorships, etc. As ESPN founder Bill Rasmussen points out, "The games are better, and well the athletes are just amazing and it all happens 24 hours a day. America's sports fans are insatiable."[18] For better or worse, sports are everywhere. The size of sport and the sports industry can be measured in different ways. Let us look at the industry in terms of attendance, media coverage, employment, and the global market.

Attendance

Not only does sport spawn legions of "soccer moms and dads" who faithfully attend youth sport events, but also for the past several years, fans have been flocking to major league sports in record numbers. The NFL achieved peak attendance in 2007, averaging 68,702 fans per game and a 99.9 percent capacity. Although the League experienced a slight decline from 2008 to 2011, the League has been able to retain a 95 percent plus capacity. The 2013 season reflected a 96.5 percent capacity and an average game attendance of 68,373. The NFL continues to experience what many would call another prosperous year, with paid attendance of 17,304,523 fans attending. In addition, the NFL extended its television contracts through 2022, embarking on deals that will generate upwards of $3 billion a year.[19]

The NFL, both on and off the field, continues to strengthen the very foundation of the game. The League strives to make changes that are having a positive impact on the delivery of the game, both to consumers in person and via media outlets. According to NFL Commissioner Roger Goodell, NFL numbers are up; up in overall fan engagement, in most cases, dramatically, and interest in the NFL is expanding as they continue to grow internationally.[20] In fact, for the 2014 season, the NFL announced that two games would be played in London, both games sold out months in advance.

The NBA also had strong attendance in recent years. In the 2012–2013 season over 17 million fans turned out to see the action and arenas averaged 17,274 per game. This was complementary to the 2011 season where the NBA noted that its three national TV partners all had their highest viewer ratings ever. According to the League, TNT saw a 42 percent increase, while ABC was up 38 percent and ESPN saw a 28 percent jump. Turner Sports noted its 1.6 rating was its highest in 27 years of NBA coverage and that it televised three of the five most-watched NBA regular-season games ever on cable this season. Despite fears of a labor stoppage after the season, the NBA reported success across many platforms. Arena capacity was 90.3 percent, its seventh straight year of 90 percent or better. Merchandise sales jumped more than 20 percent and NBA.com saw an increase of more than 140 percent in video views.[21]

After procuring four years of record attendance through 2008, Major League Baseball had multiple years of attendance declines; however, in the 2011 season, the League was able to overcome a very slow start, endured inclement weather, a slowed economy, and even the influx of high definition TVs to achieve the fifth highest attendance mark ever. A total of 74,859,268 fans attended Major League Baseball games in the 2012 regular season, representing a 1.9 percent increase from 2011. *Sports Illustrated* writer Tom Verducci noted "baseball is consumed in so many ways that hardly existed, if at all, in its pre-strike popularity era: fantasy leagues, web apps, satellite radio, websites and the plethora of television viewing options on fantastic-looking displays,"[22] all impact the game. Attendance remains a vital revenue stream and measure of interest, but now it is part of a much more diverse picture of how baseball is consumed.

Street & Smith's *Sports Business Daily* reported that the National Hockey League averaged 17,445 fans per game for the 2012 season, up 1.8 percent from 2011 and up 2.8 percent from 2010. The Canadiens secured the highest league attendance totals including totals that were at 100 percent capacity. A total of 872,193 patrons attended in 2012 equating to a 21,273 per game average.[23]

Media coverage

Although millions of Americans attend sporting events each year, even more of us watch sports on network and cable television or listen to sports on the radio. For example, the 2014 Super Bowl XLVII featuring the Seattle Seahawks and Denver Broncos was watched by an estimated 111.5 million viewers and had an estimated 26.1 million tweets, exceeding the 2013 numbers where the New York Giants victory over the New England Patriots was watched by more than 111.3 million people. These 2013 and 2014 numbers surpass the 2011 Super Bowl and 1983 finale of "M-A-S-H" to become the most-watched program in U.S. television history.

Today, in the U.S. 290 million people own at least one TV, while worldwide more than 35 percent of consumers own an HD TV. According to Nielsen's television data collected from 38 key markets around the world (including the host nation China, the United States, Brazil, South Africa, Italy, and Australia), just more than 4.4 billion viewers worldwide – almost 70 percent of the world's population – watched some part of the 2008 Olympics.[24] In fact, an estimated audience of 2 billion watched the Beijing Olympics Opening Ceremony. Viewing levels varied across regions and markets, impacted by factors such as time zone and broadcast time differences. In contrast to the Beijing Summer Olympics, the Sochi Games only drew an average of 21.4 million viewers in primetime. In comparison, NBC's coverage of the Vancouver Winter Olympic Games drew a total viewing population of 32.6 million, 56 percent female versus 44 percent male. This secured an average audience of roughly three times the size of its nearest rival, Fox, and, according to the Nielsen company in 2012, the coverage held seven of the eight top stops for the week.

During the most recent Summer Olympic Games, Nielsen reported that NBC's coverage of the London Olympic Games drew more than 219 million American viewers over the span of 5,535 hours of broadcasting. These figures eclipse those of the 2008 Beijing Olympics (also on NBC), which were watched by a mere 215 million American viewers.

ESPN, the original sports-only network launched in 1979, was highlighted by record consumption of ESPN's core television business in 2011 and 2012. On television and across digital platforms, ESPN was able to secure a series of value-rich agreements with the NFL, NCAA, Wimbledon, Pac-12, and Indy 500. With its long-term and wide-ranging pact with its largest distributor, Comcast, ESPN was able to marry compelling content with evolving technology, i.e., notably the WatchESPN. In addition, they aired a significantly higher number of regular season and college bowl games. The array of ESPN programs serves the sports fan of today on the move in the USA and around the world. ESPN's results demonstrated that sports fans' need for the latest and best information – wherever they are – remains unabated. In the most recent survey across ESPN media platforms, which includes all ESPN networks, 113 million people interacted with ESPN during the average week in 2013,[25] an average of 675,000 viewers.

However, ESPN is facing more competition than ever. In 2013, ESPN saw a significant decrease in primetime ratings, 32 percent. Competitors such as Fox Sports and NBC Sports are strengthening their position in the marketplace. In addition, broadcasts such as those presented on Golf Channel, NFL Network, Fox Soccer, and NBCSN have experienced increases in viewership.[26] According to The Media Audit report (2009), a number of sports events including professional football, baseball, and hockey are on the upswing, and it suggests that while many Americans are uncertain about jobs and the economy, their interest in following sports remains strong.[27]

Among the report's findings, 61 percent of U.S. adults regularly follow professional football on radio or TV, a figure that is up from 57.9 percent four years ago. Among professional baseball fans, 51.2 percent regularly follow the sport, compared with 49.5 percent in 2005. Professional ice hockey experienced the most significant increase among sports fans. Among U.S. adults, 22.7 percent frequently follow the sport on TV or radio today, compared with 14.4 percent in 2005. The figure represents a 58 percent increase over four years. The study further reveals that the higher their income, the more likely adults are to follow sports. For example, 71.6 percent of adults earning $100,000 or more in household income regularly follow professional football, a figure that is 18 percent higher when compared with all U.S. adults. Similarly, 61.6 percent of high-income-earning individuals regularly follow professional baseball on TV or radio, a figure that is 20 percent higher than for all U.S. adults. Furthermore, 29.3 percent of affluent adults follow professional ice hockey compared with 22.7 percent of the general U.S. population.

In college sports, the percent of adults who regularly follow college football on radio or TV increased from 44.6 percent in 2005 to 45.9 percent today. However, the same study revealed that while only 22.1 percent of U.S. adults frequently attend college or professional sporting events, the figure remains flat from 22 percent in 2005. Traditional networks are trying to keep pace with the demand for sports programming. The four major networks devote in excess of 2,000 hours to sports programming annually and a family with cable has access to 86,000 hours of sports TV. Sports fees paid by cable, satellite, and telco companies reached 17.2 billion in 2012.[28]

In addition, according to a Kantar's Global Sports Media Consumption Report (2013), about 170 million adults (71 percent of the U.S. population) label themselves sports fans, and 97 percent of them watched sports on TV in 2012.[29] The majority (97 percent) of these TV sporting events are watched live and therefore the race is on between networks to secure prominent sporting events. In 2011, NBC spent a record $4.38 billion to secure the broadcast and cable rights for the Olympic Games through 2020. NBC extended its stronghold on the Olympics by winning the broadcast rights over rivals Fox and ESPN. Fox bid $3.4 billion for four Games and $1.5 billion for two, while ESPN offered $1.4 billion for two. Add to this deal the NCAA's $10.8 billion dollar basketball tournament deal, the NCAA conferences multiplying their old deals times four, a $4.4 billion NASCAR deal with NBC, the NHL tripling their previous contract, and the astronomical procurement of the NFL, where networks will provide over $3 billion per year, and you can see the value of sports to the league and the networks.

These numbers show no signs of slowing down in the future. The huge demand for sports broadcasting has led to the introduction of more sport-specific channels. New sports networks such as the Sky Sports F1, College Sports Television (www.cstv.com), Fox Sports 1, Blackbelt TV, the Tennis Channel, and the NFL Network have emerged because of consumer demand. In fact even the WWE is contemplating the release of its own network. Presently, worldwide there are in excess of 300 sport channels. This practice of "narrowcasting," reaching very specific audiences, seems to be the future of sports media.

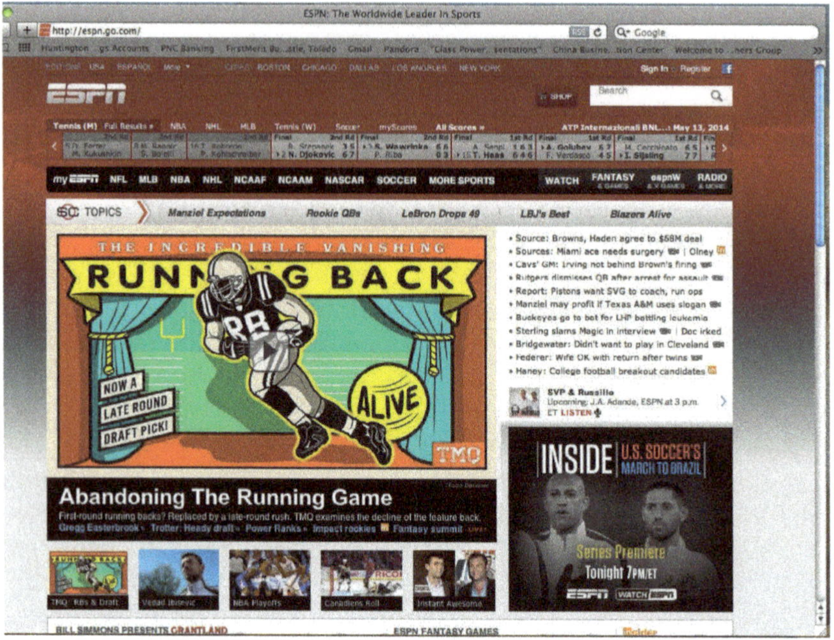

Web 1.1 The growth of sports information on the Web

Source: www.espn.go.com.

In addition to traditional sports media, pay-per-view cable television is growing in popularity. Satellite stations, such as DIRECTV, allow spectators to subscribe to a series of sporting events and play a more active role in customizing the programming they want to see. For example, DIRECTV offers NFL Sunday Ticket, Willow Cricket, NASCAR HotPass, NBA League Pass, or the NHL Center Ice to afford consumers instant viewing gratification. Packages such as NHL Center Ice allow subscribers to choose from 40 out-of-market (i.e., not local) regular season NHL games per week for an additional fee.

Employment

Another way to explore the size of the sports industry is to look at the number of people the industry employs. *The Sports Market Place Directory*, an industry directory, has more than 15,600 listings, 80,000 contact names, and 9 indexes for sports people and organizations.[30] A *USA Today* report estimates that there are upward of 4.5 million sports-related jobs in sales, marketing, entrepreneurship, administration, representation, and media.[31] Some estimates range as high as 6 million jobs. In addition to the United States, the United Kingdom employs some 400,000 people in their $6 billion a year sports industry.[32] Consider all the jobs that are created because of sports-related activities such as building and staffing a new stadium. Sports jobs are plentiful and include but are not limited to event suppliers, event management and marketing, sports media, sport sales, sports sponsorship, athlete services, sports commissions, sports lawyers, manufacturers and distribution, facilities and facility suppliers, teams, leagues, college athletics, and finance.

The number of people working directly and indirectly in sports will continue to grow as sports marketing grows. Sports marketing creates a diverse workforce from the players who create the competition, to the photographers who shoot the competition (see Appendix A for a discussion of careers in sports marketing).

Global markets

Not only is the sports industry growing in the United States, but it is also growing globally. As the following hyperlink on international sports marketing discusses, the NBA is a premier example of a powerful global sports organization that continues to grow in emerging markets: http://www.nba.com/global/nba_global_regular_season_games_london_mexico_city_2013_06_24.html.

The structure of the sports industry

There are many ways to discuss the structure of the sports industry. We can look at the industry from an organizational perspective. In other words, we can understand some things about the sports industry by studying the different types of organizations that populate the sports industry such as local recreation commissions, national youth sports leagues, intercollegiate athletic programs, professional teams, and sanctioning bodies. These organizations use sports marketing to help them achieve their various organizational goals. For example, agencies such as the United States Olympic Committee (USOC) use marketing to secure the funding necessary to train and enter American athletes into the Olympic Games and Pan American games.

Photo 1.1 Fans in grandstand.

Source: Shutterstock.com.

Figure 1.1 Simplified model of the consumer–supplier relationship in the sports industry

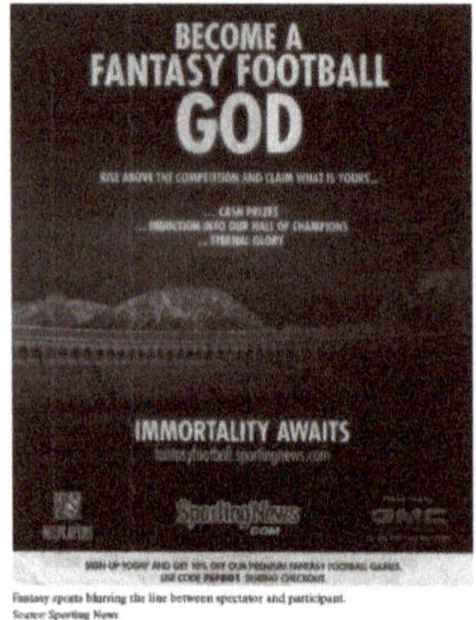

Ad 1.2 Fantasy sports blurring the line between spectator and participant

Source: Sporting News

The traditional organizational perspective, however, is not as helpful to potential sports marketers as a consumer perspective. When we examine the structure of the sports industry from a consumer perspective, the complexity of this industry and challenge to sports marketers becomes obvious. Figure 1.1 shows a **simplified model of the consumer–supplier relationship**. The sports industry consists of three major elements: consumers of sport, the sports products that they consume, and the suppliers of the sports product. In the next sections, we explore each of these elements in greater detail.

The consumers of sport

The sports industry exists to satisfy the needs of three distinct types of consumers: spectators, participants, and sponsors.

The spectator as consumer

If the sporting event is the heart of the sports industry, then the spectator is the blood that keeps it pumping. **Spectators** are consumers who derive their benefit from the observation of the event. The sports industry, as we know it, would not exist without spectators. Spectators observe the sporting event in two broad ways: they attend the event, or they experience the event via media chosen media outlet, i.e., radio, television, Internet.

As Figure 1.2 illustrates, there are two broad types of consumers: individual consumers and corporate consumers. Collectively, this creates four distinct consumer groups. Individuals can attend events in person by purchasing single event tickets or series (season) tickets. Not only do individuals attend sporting events, but so too do corporations. Today, stadium luxury boxes and conference rooms are designed specifically with the corporate consumer in mind. Many corporate consumers can purchase special blocks of tickets to sporting events. At times, there may be a tension between the needs of corporate consumers and individual consumers. Many believe that corporate consumers, able to pay large sums of money for their tickets, are pushing out the individual consumer and raising ticket prices.

Both individual spectators and corporations can also watch the event via a media source. The corporate consumer in this case is not purchasing the event for its own viewing, but, rather, acting as an intermediary to bring the spectacle to the end user groups or audience. For example, CBS (the corporate consumer) purchases the right to televise the Masters Golf Tournament. CBS then controls how and when the event is experienced by millions of individual spectators who comprise the television audience.

Historically, the focus of the sports industry and sports marketers was on the spectator attending the event. The needs of the consumer at the event were catered to first, with little emphasis on the viewing or listening audience. Due to the growth of media influence and the power of the corporate consumer, the focus has changed to pleasing the media broadcasting the sporting event to spectators in remote locations. Many season ticket holders are dismayed each year when they discover that the starting time for events has been altered to fit the ESPN schedule. In fact, the recent NFL deals provide networks with the opportunity to interchange delivery schedules across conferences. Because high ratings for broadcasted sporting events translate into breathtaking deals for the rights to collegiate and professional sports, those who present sporting events are increasingly willing to accommodate the

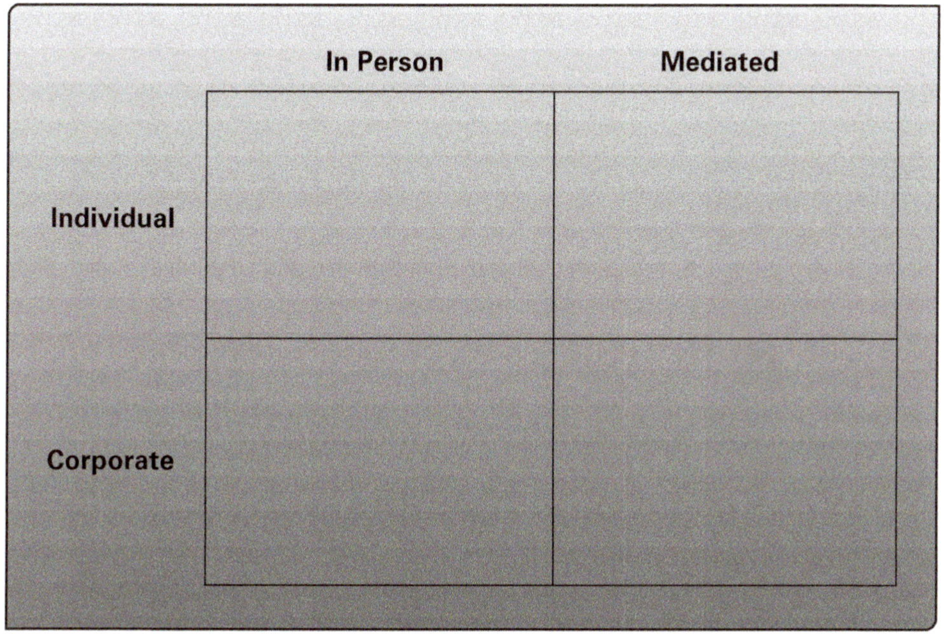

Figure 1.2 Individual vs corporate consumer

needs of the media at the expense of the on-site fan. The money associated with satisfying the needs of the media is breathtaking. For example, in 2011, the NFL agreements secured from the terrestrial networks, FOX, NBC, CBS, and ESPN, combined for a total of $20.4 billion per year. The 2014–2022 totals equate to the same networks paying $39.6 billion per year.[33] That number is continuing to grow, as seen in Table 1.2. Identifying and understanding the different types of spectator consumption is a key consideration for sports marketers when designing a marketing strategy.

The participant as consumer

In addition to watching sports, more people are becoming active **participants** in a variety of sports at a variety of competitive levels. Table 1.3 shows "core" participation in sports and fitness activities. As the number of participants grows, the need for sports marketing expertise in these areas also increases.

As you can see, there are two broad classifications of sports participants: those that participate in unorganized sports and those that participate in organized sports.

Table 1.2 NFL media rights

CBS (AFC)	2014–2022	$1.08B
DirecTV (Sunday Ticket)	2011–2014	$1B
ESPN (Monday Night)	2014–2022	$1.9B
FOX (NFC)	2014–2022	$720.3M
NBC (Sunday Night)	2014–2022	$1.05B
TOTAL		$5.75B

Source: http://espn.go.com/nfl/story/_/id/7353238/nfl-re-ups-tv-pacts-expand-thursday-schedule

Table 1.3 Most popular sports and fitness activities based on core participation (age 6 and above; U.S. residents)

Rank	Activity	# Of Participants
1	Walking for Fitness	114.1 million
2	Bowling	55.9 million
3	Treadmill	53.1 million
4	Running/Jogging	49.4 million
5	Hand Weights	45.9 million
6	Billiards/Pool	39.4 million
7	Bicycling	39.3 million
8	Freshwater Fishing	38.9 million
9	Weight/Resistance Machines	38.6 million
10	Dumbells	37.4 million

Source: Sports & Fitness Industry Association, www.sfia.org

Unorganized sport participants/organized sport participants

Amateur

Youth recreational instructional

Youth recreational elite

Schools

Intercollegiate

Professional

Minor/secondary

Major

Unorganized sports are the sporting activities people engage in that are not sanctioned or controlled by some external authority. Kids playing a pick-up game of basketball, teenagers skateboarding, or people playing street roller hockey, as well as fitness runners, joggers, and walkers are only a few of the types of sporting activities that millions of people participate in each day. The number of people who participate in unorganized sports is difficult to estimate. We can see how large this market is by looking at the unorganized sport of home fitness. According to a survey published by the National Endowment for the Arts, American households spend $130 annually on sports or exercise equipment. In addition, the average purchase price of a multi-purpose home gym station was $640 while the average cost of a treadmill was $2000.[34]

We can see that the size of the market for unorganized sports is huge, and there are many opportunities for sports marketers to serve the needs of these consumers.

Organized sporting events refer to sporting competitions that are sanctioned and controlled by an authority such as a league, association, or sanctioning body. There are two types of participants in organized events: amateur and professional.

Amateur sporting events refer to sporting competitions for athletes who do not receive compensation for playing the sport. Amateur competitions include recreational youth sports at the instructional and elite (also known as "select") levels, high school sports controlled at the state level through leagues, intercollegiate sports (NCAA Division I–III, NAIA, and NJCAA), Olympics, and adult community-based recreational sports. **Professional sports** are also commonly classified by minor league or major league status.

Sponsors as consumer

Other equally important consumers in sports marketing are the many business organizations that choose to sponsor sports. In **sports sponsorship**, the consumer (in most cases, a business) is exchanging money or product for the right to associate its name or product with a sporting event, creating a commercial competitive advantage for both parties. The decision to sponsor a sport is complex. The sponsor must not only decide on what sport(s) to sponsor, but must also consider what level of competition (recreational through professional) to sponsor. They must choose whether to sponsor events, teams, leagues, or individual athletes.

Although sponsorship decisions are difficult, sponsorship is growing in popularity for a variety of reasons. As Pope discusses in his excellent review of current sponsorship thought and practices,[35] sponsorship can help achieve corporate objectives (e.g., public awareness, corporate image building, and community involvement), marketing objectives (e.g., reaching target markets, brand positioning, and increasing sales), media objectives (e.g., generate awareness, enhance ad campaigns, and generate publicity), and personal objectives (management interest). According to IEG, lingering effects of scattered economic crises throughout the world and a yet-to-stabilize recovery in the U.S. have impeded sponsorship spending worldwide. However, despite these adverse impacts, a growth of 4.1 percent globally and 4.5 percent in North America was estimated in 2014. Sponsorship spending continued to reach a new plateau, $20.6 billion being spent in the U.S. and an estimated $55.3 billion worldwide. Projections for future growth are highly dependent upon the unprecedented recognition at the highest levels of corporations that sponsorship is a potent answer to the challenge of how to build attention, support, and loyalty for brands in an environment that is otherwise hostile to marketing communications.[36]

The sports product

Perhaps the most difficult conceptual issue for sports marketers is trying to understand the nature of the sports product. Just what is the sports product that participants, spectators, and sponsors consume? A **sports product** is a good, a service, or any combination of the two that is designed to provide benefits to a sports spectator, participant, or sponsor.

Goods and services

Goods are defined as tangible, physical products that offer benefits to consumers. Sporting goods include equipment, apparel, and shoes. We expect sporting goods retailers to sell tangible products such as tennis balls, racquets, hockey equipment, exercise equipment, and so on. By contrast, **services** are defined as intangible, nonphysical products. A competitive sporting event (i.e., the game itself) and an ice-skating lesson are examples of sport services.

Sports marketers sell their products based on the **benefits** the products offer to consumers. In fact, products can be described as "bundles of benefits." Whether as participants, spectators, or sponsors, sports products are purchased based on the benefits consumers derive. Ski Industry America, a trade association interested in marketing the sport of snowshoeing, understands the benefit idea and suggests that the benefits offered to sports participants by this sports product include great exercise, little athletic skill, and low cost (compared with skiing). It is no wonder snowshoeing has recently emerged as one of the nation's fastest growing winter sports.[37]

Spectators are also purchasing benefits when they attend or watch sporting events. For example, the 2014 Super Bowl was the most watched event in U.S. television history, attracting 111.5 million viewers. The game provides consumers with benefits such as entertainment, ability to socialize, and feelings of identification with their country's teams and athletes.

Moreover, organizations such as Federal Express, which paid $205 million over 27 years for the naming rights to the Washington Redskins sports complex that opened in 1999, believe the association with sports and the subsequent benefits will be worth far more than the investment.[38] The benefits that organizations receive from naming rights include enhanced image, increased awareness, and increased sales of their products.

CAREER SPOTLIGHT

Chris Ferris, Associate Athletic Director for Marketing & Promotions
University of Pittsburgh

Mr. Ferris joined the Pittsburgh Athletic Department in 1994 when he served as a student equipment manager. The following year, he worked as an undergraduate intern with the media relations and marketing departments. He is also a 1998 graduate of Pittsburgh with a Bachelor's degree in business and communications and earned his Master's Degree at the University of Pittsburgh's Katz Graduate School of Business.

1. **What is your career background? How did you get to where you are today?** I started in athletics as a football equipment manager. Afterwards, I volunteered and interned with both the Media Relations and Marketing Departments. Volunteering and interning were key. The opportunities allowed me to learn about the industry, meet some terrific people, and give people in our organization see me work. Once given my first opportunity as assistant director of marketing, I continued to work as enthusiastically as possible while continuing to volunteer for any additional projects within the department. Once again, this enabled me to grow as a professional.

2. **What is your role as Associate A.D. for Marketing & Promotions?** Our marketing department and Pitt manages and oversees:
   a. Licensing and merchandising
   b. Advertising and ticket sales
   c. Corporate ticket sales, group ticket sales, and promotions
   d. Game presentation
   e. Internet services
   f. PantherVision production
   g. Pitt Panthers television

   Additionally, I work very closely with our multi-media rights holder and our ticket operations team

3. **Why did you choose the University of Pittsburgh, for both academic as well as your career path?** The University of Pittsburgh is an amazing place. Our leadership at the University and in our Athletic department are both committed to being the best and providing the best experience for our students and student-athletes. I believe in our leaders and people and I believe in our leaders and professions.

4. **What made you get into marketing? What do you like about it best?** Volunteering and interning exposed me to many different areas of Intercollegiate Athletics. Marketing gives me an opportunity to work with people both internally within the university and externally. I really enjoyed having what I believe is the best of both worlds; dealing with students, faculty, and staff while also having the opportunity to work with external sponsors and partners.

5. **How large is your full-time marketing staff?** Seven people.

6. **What are the main marketing challenges facing Pitt Athletics?** These can be sport specific. Our goals are to sell-out all of our venues for all of our teams.

7. **What is your ultimate goal for your career?** First, make positive impacts on our teams, coaches, and fans. Second, serve as an athletic director.

Different types of sports products

Sports products can be classified into four categories. These include sporting events, sporting goods, sports training, and sports information. Let us take a more in-depth look at each of these sports products.

Sporting events

The primary or core product of the sports industry is the **sporting event**. By primary product we are referring to the competition, which is needed to produce all the related products in the sports industry. Without the game there would be no licensed merchandise, collectibles, stadium concessions, and so on. You may have thought of sports marketing as being important for only professional sporting events, but, as is evident by the increased number of media outlets and broadcasts, the marketing of collegiate sporting events and even high school sporting events is becoming more common.

Historically, a large distinction was made between amateur and professional sporting events. Today, that line is becoming more blurred. For example, the Olympic Games, once considered the bastion of amateur sports, is now allowing professional athletes to participate for their countries. Most notably, the rosters of the Dream Teams of U.S. Basketball fame and the U.S. Hockey team are almost exclusively professional athletes. This has been met with some criticism. Critics say that they would rather give the true amateur athletes their chance to "go for the gold."

Athletes

Athletes are participants who engage in organized training to develop skills in particular sports. Athletes who perform in competition or exhibitions can also be thought of as sports products. David Beckham, Chamique Holdsclaw, and Phil Mickelson are thought of as "bundles of benefits" that can satisfy consumers of sport both on and off the court.

One athlete to achieve this "superproduct" status is the multimillion dollar phenomenon named Eldrick "Tiger" Woods. Tiger seemed to have it all. He was handsome, charming, young, multiethnic, and most important – talented. Tiger's sponsors certainly think he was worth the money. However, poor choices and inappropriate behavior attracted controversy. Controversy has required the likes of Nike, Buick, NetJets, and American Express to rethink their level of affiliation, impacting Tiger's multimillion dollar sponsorship deals.

Sports marketers must realize that the "bundle of benefits" that accompanies an athlete varies from person to person and has affiliated risk. The benefits associated with Allen Iverson are different from those associated with Kevin Garnett or golfer Michelle Wei. Regardless of the nature of the benefits, today's athletes are not thinking of themselves as athletes but as entertainers.

Arena

A final sports product that is associated with the sporting event is the site of the event – typically an arena or stadium. Today, the stadium is much more than a place to go watch the game. It is an entertainment complex that may include restaurants, bars, picnic areas, and luxury boxes. Today's teams are not only trying to create more visually appealing buildings, but they're interested in making attending the game an all-encompassing entertainment experience. In fact, stadium seating is becoming a "product" of its own.

For example, some of the following changes already seen at today's venues will soon become the norm. Things such as free Wi-Fi, mobile apps, fantasy stats on video boards, TVs in seats and bathrooms, customizable instant replays, bars overlooking fields, holograms on the fields instead of players, and improved access are the wave of the future. Companies like Cisco offer Stadium Wi-Fi packages made specifically for sports arenas that have an immense amount of internet usage in a confined area. Cisco plans on placing antennas in specific places in the stadium for optimal performance for people to use their smart phones with optimal speeds.[39]

In another example, it might seem like a stretch to think that a roller coaster will pop up over a baseball field's outfield fence, but some type of amusement park ride – Detroit's Comerica Park already has a Ferris wheel – that provides unique views of the game (and can keep the kids entertained) seems inevitable.[40]

Sporting goods

Sporting goods represent tangible products that are manufactured, distributed, and marketed within the sports industry. The sporting goods and recreation industry was a $79.1 billion industry in 2013.[41] The segments and their relative contribution to the industry sales figure include sports equipment ($21.5 billion), exercise equipment ($4.7 billion), sports apparel ($31.8 billion), athletic footwear ($13.6 billion), and licensed merchandise ($7.5 billion). The largest product category, in terms of sales, was firearms and hunting (10 percent), industrial exercise equipment (9 percent), running footwear (6 percent), and fishing (5 percent).[42] Although sporting goods are usually thought of as sports equipment, apparel, and shoes, there are a number of other goods that exist for consumers of sport. Sporting goods also include licensed merchandise, collectibles, and memorabilia.

Licensed merchandise

Another type of sporting goods that is growing in sales is licensed merchandise. **Licensing** is a practice whereby a sports marketer contracts with other companies to use a brand name, logo, symbol, or characters. In this case, the brand name may be a professional sports franchise, college sports franchise, or a sporting event. Licensed sports products usually are some form of apparel such as team hats, jackets, or jerseys. Licensed sports apparel accounts for 60 percent of all sales. Other licensed sports products such as novelties, sports memorabilia, trading cards, and even home goods are also popular.

The Licensing Letter reports that sales of all licensed sports products reached $17.5 billion worldwide in 2012. In fact, sport licensing generates $800–$900 million in royalty revenue annually. Growth is expected to continue based on research from the National Sporting Goods Manufacturers Association and the Sports Licensing Report. U.S. retail sales of licensed products for the four major professional sports leagues

(NBA, NFL, MLB, and NHL) has more than doubled since the 1990s, from $5.35 billion in 1990 to $13.5 billion in 2012.[43]

Through this period, the various major professional sports leagues developed a sprawling network of licensing arrangements with more than 600 companies. Another 2,000 companies have arrangements with the various college and university licensing groups. As far as the retail distribution of product, a network of "fan shops" grew to more than 450 in number and licensed products found their way into sporting goods stores, department stores, and eventually, the mass merchants. To compete, most of the major sporting goods chains and many department stores developed separate areas devoted exclusively to licensed goods.[44] Sales of licensed sports products will continue to grow as other "big league" sports gain popularity. For example, NASCAR has seen the sale of licensed goods increase from $60 million in 1990 to $500 million in 1994 and to an estimated $1.2 billion in 2013 (see NASCAR.com).

Collectibles and memorabilia

One of the earliest examples of sports marketing can be traced to the 1880s when baseball cards were introduced. Consider life before the automobile and the television. For most baseball fans, the player's picture on the card may have been the only chance to see that player. Interestingly, the cards were featured as a promotion in cigarette packages rather than bubble gum. Can you imagine the ethical backlash that this practice would have produced today?

Although the sports trading card industry reached $1.2 billion in 1991, industry wide yearly sales plummeted to $700 million in 1995 and are now stable at between

Photo 1.2 The sports collector's dream – the Baseball Hall of Fame. The Baseball Hall of Fame's plaque gallery, housing plaques for all Hall of Famers, November 26, 2011 in Cooperstown, NY.

Source: Shutterstock.com

$400 and $500 million.[45] What caused this collapse? One answer is too much competition. David Leibowitz, an industry analyst, commented that "With the channel of distribution backed up and with too much inventory, it was hard to sustain prices, let alone have them continue to rise." At the beginning of the 1980s there were only a few major card companies (Topps, Donruss, and Fleer) but by the early '90s there were sets of cards produced by six different companies, more in the market than ever before. This flooded market and the cartoon fad cards have hurt the sports trading card industry. Other problems include labor problems in sports, escalating card prices, and kids with competing interests.

There is, however, some evidence that the industry will rebound. Citing a glut in the marketplace and the desire to regain some control over the baseball card industry, Major League Baseball declined to renew Donruss' license, leaving Topps and Upper Deck as the only producers. Perhaps the biggest boost will be selling and trading cards on the Internet.[46] The first major company in this market was the industry leader, Topps. Each week on etopps.com the company promotes three new limited edition cards or IPOs (Initial Player Offerings). The buyer can then purchase the card and takes physical possession, sell the card in an auction, or hold the card until it appreciates in value. The new product has been a huge success for Topps and could be the future of the card industry.

Personal training for sports

Another growing category of sports is referred to as **personal training**. According to the United States Bureau of Labor Statistics (BLS), employment opportunities for fitness workers are expected to increase more than 29 percent over the 2008 to 2018 decade.[47] Much of this growth is attributed to increasing awareness of the health benefits of regular exercise. However, these products are produced to benefit participants in sports at all levels and include fitness centers, health services, sports camps, and instruction.

Fitness centers and health services

When the New York Athletic Club was opened in 1886, it became the first facility opened specifically for athletic training. From its humble beginning in New York, the fitness industry has seen an incredible boom. "Pumping iron" was a common phrase in the 1970s and early 1980s. Moreover, the 1970s aerobics craze started by Dr. Ken Cooper added to the growth of health clubs across the United States.

It is no secret that a physically fit body is becoming more important to society. The growth of the fitness industry follows a national trend for people to care more about their health. In 1993, there were 11,655 clubs in the United States billed as "health and fitness" centers. In 2012, this number had grown to a record high of 29,960 clubs. Moreover, health club membership climbed to a record high 51.4 million people.[48] Why are people joining health clubs in record numbers? According to a study conducted by the International Health, Racquet, and Sportsclub Association, the factors that will continue to support the growth of health club membership in the United States include the following:

1. The growing number of health clubs that make it more convenient for consumers.
2. The continued and increased promotion of the benefits of exercise by organizations like the U.S. Surgeon General.
3. More Americans are concerned about the adverse effects of poor exercise and eating habits.[49]

Sports camps and instruction

Sports camps are organized training sessions designed to provide instruction in a specific sport (e.g., basketball or soccer). Camps are usually associated with instructing children; however, the "fantasy sports camp" for aging athletes has received considerable attention in the past few years. Fantasy sports camps typically feature current or ex-professional athletes, and the focus is more on having fun than actual instruction. Nearly every major league baseball team now offers some type of fantasy camp for adults. For example, Chicago White Sox Fantasy Baseball Camp allows you (if you're over 21 years old) to be a major leaguer for a week. The experience consists of social activities, games, and instruction with former major league players, but this does not come cheap. The price for participating is roughly $4,200 per person.

Along with camps, another lucrative sports service is providing personal or group instruction in sports. The difference between instruction and camps is the ongoing nature of the instruction versus the finite period and intense experience of the camp. For example, taking golf or tennis lessons from a professional typically involves a series of half-hour lessons over the course of months or sometimes years. Contrast this with the camp that provides intense instruction over a week-long period.

Sports information

The final type of sports product that we discuss is sports information. **Sports information** products provide consumers with news, statistics, schedules, and stories about sports. In addition, sports information can provide participants with instructional materials. Sports-specific newspapers (e.g., *The Sporting News*), magazines (e.g., *Sports Illustrated*), Internet sites (e.g., cnnsi.com), television (e.g., The Golf Channel), and radio (e.g., WFAN) can all be considered sports information products. All these forms of media are experiencing growth both in terms of products and audience. Consider the following examples of new sports information media. ESPN launched its new magazine in March 1998 to compete with *Sports Illustrated*, which leads all sports magazines with a circulation of more than 3.2 million. The current circulation for *ESPN The Magazine* is 2.1 million, but all indications are that there is room at the top for two sports magazine powerhouses.[50]

The fastest growing source of sports information is on the World Wide Web, through use of computers, tablets, and smartphones. A look at the top sports Web sites is shown in Figure 1.3. Today, consumers are more connected than ever, with more access and deeper engagement, thanks to the proliferation of devices and platforms. The playing field for the distribution of sports content has never been deeper or wider. In fact, social media exchanges are now standard practice in our daily lives. Not only do consumers have more devices to choose from, but they own more devices than ever. Connected devices such as smartphones and tablets have become constant companions to consumers on the go and in the home. The rapid adoption of second screen alternatives has revolutionized shopping and viewing experiences. Sports-related content publishers and advertisers seeking to reach sports enthusiasts have more options than ever to connect with fans as they consume all things sports. Case in point: it's likely that at least one billion sports fans worldwide viewed events, got updates, and checked results of the 2012 London Olympics on digital devices, including PCs, mobile phones, and tablets.[51]

A study conducted by Burstmedia (2012) revealed sports fans use tablets and/or smartphones to access online sports-related content while engaged in a number

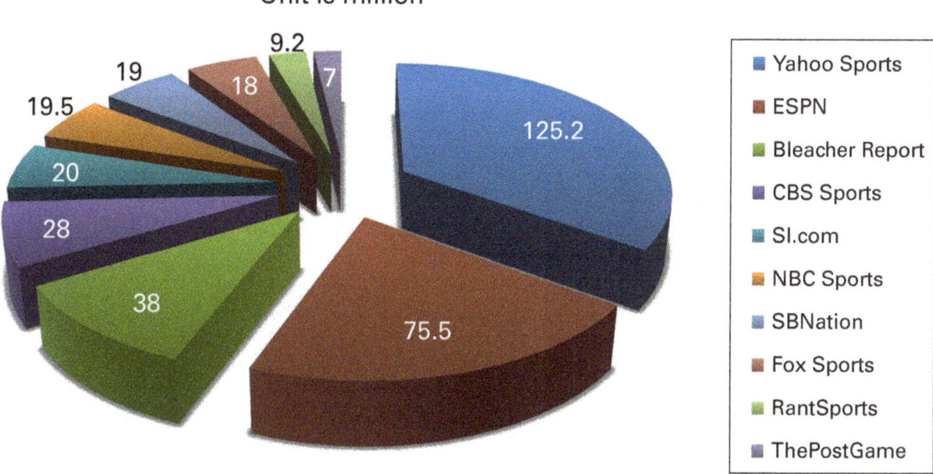

Figure 1.3 Top sports Web sites

Source: Adapted from: http://www.ebizmba.com/articles/sports-websites. Please note this is a snapshot of the current information at the time.

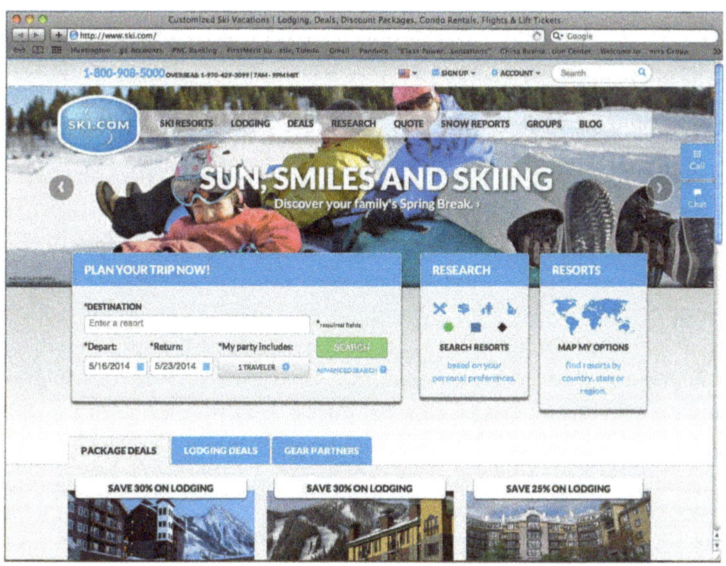

Web 1.2 Ski.com provides information for ski enthusiasts

Source: Courtesy ski.com

of activities, ranging from watching sports content on television (35.7 percent) to browsing web content on a desktop/laptop computer (19.4 percent), and/or attending a live sporting event in person (7.4 percent).[52] Tablets and smartphones are emerging as sports content consumption platforms. The study revealed that among all sports fans, 31.6 percent use tablets (e.g., an iPad) and 42.9 percent use smartphones (e.g., an iPhone) to access online sports content and video at least occasionally. In addition, 17.1 percent use tablets and 23.8 percent use smartphones to watch a live sporting event or game. Furthermore, Nielsen's 2011 study on consumer usage identified 31 percent of tablet and smartphone users who downloaded an app in the past 30 days, downloaded a sports-related app.[53] Sports fans have been leading the charge and finding new ways to share information and socialize, using the Web as a daily source of information. Due to the tremendous amount of information that sports fans desire (e.g., team stats, player stats, and league stats) and the ability of the Web to supply such information, Web portals and sports marketing make a perfect fit. Sports fans are the biggest consumers of media via cross-platform devices. According to ESPN's Glenn Enoch, sport consumers have an urgent need to stay connected to sports all day, whether it is game-casting or managing fantasy leagues, or just keeping up with headlines; that's what makes sports fans different, the demand to access information.[54] One example of the success of providing sports information via the World Wide Web is www.ESPN.com (ESPN's Web site).

ESPN's multilayered Web portal affords consumer access and tracks consumer behavior across the growing list of media and Web platforms. According to Julie Roper, ESPN Director of Advertising Analytics, "It used to be just about high ratings and reach, and that was enough, now, there's a lot more accountability, so we have gotten much more granular." Considering the global nature of sport, looking across the multiplatform universe is essential. That is why ESPN developed the following seven cross media principles to further solidify and integrate multimedia and Web platform usage and analysis.

ESPN's seven cross-media principles

1. **New media create new strata of users:** When a technology is introduced, some will adopt it but most do not. There is no foreseeable future when every person has and uses every available device.
2. **No new metrics:** Measuring new media does not require new metrics – it requires metrics that unite behavior across different platforms. They may be called different things in different media, but they have the same meaning: How many, how often and how long.
3. **Users and usage:** "How many" is not the same as "How long." Both users and usage are valuable metrics in analyzing cross-media behavior, but mean different things and must be considered separately.
4. **A heavy user is a heavy user:** The heavier user of one medium tends to be a heavier user of other media as well.
5. **Cross-media usage is not zero-sum:** Doing one behavior more does not mean doing another behavior less. Media usage is no longer constrained to limited locations and opportunities – people can consume media throughout the day, wherever they are. We call this "new markets of time." TV viewing continues to grow because the media pie is getting larger.
6. **Simultaneous usage is widespread but limited:** While people do consume multiple media at the same time, it represents only a small amount of total media usage – just minutes per day.
7. **Best available screen:** People are using different platforms at different times and in different places for different purposes. Cross-media behavior isn't about convergence – it is about the opportunity to follow the consumer throughout the day, fulfilling specific needs and building touch points.

Source: Article author: Mike Reynolds. Rightshold: ESPN.

http://www.multichannel.com/technology/espn-espouses-seven-principles-cross-media-research/124879.

The multidimensional nature of the sports product

As you can see from our previous discussion, there are a wide variety of sports products. Our earlier definition of the sports product incorporated the distinction between goods and services. Although this is a traditional approach to categorizing consumer products, the complexity of the sports product makes the goods–services classification inadequate. Consider the rich diversity of the sports products that we have just considered. Everything from a hockey puck to the NCAA championship game of the Final Four in basketball is included in our definition. Because of this diversity and complexity, we have added an additional dimension to the sports product known as the body mind continuum. The body mind continuum is based on the notion that some sports products benefit consumers' minds, while other products act on consumers' bodies. Figure 1.4 illustrates the multidimensional nature of sports products using two dimensions: goods services and body mind. These dimensions make up the **sports product map**.

As you can see, we have positioned some sports products on this map. Exercise equipment is shown as a good that works on the body of the consumer. At the other end of the map, attending or watching a sporting event is considered a service that acts on the mind of consumers. Perhaps we can best describe the differences based on the mind–body and goods–services dimension by exploring sports camps. Sports camps for children are primarily instructional in nature. The primary product being sold is the opportunity for kids to practice their physical skills. However, the fantasy camp targeting adults is a product that acts more on the mind than body. The adults are purchasing the "fantasy" to interact with professional athletes rather than the physical training.

Understanding where sports products fall on this map is critical for sports marketers. Marketers must understand how they want their sports product to be perceived by consumers so they can understand what benefits to stress. For example, the marketers of a sporting event may want to sell the intangible excitement or the tangible features of the arena. This strategic decision is based on a number of factors that will be considered in detail throughout this text.

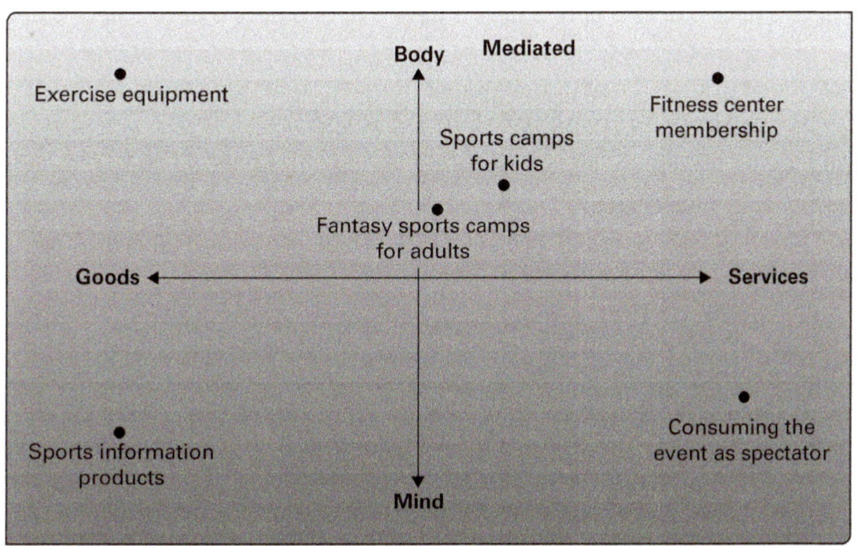

Figure 1.4 The multidimensional nature of sports products using two dimensions: Goods–Services and Body–Mind

Producers and intermediaries

Producers and intermediaries represent the manufacturers of sports products or the organizations that perform some function in the marketing of sports products. Organizations or individuals that perform the function of producer or intermediary include team owners, sanctioning bodies, agents, corporate sponsors, media, and sporting goods manufacturers. In the following paragraphs, we take a look at each of these producers and intermediaries as they relate to the various sports products.

Sports labor

Owners of professional sports franchises, partnerships that own sporting events and universities that "own" their athletic teams all represent producers of sporting events. One of the unique aspects of the sports industry is that oftentimes business people purchase a team because they always dreamed of becoming involved in sports. Typically, sports owners are entrepreneurs who have made their riches in other businesses before deciding to get involved in the business of sports. All too often these owners may be realizing a dream, but fail to realize a profit. Just think of the risks in owning your own team. Pro sports teams have seasonal revenue streams, few chances to expand, and frequent labor problems, and are dependent on the health of just a select few employees.

Many sports-related financial ownership deals – be it racehorses, minor league baseball teams, or indoor soccer franchises – score high on appeal and low on profits, unless the team spigot is affiliated with one of the premiere teams or leagues. J. W. Stealey, former owner of the Baltimore Spirit (now Blast) professional indoor soccer team, exemplifies the typical sports owner. He says, "Sports has always been my life. Owning a team is, to be honest, an ego kind of a deal, with all the attention from the media and involvement with the players." However, there is just one catch. "Although I keep expecting us to turn a profit, we never have."[55] However, on the opposite end of the spectrum are teams like Real Madrid, which generated $650 million in revenues during the 2011–2012 season and was identified as the world's most valuable sports team worth $3.3 billion.[56]

As Mark Cuban, who bought the majority share of the Dallas Mavericks for $285 million has openly admitted, "having paid $200 million plus for my franchise, I want, and need, the NBA running on all cylinders in order to maximize the return on my investment."[57] Even though many franchises struggle to generate profitable year to year revenues, astonishlngly, valuation numbers of the high demand sport ogranization often see double-digit increases.

Most professional sports teams are owned by individual investors who have staked their personal fortunes to buy their franchises, which they often operate as a public trust. The Washington Redskins, Wizards, and Capitals are owned by individuals and their investment teams. Corporate ownership of a major league sports team is rare, but exists. The Chicago Cubs are owned by the Tribune Company and the Atlanta Braves are owned by Time Warner. However, several recent corporate ownerships of professional sports teams have fizzled, including the Disney Company's ownership of the then-Anaheim Angels and the Mighty Ducks. The Los Angeles Dodgers were owned for several years by News Corp., before the company sold the team to an investor group from Boston, who recently sold the team to Guggenheim Baseball Management which includes former Los Angeles Laker Magic Johnson. Interestingly, the NFL forbids corporate ownership of franchises.

Sanctioning bodies

Sanctioning bodies are organizations that not only market sports products, but also, more importantly, delineate and enforce rules and regulations, determine the time and place of sporting events, and provide athletes with the structure necessary to compete. Examples of sanctioning bodies include the NCAA, NFL, NHL, IOC (International Olympic Committee), and MLB. Sanctioning bodies can be powerful forces in the sports industry by regulating the rules and organizing the structure of the leagues and sporting events.

The PGA (Professional Golf Association) of America is one of the largest sanctioning bodies in the world. It is comprised of more than 22,000 members that promote the game of golf to "everyone, everywhere." In addition to marketing the game of golf, the PGA organizes tournaments for amateurs and professional golfers, holds instructional clinics, and hosts trade shows.[58] Although the PGA has a long history of advancing golf, other sport sanctioning bodies are surrounded by controversy. Kevin Iole of the *Las Vegas Review Journal* describes boxing's woes as follows. "Imagine convicted mob boss John Gotti at the helm of the Internal Revenue Service and you have a sense of what it's like in boxing with the WBA, WBC, WBO and IBF controlling world titles. A surgeon general's warning should be slapped on the side of every one of their title belts: Sanctioning bodies are hazardous to boxing's health."[59]

NASCAR is another of the most influential and powerful sanctioning bodies in sport. Ever since NASCAR began **sanctioning** stock car races, there have been cries of foul play and that NASCAR has somehow influenced the outcome of a race. One of NASCAR's roles is the car inspection process prior to races and this has always raised questions. Allegations of wrongdoing go all the way back to the early days of the sport. For example, legendary Junior Johnson's so-called banana car in 1966, a Ford that NASCAR said was legal but others say was given a free pass through inspection because the series was trying to bring the manufacturer back into racing. On the track, skeptics say NASCAR deliberately uses yellow flags to close up the field for a tight finish. True or false, there is no doubt of the clout of NASCAR.

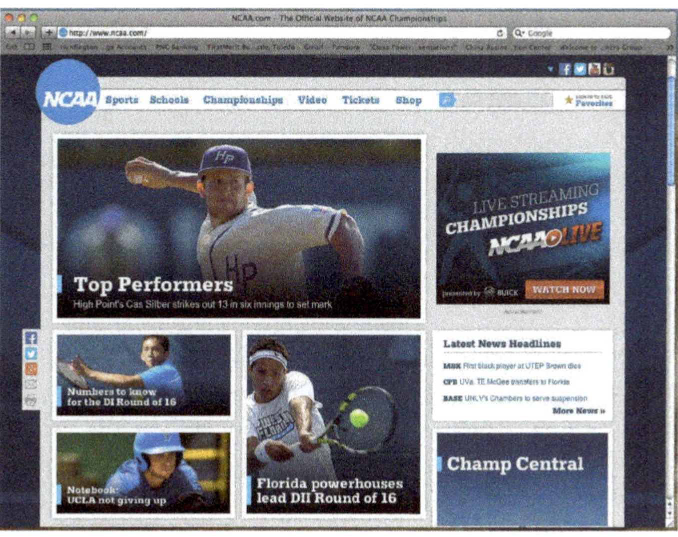

Web 1.3 NCAA: One of the most powerful sanctioning bodies

Source: http://www.ncaa.com/

Sponsors

Sponsors represent a sport intermediary. As we discussed, corporations can serve as a consumer of sport. However, corporations also supply sporting events with products or money in exchange for association with the event. The relationship between the event, the audience, and the sponsor is referred to as the event triangle.[60]

The basis of the event triangle is that the event, the audience, and the sponsor are all interdependent or depend on each other to be successful. All three groups work in concert to maximize the sport's exposure. The events showcase talented athletes and attract the audience who watch the event in-person or through some medium. The audience, in turn, attracts the sponsor who pays the event to provide them with access to the audience. In addition, the sponsor promotes the event to the audience, which helps the event reach its attendance goals. It is safe to say that sponsors represent an important intermediary or link between the event and the final consumers of sports – the audience.

Media

Earlier in this chapter, we commented on the growth of media in bringing sporting events to consumers. In fact, the media, which is considered an intermediary, may be the most powerful force in sports today and is getting stronger. The primary revenue generator for these networks is selling prime advertising time. As the price of advertising time rises, so does the cost of securing broadcast rights; however, the networks are willing to pay.

Sports organizations cannot survive without the mass exposure of the media, and the media needs sports to satisfy the growing consumer demand for this type of entertainment. As the demand for sports programming increases, innovations in media will emerge. For example, the growing number of consumers utilizing smartphones, tablet computers as well as other digital platforms to augment the spectator experience has created new activation platforms for properties and sponsors.[61] Today's consumers want to be engaged, demanding up-to-the-minute platforms that provide exclusive content, statistics, and interactive forums based upon live, on the field, action. Engagement not only extends brand support but also provides consumers with the opportunity to have real-time interaction enabling the procurement of exclusive content and an aforementioned sense of belonging.[62] All the while, professional and collegiate leagues, teams, and sponsors struggle to stay abreast of these "second screen" alternatives. Whether consumers are spectating in person or live at the event, they are using digital platforms to deepen their level of engagement and drive value for sponsors.

Agents

Another important intermediary in bringing the athlete to the consumer is the sports **agent**. From a sports marketing perspective, sports agents are intermediaries whose primary responsibility is leveraging athletes' worth or determining their bargaining power. The first "super-agent" in sports was Mark McCormack (see box, Sports Marketing Hall of Fame). Prior to his emergence, agents had never received the exposure and recognition that they enjoy today. Interestingly, it is not the agents themselves who have provoked their current rise to prominence, but rather the increased bargaining power of their clients.

The bargaining power of the athletes can be traced to two factors. First, the formation of new leagues in the 1970s, such as the American Basketball Association (ABA) and the World Hockey Association (WHA), resulted in increased competition to sign the best athletes. This competition drove the salaries to higher levels than ever before and made agents more critical. Second, free agency and arbitration have given players a chance to shop their talents on the open market and question the final offer of owners. In addition, owners are now able to pay players the higher salaries because of the multibillion dollar national television contracts and cable television revenues.

Although most people associate agents with contract negotiations, agents do much more. Here are some of the other responsibilities of the agent:[63]

- Determines the value of the player's services
- Convinces a club to pay the player the aforementioned value
- Develops the package of compensation to suit the player's needs
- Protects the player's rights under contract (and within the guidelines set by the collective bargaining agreement)
- Counsels the player about post-career security, both financial and occupational
- Finds a new club upon player free agency
- Assists the player in earning extra income from endorsements, speeches, appearances, and commercials
- Advises an athlete on the effect their personal conduct has on their career

SPORTS MARKETING HALL OF FAME

Mark McCormack

Many people trace the beginnings of modern sports marketing to one man – Mark McCormack. In 1960, Mark McCormack, a Cleveland lawyer, signed an agreement to represent Arnold Palmer. With this star client in hand, McCormack began the International Management Group, better known as IMG. Today, IMG is a multinational sports marketing organization that employs over 3,000 people, has sales of over $1 billion, and represents some of the finest professional athletes in the world.

In addition to his contribution to sports marketing in the United States, McCormack has globalized sports marketing. He opened an Asian office of IMG in Tokyo in 1969, led in the sponsorship of events in Europe, and continues to expand into the Middle Eastern markets. One example of McCormack's enormous reach into international markets is IMG's Trans World International. TWI is the largest independent producer of sports programming in the world. One of its shows, Trans World Sports, is viewed in more than 325 million homes in over 76 countries. Along with representing athletes and producing sports programming, IMG runs several sports academies that serve as training facilities for elite athletes. Additionally, IMG manages and creates sporting events such as the Skins Game, Superstars Competition, and CART races. Unfortunately for the sports world, Mr. McCormack died in May 2003 at the age of 72.

Source: Susan Vinella, "Sports Marketing Pioneer Dead at 72"; "IMG's McCormack Hailed as Visionary," *Plain Dealer*, May 17, 2003, a1; Eric Fisher, "IMG Founder McCormack Spiced Up the Sports World," *The Washington Times*, May 18, 2003, c3.

Sports equipment manufacturers

Sports equipment manufacturers are responsible for producing and sometimes marketing sports equipment used by consumers who are participating in sports at all different levels of competition. Some sporting equipment manufacturers are still associated with a single product line, whereas others carry a multitude of sports products. For example, Platypus Sporting Goods only manufactures cricket balls. However, Wilson manufactures football, volleyball, basketball, golf, tennis, baseball, softball, racquetball or squash, and youth sports equipment.

Although it is obvious that equipment manufacturers are necessary to supply the equipment needed to produce the competition, they also play an important role in sports sponsorship. Sports equipment manufacturers become sponsors because of the natural relationship they have with sports. For instance, Rawlings, one of the best known baseball glove manufacturers, sponsors the American and National League Golden Glove Award, which is given to the best defensive players in their position. Molten sponsors the NCAA Volleyball Championship by supplying the official game balls. In addition, Spalding is the official game ball of the WNBA.

Basic marketing principles and processes applied to sport

The sports marketing mix

Sports marketing is commonly associated with promotional activities such as advertising, sponsorships, public relations, and personal selling. Although this is true, sports marketers are also involved in product and service strategies, pricing decisions, and distribution issues. These activities are referred to as the **sports marketing mix**, which is defined as the coordinated set of elements that sports organizations use to meet their marketing objectives and satisfy consumers' needs.

The basic marketing mix elements are the sports product, price, promotion, and distribution. When coordinated and integrated, the combination of the basic marketing mix elements is known as the marketing program. The marketing mix or program elements are controllable factors because sports marketing managers have control over each element. In the following sections, we take a closer look at the four marketing mix elements as they apply to the sports industry.

Product strategies

One of the basic sports marketing activities is developing product and service strategies. In designing product strategies, decisions regarding licensing, merchandising, branding, and packaging are addressed. In addition, sports marketing managers are responsible for new product development, maintaining existing products, and eliminating weak products. For instance, the Anaheim Ducks recently changed their name from the Mighty Ducks and also sported new uniforms with different colors and a redesigned logo. This product decision was a result of cutting the ties with former owner, The Walt Disney Co. The team kept Ducks in its nickname after a poll of season ticketholders provided research to support the retention of the name. "A brand image is so hard to build," new owner Henry Samueli said. "If you have to change the name, then you're wiping out 13 years of brand history, not only in Orange County but in the whole country."[64]

Because so much of sports marketing is based on services rather than goods, understanding the nature of services marketing is critical for the sports marketing manager. Services planning entails pricing of services, managing demand for services, and evaluating service quality. For instance, sports marketing managers want to know fans' perceptions of ticket ushers, concessions, parking, and stadium comfort. These service issues are especially important in today's sports marketing environment because fans equate value with high levels of customer service.

Distribution strategies

Traditionally, the role of distribution is finding the most efficient and effective way to get the products into the hands of the consumers. Issues such as inventory management, transportation, warehousing, wholesaling, and retailing, are all under the control of distribution managers. The advent of sporting goods superstores such as Dick's Sporting Goods or the Sports Authority, offering sports memorabilia on the Home Shopping Network, and marketing sports products on the Internet (e.g., finishline.com) are examples of the traditional distribution function at work. Sports marketing managers are also concerned with how to deliver sports to spectators in the most effective and efficient way. Questions such as where to build a new stadium, where to locate a recreational softball complex, or how to distribute tickets most effectively are potential distribution issues facing sports marketers.

Pricing strategies

One of the most critical and sensitive issues facing sports marketing managers today is pricing. Pricing strategies include setting pricing objectives, choosing a pricing technique, and making adjustments to prices over time.

The price of tickets for sporting events; fees for personal seat licenses, pay-per-view, and television sports programming; and the rising costs of participating in recreational sports such as golf, are all examples of how the pricing function affects sports marketing.

Promotion strategies

Just ask someone what comes to mind when they think of sports marketing, and the likely response is advertising. They may think of athletes such as Maria Sharapova or Peyton Manning endorsing a product or service. Although advertising is an element of promotion, it is by no means the only one. In addition to advertising, promotional elements include communicating with the various sports publics through sponsorships, public relations, personal selling, or sales promotions. Together these promotional elements are called the promotion mix. When designing promotional strategies, sports marketers must consider integrating their promotions and using all aspects of the promotion mix.

The exchange process

Understanding the exchange process is central to any successful marketing strategy. As generally defined, an **exchange** is a marketing transaction in which the buyer gives something of value to the seller in return for goods and services. For an exchange to occur, several conditions must be satisfied:

- There must be at least two parties.
- Each party must have something of value to offer the other.
- There must be a means for communication between the two or more parties.

- Each party must be free to accept or decline the offer.
- Each party must believe it is desirable to deal with the other(s).

Traditionally, a marketing exchange consists of a consumer giving money to receive a product or service that meets their needs. Other exchanges, not involving money, are also possible. For example, trading a Pedro Martinez rookie baseball card for a Derek Jeter card represents a marketing exchange between two collectors.

Examples of elements that make up other exchanges appear in Figure 1.5. The two parties in the exchange process are called exchange players. These two participants are consumers of sport (e.g., spectators, participants, or sponsors) or producers and intermediaries of sport. Sports spectators exchange their time, money, and personal energy with sports teams in exchange for the entertainment and enjoyment of watching the contest. Sports participants exchange their time, energy, and money for the joy of sport and the better quality of life that participating in sports brings. In sponsorships, organizations exchange money or products for the right to associate with a sporting event, player, team, or other sports entity.

Although these are rather elementary examples of the exchange process, one of the things that makes sports marketing so unique is the complex nature of the exchange process. Within one sporting event, multiple exchanges will occur. Consider a Sprint Cup NASCAR event. There are exchanges between spectators and the track ownership (i.e., money for entertainment); spectators and product vendors who are licensed by NASCAR (i.e., money for goods associated with racing); track owner and NASCAR sanctioning body (i.e., money for organizing the event and providing other event services); media and NASCAR (i.e., event broadcast coverage for money); product sponsors and driving team owner (i.e., promotional benefits for money); and track owner and driving team owner (i.e., producer of the competition for money). As you may imagine, trying to sort out all these exchanges, much less determine the various marketing strategies involved in each exchange, is a complicated puzzle that can only be solved by having a full understanding of the industry within each sport. Although the nature of each sporting event and industry is slightly different, designing a marketing strategy incorporates some fundamental processes that span the sports industry.

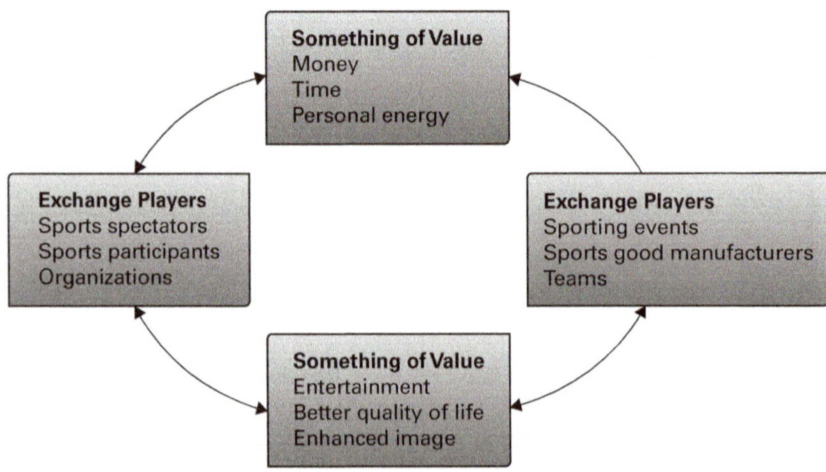

Figure 1.5 Model of the sports marketing exchange process

The strategic sports marketing process

Sports marketers manage the complex and unique exchange processes in the sports industry by using the strategic sports marketing process. The **strategic sports marketing process** is the process of planning, implementing, and controlling marketing efforts to meet organizational goals and satisfy consumers' needs.

To meet these organizational goals and marketing objectives, sports marketers must first anticipate consumer demand. Sports marketers want to know what motivates consumers to purchase, how they perceive sports products or services, how they learn about a sports product, and how they choose certain products over others.

One way sports marketers anticipate demand is by conducting marketing research to gather information about the sports consumer. Another way that sports marketers anticipate demand is by monitoring the external environment. For instance, marketing research was used to determine the feasibility of locating a new NASCAR speedway in Northern Kentucky. According to developer, Jerry Carroll, "The report was two volumes and it not only said a major racetrack would work in this area, but it would be a grand slam." In addition, Carroll anticipated demand by examining the external environment. He found out that there are about 51 million people within a 300-mile radius of the proposed track and that "NASCAR fans and other racing fans, don't think anything of driving 300 miles for a race."[65] Thus far, the research has proven to be true as the Kentucky Speedway has been a huge success since opening its door for the 2000 season.

Next, sports marketers examine different groups of consumers, choose the group of consumers in which to direct the organization's marketing efforts, and then determine how to position the product or service to that group of consumers. These market selection decisions are referred to as segmentation, targeting, and position. The final aspect of the planning phase is to offer products that are promoted, priced, and distributed in ways that appeal to the targeted consumers. The following article illustrates how many of the professional sports leagues have recently attempted to target women and design products that will appeal to the female fan.

GIRLS GET THEIR GAME ON – WITH GREAT GEAR: SPORTS TEAMS CATER TO WOMEN FANS WITH NEW LINES OF FEMININE FASHION

Pink it and shrink it. Just a few years ago, that was the idea. That's the amount of thought professional sports leagues put into the products they offered their women fans. They'd just take the popular men's stuff – the boxy t-shirts, player jerseys, boodies and such – make them smaller and turn them out in quintessential girlie color. How quaint.

As Super Bowl Sunday approaches, football's women fans will have the widest choice ever of fashion forward clothes to support their teams in trendy fits and fabrics.

If you haven't been shopping lately for team fashions, be aware: There's been a revolution.

Pro sports leagues have been madly licensing stylish clothes and new accessories to grab more of the multi-billion dollar team fashion market.

All of the big four professional leagues – baseball, football, hockey and basketball – have seen growth in their fem fan base in recent years.

This explains the availability of nail polish in authorized Major League Baseball team colors, maternity tops with "future fan" printed over the baby bump and a footwear plan under development by the National Football League to license stilettos in the same shades as team football jerseys.

"Our women's business has grown twelvefold since 2001 and doubled since 2004," says Tracey Bleczinski, the NFL's apparel vice president.

"For women, shopping is a pastime and an activity. They're constantly looking for what's new. What's trending," she says. Hence the planned entry into team high heels (and wedges and boots). She says 44 percent of NFL fans today are women.

Major League Baseball has the largest percentage of women fans (45.5 percent) of all pro sports, says MLB spokesman Matt Bourne, and "all the sports leagues have recognized there's an opportunity there" to sell them feminine merchandise to support their teams.

Judging from the items on this page, these include rhinestones, fitted Ts, jewelry, totes and, yes, even team logo'd Mediterranean Sea bath salts to calm you after a particularly painful loss by the team whose logo is emblazoned on your chest, cap, ponytail holder and wristband.

"They are a fan and it doesn't make them less of a fan to wear something with some sequins or a little more fitted . . . a little more glitz and glam," says the National Hockey League's marketing executive vice president Brian Jennings.

"Overall, our women viewers are up 45 percent this season over last," says Lisa Piken, the National Basketball Association's senior director of apparel licensing.

Source: Ellen Warren; Courtesy of Chicago Tribune; http://articles.chicagotribune.com/2011-01-28/lifestyle/sc-cons-0127-warren-shopping-super-bo20110127_1_women-fans-sports-leagues-team-colors.

Summary

The sports industry is experiencing tremendous growth, and sports marketing is playing an important role in this emerging industry. Chapter 1 provided a basic understanding of sports marketing and the sports industry. Sports marketing is "the specific application of marketing principles and processes to sport products and to the marketing of non-sports products through association with sport." The study and practice of sports marketing is complex and interesting because of the unique nature of the sports industry.

Today sports organizations define their businesses as entertainment providers. In addition, sports organizations know that to be successful in the competitive environment of sports, they must practice a marketing orientation. An organization with a marketing orientation concentrates on understanding consumers and providing sports products that satisfy consumers' needs.

Sports marketing will continue to grow in importance as sports become more pervasive in the U.S. culture and around the globe. This phenomenal growth of the sports industry can be seen and measured in a number of ways. We can identify growth by looking at the increasing numbers of sport spectators, the growth of media coverage, the increase in sports participation, rising employment opportunities, and the growth in sports internationally. To better understand this growing and complex industry, a simplified model of the consumer–supplier relationship was presented.

The simplified model of the consumer–supplier relationship in the sports industry consists of three major elements: consumers of sport, sports products, and producers and intermediaries. Three distinct types of sports consumers are identified in the model. These consumers of sport include spectators who observe sporting events, participants who take part in sporting events, and sponsors who exchange money or product for the right to be associated with a sporting event. The spectators, participants, and sponsors use sports products.

A sports product is a good, service, or any combination of the two that is designed to provide benefits to a sports consumer. The primary sports product consumed by sponsors and spectators is the sporting event. Products related to the event are athletes such as Derek Jeter and arenas such as the Staples Center, which both provide their own unique benefits. Other categories of sports products common to the sports industry include sporting goods (e.g., equipment, apparel and shoes, licensed merchandise, collectibles, and memorabilia), personal training services for sports (e.g., fitness centers and sports camps), and sports information (e.g., news and magazines). Because there are a variety of sports products, it is useful to categorize these products using the sports product map.

Producers and intermediaries represent the third element of the simplified model of the consumer–supplier relationship in the sports industry. Producers include those organizations or individuals that help "manufacture" the sporting event, such as owners, sanctioning bodies, and sports equipment manufacturers. Intermediaries are also critical to the sports industry because they bring the sport to the end user of the sports product. Sponsors, the media, and agents are the three intermediaries presented in this chapter.

Although sports marketers must have a thorough understanding of the sports industry to be successful, the tool of their trade is the sports marketing mix. The sports marketing mix is defined as the coordinated set of elements that sports organizations use to meet their marketing mix objectives and satisfy consumers' needs. The elements of the marketing mix are sports products, distribution or place, pricing, and promotion.

In addition to the marketing mix, another central element of marketing is the exchange process. The exchange process is defined as a marketing transaction in which the buyer gives something of value to the seller in return for goods and services. One of the things that makes the sports industry so unique is the complex nature of the exchange process and the many exchanges that take place within a single sporting event.

To manage the complexities of the sports industry and achieve organizational objectives, sports marketers use the strategic sports marketing process. The strategic sports marketing process consists of three major parts: planning, implementation, and control. The planning process begins by understanding consumers' needs, selecting a group of consumers with similar needs, and positioning the sports product within this group of consumers. The final step of the planning phase is to develop a marketing mix that will appeal to the targeted group of consumers and carry out the desired positioning. The second major part of the strategic sports marketing process is putting the plans into action or implementation. Finally, the plans are evaluated to determine whether organizational objectives and marketing goals are being met. This third, and final, part of the strategic sports marketing process is called control.

Key terms

- agent
- amateur sporting event
- benefits
- exchange
- goods
- licensing
- marketing myopia
- marketing orientation
- organized sporting events
- participants
- personal training
- producers and intermediaries
- professional sports
- sanctioning
- services
- simplified model of the consumer–supplier relationship
- spectators
- sport
- sporting event
- sporting goods
- sports equipment manufacturers
- sports information
- sports marketing
- sports marketing mix
- sports product
- sports product map
- sports sponsorship
- strategic sports marketing process
- unorganized sports

Review questions

1. Define sports marketing and discuss how sports are related to entertainment.
2. What is a marketing orientation, and how do sports organizations practice a marketing orientation?
3. Discuss some of the ways that the sports marketing industry is growing?
4. Outline the simplified model of the consumer–supplier relationship in the sports industry.
5. What are the three distinct types of sports consumers? What are the different types of spectators? How are sports participants categorized?
6. Define sports products. What are the different types of sports products discussed in the simplified model of the consumer–supplier relationship in the sports industry?
7. Describe the different producers and intermediaries in the simplified model of the consumer–supplier relationship in the sports industry.
8. What are the basic elements of the sports marketing mix?
9. What is the marketing exchange process, and why is the exchange process critical for sports marketers?
10. Define the strategic sports marketing process, and discuss the various elements in the strategic sports marketing process.

Exercises

1. Provide five recent examples of sports marketing that have been in the news and describe how each relates to our definition of sports marketing.
2. How does sport differ from other forms of entertainment?
3. Provide an example of a sports organization that suffers from marketing myopia and another sports organization that defines its business as entertainment. Justify your choices.
4. Attend a high school, college, and professional sporting event and comment on the marketing orientation of the event at each level of competition.
5. Provide three examples of how you would *measure growth* in the sports marketing industry. What evidence

do you have that the number of people participating in sports is growing?

6. Discuss the disadvantages and advantages of attending sporting events versus consuming a sporting event through the media (e.g., television or radio).
7. Develop a list of all the sports products produced by your college or university. Which are goods and which are services? Identify ways in which the marketing of the goods differs from the services.
8. Choose any professional sports team and describe how it puts the basic sports marketing functions into practice.

Internet exercises

1. Using Internet sites, support the growth of the sporting goods industry.
2. Compare and contrast the Internet sites of three professional sports teams. Which site has the strongest marketing orientation? Why?

Endnotes

1 American Marketing Association, http://www.marketingpower.com/AboutAMA/Pages/DefinitionofMarketing.aspx, accessed May 10, 2014.

2 Kristi Lee Covington-Baker, 2007, *A History of Sports Marketing and the Media*, UMI Microform 1450380, Proquest Information and Learning Company.

3 Ibid.

4 David Biderman, "The Stadium-Naming Game," *The Wall Street Journal* (February 3, 2010).

5 Kristie McCook, Douglas Turco, and Roger Riley, "A Look at the Corporate Sponsorship Decision Making Process," *Cyber-Journal of Sport Marketing* [Online], vol. 1, no. 2 (1997).

6 Colby Weikel, 1998, *Sports Marketing: A Take on the History and the Future*, manuscript, UNC. Available from: http://www.unc.edu./~andrewsr/ints092/weikel.html.

7 David Arthur, Garry Dolan, and Michael Cole, "The Benefits of Sponsoring Success: An Analysis of the Relationship between Television Exposure and the Position of the Motorcycle Rider," *Cyber-Journal of Sport Marketing* [Online], vol. 2, no. 2 (1998). Available from: http://fulltext.ausport.gov.au/fulltext/1998/cjsm/v2n2/arthur22.htm.

8 Nigel Pope, "Overview of Current Sponsorship Thought," *Cyber-Journal of Sport Marketing* [Online], vol. 2 (1998). Available from: www.cjsm.com/vol2/pope21.htm.

9 Kristi Lee Covington-Baker, 2007, *A History of Sports Marketing and the Media*, UMI Microform 1450380, Proquest Information and Learning Company.

10 http://www.merriam-webster.com/dictionary/sport, accessed May 10, 2014.

11 John Mossman, "Denver to Host 2005 NBA All-Star Game," *The Associated Press* [Online], (June 17, 2003).

12 David Barboza, 2000, "Michael Jordan Movie Is Sports Marketing in New and Thinner Air," *The New York Times* (May 1, C16).

13 WWE 2013 Annual Report, 2013, *W Then W Now W Forever*. Available from: http://ir.corporate.wwe.com/Cache/1001184723.PDF?Y=&O=PDF&D=&FID=1001184723&T=&IID=4121687, accessed June 19, 2014.

14 Ajay K. Kohli and Bernard Jaworski, "Marketing Orientation: The Construct, Research Propositions, and Managerial Implications," *Journal of Marketing*, vol. 54, no. 2 (1990), pp. 1–18.

15 Jeffery Derrick, "Marketing Orientation in Minor League Baseball," *Cyber-Journal of Sport Marketing* [Online], vol. 1, no. 3 (1997). Available from: http://fulltext.ausport.gov.au/fulltext/1997/cjsm/v1n3/derrick.htm.

16 Hervé Collignon, Nicolas Sultan, and Clément Santander, *The Sports Market: Major Trends and Challenges in an Industry Full of Passion*. [Homepage of A.T. Kearney, Inc., 2011], [Online]. Available from: http://www.atkearney.com/documents/10192/6f46b880-f8d1-4909-9960-cc605bb1ff34.

17 *Plunkett's Sports Industry Almanac*, 2013, Plunkett Research Ltd. Available from: http://www.plunkettresearch.com/.

18 Michele Himmelberg, "The Sporting Life; Long Hours, Low Pay, Starting at the Bottom, What Fun!," *Orange County Register* (June 14, 1999), c1; Don Walker, "Money Game: Sports Becoming Big Business," *Journal Sentinel* (2000). Available from: www.jsonline.com/news/gen/jan00/csports23012200.asp.

19 NFL Attendance, 2013. Available from: http://espn.go.com/nfl/attendance, accessed June 19, 2014.

20 Michael D. Smith, Roger Goodell State of the League Press Conference Transcript (February 2, 2013). Available from: http://profootballtalk.nbcsports.com/2013/02/02/

roger-goodell-state-of-the-league-press-conference-transcript/, accessed June 19, 2014
21 *NBA Attendance Report*, 2013. Available from: http://espn.go.com/nba/attendance/_/year/2013, accessed June 19, 2014.
22 Scott Kendrick, 2011, *Top 5 Reasons why MLB Attendance is down on 2011*. Available from: http://sportsillustrated.cnn.com/. See also: Tom Verducci, 2001, "The Good – and Bad – News about MBL's Attendance Figures" (May 3, 2011). Available from: http://sportsillustrated.cnn.com/2011/writers/tom_verducci/05/03/bud.selig.attendance/, accessed June 6, 2014.
23 Street & Smith's *Sports Business Daily*, "NHL Finishes Regular Season With Attendance Up 1.8%; Isles See 19.3% Increase," *Sport Business Journal* (April 11, 2012). Available from: http://www.sportsbusinessdaily.com/Daily/Issues/2012/04/11/Research-and-Ratings/NHL-EC-gate.aspx?hl=nhl%20attendance&sc=0.
24 *Who Were the Real Winners of the Beijing Olympics?* 2008, Just Ask Nielsen Study.
25 *ESPN Upfront* (2013). Available from: http://www.espncms.com/upfront2013/.
26 Jason Cruz, 2013, *ESPN Ratings Down as Fox 1 Sports Prepares for Launch*. Last update – July 9. Available from: http://mmapayout.com/2013/07/espn-ratings-down-as-fox-sports-1-prepares-for-launch.
27 Bob Jordan, 2009, *The Media Audit*. Last update–October. Available from: www.themediaaudit.com.
28 *Sports Costs Not the Only Reason for Rising Multichannel Bill*, SNL Kagan Whitepaper, (January 2013).
29 Kantar Media Sports, *Global Sports Media Consumption Report: A Study of Sports Media Consumption and Preferences in the US Market* (May 2013). Perform, London.
30 *Sports Market Place Directory*, 2014, Grey House Publishing, Armenia, NY.
31 Michele Himmelberg, "The Sporting Life: Long Hours, Low Pay, Starting at the Bottom, What Fun!" *Orange County Register* (June 14, 1999).
32 Nick Pandya, "Sporting a New Career," *The Guardian* (1999).
33 "NFL Renews Television Deals," *ESPN/Associated Press* (December 14. 2011).
34 B. Nichols, 2011, *Time and Money: Using Federal Data to Measure the Value of Performing Arts Activities*. NEA Research Note 102, National Endowment for the Arts, Washington, DC.
35 Nigel Pope, "Overview of Current Sponsorship Thought" [Online]. *Cyber-Journal of Sport Marketing*, vol. 2, no.1. (1998). Available from: http://fulltext.ausport.gove.au/fulltext/1998/cjsm/v2n1/pope21.htm.
36 *IEG Sponsorship Report*, 2013, IEG, Chicago, IL.
37 Geoffrey Smith, "Sports: Walk, Don't Schuss," *Businessweek* (December 7, 1997).
38 Skip Rozin, "Welcome to U.S. Widget Stadium," *Businessweek* (September 10, 2000).
39 *Cisco Won't Deny Sports Fans from Fast Internet*, 2011. Last update – July. Available from: www.electronicbytes.net.
40 Kevin Baumer, "14 Innovations that will make Sports Stadiums of the Future Unrecognizable," *Business Insider* (March 9, 2011).
41 SFIA, 2013, *Participation Topline Report*, Sport & Fitness Industry Association in conjunction with Sport Marketing Surveys, Silver Spring, MD.
42 Ibid.
43 *Sports Licensing Report*, 2010, EPM Communications, Inc. and *The Licensing Letter*, 2012.
44 *1998 State of the Industry Report*, 1998, Sporting Goods Manufacturers Association, Silver Spring, MD.
45 T. Corwin,"Sports-Card Dealers Strike Out; Web Traders Hurting Bricks-and-Mortar Stores, Owners Say," *The Plain Dealer* (2000), 1C.
46 Ibid.
47 *American Academy of Personal Training Employment Outlook*, 2013. Last update – October 5. Available from: http://www.aapt.edu/employment.html.
48 *IHRSA's Annual Health Club Consumer Study*, 2012, International Health, Racquet & Sportsclub Association. Available from: http://www.ihrsa.org/consumer-research, accessed June 6, 2014.
49 "U.S. Health Club Industry Reaches a Record High," *Club Industry* (May 1, 2003).
50 Russell Adams, "Top Sports Titles Find There's Room for Two" [Online], *Sports Business Journal* (September 22, 2013). Available from: www.sportsbusinessjournal.com/article.cms, accessed May 10, 2014.
51 "The London Olympics: Marketers in the Starting Blocks," *eMarketer* (June 28, 2012). Available from: http://www.emarketer.com/Article.aspx?R=1009159&ecid=a6506033675d47f881651943c21c5ed4, accessed June 6, 2014.
52 "Sports Fans and Digital Media: A Scorecard on Preferences and Behaviors," *Burstmedia Online Insights* (September 1, 2012). Available from: http://www.burstmedia.com/pdf/burst_media_online_insights_2012_09.pdf, accessed June 10, 2014.
53 Stephen Master, "Experts Discuss Sports &

Mobile: The Perfect Marriage," *NielsenWire* (October 10, 2011).

54 Terry Lefton, "ESPN Well Researched Sales Pitch, Street & Smith's Sports Business Journal," *Sports Business Daily* (January 2, 2012). Available from: http://www.sportsbusinessdaily.com/Journal/Issues/2012/01/02/In-Depth.aspx, accessed June 6, 2014.

55 Jill Fraser, "Root, Root, Root for Your Own Team," *Inc.* (July 1, 1997).

56 "Forbes Announces the World's 50 Most Valuable Sports Teams," *Forbes Inc.* (July 2013)

57 Angelo Bruscus, "Cuban Swears by the Bottom Line," *Seattle Post Intelligence Reporter* (June 20, 2007).

58 *The Role of the PGA in America*. Available from: www.pga.com/FAQ/pga_role.html, accessed May 8, 2014.

59 Kevin Iole, "Sanctioning Bodies Endanger Boxing," *Las Vegas Review Journal* (April 29, 2006) [Online]. Available from: http://www.reviewjournal.com/ivrj_home/. . .07477, accessed May 10, 2014.

60 Phil Schaaf, *Sports Marketing: It's Not Just a Game Anymore* (Prometheus Books, Amherst, MA, 1995).

61 IEG Sponsorship Report, *IEG Sponsorship Report – Activation, Double Vision: Activating Through the Second Screen* (July 2, 2012).

62 Mark Lyberger, "Twitter Wins Gold at the First Social Media Olympics," *PR Moment* (August 16, 2012). Available from: http://www.prmoment.com/1111/twitter-wins-gold-at-first-social-media-olympics-says-mark-r-lyberger-kent-state-university.aspx.

63 *Frequently Asked Questions* [Homepage of Sim-Gratton, Inc.], [Online]. Available from: www.home.istar.ca/~simagenty/faq.html, accessed June 10, 2009.

64 "Mighty No More: Ducks Change Name, Uniforms, Logo," *National Hockey League Newswire* (June 22, 2006).

65 Andrea Tortora, "NASCAR Track City's Future?" *The Enquirer* (November 16, 1997).

CHAPTER 2

Contingency framework for strategic sports marketing

After completing this chapter, you should be able to:

- Understand the contingency framework for strategic sports marketing.
- Describe the strategic sports marketing process.
- Describe the major internal contingencies and explain how they affect the strategic sports marketing process.
- Describe external contingencies and explain how they affect the strategic sports marketing process.
- Discuss the importance of monitoring external contingencies and environmental scanning.
- Explain and conduct a SWOT analysis.
- Define the internal and external contingencies and relate them to the strategic sports marketing process.

The foundation of any effective sports organization is a sound, yet flexible, strategic framework. The process should be systematic and well organized, but must be readily adaptable to changes in the environment, as the following article illustrates. Each strategic marketing process may have unique characteristics, but the fundamentals are all the same. To help make sense of the complex and rapidly changing sports industry, we use a contingency framework to guide the strategic sports marketing process. For the remainder of this chapter, let us look at an overview of this process.

NBA RELEASES 2011–12 REGULAR SEASON SCHEDULE

The wait is over. The highly anticipated 66-game NBA regular season schedule has officially been released. Schedules for every team are now posted on their websites. All in all, the schedule features 42 back-to-back-to-back games, with the L.A. Lakers having given the honor to commence their season in such manner, while the defending champs Dallas Mavericks will play on consecutive nights a whopping 20 times. From NBA.com:

NBA fans have 66 games per team crammed into four months, with basketball guaranteed almost every night of the week. If the NBA was dark for the lockout, the league will more than make up for that inactivity with this condensed and somewhat crazed 2011–12 schedule.

Honestly, it doesn't get busier than this. Whether "busy" means "better," we'll see. But there will be basketball, and plenty of it, between Christmas Day and late April. Back-to-back games will become the new norm for all teams, along with four-games-in-five-nights. And games on three consecutive nights, which every team must endure at least once, will challenge hamstrings and lungs.

"Those back-to-back-to-backs will be tough for every team," said the Hawks' Josh Smith. "We're a young team, but we get tired, too."

Not every team will play each other at least twice; such is the casualty of the lockout. The number of meetings between conference teams was also trimmed. But for the most part, the league made sure the popular teams would meet more than once. There was no chance, for example, the Heat wouldn't see the Lakers. Remember, the league is trying to reel in the audience, not chase it away. Therefore, you will see the games you want to see.

There are 42 back-to-back-to-back games in the overall schedule. Each team has at least one of these "triples," some more than one. There were 64 triples in 1999 in a 50-game season, which makes this season less taxing in that regard. In all, the 30 teams have 529 back-to-back games.

The schedule-makers had the complex and touchy job of trying to satisfy the networks, teams and fans, a process slightly less tricky than getting the union and owners to agree on a labor deal.

Anyway, it's necessary to examine the contenders and the schedule challenges they face. Let's begin.

The Celtics

They may be proud and championship-tested and veteran-smart and all that. But they're also gray at the temples. And the schedule will be an endurance test for the Celtics and others with a nucleus (Ray Allen, Kevin Garnett and Paul Pierce in Boston's case) well into their 30s. Ice bags and muscle relaxers will be plentiful and handy to keep the Celtics fresh as possible for the playoffs.

Their triple: April 13–15 at Toronto, New Jersey and Charlotte, which is actually mild from a competitive standpoint.

Their back-to-backs: 19, a bit on the high side, but nothing cruel in terms of overnight travel distances.

Their killer stretch: They play nine of 10 on the road in March, just when the body begins to ache and the postseason is in sight.

Key games: Miami and Chicago four times each, Thunder, Mavericks and Lakers twice.

The Bulls

With Derrick Rose coming off an MVP season and the Bulls certainly wiser from being bounced from the playoffs by Miami, Chicago hopes to make a habit of deep postseason runs. Well, we'll know more about the Bulls right away, with seven of their first nine games on the road. But they only play the Lakers and Thunder once each.

Their killer stretch: A nine-game road swing from late January through mid-February, with stops in Miami, Philly, New York and ending in Boston. Some nights will feel like playoff nights for sure.

The Mavericks

The defending champs, who have their fair share of age, must cope with 20 back-to-backs, although their triple (Suns, Kings, Warriors) isn't gruesome. They play the Thunder and Lakers four times each, Heat and Celtics twice.

Their killer stretch: Right before the All-Star break, when they play at Philly and New York, then return home for Boston and the Lakers.

The Lakers

They open with a triple, although the Christmas blockbuster with the Bulls is followed by the Kings and Jazz, providing the Lakers somewhat of a cushion. But remember this: Andrew Bynum won't be around; he must sit the first five games for cheap-shotting J.J. Barea last spring.

The Lakers must also pay a personal price for being the league's marquee team, having to work Christmas, New Year's Eve and New Year's Day. There are three games with the Thunder and 2 with Miami.

Their killer stretch: In January, home vs. Dallas, then on the road against Miami and Orlando. That's a tough stretch only if Dwight Howard is still in Orlando.

The Heat

Last season the Big Three had a rough start to their new and controversial era, stumbling out of the gate at 9–8 and causing all sorts of water-cooler and Internet conversation. Well, only five of their first 12 games are against returning playoff teams. And yeah, LeBron James and Dwyane Wade and Chris Bosh sort of know each other a little better now. They play the Thunder twice, Celtics and Bulls four times each. The Heat play 18 of their final 29.

The Dilemma: There are two off days between road games in Indiana and Cleveland. Does Miami and LeBron dare spend those days walking the streets of Cleveland?

Their killer stretch: They play Boston twice, Philly, Oklahoma City, Chicago and Memphis in a six-game April span.

The Knicks

The Garden is undergoing a pricey renovation, where the architects made the insensitive decision to eliminate the Willis Reed tunnel. Hopefully for the Knicks' sake, they create a new landmark soon enough. Anyway, home will feel like home, since the Knicks play no more than four straight on the road all season. There are 19 back-to-backs.

Speaking of home: There will be no "homecoming" for Carmelo Anthony or Amar'e Stoudemire, since the Knicks won't visit Denver or Phoenix.

Their killer stretch: At Boston, then the Mavericks and Spurs in March.

The Thunder

This will be the first full season with Kevin Durant, Russell Westbrook andKendrick Perkins, who figured to be joined by an improving surrounding cast. That should be enough for basketball to overtake football in Oklahoma pretty quickly.

The Rematch: They play at Memphis just three games into the new season. Surely you recall that epic seven-game playoff series?

Their killer stretch: In February, when they'll see the Celtics, Lakers, at Philly and Orlando, then the Hawks and Mavericks.

Those are the meatier parts of the schedule. But there are other diversions. The Nets' final game in New Jersey is April 23 against the Sixers before moving on to Brooklyn next season.

Deron Williams, meanwhile, will return to Utah, the site of his forced exit last year, on January 14. Also, make sure to catch Chris Paul in New York on February 17.

Unless, of course, Paul is a Knick by then.

Source: Slamonline.com; http://www.slamonline.com/online/nba2011/12/nba-releases-2011–2012-regular-season-schedule/.

Photo 2.1 After the lockout, the NBA is still thriving. Chris Bosh #4 participates in an NBA basketball game at the Air Canada Centre on January 24, 2010 in Toronto, Canada. The Toronto Raptors beat the Los Angeles Lakers 106–105.

Source: Shutterstock.com

Contingency framework for strategic sports marketing

Sports marketing managers must be prepared to face a continually changing environment. As Burton and Howard pointed out, "marketers considering careers or already employed in sports marketing must be prepared for unexpected, often negative actions that jeopardize a sports organization's brand equity."[1] Think about what can happen over the course of an event or a season. The team that was supposed to win the championship cannot seem to win a game or the likely cellar dwellers end up contending for championships. Take, for example, the Detroit Tigers. They lost 406 games from 2002 through 2005 and their last winning season was 1993. Suddenly they win the American League Championship and go to the World Series in 2006 and 2012. The New Orleans Saints also provide a great example of a team who faced tremendous odds after suffering displacement from Hurricane Katrina and went on to unexpectedly make the 2006 NFL playoffs and win the Super Bowl in 2010. In fact, Hurricane Katrina and its impact on the city of New Orleans and the Saints ranks as one of the most compelling examples of the changing environment that marketers cannot plan for.

Other unexpected events become commonplace in the sports marketing landscape. The star player gets injured halfway through the season. Attendance at the sporting event is affected by poor weather conditions. Leagues are shut down by lockouts. Team owners threaten to move the franchise, build new stadiums, and change personnel. All this affects the sports marketing process.

At the collegiate level, a different set of situations may alter the strategic marketing process. For example, players may be declared ineligible because of grades, star players may leave school early to join the professional ranks, programs may be suspended for violation of NCAA regulations, or conferences may be realigned.

Sports marketers need to be prepared for either positive or negative changes in the environment. These factors are out of the sports marketer's control, but they must be acknowledged and managed. Sports marketers must be prepared to cope with these rapid changes. One model that provides a system for understanding and managing the complexities of the sports marketing environment is called the **contingency framework for strategic sports marketing**.

Contingency approaches

Contingency models were originally developed for managers who wanted to be responsive to the complexities of their organization and the changing environments in which they operate.[2] Several elements of the contingency framework make it especially useful for sports marketers. First, sports marketers operate in unpredictable and rapidly changing environments. They can neither predict team or player success nor control scheduling or trades. A quote by former New York Mets Marketing Vice President Michael Aronin, who spent 13 years with Clairol, captures the essence of this idea: "Before, I had control of the product, I could design it the way I wanted it to be. Here the product changes every day and you've got to adapt quickly to these changes."[3]

Second, the contingency approach suggests that no one marketing strategy is more effective than another. However, one particular strategy may be more appropriate than another for a specific sports organization in a particular environment. For example, sports marketers for the Boston Red Sox have years of tradition on their side that influence their strategic planning. This marketing strategy, however, will not necessarily meet the needs of the relatively new teams such as the Montreal Impact (2012), Portland Timbers (2011), Vancouver Whitecaps FC (2011), and Philadelphia Union (2010) of MLS. Likewise, strategies for an NCAA Division I program are not always appropriate for a Division II program. The contingency framework can provide the means for developing an effective marketing strategy in all these situations.

Third, a contingency model uses a systems perspective; one that assumes an organization does not operate in isolation but interacts with other systems. In other words, although an organization is dependent on its environment to exist and be successful, it can also play a role in shaping events outside the firm. Think about the Chicago Blackhawks and all the resources required from the environment to produce the core product – entertainment. These resources include professional athletes, owners, management and support personnel, and minor league franchises to supply talent, facilities, other competitors, and fans. The different environments that the Chicago Blackhawks actively interact with and influence include the community, the NHL, sponsors, employees and their families, and the sport itself. Understanding the relationship between the organization and its many environments is fundamental to grasping the nature of the contingency approach. In fact, the complex relationship that sports organizations have with their many publics (e.g., fans, government, businesses, and other teams) is one of the things that makes sports marketing so complicated and so unique.

One way of thinking about the environments that affect sports organizations is to separate them on the basis of internal versus external contingencies. The external contingencies are factors outside the organization's control; the internal are considered controllable from the organization's perspective. It is important to realize that both the internal and external factors are perceived to be beyond the control, though not the influence, of the sports marketer.

The essence of contingency approaches is trying to predict and strategically align the strategic marketing process with the internal and external contingencies. This alignment is typically referred to as strategic fit or just "fit." Let us look at the contingency approach shown in Figure 2.1 in greater detail.

The focus of the contingency framework for sports marketing, and the emphasis of this book, is the strategic sports marketing process. The three primary components of this process are planning, implementation, and control. The planning phase begins with understanding the consumers of sports. As previously discussed, these consumers may be participants, spectators, or perhaps both. Once information regarding the potential consumers is gathered and analyzed, **market selection decisions** can be made. These decisions are used to segment markets, choose the targeted consumers, and position the sports product against the competition. The final step of the planning phase is to develop the sports marketing mix that will most efficiently and effectively reach the target market.

Effective planning is merely the first step in a successful strategic sports marketing program. The best-laid plans are useless without a method for carrying them out and monitoring them. The process of executing the marketing program, or mix, is referred to as implementation. The evaluation of these plans is known as the control phase of the strategic marketing plan. These two phases, implementation and control, are the second and third steps of the strategic sports marketing process.

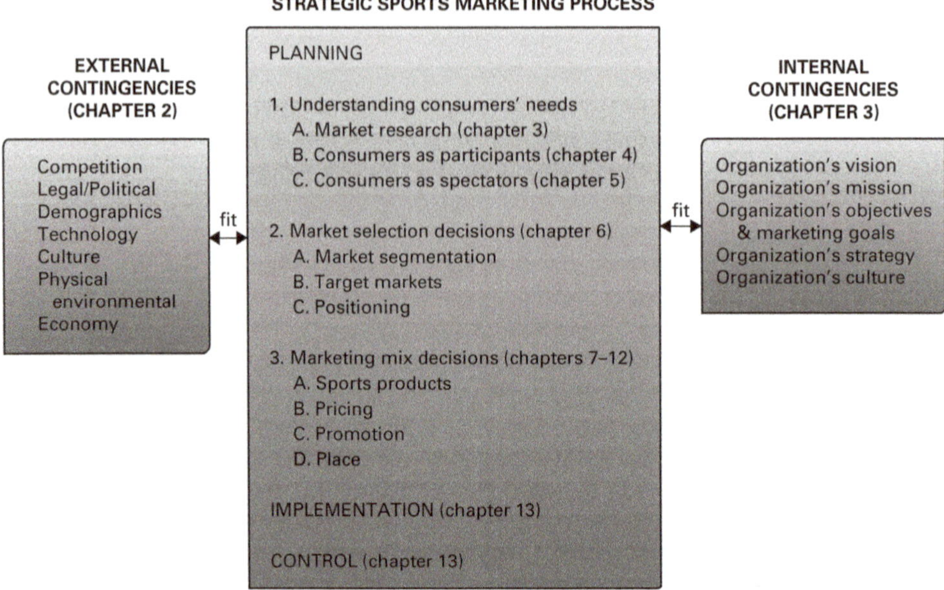

Figure 2.1 Contingency framework for strategic sports marketing

As you can see from the model, a contingency framework calls for alignment, or fit, between the strategic marketing process (e.g., planning, implementation, and control) and external and internal contingencies. Fit is based on determining the internal strengths and weaknesses of the sports organizations, as well as examining the external opportunities and threats that exist. **External contingencies** are defined as all influences outside the organization that can affect the organization's strategic marketing process. These external contingencies include factors such as competition, regulatory and political issues, demographic trends, technology, culture and values, and the physical environment. **Internal contingencies** are all the influences within the organization that can affect the strategic marketing process. These internal contingencies usually include the vision and mission of the organization, organizational goals and strategies for reaching those goals, and the organizational structure and systems.

The **strategic sports marketing process** was defined in Chapter 1 as the process of planning, implementing, and controlling marketing efforts to meet organizational goals and satisfy consumers' needs (see also Figure 2.2) and is the heart of the contingency framework. The **planning phase**, which is the most critical, begins with understanding the consumers of sport through marketing research and identifying consumer wants and needs. Next, market selection decisions are made, keeping the external and internal contingencies in mind. Finally, the **marketing mix**, also known as *the four Ps*, is developed and *integrated* to meet the identified sports consumer needs.

Once the planning phase is completed, plans are executed in the **implementation phase**. In this second phase of the strategic sports marketing process, decisions such as who will carry out the plans, when the plans will be executed, and how the plans will be executed are addressed. After implementing the plans, the third phase is to evaluate the response to the plans to determine their effectiveness. This is called the **control phase**. The strategic sports marketing process and its three phases will be described in detail in the remainder of the book. Let's turn to a discussion of the internal and external contingencies for the rest of this chapter.

PLANNING PHASE

Step 1: Understanding Consumers' Needs
A. Marketing research
B. Consumers as participants
C. Consumers as spectators

Step 2: Market Selection Decisions
A. Marketing segmentation
B. Target markets
C. Positioning

Step 3: Marketing Mix Decisions
A. Sports products
B. Pricing
C. Promotion
D. Place

IMPLEMENTATION PHASE

CONTROL PHASE

Figure 2.2 Strategic sports marketing process

Internal and external contingencies

A complex relationship exists between internal contingencies and the strategic marketing process. Sports marketers must ensure that the marketing strategies are aligned with the broader organizational purpose. Factors controlled by the organization such as its vision and mission, organizational objectives, and organizational culture must be considered carefully. Additionally, this organizational strategy is often based on changes that occur in the environment. It is at this point that external and internal contingencies must complement one another. Let's take a further look at the various factors that make up the internal and external contingencies and gain an appreciation for just how much they can influence the strategic marketing process.

Internal contingencies

Internal contingencies are all influences within and under the control of the sports organization that can affect the strategic sports marketing process. Typically, the internal or controllable factors, such as designing the vision and mission, are the function of top management. In other words, these organizational decisions are usually made by top management rather than sports marketing managers. The more marketing-oriented the organization, the more the marketing function becomes involved in the initial development and refinement of decisions regarding the internal contingencies. Irrespective of their involvement, sports marketers should have an understanding of internal contingencies and how they influence the strategic marketing process. Let us describe some of the internal contingencies that sports marketers must consider within the contingency framework.

Vision and mission

One of the first steps in developing a strategic direction for an organization is shaping a vision. The **vision** has been described as a long-term road map of where the organization is headed. It creates organizational purpose and identity. A well-written vision should be a prerequisite for effective strategic leadership in an organization. The vision should address the following:

- Where does the organization plan to go from here?
- What business do we want to be in?
- What customer needs do we want to satisfy?
- What capabilities are required for the future?

As you can see, the organizational questions addressed in the vision are all oriented toward the future. The mission, however, is a written statement about the organization's present situation. The purpose of a written mission statement is to inform various stakeholders (e.g., consumers, employees, general public, and suppliers) about the direction of the organization. It is particularly useful for motivating employees internally and for communicating with consumers outside the organization. Here are examples of mission statements constructed by Under Armour Performance gear[4] and the Kent State University Athletic Department.[5]

Mission of Under Armour

To make all athletes better through passion, science and the relentless pursuit of innovation.

Mission and objectives of Kent State University Athletic Department

The Intercollegiate Athletic program at Kent State University competes at the highest National Collegiate Athletic Association (NCAA) Division I level (FBS for football) and provides select men and women with the opportunity, challenge and support to achieve their full academic and athletic potential, while operating as an integral part of the University's educational mission.

Intercollegiate Athletics intends to intensify its pursuit of its nine major categories of objectives within the current planning horizon:

- Support and enhance University mission and objectives by furnishing an academic support system that enables student athletes to graduate in a timely fashion and at a higher rate than in the overall University undergraduate population.
- Prepare student athletes to be responsible citizens who make positive contributions to society.
- Facilitate competition in the Mid-American Conference (MAC) at an echelon meriting regional and national post-season play.
- Comply with the spirit and letter of MAC and NCAA rules and support the associations', as well as the University's, principles of sportsmanship and ethical conduct.
- Employ and develop coaches who are also teachers and role models devoted to the welfare of student athletes.
- Achieve gender equity and be proactive regarding the intent of affirmative action in the recruitment and retention of student athletes and the hiring of coaches and athletic staff.

- Augment attendance and revenue, so as to encourage esprit de corps and stimulate monetary contributions from alumni, friends and corporations.
- Operate in financial solvency.
- Represent the University in an exemplary fashion to alumni, friends, prospective students, and the general public, as well as play an active role in the community of Northeastern Ohio.

These mission statements address several key questions:

- What business are we currently in?
- Who are our current customers?
- What is the scope of our market?
- How do we currently meet the needs of our customers?

In addition to addressing these four key questions, the mission statements for Under Armour and the Kent State University Athletic Department also contain statements about the core values of the organization. In fact, these core values are fundamental to carrying out the vision and mission of the organization.

How do mission and vision influence the strategic sports marketing process? Both vision and mission define the consumers of sport in broad terms. For example, Under Armour sees its customers from a global perspective. Also, vision and mission define the products and services that are being marketed to consumers. The vision and mission also help to identify the needs of consumers and ultimately guide the marketing process in meeting these needs.

Nike provides an excellent illustration of the dependent relationship among vision, mission, and the strategic marketing process. Originally, the product was aimed toward the serious track athlete who wanted a low-priced, high-quality performance shoe for competition. By 1969, Nike had begun to build a strong brand reputation as the shoe for competitive athletes. Over time, however, Nike redefined and broadened its vision and mission. In 1978, footwear represented 97 percent of Nike's total sales. Today, this percentage has decreased to roughly 67 percent as Nike produces footwear and apparel to meet the needs of almost every consumer in global markets. Nike's strategic decision to sell more than just high-performance footwear aimed only at serious athletes has changed the entire marketing mix. Now, more Nike products are being sold at more places than ever before. In fact, Nike's mission is "to bring inspiration and innovation to every athlete in the world."[6]

Organizational objectives and marketing goals

Organizational objectives

The **objectives** of the organization stem from vision and mission. They convert the vision and mission into performance targets to be achieved within a specified timeframe. Objectives can be thought of as signposts along the road that help an organization focus on its purpose as stated in the mission statement. More specifically, an objective is a long-range purpose that is not quantified or limited to a time period.

Organizational objectives are needed to define both financial and strategic direction. Organizational leaders typically develop two types of objectives: financial objectives and strategic objectives. Financial objectives specify the performance that an organization wants to achieve in terms of revenues and profits. Achieving these financial performance objectives is critical to the long-term survival of the organization. Some examples of financial objectives include the following:

- growth in revenues;
- increase in profit margins; and
- improved return on investment (ROI).

Strategic objectives are related to the performance and direction of the organization. Achieving strategic objectives is critical to the long-term market position and competitiveness of an organization. Whereas strategic objectives may not have a direct link to the bottom line of an organization, they ultimately have an impact on its financial performance. Here are a few examples of general strategic objectives:

- increased market share;
- enhanced community relations efforts; and
- superior customer service.

Marketing goals

Marketing goals guide the strategic marketing process and are based on organizational objectives. A **goal** is a short-term purpose that is measurable and challenging, yet attainable and time specific. Specific, measurable, attainable, reachable, and timely, the acronym SMART is often used to help define the framework of marketing goals.

Here is a sampling of common marketing goals:

- Increase ticket sales by 5 percent over the next year.
- Introduce a new product or service each year.
- Generate 500 new season ticketholders prior to the next season.
- Over the next six months, increase awareness levels from 10 to 25 percent for women between the ages of 18 and 34 regarding a new sports product.

Although multiple goals are acceptable, goals in some areas (e.g., marketing and finance) may conflict, and care must be taken to reduce any potential conflict. After developing marketing goals, the organization may want to examine them based on the following criteria:

- ***Suitability*** – The marketing goals must follow the direction of the organization and support the organization's business vision and mission.
- ***Measurability*** – The marketing goals must be evaluated over a specific timeframe (such as the examples just discussed).
- ***Feasibility*** – The marketing goals should be within the scope of what the organization can accomplish, given its resources.
- ***Acceptability*** – The marketing goals must be agreed upon by all levels within the organization. Top management must feel that the goals are moving the organization in the desired direction; middle managers and first-line supervisors must feel the goals are achievable within the specified timeframe.
- ***Flexibility*** – The marketing goals must not be too rigid, given uncontrollable or temporary situational factors. This is especially true when adopting the contingency framework.
- ***Motivating*** – The marketing goals must be reachable but challenging. If the goals are too easy or too hard, then they will not direct behavior toward their fulfillment.
- ***Understandability*** – The marketing goals should be stated in terms that are clear and simple. If any ambiguities arise, people may inadvertently work against the goals.
- ***Commitment*** – Employees within the sports marketing organization should feel that it is their responsibility to ensure goals are achieved. As such, managers must empower employees so everyone in the organization is committed and will act to achieve goals.

- ***People participation*** – As with commitment, all employees in the organization should be allowed to participate in the development of marketing goals. Greater employee involvement in setting goals will foster greater commitment to goal attainment.
- ***Linkage*** – As discussed earlier, marketing goals must be developed with an eye toward achieving the broader organizational objectives. Marketing goals incongruent with organizational direction are ineffective.

Organizational strategies

Organizational strategies are the means by which the organization achieves its organizational objectives and marketing goals. Whereas the organizational vision, mission, objectives, and goals are the "what," the organizational strategy is the "how." It is, in essence, the game plan for the sports organization. Just as football teams adopt different game plans for different competitors, sports organizations must be able to readily adapt to changing environmental conditions. Remember, flexibility and responsiveness are the cornerstones of the contingency framework.

In general, there are four levels of strategy development within organizations: corporate strategy, business strategy, functional strategy, and operational strategy. The relationship among these strategy levels is pictured in Figure 2.3. Notice that there must be a good fit among the levels, vertically and horizontally, for the firm to succeed.

Corporate-level strategies represent the overall game plan for organizations that compete in more than one industry. Business-level strategies define how a business unit gains advantage over competitors within the relevant industry. Functional-level strategies are those developed by each functional area within a business unit. For example, the strategic sports marketing process is the functional-level strategy developed by sports marketing managers, just as financial strategy is the purview of their finance manager counterparts. The operational-level strategies are more narrow in scope. Their primary goal is to support the functional-level strategies. Let us take a look at the relationship among the four levels of strategy at the Maloof Companies to see how a good fit among strategies can lead to enhanced organizational effectiveness; while noted conflict and disparity can adversely impact an organization's strategy and effectiveness.

The Maloof Companies[7] are a diversified group of business ventures including entertainment, sports, hotels, casinos, banking, food and beverage, and transportation

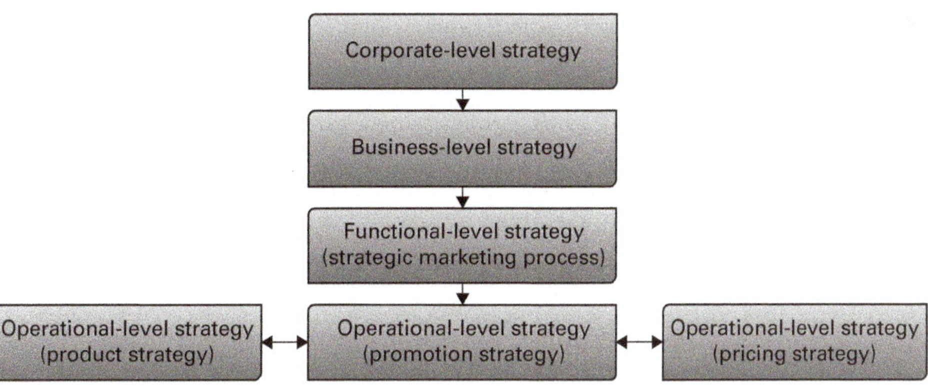

Figure 2.3 Relationship between levels of strategy

headquartered in Albuquerque, New Mexico, and operated in New Mexico, Colorado, and Nevada. The Maloof family owns the Palms, a $285 million hotel casino just off the Las Vegas strip with a 42-story tower and 447 guestrooms. In addition to their gaming business, the Maloofs have exclusive proprietorship rights to the distribution of Coors beer throughout New Mexico. The Maloof Companies also are the largest single shareholder in Wells Fargo Bank, which operates banks and branches in 23 states throughout the Western United States with over $200 billion in assets and 15 million customers.

The Maloofs are in the process of expanding their business in the entertainment industry with the development of Maloof Productions and Maloof Music. Maloof Productions is committed to developing and producing quality television and motion picture entertainment. Also of interest is that the Maloof Companies are best known for being the owners of the Sacramento Kings of the National Basketball Association (NBA) and the Sacramento Monarchs of the Women's National Basketball Association (WNBA). They acquired a minority interest in the Kings in 1998 and took majority control the following year, with Joe and Gavin operating the franchise. As part of the purchase of the Kings, they also acquired the team's sister franchise in the WNBA, the Sacramento Monarchs. The Maloofs operated the Monarchs until 2009, when the WNBA was unable to find a new owner and the team folded. In 2013, the Maloofs sold the majority share of the Sacramento Kings (65 percent) and Sleep Train Arena to a group led by TIBCO Software chairman, Vivek Ranadivé, at a valuation of more than $534 million.

Prior to the sale of the majority interest, The Maloofs, the once favored entity of Sacramento sports consumers, fell out of favor with the fans. Dissonance occurred, as sales continued to decline and rumors of moving the franchise followed. The latter topsy-turvy reign as majority owners of the team created strategic implications that hurdled the organization downward.

Traditionally, the corporate strategy for the Maloof Companies has been based on competing in all of these industries. The corporate strategy has allowed the Maloof Companies to obtain the broader organizational goals and pursue its vision and mission.

At the business level, Maloof management specified strategies for each business unit within each of the industry segments. For example, the Kings and the Monarchs would each have a unique business-level strategy, even though they are in the same industry sector – sports. These strategies were aimed at gaining competitive advantage within each relevant industry. However, each business-level strategy must support the corporate-level strategy, goals, vision, and mission.

At Maloof Corporation, there are numerous functional areas within the organization. For example, the Kings functional areas included finance and administration, general management and operations, business affairs, civic affairs, sales, and marketing. Leadership within each of these functional areas would be responsible for designing their own strategies to meet their respective business-level strategies.

Finally, within the functional areas such as sales and marketing, operational-level strategies were developed. Promotion, ticket sales, product, and pricing strategies must all be designed and coordinated to attain the sales and marketing objectives set forth in the functional-level strategy. As you can see, sports marketing managers responsible for each operational unit must be concerned with satisfying not only their own goals, but also the objectives of the broader organization.

Corporate level

Most professional sports franchises are owned by individuals or corporations that have many business interests. Sometimes these businesses are related, and sometimes the professional sports franchise is nothing more than a hobby of a wealthy owner. Today, the latter is becoming far less common as corporations include sports franchises in their portfolio. Even more rare is the sports franchise owned and operated as the primary, if not sole, source of owner income (e.g., the Mike Brown family and the Cincinnati Bengals).

There are typically two types of diversified companies – those that pursue related diversification and those that pursue unrelated diversification. In related diversification, the corporation will choose to pursue markets in which it can achieve synergy in marketing, operations, or management. In other words, the corporation looks for markets that are similar to its existing products and markets. The underlying principle in related diversification is that a company that is successful in existing markets is more likely to achieve success in similar markets. Unrelated diversification, however, refers to competing in markets that are dissimilar to existing markets. The primary criteria for choosing markets are based on spreading financial risk over different markets.

Professional sports franchises can be owned privately by one or more individuals, publicly owned corporations, or some combination of both. Corporate ownership of a major league sports team is becoming rarer. Most teams are owned by individual investors who have staked their personal fortunes to buy their franchises, which they often operate as a public trust. The Washington Redskins, Wizards, and Capitals are owned by individuals and their investment teams.

On the corporate side, the Chicago Cubs are owned by the Tribune Company and the Atlanta Braves are owned by Time Warner. However, several recent corporate ownerships of professional sports teams have fizzled, including the Disney Company's ownership of the then-Anaheim Angels and the Mighty Ducks. The Los Angeles Dodgers were owned for several years by News Corp., before the company sold the team to an investor group from Boston, who recently sold the team to the Guggenheim Baseball Management, which includes former Los Angeles Laker Magic Johnson.

Developing corporate-level strategy

Corporate-level strategies must make three types of decisions. First, top managers must determine in which markets they want to compete. Sports organizations have a core product and service, plus they also compete in ancillary markets. The core product has been defined as the game itself and the entertainment provided to consumers, whereas secondary markets include sale of licensed merchandise, fantasy sports camps, sports magazines, sports art, and so on. The leaders of a sports organization must also attempt to identify ways of capitalizing on the similarities in markets. For instance, fans for the core product often represent a natural target market for additional products and services. Companies such as Cablevision can realize the benefits of this type of vertical integration. As Scott Rosner (2010) noted, "by owning the team, playing facility and local media distribution channel, the company captures the lion's share of revenue generated by the team. It dominates the local marketplace, where fans are most passionate about the local team and can be most effectively monetized. Corporate owners with a local or regional focus are more successful than those with a national or global focus."[8]

On the international front an example may include the Singapore Sports Council's "Vision 2030". Under the Vision 2030 initiative the Ministry of Community Development, Youth and Sports (MCYS) and the Singapore Sports Council (SSC) will work with the Public–Private–People sectors to jointly develop proposals on how sport can best serve Singapore's future needs. Sports will be used as a strategy for individual development, community bonding, and nation building in the next two decades.

The second type of decision deals with enhancing the performance within each of the chosen markets. Top managers constantly need to monitor the mix of markets in which the organization competes. This evaluation might lead to decisions that involve pursuing growth in some markets or leaving others. These decisions are based on the performance of the market and the ability of the organization to compete successfully within each market.

The third type of decision involves establishing investment priorities and placing organizational resources into the most attractive markets. For a sports organization, this could involve decisions regarding stadium renovation, player contracts, or investing more heavily in merchandising. Corporate decisions within a sports organization must constantly recognize that the core product, the competition itself, is necessary to compete in related markets.

Business-level strategy

The next level of strategic decision-making is referred to as business-level, or competitive, strategies. Business-level strategies are based on managing one business interest within the larger corporation. The ultimate goal of business-level strategy decisions is to gain advantage over competitors. In the sports industry, these competitors may be other sports organizations in the area or simply defined as entertainment, in general.

One strategic model for competing at the business level contains four approaches to gaining the competitive advantage. These approaches include low-cost leadership, differentiation, market niche based on lower cost, and market niche based on differentiation. Choices of which of the four strategies to pursue are based on two issues: strategic market target and strategic advantage.

Strategic market targets can include a broader market segment or a narrow, more specialized market niche. Strategic advantage can be gained through becoming a low-cost provider or creating a real or perceived differential advantage.

The focus of low-cost leadership is to serve a broad customer base at the lowest cost to any provider in the industry. Although there may be a number of competitors pursuing this strategy, there will be only one low-cost leader. Many minor league teams compete as low-cost leaders due to the lower operating costs relative to their major league counterparts. Differentiation strategies attempt to compete on the basis of their ability to offer a unique position to a variety of consumers. Typically, companies differentiate themselves through products, services, or promotions. With differentiation strategies, companies can charge a premium for the perceived value of the sports product. Professional sports franchises attempt to differentiate themselves from competitors by providing a high-quality product on and off the field. This is done through a unique blend of sports promotion, community relations, stadium atmosphere, and a winning team.

Although low-cost leadership and differentiation strategies have mass-market appeal, the market niche strategies are concerned with capturing a smaller market segment.

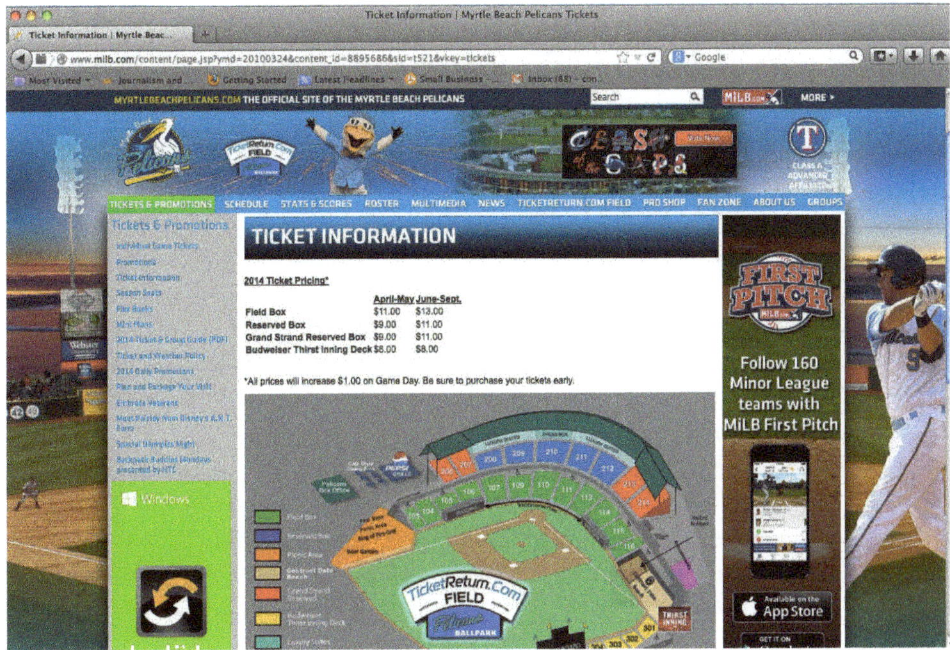

Web 2.1 Myrtle Beach Pelicans using a low-cost market niche strategy

Source: BB&T Coastal Field

These market segments may be based on consumer demographics, geographic location, lifestyle, or a number of other consumer characteristics. Within the market niche chosen, sports organizations can gain strategic advantage through a focus on low cost or differentiation. One example of the low-cost market niche strategy is the Pro Rodeo Cowboys Association (PRCA), whose events are priced inexpensively between $10 and $15.

Functional-level strategy

Each functional area of the organization (e.g., marketing, personnel, and operations) must also develop a game plan that supports the business-level and corporate-level initiatives. Again, the contingency framework calls for "fit" between each level of strategy within the organization. It is also important to coordinate among each functional area. For example, the marketing strategies should dovetail with personnel and operations strategies. The strategic marketing process discussed earlier provides the functional-level strategy for the organization's marketing efforts.

Operational-level strategy

Each strategy at the operational level must fit the broader strategic marketing process. This often requires integration across marketing functions and often, within the strategic sports marketing process, several narrower strategies must be considered. Plans must be designed, implemented, and evaluated in areas such as promotion, new product and service development, pricing, sponsorship, and ticket distribution. For example, the Los Angeles Dodgers unveiled a new operational-level promotion strategy to increase attendance by offering fans an "all you can eat" ticket. The right-field pavilion at Dodger Stadium was converted into the special section, giving around

3,000 fans as many hot dogs, peanuts, popcorn, nachos, and sodas as they wanted. Season ticket savings versus buying advance purchase single-game tickets are approximately 20 percent, $24 versus $30.[9] Numerous other major league teams are taking note and testing this idea as well.

Organizational culture

Culture is described as the shared values, beliefs, language, symbols, and tradition that is passed on from generation to generation by members of a society. Culture can affect the importance placed on sports by a region or nation, whether we participate in sports, and even the types of sports we enjoy playing or watching. A similar concept applied to organizations is called organizational culture. **Organizational culture** is the shared values and assumptions of organizational members that shape an identity and establish preferred behaviors in an organization.

As one of the internal contingencies, organizational culture influences the sports marketer in a number of ways. First, the organizational culture of a sports organization dictates the value placed on marketing. For instance, just look at the numbers of people employed and the titles of front office personnel at a variety of sports organizations. These are just two important indicators of the marketing orientation of the organization and the importance of the marketing function.

Second, organizational culture is important because it is linked with organizational effectiveness. In a study of campus recreation programs, organizational culture was found to be positively associated with organizational effectiveness. That is, a positive culture is associated with an effective organization. A positive culture rewards employees for their performance, has open communication, has strong leadership, encourages risk taking, and is adaptive. The ability to adapt to change is one of the most important dimensions from the contingency framework perspective.

Third, the organizational culture of professional sports organizations and college athletic programs not only has an impact on the effectiveness of the organization, but also can influence consumers' perceptions of the organization. For example, the Oakland Raiders, under former owner Al Davis, had an organizational culture that valued risk taking and doing anything necessary to get the job done. This organizational culture translated to the team's successful and ruthless performance on the field. Subsequently, the fans began to adopt this outlaw image. Ultimately, the black and silver bad boys of football have attracted a fan following that has come to expect this rebel image.

University athletic departments and their programs are also defined by the organizational culture. Athletic programs are known to either value education or attempt to win at all costs and be marred in scandal. Penn State University, a prestigious university known for high-quality academics, has had its image tarnished by athletics, most notably its football program. As of late, Penn State University has been characterized by its tainted image when members of both the university and football staff were accused of covering up assaults by former Assistant Coach Jerry Sandusky. In this case, actions of the athletic program have influenced consumers' perceptions of the university at large and may ultimately influence the broader university culture.

External contingencies

External contingencies are all influences outside the organization that might affect the strategic sports marketing process. External contingencies include competition; technology; cultural and social trends; physical environment; the political, legal, and regulatory environment; demographics; and the economy. Let us take a brief look at each of these factors and how they might affect sports marketing strategy.

Competition

Assessing the competitive forces in the **marketing environment** is one of the most critical components in the strategic sports marketing process. **Competition** is the attempt all organizations make to serve similar customers. Sellers realize that, to successfully reach their objectives, they must know who the competition is – both today and tomorrow. In addition, sellers must understand the strengths and weaknesses of their competitors and how competitors' strategies will affect their own planning.

For example, according to Nielsen's *Year in Sports Media Report* over 33 billion hours of national sports programming were consumed by 255 million people in the U.S. in 2013, up 27 percent from 2003.[10] Furthermore, viewership figures and advertising revenue suggests there's more to come. Much of the growth of live programming was due to the dramatically expanded coverage of college sports, on channels such as ESPNU and the Big 10 Network. The scramble to show college games, and the lucrative TV deals that scramble brings – such as the Pac-12 Conference's 12-year, $2.7 billion deal in May 2011and the University of Texas' Longhorn Network partnership with ESPN launched in August 2011 – have shaken up decades-old conference alignments and threaten the very structure of college sports.[11]

An example of many "sellers" attempting to fill the same customer need can be found in college sports broadcasting. Two digital cable networks, ESPNU and College Sports Television (CSTV), are battling for college sports fans like two prizefighters going toe-to-toe. The key to victory may be a multimedia strategy. CSTV, started in 2005, is available in more than 20 million homes, although many have access only through a digital pay tier of sports networks. To expand its reach, CSTV gets its biggest Internet showcase yet – the opportunity to broadcast the NCAA men's basketball tournament. ESPN recently launched its own network dedicated to college sports, ESPNU. In its first year, ESPNU broadcast about 300 live events ranging from Division I football to volleyball to lacrosse.[12] Table 2.1 illustrates the relative market share of the three primary players.

Table 2.1 College sports TV: the main players

Channel	Subscribers (millions)
CSTV	15
ESPNU	8
Fox College Sports	4

Source: http://www.broadcastingcable.com/news/news-articles/battle-college-sports-fans/106216.

The nature of competition

Sports marketers most often categorize their competition as product related. There are three types of product-related competition. The first of these is termed **direct competition**, the competition between sellers producing similar products and services. High school football games on a Friday night in a large metropolitan area pose direct competition in that the "product" being offered is very similar. One interesting example of direct competition is found in the game schedule of the NBA Indiana Pacers. High school basketball is so popular in Indiana that the Pacers rarely play a home game on Friday or Saturday night because of the competition posed by high school games.

Another type of product competition is between marketers of substitute products and services, the competition between a product and a similar substitute product. For example, when several professional sports teams have scheduled games that overlap, a consumer may have to choose to attend the Philadelphia 76ers (NBA), the Philadelphia Phillies (MLB), or the Philadelphia Eagles (NFL). Another example of substitute products is when spectators choose to watch a sporting event on television or listen to a radio or Web broadcast rather than attend the event.

The third type of product-related competition, called **indirect competition**, is more general in nature and may be the most critical of all for sports marketers. Marketers of sporting events at any level realize their true competition is other forms of entertainment. Professional, collegiate, and high school sporting events compete with restaurants, concerts, plays, movies, and all other forms of entertainment for the consumer dollar. In fact, a study was conducted to examine how closely other forms of entertainment are related to sports.[13] Preliminary findings suggest that respondents' most preferred entertainment activities are going out to dinner, attending parties, playing sports, watching movies, attending sporting events, attending live music or theater, watching TV, shopping for pleasure, watching sports on TV, dancing, and gambling. In addition, video games seem to be competing in the same "entertainment space" as watching sports on TV. Obviously, the toy industry has capitalized on this notion by creating a multitude of sports-related video games. Some people fear that today's interactive, virtual reality video games may replace watching "real games" on TV. Similarly, playing sports and gambling are perceived to be in the same perceptual space. Sport marketers may want to better understand the excitement and risks associated with gambling and add these attributes when marketing sports participation.

Indirect competition is present when even the popular USC and UCLA football games fail to sell out their respective home stadiums (the L.A. Memorial Coliseum and the Rose Bowl). There is simply too much entertainment competition in Southern California compared with Ann Arbor, Michigan (University of Michigan) or South Bend, Indiana (Notre Dame).

Technology

Technology represents the most rapidly changing environmental influence. New technologies affect the field of sports marketing daily. Some advances in technology have a direct impact on how sports marketers perform their basic marketing functions, whereas others aid in the development of new sports products. For example, new technologies are emerging in advertising, stadium signage, and distributing the sports product. The development of mobile apps and Internet sites remains one of the

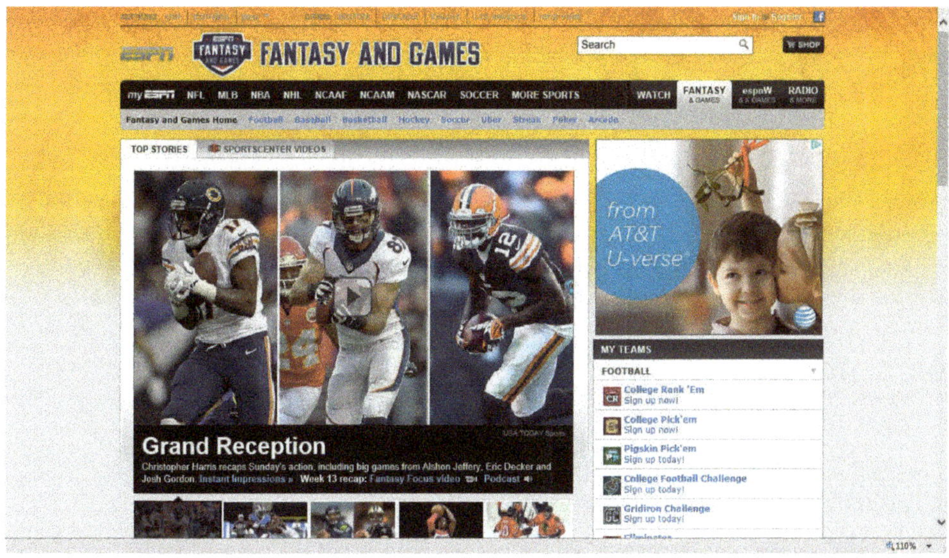

Web 2.2 ESPN.com providing sports information via the Internet

Source: ESPN.com

fastest growing technologies to affect sports marketing (see Appendix B for examples of Internet sites of interest to sports marketers). Internet sites have been developed to provide information on sports (e.g., www.nascar.com), sites of sporting events (e.g., www.daytona500.com), teams (e.g., http://www.hendrickmotorsports.com/), and individuals (e.g., www.dalejr.com). In 2014, NASCAR.com scored a Daytona 500 record with year-over-year increase of 39 percent, including an increase of 61 percent of total visits to the platform and a 131 percent increase in page views. As Colin Smith, managing director of NASCAR Digital Media noted, more people are turning to mobile devices and second screen platforms to consume NASCAR content.[14] ESPN.com is still the king of sports information on the Internet and part of sports fans' daily routines securing 62,500,000 unique visitors each month in 2011.[15]

In addition, the Internet has emerged as another popular way to broadcast live events to fans. Beginning in 1995 AudioNet, Inc. (www.Audionet.com) was one of the pioneers of live game broadcasts via the Internet and video streaming. Today each of the major leagues offers its fans opportunities to follow games online. Major League Baseball's premium package allows fans to watch up to six games live and includes a "Player Tracker" that alerts the subscriber when his or her favorite player steps to the plate. Season-long access is a reasonable $129.99.

The University of Nebraska game against San Jose State on September 2, 2000, was the first ever intercollegiate football game to be video webcast. The webcast resulted in more than 200,000 video streams around the world. Nebraska Athletic Director Bill Byrne summed it up nicely by stating that "we believe the Internet brings us one step closer to our fans, particularly those who are miles from home and have limited access to our normal radio and TV broadcasts."[16] Today, people not only are recording shows to be viewed later, but they can also call up their shows from on-demand channels, or watch them on their laptops, phones, or tablets.[17] Back in 2007, the NCAA Men's Basketball Championship was an example of how far things had come in a few years. March Madness® on Demand allowed fans to watch live game broadcasts of

CBS Sports television coverage of the NCAA Championship on their computer for free. Today, events like the Super Bowl and March Madness are communal. They afford even geographically restricted consumers the opportunity to watch events simultaneously, engaging in the interactive and immediate nature of the mediums, further optimizing and extending the mobile-specific experiences of their audiences.

In addition to providing information and game coverage to consumers, the Internet has emerged as a popular alternative to purchasing tickets at a box office. For example, MLB Advanced Media, LP (MLBAM), the interactive media and Icompany of Major League Baseball, serves as the Internet provider of tickets for MLB, while StubHub, owned by eBay, serves as the official MLB reseller. According to the *Sports Business Journal*, more than 8 million tickets were resold on StubHub during the 2011 season. However, average ticket prices on StubHub have dropped from a high of $104 in 2007 to $82 in 2011.[18]

The accompanying article presents an excellent look at some technologies that have, or will, dramatically altered the way spectators consume sport.

ON THE INDUSTRY'S RADAR

We asked executives in the sports facilities industry to identify the trends they're watching and to give their predictions on where the industry is headed. The following are highlights of what they had to say.

Food/concessions

Marc Bruno

President

Aramark Sports & Entertainment

• Technology takes off: One of the most visible trends in 2012 will be the continuing integration of mobile technology into the food delivery process. As smartphones, tablets and similar devices continue to grow in popularity, mobile food ordering applications will allow guests to order food and retail items, and customize their offerings, while providing food and beverage providers with new promotional channels to engage guests.

• Fans become foodies: Fans' tastes have become more sophisticated, which will lead to expanding the presence of specialty foods, like ethnic cuisine, street food, food trucks, gluten-free and allergen-free items, and healthy fare, to ensure menus have something for everyone. Look for an elevated dining experience, where simple comfort foods have been turned into premium quality fare.

• Going local beyond the farm: Fans are also more mindful of where their food comes from and greater emphasis is being placed on connecting with the local culinary scene by working with local farmers and featuring microbrews and craft beers. PNC Park's pierogi stacker sandwich in Pittsburgh is a local culinary specialty and there are growing opportunities to partner with local restaurateurs and celebrity chefs.

Stadium/arena merchandising

Jeff Hess

Vice president of retail

Delaware North Companies Sportservice

Fans at a stadium today expect selection, value and convenience. Demand for women's and children's apparel and merchandise will continue to grow, and fans will increasingly purchase team-branded items for their homes, cars and electronic accessories.

For stadiums and arenas, that will mean maximizing retail space to enhance fans' emotional connection to the game. Teams and their partners become mainstream retailers and not simply concessionaires. It will be increasingly important to follow fashion and retail trends and provide customers with a targeted selection of merchandise.

To provide the space needed, some venues are already developing large, iconic stores for a more exciting and memorable shopping experience. The large stores feature dramatic décor with eye-popping visuals and lighting. . . . In addition, leveraging licensed partners to create brand- or item-specific shops and portable kiosks will create a more personal shopping experience.

Targeted marketing programs and new e-commerce technology and mobile applications will increasingly be used to reach fans beyond the gates of the venue. Customized merchandise will be available throughout the stadium, and on non-game days, to offer the convenience fans will look for.

Technology

Bob Jordan

Managing partner

Venue Research and Design

Technology is developing at a much faster pace than the design and operation of the sports facilities. Fans attending the events will be video centric and it will be a BYOD (bring your own device) environment. The infrastructure will be the impediment to adoption of the technology and will be the focus as each facility moves into the future. This will require a change in some of the design philosophies in facilities. Video devices, wireless devices, structured cabling, switching and routing, and headend and demarc gear are all devices that require coordination and square footage.

The fan is expecting the visual of the living room with the communal vitality of the event. This will be a two-way experience with an unrestricted social media experience and an enhanced and memorable event. Fans are the early adopters of technology. They will also be the early exit if the brand is unable to deliver. The fans will be both a consumer and creator of content.

Using a remote method to order food, the fan base is asking for greater convenience. Removing the human interaction of a cashier translating your order to a register and then filling that order while you wait is desired. The implications are to design outlets that are not relying on the standard queues. Facilities will also have to deal with the fact of BYOD such as battery life and where does the fan set the device.

Venue design

Earl Santee

Senior principal

Populous

The booming era of new stadiums began nearly three decades ago. While we believe the vast majority can be viable for decades to come, they do need to evolve to be economically viable, socially engaging and relevant to new generations. One trend we expect to continue is the ever-increasing expectations of patrons to personally control their game-day experience, to enjoy ease of movement, and to be entertained with new experiences.

A key element of new experiences

is technology integration. It has increased dramatically in recent years, and we believe it will be integral to the future of sports design. Likewise, sponsors and corporate partners are looking for fresh alternatives to static advertising. Populous is helping integrate sponsors into facility design with sponsor-activated fan zones, interactive media and new kinds of experiences that are tailored to engage fans and express strong brand personalities.

Lastly is the growing importance of urban planning. The substantial community and private investments required by these large structures demand greater justification than simply a suitable place for watching a sporting event. Going forward, existing stadiums and arenas must include a much broader community vision for benefiting the surrounding area with economic growth and regeneration opportunities.

Premium seating

Jason Gonella

Vice president of sales

Rose Bowl Revitalization Project

The premium seating buying mantra has gone from exuberance and flashiness – where bigger and closer are best, with limited or no concern for cost as the standard 5–10 years ago – to now the model has changed due to the customer approach to be a more conservative value-based efficiency and return on investment.

- Product trends: All inclusive pricing is here to stay on club seating and the wave of the future for suites on both the consumer and building side of the sale. Value-added selling is prevalent in every aspect of the economy now. Adding food, access to special events that once were incremental, is the wave of today and I cannot see that changing. Product diversity is also critical; the one-size-fits-all mentality [has] passed us by. . . . The placement of the products has not changed too much, closer is better in almost all cases, but exclusivity to lounges and special events is more important than ever – people need more of a reason to buy than they ever have in the past. Season-ticket selling and packaging today, especially in the indoor sports and baseball, is so competitive with club-seat selling, it has become a real challenge to differentiate to the buyer where the value is in these seats. The smaller club-seat buyer has to be made to feel extremely special these days.
- Things to do: Pricing appropriately and packaging and locating the products effectively are the key to the success. Additionally, creating that sellout, high-demand mentality is critical as well. If the buyer senses the demand is soft or supply is high, one will be in a tough position to get sales in this economy.

Source: Article Author: Don Muret; rightsholder: *Sports Business Journal*; http://m.sportsbusinessdaily.com/Journal/Issues/2012/01/16/In-Depth/Trends.aspx.

Items that utilize statistical algorithms and integrate the advantages and uses of digital technologies, e.g. real-time motion tracking, are becoming more prevalent. In fact, many major American sports leagues now employ at least one full-time "number cruncher" to perform statistical analysis for league, teams, and players.[19] Teams and leagues have has also formed partnerships with high-tech companies. The leagues and teams recognize the value these technological partnerships provide. For example, the NBA has teamed up with the likes of Synergy Sports Technology and StratBridge. Synergy Sports Technology's professional online/offline products are used to provide key features, high volume video streaming, and analytics while StratBridge provides the StratTix inventory management tool to further enhance ticket sales efforts for the NBA. Throughout the year, NBA teams will be able to utilize the latest technology for managing ticket inventory, including access to graphical representations of sold and available in-arena seating, complete analysis of ticket sales and individual seating information for every game, and use of StratTix Premium service to access up-to-the-minute sales information at any time.

Interestingly, many owners have emerged from high-tech companies who are using their technology experience and strength to benefit their sports franchises. Examples of high-tech owners include but are not limited to: Charles Wan of the New York Islanders and chairman of Computer Associates International; Paul Allen of the Seattle Seahawks, Portland Trail Blazers, and Seattle Sounders, and co-founder of Microsoft; Robert J. Pera of the Memphis Grizzlies, who was a former hardware engineer for Microsoft before founding Ubiquiti Networks; Everett R. Dobson of the Oklahoma City Thunder and CEO of Dobson Technologies; Ted Leonsis of the Washington Capitals, Washington Wizards, and America Online; Daniel Snyder of Washington Redskins and Web marketer; Ken Kendrick of the Arizona Diamondbacks and Datatel; the late Hiroshi Yamauchi, former Nintendo President/Owner of Seattle Mariners who in fact sold the team to Nintendo in 2004; Mark Cuban of the Dallas Mavericks and founder of broadcast.com; while more recent emerging collaborations include TIBCO's Chief Vivek Ranadivé utilizing their spotfire technology with the Golden State Warriors and more recently the Sacramento Kings; and former Microsoft CEO Steve Ballmer, who recently bid $2 billion to acquire the Los Angeles Clippers.

So far, our discussion of technology is based more on how technology influences spectators and the distribution of sport. How do technologically advanced products affect sports participants and their performance? Although most sporting goods have experienced major technological improvements since the early 1990s, two sports that live and die by technology are golf and tennis. In the golf industry, one company that positions itself based on cutting-edge technology is E21. E21 holds the exclusive right to manufacture golf products using proprietary E21 Scandium metal alloys. Through a sophisticated multi-technology production path, E21 manufactures shafts, drivers, and other clubs with marked improvements in distance, accuracy, and feel over competing products. In recent months a number of high-profile golf professionals have switched to or began testing E21's Eagle One shafts. E21 Scandium products are 55 percent lighter and offer 25 percent strength to weight advantage over titanium alloys, the current standard in the golf equipment industry. The advanced dynamics of E21 alloys and the material economics offer a performance-enhanced alternative to manufacturing driver clubs with titanium, the largest segment of the annual $5.5 billion U.S. golf equipment marketplace.[20]

Technology is even becoming a unique way to differentiate in the highly competitive sports apparel market. For example, Textronics, Inc., a pioneer in the field of electronic textiles, has produced NuMetrex, a brand of clothes that monitor the body. The NuMetrex Heart Sensing Sports Bra was named 2006 Sports Product of the Year by the Sporting Goods Manufacturers Association. The garment features electronic sensing technology that is actually integrated right into the knit of the fabric, which picks up the heart's electrical pulse and radios it to a wristwatch via a tiny transmitter in the bra. It offers a new level of comfort and convenience for women wishing to monitor

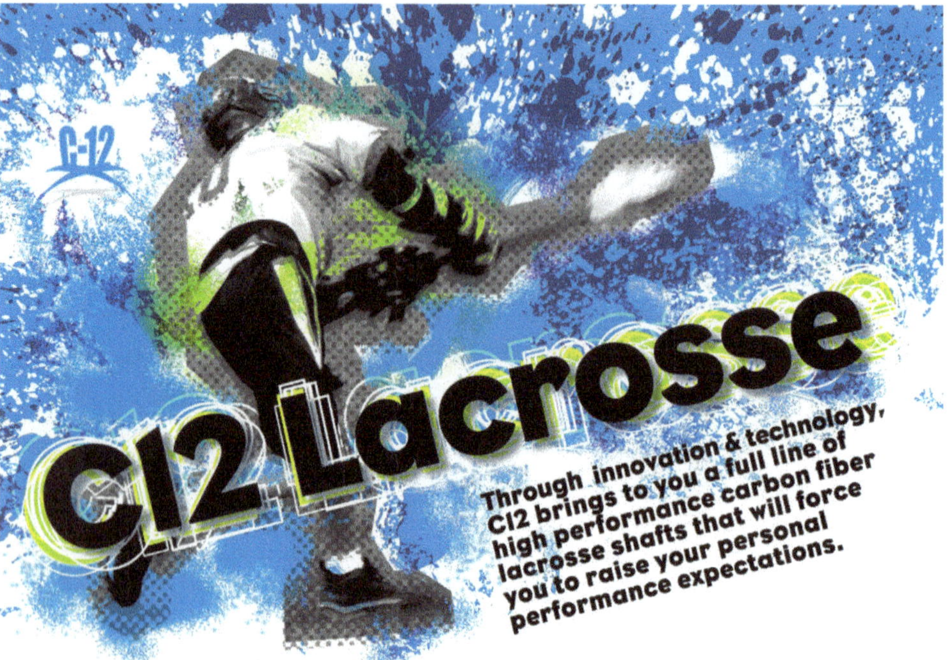

Web 2.3 C-12 Lacrosse showing its latest advances in lacrosse technology

Source: C-12 Lacrosse

their heart rate while they exercise.[21] Other recent product of the year winners include: KVA Stainless for its patented technologies to produce stainless steel bike tubing (2011) and TaylorMade R11S Driver for its innovative tuning characteristics (2012).

Global brands Nike and Apple Computer are continuously improving upon product developments that link technology and sport. In 2006, Nike and Apple Computer revealed their collaborative Nike+iPod Sport Kit, a shoe/MP3 player/personal trainer that could bring runners around the world together – virtually – enabling them to train on a level beyond the asphalt. The original product consisted of a shoe equipped with sensors under the sole insert and a tricked-out iPod nano. Today this technology works with iPod nano, or directly with a 2nd, 3rd, 4th iPod touch, iphone 3GS, iphone 4, or iphone 5 or a Nike+Sportwatch. The sensors will transfer dynamic workout information to the iPad device. Data, such as time, distance, pace, and calories burned, determined by a person's physiological makeup and the amount of steps the sensor picks up, are stored for later retrieval on the iPad device. The newly integrated personal trainer platforms allow further integration of the data with GPS, nutrition, and fitness applications.[22]

Although some marketers have a hard time grasping the special language of technology, they still agree that a whole new culture of technology has emerged. Owners such as Mark Cuban of the Dallas Mavericks acknowledges that the Mavericks constantly strive to push the tech envelope; to make the exchange more valuable to their fans and customers.[23] Cisco President and CEO John Chambers states, "Technology is changing every aspect of our life experiences and for Cisco, this is an opportunity to harness the power of our own innovative technologies to create a truly unique experience that transcends sports, connects communities, and takes the fan experience to a whole new level."[24]

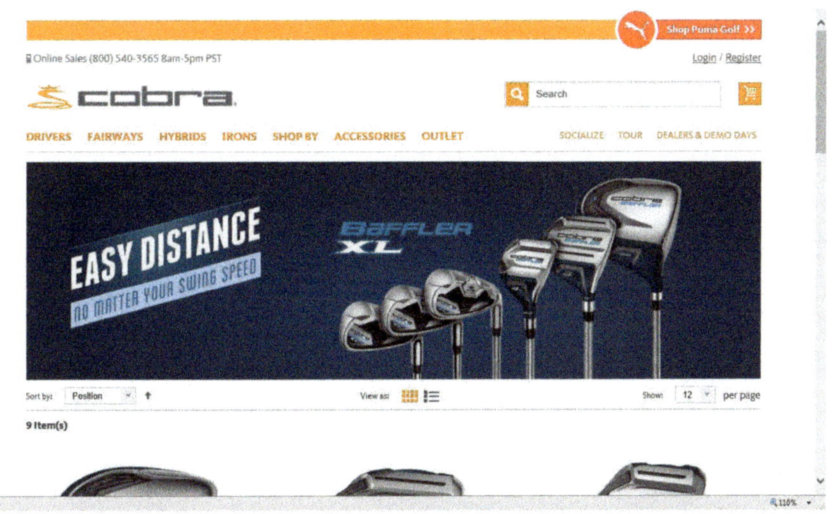

Ad 2.1 Cobra stresses an improved performance based on their technological product improvements.

Source: COBRA GOLF

Cisco stadium underscores the commitment to creating a new standard for sports venues. As the official technology partner of the Oakland A's, Cisco provided networking and communication products and services to transform the way that the A's team and ballpark operations will be managed. Cisco Field encompasses state-of-the-art technology, featuring an integrated IP network built on Cisco technology and is the platform for a multitude of applications that help take the fans' experience to the next level. For example, digital signs ensure "smart" traffic flow; fans can purchase merchandise or concessions while in their seat by ordering from a mobile device; onsite ticket kiosks enable fans to upgrade seats in real-time. Luxury suites have the opportunity to include multimedia amenities for premium video content, and Cisco TelePresence technology may even enable new forms of player-to-fan communications.

In 2010, Popular Mechanics looked at 30 NFL stadiums and identified five technologies that lead the league in innovation. Topping off the list was the Dallas Cowboys Stadium. Who would have expected Cowboys owner Jerry Jones to ignore the cliché that everything is bigger in Texas? The Lone Star State's venue has a seating capacity of over 100,000, a $1.2 billion price tag, and houses a pair of 2100 inch HDTVs. The $40 million screens span 60 yards and are five times the size of the screens at Atlanta's Turner Field. The second item on the list was innovation at the University of Phoenix Stadium, home of the Arizona Cardinals, and the introduction of a retractable field, yes we said field. The notion to install the departing lawn began with the owner's desire to play games on natural grass. Third on the list was the architectural framework of Quest Field, home to the Seattle Seahawks. Decibels were an important part of the equation for Seahawks owner and Microsoft co-founder Paul Allen. The design resulted in 135 decibels, nearly as loud as a jet plane, creating one of the loudest stadiums in professional football. Fourth on the list was one giant sunroof of Reliant Stadium in Houston, Texas. The facility was an answer to fans' cry to view football outdoors. The fifth recognized advancement was associated with the development of the New Meadowlands Stadium, home to the New York Giants and the New York Jets, and its efforts to make the stadium "sustainable". The new venue will create less pollution, conserve water and energy, and reduce the environmental impact of its operation.[25]

In other stadium technology advancements, numerous sporting events, e.g. football, baseball, and golf events, accept MasterCard® PayPass™, a "contactless" payment option giving fans the chance to pay for their purchases under $25 with a simple tap of their PayPass-enabled card or device on specially equipped merchant terminals. With MasterCard PayPass, sports fans spend less time standing in line or fumbling for cash at concession stands, and more time catching the on-field action.[26] The concept continues to expand. Enhancements as well as the future of use of the product is not only inviting to Mastercard but to organizations such as Apple, MLB, and the NFL.

Computer-driven video sport is another area of technological impact. Douglas Lowenstein, president of Entertainment Software Association, believes "The video game industry is entering a new era, an era where technology and creativity will fuse to produce some of the most stunning entertainment of the 21st century. Decades from now, cultural historians will look back at this time and say it is when the definition of entertainment changed forever."[27]

Video sports games, a subset of the video gaming industry, are called simulations because of their lifelike approximation of real sporting events. In fact, the danger for franchises lies in fans caring more about these games and simulations than they do the "real" sports. Nearly 67 percent of American homes either own a console, such as Xbox 360, PlayStation 3, and Wii, and/or use their PC to run entertainment software.[28] Sport gaming accounts for approximately 28 percent percent of video games sold. Stated differently, sports games account for approximately $20 billion of the $74 billion spent worldwide on games for systems like Wii, PlayStation, and Xbox.[29] The sport video games today are much more interactive than the "pong" environments of the past. Conceptually, today's games include multiplayer online platforms that provide free-to-play interactive experiences with state of the art motion controls. The leading interactive sports software brand in the world is Electronic Arts (EA) Sports (www.easports.com), with games including FIFA Soccer, Madden NFL, NFL Blitz, NHL Hockey, Fight Night Champion, NBA Live, Tiger Woods PGA Tour, and NCAA Football. In fact, versions of games such as EA Sports Madden and FIFA have had sales of approximately $93 million and $90 million respectively since their inception. EA has been a dominant player in the market; however, as Table 2.2 demonstrates, it has not been without competition. In fact, since its inception Wii sport-related games platforms have been the top four individual bestselling sport game consoles. Paul Allen, co-founder of Microsoft and owner of the Portland Trail Blazers, believes "the only thing holding back sports simulation products is the level of reality that can be achieved."

Video sports participation is not just limited to the couch potato or kids in the living room. Pro gaming leagues are now becoming the rage and viable sports entities of their own. CPL, or the Cyberathlete Professional League, which h as been around since 1997, has awarded more than $3 million in prize money. Television deals are even being struck. For instance, Major League Gaming has a contract with the USA Network, and ESPN has a show called Madden Nation, which shows gamers playing Madden NFL. There is even the World Cyber Games, which is the largest global electronic sports tournament that includes multiple divisions and represents a variety of nations.

Cultural and social trends

Perhaps the most important aspects of any culture are the shared and learned values. **Cultural values** are widely held beliefs that affirm what is desirable by members

Table 2.2 Top 10 sports video games (ranked by total U.S. units sold)

Title	Release Year	Publisher
1. FIFA 13	2012	2KSports
2. Grand Slam Tennis 2	2012	EA Sports
3. NBA 2K13	2012	2K Sports
4. MLB 12 The Show	2012	Sony Computer Entertainment
5. NHL 13	2012	EA Sports
6. Madden NFL 13	2012	EA Sports
7. SSX	2012	EA Sports
8. UFC 3 Undisputed	2012	THQ
9. F1 2012	2011	Codemasters
10. NFL Blitz	2012	EA Sports

Source: www.complex.com/video-games/2012/12/the-10-best-sports-video-games-of-2012/fifa-13.

of a society. Several of the core values of interest to sports marketers include individualism, youthfulness, achievement and success, and family.

Sports are symbolic of many core values. In fact in reference to America, what could be more American than baseball, our national pastime? ESPN used this rich tradition in a series of television advertisements promoting its Major League Baseball coverage. These advertisements claim "It's baseball – you're American – watch it."

All these core values are directly or indirectly relevant to sports marketing. For instance, certain sports or sporting events stress individualism. Individualism is based on nonconformance or the need to be unique. Nothing could be more directly linked to individualism than the X-treme Games, featuring sports such as skateboarding and street luge. The central or underlying values inherent in all sports are achievement and success. Virtually every sports marketing theme is either directly or indirectly linked to the achievement and success of an individual athlete or a team.

Youthfulness is another core value that is continually stressed by sports marketers. People participate in sports and watch sports to feel young and have fun. Those in the mature market are making strides at staying in shape; they are also watching their own age cohorts still participating in sports at a professional level via any number of senior tours (men's and women's golf, tennis, and bowling). In addition, products like Just for Men are endorsed by sports legends Emmitt Smith, Keith Hernandez, Walt "Clyde" Frazier, and Michael Waltrip, who all use the product to "stay looking great."

Another core value is family and the need to feel a sense of belonging. Engagement in culture and sport can take many forms. According to a recent study, team sports, which foster a sense of "group identity," continue to play an important role in the lives of American children. According to the 2013 SFIA US Trends in Team Sports Report, team sports bring us together as young children, teaching us to socialize, solve problems, resolve disputes, experience the benefits of hard work, understand the different personalities and gain self-confidence and direction.[30] They are a significant part of the fabric of American culture. In fact, after two years of negative participation growth for most of the mainstream sports, 2011 demonstrated a turnaround in sports like tackle football, soccer, basketball, and baseball, while sports such as lacrosse, rugby, and volleyball continued to experience strong growth. Basketball leads total team participation with 26,304, 000 participants, a 9.6 percent increase from 2010. Baseball was second with 14,558,000 and soccer was third with 14,075,000. Rugby with roughly 1,130,000 participants had the single largest yearly growth of 50.7 percent

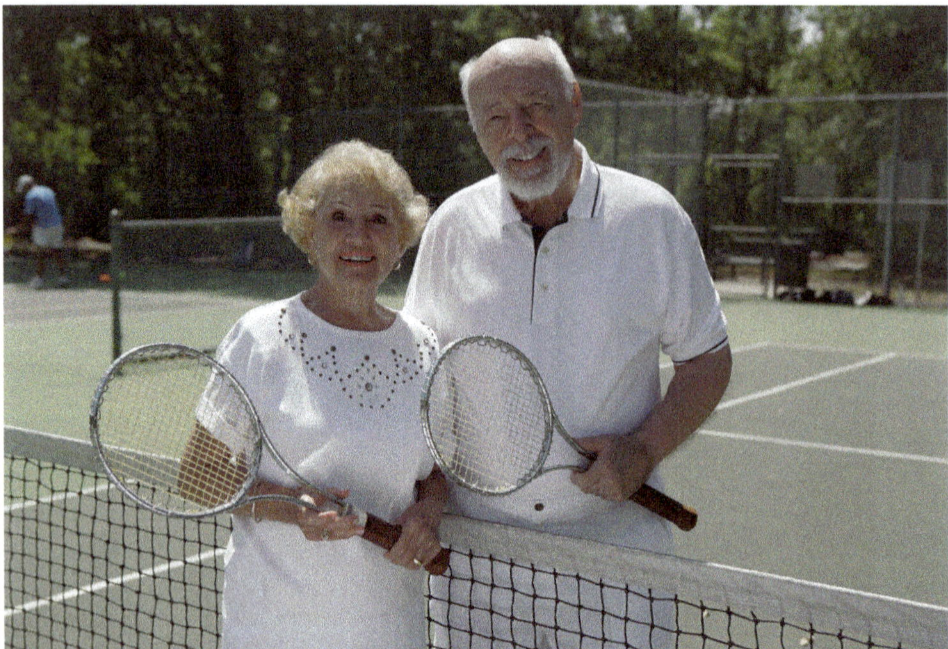

Photo 2.2 The mature market: staying young and having fun in record numbers

Source: Shutterstock.com

while lacrosse had the second most pronounced yearly growth with a 37.7 percent growth equating to 1,648,000 participants. Tackle football saw a slight growth of 1.6 percent equating to 6,905,000 participants. The declining sports included wrestling (29.9 percent), fast pitch softball (9.4 percent), and track and field (2.7 percent).

Physical environment

The **physical environment** refers to natural resources and other characteristics of the natural world that have a tremendous impact on sports marketing. For instance, the climate of a region dictates the types of sports that are watched and played in that area. In fact, various sports were developed because of the physical characteristics of a region. Skiing and hockey in the north and surfing on the coasts are obvious examples. Sports marketers attempt to control the physical environment for both spectators and sports participants. For example, Reliant Stadium has a 50/80 rule. The 50/80 rule is a guideline to help fans prepare for game day. The organization makes the roof decisions on a case-by-case basis each game by considering numerous factors, including environment and weather. The organization will consider opening the roof when game time temperature is projected to be between 50 and 80 degrees, therefore providing an optimal viewing and playing environment. The goal of the 50/80 rule is to provide the most comfortable environment possible for spectators to enjoy a Houston Texans game.

Artificial turf replaced natural grass surfaces in stadiums in the late 1960s. In the new millennium, all new stadiums being built have switched back to natural grass. Grass not only seems to be easier on the athletes in terms of avoiding potential injuries, but fans also seem to appreciate the "natural" look of grass. Likewise, domed stadiums seem to have run their (un)natural course, with Minneapolis being a rare exception.

The newer stadiums are all open-air venues, which have greater appeal for spectators. An interesting example of state-of-the-art stadium technology designed to control the physical environment is the new Cardinals Stadium in Arizona with the first roll-out playing surface. At the touch of a button, the grass field slides in and out of the stadium along 13 steel rails. The purpose of the sliding field is threefold: it eliminates indoor watering and related humidity problems; allows the field to soak up direct sunlight; and leaves behind 152,000 square feet of unobstructed floor space for things such as concerts, conventions, and expos.[31]

In addition to the climate, the physical environment of sports marketing is concerned with conservation and preserving natural resources. This trend toward conservation is most often referred to as "green marketing." Marketing ecologically responsible products and being conscious about the effects of sports on the physical environment is one of the concerns of green marketing. For instance, many golf course management groups have come under attack from environmentalists concerned about the effect of phosphate-based chemicals used in keeping golf courses green. Other groups have criticized the sport of fishing as cruel and unusual punishment for the fish.

Political, legal, and regulatory environment

Sports marketers are continually faced with **political, legal, and regulatory environments** that affect their strategic decisions. Politics have always played a major role in sports and are becoming an increasingly important part of the sports landscape. In professional sports, politicians are involved in promoting or discouraging passage of stadium tax issues. Since 1953, most stadiums have been owned by city governments. The question is, "How far does one go in sacrificing taxpayers' wealth to promote civic pride?" Additional evidence of the relationship between government and sports marketing is the growing number of sports commissions. Since 1980, the number of sports commissions, designed to attract sporting events to cities, states, or regions, has increased; in fact, the National Association of Sports Commissions has grown from 491 to more than 671 members in the past five years.[32]

The legal environment of sports has certainly taken on a life of its own in the new millennium. Sports officials (i.e., league commissioners, judges, sports arbitrators, coaches, and athletic directors) are continually confronted with legal challenges that arise on and off the playing field. These officials must be adept at interpreting the language of collective bargaining, recruiting student-athletes, understanding Title IX, avoiding antitrust issues, licensing team logos, and handling other sports law issues.

One of the most famous pieces of legislation, passed in 1972 under President Richard Nixon, was Title IX. Simply, Title IX states that "no person in the United States shall, on the basis of sex, be excluded from participation in, be denied the benefits of, or be subjected to discrimination under any education program or activity receiving Federal financial assistance." Interestingly, the law that has had the most dramatic impact on the growth of women's sports participation does not even mention the word "sports." Perhaps the most famous Title IX decision was a 1997 ruling by the U.S. Supreme Court in the *Brown University v. Cohen* case. The courts ruled that Brown University did not meet any part of the three-step Title IX compliance.

This three-part test includes the following:

1. Are opportunities for female and male athletes proportionate to their enrollment?
2. Does the school have a history of expanding athletic opportunities for the underrepresented sex?

3. Has the school demonstrated success in meeting the needs of those students?

Unfortunately, Title IX implementation has led to reduction in men's sports programs. Rather than adding women's sports programs, universities have chosen to cut men's sports such as baseball and wrestling to address the problem of proportionality.

As mentioned earlier, sports legal issues involve much more than Title IX and antitrust issues. Recent examples of sports legal issues in the news include cases of breach of contract, player-on-player/coach/fan violence, and trademark infringement. Former NBA commissioner David Stern handed down a total of $1,225 million in fines and 48 games in suspensions in the 2012–2013 season. The NBA has been a strict enforcer of policies and fines since the Pacer–Pistons brawl in 2004. In arguably the most violent fight in NBA history, with less than one minute left in the game the Indiana Pacers scuffled with the Detroit Piston players and ultimately rushed the stands, involving some drunken Detroit Pistons fans.

Due to the billions of dollars of sports-licensed merchandise sold each year, a more common form of legal issue in sport is a trademark violation. In one example, American Media, Inc. (parent company of the *National Enquirer* and *Globe*) was sued by the U.S. Olympic Committee (USOC) for using images of Olympic athletes without their consent and using the word "Olympics" in a publication entitled *Olympics USA*. Similarly, the IOC has filed a lawsuit against 1,800 Internet sites abusing the Olympic name. In yet another example, Callaway Golf recently stopped the sale of counterfeit clubs on eBay.com.

A regulatory body or agency is responsible for enacting laws or setting guidelines for sports and sports marketers. Regulatory agencies can be controlled by either governmental or nongovernmental agencies. One example of a nongovernmental regulatory body that has tremendous control over sports and sports marketing practices is the Fédération Internationale de Football Association (FIFA). FIFA is the international federation for the world's most popular sport, soccer. FIFA, which was formed in 1904, promotes soccer through development programs for youth and supervises international competition to ensure the rules and regulations of the game are being followed. In addition, FIFA is responsible for maintaining the unified set of rules for soccer called the *Laws of the Game*.

Although FIFA is concerned with regulating the game itself, it also controls many facets outside the game that have an impact on sports marketing. For example, FIFA is committed to improving stadiums for the fans and protecting them against the rising costs of attendance. Another example of FIFA's control over sports marketing is that virtual advertising – super-imposing marketing messages on the field during televised broadcasts – is forbidden.

In addition, FIFA works with ISL Marketing to secure sponsors for major soccer events, such as the World Cup. As a regulatory agency, FIFA attempts to make sure that the sponsors do not intrude in any way on the integrity of the game. FIFA does not attempt to influence how companies do their own business; however, they do their best to ensure that sponsors do not influence the game itself.

FIFA's focus is to make a difference in people's lives while creating balance and understanding of who they serve. Their mission – develop the game, touch the world, build a better future – articulates both a challenge and an opportunity. Their promise to strive for the game, for the world; reflects FIFA's emphasis and responsibility to not only promote its core product soccer, but to reach out to its world stakeholders by extending the core, using football as a symbol of hope and integration. FIFA President Joseph Blatter describes the delicate but beneficial relationship between FIFA, its consumers, and sponsors as follows: "We see it as our duty to take on the social responsibility that comes hand in hand with our position at the helm of the world's most loved sport. Join us in uniting forces to develop the game, touch the world and build a better future!"[33]

As sport continues to grow so do the regulatory and marketing concerns that affect its strategic framework. Commercial exploitation and the perceived inequalities that accompany its presence are prevalent in today's sport environment. Hence, so are the law suits that contest its framework. Governing agencies struggle to stay abreast of reform challenges. For example, in a recent landmark decision handed down on August 8, 2014, a federal judge ruled in favor of the plaintiff in the Ed O'Bannon v. NCAA antitrust case, knocking down the restrictions against college athletes profiting off their name, image and likeness. The injunction will not preclude the NCAA from implementing rules capping the amount of compensation however, the NCAA will not be permitted to set this cap below the cost of attendance. The landmark decision will have a significant impact upon the future regulatory environment and as the accompanying blogger illustrates, sanctioning bodies can often struggle to retain control.

BIG-TIME COLLEGE SPORTS IS AN OUT-OF-CONTROL MONSTER

The June 10th issue of *Sports Illustrated* had a very telling story about the state of college sports in this country. The article, titled *Go For It On Fourth and Multiply*, by Stewart Mandel and Andy Staples, highlights the mushrooming staffs of big-time college football programs in this country. For example, the University of Alabama last year employed 24 non-coaching support staff members for the football team alone. Those support staff members were paid $1.6 million. The 24 staff members, in areas such as operations, player personnel, football analysis, strength and conditioning, athletic relations, and video, are in addition to the head coach, nine assistant coaches and four graduate assistant coaches. The cost for the coaching staff is around $10 million more. Nick Saban, Alabama's head coach, is making more than $5 million a year by himself.

And I haven't even mentioned the millions of dollars going towards new or upgraded luxury locker rooms and training facilities for these programs.

Alabama brings millions of dollars of revenue in every year from television and radio contracts, ticket sales, sponsorships, etc. They're rolling in the dough, primarily because they don't have to compensate the athletes responsible for these revenue streams at anything close to their fair marketplace value.

To be sure, Alabama is far from the only school caught up in this big-time college sports arms race. Top football and basketball programs across the country are doing much the same thing. The issue at hand is do these sports operations more closely resemble pro sports enterprises (which should be taxed as such) or extracurricular activities designed to enhance the educational experience of athletically-inclined college students?

Obviously, that's a rhetorical question, yet Alabama, along with about 75 other big-time sports universities, are allowed to operate their highly-commercialized athletic departments under their school's non-profit educational institution umbrella.

The reality is, the mission of big-time college sports factories is far from the NCAA's stated purpose of integrating "intercollegiate athletics into higher education so that the educational experience of the student athlete is paramount."

"If you don't have some parameters in place, you could eventually have a football staff member for every two or three [players], and I don't think that's healthy for the industry," says Greg Byrne, University of Arizona's athletic director. Nevertheless, Arizona and other Division I colleges continue to play along, seemingly stuck in a high-stakes game of "Keeping Up With the Jones'." For their part, the NCAA is afraid to clamp down too much on this steady expansion of college sports behemoths. They're afraid if they push too hard, or penalize too much, the Alabamas, and Ohio States of the world will tell the the NCAA to take a hike, and then form their own governing body apart from the NCAA.

Where this all ends is hard to predict. But we do know that big-time college sports is filled with hypocrisy. Many NCAA administrators, college and university presidents, athletic directors, and coaches constantly talk about their educational values and the importance of 'student-athletes' getting an education. But their actions speak louder than their words. Every decision they make seems to be driven by revenue-at-all-costs and/or win-at-all-costs motives, not educational ethos.

At some point, that has to change.

– Ken Reed, Sports Policy Director, League of Fans

Source: Ken Reed; http://leagueoffans.org/2013/06/11/big-time-college-sports-is-an-out-of-control-monster/. Courtesy Ken Reed.

Demographics

Assessing the **demographic environment** entails observing and monitoring population trends. These trends are observable aspects of the population such as the total number of consumers and their composition (i.e., age or ethnic background) or the geographic dispersion of consumers. Let us look at several aspects of the demographic profile of the United States, including size of the population, age of the population, shifts in ethnic groups, and population shifts among geographic regions.

Size of the population

Currently, the world population is 7,053,112,673. The U.S. population, which is the world's third largest behind China and India, stands at over 314 million. Both are growing at a rapid pace. It is estimated that by the year 2020, the U.S. population will increase to as much as 336 million while the world population is expected to grow at a rate of roughly 76 million per year.[34] This is of special interest to marketers of sports entities who are considering expansion into international markets.

Age

Age is one of the most common variables used in segmenting and targeting groups of consumers. As such, sports marketers must continually monitor demographic shifts in the age of U.S. consumers. The "graying of America" has and will continue to exert a huge influence. Many Americans are now living into their 70s, 80s, and beyond. In fact, to date in the U.S., the growth in the number and proportion of older adults is unprecedented. Two factors – Americans are living longer lives than in previous decades and aging baby boomers encompass a proportionally larger demographic segment – combine to impact this growth. By 2030, older adults will account for roughly 20 percent of the U.S. population, doubling the population of Americans aged 65 years to about 72 million. In 2030, when the last baby boomer turns 65, the demographic landscape of our nation will have changed significantly, hence one of every five Americans – about 72 million people – will be an older adult. By 2050, it is anticipated that Americans aged 65 or older will number nearly 89 million people, more than double the number of older adults in the United States in 2010.[35]

Studies show that by the year 2015, mature adults will make up almost 25 percent of the entire population; this number will grow even larger to comprise nearly 89 million people or one-third of the population by the year 2050. This means that in about 50 years, one out of every three Americans will be 55 years of age or older, more than double the number of adults in 2010.[36] Apparently, with new technological advances bringing about breakthroughs in medicine, a lower mortality rate, and preventive approaches to health, Americans are living longer.

Moreover, the 79-million-strong baby boom generation has already entered midlife and will soon age. In fact, if you add 65 years to January 1, 1946 you get January 1, 2011; therefore, the retirement age of the baby boomer has arrived. Four out of every 10 adults in the United States are baby boomers. In 2012, baby boomers ranged from 48 to 66. Also of significance is the baby bust generation (children of baby boomers) that follows in the wake of its parental tidal wave. In 2012, there were an estimated 20.23 million children under five years of age, compared with the 16 million in 1980.[37]

Shifts in ethnic groups

The United States has been called a melting pot because of its diversity and multiethnic population providing promise that all immigrants can be transformed into Americans, forging a new alloy built upon freedom, civic responsibility, and the crucible of democracy. Today, the number of white Americans is diminishing. Immigrants today come not from Europe but overwhelmingly from Asia and Latin America and account for 60 percent of the nation's population growth in the last decade. According to the U.S. Census Bureau, the Hispanic population increased by 15.2 million between 2000 and 2010, accounting for over half of the 27.3 million increase in total population. Today, roughly 45 percent of American children under the age of five belong to minority groups. By 2050, non-Hispanic whites will account for only 54 percent of the U.S. population. In terms of sheer size, just over 102 million people represent either the African American, Asian, or Hispanic ethnic groups. All three of these ethnic groups have rising income levels, which translate into more purchasing power.[38] Although all minority groups are growing, the fastest-growing segment has been Hispanics. Hispanic buying power is expected to reach $1.3 trillion by 2015.[39] The next fastest-growing minority was Asian Americans, who represent 14.4 million people. African Americans remain the second largest minority group, with nearly 38 million people and $572 billion in annual buying power.

These ethnic groups are important subcultures that share a portion of the larger (white) American culture, but also have unique consumption characteristics. There

MLB FORMS DIVERSITY COMMITTEE

NEW YORK -- Major League Baseball has created a task force that will study how to increase diversity in the game, especially among black players.

Commissioner Bud Selig announced the committee Wednesday.

In less than a week, baseball will celebrate the 66th anniversary of Jackie Robinson breaking the color barrier. A new movie titled "42" focuses on the Hall of Famer.

The 18-member committee includes representatives from club ownership, the players' union, minor league and college baseball, the MLB scouting bureau and other areas. Hall of Famer Frank Robinson and former major league manager Jerry Manuel are among the members.

MLB says about 8.5 percent of players on this year's opening day rosters identified themselves as African-American or black. That's around half the number from the mid-1970s through the mid-1990s.

"As a social institution, Major League Baseball has an enormous social responsibility to provide equal opportunities for all people, both on and off the field," Selig said in a statement.

Tampa Bay Rays owner Stuart Sternberg and Detroit Tigers president Dave Dombrowski will help run the committee. Southern University coach Roger Cador, Chicago White Sox executive vice president Ken Williams, MLB senior vice president of baseball operations Kim Ng, union official and former big leaguer Tony Clark and Arizona Diamondbacks president Derrick Hall are among the other members.

MLB runs the Reviving Baseball in Inner Cities (RBI) program and has seven Urban Youth Academies that are either running or are in development.

"I am proud of the work we have done thus far with the RBI program and the MLB Urban Youth Academies, but there is more that we must accomplish," Selig said.

"We have seen a number of successful efforts with existing MLB task forces, and I believe we have selected the right people to effectively address the many factors associated with diversity in baseball," he said.

Source: Associated Press; URL: http://espn.go.com/mlb/story/_/id/9158114/mlb-forms-task-force-study-how-increase-diversity. Used with permission of Bloomberg L.P.

are a number of benefits in developing a marketing mix that appeals to specific ethnic groups. The accompanying article describes how Major League Baseball has recognized the value of ethnic marketing tactics.

Population shifts

The latest count of the U.S. population highlighted that the demographic center of gravity continued to shift away from the Northeast and Midwest. Through 2020, the greatest population shift will be evident in the South and West. More than one-third of the total United States population is projected to reside in the South during the years 1995 to 2025. In fact, the South will be the most populous region during the next 30 years. Over the next 30 years the West is projected to grow nearly twice the r average. The Northeast and Midwest are expected to grow at half of the U.S.

While the nation's population grew approximately 10 percent in 2010, the faste gains occurred in the South (14.3 percent) and West (13.8 percent). Texas has g by approximately 4.3 million people in the last decade, where Houston and Dall Fort Worth accounted for more than half of the State's growth. Other Southern stars included Florida, with the third largest increase, Georgia fourth, North Carolina fifth, and Arizona the sixth. By percentage, rather than actual numbers, Nevada was the fastest growing Western state in the last decade. Interestingly in the Midwest, the only state which had a declining population in the last decade was Michigan. South Dakota was found to be the fastest growing state in the Midwest which grew by 7.9 percent. In the Northeast, New Hampshire had the region's largest percentage increase for the fifth straight decade, growing 6.5 percent. New York and New Jersey posted the highest numeric gains in the Northeast, gaining 401,645 and 377,544 respectively.[40]

There is no definitive explanation for this shift, although some believe it is due to the previously discussed aging of America or the growth of employment opportunities in these areas. Keep in mind that, until 1957 when the Brooklyn Dodgers moved to Los Angeles, there were no Major League Baseball teams west of St. Louis.

Along with exploring population shifts by state, sports marketers must assess the dispersion of people within an area. Are people moving back to urban areas, or is the "flight to the suburbs" still occurring? The 2000 and 2010 censuses showed the greatest growth to be in suburban areas. There are still fewer people living in or moving back to the central city. These measures of population dispersion are having an impact on where new professional teams are locating and where new stadiums are being built.

The economy

The economic environment is another important but uncontrollable factor for sports marketers to consider. Economic factors that affect sports organizations can be described as either macroeconomic or microeconomic elements. A brief explanation of each follows.

Macroeconomic elements

Economic activity is the flow of goods and services between producers and consumers. The size of this flow and the principal measure of all economic activity is called the gross national product (GNP). The business cycle, which closely follows the GNP, is one of the broadest macroeconomic elements. The four stages of the business cycle are as follows:

- ***Prosperity*** – The phase in which the economy is operating at or near full employment, and both consumer spending and business output are high.
- ***Recession*** – The downward phase, in which consumer spending, business output, and employment are decreasing.
- ***Depression*** – The low phase of the business cycle, in which unemployment is highest, consumer spending is low, and business output has declined drastically.
- ***Recovery*** – The upward phase when employment, consumer spending, and business output are rising.

Each cyclical phase influences economic variables, such as unemployment, inflation, and consumers' willingness to spend. Decisions about the strategic sports marketing process are affected by these fluctuations in the economy. Ticket sales may boom during times of economic growth. In addition, the growth period may have an even greater impact on corporate demand for luxury boxes and season tickets. If the country is in either a recession or a depression, consumers may be reluctant to purchase nonessential goods and services such as sporting goods or tickets to sporting events. Mistakenly, the sports industry sometimes seems to operate under the "ignorance is bliss" philosophy when it comes to the economy. As Steve Wilstein points out, "salaries for athletes kept rising, TV deals soared, and ticket prices spiraled ever upward as if the leagues were living in their own fantasyland, immune to economic cycles."[41] Although Wilstein believes the sports that are hardest hit by the economy are those already on the periphery (e.g., the Women's Professional Bowling Tour), even the major sports are hit hard by a poor economy.

Although the relationship between the purchase of sporting goods and tickets to sporting events is likely to be associated with good economic times, this may not always be the case. During a recession or depression, sports may serve as a rallying point for people. Consumers can still feel good about their teams, even in times of economic hardship. This is one of the important, but sometimes neglected, societal roles of sport.

Microeconomic elements

Whereas **macroeconomic elements** examine the big picture, or the national income, **microeconomic elements** are those smaller elements that make up the big picture. One of the microelements of concern to sports marketers is consumer income level. As economist Paul Samuelson points out, "Mere billions of dollars would be meaningless if they did not correspond to the thousand and one useful goods and services that people really need and want."[42] Likewise, having sports products would be meaningless if consumers could not afford to purchase them. A primary determinant of a consumer's ability to purchase is income level.

Consumer income levels are specified in terms of gross income, disposable income, or discretionary income. Of these types of income, discretionary is of greatest interest to sports marketers. This is the portion of income that the consumer retains after paying taxes and purchasing necessities. Sports purchases are considered a non-necessity and, therefore, are related to a consumer's or family's discretionary income. According to a new analysis by The Conference Board, slightly more than half (51 percent) of American households have some discretionary income they can spend on non-necessities.[43] In addition, the number of families with discretionary income is expected to rise slightly over the next decade.

Sports advocates argue that new stadia and consumer spending on sports support local economic growth. The local economic benefits from a major professional sports team are typically derived from four major sources of spending: (1) attendance (tickets and parking) at the games; (2) concession items sold at the games such as food and merchandise; (3) spending before and after the events for other consumption items such as meals; and (4) taxes paid to local government on spending for the previous three categories. Others argue that spending on sport has little impact and that professional sport is an economic drain. The following quote summarizes this notion.

> People have a limited amount of discretionary income. They may use it on attendance at professional sporting events. In the absence of pro sports, they will spend the money elsewhere – lower-level sporting events, the movies, etc. The same is true for large corporations. If they don't buy sky boxes, they will entertain their clients elsewhere

(i.e., restaurants). Sports facilities generate very few jobs. For a local economy, player management (and that may come from outside) and low-level game day employment (vendors, etc.. . .). A modest factory or a small research facility has far more impact.[44]

Monitoring the external contingencies

As discussed, external contingencies are dynamic, and sports marketers must keep abreast of these continually changing influences. A systematic analysis of these external factors is the first step taken by sports marketers using the contingency framework. In addition, as the sports industry becomes more competitive, one of the keys to success will be identifying new market opportunities and direction through assessing the external contingencies. The method used to monitor the external contingencies is known as environmental scanning.

Environmental scanning

An outward-looking, environmental focus has long been viewed as a central component of strategic planning. In fact, it has been argued that the primary focus of strategic planning is "to look continuously outward," to have foreseeability, and to keep the organization in step with the anticipated changes in the external environment. This process of monitoring external contingencies is called environmental scanning. More formally, **environmental scanning** is a firm's attempt to continually acquire information on events occurring outside the organization so it can identify and interpret potential trends.[45]

A sports organization can do several things to enhance its environmental scanning efforts. First, the organization can identify who will be responsible for environmental scanning. The only way to move beyond the pressures of daily business activities is to include environmental scanning responsibilities in the job description of key members of the organization.

Second, the organization can provide individuals conducting the environmental scan with plenty of information on the three Cs: customers, competition, and company. Your scanners cannot correctly monitor the environment without having a solid base of information about the following: customer expectations and needs; the strengths, weaknesses, distinctive competencies, and relative market positioning of the competition; and the strengths, weaknesses, distinctive competencies, and relative market positioning of your own company – as well as the major developmental opportunities that await exploitation.

Third, the organization can ensure integration of scanned information through structured interactions and communication. All too often, information needed to recognize new market opportunities is identified but never gets disseminated among the various functional areas. That is, marketing, finance, and operations may all have some information, or pieces to the puzzle, but unless these individuals share the information, it becomes meaningless. Organizations with the most effective environmental scanning systems schedule frequent interactions among their designated scanners.

Fourth, the organization can conduct a thorough analysis of ongoing efforts to improve the effectiveness of environmental scanning activities. This systematic study consists of evaluating the types of scanning data that are relevant and available to managers. This focus on previous environmental scanning efforts can often lead to the identification of new market opportunities.

Fifth, the organization can create a culture that values a "spirit of inquiry." When an organization develops such a spirit, it is understood that the environmental scanning process is necessary for success. In addition, it is understood that environmental scanning is an ongoing activity that is valued by the organization.

Environmental scanning is an essential task for recognizing the external contingencies and understanding how they might affect marketing efforts. However, there are two reasons why environmental scanning practices may fail to identify market opportunities or threats. First, the primary difficulty in effectively scanning the environment lies in the nature of the task itself. As scanning implies, sports marketers must look into the future and predict what will likely take place. To make matters even more difficult, these predictions are based on the interaction of the complex variables previously mentioned, such as the economy, demographics, technology, and so on. Second, predictions about the environment are based on data. Sports marketers are exposed to enormous amounts of data and only with experience can individuals selectively choose and correctly interpret the "right data" from the overwhelming mass of information available to them.

Assessing the internal and external contingencies: SWOT analysis

To this point, we have looked at both the external and internal contingencies. To guide the strategic sports marketing process, an organization conducts a SWOT analysis. SWOT is an acronym for strengths, weaknesses, opportunities, and threats. The strengths and weaknesses are controllable factors within the organization. In other words, a firm must evaluate its strengths and weaknesses based on the internal contingencies. The opportunities and threats are assessed as a result of the external contingencies found in the marketing environment. These elements may be beyond the control of the sports organization.

The strategic sports marketing process must first examine its own internal contingencies. These internal strengths and weaknesses include human resources, financial resources, and whether organizational objectives and marketing goals are being met with the current marketing mix. Products and services, promotional efforts, pricing structure, and methods of distribution are also characterized as either strengths or weaknesses.

After assessing the organizational strengths and weaknesses, the firm identifies external opportunities and threats found in the marketing environment. As discussed earlier in the chapter, sports marketing managers must monitor the competition; demographic shifts; the economy; political, legal, and regulatory issues; and technological advances. Each of these external factors may affect the direction of the strategic marketing process.

The intent of conducting a SWOT analysis is to help sports marketers recognize or develop areas of strength capable of exploiting environmental opportunities. When sports marketers observe opportunities that match a particular strength, a strategic window is opened. More formally, **strategic windows** are limited periods of time during which the characteristics of a market and the distinctive competencies of a firm fit together well and reduce the risks of seizing a particular market opportunity. For example, IMG, a leading sports and entertainment marketing company, has created "IMG X Sports" to capitalize on the growing popularity in extreme and lifestyle sports and IMG College to capitalize on the growing popularity of college sports. In addition

Ad 2.2 NCAA capitalizes on the new opportunities based on the growth in women's sports.

Source: NCAA © National Collegiate Athletic Association, 2012

to capitalizing on strengths, sports marketers develop strategies that eliminate or minimize organizational weaknesses.

At this stage, you should have a broad understanding of how each of the external contingencies may affect your marketing plan. Table 2.3 provides a common list of questions to consider when developing the opportunities and threats (OT) portion of your SWOT analysis.

Table 2.3 Assessing external contingencies

1. Social – What major social and lifestyle trends will have an impact on the sports participants or spectators? What action has the firm been taking in response to these trends?
2. Demographics – What impact will forecast trends in size, age, profile, and distribution of population have on the firm? How will the changing nature of the family, the increase in the proportion of women in the workforce, and changes in ethnic composition of the population affect the firm? What action has the firm taken in response to these developments and trends? Has the firm reevaluated its traditional sports products and expanded the range of specialized offerings to respond to these changes?
3. Economic – What major trends in taxation and in income sources will have an impact on the firm? What action has the firm taken in response to these trends?
4. Political, Legal, and Regulatory – What laws are now being proposed at federal, state, and local levels that could affect the strategic marketing process? What recent changes in regulations and court decisions have affected the sports industry? What action has the firm taken in response to these legal and political changes?
5. Competition – Which organizations are competing with us directly by offering a similar product? Which organizations are competing with us indirectly by securing our customers' time, money, energy, or commitment? What new competitive trends seem likely to emerge? How effective is the competition? What benefits do our competitors offer that we do not?
6. Technological – What major technological changes are occurring that affect the sports organization and sports industry?

Summary

Chapter 2 provides an overview of the contingency framework for the strategic sports marketing process. Although there are many ways to think about constructing a sports marketing plan, it is best to lay a foundation that is prepared for the unexpected. The contingency framework is especially useful for sports marketers because of the complex and uncertain conditions in which the sports organization operates. The unexpected changes that occur over the course of a season or event may be positive or negative. The changes that occur may be either controllable or uncontrollable events that affect the sports organization. The contingency framework includes three major components: the internal contingencies, the external contingencies, and the strategic sports marketing process. Uncontrollable occurrences are typically in the marketing environment and are referred to as external contingencies, whereas internal contingencies are within the control of the organization (sometimes beyond the scope of the marketing function). The heart of the contingency framework is the strategic sports marketing process, which is defined as the process of planning, implementing, and controlling marketing efforts to meet organizational goals and satisfy consumers' needs.

Internal contingencies, thought of as managerial, controllable issues, include the vision and mission of the sports organization, organizational objectives and marketing goals, organizational strategies, and organizational culture. The vision and mission of the sports organization guide the strategic sports marketing process by addressing questions such as: What business are we in? Who are our current customers? What is the scope of our market? How do we currently meet the needs of our customers? The organizational objectives and marketing goals stem from the vision and mission of the sports organization. The objectives of the organization are long term and sometimes unquantifiable. Alternatively, marketing goals are short term, measurable, and time specific. It is extremely important to remember that the marketing goals are directly linked to decisions made in the strategic sports marketing process. Another internal contingency that influences the strategic sports marketing process is organizational strategy. The organizational strategy is how the sports organization plans on carrying out its vision, mission, objectives, and goals. There are four different levels of strategy development within the organization. These include corporate-level strategies, business-level strategies, functional-level strategies, and operational-level strategies. Marketing is described as a functional-level strategy. The operational-level strategies such as pricing and promotion must fit the broader strategic sports marketing process. A final internal contingency is the organizational culture or the shared values and assumptions of organizational members that shape an identity and establish preferred behaviors in an organization.

The external contingencies that affect the strategic sports marketing process include competition; technology; cultural and social trends; physical environment; political, legal, and regulatory environment; demographic trends; and the economy. As with any industry, understanding competitive threats that exist is critical to the success of all sports organizations. Competition for sporting events and sports organizations comes in many forms. Typically, we think of competition as being any other sporting event. However, other forms of entertainment are also considered competitive threats for sports organizations. Technological forces represent another external contingency. Advances in technology are changing the way that consumers watch sports, play sports, and receive their sports information. Cultural and social trends must also be carefully monitored. Core values, such as individualism, youthfulness, and the need for belonging, can have an impact on the target markets chosen and how sports products are positioned to spectators and participants. The physical environment, such as the climate and weather conditions, is another external contingency that can have a tremendous influence on the success or failure of sporting events. Another of the uncontrollable factors is the political, legal, and regulatory environment. Proposed legislation, such as the banning of all tobacco advertising and sponsorship at sporting events, could have a tremendous impact on the motor sports industry. Demographic trends are another critical external contingency that must be monitored by sports marketers. For instance, the graying of America will bring about changes in the levels of participation in sports and the types of sports in which the "mature market" will participate. Finally, economic conditions should be considered by sports marketers. Sports marketers must monitor the macroeconomic elements, such as the national economy, as well as microeconomic issues, such as the discretionary income of consumers in the target market.

Because the marketing environment is so complex and dynamic, sports marketers use a method for monitoring external contingencies called environmental scanning. Environmental scanning is the sports organization's attempt to acquire information continually on events occurring outside the organization and to identify and interpret potential trends. Sports marketers must continually monitor the environment to look for opportunities and threats that may affect the organization.

External and internal contingencies are systematically considered prior to the development of the strategic marketing process. The process that many organizations use to analyze internal and external contingencies is called a SWOT analysis. SWOT is an acronym for strengths, weaknesses, opportunities, and threats. The strengths and weakness are internal, controllable factors within the organization that may influence the direction of the strategic sports marketing process. For example, human resources within the organization may represent strengths or weaknesses within any organization. However, the opportunities and threats are uncontrollable aspects of the marketing environment (e.g., competition and the economy). The purpose of conducting a SWOT analysis is to help sports marketers recognize how the strengths of their organization can be paired with opportunities that exist in the marketing environment. Conversely, the organization may conduct a SWOT analysis to identify weaknesses in relation to competitors.

Key terms

- competition
- contingency framework for strategic sports marketing
- control phase
- cultural values
- culture
- demographic environment
- direct competition
- economic activity
- environmental scanning
- external contingencies
- goal
- implementation phase
- indirect competition
- internal contingencies
- macroeconomic elements
- market selection decisions
- marketing environment
- marketing mix
- microeconomic elements
- objectives

- organizational culture
- organizational strategies
- physical environment
- planning phase
- political, legal, and regulatory environment
- strategic sports marketing process
- strategic windows
- technology
- vision

Review questions

1. Describe the contingency framework for strategic sports marketing. Why is the contingency approach especially useful to sports marketers?
2. Outline the strategic marketing process, and comment on how it is related to the external and internal contingencies.
3. Define the marketing environment. Are all elements of the marketing environment considered uncontrollable? Why or why not?
4. What is environmental scanning? Why is environmental scanning so important? Who conducts the environmental scan, and how is one conducted?
5. Define competition. What are the different types of competition?
6. How has technology influenced the sports marketing industry? Discuss how "out-of-market" technology benefits sports spectators.
7. Identify several cultural and social trends in our society and describe their impact on sport and sports marketing.
8. What are the core American values, and why are they important to sports marketers?
9. How does the physical environment play a role in sports marketing? How can sports marketers manipulate or change the physical environment?
10. Define the political and regulatory environment. Cite several examples of how this can influence or dictate sports marketing practices.
11. Describe the different demographic trends of interest to sports marketers. How will these demographic trends influence the strategic marketing process?
12. Differentiate between macro- and microeconomic elements. Which (macro- or microelements) do you feel plays an important role in sports marketing? Why?
13. How can sports marketers assess the external environment? What are some sources of secondary data that may assist in understanding the current and future external environment?

Exercises

1. Interview the marketing manager of a local college or professional sports organization and develop a list of the uncontrollable factors that were unexpected throughout the last season.
2. Interview the marketing manager of a sporting goods retailer or sports organization about the company's strategic sports marketing process. Ask how the external and internal contingencies affect planning.
3. Find two sports organizations that, in your opinion, have effective mission and vision statements. How do they promote these statements and how are they reflected in the organization?
4. Describe all the ways the changing marketing environment will have an impact on NASCAR racing. How should NASCAR prepare for the future?
5. Your university's athletic program has a number of competitors. List all potential competitors and categorize

what type of competition each represents.

6. Find examples of how technology has influenced the sporting goods industry, a professional sports franchise, and the way spectators watch a sporting event. For each example indicate the technology that was used prior to the new technology.
7. Develop advertisements for athletic shoes that reflect each of the core American values discussed in this chapter.
8. Interview five international students and discuss the core values used by sports marketers in their culture. Do these values differ from the core American values? For example, do the British value individualism more or less than Americans? What evidence do the students have to support their claims?
9. How does the physical environment of your geographic area or location play a role in sports marketing?
10. Describe how changing demographic trends have led to the development of new sports leagues, the shifting of professional sports franchises, and new sports products. Provide three specific examples of each.

Internet exercises

1. Experience a portion of any sporting event via Internet broadcast. What did you enjoy the most about this experience, and what could be done to improve this technology?
2. Find three sports products on the Internet that stress technological innovation. Do the companies communicate their technological advantages differently?
3. Search the Internet for articles or sites that discuss the pros and cons of the banning of tobacco advertisements at sporting events.
4. Go to the Internet and find census data to support what sports fans in 2020 might look like from a demographic perspective.

Endnotes

1 Rick Burton and Dennis Howard, "Recovery Strategies for Sports Marketers: The Marketing of Sports Involves Unscripted Moments Delivered by Unpredictable Individuals and Uncontrollable Events," *Marketing Management*, vol. 9, no. 1 (Spring 2000), 43.

2 W. Richard Scott, *Organizations: Rational, Natural, and Open Systems* (Upper Saddle River, NJ: Prentice Hall, 1987), 87–89.

3 Bernard J. Mullin, Stephan Hardy, and William Sutton, *Sport Marketing* (Champaign, IL: Human Kinetics Publishers, 1993), 16.

4 "Under Armour Mission," Under Armour. Available from: http://www.uabiz.com/company/mission.cfm, accessed July 6, 2010.

5 "Kent State Intercollegiate Athletics Mission Statement and Objectives," Kent State University. Available from: http://www.kentstatesports.com/athleticDepartment/missionStatement, 2012.

6 Nike Mission Statement. Available from: http://www.nike.com/nikebiz/nikebiz.jhtml?page=4.

7 Maloof Family Information. Available from: http://www.arcoarena.com/default.asp?lnopt=4&pnopt=0.

8 Scott Rosner, "Team Ownership Could Fade with Comcast–NBC Universal Deal," *Sports Business Journal* (March 2010).

9 "Food for Thought: Dodgers Offer All-You-Can-Eat Seats," *The Associated Press State & Local Wire* (January 12, 2007).

10 Nielsen, 2014, *Year in Sports Media Report 2013* (February 2). Available from: http://www.nielsen.com/us/en/reports/2014/year-in-the-sports-media-report-2013.html.

11 Sam Mamudi, "Study Shows Sports TV Success," *SportsWatch* (January 24, 2012).

12 Ken Kerschbaumer, "Battle for College Sports Fans," *Broadcasting & Cable* (March 14, 2005) p. 23; "First and Ten for a TV Upstart," *Business Week* (December 18, 2006) p. 48.

13 Shank, M. D., and Verderber, K., 1999, "Understanding the Nature of Sports Competition," International Conference on Sport & Society, Marquette, MI, June.

14 NASCAR.com. "NASCAR Digital Media Records Historic Day." Available from: http://www.nascar.com/en_us/news-media/articles/2014/2/24/nascar-digital-media-records-historic-day.html, released February 24, 2014; accessed February 28, 2014.

15 "Top 15 Most Popular Websites," *The eBusiness* (February 2012).

16 Ken Kerschbaumer, "Cornhusker Fans Surf for Tackles," *Broadcasting and Cable* (August 28, 2000).

17 Rich Heldenfels, "Watching TV is Different Experience Today," *Akron Beacon Journal* (February 2012).

18 Bill King and Eric Fisher, "A Secondary Look at Ticketing: Teams Face a Secondary Market that has Redefined the Ticket Business: Like it or Loathe it, it's the World They Helped Create," *Sports Business Journal* (October 2011).

19 Eric Fisher, "Numbers Game," *Sports Business Journal* (September 27, 2010).

20 "Golf Company Featured on the Golf Channel," *Market Wire* (November 21, 2006), E21.

21 "Textronics Expands into UK with NuMetrex Clothes That Monitor the Body," *Business Wire* (September 12, 2006).

22 Wesley Cropp, "Shoes Going Very High Tech," *The Daily Iowan* (July 19, 2006).

23 Blog Maverick, The Mark Cuban WebLog. Available from: http://blogmaverick.com/, accessed February 25, 2014.

24 "Cisco and Athletics Announce Cisco Field; State-of-the-Art Technology to Take Fan Experience to New Level" (November 14, 2006). Available from: http://newsroom.cisco.com/dlls/2006/corp_111406.html?CMP=ILC-001&POSITION=SEM&COUNTRY_SITE=us&CAMPAIGN=HN&CREATIVE=STADIUM&REFERRING_SITE=GOOGLE&KEYWORD=null.

25 Jeremy Repanich, "Top 5 Technologies in NFL Stadiums," *Popular Mechanics* (2011).

26 "Twelve Baseball Parks to Use MasterCard PayPass Technology This Season," (September 27, 2006). Available from: http://www.finextra.com/fullpr.asp?id=11531.

27 "Essential Facts about the Computer and Video Game Industry," 2006, Entertainment Software Association. Available from: http://www.theesa.com/archives/files/Essential%20Facts%202006.pdf.

28 Chris Morris, "Average Vidgamer Older, More Affluent," *Technology News* (June 2010).

29 "2013 Sales and Usage Data, Essential Facts About the Computer and Gaming Industry," Entertainment Software. Available from: http://www.theesa.com/facts/pdfs/esa_ef_2013.pdf, accessed February 25, 2014.

30 Sport and Fitness Industry Association, 2013. SFIA US Trends in Team Sports Report, Silver Springs, MD, 2013.

31 Scott Wong, "New-Age Stadium Is on a High-Tech Roll," *The Arizona Republic* (August 10, 2006).

32 *NASC Playbook 2013*, National Association of Sports Commissions, December. Available from: http://issuu.com/nasc92/docs/playbook_dec13_final_hires, accessed June 17, 2014.

33 "For the Good of the Game," 1996, FIFA. Available from: http://www.fifa.com/aboutfifa/federation/mission.html.

34 http://www.census.gov/population/pop-profile/dynamic/PopDistribution.pdf.

35 *The State of Aging and Health in America 2013*, National Center for Chronic Disease Prevention and Health Promotion Division of Population Health, Department of Health and Human Services, Washington, DC. Available from: http://www.cdc.gov/features/agingandhealth/state_of_aging_and_health_in_america_2013.pdf, accessed June 17, 2014.

36 Ibid.

37 U.S. Census Bureau, 2013, *State and Country Quick Facts*. Available from: http://quickfacts.census.gov/qfd/states/00000.html, accessed June 17, 2014.

38 "Minorities Getting Closer to the Majority," *CNN* (May 11, 2006). Available from: http://www.cnn.com/2006/US/05/10/hispanics/index.html.

39 Shannon Bryant, "Hispanic Buying Power Projected to Reach $1.3 Trillion in 2015," *Marketing Forecast* (January 2010).

40 Teresa Burney, "Go West . . . and South: A Shift in US Population," *Builder Magazine* (April 2011).

41 Steve Wilstein, "Think the NBA Can't Go Belly Up? Think Again," *Associated Press*, (September 26, 2003). Available from: http://news.mysanantonio.com.

42 Paul A. Samuelson, *Economics*, 10th ed. (New York: McGraw Hill, 1976).

43 Lynn Franco, *The Marketers Guide to Discretionary Income* (The Conference Board Inc., New York, NY, November, 2007).

44 Brian Reich, "Baseball and the American City" (April 30, 2001). Available from: http://www.stadiummouse.com/stadium/economic.html.

45 Matthew D. Shank and Robert A. Snyder, "Temporary Solutions: Uncovering New Market Opportunities in the Temporary Employment Industry," *Journal of Professional Services Marketing*, vol. 12, no.1 (1995), 5–17.

PART II

Planning for Market Selection Decisions

CHAPTER 3

Research tools for understanding sports consumers

After completing this chapter, you should be able to:

- Discuss the importance of marketing research to sports marketers.
- Explain the fundamental process for conducting sports marketing research.
- Identify the various research design types.
- Describe the process for questionnaire development.
- Understand how to prepare an effective research report.

As the following RailCats, Scarborough Sports Marketing, Sponsorship Research and Strategy (SRS), IEG, Taylor (NASCAR), ESPN, and sponsorship ROI studies illustrate, marketing research is a fundamental tool for understanding and ultimately satisfying customers' needs. As described in Chapter 1, one way of demonstrating a marketing orientation is to gather information used for decision making. Another way of establishing a marketing orientation is to disseminate information and share the marketing information with those responsible for making decisions. Marketing research is viewed as an essential element in marketing-oriented organizations.

The information gathered through marketing research can be as basic as where consumers live, how much money they make, and how old they are. Research also provides information for decision makers in identifying marketing opportunities and threats, segmenting markets, choosing and understanding the characteristics of target markets, evaluating the current market positioning, and making marketing mix decisions.

More specifically, marketing research may provide answers to questions such as the following:

- What new products or services would be of interest to consumers of sport?
- What do present and potential consumers think about our new ad campaign?
- How does the advertising and promotion mix affect purchase decisions?
- What are the latest changes or trends in the sport marketplace?
- How are consumers receiving sports information and programming?
- What are sports fans spending, and what are they buying?
- Who are the biggest sponsors of professional sports leagues or college sports?
- How interested are fans in my team, my players, and in the sport itself?
- How do consumers perceive my team, league, or event relative to competitors?
- What is the best way to promote my sports product or service?
- Who participates in sports, and in what sports are they participating? Also, where are they participating, and how often?
- Are current consumers satisfied with my sports products and services? What are the major determinants of customer satisfaction?
- What price are consumers willing to pay for my sports product or service?
- What image does the team, player, or event hold with current consumers and potential consumers?

MARKETING RESEARCH IN ACTION: THE GARY SOUTHSHORE RAILCATS

Since their inception the Gary Southshore RailCats have utilized market research to enhance the strategic planning and business success of the organization. The Southshore RailCats, currently a member of the modern American Association of Independent Professional Baseball, conducted a detailed study prior to their first official game to gather information that would guide the planning phase of their strategic marketing process. At the time, under the ownership of Victory Sports Group LLC., CEO Mike Tatoian and with the assistance of former General Manager Roger Wexelberg, the Southshore RailCats were able to successfully combine the power of sports and grass roots marketing to provide an exciting and memorable experience while adding to the quality of life in Northwest Indiana. The RailCats' mission is to provide Northwest Indiana with an exceptional level of fun, affordable family entertainment in a safe and enjoyable atmosphere. To ensure that fans received this opportunity the organization sought to identify and determine if marketing services and investment opportunities were of an investment scale to which a capable private operator under a contractual agreement set-forth can achieve economic success. The goal of the RailCats organization was to offer marketing/sponsorship of such services and facilities at a reasonable cost to the consumer public, therefore validating rights fee expenditures. A self-administered survey of area consumers (N=1034) served as the primary data collection instrument to examine the identified research objectives. The survey was segmented into seven categories: interest levels, awareness, attendance/purchase characteristics, media/entertainment choices, level of importance, fan characteristics, and demographics. The intention of the research was to assist the Southshore RailCats to make informed decisions consistent with common organizational goals. In addition, the study was designed to look at how survey responses differed according to fan demographics. For instance, are males more likely than females to attend a RailCats game in the future?

Some of the contents of the survey included information specific to:

- I am planning to attend a RailCats game this coming season.
- I am more likely to a attend a game on a weekend than weekday
- I prefer to attend games that have promotional give-aways
- The quality of play will influence my attendance to a RailCats game
- The RailCats organization is actively involved in the community
- Which of the following best describes with whom you may attend a RailCats game?
- If available, would you purchase a mini season ticket plan for the upcoming XXXX season?
- Please identify the number of games you would prefer to purchase.
- Please rank from most likely to least likely the following items that may influence your attendance to a RailCats game (day of game, fireworks, opponent, premium giveaways, theme nights)
- Please rank preference of media sources for information of local sports teams
- What is your zip code?
- What is your gender?
- What year were you born?

Source: Center for Sport Recreation and Tourism Development, KSU /Gary Southshore RailCats Feasibility Study.

These are just a few of the questions that may be addressed through marketing research. As the following press release highlighting research conducted by Scarborough Sports Marketing (2012) illustrates, sport and entertainment organizations utilize a variety of research techniques to assess consumer behaviors. The following narrative of market research conducted by Scarborough Research illustrates the varying demographics of Major League Baseball.

HITTING A HOME RUN WITH THE DIGITAL GENERATION

NEW YORK (April 3, 2012) – The Major League Baseball (MLB) season has already opened in Japan with Seattle and Oakland, and fans (view infographic) are excited for MLB opening day here in the States on April 4, when the defending champions, the St. Louis Cardinals, visit the Miami Marlins at their brand new stadium. Scarborough Sports Marketing, a consumer marketing firm specializing in sports and fan insights, defines "Fans" as American adults who say they are "very, somewhat or a little bit" interested in a given sport. "Avid Fans" are American adults who say they are "very" interested in a given sport.

According to the new Scarborough Sports Marketing study, nearly half (49%, 115M) of all American adults are MLB Fans and 15% (36M) are Avid Fans. The study also reveals that there is ample opportunity to turn young fans into lifelong MLB enthusiasts as 44% of Generation Y is MLB Fans and 13% is Avid Fans.*

"Generation Y makes up 20% of the American adult population – that's 46 million people," says Bill Nielsen, Vice President of Sales for Scarborough Sports Marketing. "Major League Baseball, MLB teams and advertisers understand how critical it is to continue to reach out to this younger demographic in an effective and efficient way, to build long-term affinity for the sport."

Almost a third (30 percent) of Gen Y MLB Fans are willing to spend $25–49 on a single game MLB ticket and 12% are interested in purchasing season tickets. Gen Y MLB Fans are also 37% more likely than all MLB Fans to have bought MLB apparel with a team logo in the past 12 months. Retail spaces also offer an opportunity for fan outreach as more than half (56%) of Gen Y MLB Fans shopped at a sporting goods store in the past three months.

Where can Gen Y MLB Fans be reached? They are 54% more likely than all MLB Fans to have used a mobile device to read a newspaper in the past 30 days, 84% more likely to have listened to internet radio in the past 30 days and 22% more likely than all MLB Fans to typically watch reality TV. Gen Y MLB Fans are more than twice as likely as all MLB Fans to have visited Twitter in the past 30 days, 59% more likely to have read or contributed to a blog in the past 30 days and 68% more likely to watch video clips online in the same time period. Gen Y MLB Fans are 131% more likely than all MLB Fans to have visited Hulu.com in the past 30 days and 65% more likely to have visited YouTube.com in the same time frame.

"Generation Y is so active on Twitter and Facebook that any modern marketing campaign is incomplete without a social component," continues Nielsen. "With youthful initiatives like the MLB Fan Cave in New York City and increased social media efforts, the league, teams and advertisers can reach younger audiences in the spaces where they are most engaged."

Gen Y MLB Fans can also be found participating in a variety of different athletic and entertainment activities. Gen Y MLB Fans are twice as likely as all MLB Fans to have played soccer, football or basketball in the past 12 months and 66% more likely to have played softball or baseball in the same time frame. They are also twice as likely to have attended an R&B/Rap/Hip-Hop concert and 49% more likely to have visited a comedy club in the past year.

Gen Y MLB Fans are 23% more likely than all MLB Fans to be Black/African American and 83% more likely to be Hispanic. The top local markets for Gen Y MLB Fans are Milwaukee (76% of Gen Y are MLB fans); Philadelphia (70%); Hartford, C.T. (66%); St. Louis (66%) and Albany, N.Y. (62%).

DMA	% of Gen Y MLB Fans
Milwaukee	76
Philadelphia	70
Hartford, C.T.	66
St. Louis	66
Albany, N.Y.	62
Boston	61
Cincinnati	60
Syracuse, N.Y.	57
Providence, R.I.	57
Minneapolis	57

Looking at the two teams that play in the season opener, Gen Y makes up 21% of the total St. Louis population and 18% of the Miami population. 72% of Gen Y St. Louis residents watched, attended or listened to a Cardinals game in the past year and 36% of Gen Y Miami residents watched, attended or listened to a Marlins game in the same time period.

Top Local Markets for Gen Y MLB Fans

*Scarborough defines the different American generations as Generation Y (age 18–29), Generation X (30–44), Baby Boomers (45–64) and the Silent Generation (65+).

Continue the dialogue with Scarborough Sports Marketing over Twitter by reaching out to @ScarbSports or @ScarboroughInfo using hashtag #OpeningDay and

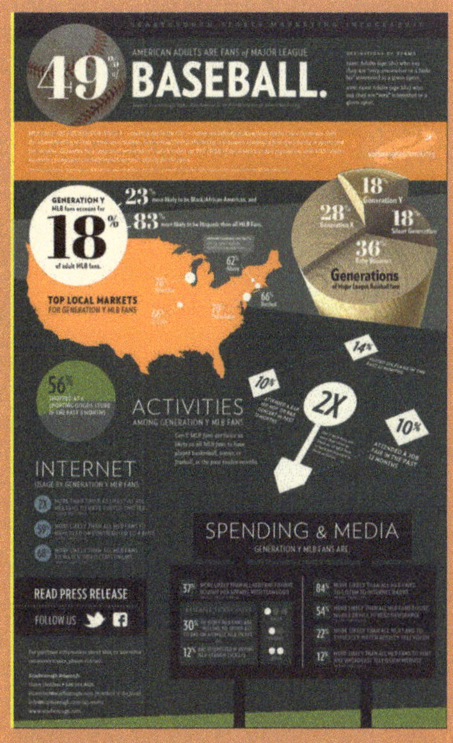

be sure to visit us on Facebook at https://www.facebook.com/ScarboroughSports.

This data is from Scarborough USA+ 2011 Release 2. Scarborough measures 210,000 adults aged 18+ annually across a wide variety of media, lifestyle, shopping and demographic categories.

If you are interested in additional Scarborough Sports Marketing reports, please contact Brad Sherer, 480.659.7395/Brad.Sherer@scarborough.com.

About Scarborough Sports Marketing

Scarborough Sports Marketing (www.scarboroughsportsmarketing.com, sports@scarborough.com) measures local and national consumer and lifestyle information by interviewing over 210,000 adults (18+) in 77 Top-Tier Markets, including all professional sports markets. Scarborough sports measurements include fan avidity; multi-media measures including sports viewing *and listening; corporate sponsorship information including fans' shopping and product/service usage; and leisure activities. Scarborough delivers twice-yearly updates of its local market reports to a diverse client base, spanning all major media, advertisers and their agencies. Scarborough Sports Marketing is a division of Scarborough Research, which is a joint venture between Arbitron Inc. and The Nielsen Company.*

Contact: Haley Dercher, 646.654.8426 / HDercher@Scarborough.com

Source: Rightsholder: Scarborough USA 2012; http://www.prnewswire.com/news-releases/hitting-a-home-run-with-the-digital-generation-145950285.html.

Marketing research as defined by the American Marketing Association (2004/2014) is: the process or set of processes that links the consumers, customers, and end users to the market through information – information used to identify and define marketing opportunities and problems; generate, refine, and evaluate marketing actions; monitor marketing performance; and improve understanding of marketing as a process. Marketing research specifies the information required to address these issues, designs the method for collecting information, manages and implements the data collection process, analyzes the results, and communicates the findings and their implications. More specifically, **sports marketing research** is the systematic process of collecting, analyzing, and reporting information to enhance decision making throughout the strategic sports marketing process.

Three key issues emerge from this definition. First, marketing research must be systematic in its approach. Systematic research is both well organized and unbiased. The well-organized nature of good research depends on adherence to the marketing research process, which is discussed later in this chapter. Researchers must also be careful not to make up their minds about the results of a study prior to conducting it; therefore, researchers must conduct the study in an unbiased manner.

Second, the marketing research process involves much more than collecting data and then reporting them back to decision makers. The challenge of research lies in taking the data collected, analyzing them, and then making sense of the data. Marketing researchers who can collect data, dump them in the computer, and spit out reports are a dime a dozen. The most valuable marketing researcher is the person who has the ability to examine the data and then make recommendations about how the information should be used (or not used) in the strategic marketing process.

Third, the importance of marketing research is found in its ability to allow managers to make informed decisions. Without the information gathered in research, management decision making would be based on guessing and luck. As Woody Hayes, Ohio State's legendary football coach, once said about the forward pass, "Three things can happen and two of them are bad!"

Finally, the definition states that marketing research is useful throughout the entire strategic sports marketing process. Traditionally, the focus of marketing research has been on how the information can be used in better understanding consumers during the planning phase of the strategic sports marketing process. It is also important to realize that marketing research is relevant at the implementation and control phases of the strategic marketing process. For example, research is used in the control phase to determine whether marketing goals are being met.

The marketing research process

As previously mentioned, marketing research is conducted using a systematic process, or the series of interrelated steps shown in Figure 3.1. Before we discuss each step in the research process in greater detail, two points should be kept in mind. First, the basic framework or process for conducting marketing research does not change, although every marketing research problem will be different. For example, the Detroit Red Wings may engage in research to understand fan satisfaction or the effectiveness of a between-period promotion. Each of these research questions is different. However, the basic marketing research process used to address each question is the same.

Second, you should understand that the steps of the research process are interdependent. In other words, defining the problem in a certain way will affect the choice of research design. Likewise, selecting a certain type of research design will influence the selection of data collection tools. Let us now examine each of the steps in the research process.

Defining the problem or opportunity

The first and most important step of the marketing research process for sports marketers is to define the problem or opportunity. **Problem definition** requires the researcher to specify what information is needed to assist in either solving problems or identifying opportunities by developing a **research problem statement**. If the research addresses the correct problem or opportunity and seeks to properly define the problem or opportunity, then the project could be successful. However, the data collected may be useless if they are not the information needed by the sports marketing manager.

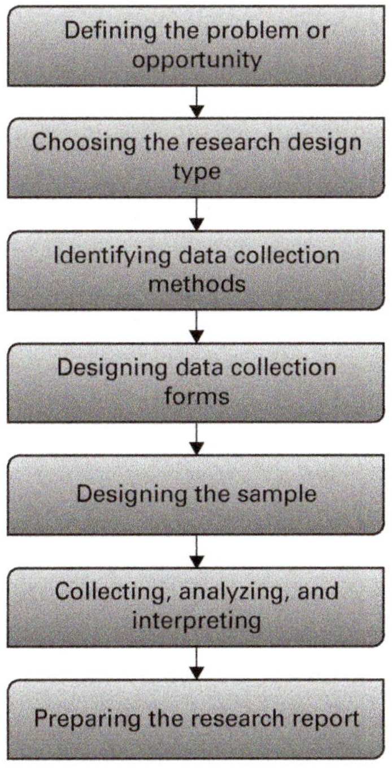

Figure 3.1 Marketing research process

Table 3.1 Issues addressed at initial research meeting

• A brief background or history of the organization or individual(s) requesting the research
• A brief background of the types of research the organization has done in the past, if any
• The information the organization wants and why (i.e., what they plan to do with the information once it is obtained)
• The targeted population of interest for this research
• The expectations in terms of the timeframe for the research and costs of conducting the study

How does the researcher identify problems or opportunities that confront the sports organization? Initially, information is gathered at a meeting between the researcher and his or her client. In this meeting, the researcher should attempt to collect as much information as possible to better understand the need for research. Table 3.1 shows a list of the typical questions or issues addressed at the first information-gathering meeting. Keep in mind that the ultimate goal of these meetings is to ensure that there is a clear understanding between the researcher and the decision makers as to the nature and role of the research and how it relates back to the need for information in the decision-making process.

Research objectives

Based on this initial meeting, the researcher should have collected the proper information to develop a set of research objectives; guidelines that establish an agenda of research activities necessary to implement the research process. **Research objectives** describe the various types of information needed to address the problem or opportunity. Each specific objective will provide direction or focus for the rest of the study.

Here is an example of the research objectives developed for the NASCAR Sponsorship Study conducted by Sponsorship Research and Strategy (SRS).[1] The purpose of the study was to provide information that would assist NASCAR sponsors in planning, evaluating, and justifying their NASCAR sponsorships. More specifically, the research objectives were as follows:

- Identify the benefits associated with NASCAR sponsorships.
- Record fan preferences for sales promotions.
- Identify lucrative market segments among NASCAR fans.
- Develop an extensive profile of NASCAR fans.
- Examine fan attitudes toward NASCAR and NASCAR sponsors.
- Analyze sponsorship effectiveness for different types of NASCAR sponsorships (e.g., car vs. league).
- Provide a comparative basis for sponsorship performance among NASCAR Nextel Cup drivers.
- Provide a comparative basis for sponsorship performance among official NASCAR sponsors in selected product categories.

How would NASCAR or any sports entity go about measuring whether these objectives have been reached? The accompanying article describes this growing concern as it relates to sponsorship ROI. As the IEG narrative illustrates, to not define evaluation tools in accordance with objectives measures and/or the failure to analyze research outcomes completely can be more dangerous than not measuring at all.

CASE STUDY
A sponsorship measurement solution

COMPLEX CHALLENGES REQUIRE NEW TOOLS

Sponsorship's impact is not one-dimensional. A partnership's ability to meet its goals depends on a series of interconnected variables.

Marketers long ago recognized that the sponsorship equation is not a simple one. They responded by reinventing the way they activate and execute partnership programs, developing big new ideas and using the latest technology to make sponsorships more relevant and engaging.

But when it comes to measurement, evaluation tools have not kept up with the pace of change. As the case study on the following pages shows, well-intentioned attempts that don't ask the right questions, or fail to analyze research outputs completely, can be more dangerous than not measuring at all, as they lead to false deductions and wrong decisions.

It also reveals that the solution does not need to be invented, merely applied.

First, brands must incorporate deep knowledge of how sponsorship works in shaping perceptions and driving changes in attitude and behavior into each step, ensuring the right partnership is targeted to the right group and activated in the right ways.

Second, marketing science—which already determines results for traditional media campaigns—must be applied to close the loop and determine ROI. The metrics, models and analyses used by brands to determine the effectiveness of their advertising can be adapted and scaled for partnerships of all types, including sports, entertainment, events and causes.

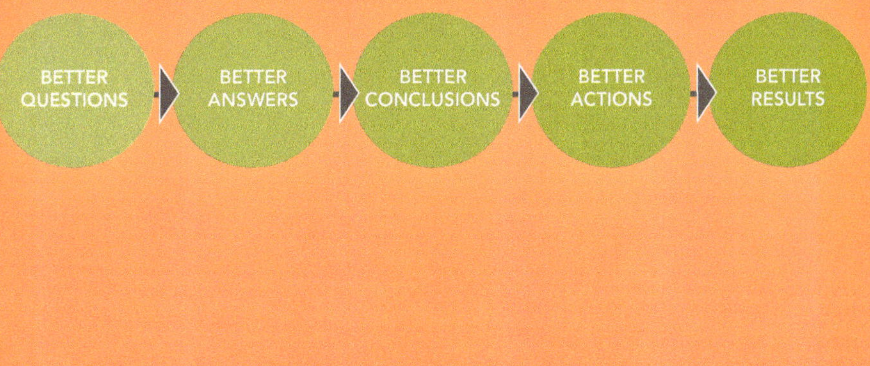

MAKING THE RIGHT DECISIONS

IEG Consulting engaged with a premium whiskey brand that was in the middle of a multi-year auto racing sponsorship to determine how the investment was performing against multiple objectives and whether it was delivering ROI. Chief among the brand's goals: acquiring one million new consumers.

In the process of gathering the necessary data to model the brand's return, the full picture of the program emerged, revealing that if true accountability and smart analytics had been incorporated from the start, the brand's objectives, execution and results would have been dramatically different.

AUDIENCE

The brand made its initial decision to sponsor motorsports based on research that showed a high percentage of whiskey drinkers among fans of the sport.

A deeper dive into the purchasing habits and lifestyles of racing fans revealed that they were much more likely to purchase non-premium brands and drank whiskey only on special occasions. In direct opposition to the sponsor brand's positioning, they were more likely to drink whiskey as a shot or mixed with soft drinks.

If the brand had the right data at the start, it could have targeted its racing efforts to build loyalty among the niche audience of its consumers to be found in the suites and skyboxes at race tracks instead of trying to convert the fans in the grandstands.

MEDIA VALUE

Broadcast reports showed that the brand received significant exposure during telecasts of races. Translating impressions into advertising equivalencies showed a 2:1 return vs. the sponsorship fee.

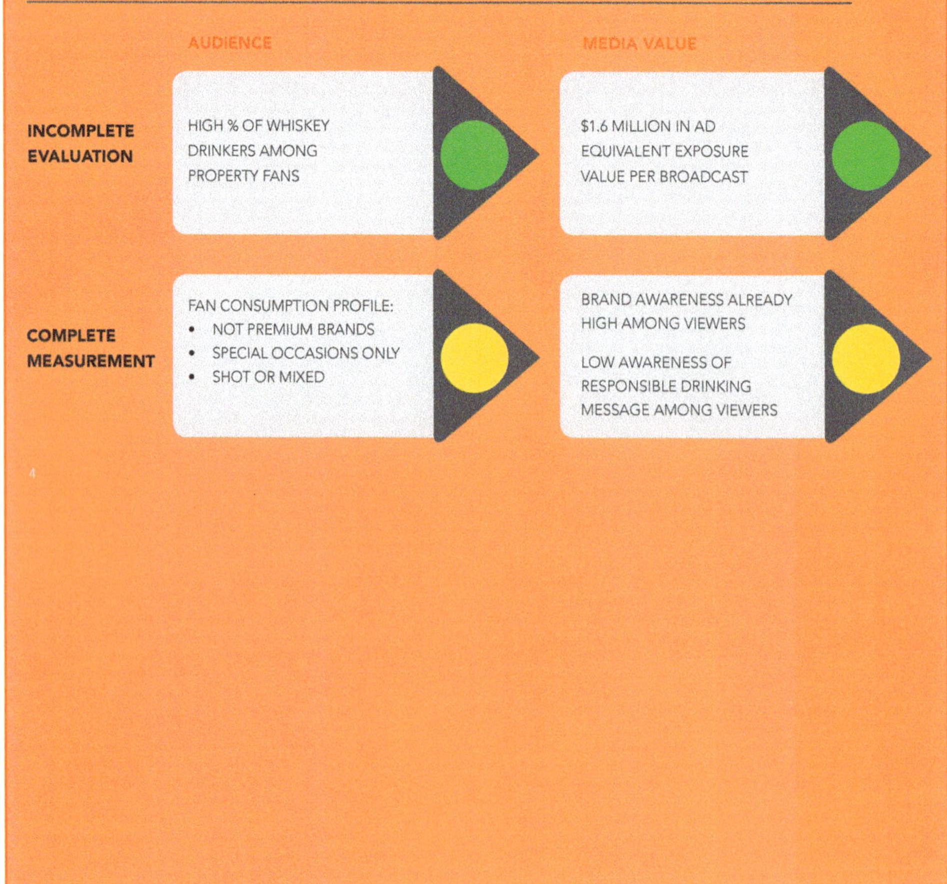

However, analysis of survey research determined that little to no awareness was generated for the responsible drinking campaign that was a focal point of the brand's messaging through signage and on-car exposure and a key goal of the sponsorship. The broadcasting of an already well-known brand name was not a primary objective.

SURVEY RESEARCH

Sixteen waves of pre- and post-race research were conducted in key markets. On the surface, a number of outputs indicated positive movement as a result of exposure to the sponsorship, including higher awareness of retail and on-premise activity and increased likelihood of associating the brand with key image attributes and benefits.

Applying historical insights from sponsorship research that indicate a greater impact with current consumers vs. non-consumers, IEG's analysis determined that this pattern repeated itself here: There was virtually no increase in awareness of promotions or positive brand associations among consumers of competitive brands. Additionally, research into activity among two other whiskey brands that also were racing sponsors indicated better results for the competitors.

ROI

Finally, survey results showed an increase in intent to purchase the brand. Additionally, the brand's overall sales increased during the term of the sponsorship.

But when modeling was applied to the drivers of business, it was clearly determined that the sponsorship was not among them. These sophisticated analytics were able to show the client that it had acquired only 10,000 new customers—not one million—as a result of its racing program.

SURVEY RESEARCH

PERCEIVED BRAND BENEFITS HIGHER AMONG FANS VS. NON-FANS

INCREASED AWARENESS OF RETAIL AND ON-PREMISE PROMOTIONS VS. BRAND AVERAGE

NO INCREASE AMONG CONSUMERS OF OTHER WHISKEY BRANDS

INCREASES NOT AS POSITIVE AS COMPETITOR BRANDS' RESULTS

ROI ANALYSIS

INCREASED INTENT TO PURCHASE AMONG SURVEY RESPONDENTS

OVERALL SALES INCREASE FOR BRAND

ONLY 10,000 NEW CONSUMERS VS. 1 MILLION GOAL

SPONSORSHIP ROI NOT AS HIGH AS OTHER MARKETING EFFORTS

LINKING SPONSORSHIP INVESTMENTS WITH BUSINESS RESULTS

Marketing science applications such as the ROI modeling used in the spirits brand case study are typically thought of in the context of traditional media campaigns. But leading brands are putting these analytics to work for partnerships ranging from six-figure single-market deals to nine-figure global platforms.

More marketers will follow suit as the accountability bar continues to rise. Nearly two-thirds of CMOs say that ROI—the direct impact of expenditures on business results—will be the primary measure of marketing effectiveness by 2015.*

Sponsorship—because it delivers true engagement—is poised to claim a better seat at the marketing table, but only if it can demonstrate its contributions to the enterprise. But measuring multifaceted engagement rather than one-dimensional reach and evaluating the complex ecosystem of sponsorship—with its ability to impact multiple audiences—requires at least the same level of data, rigor and analysis that is used to assess the other tools in the marketing arsenal.

This is not as daunting as it may sound. The techniques and analytic approaches of marketing science have become much more accessible and are flexible to the amount of data available. Much of the data needed to develop meaningful models and analyses is routinely captured by companies in the course of business.

Brands that have already taken this step know how their sponsorship investments are performing and how to make them work better.

In addition, their partnerships have gained a place in the strategic planning process, alongside other elements of the marketing mix rather than isolated and an afterthought. And, these brands are fostering better partnerships with rightsholders through a shared, fact-based understanding of the value exchange and what is needed for both to succeed.

Brands that don't take this step will see sponsorship budgets reduced in favor of marketing communications that can prove their value.

*IBM Global CMO Study, October, 2011

6

Source: From "A Sponsorship Measurement Solution," IEG October, 2011. Ukman, L. and Krasts, M.; http://www.sponsorship.com/ieg/files/07/07903e35-98d1-4f1c-b318-7524b3104222.pdf. Credit: IEG.

Table 3.2 Marketing research proposal outline

Background and History
Defining the Problem or Opportunity
Research Objectives
Research Methodology
a. Sample
b. Procedures
c. Topical areas
Time Estimate
a. Design of instrument
b. Data collection
c. Data entry
d. Data analysis
e. Final report preparation
Cost Estimate

Writing a marketing research proposal

To ensure agreement between the researcher and the client on the direction of the research, a research proposal is developed. A **research proposal** is a written blueprint that describes all the information necessary to conduct and control the study. The elements of the research proposal include background for the study; research objectives based on the need for the research, research methodology, timeframe, and cost estimates. An outline for developing a research proposal is shown in Table 3.2.

Choosing the research design type

Once the researcher is certain that the problem is correctly defined, the research design type is considered. The **research design** is the framework for a study that collects and analyzes data. Although every study is unique and requires a slightly different plan to reach the desired goals and objectives, three research design types have emerged: exploratory, descriptive, and causal designs. The type and nature of the design is highly dependent upon desired outcomes. Whatever research design or designs are ultimately chosen, it is important to remember the crucial principle in research is that the design of the research should stem from the problem.[2]

Exploratory designs

Exploratory designs are useful when research problems are not well defined. For instance, the general manager for the RailCats may say that ticket sales are down, but he is unsure why. In this case, an exploratory research design would be appropriate because there is no clear-cut direction for the research. The research is conducted to generate insight into the problem or to gain a better understanding of the problem at hand. For example, the researcher may recommend examining minor league baseball attendance trends or conducting one-on-one interviews with team management to determine their ideas about the lack of attendance. Because exploratory research design types address vague problems, a number of data collection techniques are possible. These data collection techniques will be addressed during the next phase of the research process.

Descriptive designs

If the research problem is more clearly defined, then a descriptive design is used. A descriptive design type describes the characteristics of a targeted group by answering questions such as who, what, where, when, and how often. The targeted group or population of interest to the decision maker might be current season ticket holders, people in the geographic region who have not attended any games, or a random group of people in the United States.

The RailCats study used a descriptive research design. The targeted group in this case was fans who may potentially attend RailCats home games. Characteristics of the group of interest in the study included where the fans were coming from (geographic area), how often they attended games, when they were most likely to attend games (weekends, weekdays, day, or evening), and demographics (age, race, and gender).

In addition to describing the characteristics of a targeted group, descriptive designs show the extent to which two variables differ or correlate. For example, a researcher may want to examine the relationship between game attendance and merchandising sales. Using the RailCats example, researchers wanted to understand the relationship between age of the fans and likelihood of attending games in the future. A descriptive research design type would allow us to examine the relationship or correlation between these two variables (age and future attendance).

If a positive relationship were found between age and likelihood of attending games in the future, then the older you get, the more likely you would be to attend future RailCats games. That is, as the age of the fan increases, the likelihood of going to future games also increases (see Figure 3.2a). However, a negative relationship means that as age increases, the likelihood of going to games decreases (see Figure 3.2b). Knowing the shape of this relationship will help the RailCats marketers make decisions on whom to target and how to develop the appropriate marketing mix for this group. What do you think the relationship between age and attendance would look like?

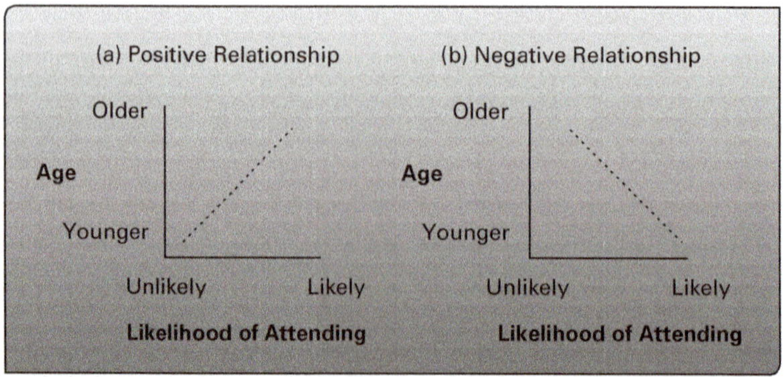

Figure 3.2 Descriptive research designs

Causal designs

Using a descriptive design, we can explore the relationship between two variables, such as age and likelihood of attending games in the future. However, what this does not tell us is that age causes the likelihood of attending to either increase or decrease. This can only be determined through a causal design.

Causal designs are useful when problems are very clearly defined. More specifically, causal designs examine whether changing the level of one variable causes the level of another variable to change. This is more commonly called a cause-and-effect relationship.

In an example of a causal design, the Southshore RailCats could conduct a study to determine whether varying the level of advertising on a local radio station has any effect on attendance. In this case, level of advertising is the independent variable and attendance is the dependent variable. The **dependent variable** is the variable to be explained, predicted, or measured (i.e., attendance). The **independent variable** is the variable that can be manipulated or altered in some way (i.e., level of advertising or perhaps whether to advertise at all).

To show cause-and-effect relationships, three criteria must be satisfied. The first criterion for causality is that the occurrence of the causal event must precede or be simultaneous to the effect it is producing. Using our example, advertising must precede or occur at the same time as the increase in attendance to demonstrate a cause-and-effect relationship.

The second criterion for causality involves the extent to which the cause and the effect vary together. This is called **concomitant variation**. If advertising expenditures are increased, then season ticket sales should also increase at the same rate. Likewise, when advertising spending is decreased, season ticket sales should also decline. Keep in mind, however, that concomitant variation does not prove a cause-and-effect relationship, but it is a necessary condition for it.

A third criterion used to show causal relationships requires the elimination of other causal factors. This means that another variable or variables may produce changes in the dependent variable. This possibility is called a spurious association or spurious correlation. In the dynamic sports marketing environment, it could be difficult to isolate and eliminate all possible causal factors. For instance, an increase in attendance may be due to the success of the team, ticket prices, and addition of other promotions (e.g., bobblehead night) rather than increased advertising. A researcher must attempt to eliminate these other potential factors, hold them constant, or adjust the results to remove the effects of any other factors.

Identifying data collection techniques

As with the previous steps in the research process, decisions regarding data collection techniques are very much a function of problem definition and research design type. If the research problem is loosely defined and requires an exploratory research design, then there are more alternatives for collecting that information. However, for well-specified problems using a causal design, the choice of data collection techniques decreases dramatically.

Data collection techniques can be broadly categorized as secondary or primary. **Secondary data** refer to data that were collected earlier but are still related to the research question. These data may come from within the sports organization or from outside the organization. For example, useful internal secondary data might include a history of team merchandise sales figures, event attendance figures, or fan satisfaction studies that were conducted previously. External secondary data, or data from outside the organization, may come from any number of the sources presented later in this chapter.

Although a researcher should always try to use existing data before conducting his or her own inquiries, it is sometimes impossible to find data relevant to the problem at hand. In that case, research must turn to the other data collection alternative, primary data. **Primary data** are information gathered for the specific research question at hand.

Before turning our discussion to the various types of primary and secondary data, it is important to note that both types of data are useful in understanding consumers. For example, sports marketers from the Chicago Bears may want to look at trends in merchandising sales for each NFL team before undertaking a study to determine why their sales have decreased. In this case, secondary data are a useful supplement to the primary data they would also need to collect.

Secondary data

As just mentioned, secondary data may be found within the sports marketing organization (internal secondary data) or from outside sources (external secondary data). External secondary data can be further divided into the following categories:[3]

- Government reports and documents
- Standardized sports marketing information studies
- Trade and industry associations
- Books, journals, and periodicals

Government reports and documents

As we discussed in Chapter 2, environmental scanning is an essential task for monitoring the external contingencies. Government reports and documents are excellent sources of data for sports marketers exploring the marketing environment. Government sources of data can provide demographic, economic, social, and political information at the national, state, and local levels. This information is generally abundant and can be obtained at no cost. There are thousands of government sources that are useful for environmental scanning. In fact, many are now published on the Internet. Let us look at a few of the most useful sources of government data.

Bureau of the Census of the U.S. Department of Commerce (www.census.gov)

The Bureau of the Census is one of the most comprehensive sources of secondary data that are readily available via the Internet. Here are some of the census documents that may be of interest: Census of Population, Census of Retail Trade, Census of Service Industries, and Census of Manufacturing Industries.

The Statistical Abstract of the United States (www.census.gov/compendia/statab/)

The *Statistical Abstract of the United States*, which is published each year by the Bureau of the Census, is an excellent place to begin a search for secondary data. In

Photo 3.1 The growing number of women's sport participants is being monitored through secondary marketing research.

Source: Elissa Unger

addition to more general statistical information on the population and economy, the *Statistical Abstract* has a section entitled "Parks, Recreation and Travel." Within this section, statistics can be found on both participants and spectators.

Chambers of Commerce

Usually, Chambers of Commerce have multiple sources of demographic information about a specific geographic area, including education, income, and businesses (size and sales volume). This type of information can be helpful to sports marketers conducting research on teams or events within a metropolitan area.

Small Business Administration (SBA) (www.sba.gov)

SBA-sponsored studies can be a valuable source for the environmental scan. The sources include statistics, maps, national market analyses, national directories, library references, and site selection.

Standardized sports marketing information studies

Although government sources of secondary data are plentiful, they are generally more useful for looking at national or global trends in the marketing environment. Standardized sports marketing information studies, such as the ESPN Sports Poll or the Sports Business Research Network (www.sbrnet.com), focus more specifically on sports consumers and markets. In fact, these sources of secondary data can provide extremely specialized information on consumers of a specific sport (e.g., golf) at a specific level of competition or interest (avid golfers). Table 3.3 shows the table of contents for a standardized study available for better understanding the golf market in North America.

Table 3.3 North American Golf Report table of contents

Executive summary
Golf supply
• Golf supply
• Golf supply by country
• Population per holes
Golf development
• Development by country
• Golf course openings
• Recent golf course openings
• New openings by state
Golf participation
• Participation by country
• Participation by state
• Number of golfers by state
Regional breakdown of supply, growth and participation in golf related goods
• Imports and exports by country

Source: http://www.golf-research-group.com/reports/report/22/content.html.

Table 3.4 Standardized sports marketing information studies

Team Marketing Report's Sports Sponsor Factbook
Team Marketing Report's Stadium Signage Report
Team Marketing Report's Inside the Ownership of Professional Sports Team
IEG's Sponsorship Report
IEG's Intelligence Reports
Sports & Media Challenges Sports Sponsorship Survey
National Sporting Goods Manufacturers' Sports Media Index
National Sporting Goods Manufacturers' Country Market Research Studies
American Sports Data's American Sport Analysis Reports
National Golf Foundation's Golf Business Publications
Gallup Poll's Sports Participation Trends
Simmons Market Research Bureau's Study of Media and Market. Sports and Leisure
ESPN Chilton Sports Poll
Yankelovich Monitor Sports Enthusiast Profile

These studies are called standardized because the procedures used to collect the information and the types of data collected are uniform. Once the information is collected, it is then sold to organizations that may find the data useful. Although the data collected are more specific than other sources of secondary data, the data may still not directly address the research question. Table 3.4 shows a sampling of the standardized sources of secondary data that may be useful to sports marketers.

Trade and industry associations

There are hundreds of associations that can be helpful in the quest for information. Sports associations range from the very broad in focus (e.g., NCAA) to the more specific (e.g., National Skating Suppliers Association). For example, the Women's Sport Foundation (www.womenssportsfoundation.org), established in 1974 by Billie Jean King, works to improve public understanding of the benefits of sports and fitness for females of all ages. To support this educational objective, the foundation has a number of publications and research reports that serve as excellent sources of secondary data. In fact, the Women's Sport Foundation now has a cyberlibrary that contains 40 plus years of information gathered on topics and issues such as business, coaching, ethics, gender equity, history, homophobia, leadership and employment, media, medical, participation, sexual harassment, special needs, and training and fitness. Here is just a small sampling of trade and sport associations:

American Marketing Association
European Association for Sport Management
Institute of Sport and Recreation Management
National Association of Sports Commissions
National Collegiate Athletic Association
National Sporting Goods Association
North American Society for Sport Management
Sport Management Association of Australia and New Zealand
Sport Marketing Association
Sports & Fitness Industry Association (formerly, SGMA)

Books and journals

A comprehensive list of journals related to sport follows the books listed here.

Books

IEG's Complete Guide to Sponsorship
Sport Marketing (Mullins, Hardy, & Sutton)
Sport Marketing: A Strategic Perspective (Shank & Lyberger)
Sport Marketing (Pitts and Stotlar)
Sport Marketing (Fullerton)
Sport Marketing: Canadian (O'Reilly)
Sport & Entertainment Marketing (Kaser)
Team Marketing Report's Newsletter
Cases in Sport Marketing (Donovan)
Cases in Sport Marketing (McDonald and Milne)
Case Studies in Sport Marketing (Pitts)
Developing Successful Sports Marketing Plans (Stotlar)
Sports Marketing: Global Marketing Perspectives (Schlossberg)
Sports Marketing: It's Not Just a Game Anymore (Schaaf)
Sports Marketing: Famous People Sell Famous Products (Pemberton)
Sports Marketing: The Money Side of Sports (Pemberton)
Sports Marketing/Team Concept (Leonardi)
The Elusive Fan: Reinventing Sports in a Crowded Marketplace (Rein, Kotler, and Shields)
Marketing of Sport (Chadwick and Beech)
Team Sports Marketing (Wakefield)
Keeping Score: An Inside Look at Sports Marketing (Carter)
Ultimate Guide to Sport Marketing (Graham, Neirotti, and Goldblatt)
Sports Marketing: Managing the Exchange Process (Milne and McDonald)

Academic journals of interest to sports marketers

European Sport Management Quarterly
International Journal of Sport Management, Recreation and Tourism
International Journal of Sports Marketing and Sponsorship
Journal of Advertising
Journal of Services Marketing
Journal of Sport & Tourism
Journal of Sport and Social Issues
Journal of Sport Behavior
Journal of Sport Management
Journal of Sport Tourism
Sports Business Journal
Sport Management Review
Sport Marketing Quarterly
The Journal of Intercollegiate Athletics
The Journal of Sport

Primary data

Data collected specifically to answer your research questions are called **primary data**. There are a wide variety of primary data collection techniques. Again, remember that your method of collecting primary data depends on your earlier choice of research design. Let us look briefly at some of the primary data collection methods and their pros and cons.

Depth interviews

Depth interviews are a popular data collection technique for exploratory research. Sometimes called "one-on-ones," depth interviews are usually conducted as highly unstructured conversations that last about an hour. *Unstructured* means that the researcher has a list of topics that need to be addressed during the interview, but the conversation can take its natural course. As the respondent begins to respond, new questions may then emerge that require further discussion.

Web 3.1 Sport Business Research is an excellent source of primary and secondary data.

Source: www.SBRNET.com

The primary advantage of depth interviews is that they gather detailed information on the research question. Researchers may also prefer depth interviews to other primary methods when it is difficult to coordinate any interface with the target population. Just think of the difficulty in trying to organize research using professional athletes as the target population. For instance, a sports marketing researcher may want to determine what characteristics a successful athlete-endorser requires. To address this research question, depth interviews may be conducted with professional athletes who have been successful endorsers, athletes who have never endorsed a product, brand managers of products being endorsed, or any other individuals who may provide insight into the research question. The responses given in these interviews then would be used to determine the characteristics of a successful endorser.

Depth interviews may also be appropriate when studying complex decision making. For example, researchers may want to find out how others influence your decision to attend a sporting event. The information gathered in the depth interviews at the initial phase of this research may then be used in the development of a survey or some other type of primary research. In yet another example, depth interviews were used in a study to understand the decision-making process used by corporate sponsors.[4]

Focus groups

Another popular exploratory research tool is the focus group. A **focus group** is a moderately structured discussion session held with eight to ten people. The discussion focuses on a series of predetermined topics and is led by an objective, unbiased moderator. Much like depth interviews, focus groups are a qualitative research tool used to gain a better understanding of the research problem at hand. For instance, focus groups may be useful in establishing a team name or logo design, deciding what food to offer for sale in the concession areas, determining how best to reposition an existing sporting goods retailer or learning what kinds of things would

Photo 3.2 Focus groups

Source: Shutterstock.com

attract children to a collegiate sporting event. Let us look at two examples of sports organizations that have used focus groups.

In 2010, a project to determine if public funding was supported by taxpayers for a new Minnesota Vikings stadium was commissioned by the Metropolitan Sports Facilities Commission, the agency that owns and operates the 28-year-old Metrodome. The commission utilized five focus groups conducted in various cities; each group was between nine and eleven participants who were identified as potential November voters, not big sports fans, and not following the Vikings stadium debate. Results show that participants would approve a variety of funding mechanisms including openness to a statewide sales tax.[5] In another example, as part of their off-season efforts to improve their team and their public image, the Mets have cut single-game ticket prices by an average of 14 percent, an attempt to increase revenues and coax spectators back to Citi Field. The team's season-ticket, ticket-plan, and group-ticket holders will receive an additional 10 percent discount. David Howard, the Mets executive vice president of business operations, said after conducting in-season market research and holding focus groups with fans, the Mets decided to make these price adjustments. "Largely what we're doing here is a result from the feedback we've received from our customers," he said. "We feel we are the people's team."[6]

Conducting focus groups, like those in the Vikings and Mets examples, requires careful planning. Table 3.5 provides questions and answers that must be considered when planning and implementing focus groups.

Projective techniques

Another source of data collection is through the use of projective techniques. **Projective techniques** refer to any of a variety of methods that allow respondents to project their feelings, beliefs, or motivations onto a relatively neutral stimulus. Projective techniques were developed by psychologists to uncover motivations or to understand personality.[7] The most famous projective technique is the Rorschach test, which asks respondents to assign meaning to a neutral inkblot. Although the Rorschach may not have value for sports marketing researchers, other projective techniques are useful. For instance, sentence completion, word association, picture association, and cartoon tests could be employed as data collection techniques. Figure 3.3 demonstrates the use of sentence completion to gain insight into consumer attitudes toward Nike. The responses to these sentences could be analyzed to determine consumer perceptions of the target market for Nike (question 1), the brand image of Nike (question 2), and product usage (question 3).

Surveys

Data collection techniques are more narrowly defined for descriptive research design types. As stated earlier, a descriptive study describes who, where, how much, how often, and why people are engaging in certain consumption behaviors. To capture this information, the researcher would choose to conduct a survey. Surveys allow sports marketing researchers to collect primary data such as awareness, attitudes, behaviors, demographics, lifestyle, and other variables of interest. For example, the Cleveland Indians handed out roughly 30,000 surveys over 14 games to understand fans' perceptions of the team's on-the-field winning prospects, the quality of the team's management and commitment to winning, and pricing issues.[8]

Table 3.5 Planning and implementing focus groups

Q.How many people should be in focus group?
A. Traditionally, focus groups are composed of 8 to 10 people. However, there is a current trend toward having minigroups of 5 to 6 people. Minigroups are easier to recruit and allow for better and more interaction among focus group participants.
Q. How many people should I recruit, if I want 8 people in my group?
A. The general rule of thumb is to recruit 25 percent more people than the number needed. For example, if you are planning on holding minigroups with 6 people, you should recruit 8. Unfortunately, some respondents will not show up for the group, even if there is an incentive for participation.
Q. What is a good incentive for participants?
A. Naturally, a good incentive depends largely on the type of individual you want to attract to your group. For example, if your group wants to target runners who might be participating in a local 10K race, $3S to $50 may be the norm, including dinner or light snacks. However, if your group requires lawyers to discuss the impact of Title IX on the NCAA, an incentive of $75 to $100 may be more appropriate. In addition to or instead of cash, noncash incentives could also serve. For example, free tickets or merchandise may work better than cash for some groups.
Q. Where should the focus group be conducted?
A. The best place to conduct focus groups is at a marketing research company that has up-to-date focus group facilities. The facility is usually equipped with a one-way mirror, videotape, microphones connected to an audio system, and an observation room for clients. In addition, more modern facilities have viewing rooms that allow the client to interact with the moderator via transmitter while the group is being conducted.
Q. How should I choose a moderator?
A. There is no rule of thumb, but research has identified a set of characteristics that seem to be consistent among good moderators. These characteristics include the following: quick learner, friendly leader. knowledgeable but not all-knowing, excellent memory, good listener, a facilitator – not a performer, flexible, empathic, a "big-picture" thinker, and a good writer. In addition, a good moderator should have a high degree of sports industry knowledge or product knowledge.[7]
Q. How many groups should be conducted?
A. The number of groups interviewed depends on the number of different characteristics that are being examined in the research. For example, Notre Dame may want to determine whether regional preferences exist for different types of merchandise. If so, two groups may be conducted in the North, two groups in the South, and so on. Using the previous example. If lawyers: were the participants in a focus group, two or three total groups may suffice. Any more than this and the information would become redundant and the groups would become inefficient.
Q. What about the composition of the group?
A. A general rule of thumb is that focus group participants should be homogenous. In other words. people within the group should be as similar as possible. We would not want satisfied, loyal fans in the same group as dissatisfied fans. Similarly, we would not want a group to be composed of both upper-level managers and the employees that report to them. In the latter case, lower-level employees may be reluctant to voice their true feelings.

Sentence Completion Test

1. People who wear Nike footwear are ______________________________ .
2. When I think of Nike, I ______________________________ .
3. I would be most likely to buy Nike shoes for ______________________________ .

Figure 3.3 Sentence completion test

An additional illustration of survey research can be found in the following NASCAR study. In the article Taylor performed market research to demonstrate how team and brands can improve how they engage fans in digital and social media outlets.[9]

DRIVERS SHOULD TAKE A SPIN ONLINE, STUDY SHOWS

NASCAR fans consume more and more information on the sport from social and digital media, but a new study by marketing and communications firm Taylor shows teams and brands can improve how they engage the fans through those outlets.

Avid NASCAR fans over the last year reported they were twice as likely to have engaged and interacted with athletes of other sports through social and digital media than they were with NASCAR drivers. The sport's teams and sponsors historically have had drivers make appearances at retail outlets in race markets but are only beginning to make drivers available online, as Roush Fenway Racing did when it hosted a Google+ Hangout with Matt Kenseth, Greg Biffle, Ricky Stenhouse Jr. and Trevor Bayne before the Daytona 500.

"We're still doing a lot of Kroger retail visits," said Ryan Mucatel, Taylor's managing partner. "How many brands are truly engaging with an active fan base online the way they could be?"

Avid NASCAR fans continue to increase their consumption of social and digital media. More than half said they visit social media sites regularly for NASCAR content and 78 percent of 18- to 34-year-olds said they turn to outlets such as Facebook and Twitter for NASCAR information. Most of them use those outlets to share NASCAR information with others, too.

The study, which is based on a survey of 1,500 self-described avid NASCAR fans, was fielded for Taylor by the global research company Toluna. It is the fifth year the firm has done the study. Taylor counts NASCAR as a client and oversaw several studies for the sanctioning body two years ago in such areas as communications and the race-day experience.

Taylor's study didn't identify the overall size of the NASCAR fan base or the percentage of casual or avid fans. It concentrated on avid fans and their consumption patterns.

Avid NASCAR fans remain loyal to sponsors, saying they are more likely to buy the products of a brand that sponsors their favorite driver.

The survey gave avid fans a list of

Taylor's NASCAR Fan Study

A snapshot of avid fans' opinions

■ Have you ever interacted with a NASCAR driver online in real-time?

Yes	9.2%
No	90.8%

■ In your opinion, how could the experience of watching a race on TV be improved?

Provide more behind-the-scenes information	40%
A broader range of commentators	19%
More explanation of what is happening on the track	37%
More explanation of what is happening off the track	24%
Less explanation of what is happening on the track	7%
Less explanation of what is happening off the track	10%
More vignettes about drivers' lives off the track	22%
More ways to follow the sport on a mobile device or tablet while I'm watching on TV	12%

■ Please select the option that best describes your reaction to the statement: I wish races were somewhat shorter.

Strongly disagree	18%
Somewhat disagree	24%
Neither agree or disagree	26%
Somewhat agree	21%
Strongly agree	11%

Source: Taylor

25 companies not in NASCAR and asked them which sponsors they would like to see get involved in the sport. The four most common answers were Nike, Google, Amazon and Apple. NASCAR and its teams have pushed to sign technology sponsors in recent years but had limited success.

In a question on how avid fans choose their favorite driver, Taylor executives were surprised to see that 41 percent of NASCAR fans in the 18- to 34-year-old demographic said they pick their driver based on who his sponsor is, while only 27 percent of all avids said they chose a driver that way.

Approximately 78 percent of avid fans said they would recommend the sport to others. That number was up from 71 percent a year earlier.

Half of avid fans said they are "more" or "much more" interested in the sport than they were a year ago, and 61 percent of 18- to 34-year-olds said they are more interested in NASCAR than they were in 2011. Among fans surveyed who are relatively new to the sport, the number that said they are "much more interested" in NASCAR jumped to 65 percent.

Source: Tripp Mickle. Rightsholder: Sports Business *Journal*.http://www.sportsbusinessdaily.com/Journal/Issues/2012/11/05/Research-and-Ratings/NASCAR-study.aspx.

Surveys that are considered "snapshots" and describe the characteristics of a sample at one point in time are called **cross-sectional studies**. For example, if a high school athletics program wanted to measure fan satisfaction with its half-time promotions at a basketball game, a cross-sectional design would be used. However, if a researcher wanted to investigate an issue and examine responses over a longer period of time, a **longitudinal study** would be used. In this case, fan satisfaction would be measured, improvements would be made to the half-time promotions based on survey responses, and then fan satisfaction would be measured again at a later time. Although longitudinal studies are generally considered more effective, they are not widely used due to time and cost constraints.

Experiments

For well-defined problems, causal research is appropriate. As stated earlier, cause-and-effect relationships are difficult to confirm. **Experimentation** is research in which one or more variables are manipulated while others are held constant; the results are then measured. The variables being manipulated are called independent variables, whereas those being measured are called dependent variables.

An experiment is designed to assess causality and can be conducted in either a laboratory or a field setting. A laboratory, or artificial setting, offers the researcher greater degrees of control in the study. For example, Major League Baseball may want to test the design of a new logo for licensing purposes. Targeted groups could be asked to evaluate the overall appeal of the logo while viewing it on a computer. The researchers could then easily manipulate the color and size of the logo (independent variables) while measuring the appeal to fans (dependent variable). All other variation in the design would be eliminated, which offers a high degree of control.

Unfortunately, a trade-off must be made between experimental control and the researchers' ability to apply the results to the "real purchase situation." In other words, what we find in the lab might not be what we find in the store. Field studies, therefore, are conducted to maximize the generalizability of the findings to real shopping experiences. For example, MLB could test the different colors and sizes of logos by offering them in three different cities of similar demographic composition. Then, MLB could evaluate the consumer response to variations in the product by measuring sales. This common approach to experimentation used by sports marketers is called test marketing.

Test marketing is traditionally defined as introducing a new product or service in one or more limited geographic areas. Through test marketing, sports marketers can collect many valuable pieces of information related to sales, competitive reaction, and market share. Information regarding the characteristics of those purchasing the new products or services could also be obtained. Over a two-year span, ESPN completed market testing of their new 3D channel, including the showing of a USC–Ohio State college football game in select theaters. With a favorable response, ESPN launched ESPN 3D in summer 2010.[10] ESPN 3D produced hundreds of events, including NCAA college football, college basketball, NBA Playoffs and Finals, Grand Slam tennis tournaments, Summer and Winter X games, the Little League World Series, MLS and international soccer, boxing, and more. However, ESPN will shut down its 3D network by the end of the 2013 year. ESPN 3D has struggled to gain traction with viewers as the adoption of 3D television sets by U.S. consumers has yet to meet the sky-high expectations of set manufacturers since being launched.[11] Another test market recently occurred in Columbus, Ohio, for the National Lacrosse League. Columbus, known as a good test market city because of its demographic composition, featured a star-studded demonstration match. If the game drew more than 5,000 spectators, the league was likely to consider Columbus as a strong possibility for a new franchise.[12] Columbus did not enter the league, but the NLL is now 10 teams strong (www.nll.com).

Although test marketer information is invaluable to a sports marketer wanting to roll out a new product, it is not without its disadvantages. One of the primary disadvantages of test marketing is cost and time. Products must be produced, promotions or ads developed, and distribution channels secured – all of which cost money. In addition, the results of the test market must be monitored and evaluated at an additional cost. Another problem related to test marketing is associated with competitive activity. Often, competitors will offer consumers unusually high discounts on their products or services to skew the results of a test market. In addition, competitors may be able to quickly produce a "me-too" imitation product or service by the time the test market is ready for a national rollout.

The problems of cost, time, and competitive reaction may be alleviated by means of a more nontraditional test market approach called a **simulated test market**. Typically, respondents in a simulated test market participate in a series of activities, such as (1) receiving exposure to a new product or service concept, (2) having the opportunity to purchase the product or service in a laboratory environment, (3) assessing attitudes toward the new product or service after trial, and (4) assessing repeat purchase behavior.

Designing data collection instruments

Once the data collection method is chosen, the next step in the marketing research process is designing the data collection instrument. Data collection instruments are

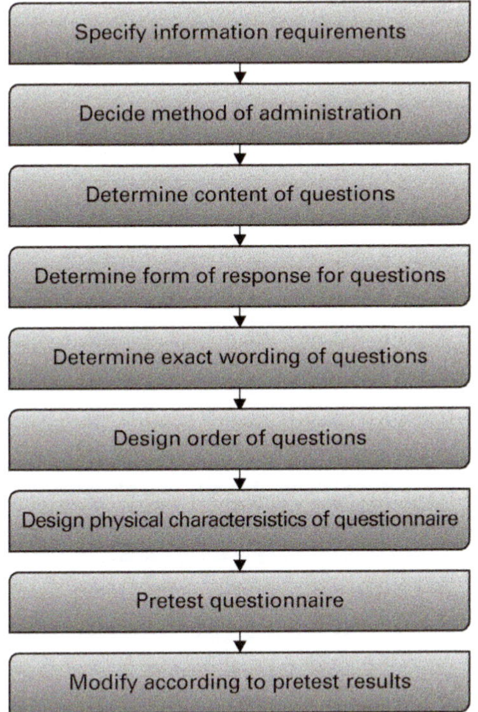

Figure 3.4 Designing a questionnaire

Source: Churchill. IM/TM – Basic Markrting Research, 3/E, 3E. © 1996 South-Western, a part of Cengage Learning, Inc.

required for nearly all types of data collection methods. Guides are necessary for depth interviews and focus groups. Data collection forms are needed for projective techniques. Even experiments require data collection instruments.

One of the most widely used data collection instruments in sports marketing is the questionnaire or survey. All forms of survey research require the construction of a questionnaire. The process of designing a questionnaire is shown in Figure 3.4.

Specify information requirements

As the first step of **questionnaire design**, the information requirements must be specified. In other words, the researcher asks what information needs to be gathered via the questionnaire. This should be addressed in the initial step of the research process if the problem is carefully defined. Remember, in the first step of the marketing research process, research objectives are developed based on the specified information requirements. The research objectives are a useful starting point in questionnaire design because they indicate what broad topic will be addressed in the study.

Decide method of administration

The method of administration is the next consideration in questionnaire design. The most common methods of administration are via mail, phone, e-mail, Web sites, or personal interview. Each method has its own unique advantages and

Table 3.6 Comparison of methods of administration

Issues	Methods of administration			
	Mail	**Telephone**	**Stadium and event interviews**	**Internet**
Costs	Inexpensive	Moderately expensive	Most expensive because of time	Inexpensive
Ability to use complex survey	Little, because self-administered	Same	Greatest because interviewer is present	Little, because self-administered
Opportunity for interviewer bias	None	Same	Greatest because interviewer is present	None
Response rate	Lowest	Moderate	Greatest	Low
Speed of data collection	Slowest	High	Medium to high	High

What is your New Year's Resolution?

a. Lose Weight
b. Spend More Time with Family & Friends
c. Quit Smoking
d. Get Out of Debt
e. Other

VOTE

Figure 3.5 New Year's resolution survey

disadvantages that must be considered (see Table 3.6). For example, if a short questionnaire is designed to measure fan attitudes toward the new promotion, then a phone survey may be appropriate. However, if the research is being conducted to determine preference for a new logo, then mail or personal interviews would be necessary.

Determine content of questions

The content of individual questions is largely governed by the method of administration. However, several other factors must be kept in mind. First, does the question address at least one research objective? Second, are several questions necessary to answer an objective? Contrary to popular belief, more is not always better. Third, does the respondent have the information necessary to answer the question? For example, respondents may not be able to answer questions regarding personal seat licenses (PSLs) if they do not have a full understanding or description of what is meant by a PSL. Finally, will the respondent answer the question?

Sometimes respondents possess the necessary information, but they elect not to respond. For instance, questionnaires may sometimes ask sensitive questions (e.g., about income levels) that respondents will not answer.

Determine form of response

After deciding on the content of the questions, the form of response should be considered. The form of the response is dependent on the degree of structure in the question. Unstructured questionnaires use a high number of open-ended questions. These types of questions allow respondents to provide their own responses rather than having to choose from a set of response categories provided by the researcher. The following are examples of open-ended questions:

- How do you feel about personal seat licenses?
- How many years have you been a season ticket holder?
- How will the personal seat license affect your attitude toward the team?

Determine exact wording of questions

One of the most rigorous aspects of questionnaire design is deciding on the exact wording of questions. When constructing questions, the following pitfalls should be avoided:

- ***Questions should not be too lengthy –*** Lengthy, run-on questions are difficult to interpret and have a higher likelihood of being skipped by the respondent.
- ***Questions should not be ambiguous –*** Clarity is the key to good survey design. For instance, "Do you like sports?" may be interpreted in two very different ways. One respondent may answer based on participation, whereas another may answer from a spectator's viewpoint. In addition, there may be ambiguity in how the respondent defines sports. Some respondents would call billiards a sport, whereas others may define it as a game.
- ***Questions should not be double barreled or contain two questions in one –*** For example, "Do you enjoy collecting and selling baseball cards?" represents a double-barreled question. This should be divided into two separate questions: "Do you enjoy collecting baseball cards?" and "Do you enjoy selling baseball cards?"
- ***Questions should not lack specificity –*** In other words, clearly define the questions. "Do you watch sports on a regular basis?" is a poorly written question in that the respondent does not know the researcher's definition of *regular*. Does the researcher mean once per week or once per day?
- ***Questions should not be technical in nature –*** Avoid asking respondents a question that will be difficult for them to answer. For instance, "What type of swing weight do you prefer in your driver?" may be too technical for the average golfer to answer in a meaningful fashion.

Determine question sequence

Now that the question wording has been determined, the researcher must determine the proper sequence of the questions. First, a good questionnaire starts with broad, interesting questions that hook the respondents and capture their attention. Similarly, questions that are more narrow in focus, such as demographic information, should appear at the end of the questionnaire. Second, questions that focus on similar topical areas should be grouped together. For example, a fan satisfaction questionnaire may include sections on satisfaction with concessions, stadium personnel, or game promotions.

Finally, proper question sequencing must consider branching questions and skip patterns. Branching questions direct respondents to questions based on answers to previous questions. For example, the first question on a questionnaire may be, "Have you ever been to a RailCats game?" If the respondents answer "yes," they might continue with a series of questions concerning customer satisfaction. If the respondents answer "no," then they might be asked to skip forward to a series of questions regarding media preferences. Because branching questions and skip patterns are sometimes confusing to respondents, these types of questions should be avoided if at all possible.

Design physical characteristics of questionnaire

One of the final steps in the questionnaire development process is to consider carefully the physical appearance of the questionnaire. If the questionnaire is cluttered and looks unprofessional, respondents will be less likely to cooperate and complete the instrument. Other questionnaire design issues include the following:

- Questionnaire should look simple and easy to fill out.
- Questionnaire should have subheadings for the various sections.
- Questionnaire should provide simple and easy-to-understand instructions.
- Questionnaire should leave sufficient room to answer open-ended questions.

Pretest

After the questionnaire has been finalized and approved by the client, the next step in the questionnaire design process is to pretest the instrument. A **pretest** can be thought of as a "trial run" for the questionnaire to determine if there are any problems in interpreting the questions. In addition to detecting problems in interpreting questions, the pretest may uncover problems with the way the questions are sequenced.

An initial pretest should be conducted with both the researcher and respondent present. By conducting the pretest through a personal interview, the researcher can discuss any design flaws or points of confusion with the respondent. Next, the pretest should be conducted using the planned method of administration. In other words, if the survey is being conducted over the phone, the pretest should be conducted over the phone.

The number and nature of the respondents should also be considered when conducting a pretest. The sample for the pretest should mirror the target population for the study, although it may be useful to have other experienced researchers examine the questionnaire before full-scale data collection takes place. The number of people to pretest depends on time and cost considerations. Although pretests slow down the research process, they are invaluable in discovering problems that would otherwise make the data collected meaningless.

Designing the sample

After the data collection instrument has been designed, the research process turns to selecting an appropriate sample. A **sample** is a subset of the population of interest from which data are gathered that will estimate some characteristic of the population. Securing a quality sample for sports marketing research is critical. Researchers rarely have the time or money to communicate with everyone in the population of interest. As such, developing a sample that is representative of this larger group of consumers is required.

To design an effective and efficient sample, a variety of sampling techniques are available. Sampling techniques are commonly divided into two categories: **nonprobability sampling** and **probability sampling**. The primary characteristic of nonprobability sampling techniques is that the sample units are chosen subjectively by the researcher. As such, there is no way of ensuring whether the sample is representative of the population of interest. Probability sampling techniques are objective procedures in which sample units have a known and nonzero chance of being selected for the study. Generally, probability sampling techniques are considered stronger because the accuracy of the sample results can be estimated with respect to the population.

Nonprobability sampling

The three nonprobability sampling techniques commonly used are convenience, judgment, and quota sampling. **Convenience sampling techniques** are also called accidental sampling because the sample units are chosen based on the "convenience" of the researcher. For example, a research project could be conducted to assess fans' attitudes toward high school soccer in a large metropolitan area. Questionnaires could be handed out to fans attending Friday night games at three different high schools. These individuals are easy to reach but may not be representative of the population of interest (i.e., high school fans in the area).

Other researchers may approach the same problem with a different data collection method. For example, three focus groups might be conducted to gain a better understanding of the fans' attitudes toward high school soccer. Using this scenario, long-time, loyal soccer fans might be chosen as participants in the three focus groups. These participants represent a **judgment sample** because they are chosen subjectively and, based on the judgment of the researcher, they best serve the purpose of the study.

A quota sampling technique may also be used to address the research problem. In **quota sampling**, units are chosen on the basis of some control characteristic or characteristics of interest to the researcher. For instance, control characteristics such as gender and year in school may be appropriate for the soccer study. In this case, the researcher may believe there may be important distinctions between male and female fans and between freshmen and seniors. The sample would then be chosen to capture the desired number of consumers based on these characteristics. Often, the numbers are chosen so that the percentage of each sample subgroup (e.g., females and juniors) reflects the population percentages.

Probability sampling

As stated earlier, the stronger sampling techniques are known as probability sampling. In probability sampling, the sample is chosen from a list of elements called a sampling frame. For example, if students at a high school define the population of interest, the sampling frame might be the student directory. The sample would then be chosen objectively from this list of elements.

Although there are many types, a simple random sample is the most widely used probability sampling technique. Using this technique, every unit in the sampling frame has a known and equal chance of being chosen for the sample. For example, Harris Interactive (http://www.harrisinteractive.com/) e-mails a random and representative sample of the U.S. population drawn from a database of more than 6.5 million respondents who have agreed to cooperate. Respondents who agree to participate are directed to the appropriate URL for each survey. The Internet-based methodology allows Harris to randomly sample a minimum of 10,000 people each month on various topics of interest to decision makers in the sports and entertainment industry. A probability sampling technique, such as simple random sampling, allows the researcher to calculate the degree of sampling error, so the researcher knows how precisely the sample reflects the true population.

Sample size

Another question that must be addressed when choosing a sample is the number of units to include in it, or the sample size. Practically speaking, sample sizes are determined largely on the basis of time and money. The more precise and confident the researchers want to be in their findings, the greater the necessary sample size.

Another important determinant in sample size is the homogeneity of the population of interest. In other words, how different or similar are the respondents? To illustrate the effect of homogeneity on sample size, suppose the RailCats are interested in determining the average income of their season ticket holders. If the population of interest includes all the season ticket holders and each person has an income of $50,000, then how many people would we need to have a representative sample? The answer, because of this totally homogeneous population, is one. Any one person that would be in our sample would give us the true income of RailCats' season ticket holders.

As you can see from this brief discussion, sample size determination is a complex process based on confidence, precision, and the nature of the population of interest, time, and money. Larger samples tend to be more accurate than smaller ones, but researchers must treat every research project as a unique case that has an optimal sample size based on the purpose of the study.

Data analysis

After the data are collected from the population of interest, data analysis takes place. Before any analytical work occurs, the data must be carefully scrutinized to ensure its quality. Researchers call this the editing process. During this process, the data are examined for impossible responses, missing responses, or any other abnormalities that would render the data useless.

Once the quality of the data is ensured, coding begins. Coding refers to assigning numerical values or codes to represent a specific response to a specific question. Consider the following question:

How likely are you to attend a RailCats' game in 20XX?

1. Extremely unlikely
2. Unlikely
3. Neither unlikely nor likely
4. Likely
5. Extremely likely

The response of *extremely unlikely* is assigned a code of 1, *unlikely* a code of 2, and so on. Each question in the survey must be coded to facilitate data analysis.

After editing and coding are completed, you are ready to begin analyzing the data. Although there are many sophisticated statistical techniques (and software programs) to choose from to analyze the data, researchers usually like to start by "looking at the big picture." In other words, researchers want to describe and summarize the data before they begin to look for more complex relationships between questions.

Often, the first step in data analysis is to examine two of the most basic informational components of the data – central tendency and dispersion. Measures of central tendency (also known as the mean, median, and mode) tell us about the typical response, whereas measures of dispersion (range, variance, and standard deviation) refer to the similarity of responses to any given question.

To give us a good feel for the typical responses and variation in responses, frequency distributions are often constructed. A frequency distribution, such as the one shown in Table 3.7, provides the distribution of data pertaining to categories of a single variable. In other words, frequency distributions or one-way tables show us the number (or frequency) of cases from the entire sample that fall into each response category. Normally, these frequencies or counts are also converted into percentages.

After one-way tables or frequency distributions are constructed, the next step in data analysis involves examining relationships between two variables. A cross-tabulation allows us to look at the responses to one question in relation to the responses to another question. Two-way tables provide a preliminary look at the association between two questions. For example, the two-way table shown in Table 3.8 explores the relationship between the likelihood of going to RailCats' games and gender. Upon examination, the two-way table clearly shows that females are less likely to attend RailCats' games in the future than males. Implications of this finding may include the need to conduct future research to better understand why females are less likely to attend RailCats' games than males and the design of a marketing mix that appeals to females.

Table 3.7 Frequency distribution or one-way table

How likely are you to attend a RailCats' game in 20XX?		
	Respondents	
	Number	**Percent**
1. Extremely unlikely	88	9.1
2. Unlikely	60	6.2
3. Neither unlikely or likely	336	34.6
4. Likely	201	20.7
5. Extremely likely	169	17.4
NA	118	12.0
Total	972	100.00

Table 3.8 Two-way table of cross-tabulation

How likely are you to attend a RailCats' game in 20XX?		
	Gender	
	Male	**Female**
1. Extremely unlikely	35	53
2. Unlikely	28	32
3. Neither unlikely or likely	178	158
4. Likely	111	90
5. Extremely likely	101	68
NA	56	62
Total	509	463

Preparing a final report

The last step in the marketing research process is preparing a final report. Typically, the report is intended for top management of the sports organization, who can either put the research findings into action or shelve the project. Unfortunately, the greatest research project in the world will be viewed as a failure if the results are not clearly communicated to the target audience.

How can you prepare a final report that will assist in making decisions throughout the strategic marketing process? Here are some simple guidelines for preparing an actionable report:

- ***Know your audience –*** Before preparing the oral or written report, determine your audience. Typically, the users of research will be upper management, who do not possess a great deal of statistical knowledge or marketing research expertise. Therefore, it is important to construct the report so it is easily understood by the audience who will use the report, not by other researchers. One of the greatest challenges in preparing a research report is presenting technical information in a way that is easily understood by all users.
- ***Be thorough, not overwhelming –*** By the time they are completed, some written research reports resemble volumes of the *Encyclopedia Britannica*. Likewise, oral presentations can drag on for so long that any meaningful information is lost. Researchers should be sensitive to the amount of information they convey in an oral research report. Oral presentations should show only the most critical findings, rather than every small detail. Generally, written reports should include a brief description of the background and objectives of the study, how the study was conducted (**methodology**), key findings, and marketing recommendations. Voluminous tables should be located in an appendix.
- ***Carefully interpret the findings –*** The results of the study and how it was conducted are important, but nothing is as critical as drawing conclusions from the data. Managers who use the research findings often have limited time and no inclination to carefully analyze and interpret the findings. In addition, managers are not only interested in the findings alone, but they also want to know what marketing actions can be taken based on the findings. Be sure you do not neglect the implications of the research when preparing both oral and written reports.

CASE STUDY
Survey shows split on racial opportunity

Twenty-five years after Martin Luther King Jr.'s life was first honored with a national holiday and nearly 50 years after the civil rights leader's "I Have a Dream" speech, black and white sports fans alike view the sports world as far more racially progressive and unifying than the rest of society, according to a recent online survey conducted for ESPN.

However, there remains a strong racial divide among those fans about the extent to which African-Americans enjoy equal opportunities in sports, as well as about the degrees of prejudice and discrimination that continue to pervade the sports landscape.

Eighty-two percent of those surveyed believe that sports provide equal opportunities for

African-Americans, compared with 55 percent who think the same is true in all other sectors of society. Of those surveyed, 73 percent give a very high rating to the sports world in terms of equal opportunities, in contrast to only 19 percent who give a very high rating to the corporate world.

As well, 72 percent believe sports do more to unite people across racial lines, while only 6 percent think sports do more to divide race relations.

However, African-Americans surveyed are less convinced than whites about the extent of the progress in the sports world. Only 36 percent of blacks – compared with 65 percent of whites – give sports high marks on the question of whether African-Americans have equal opportunities to succeed.

Most African-Americans surveyed say blacks have fewer opportunities than whites to become owners of professional sports franchises (71 percent); athletic directors at major, Division I universities (72 percent); major league baseball managers (64 percent); NFL head coaches (62 percent); or head coaches at major Division I schools (58 percent). A majority of white sports fans believe African-Americans have equal opportunities.

Charlotte Bobcats owner Michael Jordan is the only black majority owner in the four major professional sports, according to the University of Central Florida's Institute for Diversity and Ethics in Sports. Jordan bought the team from another African-American, Robert Johnson, and those two constitute the only black majority owners in the history of the four major sports.

Nevertheless, only 47 percent of white sports fans surveyed think blacks have fewer opportunities to be owners, and 44 percent believe that blacks have the same opportunities.

The online survey of 1,822 sports fans (1,213 whites, 435 African-Americans) was conducted Dec. 15 – Dec. 21 by Hart Research Associates.

An ESPN survey of coaching salaries by race indicates disparities remain. At the start of the 2010 NFL season, six out of 32 coaches were black, and the average annual salary for those coaches was $3.1 million, compared with $4.1 million for white coaches. Of the 120 major Division I college football programs, there were only 14 black coaches (and one Hispanic coach) at the start of this past season; the average annual salary for those African-American coaches was $1 million, while white coaches averaged $1.4 million.

The surveyed fans also were somewhat divided on their views about the need for the NFL's Rooney Rule, which requires consideration of minority candidates for head coaching and senior football operations positions. Of black fans polled, 57 percent believe the rule will be needed for years to come, compared with only 20 percent of white fans. Twenty-three percent of white fans indicate the rule was never needed in the first place, while only 7 percent of African-Americans feel it is unnecessary.

In conjunction with the 25th anniversary of the Martin Luther King holiday, ESPN also surveyed 100 African-American athletes about their views of the black athlete in 2010. The athletes were promised anonymity to encourage freer responses to a series of 10 questions.

"Wow, it's an honor to take this survey," said one NFL Pro Bowl player. "MLK had a huge impact on me as a kid – even though I was born a few years after he died. That's legacy, man."

"What sets Jordan apart is he's done so much more than basketball. Even the whole baseball attempt was inspiring to me. I remember thinking, 'He's the best basketball player ever, and he's walking away to try baseball just because he wants to test himself? Maybe I need to think more like that.'"

– MLB player on Michael Jordan

Asked to name the retired black athlete they could most imagine being president in 2024, the athletes' top choice was Michael Jordan, garnering 17.5 percent of votes.

"What sets Jordan apart is he's done so much more than basketball," said an MLB player. "Even the whole baseball attempt was inspiring to me. I remember thinking, 'He's the best basketball player ever, and he's walking away to try basketball just because he wants to test himself? Maybe I need to think more like that.'"

The NBA swept the top five among potential presidents, with Jordan followed by current Laker Derek Fisher and former Laker Magic Johnson (each at 12.4 percent); former Phoenix Suns great Kevin Johnson (6.2), now the mayor of Sacramento; and former Spurs superstar David Robinson (5.2).

Jackie Robinson (62.5 percent) was the top vote-getter when the athletes were asked to name the most important black athlete ever, followed by Muhammad Ali (57.3) and Jordan (54.2).

The athletes surveyed resoundingly (81 percent) believe African-American athletes need to take a more active role in the black community.

"You need more black athletes doing more positive things," said a world champion boxer. "A lot of people in the ghetto, in poor neighborhoods like where I grew up, don't believe there's life outside of the city, outside what they know. We need to be in there showing them, telling them, that there is."

Asked to identify who was the most color-blind among fans, coaches, owners and media, more than half the athletes (53.4 percent) selected coaches, followed by fans (21.8), owners (14.4) and media (10.4).

"When it's all said and done, the color that counts the most is green," said one NFL linebacker.

The athletes' answers reflected a level of suspicion regarding the media. When asked to rank five athletes by how the media treated them (1 being the kindest; 5 being the worst), the survey revealed the African-American athletes believe Steelers quarterback Ben Roethlisberger (1.6) was handled with kid gloves compared with Eagles quarterback Michael Vick (4.8). Roethlisberger was accused of sexually assaulting a 20-year-old woman, and he ultimately was given a four-game suspension by the NFL although no charges were filed against him. Vick served 21 months in prison for his role in a dogfighting ring.

Other players named in the question were pitching great Roger Clemens (2.3), who faces charges of lying before Congress when he denied steroid use; NFL wide receiver Plaxico Burress (3.5), who is currently serving a two-year prison sentence stemming from gun charges after he accidentally shot himself at a New York nightclub; and seven-time National League Most Valuable Player Barry Bonds (3.6), who is set to stand trial in March on perjury charges related to his grand jury testimony in the BALCO steroids case.

"All of those guys got raked pretty bad. But what happened to Vick wasn't right, especially compared with how the other guys on that list were treated."

– Champion boxer on Michael Vick

"All of those guys got raked pretty bad," said a champion boxer. "But what happened to Vick wasn't right, especially compared with how the other guys on that list were treated."

African-American sports fans who took part in the online survey also indicated the media had been biased in its treatment of black athletes. By a margin of 57 percent to 7 percent, the African-Americans surveyed say the media unfairly criticizes black athletes more than white athletes, while the white fans suggest there is no difference in the media's handling of various cases.

Of black sports fans surveyed, 65 percent say they admire Vick, compared with just 25 percent of the white fans. Black fans surveyed actually also seem more forgiving of Roethlisberger, with 30 percent expressing admiration, compared with just 22 percent of white fans. Asked for their views on 17 different sports figures – from NFL quarterback Tom Brady to race car driver Danica Patrick, from golfer Tiger Woods to NFL wide receiver Terrell Owens – fans overwhelmingly name Jordan as the figure they most admire (67 percent). Owens is last (18 percent), although 35 percent of black fans surveyed say they admired him, compared with just 14 percent of whites.

Provided a list of seven facts about African-Americans in sports today, sports fans of both races say they are most concerned that the graduation rate for black student-athletes is 53 percent compared with 63 percent for white student-athletes. The fan survey also touched upon the often-taboo notion of whether African-Americans are athletically superior to whites. Across the board, blacks and whites indicate they believe blacks are superior runners, have greater jumping and leaping ability, and possess more natural athletic ability than whites. In fact, 66 percent of the African-American fans surveyed associate fast runners more with black athletes than white, and 61 percent associate natural athletic ability more with blacks than whites. A very small percentage of blacks and whites associate superior athletic ability with white athletes.

The NFL is far and away the most popular sport among all fans surveyed, with Major League Baseball a distant second, followed by college football. Among black fans specifically, the NBA ranks second, followed by college football, college basketball and then MLB. Asked to rank a series of breakthrough sports moments involving African-Americans, black fans view as most significant Tony Dungy and Lovie Smith being the first African-American head coaches to reach the Super Bowl, with Dungy being the first black coach to win the title. Ranking second among blacks is Serena Williams becoming the first African-American woman to win a career grand slam in tennis. Overall, the black and white fans surveyed view Jordan becoming the first former NBA player to become the majority owner of an NBA franchise as the sports event that demonstrates the most progress in achieving King's dream of a society that provides equal opportunities for all races.

More than twice as many of the surveyed fans (32 percent to 13 percent) say the dream has been reached in sports compared with those who say it has been reached by the country as a whole. Again, though, black fans are far less convinced than whites: Regarding society in general, just 6 percent of African-Americans believe the country has fulfilled the dream, compared with 15 percent of whites; and in sports, 14 percent of the black fans indicate equality has been achieved, while 37 percent of whites think the dream has been realized.

Source: Mark Fainaru-Wada, 2011, "Survey Shows Split on Racial Opportunity," ESPN, January 11. Rightsholder: ESPN; http://sports.espn.go.com/espn/otl/news/story?id=6006813. Originally published in The Good Men Project.

Summary

Chapter 3 focuses on the tools used to gather information to make intelligent decisions throughout the strategic sports marketing process. More specifically, the chapter describes the marketing research process in detail. Marketing research is defined as the systematic process of collecting, analyzing, and reporting information to enhance decision making throughout the strategic sports marketing process.

The marketing research process consists of seven interrelated steps. These steps include defining the problem; choosing the research design type; identifying data collection methods; designing data collection forms; designing the sample; collecting, analyzing, and interpreting data; and preparing the research report. The first step is defining the problem and determining what information will be needed to make strategic marketing decisions. The tangible outcome of problem definition is to develop a set of research objectives that will serve as a guide for the rest of the research process.

The next step in the marketing research process is to determine the appropriate research design type(s). The research design is the plan that directs data collection and analysis. The three common research design types are exploratory, descriptive, and causal. The choice of one (or more) of these design types for any study is based on the clarity of the problem. Exploratory designs are more appropriate for ill-defined problems, whereas causal designs are employed for well-defined research problems.

After the research design type is chosen, the data collection method(s) is selected. Once again, decisions regarding data collection are contingent upon the choice of research design. Data collection consists of two types – secondary and primary. Secondary data refers to data that were collected earlier, either within or outside the sports organization, but still provide useful information to the researcher. Typically, sources of secondary data include government reports and documents; trade and industry associations; standardized sports marketing information studies; and books, journals, and periodicals. Primary data are information that is collected specifically for the research question at hand. Common types of primary data collection techniques include, but are not limited to, in-depth interviews, focus groups, surveys, and experiments.

The fourth step in the research process is to design the data collection instrument. Regardless of whether you are collecting data by in-depth interviews, focus groups, or surveys, data collection instruments are necessary. The most widely used data collection technique in sports marketing research is the questionnaire. As such, it is important that sports marketing researchers understand how to construct a questionnaire properly. The steps for questionnaire design include specifying information requirements, deciding the method of administration (i.e., mail, phone, and stadium interview), determining the content of questions, determining the form of response for questions, deciding on the exact wording of the questions, designing the order of the questions, designing the physical characteristics of the questionnaire, pretesting the questionnaire, and modifying it according to pretest results.

Once the data collection forms are constructed, the next step in the research process is choosing a sampling strategy. Rarely, if ever, can we take a census where we communicate with or observe everyone of interest to us in a research study. As such, a subset of those individuals is chosen to represent the larger group of interest. Sampling strategy identifies how we will choose these individuals and how many people we will choose to participate in our study.

Data analysis is the next step in the marketing research process. Before the data can be analyzed, however, they must be edited and coded. The editing process ensures the data being used for analysis are of high quality. In other words, it makes sure that there are no problems, such as large amounts of missing data or errors in data entry. Next, coding takes place. Coding refers to assigning numerical values to represent specific responses to specific questions. Once the data are edited and coded, data analysis is conducted. The method of data analysis depends on a variety of factors, such as how to address the research objectives. The last step in the marketing research process is to prepare a final report. Oral and written reports typically discuss the objectives of the study, how the study was conducted, and the findings and recommendation for decision makers.

This ESPN study clearly shows that there are major differences between how white fans and black fans view white and black athletes. According to the statistics, white fans appear to have far less interest in cheering on black athletes than they do athletes of their own skin color – *but is this assumption really accurate?* One thing that jumped out to Dr. Christopher Stankovich, founder of Advance Human Performance Systems, when looking over this report was the fact that black fans didn't dislike *any* black athletes, something that would certainly catch the attention of savvy researchers. Dr. Stankovich identified that the generalizability of these data may be compromised, therefore for discussion identifies how these data may be compromised and what limitations, if any, may be associated with the study? Also, identify how these data may be used by sport marketing professionals to enhance functions of the SSMP?

Key terms

- concomitant variation
- convenience sampling techniques
- cross-sectional studies
- data collection techniques
- dependent variable
- experimentation
- focus group
- independent variable
- judgment sample
- longitudinal study
- marketing research
- methodology
- nonprobability sampling
- pretest
- primary data
- probability sampling
- problem definition
- projective techniques
- questionnaire design
- quota sampling
- research design
- research objectives
- research problem statement
- research proposal
- sample
- secondary data
- simulated test market
- sports marketing research
- test marketing

Review questions

1. Define sports marketing research. Describe the relationship between sports marketing research and the strategic marketing process.
2. What are the various steps in the marketing research process?
3. Define problem and opportunity definition and explain why this step of the research process is considered to be the most critical.
4. What are some of the basic issues that should be addressed at a research request meeting?
5. Outline the steps in developing a research proposal.
6. Define a research design. What are the three types of research designs that can be used in research? How does the choice of research design stem from the problem definition? Can a researcher choose multiple designs within a single study?
7. Describe some of the common data collection techniques used in sports marketing research. How does the choice of data collection technique stem from the research design type?
8. What are some of the central issues that must be considered when conducting focus groups?
9. What are the pros and cons of laboratory studies versus field studies?
10. Outline the nine steps in questionnaire design. What are some of the most common errors in the wording of questions?
11. Define nonprobability sampling and probability sampling techniques. What are three types of nonprobability sampling?
12. What is a sampling frame? How do researchers decide on the appropriate sample size for a study?
13. What are some of the guidelines for preparing oral and written research reports?

Exercises

You are interested in purchasing a new minor league baseball franchise. The franchise will be located in your area. To reduce the risk in your decision making, you have requested that a sports marketing firm submit a detailed research proposal. The following questions pertain to this issue:

1. What is the broad problem/ opportunity facing you in this decision? Write the research objectives based on the problem formulation.
2. What type of research design type do you recommend?
3. The sports marketing firm has submitted the following preliminary questionnaire. Please provide a detailed critique of their work.

Age: ________ Gender: ________
Are you likely to go to a baseball game at the new stadium?
Yes ____ No ____
How many minor league games did you go to last year?
0–3 ____ 4–6 ____ 6–9 ____ 10+ ____
What types of promos would you like to see?
Beer Night ______ Straight-A Night ______ Polka Night ______

4. Now that you have looked at their survey, create a questionnaire of your own. Would any other data collection techniques be appropriate, given the research problem?

5. What sampling technique(s) do you recommend? How is the correct sample size determined, given your choice of sampling technique?

Internet exercises

1. Using secondary data sources on the Internet, find the following and indicate the appropriate URL (Internet address):

a. Number of women who participated in high school basketball last year
b. Attendance at NFL games last year
c. Sponsors for the New York City Marathon
d. Universities that offer graduate programs in sports marketing.

2. Using the Internet, find at least five articles that relate to the marketing of NASCAR.

3. Using the Internet, locate three companies that conduct sports marketing research. What types of products and services do the companies offer?

Endnotes

1 *NASCAR Sponsorship Study*, "Sponsorship Research and Strategies." Available from: http://sponsorstrategy.com/_wsn/page9.html.
2 Gilbert Churchill, *Basic Marketing Research*, 3rd ed. (Ft. Worth, TX: Dryden Press, 1996).
3 Ibid.
4 Kristie McCook, Douglas Turco, and Roger Riley, "A Look at the Corporate Sponsorship Decision Making Process," *Cyber-Journal of Sport Marketing*, vol. 1, no. 2 (1997). Available from: http://fulltext.ausport.gov.au/fulltext/1997/cjsm/v1n2/mcook.htm.
5 Jay Weiner, "New Focus Group Report, Showing Surprising Openness to Sales Tax, Could be Key to Vikings Stadium Effort" (May 4, 2010). Available from: http://www.minnpost.com/politics-policy/2010/05/new-focus-group-report-showing-surprising-openness-sales-tax-could-be-key-vi.
6 Mike Sielski, "After Losing Season, Mets Slash Ticket Prices" (November 4, 2010). Available from: http://online.wsj.com/news/articles/SB10001424052748703506904575592780665674228.
7 Gilbert Churchill, *Basic Marketing Research*, 3rd ed (Fort Worth, TX: Dryden Press, 1996).
8 "Cleveland Indians Look to Long-Term Viability through Market Research," *Akron Beacon Journal* (April 16, 1999).
9 Tripp Mickle, "Drivers Should Take a Spin Online, Study Shows," *Sports Business Journal* (November 5, 2012).
10 "ESPN 3D to Show Soccer, Football, More." Available from: www.ESPN.com (January 5, 2010).
11 Jason Dachman, "ESPN to discontinue ESPN 3D by Year's End." Available from: www.sportsvideo.org/main/blog/2013/06/breaking-news-espn-to-discontinue-3d-network/.
12 Craig Mertz, "Pro Lacrosse League to Test Local Support," *The Columbus Dispatch* (July 7, 2000), 5D.

CHAPTER 4

Understanding participants as consumers

After completing this chapter, you should be able to:

- Define participant consumption behavior.
- Explain the simplified model of participant consumption behavior.
- Describe the psychological factors that affect participant decision making.
- Identify the various external factors influencing participant decision making.
- Describe the participant decision-making process.
- Understand the different types of consumer decision making.
- Discuss the situational factors that influence participant decision making.

Think about the sports and recreational activities in which you participated during the past month. Maybe you played golf or tennis, lifted weights, or even went hiking. According to data from the National Sporting Goods Association (NSGA) provided in Table 4.1, millions of Americans participate in a variety of physical activities each year.

Table 4.1 Sport participation changes from 2013 (participants ages six and up)

2013 Sport/Recreational Activity Participation		
Ranking	**Sport**	**2013 Total Participation (in millions)**
1	Exercise Walking	96.3
2	Exercising with Equipment	53.1
3	Swimming	45.5
4	Aerobic Exercising	44.1
5	Running/Jogging	42.0
6	Hiking	39.4
7	Camping (Vacation/Overnight)	39.3
8	Bicycle Riding	35.6
9	Bowling	35.2
10	Workout at Club	34.1
11	Weightlifting	31.3
12	Fishing (Fresh Water)	27.0
13	Yoga	25.9
14	Basketball	25.5
15	Billiards/Pool	19.5
16	Target Shooting (Live Ammunition)	19.0
17	Golf	18.9
18	Hunting with Firearms	16.3
19	Boating, Motor/Power	13.1
20	Soccer	12.8
21	Tennis	12.6
22	Backpacking/Wilderness Camping	12.2
23	Baseball	11.7
24	Volleyball	10.1
25	Softball	10.0
26	Table Tennis/Ping Pong	9.8
27	Dart Throwing	9.8
28	Fishing (Salt Water)	9.5
29	Football (Touch)	8.8
30	Archery (Target)	8.3
31	Kayaking	8.1
32	Football (Tackle)	7.5
33	Football (Flag)	6.8
34	Canoeing	6.7
35	Skiing (Alpine)	6.1
36	Roller Skating (In-line)	5.7
37	Hunting with Bow & Arrow	5.7
38	Mountain Biking (off road)	5.2

Table 4.1 (continued)

2013 Sport/Recreational Activity Participation		
Ranking	**Sport**	**2013 Total Participation (in millions)**
39	Gymnastics	5.1
40	Skateboarding	5.0
41	Paintball Games	4.8
42	Target Shooting (Airgun)	4.8
43	Snowboarding	4.5
44	Water Skiing	3.6
45	Cheerleading	3.5
46	Hockey (Ice)	3.5
47	Muzzleloading	3.2
48	Wrestling	3.1
49	Lacrosse	2.8
50	Scuba Diving (Open Water)	2.7
51	Skiing (Cross Country)	2.5

Source: Courtesy of The Sporting Goods Marketing Association.

At this point you may be asking yourself, "Why are sports marketers concerned with consumers who participate in sports?" Recall from our discussion of sports marketing in Chapter 1 that one of the basic sports marketing activities was encouraging participation in sports. Sports marketers are responsible for organizing events such as the Boston Marathon, the Iron Man Triathlon, or the Gus Macker 3-on-3 Basketball Tournament in which thousands of consumers participate in sports. Moreover, sports marketers are involved in marketing the equipment and apparel necessary for participation in sports. As you might imagine, sports participants constitute a large and growing market both in the United States and internationally.

To successfully compete in the expanding sports participant market, sports organizations must develop a thorough understanding of participant consumption behavior and what affects it. **Participant consumption behavior** is defined as actions performed when searching for, participating in, and evaluating the sports activities that consumers believe will satisfy their needs. You may have noticed this definition relates to the previous discussion of marketing concepts and consumer satisfaction. Sports marketers must understand why consumers choose to participate in certain sports and what the benefits of participation are for consumers. For instance, do we play indoor soccer for exercise, for social contact, to feel like part of a team, or to enhance our image? Also, the study of participant consumer behavior attempts to understand when, where, and how often consumers participate in sports. By understanding consumers of sports, marketers will be in a better position to satisfy their needs.

The definition of participant consumption behavior also incorporates the elements of the participant decision-making process. The **decision-making process** is the foundation of our model of participant consumption. It is a five-step process that consumers use when deciding to participate in a specific sport or activity. Before turning to our model of participant consumption behavior, it must be stressed that the primary reason for understanding the participant decision-making process is to guide the rest of the strategic sports marketing process. Without a better understanding of

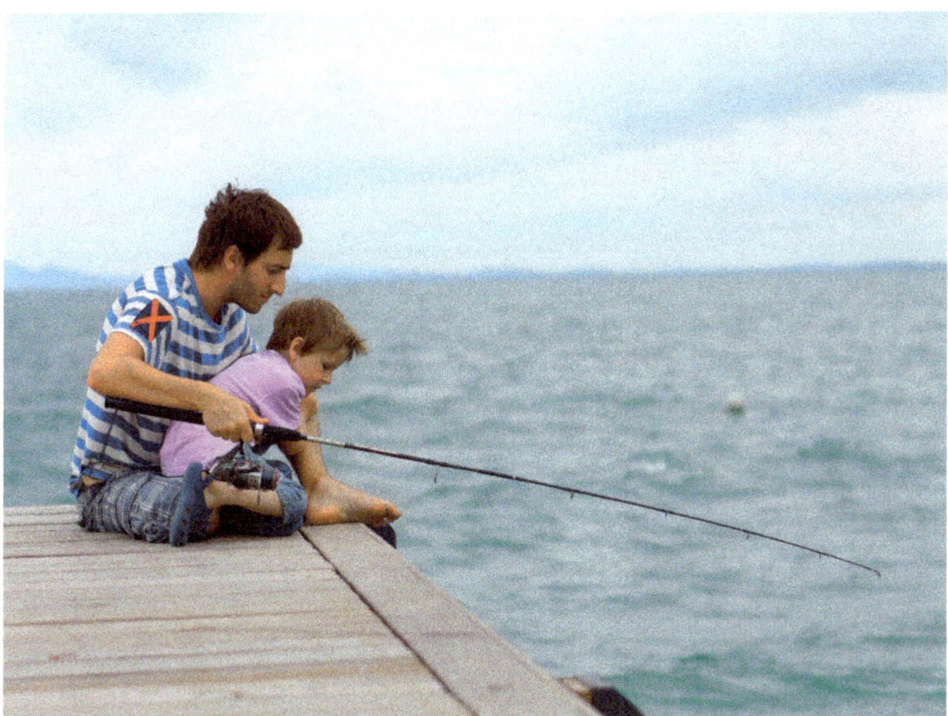

Photo 4.1 Father and son fishing together by the ocean

Source: Shutterstock.com

sports participants, marketers would simply be guessing about how to satisfy their needs.

Model of participant consumption behavior

To help organize all this complex information about sports participants, we have developed a model of participant consumption behavior that will serve as a framework for the rest of our discussion (see Figure 4.1). At the center of our model is the participant decision-making process, which is influenced by three components: (1) internal or psychological processes such as motivation, perception, learning and memory, and attitudes; (2) external or sociocultural factors, such as culture, reference groups, and family; and (3) situational factors that act on the participant decision-making process.

Participant decision-making process

Every time you lace up your running shoes, grab your tennis racquet, or dive into a pool, you have made a decision about participating in sports. Sometimes these decisions are nearly automatic because, for example, you might jog nearly every day. Other decisions, such as playing in a golf league, require more careful consideration because of the time and cost involved. The foundation of our **model of participant consumption behavior** is trying to understand how consumers arrive at their decisions.

Participant decision making is a complex, cognitive process that brings together memory, thinking, information processing, and making evaluative judgments. The five

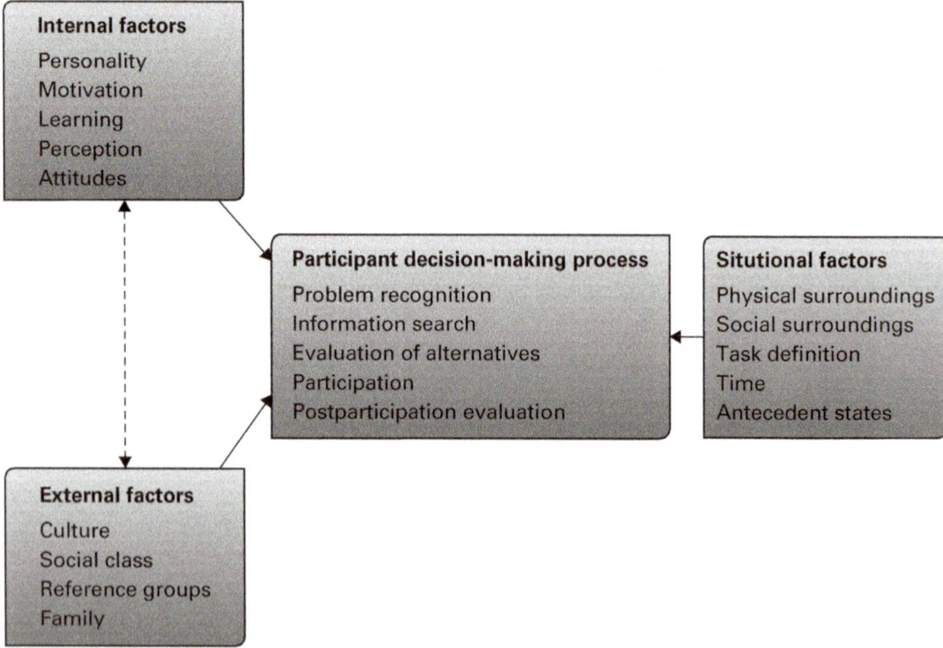

Figure 4.1 Model of participant consumption behavior

steps that make up the process used to explain participant decision making are shown in Figure 4.1. It is important to remember that every individual consumer arrives at decisions in a slightly different manner because of his or her own psychological makeup and environment. However, the five-step participant decision-making process, moving from problem recognition through post-participation evaluation, is relatively consistent among consumers and must be understood by sports marketers to develop strategies that fit with consumers' needs.

As we progress through the participant decision-making process, let us consider the case of Jack, a 33-year-old male who just moved from Los Angeles to Cincinnati. Jack has always been active in sports and would like to participate in an organized sports league. Because of work and family commitments, Jack only has the time to participate in one league. He is unsure about what sport to participate in, although he does have a few requirements. Because he is a newcomer to the city, Jack would like to participate in a team sport to meet new people. Also, he wants the league to be moderately competitive so as to keep his competitive juices flowing. Finally, he would like to remain injury free, so the sport needs to be non- or limited-contact. Let us see how Jack arrives at this important decision by using the participant decision-making process.

Problem recognition

The first step in the participant decision-making process is problem recognition. During problem recognition, consumers realize they have a need that is not presently being met. **Problem recognition** is the result of a discrepancy between a desired state and an actual state large enough and important enough to activate the entire decision-making process.[1] Stated simply, the desired state reflects the "ideal" of the participant. In other words, what is the absolute best sport for Jack to participate in, given his unique needs? If there is a difference between ideal and actual levels of participation, then the decision-making process begins.

The desire to resolve a problem and to reach goals, once recognized by consumers, is dependent on two factors: (1) the magnitude or size of the discrepancy and (2) the relative importance of the problem. Let us look at how these two factors would affect problem recognition. Jack currently jogs on a daily basis and wants to participate in a competitive, organized, and aggressive team sport. Is the discrepancy between actual state (individual, recreational, and nonaggressive) and desired state (team play, competitive, and aggressive) large enough to activate the decision-making process? Let's assume that it is and consider the second condition of problem recognition, the importance of the problem.

The second condition that must be met for problem recognition to occur is that the goal must be important enough to Jack. Some consumers may recognize the difference between participating in recreational sports versus an organized league. Would the benefits of participating in the new organized league (hopefully making some friends and being more competitive) outweigh the time, expense, and energy required to play? If the problem is important enough to Jack, then he moves on to the next stage of the decision-making process – information search.

What strategic implication does problem recognition hold for sports marketers? Generally, we would first identify the actual and desired states of sports

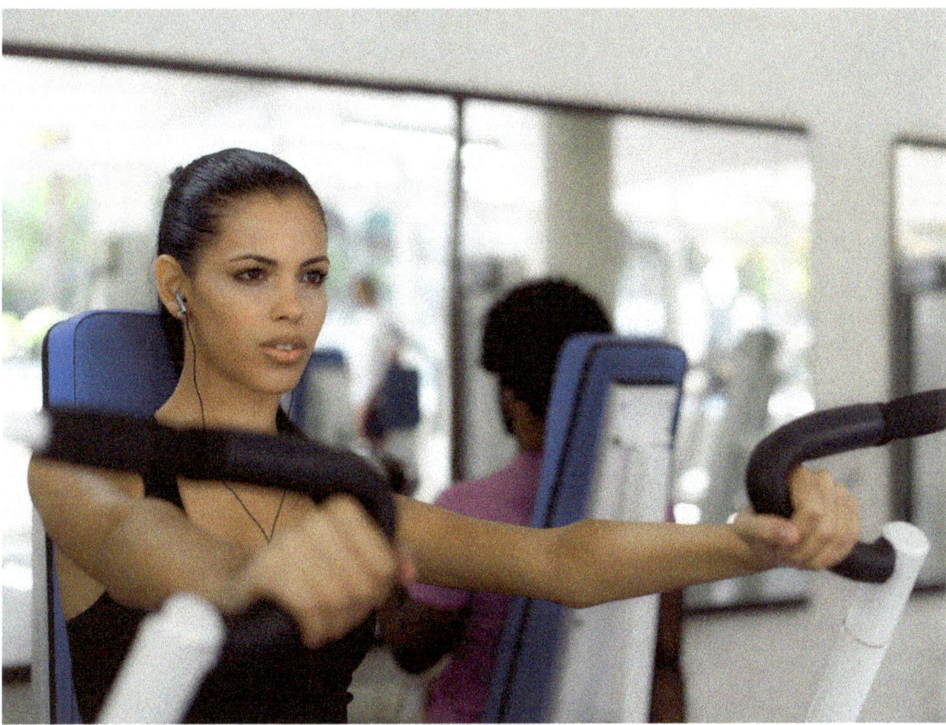

Photo 4.2 Many consumers see a discrepancy between the "ideal" and "actual" body.

Source: Shutterstock.com

participants or potential participants. Once these states have been determined, sports marketers can offer activities and events that will fill these needs and eliminate "problems." In addition, sports marketers can attempt to alter the perceived ideal state of consumers. For example, it is common for health clubs to show the "ideal" body that can be achieved by purchasing a membership and working out. Media is continually an avenue in which the ideal and actual body are forever challenged as seen in the following video: http://www.youtube.com/watch?v=rulwamsQVck.

Information search

After problem recognition occurs, the next step in the participant decision-making process is information search. **Information search** occurs when a participant seeks relevant information that will help resolve the problem. The sources of information sought by consumers can be broken down into two types: internal and external sources.

Internal sources of information are recalled from our own memories and are based on previous exposure to sports and activities. The internal information activated from memory can provide us with a wealth of data that may affect the decision-making process. Jack has spent most of his life participating in sports and recreational activities so information based on past experience is readily available. For instance, because Jack has played in an organized league in the past, he would use internal information to recall his experiences. Did he enjoy the competition of organized sport? Why did he stop participating in the sport? **External sources** of information are environmentally based and can occur in three different ways. First, Jack might ask **personal sources**, such as friends or family, to provide him with information about possible organized team sports in which to participate. Friends and family are important information sources that can have a great deal of influence on our participation choices. Second, **marketing sources**, such as advertisements, sales personnel, brochures, and Web sites on the Internet are all important information

Web 4.1 Online information source

Source: http://kayakonline.com

sources. In fact, sports marketers have direct control over this source of information, so it is perhaps the most critical from the perspective of the sports organization. The third type of external information source is called an **experiential source**. Jack may watch games in several different sports leagues to gather information. His decision is influenced by watching the level of competition.

Some participants may require a great deal of information before making a decision, whereas others require little to no information. The amount of information and the number of sources used is a function of several factors, such as the amount of time available, the importance of the decision, the amount of past experience, and the demographics and psychographics of the participants.

The extent of the information search also depends on the **perceived risk** of the decision. Perceived risk stems from the uncertainty associated with decision making and is concerned with the potential threats inherent in making the wrong decision. For individual sports participants perceived risk surfaces in many different forms. Perceived risk may be the embarrassment of not having the skill necessary to participate in a competitive league (social risks) or being concerned about the money needed to participate (economic risks). Also, an important perceived risk for many adult participants is health and safety (safety risks).

At this stage of the participant decision-making process, sports marketers must understand as much as they can about the information sources used by consumers. For instance, marketers for the Cincinnati Recreational Commission want to know the information sources for teams, what is the most effective way to provide teams with information, how much information is desired, and to whom they should provide this information. Moreover, sports marketers want to understand the perceived risks for potential participants such as Jack. This information is essential for developing an effective promotional strategy that targets both teams and individual participants.

Evaluation of alternatives

Now that the information search has yielded all the available participation alternatives that have some of the basic characteristics that appeal to Jack, he must begin to evaluate the alternatives. Jack thinks about all the organized team sports in which he might participate and chooses a subset to which he will give further consideration. The few sports given the greatest consideration are called the **evoked set** of alternatives. Jack's evoked set might consist of four sports: softball, basketball, bowling, and indoor soccer.

After consumers develop their evoked set, which is comprised of acceptable alternatives, they must evaluate each sport based on the important features and characteristics. These features and characteristics that potential consumers are looking for in a sport are called **evaluative criteria**. The evaluative criteria used by Jack include team sport, organized or league play, moderate level of competition, and moderately aggressive sport. It is important to realize that each of the four evaluative criteria carries a different weight in Jack's overall decision-making process. To continue with our example, let us say that Jack attaches the greatest importance to participating in a team sport. Next, Jack is concerned with participating in a league or organized sport. The level of aggression is the next most important criterion to Jack. Finally, the least important factor in choosing from among the four sports is the level of competition.

In complex decision making, Jack would evaluate each of the sports against each of the evaluative criteria. He would base his final decision regarding participation on which sport measures best against the various factors he deems important. The two most important criteria – team sport and league play – are satisfied for each of the four sports in the evoked set. In other words, all the sports that Jack is evaluating are team sports, and all have league play. Therefore, Jack moves on to his next criteria, level of aggression. Ideally, Jack wants to remain injury free, so he eliminates indoor soccer and basketball from further consideration. Bowling seems to be a clear winner in satisfying these criteria, and Jack is aware of several competitive bowling leagues in the area. Therefore, Jack decides to participate in a bowling league.

The **evaluation of alternatives** has two important implications for sports marketers. First, sports marketers must ensure their sports are included in the evoked set of potential consumers. To accomplish this objective, consumers must first become aware of the alternative. Second, sports marketers must understand what evaluative criteria are used by potential consumers and then develop strategies to meet consumers' needs based on these criteria. For example, marketers of bowling have determined that there are two different participant bowling markets: league or organized and recreational bowlers.

Recreational bowlers are growing in numbers and care most about the facilities at which they bowl and the related services provided. The evaluative criteria used by recreational bowlers might include the type of food served, other entertainment offered (e.g., arcade games and billiards), and the atmosphere of the bowling alley. League bowlers, however, constitute a diminishing market. This segment of bowlers cares most about the location of the bowling center and the condition of the lanes.[2]

Participation

The evaluation of alternatives has led us to what marketers consider the most important outcome of the decision-making process – the participation decision. The participation stage of the decision-making process might seem to be the most straightforward, but many things need to be considered other than actually deciding what sport to play. For instance, the consumer's needs may shift to the equipment and apparel needed to participate. Jack may decide that he needs a new bowling ball, shoes, and equipment bag to look the part of bowler for his new team. Thus, marketers working for equipment manufacturers are interested in Jack's participant consumption behavior. In addition, Jack may have to decide which bowling alley offers the best alternative for his needs. He may choose a location close to home, one that offers the best price, or the alley that has the best atmosphere. Again, these criteria must be carefully considered by sports marketers, because participants make choices regarding not only what sports they want to participate in, but also where they want to participate.

Other things might occur that alter the intended decision to participate in a given sport. At the last minute, Jack's coworkers may talk him out of playing in a competitive men's league in lieu of a co-rec, work league. There might be a problem finding an opening on a roster, which would also change Jack's decision-making process at the last moment. Perhaps the bowling team that Jack wanted to join is scheduled to play during a trip that he had planned. All these "unexpected pleasures" may occur at the participation stage of the decision-making process.

Postparticipation evaluation

You might think that the decision-making process comes to an abrupt halt after the participation decision, but there is one more very important step – **postparticipation evaluation**. The first activity that may occur after consumers have made an important participation decision is **cognitive dissonance**. This dissonance occurs because consumers experience doubts or anxiety about the wisdom of their decision. In other words, people question their own judgment. Let us suppose Jack begins participating in a competitive bowling league, and the first time he bowls, he is embarrassed. His poor level of play is far worse than that of everyone else on the team. Immediately, he begins to question his decision to participate. Whether dissonance occurs is a function of the importance of the decision, the difficulty of the choice, the degree of commitment to the decision, and the individual's tendency to experience anxiety.[3] Jack does not know his teammates well and only paid $50 to join the league, so he may decide to quit the team. However, he does not want to let his team down and ruin his chance of making new friends, so high levels of dissonance may cause him to continue with the team. In either case, the level of dissonance that Jack feels is largely based on his own personality and tendency to experience anxiety.

Another important activity that occurs after participation begins is evaluation. First, the participant develops expectations about what it will be like to play in this competitive bowling league. Jack's expectations may range from thinking about how much physical pain the sport will cause to thinking about how many new friends he will make as a result of participating. Next, Jack evaluates his actual experience after several games. If expectations are met or exceeded, then satisfaction occurs. However, if the experience or performance is poorer than expected, then dissatisfaction results. The level of satisfaction Jack experiences will obviously have a tremendous impact on his future participation and word-of-mouth communication about the sport.

Types of consumer decisions

We have just completed our discussion of Jack's decision-making process and have failed to mention one very important thing: Not all decisions are alike. Some are extremely important and, therefore, take a great deal of time and thought. Because we are creatures of habit, some decisions require little or no effort. We simply do what we have always done in the past. The variety of decisions that we make about participation in sport can be categorized into three different types of participation decision processes. The decision processes, also known as levels of problem solving, are habitual problem solving, limited problem solving, and extensive problem solving.

Habitual problem solving

One type of decision process that is used is called **habitual problem solving** (or **routinized problem solving**). In habitual problem solving, problem recognition occurs, followed by limited internal information search. As we just learned, internal search comes from experiences with sports stored in memory. Therefore, when Jack is looking for information on sports next year, he simply remembers his previous experience and satisfaction with bowling. The evaluation of alternatives is eliminated for habitual decisions because no alternatives are considered. Jack participates in bowling again, but this time there is no dissonance and limited evaluation occurs. In a sense, Jack's decision to participate in bowling becomes a habit or routine each year.

Limited problem solving

The next type of consumer decision process is called **limited problem solving**. Limited problem solving begins with problem recognition and includes internal search and sometimes limited external search. A small number of alternatives are evaluated using a few evaluative criteria. In fact, in limited problem solving, the alternatives being evaluated are often other forms of entertainment (e.g., movies or concerts). After purchase, dissonance is rare and a limited evaluation of the product occurs. Participation in special sporting events, such as a neighborhood 10k run or charity golf outing, are examples of sporting events that lend themselves to limited problem solving.

Extensive problem solving

The last type of decision process is called **extensive problem solving** (or **extended problem solving**) because of the exhaustive nature of the decision. As with any type of decision, problem recognition must occur for the decision-making process to be initiated. Heavy information search (both internal and external) is followed by the evaluation of many alternatives on many attributes. Postpurchase dissonance and postpurchase evaluation are at their highest levels with extensive decisions. Jack's initial decision to participate in the bowling league was an extensive decision due to his high levels of information search, the many sports alternatives he considered, and the comprehensive nature of his evaluation of bowling.

For many people who are highly involved in sports, participation decisions are more extensive in nature, especially in the initial stages of participating in and evaluating various sports. Over time, what was once an extensive decision becomes routine. Participants choose sports that meet their needs, and the decision to participate becomes automatic. It is important for marketers to understand the type of problem solving used by participants so the most effective marketing strategy can be formulated and implemented.

Psychological or internal factors

Now that we have looked at the participant decision-making process, let us turn our focus to the internal, or psychological, factors. Personality, motivation, learning, and perception are some of the basic **psychological** or **internal factors** that will be unique to each individual and guide sports participation decisions.

Personality

One of the psychological factors that may have a tremendous impact on whether we participate in sports, the sports in which we participate, and the amount of participation, is personality. Psychologists have defined **personality** as a set of consistent responses an individual makes to the environment.

Although there are different ways to describe personality, one common method used by marketers is based on specific, identifiable personality traits. For example, individuals can be thought of as aggressive, orderly, dominant, or nurturing.[4] Consider the potential association between an individual's personality profile and the likelihood of participating in a particular sport. The self-assured, outgoing, assertive individual may be more likely than the apprehensive, reserved, and humble person to participate

Photo 4.3 A growing number of consumers participate in high-risk sports

Source: Shutterstock.com

in any sport. Moreover, the self-sufficient individual may participate in more individual sports (e.g., figure skating, golf, or tennis) than the group-dependent individual.

In one study, Generation X-ers were found to be more interested in fast-paced, high-risk activities, such as rock climbing and mountain biking.[5] As such, action sports may be a good choice for the happy-go-lucky, venturesome personality type of the Generation X-ers. Action or extreme sports are defined as the pantheon of aggressive, non-team sports, including snowboarding, in-line skating, super modified shovel racing, wakeboarding, ice and rock climbing, mountain biking, and snow mountain biking.[6] Another example of the relationship between sports participation and personality traits can be seen in Table 4.2. As illustrated, golfers most often described themselves as responsible, family-oriented, self-confident, and intelligent. The poorest descriptors for golfers were *bitter, sick a lot, extravagant*, and *risk-averse*. Interestingly, golfers described themselves as team players, although they participate in this highly individual sport.

Although personality and participation may be linked, take care not to assume a causal relationship between personality and sports participation. Some researchers believe sports participation might shape various personality traits (i.e., sport is a character builder). Other researchers believe we participate in sports because of our particular personality type. To date, little research supports the causal direction of the relationship between personality and participation in sport.

Not only does personality dictate whether someone participates in sports, but it may also be linked with participation in particular types of sports. The violent, aggressive personality type may be drawn to sports such as mixed martial arts, football, boxing,

Table 4.2 Golfer's self-reported traits and personality characteristics

Poorest describers	Percentage	Best descriptors	Percentage
Born again	16	Practical	60
Attractive	15	Competent	61
Non-mainstream	14	Ambitious	61
Lonely	8	Sensitive	62
Fun-loving	8	Team player	63
Virgin	6	Fun-loving	64
Risk-averse	6	Intelligent	66
Extravagant	6	Confident	70
Always sick	3	Family-oriented	75
Bitter	3	Responsible	80

Source: Yankelovich Partners, "How Golfers Are Likely to Describe Themselves."

or hockey. The shy, introverted personality type may be more likely to participate in individual sports, such as tennis and running. Knowing the relationship between participation and personality profiles can help sports marketers set up the strategic sports marketing process so it will appeal to the appropriate personality segment. In addition, sports marketers of large participant sporting events use personality profiles to attract potential corporate sponsors who may want to appeal to the same personality segment.

Motivation

Why do people participate in sports? What benefits are people looking for from participating in sport, and what needs do participating in sport satisfy? McDonald, Milne, and Hong,[7] drawing on Maslow's human needs hierarchy, present evidence illustrating that consumers possess multiple and unique motivations – including achievement, competition, social facilitation, physical fitness, skill mastery, physical risk, affiliation, aesthetics, aggression, value development, self-esteem, self-actualization, and stress release – for participating in particular sport activities. Steve Jennison highlighted that "sport has the ability to enhance people's lives, improve health status, and increase participation rates to support development of a physically active city. It can also unite communities and nations through success in international competition and major events through pride, passion, and participation"[8] (Hull City). Additional studies suggest there are three basic reasons for participation in sport (see Table 4.3). Finally, studies have looked at understanding the motives for participation in a specific sport. For example, Rohm, Milne, and McDonald[9] recently explored the motives of runners (see Table 4.4 for segmentation of runners by motives).

The study of human motivation helps to better understand the underlying need to participate in sports. **Motivation** is an internal force that directs behavior toward the fulfillment of needs. In our earlier discussion of the participant decision-making process, problem recognition resulted from having needs that are not currently being met. As the definition indicates, motivation is discussed in terms of fulfilling unmet needs. Although there is no argument that all humans have needs, there is disagreement about the number of needs and the nature of them.

Table 4.3 Why people participate in sports

Personal improvement	
Release of tension or relaxation, sense of accomplishment, skill mastery, improved health and fitness, other people's respect for one's athletic skill, release of aggression, enjoyment of risk taking, personal growth, development of positive values, and sense of personal pride	
Sport appreciation	
Enjoyment of the game, sport competition, and thrill of victory	
Social facilitation	
Time spent with close friends or family and sense of being part of a group	
Why people play sport	**Why people don't play sport**
Improve fitness/skill level	No time/too busy
Make new friends	Family/home/work commitments
Sense of belonging/peer pressure	Too competitive
Fun and enjoyment	Lack motivation or confidence
Fame or money	Cost – too expensive
Achievement of goals	Physically unable

Source: George Milne, William Sutton, and Mark McDonald, "Niche Analysis: A Strategic Measurement Tool for Managers," *Sport Marketing Quarterly*, vol. 5, no. 3 (1996), 17–21.

Table 4.4 Segmentation of runners by motives

"I find running to be both relaxing and is the primary way along with a good diet that I keep up my plan for good health and fitness." – Female 50+ years old, 18 miles/week, 4 days per week

"Running is a very important because I use running to relieve stress and to think about what is bothering me. I use running to clear my head. Running is important to maintain fitness and to counteract my poor diet of late." – Male, < 25 years old, no mileage reported.

Social competitors

"Running is one of the greatest joys of life. Keeps the body, mind, and spirit soaring. Running with friends is special. Competition pushes me to new levels. Can travel to races and see new places. I can share stories with runners from all over the world." – Female, 25–39 years old, runs 40 miles per week, 5 days/week

"I just recently started running 3 yrs ago. I used to weigh 317 lbs I'm now down to 245. Before I leave work I change and go directly to a 1/2 mile track located on the way home. My running is very important; it relieves a lot of stress and is something that is within my control. I have made many acquaintances at the track. We all motivate each other. If someone misses one day everybody is aware and concerned. That alone motivates you to keep going. Besides I am trying to get down to 199lbs." – Male, 40–49, runs 24 miles/week, 6 days week

Actualized athletes

"I quit smoking at age 33, in 1978, and took up running and I will never stop running. I bike & kayak but running is my first love. It makes me feel good about myself and it gave me a lot of confidence. I've run many marathons in my past yrs and many races and you cannot describe the feeling of accomplishment at the end. It gave me the confidence to go back to school at the age of 40 and get a degree in nursing." – Female, 50+ years old, runs 30 miles, 6 days/week

"I love to run. I've always been athletic and enjoyed team sports. But running is different. It's a solitary sport. It pits me against me. I'm 42 yrs old and I know I've yet to reach my potential as a runner. My best yrs are behind me and I know I'll never be world class but I still have room to improve and I'll keep trying, training, testing. It makes me fit, it makes me happy. I love to run." – Male, 40–49 years old, runs 35 miles/week, 5 days/week

Table 4.4 (continued)

Devotees
"It is a big part of my life. It's like brushing your teeth – it's a gift I give myself every day or almost everyday. It is who I am and I never want not to run. It's the most wonderful total feeling in life. It has made me grow in so many ways and also appreciate life so much more. You can do it anywhere at any time – no expense." – Male, 50+ years old, runs 38 miles/week, 6 days/week
"It's part of who I am. Running is the most important free time activity I have besides spending time with my kids. I'm a happier person when I get my running." – Female, 25–39, runs 20 miles/week, 4 days/week

Source: Andrew J. Rohm, George R, Milne, and Mark McDonald, "A Mixed-Method Approach for Developing Market Segmentation Typologies in the Sports Industry," *Sport Marketing Quarterly*, 2006, 15, 29–39, © 2006 West Virginia University.

One popular theory of human motivation based on classification of needs is called **Maslow's hierarchy of needs** (see Figure 4.2). Maslow's hierarchy of needs consists of five levels. For video interpretation of Maslow's hierarchy of needs see: http://www.youtube.com/watch?v=zIvRITVgyKM. According to Maslow, the most basic, primitive needs must be fulfilled before the individual can progress to the next level of need. Once this higher level of need is satisfied, the individual is then motivated to fulfill the next higher level of need. Let us look at the hierarchy of needs as it relates to participation in sports.

The first and most basic level of needs in Maslow's hierarchy are called **physiological needs**. These are the biological needs that people have – to eat, drink, and meet other physiological needs. For some individuals, there may be a physiological need to exercise and have some level of activity. Once this lower order need is met, safety needs are addressed. **Safety needs** are concerned with physical safety, as well as the need to remain healthy. Sports equipment manufacturers address the need participants have for physical safety. With respect to the need for health, many

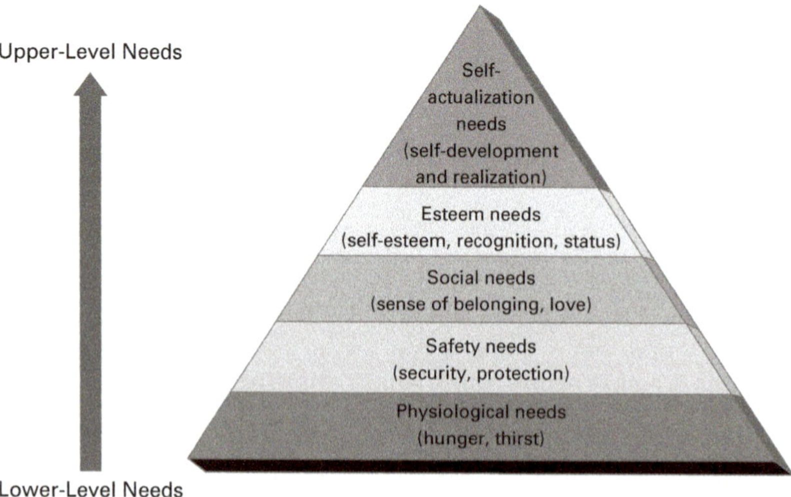

Figure 4.2 Maslow's hierarchy of needs

Source: A. H. Maslow, Motivation and Personality, 2nd ed. (New York: Harper and Row, 1970). Reprinted with permission of Pearson Education, Inc., Upper Saddle River, NJ.

participants cite that the primary reason for joining health clubs is to maintain or improve their health.

The next need level is based on **love and belonging**. Many people choose to participate in sport because of the social aspects involved. One of the early need theories of motivation includes "play" as a primary social need.[10] For some individuals, sports participation is their only outlet for being part of a group and interacting with others. The need to be part of a team and to be respected by teammates has been demonstrated in a number of studies.

As these social needs are satisfied, **esteem** needs of recognition and status must be addressed. Certainly, sport plays a major role in enhancing self-esteem and the impact of sport participation on enhanced self-esteem has been well documented. Bungee jumping provides an excellent illustration of how sport influences esteem. The president of the U.S. Bungee Association (USBA), Casey Dale, describes the motives of people who use risky activities as a self-image booster. "People are less satisfied than they used to be with being pigeonholed by what they do, so they want to change their self-image. A quick fix is to become this extreme, risk-taking individual. All of a sudden, Bill the accountant goes bungee jumping off a 20-story bridge, and all of his coworkers see him in a new light."[11]

Finally, the highest order need, **self-actualization**, should be met. This refers to the individual's need to "be all that you can be" and is usually fulfilled through

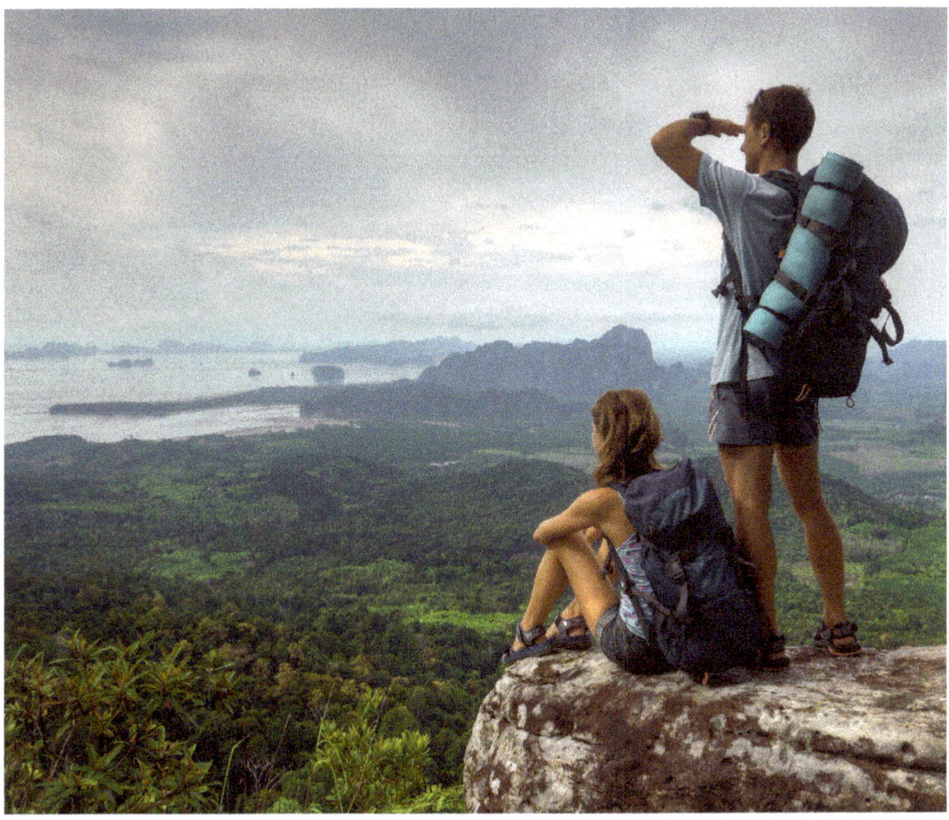

Photo 4.4 Sports participants fulfilling the need for self-actualization

Source: Shutterstock.com

participation in mountain climbing, triathlons, or any sport that pushes an individual to the utmost of his or her physical and mental capacities. For example, ultramarathons in which runners compete in 100k road races certainly test the will of all participants. Another example of self-actualization can be found in the amateur athlete who trains his or her whole life for the Olympic Games.

As a sports marketer, you may be able to enhance strategies for increasing participation if you identify and understand the needs of consumers. In some instances, participation might fill more than one need level. Consumers may satisfy physiological needs, safety needs, social needs, esteem needs, or possibly self-actualization needs. For instance, marketing a health club membership might appeal to consumers wanting to fulfill any of the need levels in the hierarchy. The members' physiological needs are being met through exercise. Safety needs might be met by explaining that the club has state-of-the-art exercise equipment that is designed to be safe for all ages and fitness levels. Social needs are addressed by describing the club as a "home away from home" for many members. The need for esteem for health club members might be easily satisfied by depicting how good they will look and feel after working out. Finally, self-actualization needs may be fulfilled by working out to achieve the ideal body.

The needs that have just been presented can be described in two ways: motive direction and motive strength. Motive direction is the way that a consumer attempts to reduce tension by either moving toward a positive goal or moving away from a negative outcome. In the case of sports participation, an individual wants to get in good physical condition and may move toward this goal by running, biking, lifting weights, and so on. Likewise, this same individual may want to move away from eating fatty foods and drinking alcohol.

Of particular interest to sports marketers is the strength of the sports participation motive. Motivational strength is the degree to which an individual chooses to actively pursue one goal over another. In sports marketing, the strength of a motive is characterized in terms of **sports involvement**. Sports involvement is the perceived interest in and personal importance of sports to an individual participating in a sport.[12]

Triathletes are an excellent example of an extreme level of sports involvement because of the importance placed on training for events. In their study, Hill and Robinson demonstrated that extreme involvement in a sport affects many aspects of the athletes' lives.[13] Participation could have positive effects, such as increased self-esteem, improved moods, and a better sense of overall wellness. Conversely, high involvement in a sport (e.g., triathlon) may produce neglected responsibilities of work, home, or family, and feelings of guilt, stress, and anxiety. Said simply, extremely involved individuals frequently have a difficult time balancing their lives.

Sports marketers are interested in involvement because it has been shown to be a relatively good predictor of sports-related behaviors. For example, a study found that level of involvement was positively related to the number of hours people participate in sports, the likelihood of planning their day around a sporting event, and the use of sports-related media (e.g., television, newspaper, or magazines).[14] Knowledge of sports involvement can help sports marketers develop strategies for both low- and high-involvement groups of potential participants.

Photo 4.5 The high involvement cyclist

Source: Shutterstock.com

Perception

Think for a moment about the image you have of the following sports: soccer, hockey, and tennis. You might think of soccer as a sport that requires a great deal of stamina and skill, hockey as a violent and aggressive sport, and tennis as a sport for people who belong to country clubs. Ask two friends about their images of these same sports, and you are likely to get two different responses. That is because each of us has our own views of the world based on past experience, needs, wants, and expectations.

Your image of sport results from being exposed to a lifetime of information. You talk to friends and family about sports, you watch sports on television, and you listen to sports on the radio. In addition, you may have participated in a variety of sports over the course of your life. We selectively filter sports information based on our own view of the world. Consumers process this information and use it in making decisions about participation.

The process by which consumers gather information and then interpret that information based on their own past experience is described as perception. **Perception** is defined as the complex process of selecting, organizing, and interpreting stimuli such as sports.[15] Ultimately, our perception of the world around us influences participant consumer behavior. The images that we hold of various sports and of ourselves dictate, to some extent, what sports we participate in. One of the primary goals of sports marketing is to shape your image of sports and sports products.

Before sports marketers can influence your perceptions, they must get your attention. **Selective attention** describes a consumer's focus on a specific marketing stimulus based on personal needs and attitudes. For example, you are much more likely to pay attention to advertisements for new golf clubs if you are thinking about purchasing a set.

Sports marketers fight with other sports and nonsports marketing stimuli for the limited capacity that consumers have for processing information. One job of the sports marketer is to capture the attention of the potential participant. But how is this done? Typically, sports marketers capture our attention through the use of novel promotions, using large and colorful promotional materials, and developing unique ways of communicating with consumers.

While sports marketers attempt to influence our perceptions, each participant brings a unique set of experiences, attitudes, and needs that affect the perceptual process. Generally speaking, consumers perceive things in ways that are consistent with their existing attitudes and values. This process is known as **selective interpretation**. For example, those who have played hockey all their life may not see it as a dangerous and violent sport, whereas others hold a different interpretation.

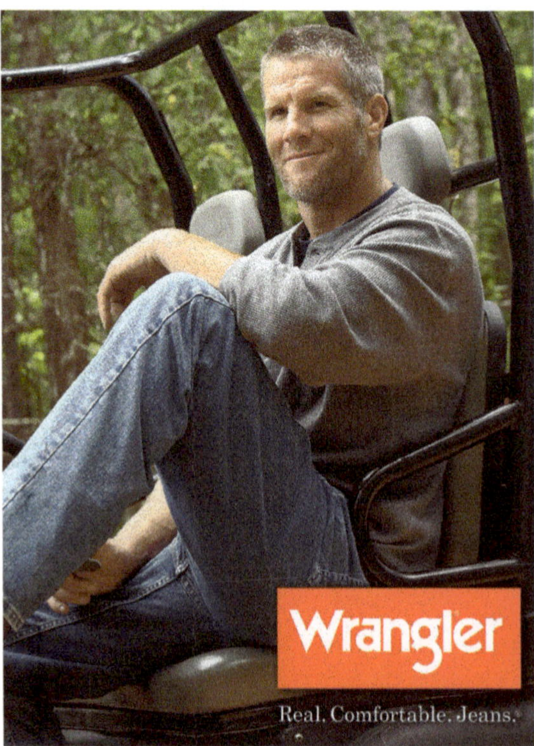

Ad 4.1 Wrangler® & Brett Farve

Source: Wrangler ®

Finally, **selective retention**, or the tendency to remember only certain information, is another of the influences on the perceptual process. Selective retention is remembering just the things we want to remember. The hockey player does not remember the injuries, the training, or the fights – only the victories.

Although sports marketers cannot control consumers' perceptions, they can and do influence our perceptions of sports through their marketing efforts. For example, a sports marketer trying to increase volleyball participation in boys ages 8 to 12 must first attempt to understand their perception of volleyball. Then the sports marketer tries to find ways of capturing the attention of this group of consumers, who have many competing sports and entertainment alternatives. Once they have the attention of this group of potential participants, a marketing mix is designed to either reinforce their perception of volleyball or change the existing image.

In addition to understanding these consumers' images of volleyball, sports marketers are also interested in other aspects of perception. For instance, how do potential participants perceive advertisements and promotional materials about the sport? What are the parents' perceptions of volleyball? Do the parents perceive volleyball to be costly? The answer to all these questions depends on our own unique view of the world, which sports marketers attempt to understand and shape.

Learning

Another psychological factor that affects our participation decisions is learning. **Learning** is a relatively permanent change in response tendency due to the effects of experience. These response tendencies can be either changes in behavior (participation) or in how we perceive a particular sport. Consumers learn about and gather information regarding participation in various sports in any number of ways. **Behavioral learning** is concerned with how various stimuli (information about sports) elicit certain responses (feelings or behaviors) within an individual. **Cognitive learning**, however, is based on our ability to solve problems and use observation as a form of learning. Finally, **social learning** is based on watching others and learning from their actions. Let us look briefly at these three theories of learning as they apply to sports participation.

Behavioral learning

One behavioral learning theory of importance to sports marketers is operant conditioning. Conditioning teaches people to associate certain behaviors with certain consequences of those behaviors. A simplified model of operant conditioning is illustrated in Figure 4.3.

Let us illustrate the model of operant conditioning using participation in snowboarding. We may decide to try snowboarding (specific behavior) as a new sport. Next and unfortunately, our behavior is punished as we continually fall down, suffer social embarrassment, and feel uncomfortably wet and cold. Finally, the likelihood of

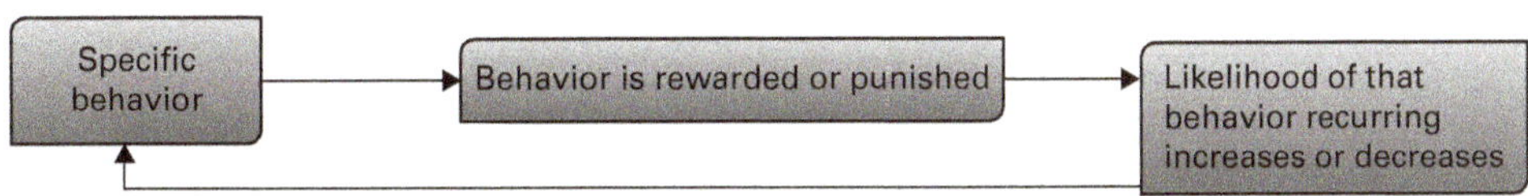

Figure 4.3 Model of operant conditioning

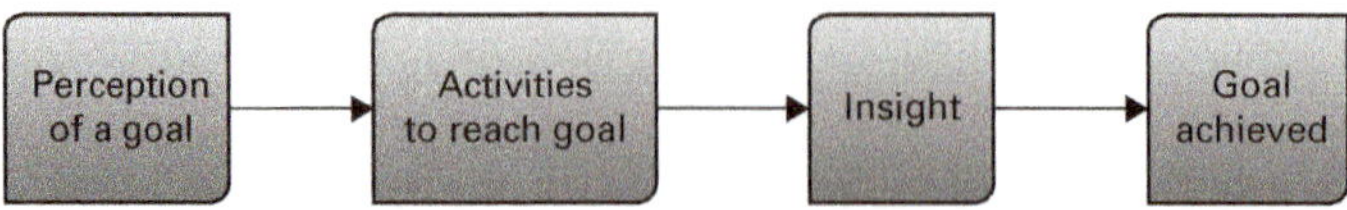

Figure 4.4 Model of cognitive learning

our engaging in this behavior in the future is decreased because of the negative consequences of our earlier attempts at snowboarding. However, if we are rewarded through the enjoyment of the sport and being with others, then we will continue to snowboard more and more.

The theory of operant conditioning lies at the heart of loyalty to a sport. In other words, if the sports we participate in meet our needs and reinforce them, then we will continue to participate in those sports. The objective of the sports marketer is to try to heighten the rewards associated with participating in any given sport and diminish any negative consequences.

Cognitive learning

Although much of what we learn is based on our past experience, learning also takes place through reasoning and thought processes. This approach to learning is known as cognitive learning. Cognitive learning is best known as learning through problem solving or insight, as shown in Figure 4.4.

Consider a goal that concerns some of us – weight loss. Once this goal is established, consumers search for activities that allow them to achieve the goal. The activities necessary to achieve weight loss might include dieting, participating in aerobics, weight training, playing basketball, or jogging. When consumers finally realize what specific activities they feel are necessary to achieve the desired goal, insight occurs. Finally, and hopefully, the goal of weight loss is achieved.

By using the concept of cognitive learning, the first focus of sports marketers is to understand the goals of potential consumers or participants. In addition, marketers must make potential participants aware of how the sport or sports product will help participants achieve their goals.

Social learning

Much of our learning takes place by watching how others are rewarded or punished for their actions. This way of learning is called social learning. As children, we watched our friends, family members, and our heroes participate in various sports. To a large extent, this early observation and learning dictates the sports in which we choose to participate later in life. In social learning, we not only see someone benefiting from sport, but we also learn how to participate in the sport ourselves.

Those individuals we choose to observe and the process of observation are called models and modeling, respectively. The job of the sports marketer is to present positive models and present sports in a positive light, so others will perceive the benefits of sports participation. For example, Venus and Serena Williams may be seen as role models for young African American athletes thinking about participating in tennis, or Peyton Manning may be a model for young men interested in football.

Attitudes

Because of the learning and perceptual processes, consumers develop attitudes toward participating in sports. **Attitudes** are learned thoughts, feelings, and behaviors toward some given object. What is your attitude toward participation in bowling? One positive aspect of bowling is the chance to interact socially with other participants. However, bowling does not burn a lot of calories and may be seen as expensive. Your overall attitude toward bowling is made up of these positive and negative aspects of the sport.

Attitudes represent one of the most important components of the overall model of sports participation because they ultimately guide the decision-making process. Our attitudes are formed on the basis of an interaction between past experience and the environment in which we live. A simple model of attitude formation or how attitudes are developed is shown in Figure 4.5.

As the model of attitude formation suggests, an attitude is based on our thinking, feeling, and actions toward a sport. These three components interact to form an overall attitude. Let us look briefly at its three components: cognitive, affective, and behavioral.

The **cognitive component** of attitude holds the beliefs that people have toward the object. Beliefs can be either a statement of knowledge regarding bowling or thoughts someone has toward bowling. They are neither right nor wrong and vary from individual to individual. For example, here are some beliefs about participation in bowling that consumers might hold:

- Bowling is expensive.
- Bowling is time consuming.
- Very few women bowl.
- Bowling is for old people. (*Note*: The largest participant group for bowling is 18- to 34-year-olds.)

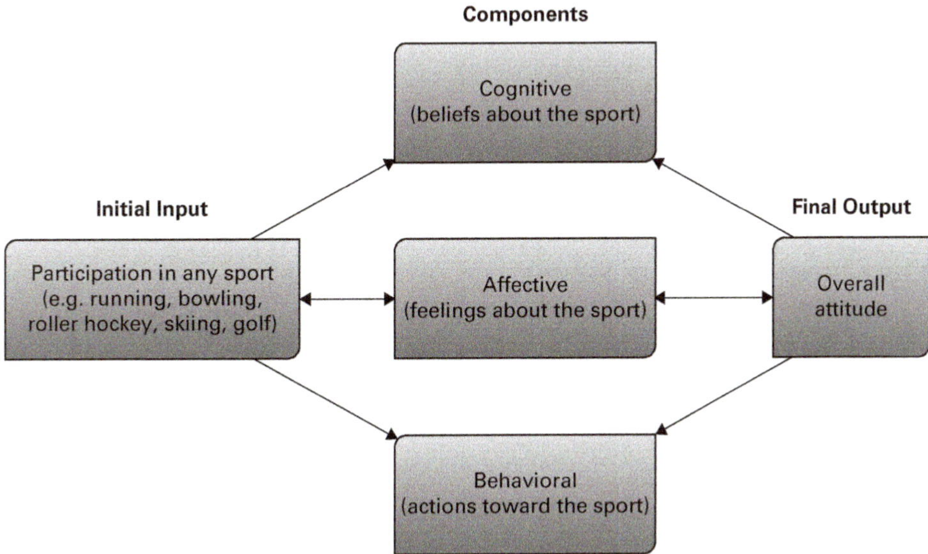

Figure 4.5 Model of attitude formation

Source: Adapted from Del Hawkins, Roger Best, and Kenneth Coney. *Consumer Behavior: Building Marketing Strategy*, 7th ed. (© 1998 The McGraw-Hill Companies, Inc., New York)

The **affective component** of attitude is based on feelings or emotional reactions to the initial stimulus. Most beliefs, such as the ones shown for cognitive attitude, have a related affective evaluation. More recently, affects, or feelings, have taken a more central role in explaining attitudes than beliefs or behaviors. In other words, some people equate attitudes with feelings that are held toward an object.[16] Here are some potential affective statements:

- I hate bowling.
- Bowling is a boring sport.

The final component is called the **behavioral component** and is based on participants' actions. In other words, does the individual participate in bowling? How often does the individual bowl? What are the individual's behavioral intentions, or how likely will he or she be to bowl in the future?

Generally, sports marketers must understand consumer attitudes to maintain or increase participation in any given sport. Only after attitudes are assessed can sports marketing strategies be formulated to improve upon or change existing attitudes. In our previous example, bowling equipment manufacturers and bowling alley management companies would need to change the beliefs that potential participants have about bowling. Additional strategies may attempt to change potential participants' feelings about bowling by repositioning the sport's current image. Finally, marketers may get potential participants to try bowling, which could lead to possible changes in their beliefs and feelings about the sport.

Sociological or external factors

Now that we have looked at the major internal or psychological factors that influence participation decisions, let us turn our attention to the sociological factors. The **sociological or external factors** are those influences outside the individual participant that affect the decision-making process. The external factors are also referred to as sociological because they include all aspects of society and interacting with others. The external factors discussed in this chapter include culture, social class, reference groups, and family.

Culture

Participating in sports and games is one of the most long-standing traditions of civilization. Since the time of the ancient Greeks, participation in sports was expected and highly valued.[17] In the United States, sports are criticized for playing too important a role in our society. Many detractors frown at public monies being spent to finance private stadiums for professional athletics or institutions of higher education spending more on a new coach than on a new president for the university. As the accompanying article illustrates, other cultures are trying to emulate sports participation patterns in the United States.

Culture is the set of learned values, beliefs, language, traditions, and symbols shared by a people and passed down from generation to generation. One of the most important aspects of this definition of culture includes the learning component. **Socialization** occurs when we learn about the skills, knowledge, and attitudes necessary for participating in sports. Sports marketers are interested in better understanding how the **consumer socialization** process takes place and how they might influence this process.

SPOTLIGHT ON INTERNATIONAL SPORTS MARKETING

Sport England

Mission Statement

Sport England created a world-leading community sport environment, as part of the legacy of the 2012 Olympic and Paralympic Games. They are building a sporting infrastructure of clubs, coaches, programmes, organizations and facilities that not only encourages new participants but also generates excellent sporting experiences that retain those already involved. If they succeed they will deliver something that no Olympic host nation has ever been able to do before – a lasting increase in grassroots participation.

The establishment of a lifelong sporting culture in their country will change sport from a minority to a majority pastime. They believe this will have a broad impact. Health, crime, social justice and enterprise and community agendas, to name but a few, will benefit at national and local levels.

Letter from Chair Richard Lewis

The sports sector accounts for more than 2.3% of total consumer spending, worth £17.74 billion. It employs 1.8% of England's total workforce, or 441,000 people. The health benefits associated with sport and physical activity are well documented, and it is no surprise that sport is increasingly viewed as a form of preventative medicine by many in primary care.

We also see local engagement stimulated through sports participation, enabling the development of more cohesive, tolerant and inclusive communities, which works well with the Government's call for more collective and individual empowerment at the local level.

In short, sport is a real positive – that's why we need it to be more than a minority interest in this country.

Unfortunately, the big numbers you see in terms of economic and social contributions are not yet replicated in regular grassroots sports participation, something we know we must change.

The current number of adults playing regular sport in England is seven million, which represents 16.6% of the country. We have increased that by over 700,000 since we won the Olympic bid, and it is good that more people are playing more sport, but are clear that there is much more to do.

We have made steady progress during my first 12 months as chair of Sport England. Our new funding strategy has invested in a wide range of projects, we have built stronger relationships with national governing bodies, and we have brought people from sporting and non-sporting organisations together nationally and locally.

Going forward, I want to provide stability for this organisation in what we recognise are challenging times, politically and economically. Our work is important – not just for its own sake, but for the broader benefits it can deliver to the country, communities and individuals alike. We are committed to delivering not just more people playing sport three times a week for thirty minutes, but building a world-leading community sport environment which retains its participants and helps those with talent to flourish.

The beneficiaries of such an environment won't just include those already immersed in sport, but also those who are yet to discover its power. All of our work – the expertise we provide, advice we give, funds we invest and relationships we build – is focused on delivering this legacy. Such ambitious targets and large levels of investment must be accompanied by effective governance and accountability. The structures in all sports organisations must provide high levels of confidence and assurance in their ability to handle public money and deliver value.

I expect Sport England to also display those standards. This is why, last year, I asked Timothy Dutton QC to investigate the World Class Payments Bureau which operated outside our usual financial controls between September 1999 and March 2007. While I was disappointed this inquiry had to take place, I was pleased to note its conclusions that there was no fraud or corruption within this organisation and the recognition that there had been a clear improvement in management and financial controls since April 2007. We are now acting on Dutton's recommendations.

In closing, I would like to thank my fellow Board Members for their advice, expertise and commitment throughout the year. Thanks in particular go to Sir Andrew Foster, Ashia Hansen MBE, Philip Lemanski and Dr Jack Rowell OBE who stood down this year after completing their fixed-term service.

We now have just two years to go until the world comes to our country to play sport. Let's work hard to make sure that more of us than ever before are taking part, at every level, long after the last elite athlete has gone home.

Richard Lewis Chair Sport England

Source: Courtesy Sport England.

A model of sports socialization is presented in Figure 4.6, which provides a framework for understanding how children learn about sports. Although the sports socialization process begins at increasingly younger ages, it extends throughout the life of the individual. Sports marketers are interested in learning how the socialization process differs on the basis of gender, income, family lifestyle, and the number of children in the family.

Socializing agents also have a tremendous impact on the process. These factors represent the direct and indirect influences on the children. Sports marketers are also interested in understanding the relative impact of each socializing agent on a child's interest in participating in sports. For instance, is watching parents or professional

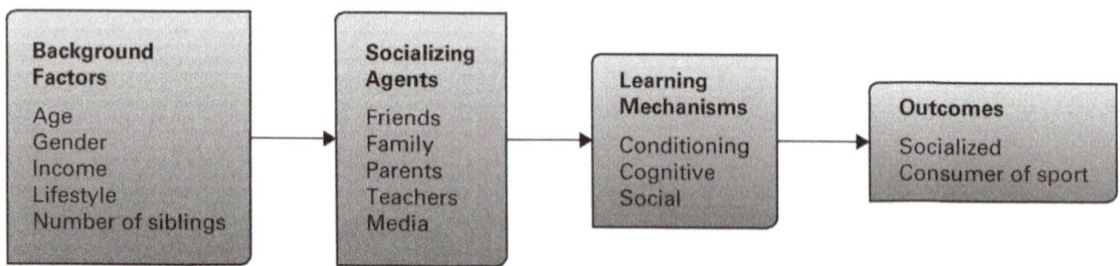

Figure 4.6 Model of consumer socialization

Source: John Mowen, *Consumer Behavior*, 3rd ed. (New York: Macmillan, 1993).

athletes a better predictor of sports participation among children? One study has shown that children look to parents first, but if they are unacceptable or unwilling role models, children turn to other people.[18]

The learning mechanisms of observation and reinforcement are just two ways that facilitate the socialization process. As discussed earlier, observation refers to looking to others as models for sports participation. For example, older siblings may serve as models for sports participation at earlier ages, whereas friends may become a more important learning mechanism as children age. Reinforcement may occur as children receive praise for participation in sport from parents, coaches, and friends.

The final element in the socialization model is the emergence of a socialized sports participant. Here, the child becomes actively engaged in sports participation. From the sports marketer's perspective, when children participate in sports at an early age, they may have better potential to become lifelong participants. Certainly, sporting goods manufacturers are interested in having children associate their brands with the enjoyment of sport at the earliest possible age.

Aside from the learning that takes place during the socialization process, values represent another important aspect of any culture. **Values** are widely held beliefs that affirm what is desirable in a culture. Whereas American priorities are often found with freedom, countries like Sweden are often more attuned to openness. America's main belief is rights for all through freedom, while Sweden's main concern is with all being accepted and resolving issues through other means such as working together to come to a solution.[19] Swedish citizens want to be able to have security and trust in their country. Several of the core values that reflect U.S. culture are shown in Table 4.5.

Some of the core American values listed in Table 4.5 have intimate ties to sports participation in the United States. Obviously, the last value mentioned, fitness and health, relates directly to our preoccupation with participating in sports. The activity value has a direct impact on the way Americans spend their leisure time, including sports participation. Likewise, achievement and success are a theme that is continually underscored as consumers participate in sports.

Table 4.5 Core American values

Core American Value	Descriptor
Achievement and success	Sense of accomplishment
Activity	Being active or involved
Efficiency and practicality	Saves time and effort; solves problems
Progress	Continuous improvement
Material comfort	Money; status
Individualism	Being themselves
Freedom	Democratic beliefs
External conformity	Adaptation to society
Humanitarianism	Overcoming adversity; supporting
Charity	Giving to others
Youthfulness	Looking and acting young
Fitness and health	Exercise and diet

Source: Leon Shiffman and Leslie Kanuk, *Consumer Behavior*, 5th ed. (Upper Saddle River, NJ: Prentice Hall, 1994).

Although they are not directly related, other core U.S. values may tangentially affect sports participation. For example, the value of individualism and being oneself may manifest itself in the types of sports or activities in which we choose to participate. Many sports, such as surfing, hang-gliding, climbing, and hiking, allow a consumer to express his or her own personality. Youthfulness is also expressed through participation in sport as consumers keep "young at heart" by staying active. Consumers may also participate in sporting events to help raise money for charities. One of the most visible charitable influences in sport today is developing breast cancer awareness. Athletes in professional, collegiate, and even youth levels will often be seen wearing pink gear to show their support for those fighting the disease.

Social class

Throughout history, people within various cultural systems have been grouped together based on social class. Whether it is the "haves" versus the "have nots" or the "upper class" versus the "lower class," social class distinctions have always been present. **Social class** is defined as the homogeneous division of people in a society sharing similar values, lifestyles, and behaviors that can be hierarchically categorized.

Important to this definition is the idea that individuals are divided into homogeneous classes, or strata. Typically, social strata are described in terms of a hierarchy ranging from lower to upper class. Consumers are grouped into the various social classes based on the interaction of a number of factors. Occupation, income, and education are usually considered the three primary determinants of social class. In addition, possessions (e.g., home and car) and affiliations (e.g., club membership, professional organizations, and community organizations) are also believed to be important factors.

Although researchers agree that there are distinct social strata, there is little agreement on how many categories there are in the hierarchy. For instance, some researchers believe a seven-tiered structure (as illustrated in Figure 4.7) explains social class in the United States. Others, however, believe in a simple two-tiered system (i.e., upper and lower).

Regardless of the class structure, sports marketers are interested in social class as a predictor of whether consumers will participate in sports and, if they do participate, the types of sports in which consumers might participate. Table 4.6 shows the relationship between average household income and participation in 22 selected sports activities.

Other research has shown that more than one in four Americans would like to have more time for leisure activities such as bowling and softball. A disproportionate number of those people who want more leisure time are lower income, blue-collar workers.[20] In addition, the U.S. Fish and Wildlife Service found that anglers are above average in income and are moderately well educated.[21]

Reference groups

Classic advertising slogans like "Be Like Mike, and "Witness" illustrate the power of reference group influence. More formally, **reference groups** are individuals who influence the information, attitudes, and behaviors of other group members. Sports participation is heavily influenced through the various reference groups to which an individual may belong. In these classic advertising campaigns hordes of children have identified with and created an association between athletes, representing a wide array of sports, and their respective sport products.

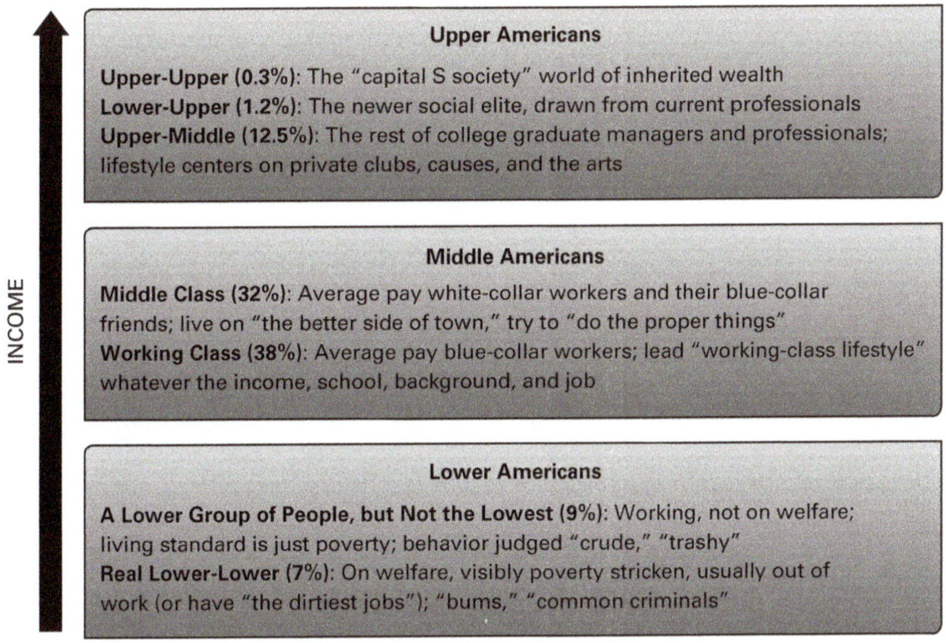

INCOME
Upper Americans
Upper-Upper (0.3%): The "capital S society" world of inherited wealth
Lower-Upper (1.2%): The newer social elite, drawn from current professionals
Upper-Middle (12.5%): The rest of college graduate managers and professionals; lifestyle centers on private clubs, causes, and the arts
Middle Americans
Middle Class (32%): Average pay white-collar workers and their blue-collar friends; live on "the better side of town," try to "do the proper things"
Working Class (38%): Average pay blue-collar workers; lead "working-class lifestyle" whatever the income, school, background, and job
Lower Americans
A Lower Group of People, but Not the Lowest (9%): Working, not on welfare; living standard is just poverty; behavior judged "crude," "trashy"
Real Lower-Lower (7%): On welfare, visibly poverty stricken, usually out of work (or have "the dirtiest jobs"); "bums," "common criminals"

Figure 4.7 The structure of social class

Source: Richard P. Coleman, "The Continuing Significance of Social Class to Marketing," *Journal of Consumer Research*, vol. 10 (December 1983), 265–280.

Table 4.6 Household incomes for select sports and activities

Activity	Household Income (in thousands)	Activity	Household Income (in thousands)
Basketball	$58	Roller hockey	$73
Bowling	$60	Running/jogging	$63
BMX bicycling	$49	Sailing	$82
Day hiking	$66	Saltwater fishing	$64
Downhill skiing	$83	Snorkeling	$83
Fitness bicycling	$71	Snowboarding	$63
Fitness swimming	$69	Soccer	$59
Fitness walking	$66	Surfing	$74
Football(tackle)	$54	Tennis	$68
Golf	$80	Tent camping	$58
Horseback riding	$65	Yoga/tai chi	$68

Source: Sports & Fitness Industry Association, www.sfia.org.

These types of reference groups, which have an impact on our participation in sports as well as on our purchase of sports products, are called aspirational groups. Although many famous athletes recognize the influence they can have on children, others refuse to accept the responsibility that reference groups can influence consumer demands (e.g., the now-retired Charles Barkley of the NBA stating, "I am not a role model").

SPORTS MARKETING HALL OF FAME

TheBabe: Babe Didrikson Zaharias

Mildred "Babe" Didrikson Zaharias was known by sports fans all over as the "best at everything." Her early success as an all-around athlete began as she played on basketball, softball, and track and field teams, named the Golden Cyclones, sponsored by the Employers Casualty Insurance Company. Babe represented the Golden Cyclones by herself in the 1932 Olympic track and field qualifying trials and entered eight of the 10 events. She ended up winning six of the events, and her legend was born. As an amateur, Babe won two gold medals and one silver in track and field events at the 1932 Olympics. She began a professional career that included stints in basketball, baseball, boxing, football, and hockey. Didrikson's most impressive sport of all, however, was golf. Returning to amateur status in golf, Babe ran up an unprecedented 17 straight wins, including a victory in the 1947 British Women's Amateur – never before won by an American. In 1949, she was one of the founding members of the LPGA.

In addition to her impressive athletic achievements, Babe was the consummate sports promoter and marketer. For example, she participated in publicity stunts such as harness racing and pitched against New York Yankee Joe DiMaggio. She published a book of golfing tips, had her own line of golf clubs through Spalding Sporting Goods, and appeared in movies such as the classic *Pat and Mike*. Through her example and performance, Babe Didrikson Zaharias legitimized women's sports. Her excellence in so many sports made her a marketer's dream. Just imagine her today.

Source: Elizabeth Lynn, *Babe Didrikson Zaharias: Champion Athlete* (New York, Chelsea House, 1989).

Celebrity athletes are not the only individuals who have an impact on sports participation. Friends and coworkers are also considered a **primary reference group** because of the frequent contact we have with these individuals and the power they have to influence our decisions. Many of us participate in sports because friends and coworkers urged us to join their team, play a set of tennis, or hit the links. Primary reference groups may exert a powerful influence among high-school athletes as participation continues to grow at this level.

Family

Another primary reference group that has one of the greatest influences on sports participation is the family. As you might guess, family plays a considerable role because sports marketers target families as spectators. But how does **family influence** affect participation in sport? Consider families of friends or your own family. It is common for family members to exert a great deal of influence on one another with respect to decisions about sports participation and activities. For example, children may either directly or indirectly get parents involved in a sport

Photo 4.6 Girls' sport participation is eroding traditional gender roles

Source: Shutterstock.com

(e.g., in-line skating, soccer, or biking) so the entire family can participate together. Conversely, parents may urge their kids to get off the couch and get involved in sports.

Traditionally, fathers have had the greatest impact on their children's (mostly their sons) sports participation. Dad might have encouraged junior to play organized football because he did or go fishing because his father took him fishing. Of course, these scenarios are vanishing, as is the traditional family structure.

Long gone are the days of the mom, dad, two kids, and a dog. Long gone is the *Leave it to Beaver* mentality where fathers are breadwinners and mothers are homemakers. Today's modern family structure typically includes dual-income families with no kids, divorced parents, single parents, or parents who are dually employed with kids.

Each of these modern family structures may influence participation in sports for both adults and children. For instance, dual-income families with no kids may have the time and the money to participate in a variety of "country club" sports. However, single or divorced parents may face time and financial constraints. Sports products such as the "10-minute workout" and 30-minute aerobic classes are targeted to working moms on the move. In addition, the tremendous increase in sales of home exercise equipment may be traced back to the constraints of the modern family structure.

HIGH SCHOOL SPORTS PARTICIPATION TOPS 7.6 MILLION, SETS RECORD

INDIANAPOLIS, IN (September 8, 2010) – Participation in high school sports increased for the 21st consecutive school year in 2009–10, eclipsing the 7.6 million mark for the first time.

Based on figures from the 50 state high school athletic/activity associations, plus the District of Columbia, that are members of the National Federation of State High School Associations (NFHS), participation for the 2009–10 school year reached a record-breaking total of 7,628,377 participants, according to the 2009–10 High School Athletics Participation Survey conducted by the NFHS.

Boys and girls participation figures also reached respective all-time highs with 4,455,740 boys and 3,172,637 girls participating in 2009–10. Boys participation increased by 33,078 this year, while the girls figure increased by 58,546.

"It is a significant achievement for our member state associations that in these difficult economic times, student participation increased for the 21stconsecutive year," said NFHS Executive Director Bob Gardner. "This reinforces the values that high school sports provide as part of the education of our students. The NFHS actively promotes participation in, and support for, the programs throughout the nation."

Based on the survey, 55.1 percent of students enrolled in high schools participate in athletics, which emphasizes and reinforces the idea that high school sports continue to have a significant role in student involvement in schools across the country.

Outdoor track and field gained the most combined participants in 2009–10, with an increase of 25,561 participants, followed by soccer with 19,597 combined participants and cross country (11,925). In girls sports, soccer gained the most participants (11,582), followed by outdoor track and field (11,445) and fast-pitch softball (9,290). Outdoor track and field led the way in boys sports with 14,116 additional participants, followed by cross country (8,156) and soccer (8,015).

The top participatory sports for boys remained the same from 2008–09: 11-player football led the way with 1,109,278 participants, followed by outdoor track and field (572,123), basketball (540,207), baseball (472,644), soccer (391,839), wrestling (272,890), cross country (239,608), tennis (162,755), golf (157,756), and swimming and diving (131,376).

Outdoor track and field continued to be the leading sport for girls with 469,177 participants. Second was basketball (439,550), followed by volleyball (403,985), fast-pitch softball (378,211), soccer (356,116), cross country (201,968), tennis (182,395), swimming and diving (158,419), competitive spirit squads (123,644) and golf (70,872).

The top 10 states based on combined participation also remained the same from last year's survey. Texas led the way with a combined total of 780,721 participants. California was second with 771,465, followed by New York (379,677), Illinois (344,257), Ohio (334,797), Pennsylvania (317,426), Michigan (313,818), New Jersey (253,097), Florida (247,428) and Minnesota (230,043).

The participation survey has been compiled since 1971 by the NFHS through numbers it receives from its member associations. The complete 2009–10 Sports Participation Survey is available here.

10 MOST POPULAR BOYS PROGRAMS

Schools		Participants	
1. Basketball	17,969	1. Football – 11-Player	1,109,278
2. Track and Field – Outdoor	16,011	2. Track and Field – Outdoor	572,123
3. Baseball	15,786	3. Basketball	540,207
4. Football – 11-Player	14,226	4. Baseball	472,644
5. Cross Country	13,942	5. Soccer	391,839
6. Golf	13,693	6. Wrestling	272,890
7. Soccer	11,375	7. Cross Country	239,608
8. Wrestling	10,363	8. Tennis	162,755
9. Tennis	9,916	9. Golf	157,756
10. Swimming and Diving	6,820	10. Swimming and Diving	131,376

10 MOST POPULAR GIRLS PROGRAMS

Schools		Participants	
1. Basketball	17,711	1. Track and Field – Outdoor	469,177
2. Track and Field – Outdoor	15,923	2. Basketball	439,550
3. Volleyball	15,382	3. Volleyball	403,985
4. Softball – Fast Pitch	15,298	4. Softball – Fast Pitch	378,211
5. Cross Country	13,809	5. Soccer	356,116
6. Soccer	10,901	6. Cross Country	201,968
7. Tennis	10,166	7. Tennis	182,395
8. Golf	9,651	8. Swimming and Diving	158,419
9. Swimming and Diving	7,171	9. Competitive Spirit Squads	123,644
10. Competitive Spirit Squads	4,879	10. Golf	70,872

This press release was written by Lauren Fellmeth, a fall intern in the NFHS Publications/Communications Department and a recent graduate of Elon (North Carolina) University.

Source: http://www.nfhs.org/content.aspx?id=3282.

Children's ability to participate in organized sport may also be hampered by the single-parent family, although women are increasingly taking on the traditional male sex role of coach, sports participant, and sports enthusiast. Also, fathers are increasingly encouraging daughters to participate in sport, another sign of changing sex roles.

Situational factors

Now that we have looked at how the psychological and sociological factors influence the participant decision-making process, let us turn to the situational factors. Unlike the psychological and sociological factors that are relatively permanent in nature, the situational factors are temporary aspects that affect participation. For instance, the culture in which we make our participation decision is considered a long-term environmental factor. Likewise, personality is a set of consistent responses that we make to our environment. However, **situational factors** are those temporary factors within a particular time or place that influence the participation decision-making process.[22]

Consider the following examples of situational influences on **participant behavior**. Your best friend is in town and, although you do not normally enjoy golfing, you do so anyway to spend time with your friend. You typically run five miles per day, but an unexpected ice storm puts a halt to your daily exercise routine. You have to study for final exams, so you settle for a 30-minute workout versus your normal 75 minutes. Each of these examples represents a different type of situational influence on participant decision making.

Consumer researchers have identified five situational influences that affect decision making. The five primary types of situational influences include physical surroundings; social surroundings; time; reason for participation, or task definition; and antecedent states. Let us briefly look at each in the context of participant decision making.

Physical surroundings

The location, weather, and physical aspects of the participation environment comprise the **physical surroundings**. In sports participation, the physical surroundings play an extremely important role in decision making. When the weather outside is good, people who might not participate in sports normally do so. Likewise, the weather can have a situational influence on where we choose to participate. The runner described in the earlier example may decide to jog indoors rather than skip the workout. In addition to the weather, location might influence our decision to participate. For example, nonskiers may be tempted to try skiing if they are attending a sales conference in Vail or Aspen. Other aspects of the physical environment, such as a perfectly groomed championship golf course or scenic biking trail, can also influence our participation decisions in a positive manner. From the perspective of the sports marketer, any attempt to increase participation must carefully consider the physical surroundings. Even the worst athletes in the world enjoy playing in nice facilities.

Social surroundings

The effect of other people on a participant during participation in a sport is another situational influence, called **social surroundings**. In other words, who we are with may have a positive or negative impact on participation decisions. The earlier golf example presented a case where the presence of a friend caused the person to participate. Likewise, golfing in the presence of unfamiliar coworkers at a corporate outing can be an unpleasant and intimidating experience. In this case, participation might be avoided altogether.

Crowds represent another social situation that is usually avoided. For example, if the tennis courts or golf courses are full, you might decide to participate in another sport that day. Biking and hiking represent two other activities where crowds are usually perceived to have a negative impact on participation. In other words, people generally do not like to bike or hike in large crowds. However, some people may take pleasure when participating among large crowds. Consider, for example, runners who feel motivated when participating in events with thousands of other runners.

Time

The effect of the presence or absence of **time** is the third type of situational influence. In today's society, there are increasing time pressures on all of us. Changes in family structure, giving rise to dual-income families and single parents, have made time for participation in sports even scarcer. Slightly more than half of all U.S. residents under the age of 50 complain of a lack of leisure time, and this percentage is even higher for dual-income families. How many times have you heard someone say, "I don't have the time to work out today"?

Because of time constraints, sports marketers are concentrating on ways to make our participation activities more enjoyable and more time effective. For example, few of us can afford to take five hours out of our day to enjoy 18 holes of golf. As such, golfing associations are always communicating ways to speed up play. Similarly, few of us feel that we have the time to drive to the gym each day. The marketers' response to this was the development of the shorter, higher intensity workout (see accompanying article) and the enormous home health equipment industry.

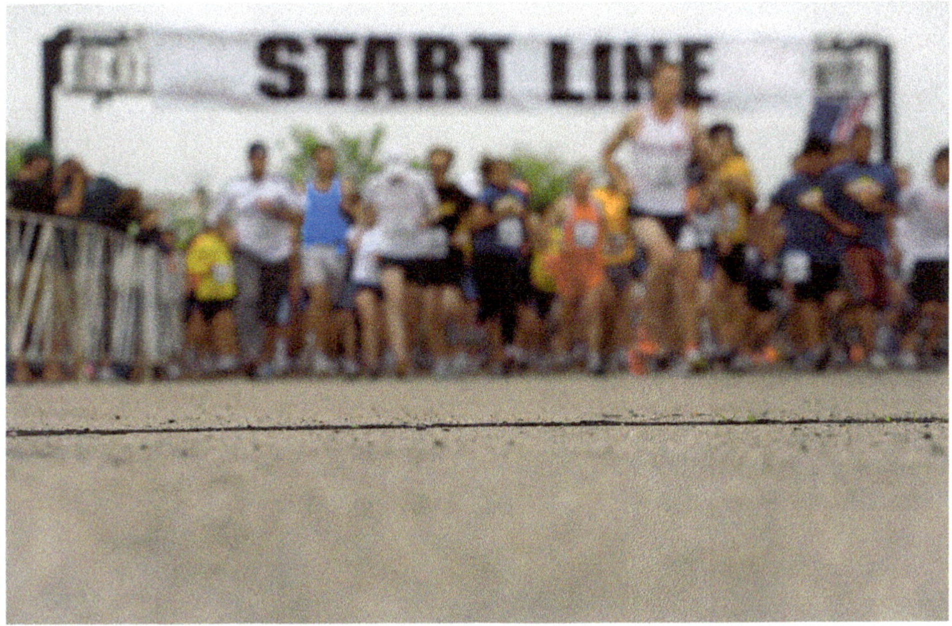

Photo 4.7 Marathon

Source: Shutterstock.com

P90X VS. INSANITY: WHICH IS THE BEST FOR YOU?

Each New Year brings about a wave of new fitness resolutions along with a surge of new gym memberships. Lately a growing number of people have been bucking tradition and ditching the cold walk to the gym in favor of at-home fitness programs.

Two of the most popular video series on the market right now are P90X and Insanity. Their infomercials are plastered over late night TV claiming to provide killer workouts and stunning results, all from the comfort of home. Each workout regimen comes packed as a set of DVDs with a predetermined workout plan and nutritional advice. Just follow the instructions to a new and improved you.

Now the only obstacle standing in the way of a killer bod is choosing which program is right for you. Both programs have significant hype and loyal followers, so I have objectively analyzed the two, so you can decide which one is the right fit.

Despite similar structure there are significant differences between P90X and Insanity. Insanity is a cardio-intense workout plan that utilizes interval training to get you the "best workout of your life" whereas P90X is a program that incorporates cardio but focuses more on strength training, using dumbbells, pull-ups, and your own body weight to provide the resistance needed to build muscle and burn calories.

P90X is a ninety-day workout regimen that claims it can significantly improve fitness in three months through intense physical training. P90X's advertising emphasizes "muscle confusion," a method of cross training and periodization achieved through switching the order of exercises and incorporating new and varied movements. Muscle confusion supposedly prevents the body from adapting to exercises over time, resulting in continual improvement without plateaus. The program provides a great all-around workout with exercises that are easy to execute.

The Insanity workouts are shorter than P90X workouts, typically lasting only 45 minutes. Each section is broken into three to four minutes of intense exercise followed by 30 seconds of rest. This may not sound like much, but the intense nature of the exercise provides maximum impact in a minimal amount of time. The fast pace and constant rotation of exercises helps make the 45 minutes fly by. While the main emphasis of the program is cardio, many of the routines are designed to incorporate core and upper body strengthening. Although it's hard to tell while you're in the middle of it, each session provides a full body workout.

Each program has its pros and cons, and choosing the best fit for you depends on what you're looking for in a workout experience. Insanity is less of a time commitment than P90X and also requires less equipment. It would be an ideal fit for anyone with a busy schedule or lack of space and resources. However, the workouts require a lot of jumping and other exercises that are tough on knees and joints. P90X is easier to modify for those just beginning to get back in shape or those with bad joints or old injuries. P90X also has a stronger emphasis on strength exercises and muscle building while Insanity is better for cardiovascular endurance and power. Those looking to bulk up and increase muscle mass might be happier with P90X while anyone looking to burn fat or increase cardiovascular endurance would like Insanity. At the end of the day it's all about personal preference and ability.

No matter what workout trend you decide to embrace and subsequently complain about, with the proper planning and commitment you'll be jacked in no time.

Source: Rebecca Anderson, *Sports & Fitness*, http://weekly.blog.gustavus.edu/2013/02/22/p90x-vs-insanity-which-is-the-best-for-you/.

Reason for participation or task definition

Another situational influence, **task definition**, refers to the reasons that occasion the need for consumers to participate in a sport. In other words, the reason the consumer participates affects the decision-making process. Some participants may use jet skis or scuba dive once a year while they are on vacation. Other consumers may participate in a fantasy baseball camp once in a lifetime.

These examples represent special occasions or situational reasons for participating. Moreover, the participation occasion may dictate the sports apparel and equipment we choose. For example, a consumer participating in a competitive softball league might wear cleats, long softball pants, and batting gloves. However, the recreational participant playing softball at the company picnic would only bring a glove.

Antecedent states

Temporary physiological and mood states that a consumer brings to the participant situation are **antecedent states**. In certain situations, people may feel worn out and lack energy. This physiological state may motivate some people to work out and become reenergized at the end of a long day of work. However, feeling tired can elicit another response in others, such as "I'm too tired to do anything today." Promotion to combat these negative antecedent states can be seen in the following link which was the Union of European Football Association "Get Active Campaign," http://www.youtube.com/watch?v=AY5AILaXDdA&feature=fvw.

Certainly, other situational mood states, such as being "stressed out," can activate the need to participate in sports or exercise. Yet feeling tired or hungry can cause us to decide against participation. At the very least, our mood can influence our decision to ride or walk 18 holes of golf.

It is important to remember that antecedent means "prior to" or "before." Therefore, the mood or physiological condition influences our decision making. For example, people who are experiencing bad moods may turn to sports to lift their spirits. Contrast this with those who feel great because they have just participated in a sporting event.

Summary

The focus of Chapter 4 is on understanding the sports participant as a consumer of sports. Sports marketers are not only concerned with consumers who watch sporting events, but also with the millions of consumers who participate in a variety of sports. To successfully market to sports participants, sports marketers must understand everything they can about these consumers and their consumption behaviors. Participant consumption behavior is defined as the actions performed when searching for, participating in, and evaluating the sports activities that consumers believe will satisfy their needs.

To simplify the complex nature of participant consumption behavior, a model was developed. The model of participant consumption behavior consists of four major components: the participant decision-making process, internal or psychological factors, external or sociological factors, and situational variables. The participant decision-making process is the central focus of the model of participant consumption behavior. It explains how consumers make decisions about whether to participate in sports and in which sports to participate. The decision-making process is slightly different for each of us and is influenced by a host of factors. However, the basis of the decision-making process is a five-step procedure that consumers progress through as they make decisions. These five steps include problem recognition, information search, evaluation of alternatives, participation, and postparticipation evaluation. The complexity of this process is highly dependent on how important the decision is to participants and how much experience consumers have had making similar decisions.

The internal or psychological factors are those things that influence our decision-making process. These psychological factors include personality, motivation, perception, learning, and attitudes. Personality is a set of consistent responses we make to our environment. Our personality can play a role in which sports we choose to participate in or whether we participate in any sports. For example, an aggressive personality type may be most likely to participate in boxing or hockey. Motivation is the reason we participate in sports. Some of the more common reasons we participate in sports are for personal improvement, appreciation of sport, or social facilitation. The strength of our motives to participate in sports is referred to as sport involvement. Another important psychological factor that influences our participation decisions is perception. Perception influences our image of the various sports and their participants as well as shaping our attitudes toward sports participation. Learning also affects our participant behavior. We learn whether to participate in sports because we are rewarded or punished by our participation (behavioral theories), because we perceive sports as a way to achieve our goals (cognitive theories), and because we watch others participating (social theories). A final internal or psychological factor that directly influences our sports participation decisions is attitudes. Attitudes are defined as learned thoughts, feelings, and behaviors toward some given object (in this case, sports participation). Our feelings (affective component of attitude) and beliefs (cognitive component) about sports participation certainly play a major role in determining our participation (behavioral component).

The external or sociological factors also influence the participant decision-making process. These factors include culture, social class, reference groups, and family. Culture is defined as the learned values, beliefs, language, traditions, and symbols shared by people and passed down from generation to generation. The values held by people within a society are a most important determinant of culture. Some of the core American values that influence participation in sports include achievement and success, activity, individualism, youthfulness, and fitness and health. Social class is another important determinant of participant decision making. Most people erroneously associate social class only with income. Our social class is also determined by occupation, education, and affiliations. Another important sociological factor is the influence of reference groups. Reference groups are individuals who influence the information, attitudes, and behaviors of other group members. For example, our friends may affect our decision to participate in a variety of recreational sports and activities. One reference group that has a great deal of influence over our attitudes and participation behavior is our family.

The final component of the model of participant behavior is situational factors. Every decision that we make to participate in a given activity has a situational component. In other words, we are always making a decision in the context of some unique situation. Five major situational influences that affect participant decision making include physical surroundings (physical environment), social surroundings (interaction with others), time (presence or absence of time), task definition (reason or occasion for participation), and antecedent states (physiological condition or mood prior to participation).

Key terms

- affective component
- antecedent states
- attitudes
- behavioral component
- behavioral learning
- cognitive component
- cognitive dissonance
- cognitive learning
- consumer socialization
- culture
- decision-making process
- esteem
- evaluation of alternatives
- evaluative criteria
- evoked set
- experiential source
- extensive problem solving (or extended problem solving)
- external sources
- family influence
- habitual problem solving (or routinized problem solving)
- information search
- internal sources
- learning
- limited problem solving
- love and belonging
- marketing sources
- Maslow's hierarchy of needs
- model of participant consumption behavior
- motivation
- participant behavior
- participant consumption behavior
- perceived risk
- perception
- personality
- personal sources
- physical surroundings
- physiological needs
- postparticipation evaluation
- primary reference group
- problem recognition
- psychological or internal factors
- reference groups
- safety needs
- selective attention
- selective interpretation
- selective retention
- self-actualization
- situational factors
- social class
- socialization
- social learning
- socializing agents
- social surroundings
- sociological or external factors
- sports involvement
- task definition
- time
- values

Review questions

1. Define participant consumption behavior. What questions does this address with respect to consumers of sport? From a marketing strategy perspective, why is it critical to understand consumer behavior?
2. Outline the components of the simplified model of participant consumer behavior.
3. Outline the steps in the decision-making process for sports participation. What are the three types/levels of consumer decision making? How do the steps in the decision-making process differ for routine decisions versus extensive decisions?
4. Define personality. Why is it considered one of the internal factors of consumption behavior? Do you think personality is related to the decision to participate in sports? Do you think personality is linked to the specific sports we choose to play?
5. Describe Maslow's hierarchy of needs. How is Maslow's theory linked to sports marketing?
6. What is meant by the term *sports involvement* from the perspective of sports participants? How is sports involvement measured and used in the development of the strategic marketing process?
7. Define perception and provide three examples of how the perceptual processes apply to sports marketing.
8. Describe the three major learning theories. Which learning theory do you believe best explains the sports in which we choose to participate? Why is learning theory important to sports marketers?
9. Describe the three components of attitude. How do these components work together? Why must attitudes be measured to increase sports participation?
10. Define culture and explain the process of sports socialization. Describe the core American values.
11. Define social class and explain the characteristics of individuals at each level of the seven-tiered structure.
12. Explain how reference groups play a role in sports participation.
13. Discuss the traditional family structure and then the nontraditional family structure. How do today's nontraditional families influence sports participation? Is this for the better or the worse?
14. Explain each of the five situational factors that influence the participant decision-making process.

Exercises

1. Trace the simplified model of participant behavior for a consumer thinking about joining a health club. Briefly comment on each element of the model.
2. Ask three males and three females about the benefits they seek when participating in sports. What conclusions can you draw regarding motivation? Are there large gender differences in the benefits sought?
3. Interview five adult sports participants and ask them to describe the sports socialization process as it relates to their personal experience. Attempt to interview people with different sports interests to determine whether the socialization process differs according to the specific sports.
4. Watch three advertisements for any sporting goods on television. Briefly describe the advertisement and then suggest which core American value(s) are reflected in the theme of the advertisement.
5. Develop a survey instrument to measure attitudes toward jogging. Have 10 people complete the survey and then report your findings. How

could these findings be used by your local running club to increase membership (suggest specific strategies)? Are attitudes and behaviors related?

6. Interview five children (between the ages of eight and 12) to determine what role the family and other reference group influences have had on their decision to participate in sports. Suggest promotions for children based on your findings.
7. Prepare a report that describes how time pressures are influencing sports participation in the United States. How are sports marketers responding to increasing time pressures?

Internet exercises

1. Using the World Wide Web, prepare a report that examines sport participation in Australia. What are the similarities and differences in the sports culture of Australia versus that of the United States?
2. Find and describe two sports Web sites that specifically appeal to children. How does this information relate to the process of consumer socialization?
3. Find and describe a Web site for a health club. How does the information relate to the consumer decision-making process to join the club?

Endnotes

1 Del Hawkins, Roger Best, and Kenneth Coney, *Consumer Behavior: Building Marketing Strategy*, 7th ed. (New York: McGraw-Hill, 1998).

2 Ian P. Murphy, "Bowling Industry Rolls Out Unified Marketing Plan," *Marketing News* (January 20, 1997), 2.

3 Del Hawkins, Roger Best, and Kenneth Coney, *Consumer Behavior: Building Marketing Strategy*, 7th ed. (New York: McGraw-Hill, 1998).

4 Raymond B. Cattell, Herbert W. Eber, and Maurice M. Tasuoka, *Handbook for the Sixteen Personality Factors Questionnaire* (Champaign, IL: Institute for Personality and Ability Testing, 1970).

5 Douglas M. Turco, "The X Factor: Marketing Sport to Generation X," *Sport Marketing Quarterly*, vol. 5, no. 1 (1996), 21–23.

6 Terry Lefton and Bernhard Warner, "Alt Sportspeak: A Flatliner's Guide," *Brandweek* (January 27, 1997), 25–27.

7 Mark A. McDonald, George R. Milne, and JinBae Hong, "Motivational Factors for Evaluating Sport Spectator and Participant Markets," *Sport Marketing Quarterly*, vol. 11 (2002), 100–113.

8 Steve Jennison, "Pride, Passion, and Participation: A Strategy for Sport and Active Recreation in Hull 2008–2013," Sport England, The Humber Sports Partnership, and Hull City Council, Hull (2008).

9 Andrew J. Rohm, George R. Milne, and Mark A. McDonald, "A Mixed-Method Approach for Developing Market Segmentation Typologies in the Sports Industry," *Sport Marketing Quarterly*, vol. 15 (2006), 29–39.

10 Henry Murray, *Exploration in Personality: A Clinical and Experimental Study of Fifty Men of College Age* (New York: Oxford University Press, 1938).

11 Rebecca P. Heath, "You Can Buy a Thrill: Chasing the Ultimate Rush," *American Demographics*, vol. 19, no. 6 (1997), 47–51. Available from: www.demographics.com/publications/ad/9 7_ad/9706_ad/ad970631.htm.

12 Fred M. Beasley and Matthew D. Shank, "Fan or Fanatic: Refining a Measure of Sports Involvement," *Journal of Sport Behavior*, vol. 21, no. 4 (1998), 435–443.

13 Ronald Paul Hill and Harold Robinson, "Fanatic Consumer Behavior: Athletics as a Consumption Experience," *Psychology & Marketing*, vol. 8, no. 2, (1991), 79–99.

14 Fred M. Beasley and Matthew D. Shank, "Fan or Fanatic: Refining a Measure of Sports Involvement," *Journal of Sport Behavior*, vol. 21, no. 4, (1998), 435–443.

15 Robert Sekuler and Randolph Blake, *Perception*, 2nd ed. (New York: McGraw-Hill, 1990).

16 John Kim, Jeen-Su Lim, and Mukesh Bhargava, "The Role of Affect in Attitude Formation: A Classical Conditioning Approach," *Journal of the Academy of Marketing Science*, vol. 26, no. 2 (1998), 143–152.

17 Harry Edwards, *The Sociology of Sport* (Homewood, IL: Dorsey Press, 1973).

18 Elizabeth Moore-Shay and Britto Berchmans, "The Role of the Family Environment in the Development of Shared Consumption Values: An Intergenerational Study," in *Advances in Consumer Research*, vol.

23. Kim Corfman and John G. Lunch, Jr., eds. (Provo, UT: Association for Consumer Research, 1996), 484–490.

19 Kristy Meyer, "Core American Values Incorporated into Everyday Life," *Content.com* (March 30, 2009).

20 "Something to Wish for: Time to Relax," *US News and World Report* (November 11, 1996), 17.

21 Diane Crispell, "Targeting Hunters," *American Demographics*, vol. 16, no. 1 (1994), 94. Available from: www.demographics.com/ publications/ad /94_ad/9401_ad/ad508.htm.

22 Russell Belk, "Situational Variables and Consumer Behavior," *Journal of Consumer Research*, vol. 2, no. 3 (1975), 157–163.

CHAPTER 5

Understanding spectators as consumers

After completing this chapter, you should be able to:

- Understand the similarities and differences between spectator and participant markets.
- Describe the eight basic fan motivation factors.
- Explain how game attractiveness, economic factors, and competitive factors relate to game attendance.
- Describe the demographic profile of spectators and explain the changing role of women as spectators.
- Understand the relationship between stadium factors and game attendance.
- Discuss the components of the sportscape model.
- Describe the multiple values of sport to the community.
- Explain sport involvement from a spectator's perspective.
- Discuss the model of fan identification.

5 Understanding spectators as consumers

In Chapter 4, we examined participants as consumers. This chapter examines another group of consumers of great importance to sports marketers – spectators. Before we turn to our discussion of spectator consumption, two key points need to be addressed. First, the model of participant consumption behavior discussed in Chapter 4 can also be applied to spectator consumption. Think for a moment about your decision to attend sporting events. Certainly, there are sociological factors that influence your decision. For instance, reference groups such as friends and family may play a major role in influencing your decision to attend sporting events. Psychological factors, such as personality, perception, and attitudes, also affect your decision to attend sporting events or which sporting events to attend. For example, the more ambitious and aspiring you are, the more likely you may be to attend sporting events. In addition, situational factors can affect your decision to attend sporting events. Maybe you were given tickets to the game as a birthday gift (e.g., task definition).

As you can see, the factors that influence participant decision making are also applicable to spectator decisions. However, the focus of this chapter is to understand why people attend sporting events and to examine what additional factors relate to game attendance. Rather than using the framework for participant consumption behavior, however, we concentrate on the wants and needs of spectators. Understanding the consumer's needs and wants, in turn, is important when developing an effective marketing mix for spectators.

Photo 5.1 Soccer crowd. Group of happy Brazilian soccer fans commemorating victory, with the flag of Brazil swinging in the air

Source: Shutterstock.com

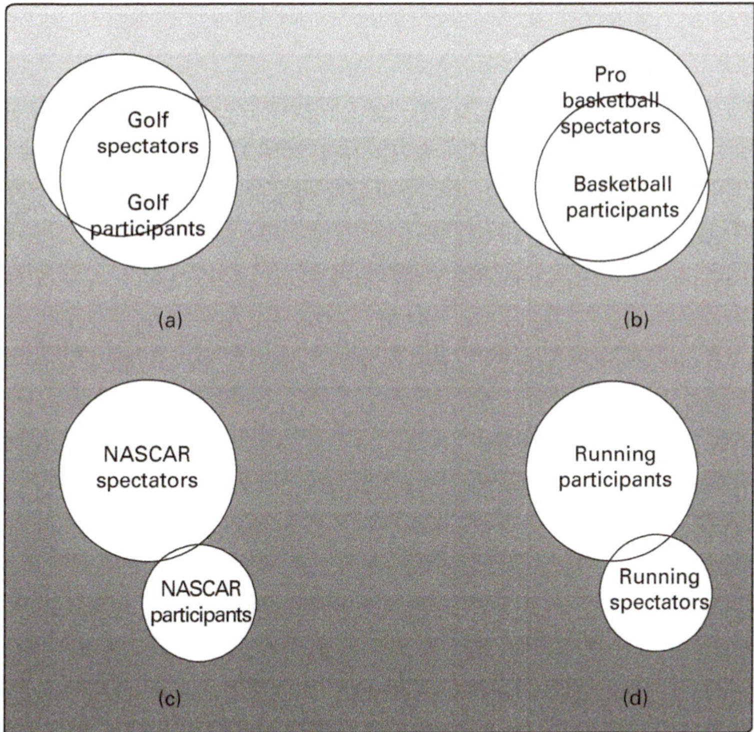

Figure 5.1 Relationship between spectator and participant markets

The second key point addresses the basis for considering spectators and participants as two separate markets. Many people who watch and attend sporting events also participate in sports and vice versa. For example, you may watch March Madness and also play basketball on a recreational basis. Research has shown, however, that two different consumer segments exist.[1] In fact, marketing to "either participants or spectators would miss a large proportion of the other group." Let us look at Figure 5.1 to illustrate the differences between spectators and participants.

Each diagram in Figure 5.1 depicts the potential relationship between spectator and consumer markets for golf, basketball, NASCAR, and running. Golf (see Figure 5.1a) represents a sport in which there is a large crossover between participants and spectators. A study conducted by Milne, Sutton, and McDonald supports this notion, finding that 84 percent of the golf participant market overlaps the golf spectator market.[2] In another study, it was found that 87.3 percent of the spectators in attendance at an LPGA event also participated in golf.[3]

A similar pattern is shown for basketball (see Figure 5.1b). The results of the study indicated an 81 percent overlap between basketball participation and watching pro basketball. Surprisingly, this same relationship did not exist for college basketball spectators. In that case, the overlap in the participation market and the college basketball spectator market was only 43 percent. The study also found that there was only a 36 percent overlap between spectators of professional basketball and spectators of college basketball – evidence that there are not only differences in spectators and participants, but also among spectators at different levels of the same sport.[4]

Web 5.1 Richard Petty Driving Experience: Allowing NASCAR fans to feel racing thrills

Source: Richard Petty Driving Experience; http://www.drivepetty.com/

The other two sports shown in Figure 5.1, NASCAR racing and running, demonstrate more extreme differences in the spectator and participant markets. There is virtually no overlap between the spectators and participants of NASCAR (see Figure 5.1c). Obviously, the NASCAR participant market is virtually nonexistent. However, new "fantasy camps" are springing up across the United States for spectators who want to try racing. For example, participants can enroll in classes at the Richard Petty Driving Experience. The "Rookie Experience" is designed for the "layperson who has a strong desire to experience the thrill of driving a Winston Cup race car." For prices starting at $440 and ranging to over $2,009, racing enthusiasts can begin to experience driving around the track at speeds up to 145 mph. Top speeds vary according to driver ability, track location, and program. Race fans can also experience a heart-pounding ride around one of the tracks with a professional instructor. Prices for the ride start at $99.00 and speeds will reach up to 165 mph. There are very few requirements, and participants soon will feel like their favorite racecar driver.[5]

Figure 5.1d depicts the potential participant and spectator markets for running. As opposed to the previous examples, the participant running market is much larger than the spectator running market. In addition to the size of the markets, there are also differences in motivations for spectators and participants. Participants, for instance, may be motivated to run for reasons of personal improvement. However, spectators are likely to watch to provide support to a family member or friend.

In addition to looking at the overlap (or lack thereof) between participants and spectators on a sport-by-sport basis, other research has explored the differences between these two groups for sports in general. Table 5.1 summarizes the findings of a study conducted by Burnett, Menon, and Smart,[6] which examined spectator and participant socioeconomic characteristics and media habits. Based on the results of this and other studies, sports participants and sports spectators seem to represent two distinct markets that should be examined separately by sports marketers.

Before we explore spectators in greater detail, it is important to note that this market can be differentiated into two groups on the basis of consumer behavior. The first

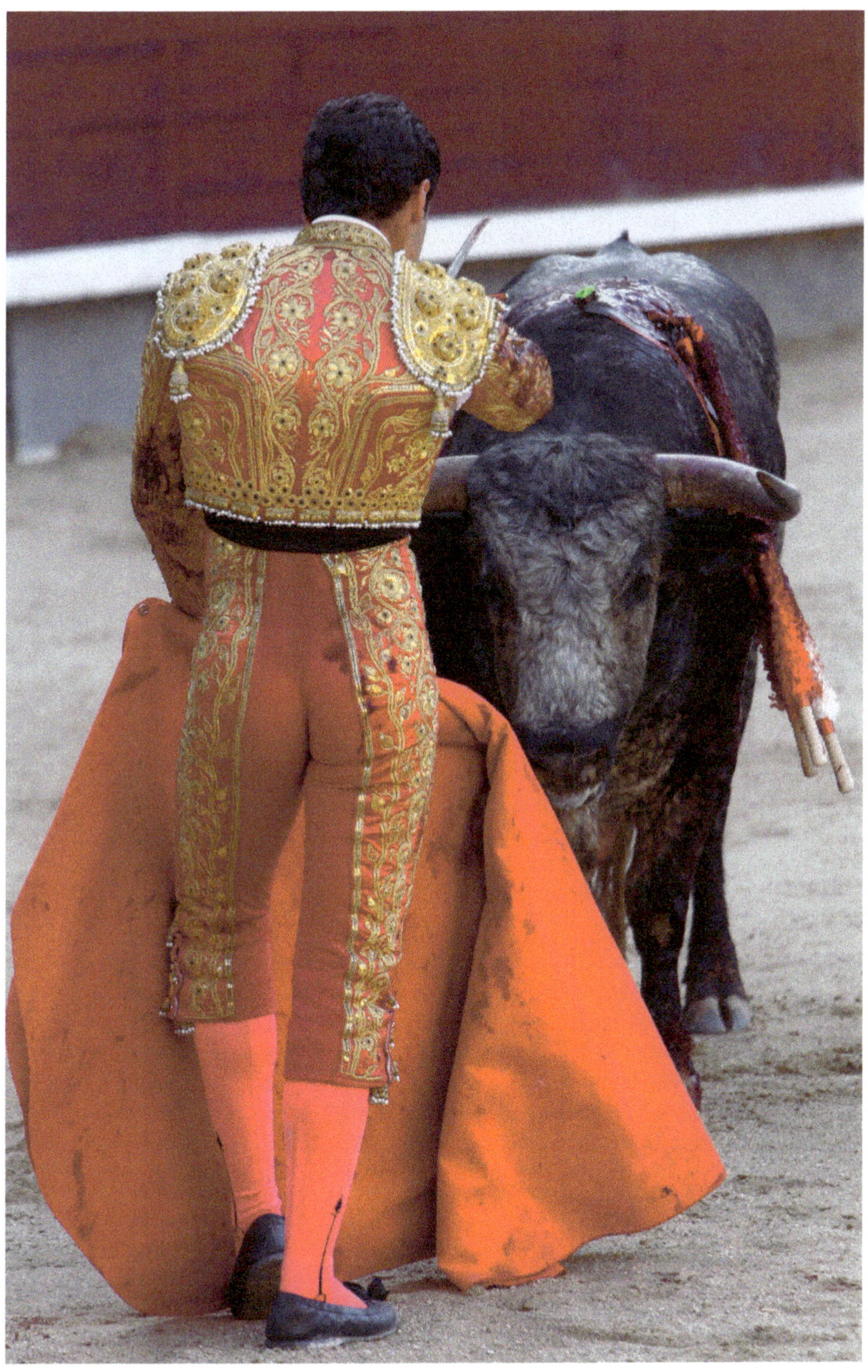

Photo 5.2 The sport of bullfighting depicts a "lack of overlap" between sports participants and sports spectators, for very few have the courage and/or the skills to master the ring

Source: Shutterstock.com

Table 5.1 Differences between spectators and participants

• Spectator and participant markets differ from each other with respect to socioeconomic characteristics and media habits.
• Consumers categorized as heavy participants were more likely to be male, better-educated, white-collar workers, minorities, and young, compared with the heavy spectator group.
• Consumers categorized as heavy participants also differ from heavy spectators with respect to media usage. Heavy participants are more likely to use business news-reporting media. In addition, heavy participants are more likely to watch intellectually appealing programming.
• Compared with male participants, male spectators exhibit an interest in a wider variety of media, especially television.
• Heavy participants and heavy spectators are different with respect to how they can be reached by advertising and how they perceive advertising.

Source: Adapted from John Burnett, Anil Menon, and Denise T. Smart, 1993, "Sports Marketing: A New Ball Game with New Rules," *Journal of Advertising Research* (September–October 1993) 21–33.

group consists of spectators who attend the sporting event. The second group of spectators consumes the sporting event through some medium (e.g., television, radio, or Internet). This chapter is primarily concerned with understanding why consumers attend sporting events and what factors influence attendance. Let us begin by looking at some of the major factors that influence the decision to attend sporting events rather than watch them from the comfort of home.

Factors influencing attendance

It is opening day in New York and the hometown Yankees are set to take on their rival the Boston Red Sox. Fred has gone to the traditional opening day parade and then attended the ball game for the past five years. The game promises to be a great one because the Yankees are returning from last year's winning season and playing the rival Red Sox. Fred will be joined at the game by his eight-year-old son and a potential business client.

As this hypothetical scenario illustrates, there are a variety of factors influencing Fred's decision to attend the season opener. He wants to experience the new stadium and watch the team that he has identified with since his childhood. As a businessman, Fred views the game as an opportunity to build a relationship with a potential client. As a father, Fred views the game as a way to bond with his son. In addition to these factors, Fred is prone to gambling and has placed a $50 bet on the home team. Finally, Fred thinks of opening day as an entertaining event that brings the whole community together and, as a lifelong resident, he wants to feel that sense of belonging.

Certainly, the interaction of the factors mentioned affected Fred's decision to attend the game. Sports marketers must attempt to understand all the influences on game attendance to market effectively to Fred and other fans like him.

A variety of studies have examined some of the major issues related to game attendance. A study conducted by Ferreira and Armstrong[7] found that eight distinct factors influence game attendance. Factor 1 had eight significant loadings: crowd density, crowd noise, popularity of sport, opportunity to watch game on TV, player's popularity, amount of advertising, rivalry, and pace. All variables loading on Factor 1 included items related to the overall popularity of sport and were collectively labeled *popularity of sport*. Factor 2 outlined items related to overall *game attractiveness*, including opposing team quality, home team quality, strategy displayed, athleticism, and skill displayed. The third factor was based on *free offerings and promotions*, such as offerings of free T-shirts, prizes, free tickets, and promotions on concessions (e.g., dime-a-dog). Factor 4 denoted *pregame and in-game entertainment* items such as band, music, and pregame activities. Factor 5, labeled *physical contact*, conveyed the degree of physical contact displayed. Factor 6 included items that related to *convenience and accessibility*, such as seating arrangement, seat location/sightlines, location convenience, and parking. Factor 7, *facility*, signified items of facility newness and niceness. Finally, Factor 8 was labeled *cost* and referenced items related to ticket prices.

Other research has shown that that weather, parking and security,[8,9,10] ticket cost,[11,12] promotional events,[13,14] team success,[15,16] attributions for team success,[17,18] and the presence of star players,[19,20] all play a role in sport consumption decisions.

Let's delve deeper into some of these critical drivers of game attendance, such as fan motivation factors, game attractiveness, economic factors, competitive factors, demographic factors, stadium factors, value of sport to the community, sports involvement, and fan identification.

Fan motivation factors

The foundation of any strategic sports marketing process is understanding why spectators attend sporting events, or **fan motivation factors**. Based on an extensive literature review, Trail et al.[21] proposed that nine different motives explain why individuals consume sport or are sport fans. Most of these motives are based on social and psychological needs: vicarious achievement, acquisition of knowledge, aesthetics, social interaction, drama/excitement, escape (relation), family, physical attractiveness of participants, and quality of physical skill of the participants. Trail and his colleagues also suggested that spectators attend games due to one or a combination of these motives.

Additional research by Wann has found eight basic motives for watching sport. The motives are categorized as self-esteem enhancement, diversion from everyday life, entertainment value, eustress, economic value, aesthetic value, need for affiliation, and family ties. It is important to note that these fundamental motives represent the most basic needs of fans. Because of this, the eight motives are often related to other factors, such as sports involvement and fan identification, which are discussed later in the chapter. Let us now examine the eight underlying motives of fans identified in a study conducted by Wann.[22]

- ***Self-esteem enhancement*** – Fans are rewarded with feelings of accomplishment when their favorite players or teams are winning. These fans more commonly are called "fair weather fans"; their association with the team is likely to increase when the team is winning and decrease when the team is doing poorly.

  The phenomenon of enhancing or maintaining self-esteem through associating with winning teams has been called BIRGing, or basking in reflected glory.[23] When BIRGing, spectators are motivated by a desire to associate with a winner and, thus, present themselves in a positive light and enhance their self-esteem. Madrigal developed a model to explain why BIRGing might occur. He found that the three antecedent conditions that are related to BIRGing are expectancy disconfirmation, team identification, and quality of the opponent. In other words, BIRGing increases when the team does much better than expected, when the fan has high levels of association with the team, and when the team upsets stronger opponents.[24]

Spectators who dissociate themselves from losing teams because that negatively affects self-esteem accomplish this through CORFing, or cutting off reflected failure. The BIRGing and CORFing behaviors even have a high-tech influence on fans. A recent study found that fans are more likely to visit their team's Web site after a victory and less likely to visit the site after a defeat.[25]

A new construct has been posited to explain why some fans, although it may sound crazy, don't want to associate themselves with a winner. In this instance, although a team might have a winning record, fans may actually dissociate themselves from the team.

Reasons for such behavior, known as CORSing (cutting off reflected success), may include rebelliousness, jealousy, loyalty (to an earlier era, a previous style of play, prior coaching/management, etc.), a need for individuality (informally seen as a need to stand apart from the crowd), and possibly a fear of success (e.g., to ascend to new heights implies a chance for a greater fall). The CORSing fans do not want to be associated with the new era of winning; rather, they prefer to stay linked to the past. By CORSing the fans are managing their self-image through an expression of individualism.[26]

- ***Diversion from everyday life*** – Watching sports is seen as a means of getting away from it all. Most people think of sports as a novel diversion from the normal routines of everyday life. In a recent article, University of Nebraska Cornhusker fans were cited as having intense emotional ties to the team, and it was stated that football served as a diversion from everyday life in Nebraska. "For several hours on a Saturday afternoon the struggling farmers of rural Nebraska – the inspiration for the school's nickname – can put aside their own problems and focus on someone else's."[27]

  In a recent example, there was great debate about whether and when Oklahoma State, undefeated at the time, should play their football game scheduled against Iowa State after a tragic plane crashed took the life of members of their coaching fraternity, the head and assistant woman's basketball coach. The game was played but ended up in an overtime upset win in favor of Iowa State. In another more national example, Major League Baseball and other sports dealt with uncertainty of when they would resume their schedules after the events of September 11. Ultimately, it was decided that play should go on to serve as diversion and to ensure that the American way of life was not disrupted.

- ***Entertainment value*** – Entertainment is closely related to the previous motive for attendance. Sports serve as a form of entertainment to millions of people. As discussed in previous chapters, sports marketers are keenly aware of the heightened entertainment value of sports. In fact, one of the unique aspects of attending a sporting event is the uncertainty associated with the outcome. The drama associated with this uncertainty adds to the entertainment value of sports. Among spectators, the entertainment value of sports is believed to be the most highly motivating of all factors. In fact, Harris Interactive Company states that "contrary to popular belief, lowering ticket prices is not the best way – or even the most profitable way – to get people into seats. Creating an entertainment experience with flexible season tickets, VIP perks, etc., is a far better alternative. In short, people want to have fun, and for an increasing number of sports attendees this may have very little to do with the actual competition."[28] A number of sports are attempting to find interesting and innovative ways to increase their entertainment value for the fans on the field of play by changing the rules of the game. College football officials felt they needed to do something to keep fans involved and entertained because five of the six major conferences averaged game times of more than 3.5 hours. Here's what the conferences have done to speed up the pace of play.[29]

First, the clock will start on kickoffs when the ball is kicked instead of when the receiving team touches the ball. This is not a big change and should have very little impact on the outcome of the game. But coaches will have to adjust, and this could shave around three or four plays off each contest.

Second, on changes of possession, the clock will start when the referee starts the 25-second play clock. This will have more of an impact on the games since 25 seconds will be able to run off the clock and teams will have to utilize their timeouts in a different fashion. Essentially, a team will be able to run the time off the clock four times during a set of downs instead of three. With teams being given only three timeouts each half, there will be one occasion when they will not be able to stop the clock.

Others feel that college football should consider adopting NFL rules to shorten game times. This includes shortening halftime to 15 minutes and not stopping the clock on first downs, which is too much of an advantage for the offensive team and allows them numerous built-in timeouts.

The NHL has also taken strides to improve the entertainment of the game through rule changes.[30] For starters, the dimensions of goaltender equipment will be reduced by more than 10 percent. In addition to a one-inch reduction (to 11 inches) in the width of leg pads, the blocking glove, upper-body protector, pants, and jersey will also be reduced. This should increase scoring and therefore increase fan entertainment.

The NHL also altered rink dimensions to increase offensive firepower. They made adjustments to the neutral-zone edges of the blue lines to position the line 64 feet from the attacking goal line and 75 feet from the end boards in the attacking zone. In addition, they added four feet in each of the offensive zones to encourage more offensive play, particularly on power plays. The NHL positioned goal lines 11 feet from the end boards, two feet closer to the end boards than before. Finally, they reduced the size of the neutral zone from 54 to 50 feet.

As the article on page 184 indicates, sometimes having a solid product on the field of play or court still doesn't translate into game attendance.

- ***Eustress*** – Sports provide fans with positive levels of arousal. In other words, sports are enjoyable because they stimulate fans and are exciting to the senses. For example, imagine the excitement felt by Indy fans when the announcer says, "Gentlemen, start your engines" or the anticipation surrounding the opening kickoff for fans at the Super Bowl.
- ***Economic value*** – A subset of sports fans are motivated by the potential economic gains associated with gambling on sporting events. Their enjoyment stems from having a vested interest in the games as they watch. Because this motive is only present for a small group of spectators, the economic factor is the least motivating of all factors. However, the number of spectators who gamble on sports continues to rise, especially among college students. Keith Whyte, executive director for the National Council on Problem Gambling, says, "college campuses bring together a lot of Internet access, a propensity for sports wagering, and most students have credit cards. We are seeing signs that it is becoming a problem."

BASEBALL SUFFERS DROP IN ATTENDANCE

Blame the weather. Why not? It's an easy target when talking about baseball's early decline in attendance, and, certainly, it's part of the explanation.

Attendance changes

Team (Gms.)	Avg. diff.
Orioles (28)	5,412
Nationals (27)	5,143
Dodgers (31)	4,381
Blue Jays (30)	3,886
Reds (29)	1,990
Athletics (28)	1,185
White Sox (24)	1,078
Angels (32)	1,028
Braves (27)	713
Padres (30)	532
Giants (31)	190
Rockies (30)	66
Mets (29)	–29
Tigers (27)	–168
Indians (30)	–252
D-backs (28)	–633
Mariners (27)	–1,055
Pirates (32)	–1,067
Cardinals (29)	–1,160
Royals (25)	–1,228
Rays (27)	–1,303
Yankees (31)	–2,576
Brewers (31)	–3,842
Rangers (26)	–3,907
Twins (27)	–4,004
Astros (31)	–4,271
Red Sox (30)	–4,554

Cubs (29)	–5,116
Phillies (30)	–6,656
Marlins (30)	–10,262

STATS LLC

Take away the crappy weather – and the crappy team almost no one wants to watch, the **Miami Marlins** – and attendance might be at the same level it was a year ago.

Instead, attendance is down more than 2 percent from the same date last season, according to MLB. And as the accompanying chart shows, five large-market teams – the **Yankees**, Rangers, **Red Sox, Cubs** and **Phillies** – rank among the nine clubs that have suffered the biggest drop-offs, according to STATS LLC.

A sixth such club, the Mets, also is down slightly, which is not exactly what you'd expect from the team hosting the All-Star Game.

Is all of that attributable to the weather?

I'm not ready to pass judgment, not when it's early June and some kids are still in school. But the attendance figures are at least cause for concern. And when you consider the obviously high no-show rates at such places as Citi Field in New York and Wrigley Field in Chicago, it's fair to ask whether the sport might have a problem.

People in baseball don't seem to think so, and better turnouts in the summer months could very well prove them correct.

Baseball already has had 26 weather-related postponements – and by May 7 had surpassed last season's total of 21. The sport also has had two weather-related suspended games, and one more would match its highest regular-season total since 1988.

Five teams in the Midwest that are experiencing significant attendance drops – the Cubs, Twins, Brewers, Royals and Cardinals – dealt with particularly nasty weather in April. Eliminate their declines, plus the Marlins' decline of more than 10,000 per game, and the overall attendance probably is flat.

Even the higher no-show rates in certain cities are offset by lower ones in places like Baltimore, which leads baseball in both total and per-game attendance gains from a year ago – 151,540 overall, 5,412 per game.

So, does baseball have a problem?

Maybe.

First off, baseball cannot view the Marlins as some kind of crazy uncle. No, the Marlins are one of 30 franchises, operating in a prominent market. They have torched their relationship with that market, only one year after opening a new ballpark that was supposed to be their salvation.

Second, a number of other teams have dealt with occasionally poor weather without experiencing huge drop-offs – or any drop-offs at all. The Reds are up 1,990 per game, the White Sox 1,078, the Rockies 66. The Indians, who already have had four games postponed or delayed because of weather, are last in the majors in attendance but down only 252 per game though the same number of dates.

The most troubling developments, meanwhile, are in the larger markets.

The Yankees are down 2,576 per game, the Red Sox 4,554, the Cubs 5,116, the Phillies 6,656. The figures might be mere snapshots in time rather than signals of larger declines – several Yankees stars are injured, the Red Sox are coming off a disappointing season, the Cubs are rebuilding, the Phillies sputtering.

Then again, the rationale for the Phillies, in particular, goes only so far: The Dodgers are up 4,381 per game and the **Angels** 1,028. And while the Dodgers are clearly benefiting from the excitement created by their new ownership, neither of those clubs is performing to expectations on the field.

Some teams view the secondary ticket market as a drag on attendance. The Yankees and Angels opted out of baseball's deal with StubHub this season, and the Cubs considered it. The Yankees felt it was difficult to sell smaller season-ticket plans when fans could buy individual game tickets at much lower prices on StubHub. So, the team created its own ticket resale market in conjunction with Ticketmaster, and the Angels did the same thing.

The larger question, though, is whether too many fans are priced out – and whether even some fans who can afford tickets would prefer the hassle-free experience of watching games at home on large-screen, high-definition televisions.

Make no mistake; baseball needs those fans in the park, even in an era when clubs are drawing record revenues from regional and national TV networks. The sheer volume of games makes baseball more dependent upon attendance than other sports. If fans stop coming to the ballpark, they eventually will stop watching the sport on television, too.

Again, it's far too early to draw sweeping conclusions, particularly when the past nine seasons have been the nine best-attended in major league history, even in a struggling economy.

Still, the early attendance figures are disturbing. The TV shots of empty seats are disturbing.

Baseball should be on alert.

Source: Article author: Ken Rosenthal. Rightsholder: Foxsports; http://msn.foxsports.com/mlb/story/attendance-down-not-just-at-miami-marlins-games-060513.

As Giuseppe Partucci noted, sport gambling has remained a popular pastime of sports fans everywhere, even despite the prolonged recent economic downturn. People turn to sports betting for a variety of reasons; some of them do it to escape their problems and relax.[31] He added that others bet on sports for a significant part of their income, so a slow down in the economy will not affect the amount they wager. In fact, according to Partucci, legal sports books in Nevada report that the volume of wagers has not declined during the recession, although the amount wagered is slightly lower. They have estimated that the total "handle" on bets they receive has declined by about 5 percent, hardly enough to cause concern.[32]

- ***Aesthetic value*** – Sports are seen by many as a pure art form. Basketball games have been compared with ballets, and many fans derive great pleasure from the beauty of athletic performances (e.g., gymnastics and figure skating).
- ***Need for affiliation*** – The need for belonging is satisfied by being a fan. Research has shown that reference groups, such as friends, family, and the community, influence

SPORTS MARKETING HALL OF FAME

David Stern

David Stern, the commissioner of the NBA since 1984, has earned his place in sports marketing history. Stern is currently called the best commissioner in sport, the best in NBA history, and perhaps the best of any sport, ever. Prior to Stern, the NBA had a shaky network reputation, plummeting attendance figures, and no television contract.

During his tenure as commissioner, Stern took a floundering NBA and turned it "into an entity that is the envy of professional sports – an innovative, multifaceted, billion-dollar global marketing and entertainment company whose future literally knows no bounds." Stern has redefined the NBA and focused his marketing efforts on licensing, special events, and home entertainment. The league has gone from the arena business to radio, television, concessions, licensing, real estate, and home video – all under Stern's leadership. When the NBA was experiencing a public relations nightmare because of the number of players believed to be on drugs, it was again Stern who cleaned up the mess.

The All-Star Weekend, the made-for-television NBA lottery, making basketball the most popular sport in America with kids, and marketing the NBA across the world are all part of the sports marketing legacy that is David Stern. In addition, Stern has helped the NBA develop an international presence in countries such as China and India making it one of the fastest internationally growing sport franchises.

David Stern has turned the NBA into a professional organization that is innovative, multifaceted, and a billion dollar empire though marketing and entertainment. Stern is also known for his contribution and commitment to social responsibility by launching the NBA Cares program. The league's players and teams donate millions of dollars and hours of community service to the youth. Here is a video clip of Stern and the NBA Cares Program. NBA Cares

Source: Adapted from E. M. Swift, 1991, "Corned Beef to Caviar," *Sports Illustrated*, June 3, 74–87. Credit line: Time, Inc.

game attendance. The more an individual's reference group favors going to a game, the more likely the person will attend games in the future. Additionally, individuals who become fans of a team later in life (adolescence and adulthood) are more likely to be influenced by friends in forming an attachment with a particular team.[33]

In addition to influencing game attendance, one study found that reference groups can also affect other game-related experiences, such as perceived quality of the stadium, perceived quality of the food service, overall satisfaction with the stadium, and perceived ticket value.[34] For instance, individuals who perceive their reference group as opposing going to games will also have less satisfaction with the stadium environment.

- ***Family ties*** – Some sports spectators believe attending sporting events is a means for fostering family togetherness. The entire family can spend time together and lines of communication may be opened through sports. Interestingly, women

SPORTS WAGERING

There are many myths associated with sports wagering in Nevada – the only state where it is legal, regulated, policed and taxed. The following are the facts about sports wagering:

- Overall, Nevada's legal sports wagering represents less than 1 percent of all sports betting nationwide. In 2011, $2.88 billion was legally wagered in Nevada's sports books; the National Gambling Impact Study Commission (NGISC) estimated that illegal wagers are as much as $380 billion annually.
- Gross revenue for Nevada's sports books was $170.0 million in 2012. While more than $3.45 billion was wagered in 2012, more than 95 percent of all bets placed were returned to patrons in winnings.
- Legal sports wagering helps bring more than 30 million visitors to Nevada each year and provides employment for thousands of people.
- Approximately two-third of all sports bets in Nevada are placed on professional, non-college sporting events.
- The FBI estimates that more than $2.5 billion is illegally wagered annually on March Madness each year.
- Comparatively, sports book operators estimate $80 million to $90 million – less than 4 percent of the illegal take – is wagered on the tournament legally through Nevada's 216[(1)] sports books.
- More bets are placed on the Super Bowl than on any other single day sporting event of the year, however more is wagered during the first four days of the men's March Madness tournament.
- According to the Nevada Gaming Control Board, approximately $98.9 million was wagered on the 2013 Super Bowl at sports books across the state, but most of that figure was returned to bettors in the form of winnings. After paying out to bettors, Nevada sports books earned $7.2 million on 2013's game.
- The Las Vegas Convention and Visitors Authority estimated that the 2012 Super Bowl weekend produced $106.2 million in non-gaming economic impact and attracted 310,000 visitors.

(1) According to Christiansen Capital Advisors (CCA), which tracks Internet gambling, online sports betting generated $4.29 billion in revenues in 2005. This is more than double the $1.7 billion generated by online sports betting in 2001. This number is current as of 6/30/12.

Source: Rightsholder: American Gaming Association; http://www.americangaming.org/industry-resources/research/fact-sheets/sports-wagering. Credit: American Gaming Association.

are more motivated than men to attend sporting events to promote family togetherness.[35] Research has also shown that "fathers" are the persons who have the greatest influence in becoming a fan of a specific team. This is especially true for individuals who became fans early in life (preteen years). In fact, brand identification in sport often occurs at an early age and is significantly linked to family influences. In the majority of these instances sport consumers become exclusive consumers, often consumers for life. These allegiances last a lifetime and these findings have important implications for sports marketers in creating opportunities for fathers to interact with children in team-related activities.[36]

Game attractiveness

Another factor related to game attendance is the perceived attractiveness of each game. **Game attractiveness** is a situational factor that varies from game to game and week to week. The perceived quality of a single game or event is based on the skill level of the individuals participating in the contest (i.e., the presence of any star athletes), team records, and league standings. In addition to these game-attraction variables, if the game is a special event (opening day, bowl game, or all-star game), game attractiveness is heightened. The more attractive the game, the more likely attendance will increase.

Economic factors

Both the controllable and uncontrollable **economic factors** can affect game attendance. The controllable economic factors include aspects of the sports marketing environment that can be altered by sports marketers, such as the price of tickets and the perceived value of the sports product. The uncontrollable economic factors are things such as the average income of the population and the economic health of the country.

Generally, the greater the perceived value of the game and the greater the income of the population, the greater the game attendance. Surprisingly, one study found that attendance has no relationship to increased ticket prices.[37] In other words, raising ticket prices does not negatively affect game attendance. Other researchers, however, have found just the opposite.[38]

Competitive factors

As discussed in Chapter 2, competition for sporting event attendance can be thought of as either direct (other sports) or indirect (other forms of entertainment). Ordinarily, the lesser the competition for spectators' time and money, the more likely they will be to attend your sporting event.

One form of direct competition of interest to sports marketers is the televised game. Television continues to be used by almost all fans to follow sports. However, according to Kantar's 2013 Global Sports Media Consumption Report well over half (59 percent) of sports fans state that their sports consumption has changed in some way in the last two years.[39] Whether it be consumption via high definition, consumption online (which now surpasses print alternatives), or the use of digital access in the use of social networking platforms, the trends of use of traditional media consumption are changing. Some of the underlying trends can only be good news to the industry. In fact, fans in the U.S. spend an average of 8 hours a week watching sport content and fans in most markets are spending more time consuming sports than ever before. The era of digital and second screen usage garners opportunity and according to Kantar's

Editor Frank Dunne, whoever said the pie doesn't get any bigger, was wrong.[40] In fact, more and more fans are consuming sport on Internet connected devices without – crucially – taking away viewers from television. Dunne noted that digital has added new layers to the experience offering more ways of viewing and discovering the alchemy, which turns digital into dollars, is the holy grail for sports rights-holders and brands. We are in an era where primary and second screen choices, as well as digital choices, continue to develop; however, many in the industry are still trying to map out a strategy and are not alive to its true potential. Sports marketers need to understand spectators' media habits and motivations to appeal to these growing segments. In addition, sports marketers want to learn whether to treat the viewing audience as a separate segment or whether it overlaps with spectators who attend games.

Some of these issues were addressed in a series of studies conducted to understand consumers' motivations for watching televised sports. Overall, the excitement, enthusiasm, and entertainment value associated with the telecasts are the primary motivating factors.[41] Interestingly, the need for watching televised sports differed by gender. Women indicated they were more motivated to watch sports for the social value and the fact that friends and family were already doing so. Men, however, were motivated to watch sports on television because they enjoy the telecasts and find them entertaining.

With respect to their viewing behavior, men are more interested in watching sports on television, want more sports coverage, watch more sports coverage, and follow it up by watching news reports of the action more frequently than do their female counterparts. In short, men appear more highly involved in televised sports.

How does consuming the game via some alternative media such as radio, webcast, or television affect game attendance? One study examined the influence of television and radio broadcasting on the attendance at NBA games. The results indicated that television broadcasts of home games would have a negative impact on attendance, with more than 60 percent of the fans indicating they would watch the game on television rather than attend. However, watching televised sports can also have a positive impact on home game attendance. For instance, the more one watches away games on television, the more one attends home games. In addition, the more one listens to the radio (for both home and away games), the greater the likelihood of attending home games.[42]

Demographic factors

Demographic factors or variables, such as population, age, gender, education, occupation, and ethnic background, are also found to be related to game attendance. Although the number of women attending sporting events is greater than ever before, males are still more likely to be in attendance. The sports that possess the male fan base include the NFL, college football, and Major League Baseball. The most avid female fans flock to figure skating, the NFL, and Major League Baseball.

In addition, male sport fans tend to be younger, more educated, and have higher incomes than that of the general population. With the exception of baseball, the majority of ticket holders at sporting events now have annual income levels of $80,000 or more. According to the most recent census data, only 15 percent of American households reach this level of income, a relatively small market segment.[43] Enthrallingly, the National Hockey League, PGA Tour, and ATP (tennis) have the greatest percentage of fans with household incomes over $50,000.[44]

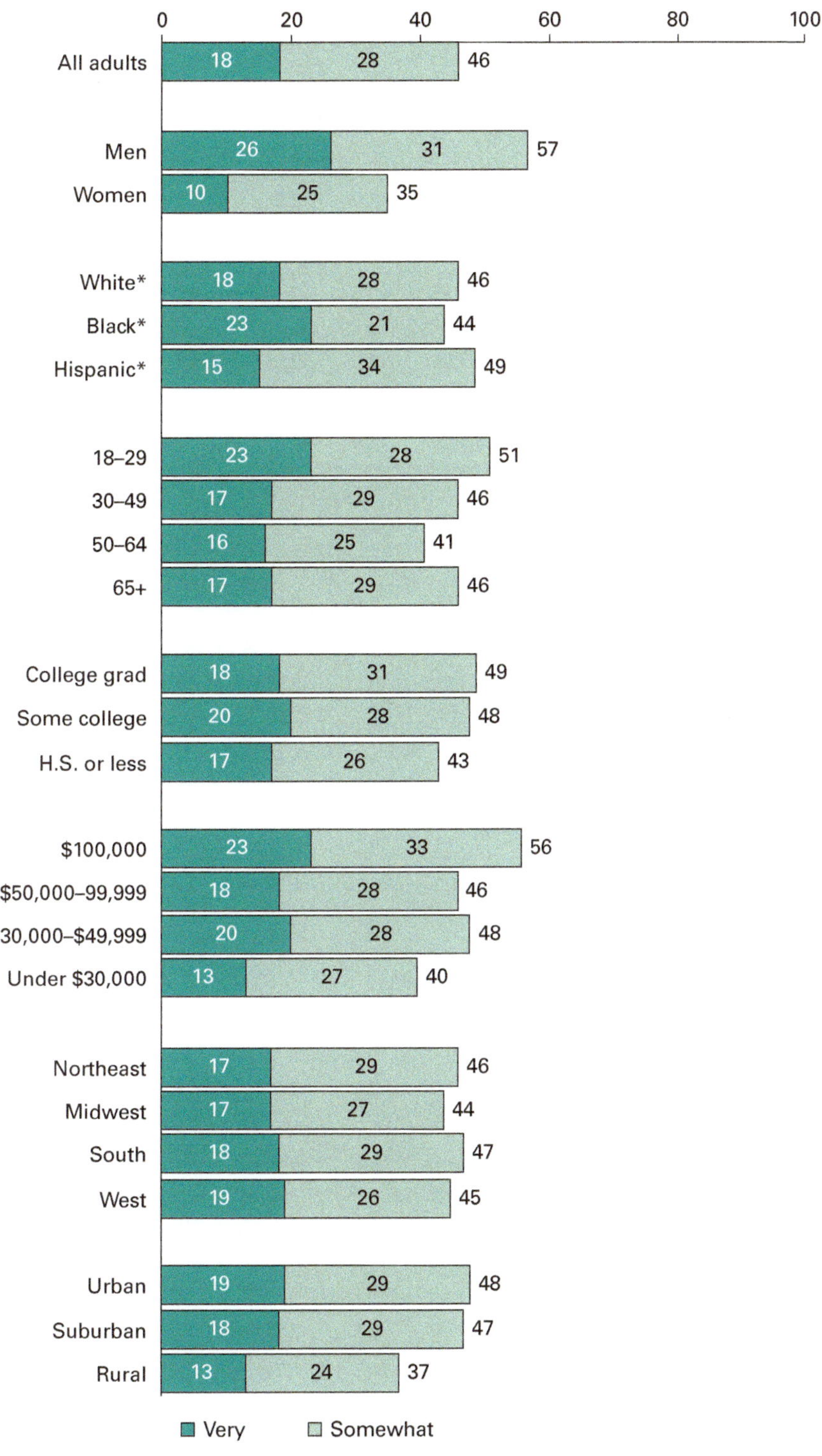

Table 5.2 Who's a sports fan?

Source: Americans to Rest of World: Soccer Not Really Our Thing, page 8; http://www.pewsocialtrends.org/2006/06/14/americans-to-rest-of-world-soccer-not-really-our-thing/

As you might imagine, it is very difficult to come up with the profile of the typical sports fan because of the varying nature of sport. However, it is important not to generalize and run the risk of neglecting a potentially huge market.[45] Table 5.2 presents the demographic profile of Americans who consider themselves sports fans.

Stadium factors

New stadiums are being built across the United States. Moreover, team owners who cannot justify or afford new stadiums are moving to cities that will build a new facility or attempt to renovate the existing stadium. Obviously, these stadium improvements are believed to affect the bottom line for team owners or for university presidents.

Stadium factors refer to variables such as the newness of the stadium, stadium access, aesthetics or beauty of the stadium, seat comfort, and cleanliness of the stadium. One study found that all these factors are positively related to game attendance. That is, the more favorable the fans' attitude toward the stadium, the higher the attendance.[46]

Similar results were found in a study conducted for *Money* magazine by IRC Survey Research Group.[47] This study looked at what 1,000 sports fans value when attending professional sporting events. The major findings, in order of importance, are:

- Parking that costs less than $8 and tickets under $25 each
- Adequate parking or convenient public transportation
- A safe, comfortable seat that you can buy just a week before the game
- Reasonably priced snack foods, such as a hot dog for $2 or less
- Home team with a winning record
- A close score
- A hometown star who is generally regarded as being among the sport's 10 best players
- Reasonably priced souvenirs
- A game that ends in less than three hours
- A wide variety of snack foods.

Interestingly, the four most important things identified in the study were unrelated to the game itself. If you make people pay too much or work too hard, they would rather stay home. Apparently, only after you are seated in your comfortable chair with your inexpensive food do you begin to worry about rooting for the home team.

In addition, spectators were concerned about having a clean, comfortable stadium with a good atmosphere. Part of the positive atmosphere is having strict controls placed on rowdy fans and having the option of sitting in a nonalcohol section of the stadium. An emerging area of some importance to new stadium design, as well as to stadium rehabilitation, is the need to provide more and larger restrooms. Because stadium atmosphere seems to be so important to fans, let us examine it in greater detail.

Sportscape

As you might have noticed, stadium atmosphere appears to be a critical issue in game attendance. Recently, studies have been conducted in the area of stadium environment or "sportscape."[48] **Sportscape** refers to the physical surroundings of the stadium that affect the spectator's desire to stay at the stadium and ultimately return to the stadium. Figure 5.2 shows the relationship between these sportscape factors and spectator behavior.

Web 5.2 New sports facilities such as the Cowboys Stadium in Dallas influence attendance.

Source: dallascowboys.com

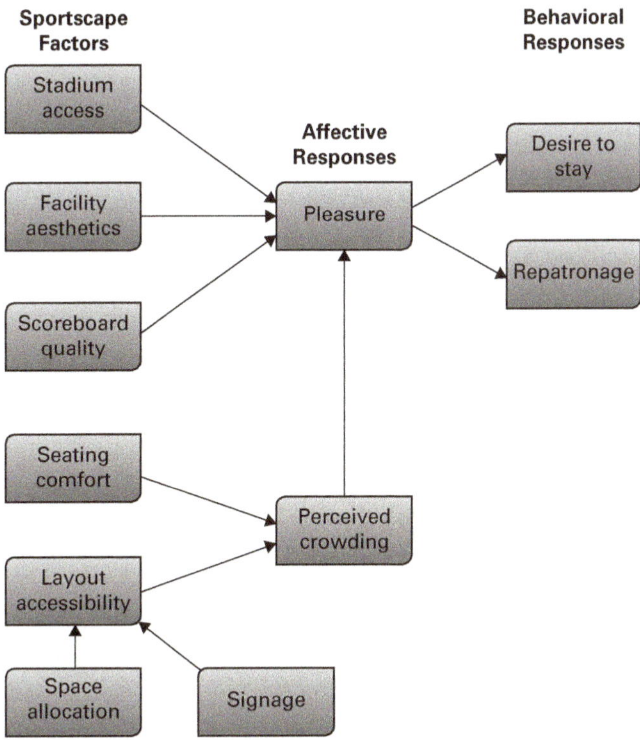

Figure 5.2 Model of sportscape

Source: K. L. Wakefield, J. G. Blodgett, and H. J. Sloan, 1996, "Measurement and Management of the Sportscape," *Journal of Sport Management*, 10(1): 16.

As shown in Figure 5.2, sportscape factors include stadium access, facility aesthetics, scoreboard quality, seating comfort, and layout accessibility. Each sportscape factor serves as input to the spectator's affective response or judgment of pleasure or displeasure with the stadium. The affective response, as we learned in Chapter 4, is the "feeling" component of attitudes. Similarly, the affective response with the sportscape is the feeling of perceived pleasure or displeasure the spectator has with the stadium. The perceptions of the stadium sportscape are linked to behavioral responses or actions of the spectator. In this case, the two behavioral responses are the desire to stay in the stadium and repatronage, or returning to the stadium for future events. Let us further examine the sportscape factors and their impact on spectators' pleasure.

Stadium accessibility

Many of us have left sporting events early to avoid traffic hassles or walked long distances to get to a game because of limited parking. For example, I recently attended a game at Wrigley Field in Chicago and, because of limited parking spaces, had to walk over three miles to get to the game. By the time I reached my seat, it was the third inning! This experience certainly resulted in displeasure with the entire game experience.

Stadium access includes issues such as availability of parking, the ease of entering and exiting the parking areas, and the location of the parking relative to the stadium. From the spectator's perspective, anything that can make it easier to get in and out of the stadium quicker will positively affect a return for future games.

Facility aesthetics

Facility aesthetics refers to the exterior and interior appearance of the stadium. The exterior appearance includes stadium architecture and age of the stadium. New stadiums, with unique architectural designs, are springing up across the United States. For example, the new Dallas Cowboys Stadium seats 80,000, making it the fourth largest stadium in the NFL by seating capacity. However, the seating capacity is expandable. The maximum capacity of the stadium, including standing room, is 110,000. The Party Pass sections are behind seats in each end zone and on a series of six elevated platforms connected by stairways. At the time of its development it was the largest domed stadium in the world, had the world's largest column-free interior and the largest high definition video screen which hangs from 20 yard line to 20 yard line. Additionally, new innovative stadia are being built around the world. Construction began in 2010 on Spartak Stadium in Moscow. Scia Engineer developed an economic, elegant, and easy-to-build steel roof design to cope with Moscow's extreme climate. Spartak Stadium is scheduled to open in 2014 and is included in Russia's bid for the 2018 FIFA World Cup. For Beijing 2008, the Swiss architects Jacques Herzog and Pierre de Meuron designed an exquisite (and expensive) structure wrapped in a delicate-looking tangle of concrete columns. (The Chinese call it "the bird's nest.") It looks like no stadium you've ever seen and has the potential to be one of the most significant pieces of architecture built anywhere in the world.

Although the external beauty adds to the stadium aesthetics, the interior can also play a major role in fan satisfaction and attendance. The interior of the stadium includes factors such as color of the stadium walls, facades, and seats; the presence of sponsors' signage; and the presence of symbols from the team's past. For example,

The Metrodome, the domed home of University of Minnesota football, was rated the poorest stadium in the Big Ten Conference because of its sterile game day atmosphere, hence its recent destruction. It was so bad that the university decided to build a standalone stadium on campus which opened in September 2009. TCF Bank Stadium, sometimes referred to as either "The Bank" or "The Gopher Hole," is the football stadium for the Minnesota Golden Gophers college football team at the University of Minnesota in Minneapolis, Minnesota. The 50,805 seat on-campus "horseshoe" style stadium is designed to support future expansion to seat close to 80,000 people. TCF Bank Stadium, which cost 288.5 million, features 39 suites, 59 loge boxes, 1,000 outdoor club seats, 300 indoor club seats, a club lounge, a 20,000-square-foot facility for the marching band, and several locker rooms. The Stadium's field is laid out in an east–west configuration, with the open end of the stadium facing campus. This layout, similar to that of Memorial Stadium, provides a view of downtown Minneapolis. Compare these design features with Fenway Park in Boston, one of the oldest and most unique stadiums in the United States and you can see how aesthetics can vary from one facility to the next. As former pitcher Bill Lee stated, "Fenway Park is a religious shrine. People go there to worship." Obviously, professional sports franchises are not the only ones who care about facility aesthetics. University marketers and athletic departments are equally concerned with their venues. In a recent article, the top 10 college football venues were ranked based on atmosphere and aesthetics, tradition, and how well the team plays at home. The number one stadium in college sport was Tiger Stadium – Louisiana State University. The rest of the best in college facilities include the following: (2) Ohio Stadium – The Ohio State University (3) Beaver Stadium – Penn State University, (4) Stanford Stadium – University of Georgia, (5) Neyland Stadium – University of Tennessee, (6) Kyle Stadium – Texas A&M University, (7) Memorial – Clemson University, (8) Memorial Stadium – University of Nebraska, (9) Bryant-Denny Stadium – University of Alabama, and (10) Ben Hill Griffin Stadium, also known as the "Swamp," at the University of Florida.[49]

Scoreboard quality

One of the specific interior design considerations that represents a separate dimension of sportscape is **scoreboard quality**. In fact, the scoreboard in some stadiums is seen as the focal point of the interior. Throughout the game, fans continually monitor the stadium scoreboard for updates on scoring, player statistics, and other forms of entertainment, such as trivia contests, cartoon animation, and music videos. Examples of scoreboard quality range from the traditional scoreboard at Fenway Park, which is manually operated, to the NFL's biggest scoreboard, at Dallas Cowboys Stadium.

Cowboys Stadium is home to the world's largest outdoor digital display. The scoreboard at Cowboys Stadium is approximately 60 yards long. The 2,100 inch display weighs in at approximately 600 tons, spans over 25,670 square feet, features back-to-back high definition LED screens, and has two small screens at each end to accommodate the stadium endzone fans. Stadium scoreboards such as those at Cowboys Stadium, Heinz Field in Pittsburgh, and AT&T Park in San Francisco are designed to create pure entertainment. Most of the entertainment will be produced like a TV show and feature in-stand giveaways, trivia contests, features on players, and facts and figures about the field. Rick Fairbend, the executive producer/broadcast manager for the Steelers, said that "[the fans] will be amazed at the whole entertainment package from now on."

Even smaller colleges like Coastal Carolina University are enjoying the benefits of custom scoreboards. Underscoring the importance of the scoreboard is Warren Koegel, athletic director at Coastal Carolina University, who believes that fans are used to high-definition TV and large-screen displays, so they made the decision to invest in top-of-the-line equipment.

Perceived crowding

As shown in Figure 5.2, seating comfort and layout accessibility are the two factors that were found to be determinants of spectators' perceptions of crowding. Perceived crowding, in turn, is believed to have a negative influence on the spectator's pleasure. In other words, spectator pleasure decreases as perceived crowding increases.

Perceived crowding not only has an impact on pleasure but also on spectator safety. For example, English football grounds are moving away from terraces (standing areas renowned for hooliganism and violence) and toward a requirement of all-seater facilities. There has been a great deal of debate about reintroducing terracing. However, based on a report that identified all-seating as the factor that contributes the most to spectator safety, the British government has no plans to bring back terraces at English football grounds.[50]

Seating comfort

Seating comfort refers to the perceived comfort of the seating and the spacing of seats relative to each other. Anyone who has been forced to sit among the more than 110,000 fans at a University of Michigan football game can understand the influence of seating on the game experience. Likewise, those who have been fortunate enough to view a game from a luxury box or club seat also know the impact of seating on enjoyment of the game. Luxury boxes often offer top of the line amenities, while the club seats provide the customer with the padded seat luxuries of a private box without the privacy. Club-level seats commonly include climate-controlled lounges, multiple TV sets, buffets, parking benefits, concierge service, and more space between rows of seats.

Chris Bigelow, president of a facility management company, contends that more seating capacity in our stadiums will not guarantee financial success in the future. Less capacity with a higher level of comfort may be a much more profitable route to attracting fans. The trend should not be for more seats in a venue but for better seating. Bigelow states, "Our culture is willing to pay for comfort."[51]

Layout accessibility

Layout accessibility refers to whether spectators can move freely about the stadium. More specifically, does the layout of the stadium make it easy for spectators to get in and out of their seats and reach the concession areas, restrooms, and so on? To facilitate access to these destinations, there must be proper **signage** to direct spectators and there must be adequate **space allocation**. Inadequate space and signage cause spectators to feel confused and crowded, leading to negative feelings about the game experience.

As stated previously, all the sportscape factors affect spectators' feelings about the game experience. These positive or negative feelings experienced by spectators ultimately affect their desire to stay in the stadium and return for other games. Although all the sportscape factors are important, research has shown that perceived crowding is the most significant predictor of spectators having a pleasurable game experience. In addition, the aesthetic quality of the stadium was found to have a major impact on spectators' pleasure with the game.[52] The findings of the sportscape research present several implications for sports marketers and stadium or facilities managers. First, stadium management should consider reallocating or redesigning space to improve perceived crowding. This might include enlarging the seating areas, walkways, and the space in and around concession waiting areas. Second, before spending the money to do major renovations or even building a new stadium to improve aesthetic quality, focus on more inexpensive alternatives. For instance, painting and cleaning alone might significantly improve the aesthetic value of an aging stadium.

UCLA has moved the Pauley Pavilion renovation process forward and has expanded and improved the building that has been a campus landmark for more than 40 years and the home court of 38 NCAA championship teams. The goal was to dedicate the restored Pauley Pavilion on October 14, 2010, to honor Coach John Wooden on his 100th birthday; unfortunately the great Coach John Wooden lived a long life that fell a little more than four months short of his 100th birthday.

Among the many enhancements being considered were a new retractable seating system to bring spectators closer to the court and new concession areas, restrooms, and modern arena technology to enhance fan experience; new and expanded locker rooms, medical treatment and media rooms, and dedicated practice facilities; and a main lobby that would serve as a central entrance and celebrate UCLA's illustrious athletic tradition. These types of changes have provided the Bruin faithful with a first-class facility that spectators feel good about, at a cost much lower than for new construction.[53]

Based on the studies conducted by Wakefield and his colleagues, there seems to be no doubt that the stadium atmosphere, or sportscape, plays a pivotal role in spectator satisfaction and attendance. Moreover, the pleasure derived from the sportscape causes people to stay in the stadium for longer periods of time. Certainly, having spectators stay in the stadium is a plus for the team, who will profit from increased concession and merchandise sales. In describing the importance of the sportscape, Wakefield states, "Effective facility management may enable team owners to effectively compete for consumers' entertainment dollars even when they may be unable to compete on the field."[54]

Value of sport to the community

Values, as you will recall, are widely held beliefs that affirm what is desirable. In this case, values refer to the beliefs about the impact of sport on the community. Based on the results of a recent study, spectators' perceptions of the impact of professional sport on a community can be grouped into eight value dimensions (see Table 5.3 for a brief description of values).

As you might expect, each value is related to spectators' game attendance and intentions to attend future games. For instance, spectators who believe sports enhance community solidarity are more likely to attend sporting events. Sport marketers should carefully consider these values and promote positive values when developing marketing strategy.

Table 5.3 Eight value dimensions of sport to the community

• ***Community solidarity*** – Sport enhances the image of the community, enhances community harmony, generates a sense of belonging, and helps people to feel proud
• ***Public behavior*** – Sport encourages sportsmanship, reinforces positive citizenship, encourages obedience to authority, and nurtures positive morality
• ***Pastime ecstasy*** – Sport provides entertainment and brings excitement
• ***Excellence pursuit*** – Sport encourages achievement and success, hardwork, and risk taking
• ***Social equity*** – Sport increases racial and class equality and promotes gender equity
• ***Health awareness*** – Sport eliminates drug abuse, encourages exercise, and promotes an active lifestyle
• ***Individual quality*** – Sport promotes character building and encourages competitive traits
• ***Business opportunity*** – Sport increases community commercial activities, attracts tourists, and helps community economic development

Source: James J. Zhang, Dale G. Pease, and Sai C. Hui, 1996, "Value Dimensions of Professional Sport as Viewed by Spectators," *Sports and Social Issues* February 21: 78–94.

CAREER SPOTLIGHT

Marc Reeves, International Commercial Director, NFL

Career questions

1. What are your roles and responsibilities? What's on your agenda?

It is essentially to grow the fan base of the NFL around the world and to increase and maximize sponsorship opportunities. We have to not only export the brand and the game that is being played here in the States, but also create new assets around the world that are locally relevant and then tie them back and grow interest in the NFL.

To understand the markets that are most ripe for growth and to work out ways to link to who our fans are. . . . In markets where the NFL is known, we need to raise awareness. In other markets, it's to get the fans to understand that the NFL is more than just the Super Bowl and cheerleaders.

2. What could the NFL do better on the global scale? What is the NFL's international vision?

We have to package the game. Make it palatable for audiences who don't understand it. We have to do a better job educating people about the game because very few people know the rules.

There are five local offices (in New York, China, Japan, Mexico, and the U.K.) and we had to figure out local sponsorships. For instance, the international game every year is being held in England right now. We have to figure out how to build local sponsorships around that and also maximize value for the existing partners of the NFL. So a lot of it will be how do we work with sponsorships and local business and then also make them a marketing function so that they are helping to grow interest in the sport.

3. What are the plans for the next five years? Is there a chance for another NFL Europa?

To grow the avid fan base of the league. We have done a lot of research that shows that there are people aware of the NFL, but there

are few avid fans depending on the countries.
No. I think we realized that fans around the world want the best product. We know based on the fact that each of the last three England NFL games sold out in 90 minutes or less.

4. What career advice do you have for people wanting to go into the sports industry?

To specifically focus on the value that you can add to any organization. And the second part is also to look beyond the obvious, like the agencies and the leagues and teams. There are a lot of great opportunities at some of the brands, tourist boards, and other areas that are involved in sports and there is a lot less competition for those jobs.

Sports involvement

In Chapter 4, involvement was examined in the context of sports participation. Measures of sports involvement have also been used to understand spectator behavior. From the spectator's perspective, **sport involvement** is the perceived interest in and personal importance of sports to an individual attending sporting events or consuming sport through some other medium. What sports are people most interested in? Just 4 percent of adults in this country rate soccer as their favorite sport to watch, compared with 34 percent who say this about football, 14 percent about basketball, and 13 percent about baseball, according to a Pew Research Center study.[55]

Fan interest and involvement in the remaining sports can be seen in Table 5.4.

Table 5.4 What's your favorite sport? Favorite sports to watch by interest in sports news

		Follow Sports	
	ALL Adults	**Very/Some-what closely**	**Not very/ Not at all closely**
	%	**%**	**%**
Football	34	45	26
Basketball	14	18	11
Baseball	13	14	12
Soccer	4	6	2
Auto racing	4	4	4
Ice skating	3	1	5
Ice hockey	3	3	3
Golf	2	2	3
Tennis	2	2	2
Boxing	2	1	2
Westling	1	1	1
Other	5	2	8
None	12	1	20
Don't know	1	*	1
	100	100	100
Number of respondents	2,250	1,029	1,216
			Pew Research Center

Source: Americans to Rest of World: Soccer Not Really Our Thing, page 9; http://www.pewsocialtrends.org/2006/06/14/americans-to-rest-of-world-soccer-not-really-our-thing/

Detailed studies have looked at the involvement levels of golf spectators, baseball spectators, Division I women's basketball spectators, and sports spectators in general.[56] In addition, a study has examined the cross-cultural differences in sport involvement (see Spotlight on International Sports Marketing). Generally, these studies have shown that higher levels of spectator involvement are related to the number of games attended, the likelihood of attending games in the future, and the likelihood of consuming sport through media, such as newspapers, television, and magazines. Also of importance, high-involvement spectators were more likely to correctly identify the sponsors of sporting events.

SPOTLIGHT ON INTERNATIONAL SPORTS MARKETING

A comparative analysis of spectator involvement: United States vs. United Kingdom

As the field of sports marketing expands into international markets, the success of U.S. sports entities will depend on understanding the core consumer abroad – the international sports fan. Recently, a study was conducted to better understand the domestic and U.K. sports fan by measuring sports involvement and by exploring the relationship between sports involvement and sports-related behaviors.

The findings indicated that there are two dimensions of sports involvement that are consistent across the U.S. and U.K. sample. The cognitive dimension refers to the way that consumers think about sports, and the affective dimension is the way that consumers feel about sports. Both the cognitive and affective factors were positively related to viewing sports on television, reading about sports in magazines and newspapers, attending sporting events, and participating in sports. That is, higher levels of involvement are related to more viewing, reading about, and attending sporting events.

There were some differences in the responses of people from the United States and the United Kingdom. People from the United Kingdom spent less time each week watching sports on television; however, they were more likely to read the sports section of the newspaper on a daily basis. Compared with the U.S. sample, people from the United Kingdom were less interested in local sports teams as opposed to national teams. Finally, the British respondents were more likely than their American counterparts to perceive sports as necessary, relevant, and important.

There were no significant differences in the responses of people from the two countries concerning (1) the likelihood of planning your day around watching a sporting event, (2) hours spent reading sports-related magazines, and (3) participation in sports-related activities.

Source: Adapted from Matthew Shank and Fred Beasley, 1998, "A Comparative Analysis of Sports Involvement: U.S. vs. U.K.," Advertising and Consumer Psychology Conference, Portland, OR, May.

Fan identification

Sports involvement was previously defined as the level of interest in and importance of sport to consumers. A concept that extends this idea to a sports organization is fan identification. Two contrasting examples of fan identification were seen with the movement of NFL franchises. When the Cleveland Browns moved to Baltimore, Browns fans became irate, holding protests and filing lawsuits to try to stop the team's move.[57] However, when the Houston Oilers moved to Nashville relatively little fan resistance was observed, indicating low levels of fan identification.

Sports marketers are interested in building and maintaining high levels of fan identification for organizations and their players. If high levels of identification are developed, a number of benefits can be realized by the sports organization. Before examining the benefits of fan identification, let us take a closer look at what it is. **Fan identification** is defined as the personal commitment and emotional involvement customers have with a sports organization.[58] A conceptual framework was developed by Sutton, McDonald, Milne, and Cimperman for understanding the antecedents and outcomes of fan identification.[59] The model is shown in Figure 5.3.

Managerial correlates are those things such as team characteristics, organizational characteristics, affiliation characteristics, and activity characteristics that directly contribute to the level of fan involvement. Team characteristics include, most notably, the success of the team. Typically, the more successful the team, the higher the level of fan identification – because people want to associate themselves with a winner (BIRGing). However, some fans see loyalty to the team to be more important than team success. For instance, the Chicago Cubs continue to have high levels of fan identification even though they have not won the World Series since early in the twentieth century.

Organizational characteristics also lead to varying levels of fan identification. In contrast to team characteristics, which pertain to athletic performance, organizational characteristics relate to "off-the-field" successes and failures. Is the team trying to build a winning franchise or just reduce the payroll? Is the team involved in the community and community relations? Is the team owner threatening to move to another city if a new stadium is not built with taxpayers' monies? An example of the impact of team and organizational characteristics on fan identification was provided by the Florida Marlins. As soon as the team won the 1997 World Series (team characteristic that should foster high fan identification), the owner talked about

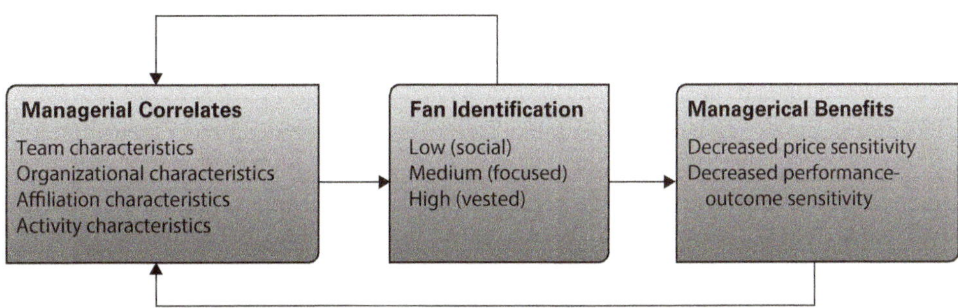

Figure 5.3 Model for fan identification

Source: William A. Sutton, *Sport Marketing Quarterly*

selling the team, and the organization traded several of its star players (organizational characteristic that will diminish fan identification).

Affiliation characteristics refer to the sense of community that a fan builds as a result of a team. According to Sutton et al., "The community affiliation component is . . . defined as kinship, bond, or connection the fan has to a team. Community affiliation is derived from common symbols, shared goals, history, and a fan's need to belong."[60] As discussed in the study on the impact of sports on the community, the sports team provides fans with a way to feel connected to the community and fulfill the need for affiliation. In addition, the more a fan's reference group (friends and family) favors going to games, the more the individual identifies with the team.[61]

Activity characteristics represent another antecedent to fan identification. In this case, activity refers to attending sporting events or being exposed to events via the media. As technology continues to advance, sports fans are afforded more opportunities to watch their favorite team via cable or pay-per-view, listen to games via radio, or link to broadcasts from anywhere via the Internet. With increased exposure, fan identification should be enhanced.

The interaction of the four preceding factors will influence the level of fan identification. An individual's level of identification with a team or player can range from no identification to extremely high identification. However, for simplicity, Sutton et al. describe three distinct categories of fan identification.[62]

Low identification

Fans who attend sporting events primarily for social interaction or for the entertainment benefit of the event characterize low-level identification. These "social fans" are attracted by the atmosphere of the game, promotions or events occurring during the competition, and the feelings of camaraderie that the game creates. Although this is the lowest level of fan identification, if fans are reinforced by the entertainment benefits of the game, then they may become more involved.

Medium identification

The next higher classification of fan involvement is called medium identification, or focused fans. The major distinguishing characteristic of these fans is that they identify with the team or player, but only for the short term. In other words, they may associate with the team, or player, if it is having an especially good year. However, when the team starts to slump or the player is traded, "focused" identification will fade. As with low-level identification, a fan that experiences medium levels of identification may move to higher levels.

High identification

The highest classification of fan involvement is based on a long-term commitment to the sport, team, or player. These vested fans often recruit other fans, follow the team loyally, and view the team as a vital part of the community. Fans classified as high involvement exhibit a number of concrete behavioral characteristics. Most important, high-identification fans are the most likely to return to sporting events. Moreover, high-involvement fans are more likely to attend home and away games, have been fans for a greater number of years, and invest more financially in being a fan.

Managerial benefits

The final portion of the fan identification model put forth by Sutton et al. describes the outcomes of creating and fostering vested fans. One outcome is that high-identification fans have decreased price sensitivity. Price sensitivity refers to the notion that small increases in ticket prices may produce great fluctuations in demand for tickets. Fans that stick with the team for the long run are more likely to be season ticket holders or purchase personal seat licenses to get the right to purchase permanent seats. Fans that exhibit low levels of identification may decide not to purchase tickets, even for small increases in ticket prices.

Another outcome of high levels of fan identification is decreased performance-outcome sensitivity. Stated simply, fans that are vested will be more tolerant of poor seasons or in-season slumps. Fans will be more likely to stick with the team and not give up prime ticket locations that may have taken generations to acquire.

Summary

In this chapter, we explored the spectator as a consumer of sport. Although there are many people who both participate in and observe sports, research suggests that there are two distinct segments of consumers.

There are a variety of factors that influence our decision to attend sporting events. These factors include fan motivation, game attractiveness, economic factors, competitive factors, demographic factors, stadium factors, value of sport to the community, sports involvement, and fan identification. Fan motivation factors are those underlying reasons or needs that are met by attending a sporting event. Researchers believe that some of the primary reasons fans attend sporting events are enhancement of self-esteem, diversion from everyday life, entertainment value, eustress (feelings of excitement), economic value (gambling on events), aesthetic value, need for affiliation, and time with family members.

Another factor that influences our decision to attend sporting events is game attractiveness. Game attractiveness refers to the perceived value and importance of the individual game based on which teams or athletes are playing (e.g., Is it the crosstown rival or is Ken Griffey, Jr. in town?), the significance of the event to the league standings, whether the event is postseason versus regular season competition, or whether the event is perceived to be of championship caliber (e.g., the four majors in golf or the NCAA Final Four). In general, the greater the perceived attractiveness of the game, the more likely we will want to attend.

Economic factors also play a role in our decision to attend sporting events. As we discussed briefly in Chapter 2, the economic factors that may affect game attendance can be at the microeconomic level (e.g., personal income) or macroeconomic level (e.g., state of the nation's economy). Although these are uncontrollable factors, the sports organization can attempt to control the rising cost of ticket prices to make it easier for fans to attend sporting events.

Competition is another important factor that influences our decision to attend sporting events or observe them through another medium. Today, sports marketers must define the competition in broad terms – as other entertainment choices such as movies, plays, and theater compete with sporting events. Interestingly, sports organizations sometimes compete with themselves for fans. For example, one study found that televising home basketball games had a negative impact on game attendance.

Demographic factors such as age, ethnic background, and income are also related to spectator behavior. There is no such thing as a profile of the typical spectator. However, spectators are more likely to be male, young, more educated, and have higher incomes than that of the general population.

Perhaps the most important factor that influences attendance is the consumer's perception of the stadium. Stadium atmosphere appears to be a critical issue in attracting fans. The stadium atmosphere, or environment, has been referred to as the sportscape. The sportscape is the physical surroundings of the stadium that affect spectators' desire to stay at the stadium and ultimately return to the stadium. The multiple dimensions of sportscape include stadium access, facility aesthetics, scoreboard quality, seating comfort, and layout accessibility.

Another factor influencing game attendance and the likelihood of attending sporting events in the future is the perceived value of sport to the community. A study found that the more value attributed to sport, the more likely people were to attend. The value dimensions of sport to the community include community solidarity (bringing the community together), public behavior, pastime ecstasy (entertainment), pursuit of excellence, social equity, health awareness, individual quality (builds character), and business opportunities.

As discussed in Chapter 4, sports involvement refers to the consumer's perceived interest in and the importance of participating in sport. Sports involvement has a related definition for those observing sporting events. High-involvement spectators are more likely to attend sporting events, read sports magazines, and plan their entire day around attending a sporting event.

A final factor related to spectator behavior is fan identification. Fan identification is the personal commitment and emotional involvement customers have with the sports organization. The characteristics of the team, the characteristics of the organization, the affiliation characteristics (sense of community), and the activity characteristics (exposures to the team) all interact to influence the level of fan identification. The higher the level of fan identification, the more likely fans are to attend events.

Key terms

- aesthetic value
- demographic factors
- diversion from everyday life
- economic factors
- economic value
- entertainment value
- eustress
- facility aesthetics
- family ties
- fan identification
- fan motivation factors
- game attractiveness
- layout accessibility
- need for affiliation
- scoreboard quality
- seating comfort
- self-esteem enhancement
- signage
- space allocation
- sport involvement
- sportscape
- stadium access
- stadium factors

Review questions

1. Describe the differences and similarities between spectators and participants of sport.
2. Discuss the spectators' eight basic motives for attending sporting events. Which of these are similar to the motives for participating in sports?
3. Provide two examples of how game attractiveness influences attendance.
4. What are the economic factors that influence game attendance? Differentiate between the controllable and uncontrollable economic factors.
5. Describe the typical profile of spectators of women's sporting events. How would a sports marketer use this information in the strategic sports marketing process?
6. Discuss, in detail, the sportscape model and how the sportscape factors affect game attendance.
7. What are the value dimensions of professional sport to the community? How would sports marketers use these values in planning the strategic sports marketing process?
8. Define sports involvement from the spectator perspective. Why is it important to understand the levels of involvement among spectators?
9. Discuss, in detail, the model of fan identification and its implications for sports marketers.
10. Explain the relationship among the eight basic fan motivation factors and the other factors that influence game attendance (i.e., game attractiveness, economic factors, competitive factors, demographic factors, stadium factors, value to the community, sports involvement, and fan identification).

Exercises

1. Go to a high school sporting event, college sporting event, and professional sporting event. At each event, interview five spectators and ask them why they are attending the events and what benefits they are looking for from the event. Compare the different levels of competition. Do the motives for attending differ by level (i.e., high school, college, and professional)? Are there gender differences or age differences among respondents?
2. Go to a sports bar and interview five people watching a televised sporting event. Determine their primary motivation for watching the sporting event. Describe other situations in which motives for watching sporting events vary.
3. Attend a women's sporting event and record the demographic profile of the spectators. What are your observations? Use these observations and suggest how you might segment, target, and position (market selection decisions) if you were to market the sport.
4. Attend a collegiate or professional sporting event. Record and describe all the elements of sportscape. How do these affect your experience as a spectator?
5. Ask 10 consumers about the value they believe a professional sports team would (or does) bring to the community. Then ask the same people about the value of college athletics to the community. Comment on how these values differ by level of competition.
6. How will marketing play a role in revitalizing the following sports: baseball, tennis, and cricket? How has marketing played a role in the increased popularity in the following sports: golf, basketball, and soccer?

Internet exercises

1. Find examples via the Internet of how sports marketers have attempted to make it easier for fans to attend sporting events.
2. Locate two Web sites for the same sport – one for women and one for men (e.g., women's basketball and men's basketball). Comment on differences, if any, in how these sites market to spectators of the sport.
3. Locate two Web sites for the same sport – one American and one international (e.g., Major League Soccer and British Premier League). Comment on differences, if any, in how these sites market to spectators of the sport.

Endnotes

1 John Burnett, Anil Menon, and Denise T. Smart, "Sports Marketing: A New Ball Game with New Rules," *Journal of Advertising Research* (September–October 1993), 21–33.
2 George R. Milne, William A. Sutton, and Mark A. McDonald, "Niche Analysis: A Strategic Measurement Tool for Managers," *Sport Marketing Quarterly*, vol. 5, no. 3 (1996), 17–22.
3 Ibid.
4 Ibid.
5 *Richard Petty Driving Experience*, http://www.1800bepetty.com/experience/Ride.aspx.
6 John Burnett, Anil Menon, and Denise T. Smart, "Sport Marketing: A New Game With New Rules," *Journal of Advertising Research*, 33 (October 1993), 21–33.
7 Mauricio Ferreira and Ketra L. Armstrong, "An Exploratory Examination of Attributes Influencing Students' Decisions to Attend College Sport Events," *Sport Marketing Quarterly*, vol. 13 (2004), 194–208.
8 R. D. Hay and C. P. Rao, "Factors Affecting Attendance at Football Games," in M. Etzel and J. Gaski (Eds.), *Applying Marketing Technology to Spectator Sports* (South Bend, IN: University of Notre Dame Press, 1982), 65–76.
9 Roger G. Noll, "Attendance and Price Setting," in Roger G. Noll (Ed.), *Government and the Sports Business* (Washington, DC: The Brookings Institute, 1974), 115–157.
10 Dominic H. Rivers and Timothy D. DeSchiver, "Star Players, Payroll Distribution, and Major League Baseball Attendance," *Sport Marketing Quarterly*, vol. 1 (2002), 164–173.
11 Hal Hansen and Roger Gauthier, "Factors Affecting Attendance at Professional Sport Events," *Journal of Sport Management*, vol. 3, (1989), 15–32.
12 James J. Zhang, Dael G. Pease, Stanley C. Hui, and Thomas J. Michaud, "Variables Affecting the Spectator Decision to Attend NBA Games," *Sport Marketing Quarterly*, vol. 4, no. 4 (1995), 29–39.
13 James R. Hill, Jeff Madura, and Richard A. Zuber, "The Short Run Demand for Major League Baseball," *Atlantic Economic Journal*, vol. 10 (1982), 31–35.
14 Mark McDonald and Daniel Rascher, "Does Bat Day Make Cents? The Effect of Promotions on the Demand for Major League Baseball," *Journal of Sport Management*, vol. 14 (2000), 8–27.
15 Robert A. Baade and Laura J. Tiehen, "An Analysis of Major League Baseball Attendance, 1969–1987," *Journal of Sport & Social Issues*, vol. 14, no. 1 (1990), 14–32.
16 J. A. Schofield, "Performance and Attendance at Professional Team Sports," *Journal of Sport Behavior*, vol. 6 (1983), 196–206.
17 S. E. Iso-Ahola, "Attributional Determinants of Decisions to Attend Football Games," *Scandinavian Journal of Sports Sciences*, vol. 2 (1980), 39–46.
18 Daniel L. Wann, Angie Roberts, and Johnnie Tindall, "The Role of Team Performance, Team Identification, and Self-Esteem in Sport Spectators' Game Preferences," *Perceptual & Motor Skills*, vol. 89 (1999), 945–950.
19 Roger G. Noll, "Attendance and Price Setting," in R. G. Noll (Ed.), *Government and the Sports Business* (Washington, DC: The Brookings Institute, 1974), 115–157.
20 J. Michael Schwartz, "Causes and Effects of Spectator Sports," *International Review of Sport Sociology*, vol. 8 (1973), 25–45.
21 Galen Trail, Dean F. Anderson, and Janet Fink, "A Theoretical Model of Sport Spectator Consumption Behavior," *International Journal of Sport Management*, vol. 1 (2000), 154–180.
22 Daniel L. Wann, "Preliminary Validation of the Sport Fan Motivation Scale," *Journal of Sport & Social Issues* (November 1995), 337–396.
23 Robert B. Cialdini, Richard J. Borden, Avril Thorne, Marcus R. Walker, Stephen Freeman, and Lloyd R. Sloan, "Basking in Reflected Glory: Three (Football) Field Studies," *Journal of Personality and Social Psychology*, vol. 34 (1976), 366–375.
24 Robert Madrigal, "Cognitive and Affective Determinants of Fan Satisfaction with

Sporting Events," *Journal of Leisure Research*, vol. 27 (Summer 1995), 205–228.

25 Filip Boen, Norbert Vanbeselaere, and Jos Feys, "Behavioral Consequences of Fluctuating Group Success: An Internet Study of Soccer-Team Fans," *The Journal of Social Psychology*, vol. 142 (2002), 769–782.

26 Richard M. Campbell, Jr., Damon Aiken, and Aubrey Ken, "Beyond BIRGing and CORFing: Continuing the Exploration of Fan Behavior," *Sport Marketing Quarterly*, vol. 13 (2004), 151–157, © 2004 West Virginia University.

27 Malcolm Moran, "For Nebraska, Football Is Personal," *USA Today* (October 27, 2000).

28 "Get Them Out to the Ballpark – and Off of the Couch," Harris Interactive, *Sporttainment News*, vol. 1, no. 3 (June 12, 2001).

29 "Rule Changes in College Football." Available from: http://www.phoenixsports.com/list_articles.php?cappers_article_id123=459&show=articles.

30 "ESPN.com – NHL – Rules: Changes Are Widespread." Available from: sports.espn.go.com/nhl/news/story?id=2114523.

31 "The True Statistics of Sports Gambling," 2011, *online sportsbetting picks*, July 25. Available from: Online-sportsbetting-picks.com/the-true-statistics-of-sports-gambling, accessed December 9, 2013.

32 Ibid.

33 Richard Kolbe and Jeffrey James, "An Identification and Examination of Influences That Shape the Creation of Professional Team Fan," *International Journal of Sports Marketing and Sponsorship*, vol. 2 (2000), 23–38.

34 Daniel C. Funk, Lynn L. Ridinger, and Anita M. Moorman, "Exploring Origins of Involvement: Understanding the Relationship Between Consumer Motives and Involvement with Professional Sport Teams," *Leisure Science*, vol. 26 (2004), 35–61.

35 Daniel L. Wann, "Preliminary Validation of the Sport Fan Motivation Scale," *Journal of Sport & Social Issues* (November 1995), 337–396.

36 Richard Kolbe and Jeffrey James, "An Identification and Examination of Influences That Shape the Creation of Professional Team Fan," *International Journal of Sports Marketing and Sponsorship*, vol. 2 (2000), 23–38.

37 Robert A. Baade and Laura J. Tiechen, "An Analysis of Major League Baseball Attendance, 1969–1987," *Journal of Sport & Social Issues*, vol. 14 (1990), 14–32.

38 Brad Edmondson, "When Athletes Turn Traitor," *American Demographics* (September, 1997).

39 Kantar Media Sports, *Global Sports Media Consumption Report* 2013, PERFORM (May 2013).

40 Ibid.

41 Walter Gantz, "An Exploration of Viewing Motives and Behaviors Associated with Televised Sports," *Journal of Broadcasting*, vol. 25, no. 3 (1981),) 263–275.

42 James Zhang and Dennis Smith, "Impact of Broadcasting on the Attendance of Professional Basketball Games," *Sport Marketing Quarterly*, vol. 6, no. 1 (1997), 23–32.

43 Noel Paul, "High Cost of Pro-Sports Fandom May Ease Attendance at Most Major Events Drop – and Ticket Prices Are Expected to Follow," *Christian Science Monitor* (November 19, 2001), p.16.

44 "2003 ESPN Sports Fan Poll Is Now Available," Sporting Goods Manufacturers Association.

45 Donna Lopiano, "Marketing Trends in Women's Sports and Fitness," *Women's Sports Foundation*.

46 Kirk L. Wakefield and Hugh J. Sloan, "The Effects of Team Loyalty and Selected Stadium Factors on Spectator Attendance," *Journal of Sport Management*, vol. 9, no. 2 (1995), 153–172.

47 Jillian Kasky, "The Best Ticket Buys for Sports Fans Today," *Money*, vol. 24, no. 10 (October 1995), 146.

48 Kirk L. Wakefield, Jeffrey G. Blodgett, and Hugh J. Sloan, "Measurement and Management of the Sportscape," *Journal of Sport Management*, vol. 10, no. 1 (1996), 15–31.

49 B Gall 2013, "Ranking the Top 25 College Football Stadiums," AthalonSports. Available from: http://athlonsports.com/college-football/college-football-2013-ranking-nations-top-25-stadiums#, accessed June 17, 2014.

50 "British Sports Minister Says 'The Terraces Are History'" (October 1997, www.nando.net/newsroom/sport.../feat/archive/102297/ssoc 45127.html).

51 Bigelow, Chris, 2005, IAVM News, International Association of Assembly Managers, Coppell, TX, formerly http://www.iaam.org/facility_manager/pages/2005_Aug_Sep/STADIUMS.HTM.

52 Kirk L. Wakefield, Jeffrey G. Blodgett, and Hugh J. Sloan, "Measurement and Management of the Sportscape," *Journal of Sport Management*, vol. 10, no. 1 (1996), 15–31.

53 Andy Hemmer, "Gardens Gets Skyboxes in Makeover," *Cincinnati Business Courier Inc.*, vol. 11, no. 48 (April 10, 1995), 1.

54 Kirk L. Wakefield, Jeffrey G. Blodgett, and Hugh J. Sloan, "Measurement and Management of the Sportscape," *Journal of Sport Management*, vol. 10, no. 1 (1996), 15–31.

55 Pew Research Study, "Americans to the Rest of the World: Soccer Not Really Our Thing" (June 14, 2006).
56 Deborah L. Kerstetter and Georgia M. Kovich, "An Involvement Profile of Division I Women's Basketball Spectators," *Journal of Sport Management*, vol. 11 (1997), 234–249; Dana-Nicoleta Lascu, Thomas D. Giese, Cathy Toolan, Brian Guehring, and James Mercer, "Sport Involvement: A Relevant Individual Difference Factor in Spectator Sports," *Sport Marketing Quarterly*, vol. 4, no. 4 (1995), 41–46.
57 Geoff Hobson, "Just Another Sunday," *The Cincinnati Enquirer* (December 7, 1996).
58 William A. Sutton, Mark A. McDonald, George R. Milne, and John Cimperman, "Creating and Fostering Fan Identification in Professional Sports," *Sport Marketing Quarterly*, vol. 6, no. 1 (1997), 15–22.
59 Ibid.
60 Ibid.
61 Ibid.
62 Ibid.

CHAPTER 6

Segmentation, targeting, and positioning

After completing this chapter, you should be able to:

- Discuss the importance of market selection decisions.
- Compare the various bases for marketing segmentation.
- Understand target marketing and the requirements of successful target marketing.
- Describe positioning and its importance in the market selection decisions.
- Construct a perceptual map to depict any sports entity's position in the marketplace.

Market selection decisions are the most critical elements of the strategic sports marketing process. In this portion of the planning phase, decisions are made that will dictate the direction of the marketing mix. These decisions include how to group consumers together based on common needs, whom to direct your marketing efforts toward, and how you want your sports product to be perceived in the marketplace. These important market selection decisions are referred to as segmenting, targeting, and positioning (STP). In this chapter, we examine these concepts in the context of our strategic sports marketing process. Let us begin by exploring market segmentation, the first of the market selection decisions.

Segmentation

Not all sports fans are alike. You would not market the Xtreme Games to members of the American Association of Retired People (AARP). Likewise, you would not market the PGA's Champions Tour to Generation Xers. The notion of mass marketing and treating all consumers the same has given way to understanding the unique needs of groups of consumers. This concept, which is the first market selection decision, is referred to as market segmentation. More specifically, **market segmentation** is defined as identifying groups of consumers based on their common needs.

Market segmentation is recognized as a more efficient and effective way to market than mass marketing, which treats all consumers the same. By carefully exploring and understanding different segments through marketing research, sports marketers determine which groups of consumers offer the greatest sales opportunities for the organization.

If the first market selection decision is segmentation, then how do sports marketers group consumers based on common needs? Traditionally, there are six common bases for market segmentation. These include demographics, socioeconomic group, psychographic profile, geographic region, behavioral style, and benefits. Let us take a closer look at how sports marketers use and choose from among these six bases for segmentation.

Bases for segmentation

The bases for segmentation refer to the ways that consumers with common needs can be grouped together. Six bases for segmenting consumer markets are shown in Table 6.1.

Demographic segmentation

One of the most widely used techniques for segmenting consumer markets is **demographic segmentation**. Demographics include such variables as age, gender, ethnic background, and family life cycle. As the accompanying article illustrates, sports fans may be segmented in a variety of ways.

Segmenting markets based on demographics is widespread for three reasons. First, these characteristics are easy for sports marketers to identify and measure. Second, information about the demographic characteristics of a market is readily available from a variety of sources, such as the government census data described in Chapter 3. Third, demographic variables are closely related to attitudes and sport behaviors, such as attending games, buying sports merchandise, or watching sports on television.

Table 6.1 Common bases for segmentation of consumer markets

Demographic	**Geographic**
• Age	• World region
• Gender	• Country
• Ethnic background	• Country region
• Family life cycle	• City
Socioeconomic	• Physical climate
• Income	**Behavioral**
• Education	• Frequency of purchase
• Occupation	• Size of purchase(s)
Psychographic	• Loyalty of consumers
• Lifestyle	**Benefits**
• Personality	• Consumer needs
• Activities	• Product features desired
• Interests	
• Opinions	

TECHNICAL REPORT – SPORT ENGLAND MARKET SEGMENTATION

The Sport England market segmentation is built primarily from the 'Taking Part' and 'Active People' surveys[1], and helps explain individual's motivations, attitudes, behaviour and barriers towards sport and active recreation. It is underpinned by key socio-demographic variables, thereby ensuring that the segments can be geographically quantified and appended to both customer records and the Electoral Roll. Therefore every adult in England can have a Sport England segment appended to them, whilst a market segment profile can be counted at any geographic level within England down to postcode.

It was this key requirement to be able to geographically quantify and append the classification to customer records which drove the methodology adopted for this project.

1 For more information on these surveys please go to www.sportengland.org/research

Key socio-demographic variables were used as the link between the sport and active recreation details in the two sport surveys. It was also this common set of indicators that enabled us to link our sport data to other datasets. This enabled us to apply the classification outside the restricted set of individuals who responded to Active People and Taking Part.

Using the 'Taking Part' survey a series of propensity models were built to predict the likelihood an individual would have to take part in an activity or have a particular motivation or attitude towards sport and active recreation. The 'Taking Part' survey was used as it contained attitude and motivation questions and therefore provided the most comprehensive insight, whilst 'Active People' insight was used to enhance our understanding of each segment. Propensity modelling is a statistical technique that assigns the probability of displaying a particular behaviour/

attitude to each demographic category. The differences in these probabilities are measured for significance by comparing across the sample population as a whole. Those models which show the most significance are subsequently extrapolated across the whole England adult population.

The key demographic variables used within this propensity modelling process were selected based on the assumption that they were available in both surveys and on Experian's consumer database of all adults. This was essential to ensure that the final sport segmentation solution could be linked to 'Active People', the Electoral Roll and geographic "bricks".

A proprietary technique known as Mosaic-Pixel grid (MPG) methodology was used to create the propensity models. This technique has been successfully employed by Experian for many years and on hundreds of other person-level segmentations. It is based on the principle that within tightly defined lifestyle and lifestage groups people do display similar traits. Mosaic identifies the postcode-based socio-demographics whilst Pixel is a person level combination of key variables that define people as unique and different to their partner, spouse, children and neighbours. Mosaic has 61 categories and Pixel in the region of 6,300 combinations, which when combined provides a grid of c.380,000 pre-defined 'cells'. It is these c.380,000 'cells' which were clustered to create the unique Sport England segments.

As part of this process the actual combination of demographic variables and behavioural and attitudinal information to be used was tested. It became evident that all the variables assessed contributed to explaining sports behaviour and attitudes. Therefore a key challenge was to match the variable classes defined in 'Taking Part' as closely as possible to those found on Experian databases. The final set of individual demographic variables used were:

- Gender (Male, Female)
- Age (18–25, 26–35, 36–45, 46–55, 56–65, 66+)
- Marital status (Single, Married, Unknown/missing)
- Tenure (Owner occupied, Private rented, Council/HA rented)
- Employment status (Employed full-time/Other, Student/ Unemployed, Employed part-time/Housewife, Retired)
- Households with children (No, Yes)

Once this large set of propensity models had been built they were analysed in two ways. Firstly, statistical analysis was undertaken to identify those models that provided the most 'significance', in terms of probability of displaying certain behaviour or attitude. Secondly, across all the models the levels of correlation were analysed, thereby identifying those models that worked well independently and also collectively to provide a rounded picture of insight. Once completed, a subset of these models which represented a cross-section of all the characteristics was selected as the clustering variables.

A cluster analysis of the Taking Part survey was then carried out using the values of the selected propensity models as the input variables, across these pre-defined 380,000 cells. "K-means clustering[2]", an industry-recognised clustering

2 Please see http://en.wikipedia.org/wiki/Cluster_analysis#K-means_clustering

technique, was used that clusters the centroids of each observation based on how 'close' they are to each other – this therefore enables the user to pre-determine the number of clusters required from the final solution.

A segmentation containing about 8–10 clusters was sought after by Sport England, with the initial solution created by Experian having 11 clusters. However, it became clear that more clusters were needed to fully explain and interpret the variety of sporting attitudes and behaviours in the population. Therefore, solutions with 15–20 clusters were looked at and a final classification of 19 clusters was selected as the one which was the "best" explanation of the data. These were analysed by average age and grouped into 4 super-groups on this basis.

Once this 19-segment solution was agreed, additional socio-demographic, attitude and behavioural datasets were profiled to provide the additional 'colour' and insight on the segments – in essence, to help provide the indices and percentiles that would bring the segments 'to life'. These datasets included the 'Active People' survey, Experian's Mosaic, TrueTouch and Financial Strategy segmentation solutions, Experian's national consumer surveys, Hospital Episodes Statistics and the Indices of Multiple Deprivation from the ONS.

This additional research and socio-demographic data is appended to the segments through the Mosaic-Pixel methodology as previously outlined. In essence, each respondent from these surveys is assigned one of the 380,000 Mosaic-Pixel cells, which in turn have been allocated to one of the 19 Sport England segments.

As earlier suggested, the segments have been constructed in a manner enabling them to be appended to the electoral roll. As such, for each segment we are able to identify the counts (and therefore percentages and indices) of actual names. We can then select those names that are over-represented for each segment and that are also perceived to encapsulate that segment – similarly, the 'marketing' phrase for each segment is defined through analysis of all the variable indices and is intended to provide a strapline for each segment.

For more information please contact the Research Team at Sport England – research@sportengland.org

Source: Sport England; http://www.sportengland.org/research/about-our-research/market-segmentation/.

Age

Age is one of the most simplistic, yet effective demographic variables used to segment markets. Not only is age easy to measure, but it also is usually related to consumer needs. In addition, age of the consumer is commonly associated with other demographic characteristics, such as income, education, and stage of the family life cycle. A number of broad age segments exist such as the children's market, the teen market, and the mature market. Care must be taken, however, not to stereotype consumers when using age segmentation. How many 10-year-olds do you know who think they are 20, and how many 75-year-olds think they are 45?

Web 6.1 A wide array of youth football programs exist that target participation in youth football and cheerleading.

Source: **Reprinted** with permission of Cleveland Browns Inc. (2014).

Children. There has always been a natural association between children and sports. However, sports marketers are no longer taking the huge children's market for granted – and with good reason. Children have tremendous influence on purchasing decisions within the family and are increasingly purchasing more and more on their own.[1]

Children, up to age 11, spend around $18 billion a year. Tweens, 8–12 year olds, 'heavily influence' more than $30 billion in other spending by parents, and 80 percent of all global brands now deploy a 'tween strategy.' As Dan Cook, Assistant Professor of Advertising and Sociology at the University of Illinois, noted in an article titled "Lunchbox Hegemony: Kids and the Marketplace, Then & Now," kids not only want things, but have acquired the socially sanctioned right to want – a right which parents are loath to violate. Layered onto direct child enticement and the supposed autonomy of the child-consumer are the day-to-day circumstances of overworked parents: a daily barrage of requests, tricky financial negotiations, and that nagging, unspoken desire to build the lifestyle they have learned to want during their childhoods.[2]

Presently, many families spend at least $2,000 a year on sports-related expenses for their children.[3] Children are participating in sports and are identifying with teams, players, and brands at younger ages each year. The 2012 Harris Poll YouthPulse study noted that young people have just as much money to spend as older adults.[4] In fact, the purchasing power of 8–24 year old citizens in America is reaching $211 billion. Thus, sports marketers have recognized the power of the kids' market. They realize children will become the fans and the season ticket holders of the future. As such, they have segmented markets accordingly.

Examples of sports marketers reaching the kids' market are plentiful. For instance, Fisher-Price, the toy company, negotiated the rights to acquire a NASCAR license to produce battery-operated race cars for children. The mini-vehicles with engine sound effects feature two gears and achieve speeds of 2.5 or 5 mph, plus reverse, and sell for more than $200.

Build-a-Bear Workshops has collaborated with multiple Major League Baseball stadiums to find new customers, targeting the 12 and under market segment. Targeting this age group affords Build-a-Bear the opportunity for youth sports fans to build their own little team mascot.

In 1998, the NFL and the NFL Players Association formed the NFL Youth Football Fund (YFF), a 501(c)3 nonprofit foundation that supports the game at the youth level and promotes positive youth development. Through this fund, hundreds of thousands of children have been given the opportunity to learn about the game of football, get physically fit, and interact positively with adult mentors, all in a safe and accessible environment.

In 2005, the National Basketball Association launched an initiative offering its teams and players to further promote global community outreach. This initiative aimed to address important social issues such as education, youth and family development, and health and wellness, all through the use of various partners and programs. To date, the league, players, and teams have donated more than $210 million to charity, provided more than 2.3 million hours of hands-on service, and built more than 760 places where kids and families can live, learn, or play in communities worldwide.[5] U.S. Fund for UNICEF President Caryl Stern recently complimented the NBA's commitment to social responsibility, noting that their strategy has been philanthropic in a strategic way. He defined the NBA as utilizing a dedicated strategy at a number of different levels, noting that it was not just writing a check; it was a way to achieve and see results.[6]

In addition, the NHL's *Hockey is for Everyone* initiative provides support to both ice and street hockey programs by teaching children how to learn, compete, and grow. The programs provide these unique hockey experiences to more than 300,000 children annually in over 30 non-profit hockey organizations and 1,600 schools and communities nationwide.

Photo 6.1 Professional sports are realizing the importance of the kids' market to their long-term success.

Source: Shutterstock.com

The children's segment is also growing in importance to those organizations marketing to kids via the Internet. For example, ToysRUs.com has introduced a new sporting goods site called SportsRUs.com with a "just for kids" area designed to help parents select sports equipment for kids ages five to 12. In another example, the President's Council on Physical Fitness and Activity has launched a Web site (www.presidentschallenge.org) to help motivate kids and families become more physically active. The NFL also incorporates marketing geared toward children, with its own official NFL kids' website, NFLRUSH.com. For example on the NFLRUSH.com site you will find the NFL's Play 60 campaign. The campaign, tailored to make the next generation of youth the most active and healthy was launched in 2007. The program focused on increasing the health and wellness of youth fans by encouraging them to become active for at least 60 minutes a day.

Teens. Just as with the youth user segment, the number of teens is also expected to rise exponentially. According to the U.S. Census Bureau, by 2015, the population of children and teens between the ages of 10 and 19 will reach 41.42 million.[7] With this potential amount of purchasing power it can be understood why sporting goods fall within the top 10 advertising categories for teens. One key to reaching this teen market is to involve them in the marketing process and engage them in the brand. What brands (or leagues, in this case) are hot with teens? Figure 6.1 shows the pro sports of interest to the teen market, including differences among males and females.

Although teens represent a sizable and important market, sports marketers must better understand this group, or it will be lost. For instance, American teens are

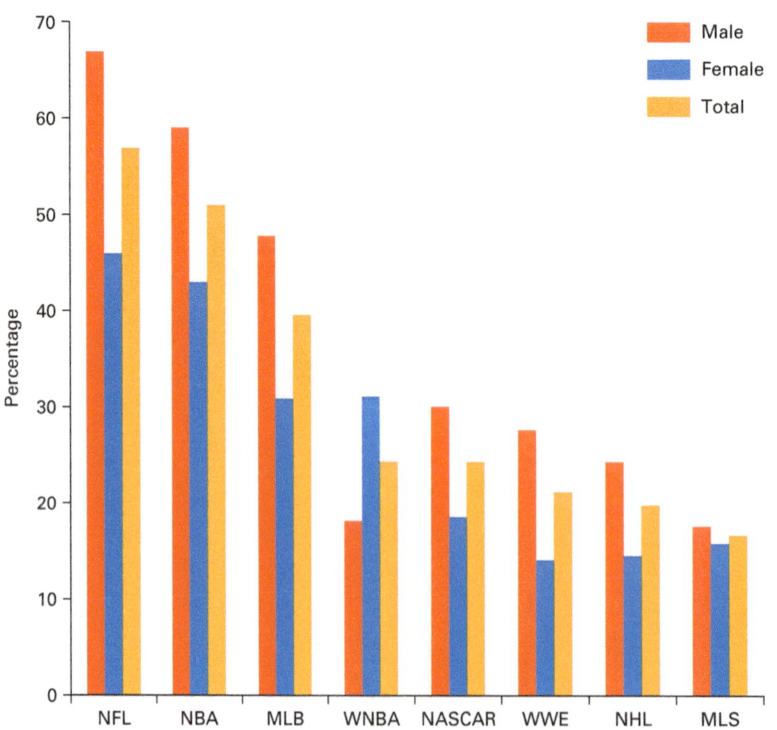

Figure 6.1 Pro-sports that appeal to teenagers: youth who say they are very or somewhat interested in the sport

Source: with permission of The Futures Company

not tuning in to major sporting events in large numbers, at least not compared with the general population. None of the traditional championships attracts a television audience that is higher than 7.3 percent of teens ages 12–17. For the Daytona 500 and the World Series, only about one in 30 television viewers are teens. The one non- traditional championship that can claim a teenage viewing audience of 11.4 percent is the X Games, but even that finds the overwhelming majority of its viewers are from outside the teen ranks.[8] Furthermore, these ratings are in spite of the fact that television viewing for teenagers is at an all time high. According to the Kaiser Foundation report, over the past five years there has been a huge increase of media use amoung young people. Teen's lives today are primarily a story of technology facilitating increased consumption. Today's multitasking teens pack 10 hours and 45 minutes worth of media content (multitasking) into a 7.38 hour day. These media frenzies occur 7½ hours a day, seven days a week.[9]

What can sport marketers do to better reach teens? As the accompanying article illustrates, thinking "outside the norm" to grasp a further understanding of their usage pattens may be the answer.

The mature market. Another market that is expected to increase at a staggering pace is the age 55 and older, mature market. According to the 2012 U.S. Statistical Abstract, mature adults, age 55-plus in 2010 totaled 75 million.[10] In fact, every day in America about 10,000 people turn 65 and by the year 2030, roughly one out of every five Americans will be aged 65 years and older.[11] These staggering numbers equal the entire populations of New York and California, Washington State, and the District of Columbia, or New York, California, and Massachusetts combined. Stereotypically, the elderly are perceived to be inactive and thrifty. Nothing could be further from the truth. The mature market is living longer and becoming more physically active. The country's largest generation of 55-plus are joining health clubs at a rate of 34 percent per year.[12] The 50-plus age group controls over 70 percent of disposable income, holds $1.6 trillion in spending power, and a net worth that's nearly twice the U.S. average. As a result, sports marketers are capitalizing on this growing market in a variety of ways.[13]

Traditionally, senior citizen discounts have been promoted in Major League Baseball. For example, the Milwaukee Brewers' minor league affiliate, the Brevard County Manatees, created the 55+ fan club, providing tickets, merchandise, and other special promotional offers to seniors. Promotions such as private meet and greet with the players and coaches were designed to strengthen the relationship between the Manatees and the teams' senior fans.[14] Other examples of sports markets being segmented by age can be seen in the growing number of "senior" sporting tours and events. The Champions Tour of the PGA has nearly the following of the regular tour events. Although not as successful as the golf tour, other professional senior tours include tennis and bowling.

Seniors are also becoming more active as sports participants. The fastest-growing participation sports for seniors, classified as age 55 and older, include exercising to music and running or walking on the treadmill. Table 6.2 shows some of the most popular sports for the maturing baby boomer market.

The Golden Age Games is the largest veterans' competition in the world open to those 55 and older. This Olympic-type event brings in more than 700 military veterans of the mature market, from 42 states as well as the U.S. Virgin Islands. Furthermore, the International Tennis Federation offers Seniors and Super-Seniors Individual and

GENERATION M2

Media in the life of 8 to 18 year olds, the Henry J. Kaiser Family Foundation, 2013.

Key findings

Over the past five years, there has been a huge increase in media use among young people.

Five years ago, we reported that young people spent an average of nearly 6½ hours (6:21) a day with media—and managed to pack more than 8½ hours (8:33) worth of media content into that time by multitasking. At that point it seemed that young people's lives were filled to the bursting point with media.

Today, however, those levels of use have been shattered.

Over the past five years, young people have increased the amount of time they spend consuming media by an hour and seventeen minutes daily, from 6:21 to 7:38—almost the amount of time most adults spend at work each day, except that young people use media seven days a week instead of five.

Moreover, given the amount of time they spend using more than one medium at a time, today's youth pack a total of 10 hours and 45 minutes worth of media content into those daily 7½ hours—an increase of almost 2¼ hours of media exposure per day over the past five years.

Media use over time

Among all 8- to 18-year-olds, average amount of time spent with each medium in a typical day:

	2009	2004	1999
TV content	4:29[a]	3:51[b]	3:47[b]
Music/audio	2:31[a]	1:44[b]	1:48[b]
Computer	1:29[a]	1:02[b]	:27[c]
Video games	1:13[a]	:49[b]	:26[c]
Print	:38[a]	:43[ab]	:43[b]
Movies	:25[a]	:25[ab]	:18[b]
TOTAL MEDIA EXPOSURE	10:45[a]	8:33[b]	7:29[c]
Multitasking proportion	29%[a]	26%[a]	16%[b]
TOTAL MEDIA USE	7:38[a]	6:21[b]	6:19[b]

Notes: See Methodology section for a definition of terms, explanation of notations, and discussion of statistical significance. See Appendix B for a summary of key changes in question wording and structure over time. **Total media exposure** is the sum of time spent with all media. **Multitasking proportion** is the proportion of media time that is spent using more than one medium concurrently. **Total media use** is the actual number of hours out of the day that are spent using media, taking multitasking into account. See Methodology section for a more detailed discussion. In this table, statistical significance should be read across rows.

Use of every type of media has increased over the past 10 years, with the exception of reading. In just the past *five* years, the increases range from 24 minutes a day for video games, to 27 minutes a day for computers, 38 minutes for TV content, and 47 minutes a day for music and other audio. During this same period, time spent reading went from 43 to 38 minutes a day, not a statistically significant change. But breaking out different types of print does uncover some statistically significant trends. For example, time spent reading magazines dropped from 14 to nine minutes a day over the past five years, and time spent reading newspapers went down from six minutes a day to three; but time spent reading books remained steady, and actually increased slightly over the past *10* years (from 21 to 25 minutes a day).

Changes in media use, 2004–2009

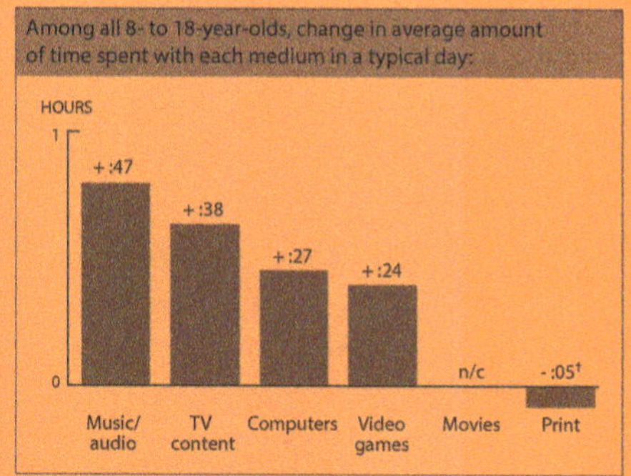

† Not statistically significant. See Appendix B for a summary of key changes in question wording and structure over time.

An explosion in mobile and online media has fueled the increase in media use among young people.

The story of media in young people's lives today is primarily a story of technology facilitating increased consumption. The mobile and online media revolutions have arrived in the lives—and the pockets—of American youth. Try waking a teenager in the morning, and the odds are good that you'll find a cell phone tucked under their pillow—the last thing they touch before falling asleep and the first thing they reach for upon waking. Television content they once consumed only by sitting in front of a TV set at an appointed hour is now available whenever and wherever they want, not only on TV sets in their bedrooms, but also on their laptops, cell phones and iPods®.

Today, 20% of media consumption (2:07) occurs on mobile devices—cell phones, iPods or handheld video game players. Moreover, almost another hour (:56) consists of "old" content—TV or music—delivered through "new" pathways on a computer (such as Hulu™ or iTunes®).

Mobile media. The transformation of the cell phone into a media content delivery platform, and the widespread adoption of the iPod and other MP3 devices, have facilitated an explosion in media consumption among American youth. In previous years, the proliferation of media multitasking allowed young people to pack more media into the same number of hours a day, by reading a magazine or surfing the Internet while watching TV or listening to music. Today, the development of mobile media has allowed—indeed, encouraged—young people to find even more opportunities throughout the day for using media, actually expanding the number of hours when they can consume media, often while on the go.

Over the past five years, the proportion of 8- to 18-year-olds who own their own cell phone has grown from about four in ten (39%) to about two-thirds (66%). The proportion with iPods or other MP3 players increased even more dramatically, jumping from 18% to 76% among all 8- to 18-year-olds.

Mobile Media Ownership, Over Time

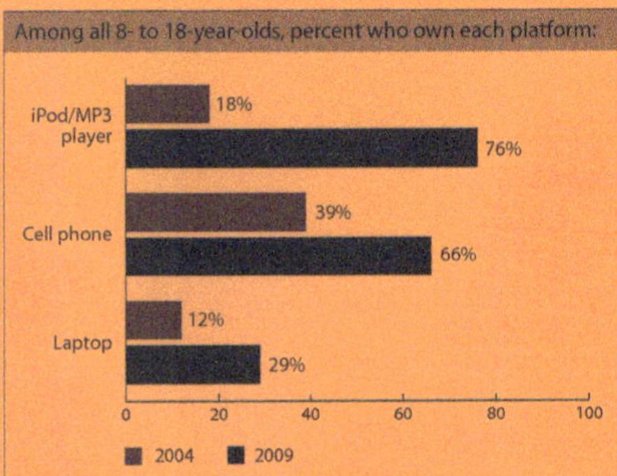

Not only do more young people own a cell phone, but cells have morphed from a way to hold a conversation with someone into a way to consume more media. Eight- to eighteen-year-olds today spend an average of a half-hour a day (:33) talking on their cell phones, and an average of 49 minutes a day (:49) listening to, playing or watching other media on their phones (:17 with music, :17 playing games, and :15 watching TV)—not to mention the hour and a half a day that 7th- to 12th-graders spend text-messaging (time spent texting is *not* included in our count of media use, nor is time spent talking on a cell phone).

These two platforms—cell phones and MP3 players—account for a sizeable portion of young people's increased media consumption. For example, total time spent playing video games increased by about 24 minutes over the past five years (from :49 to 1:13), and 20 minutes of that increase comes on cell phones, iPods and handheld video game players. Time spent listening to music and other audio has increased by more than three-quarters of an hour a day (:47) to just over 2½ hours (2:31); nearly an hour (:58) of that listening occurs via a cell phone or an iPod, and another 38 minutes is streamed through the computer, through programs like iTunes or Internet radio.

Television on new media platforms. For the first time since we began this research in 1999, the amount of time young people spend watching regularly scheduled programming on a television set at the time it is originally broadcast has declined (by :25 a day, from 3:04 to 2:39). However, the proliferation of new ways to consume TV content has actually led to an *increase* of 38 minutes of daily TV consumption. The increase includes an average of 24 minutes a day watching TV or movies on the Internet, and about 15 minutes each watching on cell phones (:15) and iPods (:16). Thus, even in this new media world, television viewing—in one form or another—continues to dominate media consumption, taking up about 4½ hours a day in young people's lives (up from a total of 3:51 in 2004). But *how* young people watch TV has clearly started to change. Indeed, today just 59% of young people's TV watching occurs on a TV set at the time the programming is originally broadcast; fully 41% is either time-shifted, or occurs on a platform other than a TV set.

Online media. In addition to mobile media, online media have begun making significant inroads in young people's lives. The continued expansion of high-speed home Internet access, the proliferation of television content available online, and the development of compelling new applications such as social networking and YouTube, have all contributed to the increase in the amount of media young people consume each day. Today's 8- to 18-year-olds spend an average of an hour and a half (1:29) daily using the computer outside of school work, an increase of almost half an hour over five years ago (when it was 1:02).

In the last five years, home Internet access has expanded from 74% to 84% among young people; the proportion with a laptop has grown from 12% to 29%; and Internet access in the bedroom has jumped from 20% to 33%. The quality of Internet access has improved as well, with high-speed access increasing from 31% to 59%.

Source: http://kff.org/other/poll-finding/report-generation-m2-media-in-the-lives/. Courtesy The Henry J. Kaiser Family Foundation.

6

Table 6.2 Most popular sports/athletic/fitness activities U.S. population, age 55+, based on total participation

Rank	Athletic Activity	Participants
1.	Fitness walking	10.3 million
2.	Treadmill exercise	8.8 million
3.	Stretching	8.2 million
4.	Hand weights	5.3 million
5.	Golf	4.9 million
6.	Freshwater fishing	4.6 million
7.	Day hiking	3.7 million
8.	Weight/resistance machines	3.6 million
9.	Stationary cycling (upright bike)	3.4 million
10.	Bowling	3.3 million
11.	Recreational vehicle camping	2.8 million
12.	Saltwater fishing	2.7 million
13.	Other exercise to music	2.6 million
14.	Dumbbells	2.5 million
15.	Stationary cycling (recumbent bike)	2.4 million

Source: Sports & Fitness Industry Association, www.sfia.org.

Team Championships held yearly in countries all over the world. The ITF Super-Senior World Team Championships, offering women's age divisions (ages 60 to75) and men's age divisions (ages 60 to 80), brings in 114 teams from 24 countries to compete.

These examples of the senior athletes are representative of the mature market worldwide and demonstrate what a vibrant, independent, and viable segment this is for sport marketers.

Gender

A number of marketing executives in the sports industry have taken note that women have become crucial to their fan bases. Female fans have been so crucial that organizations such as the FIFA, the NFL, NASCAR, MLB, NBA, and NHL have focused promotional efforts toward enhancing the female audiences, with much success. For example, some 67 million women count themselves baseball fans – that's just over *half* of baseball's audience.[15] In addition, 37 percent of basketball fans are women; and 44 percent of football fans are female. In fact, an estimated 43 million female viewers tuned in to the Super Bowl earlier this year, making it more popular than the Oscars.

The NFL has realized the importance of women fans and is developing a strategic plan to attract them and keep them interested in a traditionally male-oriented sport. Based on research conducted by the NFL, women fans do not want to be treated differently than men. NFL Commissioner Roger Goodell stated, "(Women) fans want to be treated as real fans because they love the game, understand the game, and want to have the opportunity to experience the game just as anyone else does."[16]

In 2010, ESPN also developed a strategic approach to targeting a growing female fan base, as the accompanying article indicates.

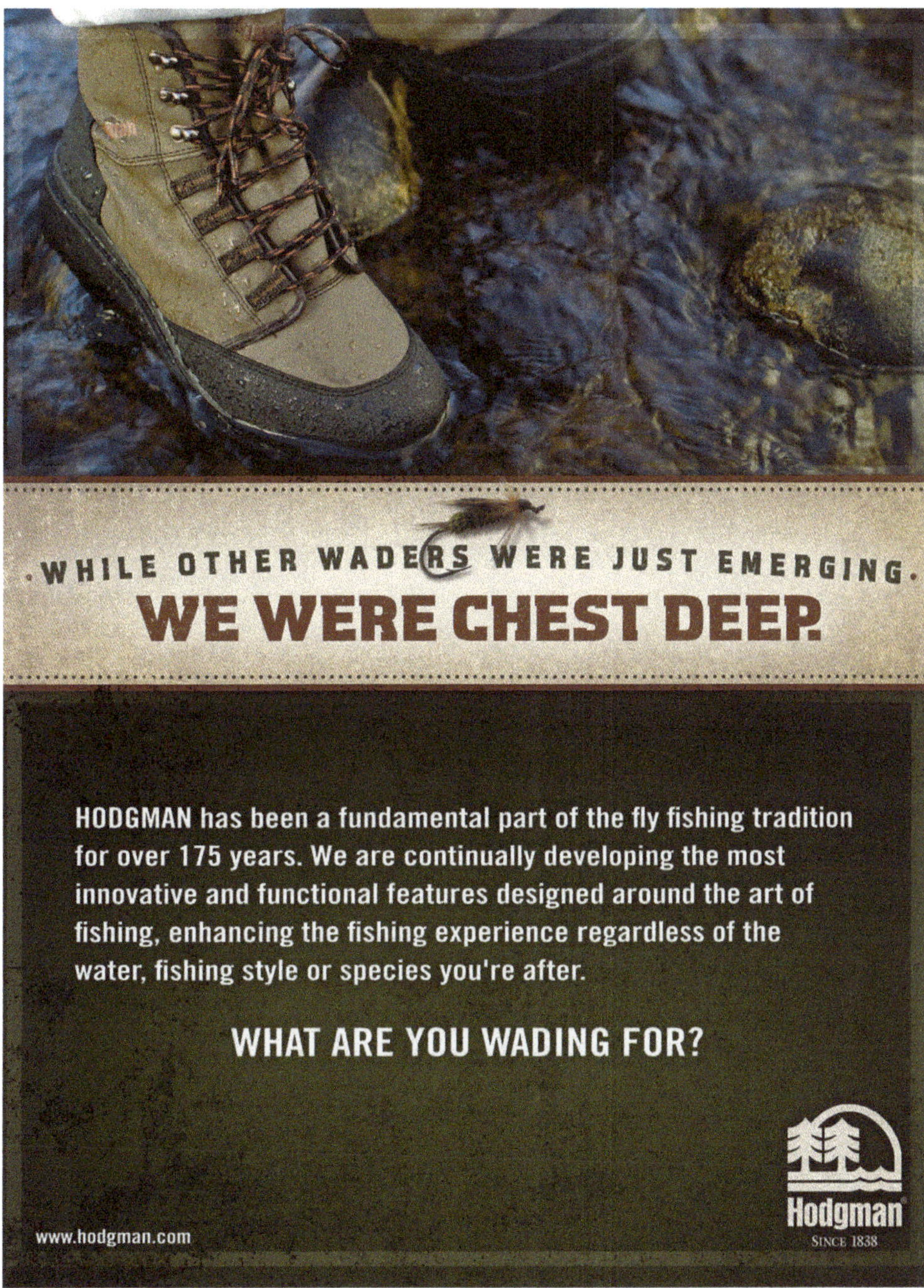

Ad 6.1 Hodgman is capitalizing on the growing mature market.

Source: Pure Fishing – Columbia

Despite the obvious male overtones of the increasingly popular mixed martial arts scene – as exhibited by the success of the Ultimate Fighting Championship – fans of the female persuasion are also flocking to the newest sporting trend to hit the pay-per-view circuit. In fact, for a sport that used to be known as little more than a glorified bar brawl, mixed martial arts fights have been branded and stamped with a marketable seal of approval by sponsors and UFC stakeholders alike.

ESPN W: A BRAND FOR FEMALE ATHLETES

In 2010, ESPN, the worldwide leader in sports, announced a bubbling business from within called espnW, a brand completely driven for and by sports-minded women. Now, before you jump to conclusions based upon the espnW name, I simply ask that you first hear me out – because it's critical to understand exactly *why* this new business is necessary for the success of female athletes.

ESPN unveiled their new "w" brand at a retreat in San Diego, California. It took place in front of some of the biggest movers and shakers in women's sports, including famous female athletes, coaches, journalists and sports marketing executives. At the event, not only did I have the chance to meet and talk to some of the women and men that I respect most in this world, but I also had the chance to share some of my opinions about what needs to happen to make the espnW business work. First, some context. . .

Since the passage of Title IX in 1972, the United States has seen a 900 percent increase in girls playing high school sports and a 450 percent increase in women playing sports at the collegiate level. This means that over the past 40 years, a female sport culture was born and lives today. Despite the incredible successes we've seen, a drop-off exists when it comes to the transition from a female athlete to a female sports fan. There are several reasons for this, but here are two major ones as to why that ESPN cares:

1) Sports media rarely covers female athletes.

Research has shown that female athletes are significantly under-represented with respect to the amount of national coverage they receive compared to men. I don't think anyone would argue with me on this – turn on SportsCenter, open ESPN The Magazine or Sports Illustrated and tell me how many articles about female athletes you see. For whatever reason, female athletes are simply not on the radar. The only time women are covered fairly is in the Sports Illustrated Swimsuit Edition or ESPN Body, sending a clear message to women: it's OK for you to play sports, but the only time you deserve national media attention is when you take off your clothes, show some skin, and act like a girl.

2) Female sports fans are on the rise

It's also important to understand the core mission that ESPN has followed faithfully since its inception: "serve the sports fan." However, the idea of a "sports fan" as a guy in front of his TV is changing - in fact, women (these are women who watch men's sports) comprise almost 40% of their total viewing audience. ESPN's internal research keeps telling them that this audience feels under-served – they don't feel as if the ESPN brand speaks to them.

The Answer: espnW

Enter: ESPN employee Laura Gentile. Back in 2007, emerging from within ESPN's own culture as a rising business star, the former Duke field hockey player started raising the possibility of offering a female-specific sports outlet that seeks to address these gaps. The team started by targeting high school girls with ESPN's *Girl Magazine* – a grassroots publication for high school athletes which is published three times per year, followed up by ESPN Rise Girl Edition online (still in Beta). The idea here is to reach a young audience early, and have them transition over time into espnW a female-specific business.

EspnW, launched a blog and more digital content that targets the 18–49-year-old woman who loves sports, which happens to comprise 50 million current and former athletes. If activated successfully, you can imagine the potential impact, not only in effectively serving a new audience, but also in acquiring new advertisers who want to reach this audience.

However, it's not going to come easy. These women are a very tricky age group. They have a lot going on in their lives – they're in graduate school, cultivating professional careers, trying desperately to stay in shape, meeting their life partners, getting married and raising children. All of a sudden, their love for "sport" falls into many different types of areas – they might follow their college teams as an alum, watch men's professional sports, play sports recreationally in the evenings, run 5K races and triathlons on the weekends, go to the gym every night, or coach kids.

As you can see, trying to interject a new entertainment habit into an already-busy woman's life is going to be quite challenging. So challenging, in fact, that some outlets have tried and failed – for example, *Sports Illustrated for Women* attempted to tap into this market between 2000–2002, but folded quickly. Then-president Ann Moore cited the downturn in the advertising economy, saying, "SI Women needed a significant investment to reach its potential," and "The investment climate was simply not on our side."

2010, was a different climate, backed with a major investment from ESPN, a Disney-owned company. In addition to the initial investment, the "w" brand secured founding sponsors Nike and Gatorade, as well as support from other brands like Under Armour, Roxy, Oakley and Lululemon, all eager to attach themselves to a "w" business. If money really is the key issue, with this level of up-front investment, on paper, it seems the espnW team can make this thing happen. But the truth is it's not that easy – the espnW team is going to have to tread very, very carefully with the public. Here's why:

First, the idea of a "w" brand is very controversial for women who are already fans of men's sports. For example, Chicago Cubs blogger cubbiejulie cited that she "hates" the idea of espnW because she believes it's going to be a "girlier" version of ESPN, promoting things like "pink hats and bedazzled t-shirts." As a sports-minded woman, she really has no need to go to a "w" network – she has everything she needs from what ESPN already offers.

But it's important to understand that espnW isn't targeting Julie who already gets what she needs from ESPN. And I can assure you – the last thing the W team would consider promoting (or wearing, for that matter) are bedazzled t-shirts.

Rather, from what I experienced, watching the unveiling of the new brand on the same stage as Billy Jean King (who received a standing ovation on opening night), as well as notables like Laila Ali, Julie Foudy, and Gretchen Bleiler, among countless other amazing women, I think it's safe to say that, at the very heart of this new business is the mission to serve current and former *female athletes*. . . a uniquely different audience, one that's been struggling for public attention for 40 years.

ESPN is also opening itself up to criticism from its current diehard male fans - the whole idea of "espnW" seems outrageous (and quite funny) to men who already feel served by the brand. . . especially if it's aimed at promoting professional female sports, which may or may not meet their needs for sports entertainment.

But it's really critical for these guys to understand that they're not the target audience, either. And on the surface, although this may seem like an easy target for a quick joke, if they ever want their sisters, daughters or granddaughters to have the opportunity to experience financial success as professional athletes, they'll need to support (or at least not mock) a major sports media company when they build opportunities for female athletes to get attention.

Last, I can say with confidence that espnW is a brand that the retreat attendees, including myself, celebrate and welcome with open arms. And I challenge you to join me. Because for once, there's a possibility that female athletes will be able to showcase their athletic achievements to the world without needing to take their clothes off.

Megan Hueter is the cofounder of WomenTalkSports.com, which, until the advent of espnW, has remained the only sports blog network that specifically promotes female athletes. Megan is also a former athlete from Haddon Heights, New Jersey who played basketball The College of New Jersey. She works full time as a public relations professional in New York.

Source: http://blogswithballs.com/2010/10/espnw-a-brand-for-female-athletes/.ESPN.com.

These widely publicized fights between experts in various martial arts are becoming a hit with women both in and out of the ring. Historically, sports enthusiasts have been male. However, stereotypes are eroding quickly as women are becoming more involved in every facet of sport. More women are participating in sports, and more women are watching sports. Moreover, every attempt is being made to make women's sports equitable with their male counterparts as the promotion of the recent female championship broadcasts demonstrate.

One example of females participating in a historically male sport is football. Nationwide, 1,531 girls played on high school tackle football teams in the 2013 season, according to a survey by the National Federation of State High School Associations.[17] Some 90 professional women's football teams in three main leagues exist across the country. The three leagues all play the same game, with minor deviations from NFL rules, but they approach the business in very different ways. A NSGA poll tracking sports participation noted that 12.1 percent of females participate in football and 21.4 percent in baseball, both male-dominated sports.[18]

THE IWFL AND THE HISTORY OF WOMEN'S TACKLE FOOTBALL

Zachary Fenell, Yahoo Contributor Network
Sep 18, 2009
Independent Women
Professional Football
Talent Agent
Web Services
Flag
Post a comment

Cassie Newall, Robyn Taylor and Nikita Payne are all all-star football players, but you will not find them on the cover of *Sports Illustrated* or profiled on ESPN because Newall, Taylor and Payne don't play for the National Football League. Rather, Newall, Taylor and Payne are three of over 1,500 football players in the Independent Women's Football League. The IWFL is a professional football league for women who play tackle football.

The origins of women's tackle football stems back to the mid 1920s when the NFL team Frankfort Yellow Jackets hired a women's football team to serve as entertainment during halftime. In 1965 talent agent Sid Friedman took women's tackle football to the next level by starting a semi-pro women's football league in Ohio. The league started with two teams, one in Cleveland and one in Akron. The league grew as more Ohio cities adopted teams. Eventually cities from Pennsylvania and New York joined the league.

By 1974 women's tackle football became so popular the National Women's Football League (NWFL) was formed. Unfortunately the NWFL was not a big financial success. Owning a women's tackle football team became a financial burden and by the end of the decade several NWFL teams folded. By 1982 the NWFL only had teams left operating in Ohio and Michigan. Professional women's football continued on as the NWFL did their best to reinvent themselves but the interest in women's football had bottomed out.

In 2000 interest in women's tackle football picked up again with the creation of the IWFL. The IWFL, a non-profit organization, aims to provide a positive, safe, and fun environment for women to play tackle football. The IWFL mission is to give women the opportunity to play professional football. The league has grown at a rapid rate too The number of teams in the IWFL has more than doubled since 2000. Currently there are 51 IWFL teams spread out across North America, including teams in big market cities like New York and Chicago.

The IWFL season is during the NFL's off season. The IWFL begins their 10 week season in April and concludes in July with the championship game and the IWFL All-Star Game. The IWFL is made possible by the league's sponsors, AWS (Athletic Web Services), Nike, Kotis Design, USA Football, and the Round Rock Convention and Visitors Bureau.

Source: http://voices.yahoo.com/the-iwfl-history-womens-tackle-football-4268395.html. Reprinted with permission from Yahoo.

6

NFL MAY BE HITTING STRIDE WITH FEMALE FANS

By Kristi Dosh | Feb 3, 2012
ESPN.com
AP Photo/Paul Spinelli

Female fans of the Giants hope this Super Bowl against the Patriots will go as well as the last.

The NFL's concerted effort over the past two years to market the game and apparel to women is showing signs of paying off, but sales of league merchandise still trail Major League Baseball and collegiate-licensed materials.

In terms of female fans, the NFL trails only college sports, according to data from The ESPN Sports Poll and the U.S. Census, with league officials saying 44 percent of all football fans are now women.

Various sources show positive indicators for the NFL:

- NFL merchandise sold to women jumped significantly over last year, according to Fanatics, the world's largest online retailer of officially licensed products. The 2011 playoff season showed a dramatic change: an 85 percent sales increase in December over 2010 and a 125 percent increase in January from the year prior.
- Although the 2011 NFL season saw a slight drop in the number of women who watched games on TV, ratings increased from a 3.7 to a 3.9 in the 18- to 34-year-old demographic, according to Nielsen.
- The number of American women participating in fantasy football doubled in 2011, according to Ipsos Public Affairs, which works with the Fantasy Sports Trade Association.

Marketing experts say women are a prized demographic for the NFL because of their value to advertisers. Ann Bastianelli, senior lecturer of marketing at Indiana University's Kelley School of Business, said 70 percent of "important family decisions" are made by women.

"When we talk about women being the decision-makers, I think a lot of people don't realize that's cars, stocks, electronics – things people might not associate women making the decisions about," said Meghann Malone, a marketing manager for marketing, advertising and public relations firm IMRE.

A growing female fan base creates a more marketable NFL for advertisers and sponsors. "A female consumer is a consumer for life," Malone said. "They're the ones more likely to become brand loyalists."

Peter O'Reilly, vice president of fan strategy/marketing for the NFL, said the league has done well in this area the last couple of years.

In 2010, the league introduced a clothing line specifically made for women called "Fit for You," featuring various choices, from junior sizes to maternity clothing. Building upon the positive response to that initiative, the league added to the line in 2011 and opened up a new section of its website just for women: www.nfl.com/women.

The new site highlights the women's apparel line and also added NFL Party, a site that promotes "homegating." NFL Party features a blog with tips and recipes.

"NFL Party was coming together with licensees to make it easy for families and people hosting parties, and certainly women are largely driving that in the home," O'Reilly said. The league considers the site a success, he said, and will increase its content.

O'Reilly also said NFLShop.com saw double-digit growth this season on merchandise geared toward women. Fanatics noted the same, particularly during the 2011 playoffs.

NexTag, the online comparison-shopping site, said women's jerseys accounted for six of the top 10 Tom Brady jerseys viewed and six of the top 10 Eli Manning jersey viewed the week before and after championship weekend. Jersey searches since Jan. 1 have been dominated by women's products, with the top five most-searched jerseys being women's Tim Tebow or Aaron Rodgers jerseys.

When the NFL women's clothing line was expanded in 2011, the league looked to the women who make up the NFL family for some help. Wives of players, coaches and owners donned gear for advertisements, which appeared in popular magazines.

"The NFL has done a really good job realizing wives and daughters of coaches are some of the best ambassadors of the game," said Heather Zeller, founder of AGlamSlam.com, a website dedicated to the intersection of fashion and sports. "They could have used Victoria's Secret models, but these are the women actually watching the game, so they're much more relatable."

One of those women is Suzanne Johnson, wife of New York Jets owner Woody Johnson, whom Zeller said has helped push NFL fashion into high fashion. "They're treating sports apparel as high fashion, and that's unique. It's a point of differentiation with other leagues," Zeller said.

Johnson helped create an NFL-themed shopping experience for women before the Jets game against the Patriots this year that looked more like a Miami night club than a sports apparel showroom. Women's Wear Daily reported that Johnson marketed the new duds to magazine editors and even convinced some of her socialite friends to wear Jets jerseys to Badgley Mischka's runway during New York Fashion Week.

Johnson appeared this week on the "Wendy Williams Show" highlighting some of her favorite Jets gear. Even with the recent successes, the NFL has a way to go to catch the retail sales leaders.

MLB led all sports with $5 billion in retail sales in 2010, with Collegiate Licensing Company behind, at $4.3 billion. The NFL lagged at about $3.3 billion.

With double-digit growth in women's merchandise in 2011 and a growing buzz, the NFL could make up some ground in the next study: "I haven't seen the other leagues in fashion magazines," Zeller said. "They've done more than just create something you can wear in the stadium on Sunday."

Kristi Dosh covers sports business for ESPN.com and can be reached at kristi@kristidosh.com. Follow Dosh on Twitter: @SportsBizMiss.

Source: Rightsholder: ESPN: Published 2/3/12; accessed 1/2/14; http://espn.go.com/espnw/news-commentary/article/7536295/nfl-finding-success-targeting-women-fans-merchandise-fashion.

6

Ethnic background

Segmenting markets by **ethnic background** is based on grouping consumers of a common race, religion, and nationality. Ethnic groups, such as African Americans (12.9 percent of the U.S. population), Hispanic Americans (15 percent of the U.S. population), and Asian Americans (4 percent of the U.S. population)[19] are increasingly important to sports marketers as their numbers continue to grow. When segmenting based on ethnic background, marketers must be careful not to think of stereotypical profiles but to understand the unique consumption behaviors of each group through marketing research.

Major League Soccer (MLS) has long espoused the philosophy of having an ethnic fan base. Commissioner Don Garber believes the MLS is "perfectly suited to capitalize on what's going on in this country. We are a nation of increasing ethnic diversity. We are a nation that's finding itself in an increasingly growing global community. And that global community is linked by one language, a language that is shared by all, and that's the sport of soccer." Garber has also helped league officials and marketing folks understand that there are increasing numbers of immigrants – particularly in Hispanic communities – to whom soccer is a cultural necessity. Garber said, "Capturing the ethnic fan" is essential in making that approach work. "It requires careful considerations. It means realizing that fans bang drums and stand throughout the game. It means courting Spanish-language media, Caribbean media, and other foreign-language interests."[20] As the accompanying article articulates, understanding any subculture goes well beyond the language.

MOVE OVER FÚTBOL. THE NFL SCORES BIG WITH LATINOS

More than 33 million Hispanics have watched professional football so far this season, making it the most-watched NFL season among Latinos. Professional football, not fútbol, delivered two of the most-watched professional sporting games in 2011 among Hispanics.

Generation Ñ

As a group, Hispanic children are growing faster than any other. History suggests today's Latino kids eventually will become the parents of fully Americanized descendants whose only link to their cultural heritage is a surname, religious practice or holiday, said Hernán Ramírez, a sociologist at Florida State University who specializes in Hispanic assimilation tells the Tampa Tribune.

More and more NFL teams are courting the lucrative Latino market in attempt to tap into an aggressive and young fan base ready to shell out consumer dollars. Since Hispanic football fans spend nearly 15 hours engaged with the NFL each week during the regular season and because more Latinos watched the Super Bowl than the World Cup Final, it is easy to understand why the NFL's strategic marketing efforts for this season's big game should enable them to make unparalleled inroads with young Americans of Hispanic descent.

"There is a prevailing sense of 'family' in football," Pro Football Hall of Fame tackle Anthony Muñoz said in an interview with the web site USA Football. "You get that in the Hispanic community, and that's what you want in a football team."

According to the NFLHispanic.com, last year's Super Bowl

was the most watched TV program ever among Hispanics, averaging ten million Hispanic viewers.

Latino Influenced Super Bowls

The NFL played its first regular-season game outside the United States in 2005 and drew over 100,000 people in Mexico City. Over the last five years, the NFL has aggressively sought to connect with Hispanics, a fan base that is large and growing at rapid pitch. The 2011 season saw one of the most aggressive positioning strategies by NFL members as more than half of the teams celebrated Hispanic heritage events at various stadiums.

The NFL vamped its push towards U.S. Hispanics in recent years. Last year's big game in Dallas offered a definitive Latino flair. According to the 2010 U.S. Census, Texas grew more than twice as fast as the nation, thanks largely to a surge among Mexican Hispanics. Dallas has the fifth largest U.S. Hispanic population that are from Mexican decent and over 1.5 million Mexicans in the Dallas–Fort Worth Metroplex are the third largest foreign born Mexican population in the U.S. per Metropolitan Statistical Areas.

On one level, the choice to host the game in Dallas was rational – the weather is ideal, the atmosphere is fun and the tourist industry can accommodate the crowd. On another and most likely more influential level, the choice is strategic. What better way to captivate the Hispanic market than to bring the game to the famed Latino football hotspot?

In an interview with the Phoenix Business Journal, Victor Villalba, head of Spanish language broadcasting for the Dallas Cowboys, stated "most games are on Sunday, which meshes with traditional Latino family get-togethers and social gatherings."

Super Bowl XLVI will showcase a full on attempt to captivate Hispanic audiences. The NFL is pushing its NFLHispanic.com website even more than ever. This site is designed as a tool to attract potential marketers to buy into their 360-degree platform approach to reach the Hispanic demographic. This approach allows brands to reach the segment at every angle from television, online, radio, print, calendar events to grass-roots efforts. Viewers can expect a markedly overt Hispanic overtone for this year's championship game.

'Show Me the Money'

The big push toward Hispanic consumers is in part due to the quality of fanship. Latinos tend to be ardent fans with strong home team convictions. High levels of extreme revelry coupled with abundant consumer dollars have motivated sports leagues to seriously re-evaluate their efforts toward the Hispanic population.

Hispanics in the United States tend to be predominantly male, on average younger that the non-Hispanic population, and tend to have higher viewership of sports. Marketing, advertising, and sponsorship dollars as well as innovative grassroots public relations initiatives have all been cultivated with the new target demographic in mind.

With the average cost for a 30-second commercial in the U.S. during the last World Cup costing $250,000 versus $3 million for the last Super bowl, professional football is

an arena that marketers and media heavyweights are investing big in.
Tags: hispanic Sports

Source: Rightsholder: Diálogo Public Relations (http://Dialogo.us/); http://www.dialogo.us/move-over-futbol-the-nfl-scores-big-with-latinos/; published January 3, 2012, accessed January 2, 2014. Credit: Diálogo Public Relations.

The NBA has also strengthened international marketing efforts. Under the umbrella program NBA Cares, the National Basketball Association has developed an initiative to reach globally to the Latin American youth population. Basketball Without Borders developed programs including building youth centers and hosting clinics in Brazil, Argentina, and Puerto Rico.

Another example of marketing to ethnic groups includes the introduction of *Deportes Hoy*, the premier Spanish-language sports daily. The sports information product will be circulated in Los Angeles, Orange, and San Diego counties (California) and will be targeted to reach everyone from the occasional to the most highly involved sports enthusiasts.[21] ESPN began to publish a monthly Spanish-language edition of *ESPN The Magazine* beginning in 2007 and a Spanish-language version of ESPN.com, demonstrating their ongoing commitment to Hispanic sports fans in the United States. Similarly, many MLB teams are also establishing Spanish-language websites corresponding with the main English site.

The Hispanic market is not the only ethnic segment of interest to sport marketers. In the United States, Asian Americans have the highest median household income of any ethnic group of $70,221, which is nearly 14.7 percent higher than that of non-Hispanic whites. With a 116 percent increase in purchasing power over the past decade, Asian Americans are the fastest growing, most educated, and a highly reachable segment in the country. Moreover, they are the nation's fastest growing ethnic group, with large population centers in major cities that are home to multiple pro sports franchises. When it comes to putting fans in the stands and merchandise in their homes and offices, Asian Americans should be a sports marketer's dream.[22] Whether it's the Hispanic market, Asian market, or any other ethnic market, sport organizations are realizing the critical nature of understanding and catering to these growing segments for all sports products and services.

Family life cycle

The family life cycle was a concept developed in the 1960s to describe how individuals progress through various "life stages," or phases of their life. A traditional life cycle begins with an individual starting in the young, single "life stage." Next, an individual would progress through stages such as young, married with no children; young, married with children; to, finally, older with no spouse. As you can see, the traditional stages of the family life cycle are based on demographic characteristics such as age, marital status, and the presence or absence of children.

Today, the traditional family life cycle is no longer relevant. In 2013, 3.6 per 1,000 people in the United States are divorced, compared with 6.8 per 1,000 people who are married, and the number of single-parent households is on the rise.[23] Changes

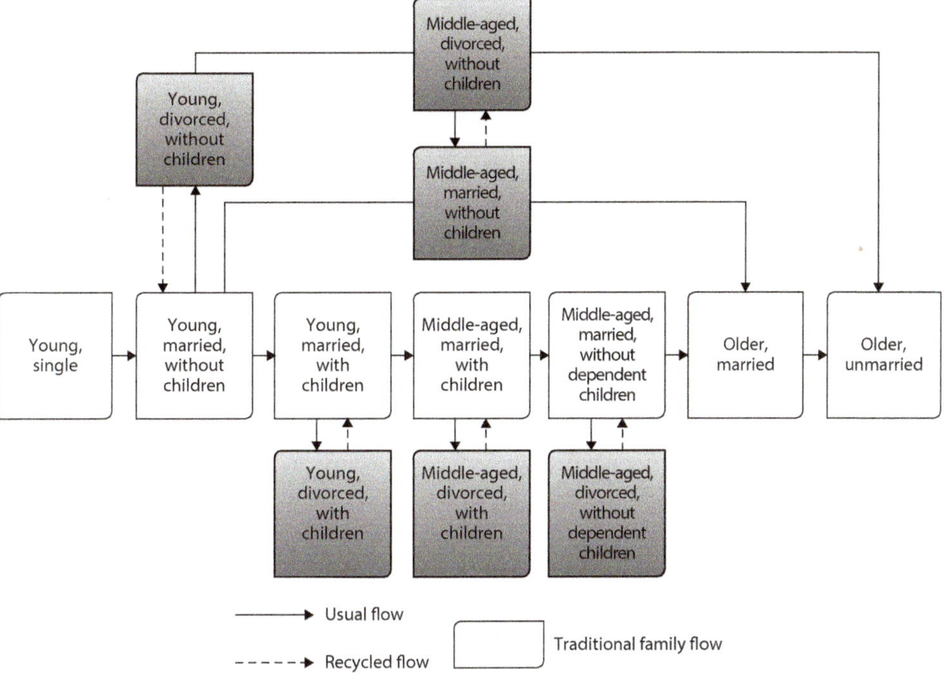

Figure 6.2 Modern family life cycle

in family structure such as these have led marketers to a more modern view of the family life cycle, shown in Figure 6.2.

Sports marketers segmenting on the basis of family life cycle have a number of options. Do they want to appeal to the young and single, the elderly couple with no kids living at home, or the family with young children? Sports that are growing in popularity, such as biking, segment markets based on a stage of the family life cycle. Just imagine the incompatible biking needs of a young, single person versus a young, married couple with children.

Professional sports have come under increased scrutiny in the past decade for their lack of family values. Rising ticket prices, drunken fans, and late games have all been cited as examples of professional sports becoming "family unfriendly." Realizing this, sports marketers have tried to renew family interest in sports and make going to the game "fun for the entire family."

There are numerous examples of sports marketers trying to become more family friendly. For instance, the addition of Homer's Landing, an area where families can picnic before, during, and after the game, has become a "hit" for the St. Louis Cardinals. The Chicago Cubs and other professional teams have initiated no-alcohol sections at their games to encourage a family environment. The NFL is taking an initiative to give professional football a G-rated family-friendly atmosphere, limiting the service of alcohol and setting up text-messaging systems for fans to report unruly behavior. The hope is for a raise in the standard of fan behavior on game days, making the environment more appropriate for families. Moreover, many sports organizations have instituted family nights, which include tickets, parking, and food for a reduced price to encourage family attendance.

Ad 6.2 Pygmy is segmentation on the basis of the family life cycle.

Source: www.pygmyboats.com

Socioeconomic segmentation

Thus far, we have discussed demographic variables such as age, gender, ethnic background, and family life cycle as potential ways to segment sports markets. Another way of segmenting markets that was found to be a good predictor of consumer behavior is through **socioeconomic segmentation**. As previously defined, **social class** is a division of members of a society into a hierarchy of distinct status classes, so that members of each class have relatively the same status and members of all other classes have either more or less status.

Although most people immediately equate social class with income, income alone can be a poor predictor of social class. Other factors such as educational level and occupation also determine social standing. Usually, income, education, and occupation are highly interrelated. In other words, individuals with higher levels of education typically have higher income and more prestigious occupations. Based on these factors (income, education, and occupation), members of a society are artificially said to belong to one of the social class categories. The traditional social class categories are upper-, middle-, and lower-class Americans. Participation in certain sports has been associated with the various social strata. For instance, golf and tennis are called "country club" sports. Polo is a sport of the "rich and famous." Bowling is usually thought of as the "blue-collar" sport of the working class.

As with sex roles, the relationship between social class and sport is now shifting. Golf is now being enjoyed by people of all income levels and sports like mixed martial arts continue to attract both blue- and white-collar populations. While there appears to be valid evidence to support the notion that sport participation is related to social class, studies of sport have found that the higher one's social class, the greater one's involvement in sports.[24] Many believe that sport and entertainment are perfectly suited to capitalize on the social qualities of a "New America." In an era where the Internet is eliminating physical and cultural boundaries and creating a larger global community, sport provides a platform to augment these "pastime" exchanges. Although these exchanges are often still tied to economic factors, i.e., what one can afford, sport serves as an escalator that provides opportunity.

Photo 6.2 Polo is a sport that has typically appealed to the upper class.

Source: Shutterstock.com

Attending a professional basketball or hockey game, once affordable for the whole family, is now a more costly endeavor, therefore today's consumers tend to weigh the pros and cons of attending against the array of entertainment alternatives, i.e. media and other forms of entertainment. Some choose to spend the money, others not, but, the opportunity for exchange still exists. In addition, as the roles of social class continue to shift so do value exchange components that affect their purchasing decisions. For in many instances season tickets options to these events, which used to be readily affordable, can only be enjoyed by wealthy corporate season ticket holders today.

Traditionally, NASCAR fans are stereotypically "good ol' boys" with "blue-collar" values. However, NASCAR has turned into a multibillion-dollar-a-year industry and a marketing success story. During this tremendous growth, the sport is moving beyond its "good-ol'-boy" mentality and reaching a new market in yuppie America. Just consider the demographics of the NASCAR fan. Approximately 42 percent of NASCAR fans earn $50,000 or more per year, compared with 39 percent of the entire U.S. population. At the other end of the wage scale, 39 percent of the U.S. population earns under $30,000, compared with 29 percent of NASCAR fans.[25]

Psychographic segmentation

Psychographic segmentation is described as grouping consumers on the basis of a common lifestyle preference and personality. Because personality alone is very difficult to measure and has not been linked to sports behavior, few sports marketing practitioners find it useful alone. The results of one recent study suggest that individuals who are most likely to identify with a team are those who are most likely to seek out and enjoy social exchanges. The researchers suggest that marketing plans should be designed to emphasize communal aspects of events and that individuals rated high on extraversion, agreeability, and materialism may be more responsive to such promotions. Psychographics, however, looks more toward lifestyle preferences and less toward specific personality measures.

Psychographic segments are believed to be more comprehensive than other types of segmentation, such as demographics, behavioral, or geodemographic. As consumer behavior researcher Michael Solomon points out, "Demographics allow us to describe *who* buys, but psychographics allows us to understand *why* they do."[26] For this reason, many sports marketers have chosen to segment their markets on the basis of psychographics. To gain a better understanding of consumers' lifestyles, marketers assess consumers' **AIO dimensions**, or statements describing activities, interests, and opinions (AIO). The three AIO dimensions are shown in Table 6.3.

Typically marketers quantify AIOs by asking consumers to agree or disagree with a series of statements reflecting their lifestyle. These statements can range from measures of general interest in sports to measures focusing on a specific sport. As seen in Table 6.3, many of these AIO dimensions relate indirectly or directly to sports. For example, sports, social events, recreation, and products may have a direct link to sports, whereas club memberships, fashion, community, and economics may be indirectly linked.

An example of psychographic segmentation in the fresh water fishing market can be seen in Table 6.4. This table illustrates a fisherman's lifestyle based on research from *SRDS: The Lifestyle Market Analyst/National Demographic and Lifestyle*. This type of information examines activities and interests of fishermen to determine what products and services might be successfully marketed to this group. For example, many

Table 6.3 AIO dimensions

Activities	Interests	Opinions
Work	Family	Themselves
Hobbies	Home	Social issues
Social events	Job	Politics
Vacation	Community	Business
Entertainment	Recreation	Economics
Club membership	Fashion	Education
Community	Food	Products
Shopping	Media	Future
Sports	Achievements	Culture

Source: *Journal of Advertising Research*

professional fresh water fishing tournaments are sponsored by investment companies to capitalize on this popular activity of fishing.

Marketers can also segment and target consumers by combining their lifestyles, obtained through AIOs, with their values. This method is called VALS, which is an acronym for values and lifestyles.[27] Values are "desirable, trans-situational goals, varying in importance, that serve as guiding principles in people's lives." The VALS model places consumers into one of eight segments based on their values. These segments range from innovators at the top to survivors at the bottom. Consumers are further segmented based on their affinity for ideals, achievement, and self-expression. For example, a consumer categorized as an innovator who values achievement would be motivated to seek products and services that convey status and success to others. Knowing this, marketers are able to tailor strategies that reach these types of consumers and impact them accordingly. Some researchers consider the VALS method to be "more elegant and fundamental" than the AIO approach.

Table 6.4 Lifestyle Analysis Report: Lifestyle Ranking Index

Sports & Leisure: Go Fresh Water Fishing,1yr (A)			
Lifestyle Category: Psychographics			
Lifestyle Title	**Count**	**Users / 100 HHs**	**Index**
Try to Buy Goods Produced by Own Country, Agr (A)	37,764,670	100.40	108
Like Spending Most Time Home with Family, Agr (A)	49,590,631	131.84	107
Advertising to Kids Is Wrong, Agr (A)	33,121,346	88.05	106
How I Spend Time Is More Important than Money, Agr (A)	44,704,816	118.85	105
Consider Myself a Spiritual Person, Agr (A)	42,487,608	112.95	105
My Faith is Really Important to Me, Agr (A)	43,215,029	114.89	105
Only Go Shopping to Buy Something I Really Need, Agr (A)	49,278,623	131.01	105
Always Look for Special Offers, Agr (A)	44,640,336	118.68	105
Rely on TV To Keep Me Informed, Agr (A)	37,577,721	99.90	105
Have a Keen Sense of Adventure, Agr (A)	34,670,003	92.17	105
Rely on Radio to Keep Me Informed, Agr (A)	20,406,883	54.25	104
Typically Avoid Watching TV Commercials, Agr (A)	35,607,315	94.66	104
Consider Myself a Creative Person, Agr (A)	45,697,334	121.49	104
Do Some Sport/Exercise Once a Week, Agr (A)	39,187,986	104.18	103
Rely on Newspaper to Keep Me Informed, Agr (A)	25,910,852	68.89	103
Prefer Specialty Store because Employee Knowledge, Agr (A)	25,746,422	68.45	101
People Have a Duty to Recycle, Agr (A)	41,615,117	110.64	101
Always Look for Brand Name, Agr (A)	25,135,001	66.82	101
Prefer to Buy Products from Specialty Stores, Agr (A)	19,425,898	51.64	100
Prefer Specialty Stores because Have Best Brands, Agr (A)	15,450,159	41.08	100
Listen Less to Non-Internet Radio because of Internet, Agr (A)	8,665,177	23.04	99
Ban Products that Pollute, Agr (A)	25,398,600	67.52	99
Would Pay More for Environmentally Friendly Products, Agr (A)	24,595,905	65.39	99
Rely On Magazines to Keep Me Informed, Agr (A)	9,967,361	26.50	99
Interested in The Arts, Agr (A)	28,021,405	74.50	99
Like to Stand Out in a Crowd, Agr (A)	15,827,240	42.08	97

Source: PRIZM 2010, Experian Marketing Solutions, Inc, 2010.

Geographic segmentation

Geographics is a simple, but powerful, segmentation basis. Certainly, this is critical for sports marketers and as long-standing as "rooting for the home team." All sports teams use **geographic segmentation**; however, it is not always as straightforward as it may initially seem. For instance, the Dallas Cowboys, Chicago Bulls, Atlanta Braves, and the Fighting Irish are all known as "America's Team."

Geographic segmentation can be useful in making broad distinctions among local, regional, national, and international market segments. International or multinational marketing is a topic of growing interest for sports marketers. For example, Major League Baseball has held regular-season games in Japan, Mexico, and Puerto Rico, and the NBA games are televised in 215 countries in 47 languages.[28] The NFL has also expanded internationally and now broadcasts games in 234 countries and territories in 31 languages.[29] As the Spotlight on International Sports Marketing indicates, the leagues are realizing that the key to growth is going global.

SPOTLIGHT ON INTERNATIONAL SPORTS MARKETING

NBA continues to grow internationally

MIAMI (AP) – Over nearly a two-week stretch in January, the Detroit Pistons play four straight "home" games. First comes Utah, then New York, followed by Boston and Orlando.

It's a most unusual run of home games - since the one against the Knicks will be played in London.

The league calls itself the National Basketball Association, though the National part hardly tells the whole story. Maybe now more than ever, the NBA continues to look for growth on the international side of the game, a stretch that seems to have started when the group of U.S. players forever to be known as the Dream Team took center stage at the 1992 Barcelona Olympics.

Commissioner David Stern has talked for years about the prospects of more NBA games, possibly even teams, abroad. On Thursday, Stern announced his plan to step down in 2014, but it's certain that at least some - probably quite a bit - of his remaining tenure will be spent on laying more groundwork for the league to keep evolving internationally.

"Look, if you said 10 years ago that we were going to be playing regular-season games in Europe, I would have probably said, 'Not a chance,'" Miami coach Erik Spoelstra said. "And last year they played two games over there. So anything's possible. The fan base continues to grow over there. It's cool to be part of a league that has become so global."

The numbers are eye-popping. The league's games are now shown in 215 countries and territories. The NBA says a total of 114 games have been played in 32 international cities across 17 foreign countries since 1988. Through social media, the league says it engages 320 million fans – that's more than the entire U.S. population - across the globe, and seems to put the NBA at the front when it comes to interest internationally among the four major U.S. leagues.

Stern says international potential is an area "of extreme importance" for the league, which is clear. The NBA has a newly opened office in Brazil, which will play host to the World Cup in 2014 and the Olympics in 2016. There's an NBA office in Mumbai now, for the growing market in India. And Stern said he wasn't even sure the league would be able to respond to all the requests from firms there to do business with the NBA.

"It's the reality of the game," Stern said. "There has been enormous improvement in the quality of the basketball around the world. In the London Olympics on 11 of the 12 teams, we had 59 current or former NBA players. That just speaks to the quality of the international competition. The quality being that international players make our game better by playing in the NBA, and then they return to play for the national teams."

Even before the league formally announced the Pistons-Knicks game in London - which will bring reigning gold medalists Tyson Chandler and Carmelo Anthony of the Knicks back to the city where they helped the U.S. win the Olympic title - fans in England were asking around about tickets.

"I think it is a good thing," Chandler said. "I think the game is slowly turning into a global game. I think it's good for everybody. It's good for the fans over there, it's good for the game, it's good for players as well, as long as it's done correctly."

The ideas for foreign growth have been a constant in the NBA, including Stern's oft-repeated hope of eventually adding a division of teams in Europe. (He has long said the idea is 10 years away, which has almost become a bit of a running joke since his prediction never changes even as the calendar flips from one year to the next.)

But in a global economy, and as the dominant force in a global game, reaching the billions of people who aren't exposed to elite-level basketball remains a top priority. That was even illustrated on Thursday, when Stern's decision to leave the commissioner's office was announced, but with the caveat that he will continue helping the NBA with certain issues - international ones in particular.

"At our urging we are going to also sit down with David, and have him continue to help us to be available to the partners or to the new commissioner after that time, to help us in particular on new projects or probably international projects," said Minnesota Timberwolves owner Glen Taylor. "We just think that his leadership will be important to our future."

Markets differ widely from one country to the next. Interest in certain players, apparently, does not.

Earlier this year, the NBA released the list of best-selling jerseys in international markets. In China, the top three were the Los Angeles Lakers' Kobe Bryant, Chicago's Derrick Rose and Miami's LeBron James, respectively. In Europe, the order was the same. In Latin America, Bryant was again No. 1, followed by James and Rose.

Notice a trend there?

"Every time I go to another country, I'm always amazed by where the game's going," James said. "I think the interest in our game just keeps growing. You're talking about billions of people in this world, and a lot of people know the NBA."

There were seven preseason games abroad this season: Istanbul, Milan,

Berlin, Barcelona, Shanghai, Beijing and Mexico City were the host cities. Each venue sold out, the NBA said.

Given the interest, and given the dollars that are out there, no one would be surprised to see more NBA games abroad - and regularly.

"I would never underestimate the creativity of the league," Spoelstra said.

Source: http://www.nba.com/2012/news/10/26/nba-international-growth.ap/index.html. Rightsholder: NBA.com.

The physical climate also plays a role in segmenting markets geographically. Classic examples include greater demand for snow skiing equipment in Colorado and surfboards in Florida. However, Colorado ski resorts have the greatest number of sports tourists who come from Florida, hardly thought of as a snow ski mecca. Therefore, segments of sports consumers may exist in unlikely geographic markets. In this example, the psychographics of the sports consumer may be more important in predicting behavior than geographic location.

Although the climate plays an important role in sports, marketers have attempted to tame this uncontrollable factor. For instance, tons of sand was shipped to Atlanta, creating beach-like conditions, for the first ever Olympic beach volleyball competition. The creation of domed stadiums has also allowed sports marketers to tout the perfect conditions in which fans can watch football in the middle of a blizzard in Minnesota or during the middle of a thunderstorm in Houston, Texas.

Behavioral segmentation

For sports marketers engaged in the strategic sports marketing process, two common goals are attracting more fans and keeping them. Behavioral segmentation lies at the heart of these two objectives. **Behavioral segmentation** groups consumers based on how much they purchase, how often they purchase, and how loyal they are to a product or service.

Interestingly, in today's professional sports environment, loyalty is an increasingly important topic. Many professional sports teams have held their fans and cities hostage, and cities are doing everything they can to keep their beloved teams. Taxpayers nationwide have paid more than $14 billion for stadiums and arenas during the past 20 years. This new construction and renovation was done largely to keep team owners satisfied and curb any threat of moving. For 2012–2013, the value of major league arenas and stadiums opening was over $10 billion. Add collegiate and minor league facility construction, and the number increased beyond $19 billion.[30]

Franchises and players within each team move so rapidly that fan loyalty becomes a difficult phenomenon to capture. The day of the lifelong fan is over. Because of this, fans may identify more with individual players or even coaches (e.g., Derek Jeter and the Yankees, Kobe Bryant and the Lakers, or Frank Beamer and Virginia Tech Football) than they do with teams. According to some sports marketing experts, next to wins, fans like to see famous faces on the field.[31] This is true even in team-dominated sports, such as football.

Fans may be more concerned with the individual performance of Albert Pujols than they are with the St. Louis Cardinals. Certainly, sports marketers have to monitor this trend of diminishing loyalty to a team. However, some sports fans show extreme loyalty by purchasing personal seat licenses (PSLs). PSLs require fans to pay a leasing fee for their seats. This fee would guarantee the consumer his or her seat for several years. The PSL, of course, demonstrates the extreme devotion of a group of fans. For example, NFL fans in Dallas had to pay PSLs of up to $150,000 just for the right to purchase season tickets at the new Cowboys Stadium.

Sports marketers have recently taken a lesson in loyalty marketing from other industries and are creating loyalty marketing programs. A study by Pritchard and Negro[32] found that these programs are effective when they build on the genuine affinity fans have for their teams, rather than rewarding attendance alone. Increasing fan interaction with players, coaches, and the entire organization through direct access or personal communication was shown to be much more important to the success of loyalty programs than rewarding attendance.

Along with behavioral segmentation based on loyalty to a team or sports product, consumers are frequently grouped on the basis of other attendance or purchasing behaviors. For instance, lifelong season ticket holders represent one end of the usage continuum, whereas those who have never attended sporting events represent the other end. A unique marketing mix must be designed to appeal to each of these two groups of consumers.

Benefits segmentation

The focus of **benefits segmentation** is the appeal of a product or service to a group of consumers. Stated differently, benefits segments describe why consumers purchase a product or service or what problem the product solves for the consumer. In a sense, benefits segmentation is the underlying factor in all types of marketing segmentation in that every purchase is made to satisfy a need. Benefits segmentation is also consistent with the marketing concept (discussed in Chapter 1) that states that organizations strive to meet customers' needs.

Major shoe manufacturers, such as Nike, focus on "benefits sought" to segment markets. In fact, Nike's mission is to bring inspiration and innovation to every athlete in the world. This includes both the elite athletes and professional performers as well as the casual performer. Some consumers desire a high-performance cross-training shoe, whereas others want a shoe that is more of a fashion statement. Nike is a fashion brand. Consumers that wear Nike products do not always buy it to participate in sport. Nike produces sportswear products from manufacturing waste therefore enhancing the development opportunities that satisfy a consumer market, i.e. sunglasses and jewelry. Nike focuses on personal benefit associated with the use of its products and the values satisfied by this product use.[33]

Golf ball manufacturers also try to design products that will appeal to the specific benefits sought by different groups of golfers. Pro V1 has enhanced aerodynamics with slightly higher flight for longer distance, soft feel, and Drop-And-Stop control. DT SoLo gives the ultimate combination of distance with soft feel and guaranteed cut-proof durability. NXT Tour has long distance off the driver and improved control with long irons. The Titleist DT Spin offers a combination of long tee-to-green distance, wound-ball spin, improved feel, and guaranteed cut-proof durability, whereas the

Titleist DT Distance offers golfers longer and straighter two-piece distance with cut-proof durability. Sports marketers really hit a home run when they design products that satisfy multiple needs (i.e., distance, feel, accuracy, durability) of consumers.

Choosing more than one segment

Although each of the previously mentioned bases for segmentation identifies groups of consumers with similar needs, it is common practice to combine segmentation variables. An example of combining segmentation approaches is found in a study of the golf participant market.[34] A survey was conducted to determine playing ability, purchase behavior, and the demographic characteristics of public and private course golfers. The resulting profile produced five distinct market segments that combine some of the various bases for segmentation discussed earlier in the chapter. These five segments are shown in Table 6.5.

Table 6.5 Five market segments for golf participants

Competitors (18.6 percent)

- Have a handicap of less than 10
- Indicate love of game
- Play for competitive edge
- Practice most often
- Most likely to play in league
- Own most golf clothing
- Are early adopters (e.g., third wedge)
- Buy most golf balls

Players (25.7 percent)

- Have handicap between 10 and 14
- Use custom club makers
- Practice a lot
- Like competition
- Exercise and companionship are important
- Most likely to take out-of-state golf vacation

Sociables (17.8 percent)

- Have handicap between 15 and 18
- Often play with family
- Purchase from off-price retailers
- Play for sociability
- Most likely to take winter vacation to warm destination

Aspirers (18.4 percent)

- Have handicap between 19 and 25
- Love to play; hate to practice
- Most inclined to use golf for business purposes
- Golf shows are important as source of information
- Competition and sociability are unimportant reason to play

Table 6.5 (continued)

Casual (19.5 percent)
• Have handicap of 26 or more
• Do not practice
• More women in this segment
• Play less frequently than other segments• Own the least golf clothing
• Purchase the fewest golf balls
• Recreation is most important factor for play
• Exercise and companionship are moderately important
• Least likely to take a golf vacation
• Most likely to shop in course pro shop

Source: Sam Fullerton and H. Robert Dodge, "An Application of Market Segmentation in a Sports Marketing Arena: We All Can't Be Greg Norman," *Sport Marketing Quarterly*, vol. 4, no. 3 (1995), 43–47.

Geodemographic segmentation

One of the most widely used multiple segment approaches in sports is **geodemographic segmentation**. Although geographic segmentation and demographic segmentation are useful tools for sports marketers, combining geographic and demographic characteristics seems to be even more effective in certain situations. For instance, many direct marketing campaigns apply the principles of geodemographic segmentation.

The basis for geodemographic segmentation is that people living in close proximity are also likely to share the same lifestyle and demographic composition. Because lifestyle of the consumer is included in this type of segmentation, it is also known as geolifestyle. Geodemographics allows marketers to describe the characteristics of broad segments such as standard metropolitan statistical areas (SMSAs) all the way down to census blocks (consisting of roughly 340 houses). The most common unit of segmentation for geodemography is the zip code. Claritias, Inc., a marketing firm leading the charge in geodemographics, established the PRIZM system in the 1970s. PRIZM is used to identify potential markets for products. PRIZM affords marketers the benefits of household-level precision in applications such as direct mail, while at the same time maintaining the broad market linkages, usability, and cost-effectiveness of geodemographics for applications such as market sizing and site selection.[35] Each unit of geography was originally classified as one of 62 PRIZM clusters. However, PRIZM NE (New Evolution) released in 2004, replaced the original PRIZM system (now referred to as PRIZM 62). PRISM NE utilizes one of 66 PRIZM clusters, which have been given names that best characterize those populations. Some examples of the PRIZM 62 cluster categories are shown in Table 6.6.

6

Target markets

After segmenting the market based on one or a combination of the variables discussed in the previous section, target markets are chosen. **Target marketing** is choosing the segment(s) that will allow an organization to most efficiently and effectively attain its marketing goals.

Table 6.6 PRIZM cluster categories and descriptions

Uppper Crust – Ranked number 1 of all 66 clusters, the upper class segment includes those who are older and wealthier without children. This group is 55 or older and takes on more management roles in the workforce. This neighborhood would be filled with more prestigious individuals who would drive cars such as Lexus LS.

God's Country – Populated by educated, upscale professionals, married executives who choose to raise their children in the far exurbs of major metropolitan areas. Their affluence is often supported by dual incomes. Lifestyles are family and outdoor centered.

Bohemian Mix – Describes most of our nation's college towns and university campus neighborhoods. With a typical mix of half locals (towns) and half students (gowns), it is totally unique. Thousands of penniless 18- to 24-year-old kids, plus highly educated professionals with a taste for prestige products beyond their means.

Winner's Circle – Sixth in American affluence and typified by new money, living in expensive new mansions in the suburbs of the nation's major metros. These are well-educated, mobile executives and professionals with teen-age families. Big producers, prolific spenders, and global travelers.

Source: *How to Use PRIZM* (Alexandria, VA: Claritas, 1996).

Sports marketers must make a systematic decision when choosing groups of consumers they want to target. To make these decisions, each potential target market is evaluated on the basis of whether it is sizable, reachable, and measurable, and whether it exhibits behavioral variation. Let us look at how to judge the worth of potential target markets in greater detail.

Evaluation of target markets

Sizable

One of the first factors to consider when evaluating and choosing a potential target market is the size of the market. In addition to the current size of the market, sports marketers must also analyze the estimated growth of the market. The market growth would be predicted, in part, through environmental scanning, already discussed in Chapter 2.

Sports marketers must be careful to choose a target market that has neither too many nor too few consumers. If the target market becomes too large, then it essentially becomes a mass, or undifferentiated, market. For example, we would not want to choose all basketball fans as a target market because of the huge variations in social class, lifestyles, and consumption behaviors.

However, sports marketers must guard against a target market that is too small and narrowly defined. We would not choose a target market that consisted of all left-handed female basketball fans between the ages of 30 and 33 who live in San Antonio and have income levels between $40,000 and $50,000. This market is too narrowly defined and would not prove to be a good return on our marketing investment.

One common trap that marketers fall into with respect to the size of the potential market is known as the majority fallacy. The **majority fallacy** assumes that the largest group of consumers should always be selected as the target market. Although in some instances the biggest market may be the best choice, usually the competition is the fiercest for this group of consumers; therefore, smaller and more differentiated targets should be chosen.

These smaller, distinct groups of core customers that an organization focuses on are sometimes referred to as a market niche. **Niche marketing** is the process

Table 6.7 Market segment vs. market niches

Segment	Niche
Small mass market	Very small market
Less specialized	Very specific needs
Top down (go from large market into smaller pieces)	Bottom up (cater to the smaller pieces of the market)

of carving out a relatively tiny part of a market that has a very special need not currently being filled. By definition, a **market niche** is initially much smaller than a segment and consists of a very homogeneous group of consumers, as reflected by their unique need. The differences between market segments and niches are highlighted in Table 6.7. Hanas (2007) provides support for the use of niche marketing in the sports industry, emphasizing that niche sport properties should be aware of their influence on several different communities. Properties need to be aware of their image, be cognizant of the image potential, and how their image may be attractive to potential sport properties. Focusing on the image intricacies, niche marketing may enable sport properties to enhance the linkage between the wants and needs of the consumer with sponsors and sponsees. For these reasons niche sport properties need to know how to best reach and connect with the different communities. Niche sport marketers should have a thorough grasp on each of these communities and what each of those communities looks like from a demographic and psychographic perspective. Organizations and sports such as professional bull riders, paintball leagues, hunting, even professional gamblers and eaters have always been present but have increased in status and popularity with fans as well as sponsors over recent years.

These niche leagues and sports have the ability to reach a small target audience and have been seen to be more aggressive in collaborating with marketers. By providing alternative platforms to marketers, they have multiplied the sponsorship opportunities.[36]

One specific example of a niche market is individuals (as opposed to corporations) who have financially invested in the sports franchise through the purchase of season tickets for many seasons. In addition to their financial investment, these loyal fans have a high emotional investment in the team. To retain these valuable consumers, sports marketers must develop a specialized marketing mix to reinforce and reward the loyalty that these fans have shown to the organization.

Reachable

In addition to exploring the size of the potential target market, its ability to be reached should also be evaluated. Reach refers to the accessibility of the target market. Does the sports marketer have a means of communicating with the desired target market? If the answer to this question is no, then the potential target market should not be pursued.

Traditional means of reaching the sports fan include mass media, such as magazines, newspapers, and television. In today's marketing environment it is possible to reach a specific target market with technology such as the Internet, specifically through social media. According to Sports Fan Graph, professional sports have recently been utilizing this avenue to promote leagues, teams, and athletes through Facebook. The NBA has over 24 million fans "likes" on Facebook, MLB 5.4 million "likes" while the

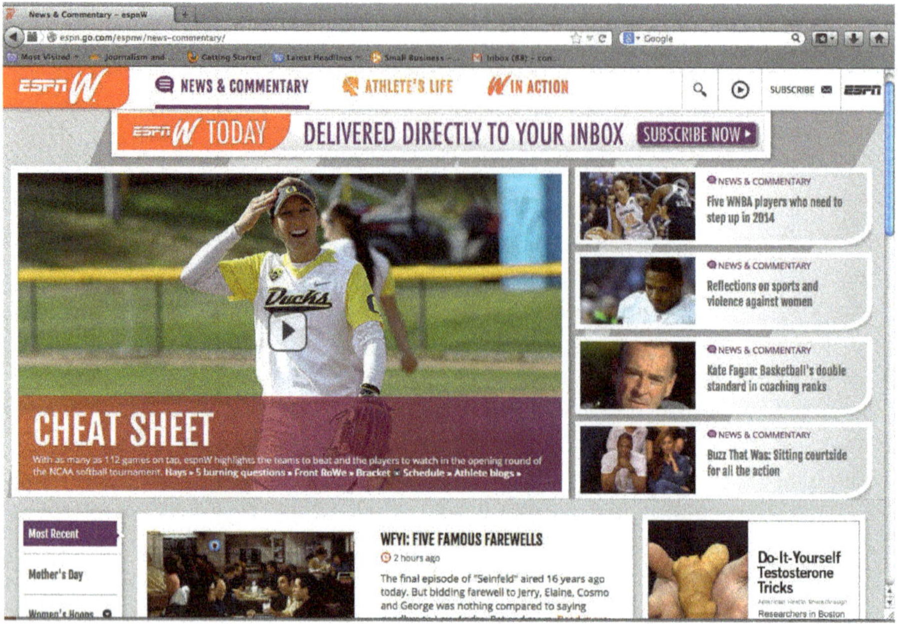

Web 6.2 Reaching women's soccer fans on the Web

Source: ESPN.com

NFL has over 10.5 million fan "likes". In fact when looking at the NFL, and including all 32 teams, almost 1 in 10 Americans have declared their support for an NFL team on Facebook[37] In addition to the Internet, satellite technology products, such as DIRECTV, are allowing sports fans across the United States access to their favorite teams. This, of course, opens new geographic segments for sports marketers to consider.

Measurable

The ability to measure the size, accessibility, and purchasing power of the potential target market(s) is another factor that needs to be considered. For a market segment to represent a good target market, sport marketers must be able to identify and then measure the number of people in that segment. If a sport marketer has no measurable criteria to identify the size or scope of that market segment, a marketer may want to reconsider basing a marketing campaign on that segment. Segments may be composed of multiple criteria; however, for segments to be measurable they should be evaluated against the following criteria:

- ***Identifiable*** – Differentiation among attribute measures must occur so they can be identified.
- **Accessible** – Market segments must be reachable through communication and distribution channels.
- ***Sustainable*** – Market segments should be sufficiently large to justify the resources required to target them.
- ***Unique needs*** – Clarify considerations and offerings as they relate to the needs of the consumer.
- ***Durable*** – Segments should be measured to identify stability and to minimize cost and the frequency of change.

One of the reasons demographic segmentation is so widespread is the ease with which characteristics such as age, gender, income level, and occupation can be assessed or measured. Psychographic segments are perhaps the most difficult to measure because of the complex interaction of personality and lifestyle.

Behavioral variation

Finally, if the target market is sizable, reachable, and measurable, sports marketers must examine behavioral variation. We want consumers within the target market to exhibit similar behaviors, attitudes, lifestyles, and so on. In addition, marketers want these characteristics to be unique within a target market. This component is the underlying factor in choosing any target market.

An example of behavioral variation among market segments is the corporate season ticket holder versus the individual season ticket holder. Although both corporate season ticket holders and individual season ticket holders may be fans at some level, their motivation for attending games and attitudes toward the team may be quite different. These variations would prompt different approaches to marketing to each segment.

How many target markets?

Now that we have evaluated potential target markets, do we have to choose just one? The answer depends largely on the organization's marketing objectives and its resources. If the firm has the financial and other resources to pursue more than one target market, it does so by prioritizing the potential target markets.

The market distinguished as the most critical to attaining the firm's objectives is deemed the primary target market. Other, less critical markets of interest are called secondary, tertiary, and so on. Again, a unique marketing mix may need to be developed for each target market, so the costs associated with choosing multiple targets are sometimes prohibitive.

Positioning

Segmentation has been considered and specific target markets have been chosen. Next, sport marketers must decide on the positioning of their sporting events, athletes, teams, and so on. **Positioning** is defined as fixing your sports entity in the minds of consumers in the target market.

Before discussing positioning, three important points should be stressed. First, positioning is dependent on the target market(s) identified in the previous phase of the market selection decisions. In fact, the *same* sport may be positioned differently to distinct target markets. As the spotlight demonstrated earlier in the chapter, the positioning of the NBA and other professional sports is changing with the opening of a new target market – women.

Second, positioning is based solely on the perceptions of the target market and how its members think and feel about the sports entity. Sometimes positioning is mistakenly linked with where the product appears on the retailer's shelf or where the product is placed in an advertisement. Nothing could be further from the truth. Position is all about how the consumer perceives your sports product relative to competitive offerings.

Third, the definition of positioning reflects its importance to all sports products. It should also be noted that sports leagues (Arena Football versus NFL), sports teams (e.g., Dallas Cowboys as "America's Team"), and individual athletes (e.g., Danica Patrick as a female athlete in a male-dominated sport, or the NFL's perennial bad boy, Michael Vick) all must be positioned by sports marketers.

How does the sports marketer attempt to fix the sports entity in the minds of consumers? The first step rests in understanding the target market's perception of the relevant attributes of the sports entity. The relevant attributes are those features and characteristics desired in the sports entity by the target market. These attributes may be intangible, such as a fun atmosphere at the stadium, or tangible, such as having cushioned seating. Golf manufacturers such as Slazenger have positioned their equipment as the "standard of excellence" and having "impeccable quality."

In another example, consider the possible product attributes for in-line skates. Pricing, status of the brand name, durability, quality of the wheels, and weight of the skate may all be considered product attributes. If serious, competitive skaters are chosen as the primary target market, then the in-line skates may be positioned on the basis of quality of the wheels and weight of the skate. However, if first-time, recreational skaters are considered the primary target market, then relevant product attributes may be price and durability. Marketers attempt to understand all the potential attributes and then which ones are most important to their target markets through marketing research.

Perceptual maps

Perceptual mapping is one of the few marketing research techniques that provides direct input into the strategic marketing planning process. It allows marketing planners to assess the strengths and weaknesses and to view the customer and the competitor simultaneously in the same realm. Perceptual mapping and preference mapping techniques have been a basic tool of the applied marketing research profession for over 20 years. It is one of the few advanced multivariate techniques that has not suffered very much from alternating waves of popularity and disfavor.[38]

Ad 6.3 47 Brand positions itself as the official licensee of the National Basketball Association.

Source: Forty Seven Brand

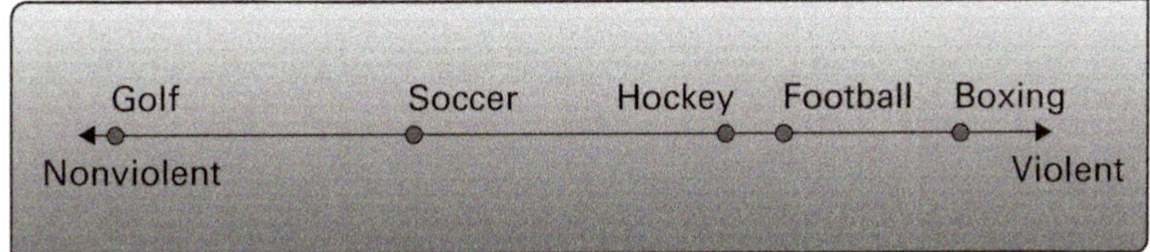

Figure 6.3 One-dimensional perceptual map of sports

Perceptual maps provide marketers with three types of information. First, perceptual maps indicate the dimensions or attributes that consumers use when thinking about a sports product or service. Second, perceptual maps tell sports marketers where different sports products or services are located on those dimensions. The third type of information provided by perceptual maps is how your product is perceived relative to the competition.

Perceptual maps can be constructed in any number of dimensions, based on the number of product attributes being considered. Figure 6.3 demonstrates a one-dimensional perceptual map, which explores the positioning of various spectator sports based on the level of perceived aggression or violence associated with the sports. This hypothetical example can be interpreted as follows: Boxing is seen as the most violent or aggressive sport, followed by football, hockey, and soccer. However, golf is the least aggressive sport. These results would vary, of course, based on who participated in the research, how aggression or violence is defined by the researchers, and what level of competition is being considered (i.e., professional, high school, or youth leagues).

6

Although it is easy to conceptualize one-dimensional perceptual maps, the number of dimensions is contingent upon the number of attributes relevant to consumers. For example, Converse positions its shoes for multiple uses like action sports, basketball, cheerleading, cross-training or fashion. New Balance, however, positions its shoes solely on the basis of running.

A study using perceptual mapping techniques found that consumers identify six dimensions of sport (shown in Table 6.8). Although it is possible to create a six-dimensional perceptual map, it is nearly impossible to interpret. Therefore, two-dimensional perceptual maps were constructed that compared 10 sports on the six dimensions identified by consumers.

Figure 6.4 shows a two-dimensional perceptual map using Dimension 4 (skill developed primarily with others versus skill developed alone) and Dimension 5 (younger athletes versus broad age ranges of participants). Interpreting this perceptual map, we see that football is considered a sport whose participants are younger athletes and skill is developed primarily with others. Compared with football, golf is seen as a sport for a broader range of participants with skills developed more on your own. Using these results, sports marketers can better understand the image of their sport from the perspective of various target markets and decide whether this image needs to be changed or maintained.

Table 6.8 Six dimensions or attributes of sports

Dimension 1	Strength, speed, and endurance vs. methodical and precise movements
Dimension 2	Athletes only as participants vs. athletes plus recreational participants
Dimension 3	Skill emphasis on impact with object vs. skill emphasis on body movement
Dimension 4	Skill development and practice primarily alone vs. primarily with others
Dimension 5	A younger participant in the sport vs. participant ages from young to older
Dimension 6	Less masculine vs. more masculine

Source: James H. Martin, "Using a Perceptual Map of the Consumer's Sport Schema to Help Make Sponsorship Decisions," *Sport Marketing Quarterly*, vol. 3, no. 3 (1994), 27–33.

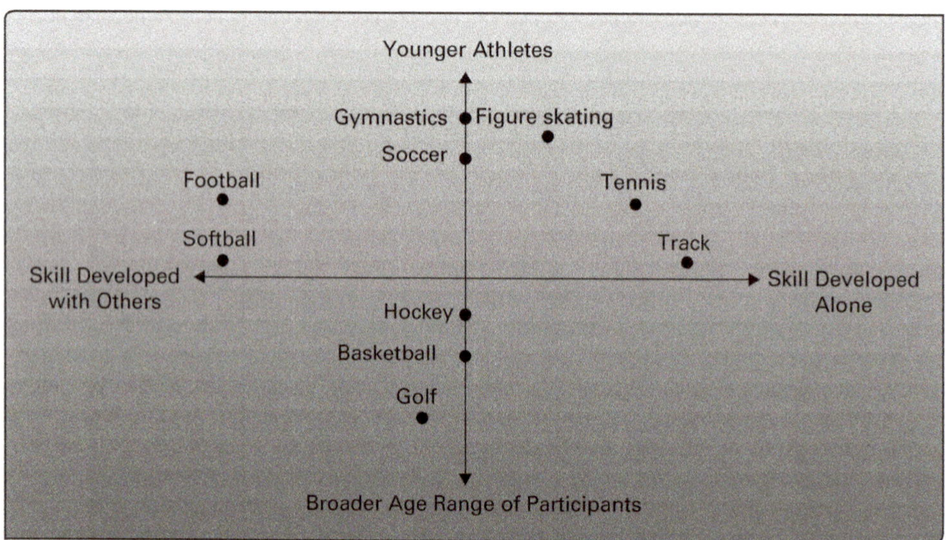

Figure 6.4 Two-dimensional perceptual map of sports

Repositioning

As suggested, sport marketers may use the results of positioning studies to change the image of their sport. For instance, professional cycling, one of the most popular sports in the world, has been marred by doping scandals in recent years. Cycling took a big hit when the "Operation Puerto" case alleged that a number of riders had accepted illegal doping substances, and that scandal was followed by the Tour de France, which was tainted by the revelation that U.S. rider and Tour winner Floyd Landis had failed both of his drug tests. Obviously this is not the image the cycling federations and the cyclists themselves wish to project. Thus, the sport of cycling was trying to **reposition** itself or change the image or perception of the sports entity in the minds of consumers in the target market.

In response to those drug allegations, and in hopes of cleaning up the reputation of the sport, Team Slipstream took a pro-active response. Team Slipstream, now Garmin-Sharp Pro Cycling Team, is a professional cycling team based in the United States, consisting of 29 riders who have subjected themselves to weekly drug testing, instead of just waiting until race day to be tested.[39] "It's ensuring [to] the public, the fans, and ourselves that our riders are clean," said team director Jonathan Vaughters, who retired from competitive racing in 2003. "It's enormously important as far as sponsors go to know that their team is not getting caught up in a scandal, and it's setting an example for young athletes."[40] Unfortunately, during this "repositioning phase" a larger scandal emerged involving Lance Armstrong. In June 2012, The United States Anti-Doping Agency charged Armstrong with having used illicit performance-enhancing drugs.[41] On August 24, 2012, the USADA announced that Armstrong had been issued a lifetime ban from competition, applicable to all sports which follow the World Anti-Doping Agency code. The USADA stripped Armstrong of his seven Tour de France titles, highlighting that Armstriong had engaged in "the most sophisticated, professionalized and successful doping programs that sport has ever seen."[42] The Armstrong scandal further diminished repositioning efforts and tarnished the industry. Therefore, cycling federations once again had to regroup, refocus, and realign their market strategies. This situation further accentuates how situations outside of a marketer's control can adversely impact market strategy.

Cycling is not the only sports entity attempting to reposition itself. Following a series of scandals with coaches and athletes, the NCAA is also experiencing image problems. And let's not forget baseball players such as slugger Barry Bonds, who has some problems of his own. Individual athletes can produce image problems for themselves, a city, as well as a sponsor. LeBron James and "The Decision" left himself, Cleveland, and Nike to re-establish an image and reposition within the sports industry. One professional sport team, albeit a temporary tenant, can even serve to reposition an entire city, as discussed in the accompanying article.

BASEBALL CONTINUES TO ASSIST STORM RELIEF EFFORTS

The devastation wrought by Hurricane Sandy has taken a toll on communities where Major League Baseball teams live alongside fans as neighbors and friends, and now many of those neighbors and friends need some help to recover and rebuild.

It takes a team to get through a crisis like the damage inflicted in late October, and baseball's team of teams, players and fans around the country, is gathering forces to help assist those in need in the wake of the "superstorm" that hit with such impact in New York, New Jersey and elsewhere on the Eastern seaboard and inland areas.

To that end, Major League Baseball announced that in conjunction with the Major League Baseball Players Association a donation of $1 million is being made to benefit the American Red Cross, the Salvation Army and Feeding America to assist in the efforts being made to help those affected most by the storm. In addition, relief efforts have by MLB, its clubs and employees been ongoing to deliver truckloads of supplies and administer help to devastated areas.

"As our thoughts and prayers remain with all those who have been impacted by this tragedy, it is a privilege for Major League Baseball to support our fans and their communities during this urgent time of need," Commissioner Bud Selig said. "All of us at Major League Baseball are grateful to our society's leaders, first responders and volunteers, and we hope that our contribution to these humanitarian organizations will assist in the vital relief efforts along the East Coast. This is a time when the resiliency of the great American spirit will prevail."

Said MLBPA executive director

Michael Weiner: "Natural disasters know no boundaries, and this one was a direct hit that affected many in the MLBPA's office personally. On behalf of the MLBPA and its members, we are honored to join with the Commissioner's Office in making this contribution to support the efforts of organizations working around the clock to help provide various forms of relief and assistance to those suffering in the aftermath of the storm, including many of our friends and neighbors in need."

The message from Major League Baseball, its players, its 30 teams and MLB.com is simple: Please donate to the **American Red Cross, the Salvation Army** and **Feeding America**. Help your neighbors and friends, and be a part of the team bringing relief where it's needed.

On Thursday, 62 more boxes filled with warm clothing and supplies were packed onto a truck at the Commissioner's Office in Manhattan and driven to hard-hit areas in New Jersey. The first stop was to a social services community center in Hoboken, a heavily flooded square-mile town on the Hudson River. From there it was down the turnpike to the Jersey Shore, where a major delivery was dropped off at The Foodbank of Monmouth and Ocean Counties, a facility whose wide coverage area was in the bulls-eye of Sandy.

Carlos Rodriguez, executive director of The Foodbank, said his operation has been inundated with help since the storm through bulk truck dropoffs, like one semi that showed up unsolicited from Indiana. The Foodbank works with more than 250 emergency food programs, pantries, soup kitchens, shelters and low-income day care centers, so they can connect to people in need and will immediately disperse the contents from MLB and clubs as cold weather sets in for many whose lives are in disarray.

"What we experienced here at the Jersey Shore was a storm within a superstorm," Rodriguez said. "We were already just trying to figure out the struggle that the economic crisis left us, and then the storm has compounded that even more. To make it worse, it's right before the Thanksgiving holiday.

"Normally, we would be serving one in 10 of the residents in Monmouth and Ocean Counties, or about 127,000 people – even before the disaster. Immediately after the disaster, we were able to open up our shops, and we've been open continuously every day, serving upwards of 460,000 meals since Hurricane Sandy. But we've had to do dual efforts – not only provide the immediate relief because of the storm, but to also make sure that those who can and *have* a table can have a Thanksgiving next week."

Rodriguez encouraged citizens to donate at **foodbankmoc.org**, as $10 allows them to provide more than 30 meals.

"We've dealt with the immediate sadness of the disaster, but I think the entire community is really gearing up to rebuild, and to recover our beloved Jersey Shore," he said. "We're in this for the long haul. Today, and now more than ever, we need to make sure The Foodbank and the network of charities that we work with stay strong, so we can make sure that Jersey stays strong."

Leo Pellegrini, director of health and human services for the City of Hoboken, oversaw the reception of many boxes off the MLB truck and said the contents would be distributed to the people in need, those who have lost their clothing and supplies.

"We've been getting a lot of supplies from members of the community and outside the state of New Jersey, so we've kind of staged this area since it was devastated by Hurricane Sandy," he said. "It was a grueling experience, but you have to thank the public safety – they came through in a big spot for us. All the community members came in and helped, especially our volunteers – going into buildings where we didn't have power for seven days. Our volunteers were delivering food to our seniors who could not go from the 14th floor all the way to the first floor."

On Nov. 9, MLB delivered several vans filled with warm-weather clothing, non-perishable food and supplies to the hard-hit area of Far Rockaway in the New York City borough of Queens. The first drop-off was at the Food Bank Distribution Center in the Mott Haven section of the Bronx, where long food lines were common from corner to corner. Then the caravan went to St. Mary Star of the Sea and St. Gertrude Parish, forming an assembly line of boxes that were then sorted into care packages for the long line there.

There was no power anywhere in sight, there were 6 p.m. ET curfews and arrests, there was looting and robberies and broken lights whenever emergency lights were set up at night. There were cries of frustration within a community looking for support.

"It's horrific," said Rosemary Lopez, associate executive director for program services at the Advocacy Center of Queens County, a group that helped MLB get supplies into the right hands. "People are suffering. To the people who follow Major League Baseball, we could really use more food, clothing, water, whatever you can spare. Out here, they just don't have it. Nothing's open. No stores, absolutely nothing."

Joanne Murray, a full-time volunteer handling the processing of relief supplies at St. Mary of the Sea, said her church has been "so blessed with people from all over the country coming through. The need is very great."

"They mostly need food, diapers, wipes, toilet paper, flashlights, batteries," Murray said. "Now we have to look at cleaning supplies, because once lights come back on, people need those. Some people are going to need financial help as well. Our parish has a big number of undocumented people here, people who can't pay their rent. We also need to fund their short-term financial needs."

With the Commissioner's Office and MLBPA headquartered in Manhattan, two storied teams in New York and about one-third of Major League cities directly affected by the storm, this obviously is a disaster that struck home for baseball. But it's one that touches every community in some way, and baseball is gathering its resources to help.

Living right in the path of the destruction, the Yankees were among the first clubs to step up to support relief efforts, pledging $500,000 to the American Red Cross and spearheading a blood drive Friday that included tickets to a 2013 game for those who made donations to the New York Blood Center.

"As a neighbor and community member, the Yankees embrace our role of stepping forward and assisting the American Red Cross, which comes to the aid of so many people through their tireless efforts," Yankees chairman Hal Steinbrenner said in a statement announcing the donation.

Clearly, it's going to take more than the hometown team to help, and baseball's all about teamwork.

One team that already has pledged its support took team concept to the sport's pinnacle: the Giants, 2012 World Series champions after an October in which they showed resilience on a baseball field that was historic – but nothing compared to the resilience needed now in areas hit hard by Sandy.

And so it was that the Giants' victory celebration – on the steps of City Hall before the crowd of about one million that attended the parade – began with thoughts and prayers for people on the other side of the country needing help.

"As we gather together as a community today to celebrate this joyous occasion," emcee Renel Brooks-Moon said as she began the presentation, "we do want to take a moment first to recognize those impacted by Hurricane Sandy and mourn the lives lost from this disaster.

"Of course, the Giants share a rich and deep history with New York, so all of us, our thoughts and prayers go out to everyone on the East Coast affected by this disaster."

Brooks-Moon then announced to the huge crowd gathered at Civic Center Plaza that Giants players are planning to make many donations – with the Giants organization matching those donations, dollar for dollar. And she urged fans to join the effort by donating to the American Red Cross.

"Just think," she said. "Everybody here today, one dollar from all of us, what that can do. That can really, really help."

It takes neighbors coming together to help, and it really can add up.

The Oakland A's – the Giants' neighbor in the Bay Area – announced that the team's **Community Fund** is accepting monetary donations to help those affected by Sandy. They'll be sending the proceeds to the Salvation Army, which is providing mobile feeding units, shelters and clean-up kits, and the Humane Society of the United States, which is helping animal rescue teams and providing supplies to animal shelters.

Team by team, fan by fan, neighbor by neighbor, baseball can help the relief effort following one of the worst natural disasters in the nation's history.

In the days and weeks ahead, baseball will be part of the healing process for the region devastated by Superstorm Sandy, and the message will continue to be spread on MLB.com and MLB Network and in every possible way in every city in Major League Baseball's vast neighborhood of teams and fans:

Please donate to the **American Red Cross, the Salvation Army** and **Feeding America.**

Source: Article authors: John Schlegel and Mark Newman; http://washington.nationals.mlb.com/news/article.jsp?ymd=20121102&content_id=40155972&vkey=news_chc&c_id=chc. Rightsholder: MLB.com.

Summary

Chapter 6 focuses on the critical market selection decisions, also referred to as segmentation, targeting, and positioning. Segmentation, the first market selection decision, is identifying consumers with common needs. Typically, the bases for segmentation of consumer markets include demographics, socioeconomics, psychographics, behaviors, and benefits. Marketers using demographic segmentation choose groups of consumers based on common ages, gender, ethnic background, and stage of the family life cycle. Geographic segmentation groups people who live in similar areas such as cities, states, regions of the country, or even countries (e.g., the United States versus international markets). Socioeconomic segmentation groups consumers on the basis of similar income levels, educational levels, and occupations. Psychographic segments are especially useful to sports marketers; they are based on consumers' lifestyles, activities, interests, and opinions. Behavioral segments are groups of consumers that are similar on the basis of consumer actions, such as how often they purchase sports products or how loyal they are when purchasing a sports product. Finally, benefits segmentation are groups of consumers attempting to satisfy similar needs by consuming the sports product together. Sports marketers may choose to segment their markets using one of the previously mentioned segmentation variables (e.g., demographics) or combine several of the bases for segmentation (e.g., geodemographic).

Once market segments have been chosen, the next market selection decision is picking a target market. Target marketing is choosing the segment or segments that will allow the organization to most effectively and efficiently achieve its marketing goals. When evaluating potential target markets, care should be taken to ensure the markets are the right size (neither too large nor too small), reachable (accessible), measurable (i.e., size, purchasing power, and characteristics of the segments can be measured), and demonstrate behavioral variation (i.e., consumers share common characteristics within the target market).

The final market selection decision is positioning. After the target market has been chosen, sports marketers want to position their products or fix them in the minds of the target markets. Positioning is based on the perception or image that sports marketers want to develop or maintain for the sports product. For example, a minor league baseball team may want to position itself as an inexpensive, family entertainment alternative. To understand how a sports product is positioned relative to its competition, perceptual maps are developed through marketing research techniques. By looking at perceptual maps, sports marketers can identify whether they have achieved their desired image or whether they need to reposition their sports product in the minds of the target market.

Key terms

- AIO dimensions
- behavioral segmentation
- benefits segmentation
- demographic segmentation
- ethnic background
- family life cycle
- geodemographic segmentation
- geographic segmentation
- market niche
- majority fallacy
- market segmentation
- market selection decisions

- mature market
- niche marketing
- perceptual maps
- positioning
- psychographic segmentation
- reposition
- social class
- socioeconomic segmentation
- target marketing

Review questions

1. Describe the key components of market selection decisions and indicate how market selection decisions are incorporated into the larger strategic marketing process.
2. What is market segmentation? Provide some examples of how sports marketers segment the sports participant market (those who play) and the sports spectator market (those that watch).
3. Discuss the various ways to segment the sports market based on demographics. Which of the demographic bases are the most effective when segmenting the sports market and why?
4. Describe, in detail, the family life cycle and how it is used as a strategic tool when segmenting sports markets. What stage of the family life cycle are you currently in? How does this affect your sports participation and spectator behavior?
5. Provide examples of sports you believe would appeal to each of the six social class categories (upper-upper through lower-lower). What sports appeal to all social class segments?
6. What are AIOs? What are VALS? Describe the similarities and differences in obtaining each, and evaluate which is more effective at segmenting consumers for sports marketers.
7. Why is developing and maintaining an international presence important for sports marketers? What further considerations, if any, need to be taken into account when attempting to segment an international market? Provide several examples of the growth of international sports marketing.
8. What is behavioral segmentation? What are some of the common behaviors that sports marketers would use for segmentation purposes?
9. Define benefits segmentation and discuss why benefits segmentation is considered to be at the core of all segmentation. What benefits do you look for when attending a sporting event? Does your answer vary from event to event?
10. Define a target market. What are the requirements for successful target markets (i.e., how should each target be evaluated)? Provide examples of sports products or services that target two or more distinct markets.
11. How many target markets should a sports marketer consider for a single product?
12. Describe positioning and discuss how perceptual mapping techniques are used by sports marketers. What is repositioning?

Exercises

1. Find two advertisements for sports products that compete directly with one another. For example, you may want to compare Nike running shoes with Reebok running shoes or King Cobra golf clubs with Taylormade golf clubs. How is each product segmented, targeted, and positioned? Are there more differences or similarities in these market selection decisions?
2. How is the health and fitness industry segmented in general?

Describe the segmentation, targets, and positioning of health and fitness clubs in your area.

3. You are hired as the director of sports marketing for a new minor league hockey franchise in Chicago, a city that already has an NHL team. Describe how you would segment, target, and position your new franchise.
4. Describe the primary target market for the following: NASCAR, the Kentucky Derby, "The Rhino" bowling ball, and the WNBA. Next, define a potential secondary target market for each of these sports products.
5. Interview five consumers who have recently attended a high school sporting event, five consumers who have recently attended a college sporting event, and five who have recently attended any professional sporting event. Ask them to identify why they attended this event and what benefits they were looking for. Were their needs met?
6. Develop a list of all the possible product attributes that may be considered when purchasing the following sports products: a tennis racquet, a basketball, and a mountain bike. After you have developed the list of attributes, ask five people which attributes they consider to be the most important for each product. Do all consumers agree? Are there some attributes that you may have omitted? Why are these attributes important in positioning?
7. How do you think the following races are positioned: Boston Marathon, "Run Like Hell" 5k Halloween Race, and the Bowling Green 10k Classic? Draw a two-dimensional perceptual map to illustrate the positioning of each race.
8. Provide examples of individual athletes, teams, and sports (leagues) that have had to develop repositioning strategies.
9. Find the Web sites for three professional sports franchises and go to their ticket section. How many special promotions do they offer? Which segment of the population is being targeted by each promotion? Are any segments excluded? If so, create a promotion targeting that segment and explain why it would be effective.
10. Choose a professional sports team that performs poorly in attendance. Locate its Facebook page on the Internet. (If you cannot find it, choose another team.) Examine the content of the page. Are any special events or promotions being planned? How many friends/fans does the team have? As far as you can tell, what kinds of people are these (i.e. college students, professionals, families, etc.)? Develop a segmentation strategy that revolves around Facebook. How would you appeal to each segment?

Internet exercises

1. Using the Internet, find the demographic profile for fans attending the LPGA (women's tour) versus the PGA (men's tour). Are there differences? Use this information to comment on the market selection decisions for the LPGA.
2. Find two Internet sites that target children interested in sports and two Internet sites that target the mature market. Note any similarities and differences between the sites.
3. Find two Internet sites for soccer. One site should focus on U.S. soccer, whereas the other focus should be international. Comment on the relative positioning of soccer in the United States versus abroad

based on information found on the Internet.

Endnotes

1 James McNeal, "Tapping the Three Kids' Markets," *American Demographics* (1998); James McNeal, "Kids in 2010," *American Demographics* (1999).
2 Dan Cook, "Lunchbox Hegemony: Kids & the Marketplace, Then & Now," *LiP Magazine* (August 20, 2001).
3 L. Coffey, "10 Ways to Get a Grip on Sports Costs for Kids (2010); Mogosport, "10 Ways to Save Money in Youth Sports" (May 23, 2011). Available from: http://mogosport.wordpress.com/tag/youth-sports/.
4 Harris Poll, *YouthPulse*, Harris Interactive (2012). Available from: http://www.harrisinteractive.com/.
5 NBA.com. *NBA Cares: Bigger than Basketball* (2013). [Online]. Available from: http://www.nba.com/2013communityreport/.
6 "NBA Care is Turning Five," Unicef United States Fund (October 30, 2010). Available from: http://www.unicefusa.org/2010/10/nba-cares-anniversary.html, accessed June 17, 2014.
7 United States Census Bureau. *Population Projections* (2013). [Online]. Available from: http://www.census.gov/population/projections/data/national/2012.
8 Street & Smith's Sport Business Journal, "What are Today's Youth Playing and Watching," *Sports Business Journal* In Depth (March 27, 2006).
9 Kaiser Foundation, "Generation M2:Media in the Lives of 8–18 Year Olds" (January 20, 2010).
10 The 2012 Statistical Abstract. Census.gov 2012, accessed June 17, 2014.
11 *The State of Aging and Health in America 2013*, National Center for Chronic Disease Prevention and Health Promotion Division of Population Health, Department of Health and Human Services, Washington D.C. Available from: http://www.cdc.gov/features/agingandhealth/state_of_aging_and_health_in_america_2013.pdf, accessed June 17, 2014.
12 http://www.suddenlysenior.com/seniorfacts.html.
13 The 2012 Statistical Abstract. Census.gov 2012, accessed June 17, 2014.
14 ManateesBaseball.com. Available from: http://www.milb.com/content/page.jsp?sid=t503&ymd=20091218&content_id=7830080&vkey=team2, accessed January 25, 2014.
15 Yael Kohen, "Game Changer," *Marie Claire* (July 18, 2012). [Online]. Available from: http://www.marieclaire.com/celebrity-lifestyle/articles/female-sports-kim-ng.
16 Scott Goldberg, "Why the NFL Struggles to Attract Female Fans," *Digital Wire Media* (December 5, 2006). Available from: http://www.dmwmedia.com/news/2006/12/05/why-the-nfl-struggles-to-attract-female-fans, accessed June 18, 2014.
17 Nancy DeVault. "Good Ol' Boys (and Girls) Play Football," *Orlando Family Magazine*. Available from: http://www.orlandofamilymagazine.com/current-issue/realatively-speaking/good-ol-boys-and-girls-play-football/, Copyright © 2014, accessed June 17, 2014.
18 National Sporting Goods Association, *NSGA Participation Report 2011*, NSGA.org.
19 Campbell Gibson and Kay Jung, "Historical Census Statistics on Population Totals By Race, 1790 to 1990, and By Hispanic Origin, 1970 to 1990, For The United States, Regions, Divisions, and States," Working Paper Series No. 56 (September 2002). Population Division, U. S. Census Bureau.
20 Don Garber, *Major League Soccer State of the League Address* (July 2000).
21 "Group Seven Communications, Inc. Launches 'Deportes Hoy,' The Premier Spanish-Language Sports Daily" (January 22, 1998). Available from: www.guide-p.infoseek.com.
22 Irvine Clark III and Ryan Mannion, "Marketing Sport to Asian American Consumers," *Sport Marketing Quarterly* (2006), pp. 15, 20–28. Available from: http://www.docstoc.com/docs/139354940/Marketing-Sport-to-Asian-American-Consumerspdf.
23 CDC, National Center for Health Statistics (November 21, 2013). Available from: http://www.cdc.gov/nchs/fastats/divorce.htm, accessed June 17, 2014.
24 Tom C. Wilson, "The Paradox of Social Class and Sport involvement," *International Review for the Sociology of Sport*, vol. 37, no. 1 (2002), 5–16.
25 NASCAR Fan Base Demographics. Scarborough Research USA (2009).
26 Michael Solomon, *Consumer Behavior*, 3rd ed. (Upper Saddle River, NJ: Prentice Hall, 1996).
27 VALS, Strategic Business Insights. Available from: http://www.strategicbusinessinsights.com/vals/, accessed June 18, 2014.
28 Christopher Dragicevich, "NBA to Become More Popular Internationally Than Domestically, Liberty Voice," *Guardian Liberty Voice* (March 18, 2014). Available from: http://guardianlv.com/2014/03/nba-to-become-more-popular-internationally-than-domestically/, accessed June 18, 2014.
29 NFL International. Available from: http://

www.nfl.com/global/programming, accessed June 18, 2014.
30 Ronald Powell, 2006, "Commercial Model May Be Stadiums Future," *Union-Tribune, San Diego* (December 28, 2006). Available from: http://www.utsandiego.com/sports/chargers/20061228-9999-1n28finance.html, accessed June 17, 2014.
31 Jon Morgan, "Orioles Makeover Likely to Put Sales in Foul Territory," *The Baltimore Sun* (August 2, 2000), 1A.
32 Mark Pritchard and Christopher Negro, "Sport Loyalty Programs and Their Influence on Fan Relationships," *International Journal of Sports Marketing and Sponsorship*, vol. 3 (2001), 317–338.
33 Nike, Inc. SWOT. Available from: www.scribd.com/doc/52065502/swot-analysis-of-nike.
34 Sam Fullerton and H. Robert Dodge, "An Application of Market Segmentation in a Sports Marketing Arena: We All Can't Be Greg Norman," *Sport Marketing Quarterly*, vol. 4, no. 3 (1995), 42–47.
35 *PRIZM NE Method Summary* (2004). Available from: http://www.uvm.edu/rsenr/gradgis/advanced/prizm_method.pdf, accessed June 18, 2014.
36 Jim Hanas, "Going Pro: What's with all these Second-Tier Sports?" *Advertising Age* (January 29, 2007).
37 "NFL Fans on Facebook." Available from: http://www.facebook.com/notes/facebook-data-science/nfl-fans-on-facebook/10151298370823859, accessed February 26, 2014.
38 William Neal, "Overview of Perceptual Mapping" (1988). Available from: http://www.sdr-consulting.com/article11.html.
39 Team Garmin-Sharp Pro Cycling Team, *Garmin* (2013). [Online]. Available from: http://www.slipstreamsports.com/.
40 Juliet Macur, "Welcoming the Testing Needle, Team Battles Cycling's Image," *The New York Times* (February 13, 2007), A1.
41 BBC Sport Cycling, "Lance Armstrong Charged by US Anti-Doping Agency" (June 29, 2012). Available from: http://www.bbc.com/sport/0/cycling/18655970, accessed February 25, 2014.
42 "Lance Armstrong Receives Lifetime Ban And Disqualification Of Competitive Results For Doping Violations Stemming From His Involvement In The United States Postal Service Pro-Cycling Team Doping Conspiracy, USADA." Usada.org, accessed November 10, 2012.

PART III

Planning the Sports Marketing Mix

CHAPTER 7

Sports product concepts

After completing this chapter, you should be able to:

- Define sports products and differentiate between goods and services.
- Explain how sports products and services are categorized.
- Define branding and discuss the guidelines for choosing an effective brand name.
- Discuss the branding process in detail.
- Examine the advantages and disadvantages of licensing from the perspective of the licensee and licensor.
- Identify the dimensions of service quality and goods quality.
- Define product design and explain how product design is related to product quality.

Think about attending a Major League Baseball game at Wrigley Field in Chicago. Inside the stadium you find vendors selling game programs, scorecards, Major League Baseball-licensed merchandise, and plenty of food and drink. An usher kindly escorts you to your seat assignment and ensures that your seat is clean before you begin to enjoy the entertainment. During the game, you are exposed to more product choices.

Every game experience presents us with a number of opportunities to purchase and consume sports products. Some of the products, such as the scorecards, represent a pure good, whereas others, such as the game itself, represent a pure service. Each sports product represents a business challenge with incredible upward and downward potential. In this chapter, we explore the multidimensional nature of sports products.

Defining sports products

A **sports product** is a good, a service, or any combination of the two that is designed to provide benefits to a sports spectator, participant, or sponsor. Within this definition, the market concept discussed in Chapter 1 is reintroduced. As you recall, the marketing concept states that sports organizations are in the business of satisfying consumers' needs. To do this, products must be developed that anticipate and satisfy consumers' needs. Sports marketers sell products based on the benefits they offer consumers. These benefits are so critical to marketers that sometimes products are defined as "bundles of benefits." For example, the sport of lacrosse has emerged as one of the nation's fastest-growing sports. Lacrosse has been tagged as "the fastest game on two feet" and those "feet" are rapidly moving across the country.[1] Colleges and High Schools are now adding Lacrosse to their athletic repertoire as the sport gains attention in the areas that knew little if anything about the game in the past. Lacrosse originated from Native Americans who often played the game as a way to train for warfare. The game may not be played for the same reasons today, but the action and intensity that is displayed is still highly competitive and exciting providing a "bundle of benefits" for the consumer.

What has caused the game to spread so quickly? There are four main factors. 1. Increased visibility in the National Media. 2. Development of a Professional League. 3. Growth of new High School and College Programs. 4. Growth of Youth Programs. Knowledge of the game is spreading, making it no longer appear to be in the dark to the general public. The game is also very appealing. It is fast-paced, full of non-stop action, provides great exercise, and is less expensive to play than many traditional sports. It is a good mix between many popular American sports such as football,

Photo 7.1 This baseball, glove, and bat represent pure goods.

Source: Shutterstock.com

Photo 7.2 This competition represents a pure service.

Source: Courtesy of Cory Hindel

basketball, and hockey. The whole of America is starting to discover Lacrosse and it is spreading just as fast as the game itself.

In addition to sports and sporting goods, athletes can also be thought of as sports products that possess multiple benefits. For example, NBA teams are currently seeking players who can perform multiple roles on the court rather than those who have more specialized skills. The player who can rebound, is great defensively, dribbles well, and can play the post is invaluable to the franchise. The classic example of the "hybrid" player with multiple skills was Magic Johnson, who played center and guard in the 1980 NBA Finals. Today's NBA stars, such as the Boston Celtics' Kevin Garnett and Miami Heat's LeBron James and Dwayne Wade, exemplify the versatile player who offers many benefits to the team.

A number of athletes offer a unique bundle of benefits both on and off the court. Consider former star center, Shaquille O'Neal. The Shaq has been a top performer, helping teams such as the Lakers earn a three-peat championship and he was one of three players in NBA history to be selected to the NBA All-Star Game for 15 seasons. In addition to Shaq's 18 seasons as a player, he was the oldest active player in the NBA, has made and appeared in several movies and raps, written his autobiography, owns his own sportswear company, starred in his own reality show titled *Shaq vs.*, and is currently an NBA analysts for TNT. The 7-foot-1-inch center has been aligned with numerous endorsement contracts, from Taco Bell to Payless Shoes to Buick, and has helped a number of nonprofit organizations. Most recently, Shaq has utilized the social network of Twitter as a way to communicate with fans and enhance his brand. All of these activities contribute to the "product" we know as Shaq.[2]

Goods and services as sports products

Our definition of products includes goods and services. It is important to understand the differences in these two types of products to plan and implement the strategic sports marketing process. Because services such as watching a game are being produced (by the players) and consumed (by the spectators) simultaneously, there is no formal channel of distribution. However, when you purchase a pure good, such as a pair of hockey skates, they must be produced by a manufacturer (e.g., Bauer), sent to a retailer (e.g., Sports Authority), and then sold to you. This formal channel of distribution requires careful planning and managing. Let us explore some of the other differences between goods and services.

Goods are defined as tangible, physical products that offer benefits to consumers. Obviously, sporting goods stores sell tangible products such as tennis balls and racquets, hockey equipment, exercise equipment, and so on. By contrast, **services** are usually described as intangible, nonphysical products. For instance, the competitive aspect of any sporting event (i.e., the game itself) or an experience such as receiving an ice-skating lesson reflects pure services.

CAREER SPOTLIGHT

Rodger Collins, President Packaged Beverages, Dr. Pepper Snapple Group

Question: From your perspective, what is most successful . . . new to the world products, new product category entries, product line extensions, product improvement, or repositioning?

Answer: At Dr. Pepper marketing is implemented in four so called buckets. The first bucket is the heavy or core user. The second bucket is the light user. The third bucket would be the line extension or innovation, such as launching Dr. Pepper Cherry and using Kiss as the spokesman. Finally a cultural approach, for example, Dr. Pepper is targeting the Hispanic community.

Question: In looking at the consumers' perspective, which of the following do you target, discontinuous innovations, dynamic continuous innovations, or continuing innovations?

Answer: We look internally, where the value of a product or service is with the correct investment. An example would be the Crush brand, which was idle until we utilized the brand exploiting the flavor line with a powerful trademark and marketed it across the country. As for the citrus beverage line Mountain Dew holds the market. We look to utilize Sun Drop which is popular in the southeast and to become a player in this product line.

Question: How does your company go about implementing the new product development process?

Answer: We have a committee that receives concepts from our marketing department on all new products. All new products are developed internally through our research and development laboratory. We have doctors in our labs developing all of our new products. As for market categories, we test and launch products depending on market segmentation and focus groups.

Question: How does your company go about dealing with problems in marketing?

Answer: All market research is considered to be on the high end. Therefore it is discounted and we approach this utilizing low end numbers. Formulas are in place in this company to actualize all numbers into useable material.

Question: Can you give me some examples of your company's products and the product life cycle?

Answer: A good example would be Snapple; a twenty year old product that started as a high end, healthy beverage. Between competitors and a lack of advertising Snapple went from a growth to a mature to a declining product. Two years ago we had a product restage with new packaging, ads, and a conversion to the use of real sugar in the beverage. This plan has completely paid off. We must be careful because this beverage line is quick to decline because of competition and copy cats. We have another beverage that is in the introduction stage. This is Mott's Medley, which competes with V8's Fusion. We are in the early stages. We have priced this beverage low, so as to create a larger customer base. The jury is out. Finally we have Dr. Pepper. A beverage that is 100 years old that we do not feel has reached the maturity stage. We feel we are still in the growth stage. We believe line extensions will allow us to continue to grow despite the cycling of the market. As for declining brands, we have been harvesting Royal Crown Cola. We have put no money into it because of the competition of Coke and Pepsi and are somewhat treading water with this beverage. We have not deleted any brands, only packaging on many different products.

Question: How much stock does your company put into fads, classics, and seasonal products?

Answer: We never look at products like fads. We look at them as innovations. If we have the ability to manufacture and the capacity to distribute with no capital upstart we will look to utilize the product. We have very limited seasonal products, but Iced Tea and Lemonade sells better in the summer.

Question: What techniques do you employ in the product diffusion process to speed the adoptions of your products?

Answer: With our new products we utilize target marketing, the internet, and social media, especially when dealing with the younger demographic. As for an older demographic we employ coupons, especially at checkouts in grocery stores with a coupon printed on the back of the receipt.

Question: Can you speak of your new Venom line of energy drinks and your managing of the products?

Answer: We developed this line and launched it in 2007 and it is in the growth category. We feel there is a large amount of potential. We are focusing on the distribution and availability of this product targeting young males. We have created a partnership with Andretti motor sports and are sponsoring Marco Andretti, a young male Indy car driver. We have also utilized exit sampling, focusing on handing out the product at big stadiums where young males are likely to attend. We have made a large investment into the development marketing and distribution of this product as we hope it will pay off in the future.

It is easy to see why soccer balls and exercise equipment are classified as pure goods and why the intangible nature of the game constitutes a pure service, but what about other sports products? For example, sporting events typically offer a variety of pure goods (such as food, beverages, and merchandise). However, even these goods have a customer service component. The responsiveness, courtesy, and friendliness of the service provider are intangible components of the service encounter.

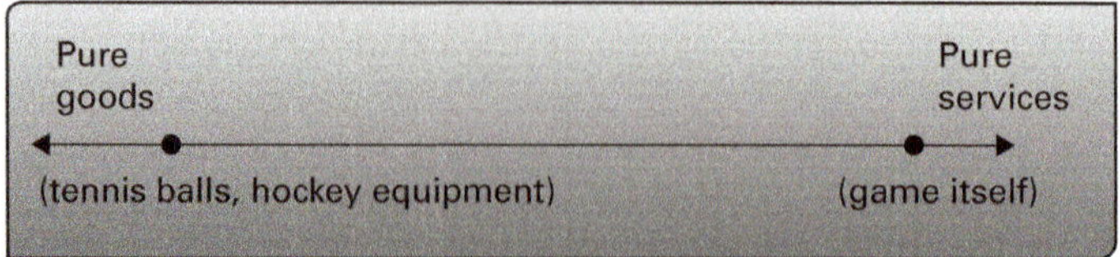

Figure 7.1 The goods–services continuum

Most sports products do not fall so neatly into two distinct categories, but possess characteristics of both goods and services. Figure 7.1 shows the goods–services continuum. On one end, we have sporting goods. At the other end of the continuum, we have, almost exclusively, sports services. For example, a sports service that has received considerable attention in the past few years is the fantasy sports camp. Sports camps from a variety of team and individual sports have sprung up to appeal to the aging athlete. For instance, the Chicago Cubs Fantasy Camp offers lifelong memories and mementos for $4,500.00. During the week, campers receive the following tangible goods: a personalized uniform with name and number, engraved Louisville Slugger bat, baseball autographed by an instructor, baseball card with the camper's picture and camp stats, a DVD of the "Big Game" vs. the former major leaguers, and a glossy 8' ×10' team photo, and an opportunity to play under the lights at Wrigley Field.

Thus far, the distinction between goods and services has been based on the tangible aspects of the sports product. In addition to the degree of tangibility, goods and services are differentiated on the basis of perishability, separability, and standardization. These distinctions are important because they form the foundation of product planning in the strategic sports marketing process. Because of their importance, let us take a look at each dimension.

Tangibility

Tangibility refers to the ability to see, feel, and touch the product. Interestingly, the strategy for pure goods often involves stressing the intangible benefits of the product. For example, advertisements for Nike's Dri-FIT performance apparel highlight not only the comfort of the product, but also the way the clothing will make you "ready to take on the challenges of wild and wicked workouts." Similarly, Formula 1 racing is paired with TAG Heuer watches in a sponsorship agreement and product line that leverages the benefits of both brands by asking "What are you made of?" By pairing with Formula 1 racing, Tag Heuer hopes to capitalize on the intangible attributes of excitement, danger, excellence, and pushing yourself to be the best.

However, the strategy for intangible services is to "tangibilize them."[3]

Standardization and consistency

Another characteristic that distinguishes goods from services is the degree of **standardization**. This refers to receiving the same level of quality over repeat purchases. Because sporting goods are tangible, the physical design of a golf ball is manufactured with very little variability. This is even truer today, as many organizations focus on how to continuously improve their manufacturing processes and enhance their product quality.

Pure services, however, reflect the other end of the standardization and consistency continuum. For example, think about the consistency associated with different individual and team athletic performances. How many times have you heard an announcer state before a game, "Which team (or player) will show up today?" Meaning, will the team play well or poorly on that given day?

The Duke University men's basketball team, under the leadership of Mike Krzyzewski, has been one of the most consistent teams in college sports over the past 25 seasons. This, however, does not guarantee they will win the night you attend the game. In recent years, teams such as the high-performing New England Patriots have had very successful regular seasons, but have faced the embarrassing distinction of being eliminated in the first round of the NFL playoffs. Historically, Buffalo Bills had the embarrassing distinction of being the only team ever to lose four consecutive Super Bowls.

Consider another example of the lack of consistency within a sporting event. You may attend a doubleheader and see your favorite team lose the first game 14 to 5 and win the second game of the day by a score of 1 to 0. One of the risks associated with using individual athletes or teams to endorse products is the high degree of variability associated with their performance from day to day and year to year. Because sports marketers have no control over the consistency of the sports product, they must focus on those things that can be controlled, such as promotions, stadium atmosphere, and, to some extent, pricing.

Perishability

Perishability refers to the ability to store or inventory "pure goods," whereby services are lost if not consumed. Goods may be inventoried or stored if they are not purchased immediately, although there are many costs associated with handling this inventory. The length of time a product may be inventoried, a product's **shelf life**, varies. Most sport and entertainment services have a limited shelf life and are perishable only during the life of the exhibition. Each exhibition has an exclusive time frame that encompasses a unique set of attributes, therefore, they cannot be renewed. Although future reproductions via video rebroadcast and match play may occur, the unique intangible characteristics cannot be renewed. For example, if one was planning to attend a 1:00 football game but has car trouble and ends up not arriving until 4:30, most likely, exception being overtime or major delay, the shelf life of the exhibition has expired. If a tennis professional is offering lessons, but no students enroll between the hours of 10:00 A.M. and noon, this time (and money) is lost. This "down time" in which the service provider is available but there is no demand is called **idle product capacity**. Idle product capacity results in decreased profitability. In the case of the tennis pro, there is a moderate inventory cost associated with the professional's salary.

Another example with much higher inventory costs is a professional hockey team that is not filling the stands. Consider the New York Islanders, the NHL team with the poorest average attendance and lowest percentage of attendance to capacity (82 percent) in the 2012 to 2013 season. The costs of producing one professional game include everything from the "astronomical" salaries of the players to the basic costs of lighting and heating the arena. If paying fans are not in the seats, the performance or service will perish, never to be recouped. As a general rule of thumb, the most perishable products in business are airline seats, hotel rooms, and athletic event tickets.

In an effort to reduce the problem of idle product capacity, sports marketers attempt to stimulate demand in off-peak periods by manipulating the other marketing mix variables. For example, if tennis lessons are not in demand from 10:00 A.M. to noon, the racquet club may offer reduced fees for enrolling during these times.

Separability

Another factor that distinguishes goods from services is **separability**. If a consumer is purchasing a new pair of running shoes at a major shoe store chain, such as The Athlete's Foot, the quality of the good (the Reebok shoes) can be separated from the quality of the service (delivered by The Athlete's Foot sales associate). Although it is possible to separate the good from the person providing the service, these often overlap. What this suggests is that manufacturers will selectively choose the retailers that will best represent their goods. In addition, manufacturers and retailers often provide detailed training to ensure salespeople are knowledgeable about the numerous brands that are inventoried.

As we move along the goods–services continuum from pure goods toward pure services, there is less separability. In other words, it becomes more difficult to separate the service received from the service provider. In the case of an athletic event, there is no separation between the athlete, the entertainment, and the fan. The competition is being produced and consumed simultaneously. As such, sport marketers can capitalize on a team or athlete when they are performing well. When things are going poorly, they may have to rely on other aspects of the game (food, fun, and promotions) to satisfy fans. The Green Bay Packers have sold the history and tradition of the team to the fans. Despite several losing seasons the team has sold out every game since 1960, with the fans braving the elements in support of their team. These fans were rewarded with another Super Bowl victory in the 2010–2011 season.

Classifying sports products

In addition to categorizing products based on where they fall on the goods–services continuum, a number of other classification schemes exist. For sports organizations that have a variety of products, the concepts of product line and product mix become important strategic considerations. Let us look at these two concepts in the context of a goods-oriented sports organization and a services-oriented sports organization.

A **product line** is a group of products that are closely related because they satisfy a class of needs, are used together, are sold to the same customer groups, are distributed through the same type of outlets, or fall within a given price range. Wilson Sporting Goods sells many related product lines such as shoes, bats, gloves, softballs, golf clubs, and tennis racquets. The total assortment of product lines that a sports organization sells is the **product mix**. Table 7.1 illustrates the relationship between the product lines and product mix for Wilson Sporting Goods. The number of different product lines the organization offers is referred to as the breadth of the product mix. If these product lines are closely related in terms of the goods and services offered to consumers, then there is a high degree of product consistency.

Nike recently increased the breadth of its product mix by adding new brands and product lines. The company acquired Converse and its famous Chuck Taylor All-Star shoes, as well as Hurley International, a surf- and skateboard apparel brand. Other new acquisitions include Cole Haan dress shoes and Umbro sports apparel. The strategic advantage of this related diversification is the use of Nike's established marketing muscle.[4] Synergy in distribution and promotion, as well as strong brand identification, should make Nike's launch into new markets a successful venture.

Table 7.1 Wilson Sporting Goods product mix

Baseball	Basketball	Football	Golf	Racquetball	Soccer
Gloves DeMarini Bats Baseballs Protective gear Bags Accessories Uniforms	Accessories Basketballs Uniforms	Footballs Tees/ accessories Youth protective uniforms NFL accessories	Irons Woods Wedges Putters Complete sets Balls Bags Gloves Accessories Retired models	Racquets Gloves Eyewear Racquetballs Footwear Bags String Accessories Apparel	Soccer balls Protective gear Bags
Volleyball	**Softball Fastpitch**	**Softball Slowpitch**	**Squash**	**Tennis**	**Badminton**
Outdoor Balls Indoor Balls Uniforms Ball carts Bags	Gloves Bats Balls Protective gear Accessories	Gloves Bats Balls Accessories	Racquets Bags String Grips	Balls Footwear Legacy footwear Accessories Platform tennis Court equipment Retired models Raquets Bags String Grips	Racquets Shuttlecocks String

Source: Wilson Sporting Goods, www.wilsonsports.com.

Joycelyn Hayward, the manager of a sporting goods store that carries Nike, summed it up best by saying, "Nike's ability to churn out innovative products and marketing plans has kept it ahead of rivals".[5]

Today, Nike is focusing on increasing their talent pool of athletes and expanding their growing product lines in new sports. For example, LeBron James joined the Phil Knight stable in 2003 for a $90 million, multiyear endorsement contract prior to playing a college or professional game. Nike certainly pinned its hopes on James to invigorate sales in the high-end market. This risk paid off as 2005 was a record year for sales and profitability for Nike who increased revenues by 12 percent from the previous fiscal year to $13.7 billion.[6] Nike, under the initial leadership of Knight, is quickly moving into international markets and these endeavors accounted for 55 percent of Nike's total of $25.3 billion of revenue in 2013.[7] Knight will always be remembered as the man who realized the true marketing power of sports celebrities.

The depth of the product lines describes the number of individual products that comprise that line. The greater the number of variations in the product line, the deeper the line. For example, the Wilson basketball product line currently features over 60 different basketballs, 6 of which are indoor and 56 of which are indoor/outdoor. Now, think about how the product concepts might relate to a more service-oriented sports organization, such as a professional sports franchise. All these organizations have gone beyond selling the core product, the game itself, and moved into other profitable

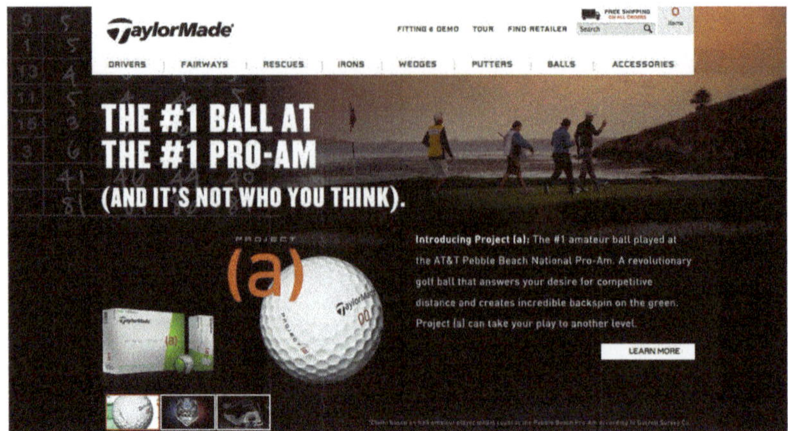

Web 7.1 TaylorMade-Adidas Golf extends their product line with Adidas golf footwear and apparel.

Source: © 2014 TaylorMade Golf Company, Inc.

areas, such as the sale of licensed merchandise, memorabilia, and fantasy camps. In essence, sports organizations have expanded their product lines or broadened their product mix.

Understanding the depth, breadth, and consistency of the product offerings is important from a strategic perspective. Sports organizations might consider adding product lines, and, therefore, widen the product mix. For example, Nike is using this strategy and capitalizing on its strong brand name. Alternatively, the sports organization can eliminate weak product lines and focus on its established strengths. In addition, the product lines it adds may be related to existing lines (product line consistency) or may be unrelated to existing lines (product line diversification).

Another strategic decision may be to maintain the number of product lines, but add new versions to make the line deeper. For instance, the MLS has 19 teams divided into Eastern and Western conferences, 16 in the U.S. and 3 in Canada, and is scheduled to grow to 20 teams in the near future. All of these product planning strategies require examining the overarching marketing goals and the organizational objectives, as well as carefully considering consumers' needs.

Product characteristics

Products are sometimes described as "bundles of benefits" designed to satisfy consumers' needs.[8] These "bundles" consist of numerous important attributes or characteristics that, when taken together, create the total product. These **product characteristics**, which include branding, quality, and design, are illustrated in Figure 7.2. It is important to note that each of the product characteristics interacts with the others to produce the total product. Branding is dependent on product quality; product quality is contingent on product design; and so on. Although these product features (i.e., branding, quality, and design) are interdependent, we examine each independently in the following sections.

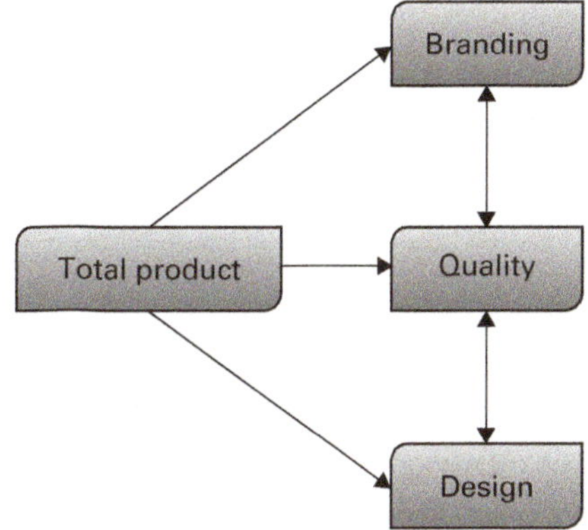

Figure 7.2 Product characteristics

SPOTLIGHT ON INTERNATIONAL SPORTS MARKETING

The 5 worst athlete-endorsed products of all time

Athletes-endorsed products are an enigmatic paradox that has plagued me for quite some time.

In layman's terms, athletes have long tried to attach their names to companies or products that have left us shaking our heads or wiping the tears of laughter from our eyes.

Raffy Palmeiro's Viagra advertisement a few years back was a fine case of both. Alas, seasoned slugger and seemingly impotent Palmeiro is not the only man who has made some downright dumb choices in marketing.

This brief list is a compilation of some of the more bizarre athlete endorsements of the past few decades.

David Robinson Doritos Raft

It's a hot August day, and the sun beats down, as you dream of Tom Brady's UGG Boot endorsements and Roethlisberger jerky.

You sit up and slowly walk toward the nearest body of water, but you're not quite sure you want to go all the way under.

Really, there's only one thing to do – grab your David Robinson Doritos raft!

What was the thought process here? David Robinson was a Navy man, but the Navy seldom uses life rafts like the one pictured above (or so I've read).

I also worry about the size of the raft itself, I doubt it could hold one of the Robinson's limbs, let alone his whole body.

Shaq Fu for Sega

Shaquille O'Neal has never been shy about trying different things. He has rapped, protected and served, acted, commentated, competed and headlined an awesome 1990s video game.

Ladies and gentlemen, I give you "Shaq Fu," the game that, well, gamers around the world regard as the worst fighting game ever created. The old mantra says not to judge a book by its cover, but anyone who judged this game by the cover was rewarded with some extra time and money.

There is a website that has dedicated itself to destroying all

7

remaining copies of the game left in existence. It's facetious to an extent, or at least, I hope.

Query of the day

What would you rather do for an hour?

A) Play several rousing rounds of Shaq Fu

B) Watch Kazam

C) Listen to Shaq's Diesel album.

D) Wait in line for Shinedown tickets?

Carson Palmer Goes "Long-Er"

Why in the world would Carson Palmer sign off on this? Who is his agent? Was Mark Sanchez unavailable?

How psyched was the guy who suggested they do the mustard as football laces pattern on the wiener when his idea was accepted? Is this why Palmer is no longer a Bengal? What was the runner up tag-line to "GO Long-er."

My stomach is rumbling!

Big Ben Does Beef Jerky Right

While Ben Roethlisberger is high in both protein and fat, his "Super Championship Edition" jerky – whatever that means – is low fat.

With Big Ben's numerous indiscretions over the past few seasons, he is somewhat of an easy target. To be entirely honest though, any athlete who endorses his own beef product should expect a few punches and pokes.

What is the obsession with quarterbacks and meaty byproduct?

Tom Brady Loves UGG Boots

Personally, I am yet to meet a man who dons UGG Boots. Then again, I am not all that worldly and seldom spend time with society types like Tom Brady.

It's hard to take shots at Tom Brady with all the success he has had in his career, and while it's possible he can transform the UGG brand into something men will actually wear, I think this will be a tough sell.

Source: Article author: Adam Dietz. Rightsholder: Bleacher Report; http://bleacherreport.com/articles/1165407-the-worst-athlete-endorsed-products-of-all-time?search_query=athlete endorsements#/articles/1434868-the-50-biggest-sports-fails-of-2012.

Branding

What first comes to mind when you hear University of Notre Dame, Green Bay, or Adidas? It is likely that the Fighting Irish name, along with the Lucky Leprechaun ready to battle, comes to mind for Notre Dame. The Packers are synonymous with Green Bay, Wisconsin, and the symbolic three stripes are synonymous with Adidas. All these characteristics are important elements of branding.

Branding is a name, design, symbol, or any combination that a sports organization (or individual athlete as is the case with David Beckham) uses to help differentiate its products from the competition. Three important branding concepts are brand name, brand marks, and trademarks. A **brand name** refers to the element of the brand that can be vocalized, such as the Nike Air Jordan, the Pittsburgh Penguins, and the UNC Tarheels. When selecting a brand name for sporting goods or a team name, considerable marketing effort is required to ensure the name symbolizes strength and confidence. Because choosing a name is such a critical decision, sports marketers sometimes use the following guidelines for selecting brand names:

- The name should be positive; distinctive; generate positive feelings and associations; be easy to remember and to pronounce. For team names, the positive associations include those linked with a city or geographic area.
- The name should be translatable into a dynamite attitude-oriented logo. As an example of a successful logo choice, consider Kansas City's Major League Soccer team, who recently changed their name from the Wizards to Sporting Kansas City. CEO and managing partner Robb Heineman stated that the name change "continues the forward-thinking and innovation. This is all about our connection to the community and us trying to be innovative in what we're trying to do."[9]
- The name should imply the benefits the sports product delivers. For example, the name communicates the product attributes the target market desires.
- The name should be consistent with the image of the rest of the product lines, organization, and city. Again, this is especially important for cities naming their sports franchises. One example of this concept in action is MLS's Columbus Crew.[10] The Crew was chosen to represent the Columbus community in a positive manner. The name suggests the hard work, do-not-quit attitude that people in the Columbus community value.
- The name should be legally and ethically permissible. That is, the name cannot violate another organization's trademarks or be seen as offensive to any group of people. For example, a great many team names with reference to (and perceived negative connotations of) Native Americans have been changed or are under scrutiny (e.g., Miami University of Ohio Redskins to RedHawks, Atlanta Braves, and Washington Redskins). The NCAA decided in 2005 to ban the use of American Indian mascots by sports teams during its postseason tournaments. Schools using American Indian mascots or nicknames would also be barred from hosting NCAA postseason tournaments.

  While choosing a team/brand name is critical to marketing success, some teams and leagues haven't fared so well in the name game. For example, the National Lacrosse League has had a history of poor team names.[11] The name Colorado Mammoth conjures up images such as big, slow, and extinct – not exactly a good fit for a professional athletic team. In addition, some of the University of California institutions such as UC Santa Cruz and UC Irvine have struggled to develop a positive association with the brand names of Banana Slugs and Anteaters, respectively.

A **brand mark**, also known as the **logo** or **logotype**, is the element of a brand that cannot be spoken. One of the most recognizable logos in the world is the Nike Swoosh. Interestingly, Carolyn Davidson was paid just $35 in 1971 to create the logo that now adorns Nike products, as well as CEO Phil Knight's ankle in the form of a tattoo. It's important for sports marketers to realize that while the Nike logo was created for the paltry sum of $35, the cost of changing logos and nicknames can swell to $250,000. Some of the incidental costs of changing your brand include: surveys of constituent groups, designing the logo, retaining a marketing firm, developing a new ad campaign to create awareness, repainting facilities, buying new stationery, replacing signage, creating new uniforms, and even developing a new mascot costume.[12]

SPOTLIGHT ON SPORTS MARKETING ETHICS

NCAA Native American mascot controversy

The world of intercollegiate athletics is an interesting stew to say the least.

It is a mixture of money, a smattering of egocentricity, a dash of concern for the student athlete, a yet smaller dash of perceived concern for said student athlete's actual academic progress towards a degree and then brought together with a healthy dose of public perception and dare I say EVEN MORE MONEY.

Back in 2005, the NCAA decided that it would institute a new rule:

It self-decided (as a PR move I believe) it would strong-arm schools with nicknames or mascots IT deemed "hostile or abusive"; they would no longer be allowed to keep these nicknames.

This was targeted at colleges and universities that were currently using a Native American derived name and/or symbols.

Most of these schools were small with no strong alumni bases or financial incentive to keep their respective name and made the change without any fanfare.

However, there were plenty of major universities that were presented with a proverbial pickle.

Schools such as Florida State (Seminoles), Utah (Utes), Illinois (Illini), and, to lesser extents, Central Michigan (Chippewa's), Miami of Ohio (Redskins) and North Dakota (Sioux).

The first three schools are traditional football and basketball powerhouses whose revenue annually adds tens of millions to their athletic department coffers as well as hefty sums reaching the NCAA itself.

From the schools above, Miami has changed its name to "Redhawks" with little to no opposition; North Dakota is in the process of dropping "Sioux" after 81 years upon losing its final appeal to the NCAA after many years while Florida State, Utah, Illinois and Central Michigan have kept their names after receiving "waivers" from the NCAA by proving they (currently) have the blessing and written approval of those respective tribes (Seminole, Illini, Ute and Chippewa).

Ironically, these schools (save CMU) produce millions of dollars in athletic revenue through large gate attendance, huge TV contracts and merchandising. Even more "ironic" is the fact that the NCAA actually profits twofold. It is giving the appearance on one hand of being thoughtful, respectful and politically correct while the other hand is taking fistfuls of dollars looking the other way. If they are going to enact any rule, then it should apply to all schools regardless of their circumstances. If not, then retract it.

The truth (in my opinion and millions of other fan-based polls) is that the NCAA should be involved in other things like policing an ever growing number of student athletes being arrested (some multiple times), making sure progress is made in the classroom and that graduation rates are strong (things it was actually set up to do in the first place).

Schools along with their alumni and communities should be able to decide for themselves what they want to be called. If a school thinks its current nickname is somehow offensive, then let it decide (such as Stanford University did in 1972 all by itself in dropping the nickname "Indians" in favor of "Cardinal").

If a school has a relationship with a certain tribe and they mutually agree that the name is acceptable, again let them decide. But to force schools to do what you want them to do and then go and break this rule yourself (as the NCAA is doing) AND then on top of that, still profit from it, this is ridiculous to say the least.

A final footnote to this article:

One school (the University of Iowa) has even gone a step further in this. They have now decided that they themselves will also police the ranks and will no longer schedule a school to any athletic event that still carries a Native American name and its most recent victim was the University of North Dakota.

Even though again UND is in the process of dropping the "Sioux" nickname, this is still not enough for the Iowa Hawkeye higher-ups. So, a potential track meet between the schools was recently cancelled.

Yet another "irony" is that Iowa plays in the same conference (the wealthy Big 10) as Illinois (Illini) and they meet in every NCAA sanctioned sport, every year.

FYI Iowa "enlightened" brass: the term "Hawkeye" originally appeared in the novel, "The Last of the Mohicans" written by James Fenimore Cooper. In the book, the character named Natty Bumppo is given the word "Hawkeye" as a nickname from the Delaware Indians.

Maybe the university should consider beefing up its own literature and history departments. Talk about hypocrites!!!

Fortunately, I graduated from a university where this was not an issue.

Our mascot was a feisty chicken bred for cock-fighting to entertain soldiers during the American Revolutionary War.

OOPPS, maybe I spoke to soon. Let's hope the NCAA and PETA don't read this...............................
shhhhhhhhhhhhhhh

Source: Rightsholder: Neil Kline; http://www.bernardgoldberg.com/ncaa-native-american-mascot-controversy/.

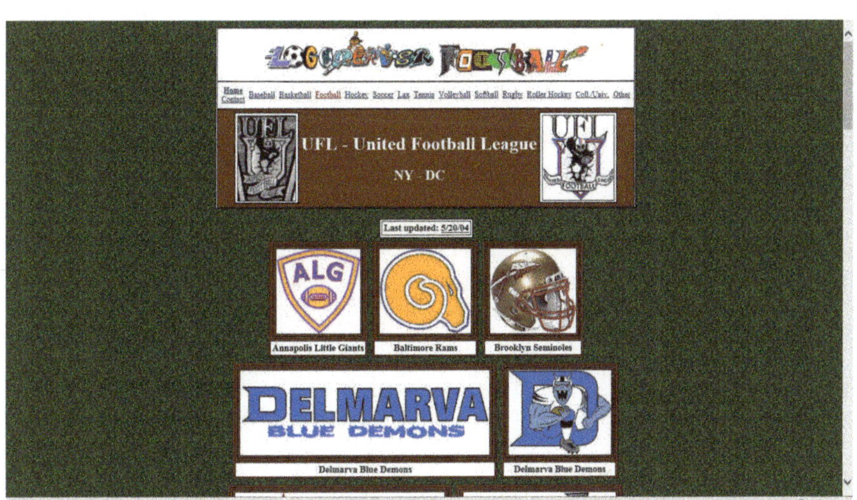

Web 7.2 Sports logos gallery on the Web

Source: http://www.baseball-almanac.com/

A **trademark** identifies that a sports organization has legally registered its brand name or brand mark and thus prevents others from using it. Unfortunately, product counterfeiting or the production of low-cost copies of trademarked popular brands is reaching new heights. Product counterfeiting and trademark infringement are especially problematic at major sporting events, such as the Super Bowl or Olympic Games. For example, Collegiate Licensing Co., a division of IMG Worldwide, which represents about 200 collegiate properties, found some 3,000 counterfeit items at football bowl games and the NCAA basketball tournament.

The branding process

The broad purpose of branding a product is to allow an organization to distinguish and differentiate itself from all others in the marketplace. Building the brand will then ultimately affect consumer behaviors, such as increasing attendance, merchandising sales, or participation in sports. However, before these behaviors are realized, several things must happen in the **branding process** shown in Figure 7.3.

First, **brand awareness** must be established. Brand awareness refers to making consumers in the desired target market recognize and remember the brand name. Only after awareness levels reach their desired objectives can brand image be addressed. After all, consumers must be aware of the product before they can understand the image the sports marketer is trying to project.

After brand awareness is established, marketing efforts turn to developing and managing a **brand image**. Brand image is described as the consumers' set of beliefs about brands, which, in turn, shape attitudes. Brand image can also be thought of as the "personality" of the brand. Organizations that sponsor sporting events are especially interested in strengthening or maintaining the image of their products through association with a sports entity (athlete, team, or league) that reflects the desired image. For instance, the marketers of Mercedes-Benz automobiles have established sponsorships with tennis events to reinforce a brand image of power, grace, and control.

Sports marketers attempt to manage beliefs that we have about a particular brand through a number of "image drivers," or factors that influence the brand image. The image drivers controlled by sports marketing efforts include product features or characteristics, product performance or quality, price, brand name, customer service, packaging, advertising, promotion, and distribution channels. Each of these image drivers contributes to creating the overall brand image. After shaping a positive brand image, sports marketers can then ultimately hope to create high levels of brand equity.

Another link in the branding process is developing high levels of brand equity. **Brand equity** is the value that the brand contributes to a product in the marketplace. In economic terms, it is the difference in value between a branded product and its generic equivalent. Consumers who believe a sport product has a high level of brand equity are more likely to be satisfied with the brand. The satisfied consumers will, in turn, become brand-loyal or repeat purchasers. Gladden, Milne, and Sutton

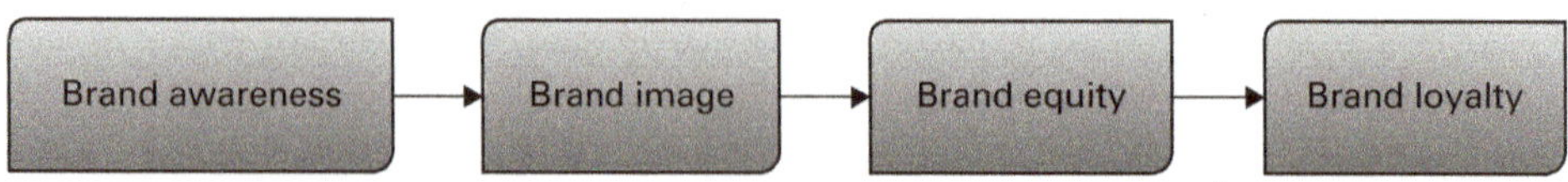

Figure 7.3 The branding process

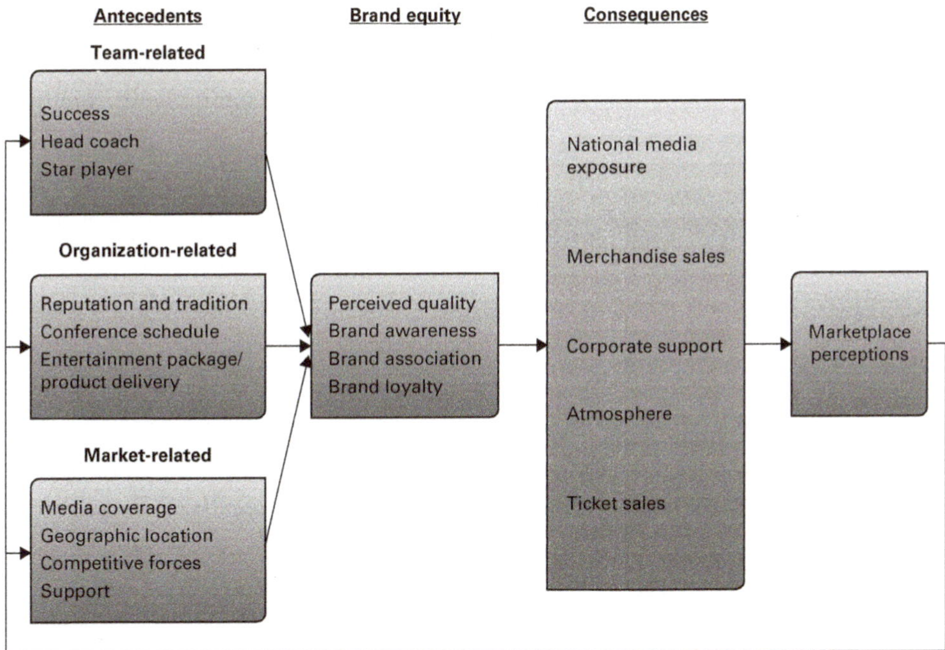

Figure 7.4 The conceptual model for assessing brand equity

have developed a unique model of assessing brand equity for the sports industry. The components of the model can be seen in Figure 7.4. The authors explain brand equity by extending the previous work of Aaker, who believes there are four major components of brand equity.[13] These are perceived quality, brand awareness, brand associations, and brand loyalty. Gladden, Milne, and Sutton describe the perceived quality of sport as the consumers' perceptions of a team's success. Obviously, this could be extended beyond the notion of a team to other sport products. Brand awareness is defined as the consumers' familiarity with a particular team or sport product. Brand associations refer to the intangible attributes of a brand or, in the case of sport, the experiential and symbolic attributes offered by an athletic team. The final component, brand loyalty, is defined as the ability to attract and retain consumers. As the authors point out, this is sometimes difficult because of the inconsistent and intangible nature of the sports product.[14]

When describing the full model of brand equity for sport, Gladden and his colleagues also discuss the antecedents and consequences of brand equity for a sports product. These antecedent conditions are particularly important for marketing managers to understand because they will have an impact on the level of brand equity. The three broad categories of antecedents include team-related factors, organization-related factors, and market-related factors.

Team-related factors are further broken down into the success of the team, head coach, and star player(s). Previous research has shown that winning or success is still a critical factor in establishing a strong brand and in achieving the desired outcomes such as merchandise sales, media exposure, and so on. Although selling an inferior core product (i.e., losing team) is never easy, it is important to underscore the notion that sports marketers must do their best to enhance those aspects of the event experience that they can control. As the accompanying article illustrates, the Miami Marlins are still making money even after a series of losing seasons.

Miami Marlins attendance reverts to old Sun Life Stadium levels

What has moving to Miami brought the Marlins? About 100 extra fans per game.

That's the current gap between this year's attendance and the average gate count for the Marlins' last season at Sun Life Stadium, the football field that owner Jeffrey Loria blamed for the team's long-standing attendance and revenue woes.

Those problems ended up following Loria to the government-owned Marlins Park, which is on track to face the worst fan rejection of a new baseball stadium in at least a generation.

"Usually you have a honeymoon effect," said J.C. Bradbury, a sports-science professor at Kennesaw State University in Atlanta who studies the business side of baseball. "It's hard to have that when the fans are predisposed not to like you."

Attendance for the Marlins hit a 15-year high with the opening of the 36,000-seat Marlins Park last year, despite lingering ire over Miami and Miami-Dade picking up most of the $634 million construction tab. But the gains didn't last long. On the heels of a losing season, Loria slashed the team's payroll by $60 million and traded most of the star players. Sales of season tickets plunged 60 percent, and the Marlins became the only Major League franchise to turn to Groupon to fill seats on Opening Day in April.

"I obviously still feel tremendously sorry about what happened last year," said Marlins president David Samson. "The goal we have with our fans every day is to get them to the point when they say, 'I remember when – I remember when I was so unhappy with the team. But now, it's a love affair.'"

At the moment, the Marlins have the worst attendance in baseball at about 17,830 people per game, according to a ranking on espn.com. That amounts to an average sales drop of 10,400 tickets from the 2012 inaugural season – a 37 percent decline.

Using attendance figures from the 1980s on posted at baseball-reference.com, The Miami Herald compared the ongoing 2013 season at Marlins Park to the second year of every new stadium built since 1989.

Only one ballpark saw a worse drop: Tampa Bay's Tropicana Field, where attendance fell 38 percent in the season after its 1998 debut.

But Marlins Park could wind up in the statistical basement by the time this season ends. During its first 55 home games, which is how many times the Marlins have played in Miami this year, Tampa Bay only saw a drop of 30 percent. Assuming the Marlins follow the same trajectory once summer ends, it will pass Tampa's record for the worst sophomore season.

Loria argued the player trades were necessary after his $100 million payroll, one of the highest in baseball, failed to deliver last year. Once the new squad gels and starts winning, front-office executives predict fans to come back in the numbers needed to spend more on the field. In April, Samson said the Marlins need attendance of about 30,000 to afford a $80 million payroll, far better than the estimated $35 million players earn now.

The Marlins are reporting an average announced attendance of 17,977 per game, helped along by Thursday's second-best tally of

25,916 thanks to a popular summer-camp promotion.

The per-game average is 109 more seats than the team's attendance for the same number of games at Sun Life in 2011. It's also enough to fill about half of Marlins Park's 36,742 seats, but actual attendance has been lower because the announced tally includes sold or distributed tickets that are not used.

Despite a strong start when then-Dolphins owner H. Wayne Huizenga brought the team to his South Florida football stadium in 1993, the Marlins have generally drawn some of the smallest crowds in the major leagues. Even when the team won the World Series in 2003, attendance was still the third worst in baseball.

Ire over Loria's trades and the team's second losing season have yet to put baseball to the real test in Miami. "I think when they see a winning team, we'll have the same enthusiasm we have for the Miami Heat," said Miami Mayor Tomás Regalado, who opposed using public funds to build the stadium. He said he has yet to attend a Marlins game there, but added, "I think the stadium is fabulous."

On Tuesday night, Luis Roblejo joined family and friends for their first Marlins game of the season. They took up five seats in a mostly empty upper deck above right field. Each wore a Marlins jersey. None bore the name of a current player.

"I'm a little bit embarrassed" about not being at the ballpark yet, said Roblejo, an IT worker in Miami. He wore an old Gaby Sanchez jersey, while his 13-year-old son, Ryan, had Hanley Ramirez's name on the back of his Marlins shirt. Both players were traded last year.

"If I had more players to identify with, I would come," Roblejo said.

To combat weak demand, the Marlins are cutting into profits with more promotions than they ever envisioned at the new ballpark. The discounting includes kids-eat-free specials on Wednesdays and $27 all-you-can-eat buffets on Saturdays. Seniors get free tickets on Thursdays. "It's a very aggressive approach to get people back into the building," said Sean Flynn, head of marketing for the team.

Ana and Juan Avila paid about $54 to bring their two children to Sunday afternoon's win over the Pittsburgh Pirates. Each ticket came with a free hot dog and soda. "It's my first game ever," said their son Juan, 9, from his seat high above right field in a nearly empty Section 140. "It's bigger than I expected."

Even with the discouraging attendance numbers, Marlins Park remains livelier than the statistics might suggest. Buying a hot dog ($6) or a Pepsi ($4.50) requires waiting in line. While the upper deck remains roped off many evenings for lack of ticket sales, the lower deck appeared more than half full during two visits to the park this week.

During Tuesday night's extra-inning loss to the New York Mets, enough spectators jumped up with raised arms to perform several laps of a respectable fan wave before it fizzled.

"The recovery from the hurt is happening quicker than we thought," said Samson, the team president. "As time passes and people realize it's a fun place to see a game, things will get better."

Source: Article author: Douglas Hanks; http://www.miamiherald.com/2013/08/01/3537432/marlins-attendance-reverts-to.html.

7

Although success is defined by wins and losses, it can also be thought of as the historical standard by which the team has been judged. Interestingly, the authors of the model also believe the head coach can be an important factor in establishing brand equity. The University of Minnesota received a tremendous boost when they hired basketball coach Tubby Smith, and The Ohio State University brand was bolstered with the hiring of former Florida head coach Urban Meyer. Similarly, a star player or players can boost brand equity, especially in the sports of baseball and basketball. For example, the LeBron phenomenon gave the struggling Cleveland Cavaliers a new image and chance to reposition their franchise with the drafting of James in 2003. However, this brand positioning strategy was changed when LeBron James and Chris Bosh signed matching 6-year $110.1 million contracts to join Dwayne Wade and the Miami Heat in 2010. Now that James will be returning to Cleveland, new brand image strategies will be developed.

The organization-related antecedents described in the model include reputation and tradition, conference and schedule, and entertainment package–product delivery. The reputation and tradition of the team off the field is believed to be a factor in building brand equity. An excellent example of problems in the front office influencing fan perceptions and brand equity is that of the hapless Arizona Cardinals. Owner Bill Bidwell has been scrutinized and criticized by the fans and media for years because of bad choices made on and off the field.

The conference affiliation and schedule are also organizational factors influencing image. Gladden et al. believe college and professional teams who play in tougher conferences with long-standing rivals will create greater benefits for the team's equity in the long term. This must certainly hold some truth as college teams and conferences are constantly realigning. Starting back in 2011, the Big Ten, Pac-10, Big 12, WAC, and the MWC all had new looks. The projected conference changes for 2013 and 2014 include the following: Syracuse and Pittsburgh moving to the ACC; Memphis, San Diego State, SMU, Boise State, Houston, and UCF all moving to the Big East; FIU, Old Dominion, UAB, Louisiana Tech, North Texas, UTEP, and UTSA all moving to the Conference USA, with Charlotte planned to join in 2015; San Jose State, Utah State, Idaho, and New Mexico State will all be independents; Georgia State moving to the Sun Belt Conference; Maryland and Rutgers are moving to the Big Ten in 2014; and the dissolution of the WAC for football in 2013.

Finally, the entertainment aspect of sport created and managed by the organization will affect brand equity. As mentioned previously, this is one of the controllable elements of the largely uncontrollable sports industry.

The market-related antecedents are those things such as media coverage, geographic location, competitive forces, and support. Media coverage refers to the exposure the sport product receives in the media via multiple outlets such as radio, TV, newspaper, and the Internet. Obviously, the images portrayed in the media and amount of coverage can have a huge bearing on all aspects of brand equity. Geographic location is also related to equity in that certain areas of the United States are linked with certain types of sport. As described in Milne and McDonald,[15] "it may be easier to establish brand equity for a Division I men's basketball team in Indiana than it would be in Idaho." Competition must also be considered a market factor, and the authors of the model describe it as the most influential in creating equity. In some instances, competition can enhance the value of a brand, but more typically competitive forces vying for similar consumers will weaken equity and its outcomes. Fan support is the final market force influencing equity. Quite simply, the greater the number of loyal fans or supporters means the greater the brand equity.

Although the preceding discussion has focused on the antecedents of brand equity to a sports product, the model also describes the related outcomes or consequences of establishing a strong brand. More specifically, the authors believe higher levels of brand equity will lead to more national media exposure, greater sales of team merchandise, more support from corporate sponsors, enhanced stadium atmospherics, and increased ticket sales.

How can marketers assess the equity of a brand such as the Yankees or Nike? One popular technique to measure brand equity evaluates a brand's performance across seven dimensions. Brand equity is then calculated by applying a multiple, determined by the brand's performance on the seven dimensions, to the net brand-related profits. These dimensions include leadership or the ability of the brand to influence its market, stability or the ability of the brand to survive, market or the trading environment of the brand internationality or the ability of the brand to cross geographic and cultural borders, trend or the ongoing direction of the brand's importance to the industry, support or the effectiveness of the brand's communication, and protection of the owner's legal title.[16]

Although there are a number of ways to measure brand equity in consumer goods, there have been very few attempts to look at the equity of sports teams. One exception was a study that measured the brand equity of MLB franchises.[17] To measure brand equity, the researchers first calculated team revenues for each franchise. These revenues are based on gate receipts; media; licensing and merchandise; and stadium-oriented issues, such as concessions, advertising, and so on. The franchise value is then assigned a multiple based on growth projections for network television fees. Next, the total franchise value is subtracted from the value of a generic product to determine the brand equity. Because there is no such thing as a generic baseball team, the researchers used the $130 million fee paid by the two new expansion teams at the time of the study, Tampa Bay and Arizona. This $130 million fee, though low when compared with today's standards, represents the closest estimate to an unbranded team, because the new teams had yet to begin play.

Interestingly, only seven of the 30 MLB teams show any brand equity. Based on the research, the following teams have positive brand equity (in rank order): New York Yankees, Toronto Blue Jays and New York Mets, Boston Red Sox, Los Angeles Dodgers, Chicago White Sox, and Texas Rangers. The teams with the lowest brand equity include the Pittsburgh Pirates and Seattle Mariners. Given the fact that many of these "brands" have been around for decades, the brand equity for MLB franchises is surprisingly low.

Although the previous study used an economic basis for determining brand equity, other research has employed less precise, qualitative approaches. For example, a panel of sporting goods industry experts was asked to name the most powerful brands in sport. In this study of equity, sports brands were defined as those who directly manufacture sporting apparel, equipment, and shoes. Nike is in a league of its own when it comes to branding. Ever since the introduction of the Air Jordan basketball shoe, Nike has grown geometrically since the days when Phil Knight (founder) sold shoes out of the trunk of his car.

Brand loyalty is one of the most important concepts to sports marketers, because it refers to a consistent preference or repeat purchase of one brand over all others in a product category. Marketers want their products to satisfy consumers, so decision making becomes a matter of habit rather than an extensive evaluation among competing brands.

SPORTS MARKETING HALL OF FAME

Phil Knight

Knight was a middle-distance runner for the University of Oregon track team, where he encountered Coach Bill Bowerman's obsession with improving running shoes.

When Knight studied at the Graduate School of Business at Stanford, a professor, Frank Shallenberger instructed his students to write a paper on how they would create a new company.

With his experience of Bowerman in his mind, Phil Knight's paper argued how profits could be generated by importing cheap but well-made running shoes from Japan.

He put his theory into practice and Phil Knight and Bowerman each invested $500 in purchasing Tiger shoes from Japan. They founded Blue Ribbon Sports, Inc. (either in 1962 or 1963 – I have seen both dates reported).

In their first year they cleared $364, but by 1969 sales had rocketed to a million dollars. The company was renamed Nike in 1972.

They developed the "swoosh" logo and cultivated endorsers that included Michael Jordan, Tiger Woods and Pete Sampras.

In spite of receiving a lot of negative publicity because of their use of child labor in the Far East, by 2004 Nike was selling goods worth around $12bn annually and employing 24,000 staff worldwide.

In November 2004 Phil Knight announced he was stepping down as chief executive, but will remain chairman of the board of directors.

On the Nike website, Phil Knight states his personal philosophy:

"There is an immutable conflict at work in life and in business, a constant battle between peace and chaos. Neither can be mastered, but both can be influenced. How you go about that is the key to success."

Source: http://www.biogs.com/famous/knightphilip.html. © 2002–2014 Danny Rosenbaum All Rights Reserved.

In sports marketing, teams represent perhaps one of the most interesting examples of loyalty. It is common to hear us speak of people as being "loyal fans" or "fair-weather fans." The loyal fans endure all the team's successes and hardships. As the definition implies, they continue to prefer their team over others. Alternatively, the fair-weather fan will jump to and from the teams that are successful at the time.

What are the determinants of fan loyalty to a team? Psychologist Robert Passikoff believes the interaction of four factors creates fan loyalty.[18] The first factor is the *entertainment value* of athletics. As we discussed in Chapter 5, entertainment value is one of the underlying factors of fan motivation. In addition, entertainment was discussed as one of the perceived values of sports to the community. The second component of fan loyalty is *authenticity*. Passikoff defines authenticity as the "acceptance of the game as real and meaningful." *Fan bonding* is the third component of fan loyalty. *Bonding* refers to the degree to which fans identify with players and the team. The bonding component is similar to the concept of fan identification discussed in Chapter 5. The fourth and final component of fan loyalty is the *history and tradition* of the team. For example, the Cincinnati Reds are baseball's oldest team and,

Table 7.2 Psychological commitment to team scale

1.	I might rethink my allegiance to my favorite team if this team consistently performs poorly
2.	I would watch a game featuring the [name of team] regardless of which team they are playing
3.	I would rethink my allegiance to the [name of team] if the best players left the team (i.e. transfer, graduate, etc.).
4.	Being a fan of the [name of team] is important to me.
5.	Nothing could change my allegiance to the [name of team].
6.	I am a committed fan of the [name of team].
7.	It would not affect my loyalty to the [name of team] if the athletic department hired a head coach that I disliked very much.
8.	I could easily be persuaded to change my preference for the [name of team].
9.	I have been a fan of the [name of team] since I began watching collegiate football.
10.	I could never switch my loyalty from the [name of team] even if my close friends were fans of another team.
11.	It would be unlikely for me to change my allegiance from the [name of team] to another team.
12.	It would be difficult to change my beliefs about the [name of team].
13.	You can tell a lot about a person by their willingness to stick with a team that is not performing well.
14.	My commitment to the [name of team] would decrease if they were performing poorly and there appeared little chance their performance would change.

although they may be lacking in other dimensions of loyalty, they certainly have a long history and tradition with the fans in the greater Cincinnati area.

To measure fan loyalty, self-identified fans are asked to rate their hometown teams on each of the four dimensions. Interestingly, the fan loyalty measure does not specifically include a team performance component. Contrary to popular belief, Passikoff believes winning and loyalty do not always go hand in hand.

Another way to operationalize the loyalty construct has been developed by researchers Dan Mahony and his colleagues.[19] They believe that loyalty can be thought of as having two distinct components: attitudinal loyalty and behavioral loyalty. Attitudinal loyalty can be expressed as an individual's psychological commitment to the team (or PCT). To better understand how to measure PCT and what it means, Table 7.2 shows the scale developed by Mahony.

In our society, loyalty to sports teams, at the high school, college, and professional levels, is perhaps higher than it is for any other goods and services we consume. Unfortunately, team loyalty at the professional level is beginning to erode because of the constant threat of uprooting the franchise and moving it to a new town. This is perhaps one reason for the increased popularity of amateur athletics. Colleges will not threaten to move for a better stadium deal, and athletes do not change teams for better contracts (although they do leave their universities early for professional contracts). Historically, fan loyalty has been defined in four ways: Pure entertainment – how well a team performs or how exciting the play; fan bonding – respect and admiration of players; history and tradition – is the game and the team part of community beliefs and rituals; and authenticity – how well they play as a team or how well the stadium or managers/players present themselves in the community. To increase fan loyalty, many teams are establishing fan loyalty programs, pairing new technology with existing marketing principles. Technology facilitates engagement with fans during games through a variety of scoreboard and fan chatter platforms. These platforms could be expanded to all team branded touch points that a fan may encounter. These points include sports websites, fantasy sports systems, and stores and bars in which sports fans purchase products.[20]

The loyalty programs are driven by a card that is swiped at kiosks when fans enter a stadium or event. The fans benefit by earning points that can be redeemed for rewards such as free tickets, merchandise, and concessions. The teams benefit by collecting valuable information on their fan base that can later be used to direct strategic marketing decisions. Major League Baseball seems to have taken the lead in fan loyalty efforts, including the most successful program with the Arizona Diamondbacks.[21]

Non-sport organizations also seek to develop customer loyalty through sport. In a Turnkey Intelligence survey conducted exclusively for *Sport Business Journal* and Sport Business Daily respondents were screened and analyzed based on their general avidity levels.[22] Results revealed that overall official brands got a good ride with NASCAR. For example, Subway who was not even an official sponsor but a part-time sponsor on driver Carl Edwards' car, received the highest percentage of recognition among respondents in the quick-service restaurant category. In addition, according to NASCAR's Brian Moyer, managing director of market and media research, Nationwide, the insurance company who titles NASCAR's second-tier circuit, did a good job of diversifying their partnership by tying-in and integrating Dale Earnhardt Jr. and Danica Patrick with the Code Spotter and their Dash-4-Cash promotions.[23] Gatorade also received high marks specifically integrating the success of their partnership with Kroger for the Dayton 500, creating custom labels highlighting three flavors which integrated the race and Driver Johnson. Other notable winners with NASCAR fans were Coca-Cola, Visa, Chevrolet, Bank of America, and UPS.

Licensing

The importance of having a strong brand is demonstrated when an organization considers product licensing. **Licensing** is a contractual agreement whereby a company may use another company's trademark in exchange for a royalty or fee. A branding strategy through licensing allows the organization to authorize the use of brand, brand name, brand mark, trademark, or trade name in conjunction with a good, service, or promotion in return for royalties. According to author Steve Sleight, "Licensing is a booming area of the sports business with players, teams, event names, and logos appearing on a vastly expanding range of products."[24] For example, the NFL has approximately 175 licensees selling more than 2,500 products such as apparel, sporting goods, basketball cards and collectibles, home furnishings, school supplies, home electronics, interactive games, home video, publishing, toys, games, gifts, and novelties.[25]

Since the emergence of NFL Properties in 1963, licensing has become one of the most prevalent sports product strategies. In 2012, sales of licensed products generated an estimated $5.454 billion in royalties, a gain of 2.5 percent over 2011, for an estimated retail value of $112.1 billion.[26] Sports accounted for an estimated $12.6 billion in retail sales and collegiate merchandise accounted for an additional $3.8 billion, royalties were $685 million and $206 million, respectively.[27] Major League Baseball retained top spot as the largest sports licensing agency; however, the

Photo 7.3 Future Redbirds in their St. Louis Cardinals licensed baby gear

Source: Matthew Shank

National Football League, National Basketball Association, collegiate products, WWE, NHL and NASCAR all topped the billion dollar mark. Additionally, the PGA and Major League Soccer are growing markets that together account for $1.19 billion in sales.

Let's take a look at the top five properties and their plans for strategic growth.

1. **Major League Baseball, $5.28 billion:** The 30 clubs that make up Major League Baseball scored more than 74 million fans during the 2013 championship season, producing the sixth largest total attendance in the history of the league. MLB was also bolstering its number of licensing deals. MLB announced a variety of exclusive multi-year deals with newcomers in 2013. MLB forged a multi-year agreement with Pandora jewelry introducing a collection of Pandora charms representing the Leagues' 30 MLB clubs.[28] In addition MLB and Wines by Design (WBD) announced a new relationship to feature limited edition, collectible baseball wines. Howard Smith, Senior Vice President of Licensing noted that WBD would be introducing wines from a variety of winemakers and tailor each to individual teams for their fans to enjoy throughout the season.[29] These deals helped MLB retain the top spot in sport licensing sales and further complement previous enactments such as Topps, the first exclusive baseball card company of MLB in nearly 30 years, as well as others including Ballpark Classics for ballpark-themed tabletop baseball games; ballpark-branded grass seed blends and fertilizers from The Scotts Miracle-Gro Company; and Tommy Bahama in a multi-year deal for a series of collector's edition Major League Baseball team shirts.
2. **National Football League, $3.25 billion:** The NFL split a key part of its licensing deal between Nike and New Era in the hopes of enhancing future revenue. The five-year multimillion-dollar deals with those companies and five others

began in 2012 and many analysts believe they could be worth $1 billion to the U.S. sport league.[30] The goal was to provide the fans with a wider breath of merchandise and under the new agreement Nike secures the license for uniforms and gear worn by players and coaches, while New Era is the on field hat provider.[31] The NFL also extended agreements with Under Armour (sponsor of the NFL Combine), GIII (outerwear), VF (T-shirts and fleece), and Outerstuff (youth apparel).[32] Other key NFL initiatives focus on Back To Football, women's merchandise, tailgating, cross promotion with NFL sponsors (for example, Proctor & Gamble's Gillette razor blades). NFL-licensed product is sold at GSI/NFLShop.com, team stores, and national retailers such as Kohl's.

3. **National Basketball Association, $3 billion:** Key licensing properties include NBA, WNBA, NBA Development League, and USA Basketball. With the start of every new season, the NBA introduces new uniforms and new products. To celebrate the Los Angeles Lakers' 15th championship, NBA unveiled a line of commemorative merchandise. The line was highlighted by an Adidas anniversary jacket, which featured 15 individual patches, each one representing a championship year. The Lakers wore the jacket on-court opening night when the team received their championship rings. The collection was sold at Champs Sports, NBA Store on Fifth Avenue, and NBAStore.com. Other new products include the launch of new trading cards from the NBA's new exclusive trading card partner, Panini, and the launch of a new trading card game called Adrenalyn. In 2013, the NBA signed a three-year, $100 million deal with technology guru Samsung. The agreement will put the company's tablets and televisions courtside. The NBA is also expected to create content customized for Samsung devices.
4. **The Collegiate Licensing Company, $4.62 billion:** Top collegiate properties include Texas, Alabama, Notre Dame, Michigan, and Kentucky as well as the NCAA, the Tournament of Roses, the BCS, and the South Eastern Conference (SEC). Women's, youth, and housewares will continue to be growth categories in the college market. Vintage-inspired products and the use of vintage college logos through the College Vault program will also continue to be a source of growth. Electronic Arts' NCAA Football title, which launches its 20th anniversary game in 2012, remains the top revenue-producing college product, with exciting new developments such as FTDs College Rose program, Nocona Boots, and projects in the electronic and digital space. Wal-Mart continued to be the largest retailer of collegiate licensed product. College-branded merchandise at Old Navy and Justice proved successful, and new programs with other non-traditional college retailers are in development. Online retailers such as Fanatics and Dreams continue to be key partners in reaching displaced college fans. College Colors Day, a fan holiday created by The Collegiate Licensing, will continue to provide a strong marketing platform for retailers during the critical back-to-school selling period, with other retail marketing programs such as Saturdays Since, I Love College Hoops, and others providing retailers solid platforms for raising consumer awareness and driving sales of college merchandise. (Note: Collegiate Licensing Company, clients includes all major schools except the Ohio State University, Michigan State, University of Southern California and Oregon.)
5. **NASCAR, $1.3 billion:** The key licensing properties for NASCAR and its teams were a variety of initiatives aimed at core fans, new young fans, and those with a love of technology. Historically NASCAR fans see licensed NASCAR products as money well spent. [33] While Dale Earnhardt Jr. has dominated NASCAR

merchandise sales over the past decade, other newcomers, such as Danica Patrick, Austin Dillon, Ricky Stenhouse Jr., Trevor Bayne and Kyle Larson provide a new set of inventory in the collectibles and merchandise markets. In fact, after her procurement of pole position in 2013, Patrick merchandise soared, setting off a flurry of buying activity.[34] Traditional licensing products include apparel, die-cast, and collectibles. In fact, NASCAR die-cast collecting has become a bona fide hobby. However, the economic downturn and a saturated licensing market have raised concerns of how NASCAR teams can stack up in the future. Therefore, NASCAR announced the formation of the NASCAR Teams Licensing Trust to coordinate merchandise sales of the top 11 teams.[35] In addition, other new programs were announced in the electronics category with products such as Right Way Dale Earnhardt Jr. Spotter GPS, Centon NASCAR flash drives and new remote-control cars and slot car racing sets by Jada and SCX. Expansion of the NASCAR hologram program consisted of continued protection for the sport and the fans who buy licensed products coupled with an online NASCAR Superstore giveaway for each code registered. NASCAR's licensing business will continue to focus on avid fans and expand its product lines for new young fans. There will be special emphasis on a video game strategy, outdoor programs, the launch of the NASCAR Hall of Fame and expanded retail. The demand for NASCAR merchandise still goes up after a victory, and many suggest that NASCAR should be proactive and make a more concerted effort to hark back to its dirty fingernail roots redefining the win on Sunday, sell on Monday mentality.[36]

Advantages to the licensee

- The licensee benefits from the positive association with the sports entity. In other words, the positive attributes of the player, team, league, or event are transferred to the licensed product or service.
- The licensee benefits from greater levels of brand awareness.
- The licensee benefits by saving the time and money normally required to build high levels of brand equity.

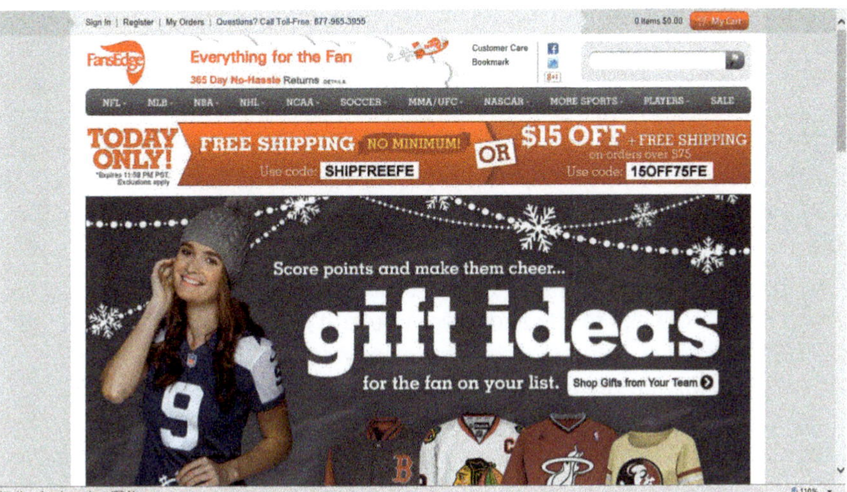

Web 7.3 Licensed merchandise on the Web

Source: FansEdge™, Incorporated

- The licensee may receive initial distribution with retailers and potentially receive expanded and improved shelf space for their products.
- The licensee may be able to charge higher prices for the licensed product or service.

Disadvantages to the licensee

- The athlete, team, league, or sport may fall into disfavor. For example, using an athlete such as Terrell Owens is risky given his past behavior, off the field as well as on the field.
- In addition to the licensee, the licensor also experiences benefits and risks due to the nature of the licensing agreement.

Advantages to the licensor

- The licensor is able to expand into new markets and penetrate existing markets more than ever before.
- The licensor is able to generate heightened awareness of the sports entity and potentially increase its equity if it is paired with the appropriate products and services.

Disadvantages to the licensor

- The licensor may lose some control over the elements of the marketing mix. For instance, product quality may be inferior, or price reductions may be offered frequently. This may lessen the perceived image of the licensor.

Based on all these considerations, care must be taken in choosing merchandising–licensing partnerships. Certainly, "the manufacturer of the licensed product should demonstrate an ability to meet and maintain quality control standards, possess financial stability, and offer an aggressive and well-planned marketing and promotional strategy."[37]

In addition to carefully choosing a partner, licensors and licensees must also be on the lookout for counterfeit merchandise. One estimate has it that $1 billion worth of counterfeit sports products hit the streets each year. For instance, the NFL typically confiscates $1 million worth of fake goods during Super Bowl week. The licensing affiliate Locog had targeted in excess of $110 million from merchandising sales for the London 2012 Olympics, while the Beijing organizing committee targeted income of $70 million from merchandising Olympic products for the 2008 Games and in previous games an estimated $17 million in bad goods were sold. In an attempt to stop or reduce counterfeit merchandise, Olympic officials have previously used a new DNA technology in which an official Olympic product has a special ink containing the DNA of an athlete. A handheld scanner determines whether the tag matches the DNA and whether the merchandise is legitimate.[38]

This problem has become so pervasive that the leagues now have their own logo cops who travel from city to city and event to event searching for violations. In addition to this form of enforcement, the Coalition to Advance the Protection of Sports Logos (CAPS; see http://www.capsinfo.com/) was formed in 1992 to investigate and control counterfeit products. Since 1993, CAPS has been involved in the seizure of more than nine million pieces of counterfeit merchandise featuring the logos of various professional sports leagues and teams, colleges, and universities – valued at more than $329 million. How can consumers guard against fakes? CAPS offers the following suggestions to consumers who are purchasing sports products:[39]

- ***Look for quality*** **–** Poor lettering, colors that are slightly different from the true team colors and background colors bleeding through the top color overlay are all signs of poor product quality.
- ***Verification*** **–** Counterfeiters may try to fake the official logo. Official items will typically have holograms on the product or stickers with moving figures, and embroidered logos should be tightly woven.
- ***Check garment tags*** **–** Poor-quality merchandise is often designated by split garment tags. Rarely, if ever, will official licensed products use factory rejects or seconds.

Quality

Thus far, we have looked at some of the branding issues related to sports products. Another important aspect of the product considered by sports marketers that will influence brand equity is quality. Let us look at two different types of quality: service quality and product quality.

Quality of services

As sports organizations develop a marketing orientation, the need to deliver a high level of service quality to consumers is becoming increasingly important. For instance, at NFL Properties (NFLP), service quality is taken to the highest levels. NFLP is highly committed to understanding the individualized needs of each of its sponsors. Every sponsor of the NFL receives the name of a primary contact at NFLP whom they can call at any time to discuss their marketing needs. They also recognize that each sponsor is in need of a unique sponsorship program, given their vastly different objectives and levels of financial commitment to the NFL.[40]

Although NFLP is an excellent example of an organization that values service quality, we have yet to define the concept. **Service quality** is a difficult concept to define, and as such, many definitions of service quality exist. Rather than define it, most researchers have resorted to explaining the dimensions or determinants of service quality. Unfortunately, there is also little agreement on what dimensions actually comprise service quality or how best to measure it.

Lehtinen and Lehtinen say service quality consists of physical, interactive, and corporate dimensions.[41] The physical quality component looks at the tangible aspect of the service. More specifically, physical quality refers to the appearance of the personnel or the physical facilities where the service is actually performed. For example, the physical appearance of the ushers at the game may affect the consumer's perceived level of service quality.

Interactive quality refers to the two-way flow of information that disseminates from both the service provider and the service recipient at the time of the service encounter. The importance of the two-way flow of information is why many researchers choose to examine service quality from a dyadic perspective. This suggests gathering the perceptions of service quality from stadium employees, as well as fans.

The image attributed to the service provider by its current and potential users is referred to as corporate quality. As just discussed, product performance and quality is one of the drivers of brand image. Moreover, Lehtinen and Lehtinen also cited customer service as one of the image drivers. This suggests a strong relationship between corporate quality, or image of the team, and consumers' perceptions of service quality.

Groonos describes service quality dimensions in a different manner.[42] He believes service quality has both a technical and functional component. Technical quality is described as "what is delivered." Functional quality refers to "how the service is delivered." For instance, "what is delivered" might include the final outcome of the game, the hot dogs that were consumed, or the merchandise that was purchased. "How the service is delivered" might represent the effort put forth by the team and its players, the friendliness of the hot dog vendor, or the quick service provided by the merchandise vendor. This is especially important in sports marketing, as "the total game experience" is evaluated using both the "what" and "how" components of quality.

The most widely adopted description of service quality is based on a series of studies by Parasuraman, Zeithaml, and Berry.[43] They isolated five distinct dimensions of service quality. These **dimensions of service quality** comprise some of its fundamental areas and consist of reliability, assurance, empathy, responsiveness, and tangibles. Because of their importance in service quality literature, a brief description of each follows.

Reliability refers to the ability to perform promised service dependably and accurately. **Assurance** is the knowledge and courtesy of employees and their ability to convey trust and confidence. **Empathy** is defined as the caring, individualized attention the firm provides its customers. **Responsiveness** refers to the willingness to help customers and provide prompt service. **Tangibles** are the physical facilities, equipment, and appearance of the service personnel.

To assess consumers' perceptions of service quality across each dimension, a 22-item survey instrument was developed by Parasuraman, Zeithaml, and Berry. The instrument, known as SERVQUAL, requires that the 22 items be administered twice. First, the respondents are asked to rate their expectations of service quality. Next, the respondents are asked to rate perceptions of service quality within the organization. For example, "Your dealings with XYZ are very pleasant" is a perception (performance) item; whereas the corresponding expectation item would be "Customers' dealing with these firms should be very pleasant."

From a manager's perspective, measuring expectations and perceptions of performance allows action plans to be developed to improve service quality. Organizational resources should be allocated to improving those service quality areas where consumer expectations are high and perceptions of quality are low.

The original SERVQUAL instrument has been tested across a wide variety of industries, including banking, telecommunications, health care, consulting, education, and retailing. Most important, McDonald, Sutton, and Milne adapted SERVQUAL and used it to evaluate spectators' perceptions of service quality for an NBA team. The researchers fittingly called their adapted SERVQUAL instrument **TEAMQUAL**.[44]

In addition to finding that the NBA team exceeded service quality expectations on all five dimensions, the researchers looked at the relative importance of each dimension of service quality. More specifically, fans were asked to allocate 100 points among the five dimensions based on how important each factor is when evaluating the quality of service of a professional team sport franchise. As the results show in Table 7.3, tangibles and reliability are considered the most important dimensions of service quality. Tangibles, as you will recall from Chapter 5, form the foundation of the sportscape, or stadium environment. This study provides additional evidence that the tangible factors, such as seating comfort, stadium aesthetics, and scoreboard

Table 7.3 Importance weights allocated to the five TEAMQUAL dimensions

Dimensions	Allocation
Reliability – ability to perform promised services dependably and accurately	23%
Assurance – knowledge and courtesy of employees and their ability to convey trust and confidence	16
Empathy – the caring, individualized attention provided by the professional sports franchise for its customers	18
Responsiveness – willingness to help customers and provide prompt service	19
Tangibles – appearance of equipment, personnel, materials, and venue	24

Source: Mark A. McDonald, William A. Sutton, and George R. Milne, "TEAMQUAL: Measuring Service Quality in Professional Team Sports," *Sport Marketing Quarterly*, vol. 4, no. 2 (1995).

quality, play an important role in satisfying fans. Understanding fans' perceptions of TEAMQUAL is critical for sports marketers in establishing long-term relationships with existing fans and trying to attract new fans. As McDonald, Sutton, and Milne point out, "Consumers who are dissatisfied and feel that they are not receiving quality service will not renew their relationship with the professional sport franchise."

On the sports participation side, an excellent study was conducted to explore the determinants of service quality in the sport recreation industry or recreation center. The researchers, Ko and Pastore,[45] suggest that service quality is multidimensional and consists of four primary factors. Factor one is program quality, which refers to the range of programs, such as the variety of recreation and fitness programs offered, operating time or whether programs start and finish on time, and whether participants can get up-to-date information on programs. Factor two, interaction quality, is the level of customer to employee interaction and also customer to customer relationships. Outcome quality is the third factor and is based on physical change, or does the participant realize the health benefit he or she wished to obtain; valence, which refers to post consumption or whether the overall experience was a good or bad one; and sociability, or the social interaction, which motivates many participants to engage in physical activity. The final factor, environment quality, is the ambient condition, design, and equipment quality. All of these refer to the tangible, physical environment in which the consumption takes place.

Quality of goods

The quality of sporting goods that are manufactured and marketed has two distinct dimensions. The first **quality dimension of goods** is based on how well the product conforms to specifications that were designed in the manufacturing process. From this standpoint, the quality of goods is driven by the organization and its management and employees. The other dimension of quality is measured subjectively from the perspective of consumers or end users of the goods. In other words, does the product perform its desired function? The degree to which the goods meet and exceed consumers' needs is a function of the organization's marketing orientation.

From the sports marketing perspective, the consumer's perception of **product quality** is of primary importance. Garvin found eight separate quality dimensions, which include performance, features, reliability, conformance, durability, serviceability, aesthetics, and perceived quality (see Table 7.4).

Whether it is enhancing goods or service quality, most sports organizations are attempting to increase the quality of their product offerings. In doing so, they can

Table 7.4 Quality dimensions of goods

Quality dimensions of goods	Description
Performance	How well does the good perform its core function? (Does the tennis racquet feel good when striking the ball?)
Features	Does the good offer additional benefits? (Are the golf clubheads constructed with titanium?)
Conformity to specifications	What is the incidence of defects? (Does the baseball have the proper number of stitches or is there some variation?)
Reliability	Does the product perform with consistency? (Do the gauges of the exercise bike work properly every time?)
Durability	What is the life of the product? (How long will the golf clubs last?)
Serviceability	Is the service system efficient, competent, and convenient? (If you experience problems with the grips or loft of the club, can the manufacturer quickly address your needs?)
Aesthetic design	Does the product's design look and feel like a high-quality product? (Does the look and feel of the running shoe inspire you to greater performance?)
Perceived quality	Is the product perceived to be long lasting? Does the product have a good reputation?

Source: Adapted from D. A. Garvin, "Competing on the Eight Dimensions of Quality," *Harvard Business Review* (November–December 1987), 101–109.

better compete with other entertainment choices, more easily increase the prices of their products, influence the consumer's loyalty, and reach new market segments willing to pay more for a higher quality product.

Some sports franchises have been criticized for attempting to increase the quality of their overall products, while driving up the price of tickets. Unfortunately, it is becoming more costly for the "average fan" to purchase tickets to any professional sporting event. Sports marketers have targeted a new segment (corporations) and overlooked the traditional segments.

Other criticisms have been directed at the NCAA and professional sports for making it too easy for athletes to leave school and turn professional. The National Basketball Association announced that 56 players, including 49 players from U.S. colleges and institutions and 7 international players, have filed as early entry candidates for the 2012 NBA Draft. This exodus of stars may have detrimental effects on "product quality" at the high school and college levels. The NFL requires draftable college players to exhaust eligibility (either 4 or 5 years) and non-college players become automatically eligible for selection in the next principal draft that is conducted after four NFL regular seasons have begun and ended following either his graduation from high school or graduation of the class in which one entered high school.[46] Even under the NFL's "Special Eligibility" route, requiring players to request special permission to enter the league, the players must still be three seasons removed from their high school graduation.[47] The reason for this rule is that it's believed that younger college players are not fully developed physically and are not ready for the physical demands of professional football.[48] The most famous challenge to this ruling, in which the courts ultimately upheld the policies of the NFL, was former Ohio State standout Maurice Clarett. Clarett challenged the ruling of the NFL and entered the 2004 draft. Federal Judge Shira Scheindlin initially ruled that the NFL could not bar Clarett from participating in the 2004 NFL Draft. This decision was later overturned by the United

States Court of Appeals for the Second Circuit, and Clarett's higher appeal was refused by the Supreme Court.

From a marketing standpoint, the fans are also suffering and may experience dissatisfaction when college players and high school players turn pro early. Teams no longer stayed together long enough to get and capture the imagination of fans. Former Atlantic 10 Commissioner Linda Bruno stated, "It seems as soon as college basketball hooks on to a star, he's suddenly a part of the NBA. Athletes leaving early have definitely hurt the college game." University of Louisville's head basketball coach Rick Pitino, whose opinion is widely respected, adds, "Quite frankly, I think college basketball is in serious trouble." Interestingly, the early departures that are making the college game less appealing are doing nothing to strengthen the quality of the NBA. The NBA is saturated with players whose games never had a chance to grow or, as former Stanford Coach Mike Montgomery put it, "will have to be nurtured through [their] immaturity."[49]

A final product feature related to perceptions of product quality is product warranties. **Product warranties** are important to consumers when purchasing expensive goods or hedonic purchases because they act to reduce the perceived risk and offset consumer sensitivity, i.e., fear of replacement, associated with cognitive dissonance. Traditional warranties are statements indicating the liability of the manufacturer for problems with the product. For example, Spalding's line of Neverflat balls has a product redesign with a new membrane, a redesigned valve, and the addition of NitroFlate, a substance added to the ball during inflation that forms a barrier preventing seepage. Spalding has produced balls it says will not leak air for at least a year. It is backing that claim with a money-back guarantee.

Interestingly, warranties are also being developed by sports organizations. The New Jersey Nets offered their season ticket holders a money-back guarantee if they were dissatisfied with the Nets' performance. With the price of tickets skyrocketing for professional sporting events, perhaps these service guarantees will be the wave of the future. The Indiana Ice of the U.S. Hockey League offered their fans a similar deal. The Ice are so convinced local hockey fans will enjoy seeing the under-20 amateur team play next season, franchise officials are offering a money-back guarantee on season tickets.

Product design

Product design is one competitive advantage that is of special interest to sports marketers. It is heavily linked to product quality and the technological environment discussed in Chapter 2. In some cases, product design may even have an impact on the sporting event. For example, the latest technology in golf clubs does allow the average player to improve his or her performance on the course. The same could be said for the new generation of big sweet spot, extra-long tennis racquets. In another example, the official baseball used in the major league games was believed to be "juiced up." In other words, the ball was livelier because of the product design. As a result of this "juiced up" ball, home run production increased, much to the delight of the fans. From a sports marketing perspective, anything that adds excitement and conjecture to a game with public relation problems is welcomed. In the end, what matters is not whether the ball is livelier, but that the game is.

Baseballs are not the only products that are having an impact on the outcome of sporting events, and equipment changes aren't the only way to think about product

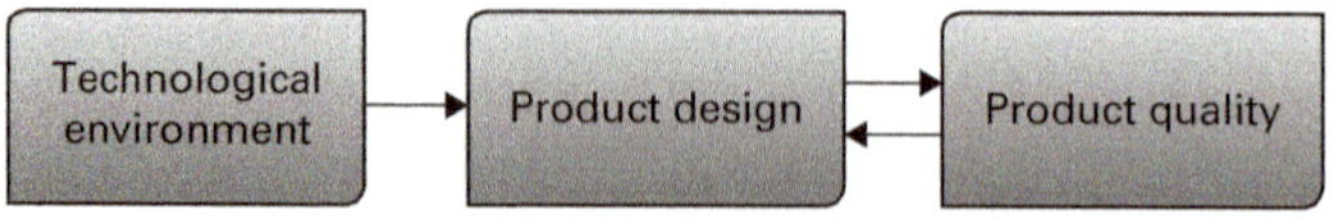

Technological environment → Product design ⇄ Product quality

Figure 7.5 Relationship among product design, technology, and product quality

design or redesign. Baseball is constantly looking for ways to make games shorter and thus more attractive to fans. In a recent rule change, the time a pitcher is allotted to deliver the ball with no runners on base has changed from 20 to 12 seconds. The price for each violation is a ball. It is hoped that this minor product redesign will have a major impact. Historic rule changes that have had a significant impact on the sport product include the designated hitter in baseball, the shot clock in basketball, or (in 1912) when hockey moved from seven to six players on the ice at one time.

Product design is important to sport marketers because it ultimately affects consumers' perceptions of product quality. Moreover, organizations need to monitor the technological environment to keep up with the latest trends that may affect product design. Let us look at this relationship in Figure 7.5.

As you would imagine, the technological environment has a tremendous impact on product design decisions. In almost every sporting good category, sports marketers communicate how their brands are technologically superior to the competition.

The golf equipment industry thrives on the latest technological advances in ball and club design. Bicycle manufacturers stress the technological edge that comes with the latest and greatest construction materials. Tennis racquets are continually moving into the next generation of frame design and racquet length. NordicTrack exercise equipment positions itself as technologically superior to other competing brands. Nike is continually developing new lines of high-tech sports gear in its state-of-the-art Sports Research Lab, which aided in the development of the Nike+ wireless system, allowing Nike footwear to communicate with an iPod nano for the ultimate personal running and workout experience. "The most common feedback we are receiving from Nike+ users is that the experience has changed the way they approach running," says Brent Scrimshaw, vice president of EMEA Marketing.[50] "Whether it's the instant feedback they hear over their music or the ability to set goals and challenge friends on nikeplus.com, Nike+ is encouraging people who never ran to run, and motivating people who run to run more." In this case, the claim is that product design is actually influencing not only performance, but motivation to perform.

The product design of sporting goods, in turn, influences consumer perceptions of product quality. By definition, **product design** includes the aesthetics, style, and function of the product. Two of the eight dimensions of the quality of goods are incorporated in this definition, providing one measure of the interdependency of these two concepts.

The way a good performs, the way it feels, and the beauty of the good are all important aspects of product design. Again, think of the numerous sporting goods that are purchased largely on the basis of these benefits. Consumers purchase golf clubs because of the way they look and feel. Tennis shoes are chosen because of the special functions they perform (cross-trainers, hiking, or basketball) and the way they look (colors and style).

Color has historically been an important factor in the design of almost all licensed merchandise. Recent trends show that in hats, jerseys, and jackets, anything that's black is "gold." The Oakland Raiders' silver and black are always near the top in NFL

Photo 7.4 Bike manufacturers must stress the importance of product design and technology.

Source: Shutterstock.com

merchandise sales regardless of the team's record on the field. The Toronto Blue Jays adopted logo incorporates black and moves away from the reds and blues of the past. Although fans associate certain colors with their favorite teams (e.g., Dodger Blue or the Cincinnati Reds), MLB markets licensed products that deviate from the traditional colors. Baby blues, pinks and camouflage are replacing the traditional team colors, and fans seem to be responding. Examples like these illustrate that color alone may be a motivating factor in the purchase of many sports products. Sports marketers, therefore, must consider color to be critical in product design.

Figure 7.5 also shows that product quality may influence product design to some extent. Sports organizations are continually seeking to improve the levels of product quality. In fact, having high-quality goods and services may be the primary objective of many firms. As such, products will be designed in the highest quality manner with little concern about the costs that will be ultimately passed on to the consumers.

Some major league sports organizations (e.g., New York Yankees and Detroit Red Wings) will design their teams to achieve the highest quality levels without cost consideration.

As new technologies continue to emerge, product design will become increasingly important. Organizations with a marketing orientation will incorporate consumer preferences to ensure their needs are being met with respect to product design for new and existing products. What will the future bring with respect to product design, technology, and the need to satisfy consumers? One hint comes to us via the athletic shoe industry. With advances in technology, customized shoes are now being produced for professional athletes. Gone are the days when recreational athletes could wear the same shoes as their professional counterparts. Today's professional athletes are demanding custom fit and high-tech shoes, and weekend athletes will soon require the same. Companies such as Nike are now customizing certain features of their shoes to the mass market under the Nike ID (individualized design) name. While other companies such as Under Armour, who made headlines at the 2014 Olympics in Sochi for seemingly all the wrong reasons, i.e., speed skating apparel deemed inferior, remained committed to its customers and ended up being vindicated, also cementing its place at the next two Olympics.

Another perspective on the future of product design is that the design of products will stem from demand and changes in the marketing environment. One such change is the emergence of a viable market for women's sports products. For instance, ski and snowboard companies are now turning their attention to women's products based on a growing number of women hitting the slopes. Historically, the only difference in men's and women's ski products was the color, but today there are product design changes that truly address women's needs. Skis for women are softer and lighter. Boots are more cushioned and designed to fit the foot and calf muscles of the female skier. All of these product changes try to capitalize on the marketing environment and satisfy the needs of a growing target market.[51]

Summary

Sports products are defined as goods, services, or any combination of the two that are designed to provide benefits to a sports spectator, participant, or sponsor. Within the field of sports marketing, products are sometimes thought of as bundles of benefits desired by consumers. As discussed in Chapter 1, sports products might include sporting events and their participants, sporting goods, and sports information. The definition of sports products also makes an important distinction between goods and services.

Goods are defined as tangible, physical products that offer benefits to consumers. Conversely, services are intangible, nonphysical products. Most sports products possess the characteristics of both goods and services. For example, a sporting event sells goods (e.g., concessions) and services (e.g., the competition itself). The classification of a sports product as either a good or a service is dependent on four product dimensions: tangibility, standardization and consistency, perishability, and separability. Tangibility refers to the ability to see, feel, and touch the product. In other words, tangibility is the physical dimension of the sports product. Standardization refers to the consistency of the product or the ability of the producer to manufacture a product with little variation over time. One of the unique and complex issues for sports marketers is dealing with the inconsistency of the sports product (i.e., the inability to control the performance of the team or athlete). Perishability is the ability to store or inventory product. Pure services are totally perishable (i.e., you cannot sell a seat after the game has been played), whereas goods are not perishable and can be stored or warehoused. Separability, the final product dimension, refers to the ability to separate the good from the person providing the service. In the case of an athletic event, there is little separation between the provider and the consumer. That is, the event is being produced and consumed simultaneously.

Along with classifying sports products by the four product dimensions, sports products are also categorized based on groupings within the sports organization. Product lines are groups of products that are closely related because they satisfy a class of needs. These products are used together, sold to the same customer groups, distributed through the same types of outlets, or fall within a given price range. The total assortment of product lines is called the product mix. The mix represents all the firm's products. Strategic decisions within the sports organization consider both the product lines and the entire product mix. For instance, an organization may want to add product lines, eliminate product lines, or develop new product lines that are unrelated to existing lines.

Products can also be described on the basis of three interrelated dimensions or characteristics: branding, quality, and design. Branding refers to the product's name, design, symbol, or any combination used by an organization to differentiate products from the competition. Brand names, or elements of the brand that can be spoken, are important considerations for sports products. When choosing a brand name, sports marketers should consider the following: the name should be positive and generate positive feelings, be translatable into an exciting logo, imply the benefits that the sports product delivers, be consistent with the image of the sports product, and be legally and ethically permissible.

The broad purpose of branding is to differentiate your product from the competition. Ultimately, the consumer will (hopefully) establish a pattern of repeat purchases for your brand (i.e., be loyal to your sports product). Before this can happen, sports marketers must guide consumers through a series of steps known as the branding process. The branding process begins by building brand awareness, in which consumers recognize and remember the brand name. Next, the brand image, or the consumers' set of beliefs about a brand, must be established. After the proper brand image is developed, the objective of the branding process is to develop brand equity. Brand equity is the value that the brand contributes to a product in the marketplace. Finally, once the brand exhibits high levels of equity, consumers are prone to become brand loyal, or purchase only your brand. Certainly, sports marketers are interested in establishing high levels of awareness, enhancing brand image, building equity, and developing loyal fans or customers.

One of the important sports product strategies that is contingent upon building a strong brand is licensing. Licensing is defined as a contractual agreement whereby a company may use another company's trademark in exchange for a royalty or fee. The licensing of sports products is experiencing tremendous growth around the world. Advantages to the licensee (the organization purchasing the license or use of the name or trademark) include positive association with the sports entity, enhancing brand awareness, building brand equity, improving distribution and retail relationships, and having the ability to charge higher prices. Disadvantages to the licensee are the possibility of the sports entity experiencing problems (e.g., athlete arrested or team performing poorly or moving). However, the licensor (the sports entity granting the permission) benefits by expanding into new markets, which creates heightened awareness. Yet the licensor may not have tight controls on the quality of the products being licensed under the name.

Quality is another of the important brand characteristics. The two different types of quality that affect brand image, brand equity, and, ultimately, loyalty, are the quality of services and the quality of goods. The quality of services, or service quality, is generally described on the basis of its dimensions. Parasuraman, Zeithaml, and Berry describe service quality as having five distinct dimensions: reliability, assurance, empathy, responsiveness, and tangibles. Reliability refers to the ability to perform a promised service dependably and accurately. Assurance is the knowledge and courtesy of employees and their ability to convey trust and confidence. Empathy is defined as the caring, individualized attention the firm provides its customers. Responsiveness refers to the willingness to help customers and provide prompt service. Tangibles are the physical facilities, equipment, and appearance of the service personnel. Using this framework, sports researchers have designed an instrument called TEAMQUAL to assess the service quality within sporting events.

The quality of goods is based on whether the good conforms to specifications determined during the manufacturing process and the degree to which the good meets or exceeds the consumer's needs. Garvin has conceptualized the quality of goods from the consumer's perspective. He found eight separate dimensions of goods quality, including performance, features, conformity to specifications, reliability, durability, serviceability, aesthetic design and perceived quality.

Product design is the final characteristic of the "total product." Product design is defined as the aesthetics, style, and function of the product. It is important to sports marketers in that it ultimately affects consumers' perceptions of product quality. For a sporting event, the product design might be thought of as the composition of the team. For sporting goods, product design has largely focused on the development of technologically superior products. In fact, the technological environment is believed to directly influence product design. Product design, in turn, enjoys a reciprocal relationship with product quality. In other words, product design affects perceptions of product quality and may influence product design.

Key terms

- assurance
- brand awareness
- brand equity
- brand image
- brand loyalty
- brand mark
- brand name
- branding
- branding process
- dimensions of service quality
- empathy
- goods
- idle product capacity
- licensing
- logo
- logotype
- perishability
- product design
- product characteristics
- product line
- product mix
- product quality
- product warranties
- quality dimensions of goods
- reliability
- responsiveness
- separability
- service quality
- services
- sports product
- standardization
- tangibility
- tangibles
- TEAMQUAL
- trademark

Review questions

1. Define sports products. Why are sports products sometimes called "bundles of benefits"?
2. Contrast pure goods with pure services, using each of the dimensions of products.
3. Describe the nature of product mix, product lines, and product items. Illustrate these concepts for the following: Converse, Baltimore Orioles, and your local country club.
4. What are the characteristics of the "total product"?
5. Describe branding. What are the guidelines for developing an effective brand name? Why is brand loyalty such an important concept for sports marketers to understand?
6. Describe how an athlete's image has an impact upon brand development.
7. Define licensing. What are the advantages and disadvantages to the licensee and licensor?
8. Describe service quality and discuss the five dimensions of service quality. Which dimension is most important to you as a spectator of a sporting event? Does this vary by the type of sporting event?
9. Describe product quality and discuss the eight dimensions of product quality. Which dimension is most important to you as a consumer of sporting goods? Does this vary by the type of sporting good?
10. How are product design, product quality, and technology interrelated?

Exercises

1. Think of some sports products to which consumers demonstrate high degrees of brand loyalty. What are these products, and why do you think loyalty is so high? Give your suggestions for measuring brand loyalty.
2. Interview the individuals responsible for licensing and licensing decisions on your campus. Ask them to describe the licensing process and what they believe the advantages are to your school.
3. Construct a survey to measure consumers' perceptions of service quality at a sporting event on campus. Administer the survey to 10 people and summarize the findings. What recommendations might you make to the sports marketing department based on your findings?
4. Go to a sporting goods store and locate three sports products that you believe exhibit high levels of product quality. What are the commonalities among these three products? How do these products rate on the dimensions of product quality described in the chapter?

Internet exercises

1. Search the Internet for a sports product that stresses product design issues on its Web site. Then locate the Web site of a competitor's sports product. How are these two products positioned relative to each other on their Web sites?
2. Search the Internet for three team nicknames (either college or professional) of which you were previously unaware. Do these team names seem to follow the suggested guidelines for effective brand names?

Endnotes

1 Kevin Burke. "Lacrosse: The Fastest Growing Sport in the Country" (2008). Available from: http://blog.dc.esri.com/2008/01/24/lacrosse-the-fastest-growing-sport-in-the-country/.

2 Shaquille O'Neal, http://cbs.sportsline.com/u/fans/celebrity/shaq; "Athletic Shoes by Shaquille O'Neal Now Available Only at Payless ShoeSource," *PR Newswire, Financial News* (January 14, 2004).

3 Christopher Lovelock, *Services Marketing* (Englewood Cliffs, NJ: Prentice Hall, 1984).
4 Boaz Herzog, "Rising with a Swoosh," *The Sunday Oregonian* (September 21, 2003), D1.
5 Joycelyn Hayward, Sporting Goods Store Manager. Personal Statement.
6 Nike Annual Report & Notice of Annual Meeting, Form 10-K, 2013.
7 Nike Annual Report & Notice of Annual Meeting, Form 10-K, 2013.
8 See, for example, Courtland Bovee and John Thill, *Marketing* (New York: McGraw-Hill, 1992), 252.
9 Terez Paylor, "Wizards Change Name to Sporting Kansas City," *Kansas City Star* (November 17, 2010). (http://www.kansas.com/2010/11/17/1593465/wizards-change-name-to-sporting.html)
10 *The Columbus Crew*, www.thecrew.com.
11 Andrew Lupton, "The NLL Fails to Excel at the Team Name Game," *National Post* (f/k/a *The Financial Post*) (Canada),(January 8, 2007), p. S2.
12 Marcus Nelson, "Want a New Look? There's a Price," *The Palm Beach Post* (October 24, 2003).
13 David Aaker, *Managing Brand Equity* (New York: The Free Press, 1991).
14 James Gladden, George Milne, and William Sutton, "A Conceptual Framework for Assessing Brand Equity in Division I College Athletics," *Journal of Sports Management*, vol. 12, no. 1 (1998), 1–19.
15 George R. Milne and Mark A. McDonald, *Sport Marketing: Managing the Exchange Process* (Sudbury, MA: Jones & Bartlett, 1999).
16 Louis E. Boone, C. M. Kochunny, and Dianne Wilkins, "Applying the Brand Equity Concept to Major League Baseball," *Sport Marketing Quarterly*, vol. 4, no. 3 (1995), 33–42.
17 Ibid.
18 John Lombardo, "MLB Makes It 5 Firsts in a Row in Brand Keys Fan Loyalty Survey," *Street and Smith's Sports Business Journal*, vol. 8, no. 10 (August 25–31, 2003), 28.
19 Daniel F. Mahony, Robert Madrigal, and Dennis Howard, "Using the Psychological Commitment to Team (PCT) Scale to Segment Sport Consumers Based on Loyalty," *Sport Marketing Quarterly*, vol. 9 (2000), 15–25.
20 Michael Manoochehri, "Information Systems & Service Design" (2009). Available from: http://courses.ischool.berkeley.edu/i228/f10/files/A4_Michael_Manoochehri_0.pdf.
21 Jeff Summers, "Diamondbacks' Fan Loyalty Programs," *Bleacher Report* (April 21, 2010).
22 David Broughton, "Official Brands Get a Good Ride with NASCAR', *Sport Business Journal* (November 28–December 4, 2011).
23 Ibid.
24 Steve Sleight, *Sponsorship: What Is It and How to Use It* (London: McGraw-Hill, 1989).
25 Scott Sillcox, "Licensed Sports Products and the Ebb and Flow of Time: What Can Change in 10 Short Years," *licensedsports.blogspot.com*, accessed March 3, 2014.
26 Licensing.org, "Licensing Industry Revenue Rises for Second Consecutive Year," June 18, 2013.
27 Ibid.
28 PR Newswire, "PANDORA Jewelry and Major League Baseball Properties Form a New Relationship," *PR Newswire.com*, accessed March 4, 2014.
29 MLB.com, "Wines by Design Announces Wine Licensing Agreement with Major League Baseball Properties with an MLB All-Star Wine Release," *MLB.com*, accessed March 5, 2014.
30 Reuters, "NFL signs Apparel Licenses with Nike, Six Others," *reuters.com*, accessed March 5, 2014.
31 Ibid.
32 Ken Belson, "Nike to Replace Reebok as NFL's Licensed-Apparel Maker," *New York Times* (October 12, 2010), accessed March 5, 2014.
33 Hlglicensing.com, Licensors, NASCAR Demographics, accessed March 6, 2014.
34 Kurt Badenhausen, "Danica Patrick Merchandise Flying Off Shelves Since Winning Daytona 500 Pole," *Forbes.com* (February 24, 2013), accessed March 4, 2014.
35 Dave Caldwell, "With Merchandise Sales Down, Nascar Has High Hopes for Tiny Cars," *New York Times Business Daily* (August 21, 2010), accessed June 20, 2014.
36 Ibid.
37 Eddie Baghdikian, "Building the Sports Organization's Merchandise Licensing Program: The Appropriateness, Significance, and Considerations," *Sport Marketing Quarterly*, vol. 5, no. 1 (1996), 35–41.
38 Elliott Harris, "Spitting Image: Ink with DNA Could Put Counterfeiters on Spot at Olympics," *Chicago Sun Times* (June 8, 2000), 133.
39 Robert Thurow, 1996, "Busting Bogus Merchandise Peddlers with Logo Cops," *The Wall Street Journal* (October 24, 1997), B1, B14.
40 Rick Burton, "A Case Study on Sports Property Servicing Excellence: National Football League Properties," *Sport Marketing Quarterly*, vol. 5, no. 3 (1996), 23.
41 Jarmi R. Lehtinen and Uolevi Lehtinen, *Service Quality: A Study of Quality Dimensions* (Helsinki: Service Management Institute, 1982).

42 Christian Groonos, "A Service Quality Model and Its Marketing Implications," *European Journal of Marketing*, vol. 18 (1982), 36–44.
43 A. Parasuraman, Valarie Zeithaml, and Leonard Berry, "A Conceptual Model of Service Quality and Its Implications for Future Research," *Journal of Marketing*, vol. 49 (1985), 41–50.
44 Mark A. McDonald, William A, Sutton, and George R. Milne, "TEAMQUAL: Measuring Service Quality in Professional Team Sports," *Sport Marketing Quarterly*, vol. 4, no. 2 (1995), 9–15.
45 Yong Jae Ko and Donna L. Pastore, "Current Issues and Conceptualizations of Service Quality in the Recreation Sport Industry," *Sport Marketing Quarterly*, vol. 13, no. 3. (2004).
46 See National Football League Eligibility Rules, NFL Regional Combines, https://www.nflregionalcombines.com/Docs/Eligibility%20rules.pdf, accessed June 20, 2014.
47 Ibid.
48 Chad Walters, "NBA and NFL Draft Eligibility Restrictions – Why?" *Lean Blitz* (February 15, 2013).
49 Jack McCallum, "Going, Going, Gone," *Sports Illustrated*, vol. 84, no. 20 (May 20, 1996), 52.
50 Aaron Reed, "Nike+ Motivates Athletes to 'Run Like You've Never Run Before' in New Commercial," SYS-CON Media (April 20, 2007). Available from: http://java.sys-con.com/read/364540.htm.
51 "Ski Industry Focusing on Women," *sportsbusinessnews.com* (January 30, 2004).

Managing sports products

After completing this chapter, you should be able to:

- Describe the characteristics of new products from an organizational and consumer perspective.
- Explain the various stages of the new product development process.
- Discuss the phases of the product life cycle and explain how the product life cycle influences marketing strategy.
- Determine the factors that will lead to new product success.
- Discuss the diffusion of innovations and the various types of adopters.

The article on Nike Fuel Bands provides an interesting illustration of a new sports product that is taking off in the North American market. There is obviously nothing new about fitness, or even wristbands, but when combined they create an exciting new sport product. Nike will have to keep this in mind when executing a marketing strategy for this emerging new sport product

NIKE ANNOUNCES NEW NIKE+ FUELBAND – MEASURING MOVEMENT TO MAKE LIFE A SPORT

New York (January 19, 2012)

NIKE, Inc. (NYSE:NKE) announced today the NIKE+ FuelBand, an innovative wristband that tracks and measures everyday movement to motivate and inspire people to be more active. Activities can now be measured through a new metric called NikeFuel: the more active you are, the more NikeFuel you earn.

NIKE, Inc. President & CEO Mark Parker unveiled NIKE+ FuelBand at an event in New York attended by seven-time Tour de France champion Lance Armstrong, Oklahoma City scoring champion and all-star Kevin Durant and 2011 IAAF women's 100-meter World Champion Carmelita Jeter.

"The NIKE+ FuelBand is a way for Nike to further evolve the exciting possibilities of merging the physical and digital worlds," said Parker. "Nike has always been about inspiring athletes, and the NIKE+ FuelBand will help motivate them in a simple, fun and intuitive way."

Designed to be worn throughout the day, the ergonomic, user-friendly NIKE+ FuelBand uses accelerometers to provide information about different activities through movement of the wrist via a LED dot matrix display. Four metrics are available: Time, Calories, Steps and NikeFuel. Unlike calorie counts, which vary based on someone's gender and body type, NikeFuel is a normalized score that awards equal points for the same activity regardless of physical makeup.

Users set a daily goal of how active they want to be, and how much NikeFuel they want to achieve. The NIKE+ FuelBand displays a series of 20 LED lights that go from red-to-green as the user gets closer to their goal. The FuelBand syncs with the Nike+ website through a built-in USB, or wirelessly through Bluetooth to a free iPhone app, to record activity and track progress every day. The app interface also provides encouragement and motivation as goals are achieved.

Armstrong said, "What's great about the idea of NikeFuel and the FuelBand is the way it provides real information and numbers to show how much people are doing all day, every day. That's what will get people challenging themselves to do more and better their own scores. It's a tool to get people more active."

"NikeFuel means everyone can get recognition for activities they do," said Durant. "It provides a scoreboard for your day and gets everyone moving." Jeter said, "You don't have to be an elite athlete to appreciate how NikeFuel can motivate you. It's an easy way to get credit for activities and compare how you do with others, even if you take part in different sports.

The Nike+ Fuelband will be available for preorder starting

January 19th in the US at Nikestore.com for a suggested retail price of $149 (US).

To use Nike+ FuelBand, the following is needed:

A Macintosh or PC with built-in USB. Mac OS v 10.4 or later, Windows 7 or Windows Vista (SP2) or Windows XP (SP2)

Internet access. Broadband is recommended. Optional mobile app available in the iTunes App store; for updates on compatible mobile devices, visit Nikeplus.com

Source: Nike, Inc; http://nikeinc.com/news/nike-fuelband-makes-life-a-sport#/inline/6742.

New sports products

Although it might seem as if new products are easy to describe and think about, "new" is a relative term. Think about purchasing season tickets to your favorite college basketball team for the first time. You might consider this a new product even though the tickets have been available for many years. In other instances consumers may be exposed to a sport that utilizes a combination of techniques they are familiar with to create "new" and exciting alternatives, such as Bossaball.

Bossaball combines elements of different sports on a pitch of trampolines and bouncy inflatables. The popularity of Xtreme sports, soccer, and volleyball around the globe suggest the time could be right for this new product. There is obviously nothing new about volleyball, soccer, and jumping on a trampoline, but when combined they create an exciting new sport. The founders of Bossaball will have to keep this in mind when developing a marketing strategy for this emerging sports product. This sports product is new to spectators and participants alike.

Web 8.1 The new sport of Bossaball combines volleyball, football, gymnastics, and capoeira.

Source: www.Bossaballsports.com

Regardless of how you define "new products," they are critical to the health of any sports organization for two reasons. First, new products are necessary to keep up with changing consumer trends, lifestyles, and tastes. Second, as unsuccessful sports products are dropped from the product mix, new products must be introduced continually to maintain business and long-term growth.

One of the key considerations for any sports organization is to continually improve the products it offers to consumers. New products seek to satisfy the needs of a new market, enhance the quality of an existing product, or extend the number of product choices for current consumers. Before discussing the process for developing new products, let us look at the different types of **new sports products**.

SPORTS MARKETING HALL OF FAME

Bill Rasmussen

Bill Rasmussen is hardly a household name, but all you have to do is mention four letters – ESPN – and his place in sports marketing history is secured. ESPN's founder developed the 24-hour sports programming channel in the fall of 1979. At that time, Rasmussen was simply looking for a way to broadcast the University of Connecticut basketball games when he happened upon satellite technology.

Today, ESPN reaches more than 99 million households and has more than 5,100 live and/or original hours of sports programming presented annually for more than 65 sports. A second channel, ESPN2, also reaches over 93 million households and has more than 4,800 live and/or original hours of sports programming. ESPN2 also has the distinction of being the fastest network to ever reach 90 million viewers. Combined ESPN has more than 50 business entities, which include ESPN on ABC, six domestic cable television networks (ESPN, ESPN2, ESPN Classic, ESPNEWS, ESPN Deportes, ESPNU), ESPN HD and ESPN2 HD (high-definition simulcast services of ESPN and ESPN2, respectively), ESPN Regional Television, ESPN International (31 international networks and syndication), ESPN Radio, ESPN.com, *ESPN The Magazine*, ESPN Enterprises, and ESPN Zones (sports-themed restaurants). Other new and fast-growing businesses include ESPN360 (broadband), Mobile ESPN (wireless), ESPN On Demand, ESPN Interactive, and ESPN PPV. Amazingly, this media giant continues to expand with all these networks and new products, because of Bill Rasmussen's desire to bring U Conn basketball to the people of Connecticut.

Source: Richard Hoffer, "Bill Rasmussen," *Sports Illustrated* (September 19, 1994), 121. Courtesy of Time, Inc.

Types of new products

As noted previously, there is no universally accepted definition of new products. Instead, new products are sometimes described from the viewpoint of the sports organization versus the consumer's perspective. The organization's definition of a new product is based on whether it has ever produced or marketed this particular product in the past. This can be important for organizations trying to understand how the new sports product "fits" with their existing products.

However, newness from the consumer's perspective is described as any innovation the consumer perceives as meaningful. In other words, the new product could be a minor alteration of an existing product or a product that has never been sold or marketed by any organization. Looking at new products from the consumer's viewpoint helps sports organizations understand the most effective way to market the product. Let us examine the types of new products from the organizational and consumer perspectives in greater detail.

Newness from the organization's perspective

New-to-the-world products

Brand-new sports innovations, such as the first in-line skates, the first sailboard, or the advent of arena football in 1987, all represent **new-to-the-world products**. These products were new to the organization selling the product as well as to the consumers purchasing or using the product.[1]

Another interesting, new-to-the-world sports product is the wireless ballpark. Raley Field, home of the AAA Sacramento River Cats baseball team, has become one of professional sports' most technologically advanced venues. The River Cats were among the first teams to implement wireless Internet access to customers in suites and the exclusive "Solon Club." The stadium is now wired for all fans who are able to operate laptop computers, PDAs, and other wireless devices from their seats for access to up-to-the-minute stats and replays. Additionally, fans can order food or tickets for future games right from their seat.[2]

New product category entries

Sports products that are new to the organization, but not to the world, are referred to as **new product category entries**. For example, IMG, a sports, entertainment, and media company, acquired Host Communications in November of 2007. Several months earlier IMG acquired the Collegiate Licensing Company and collectively these two companies formed the foundation for IMG College, a division of IMG Worldwide, which provides unparalleled expertise and resources to the collegiate market through the use of licensing and multimedia rights services. IMG further expanded this platform with the acquisition of ISP Sports on July 28, 2010. This acquisition made IMG College the leading representative of colleges and universities in their efforts to maximize their revenue through media and marketing rights deals.

New Balance, known only for its footwear, acquired Brine, Inc., a recognized industry leader in soccer, lacrosse, field hockey, and volleyball. "Brine's history of manufacturing high-performance team sports products will enable us to broaden our offerings at the global level," said Jim Davis, chairman and CEO of New Balance. "Brine's motto, 'Find Your Game,' speaks directly to their long-standing support of game improvement products and programs, and fits in well with New Balance's philosophy of promoting personal athletic achievements."[3]

In another example, the athletic footwear landscape was significantly altered when German-based manufacturer Adidas announced it would be acquiring all outstanding shares of Reebok. Under the terms of the deal, Adidas bought Reebok for $3.8 billion in 2006. For Adidas, the merger strengthens its presence in global athletic footwear, apparel, and hardware markets – allowing for a more competitive vantage point, a more defined brand identity, a wider product offering, and a stronger presence in professional athletics. These products are not new to the sports consumers, but they are new acquisitions for the organizations.

Product line extensions

Product line extensions refer to new products being added to an existing product line. For instance, the addition of expansion teams in Major League Baseball, or Daiwa's new Dendoh Marine Power Assist fishing reels, precision engineered with Daiwa's unique Power Lever for instant control of winding speed and power, are product line extensions. The NBA D-League is also a product line extension of the original National Basketball Association. The league is currently fielding 17 teams across the United States and until summer 2005, was known as the National Basketball Development League (NBDL). The NBA D-League started with eight teams in the fall of 2001.

In another example of a product line extension, New Balance footwear launched Custom US574 in 2011. The Custom US574 puts New Balance's best-known and best-loved silhouettes in the hands of consumers to style the way they want. Consumers pick the color ways and fabrics and then the shoe is shipped directly to the consumer in 4–5 business days.

Product improvements

Product improvements refer to current products that have been modified and improved, such as the new shoe addition to the long line of the Jordan Brand with the release of the Air Jordan 10 "Powder Blue" retro sneaker, 20 years after the first Jordan 10s hit shelves. According to Forbes, like all the Jordan retro releases, Powder Blue was highly anticipated and first-day sales hit $35 million.[4] For perspective, in all of 2013, Adidas sold $40 million in the U.S. of the signature shoes of its top star, Derrick Rose. Other notable Jordan lines include: the Jordon Melo M10 YO TH, retailing at $200 and the retro Jordan IX Kilroy Pack, retailing at $160, and are labeled product improvements. The shoes have a revived marketing campaign, made popular during Jordan's first retirement. The collection started with the Jordan namesake, followed with the Fonte Montanas, and continues with its third installment of the Bentley Ellis shoes.

Another example of a product improvement is the Wilson Six.One Tour BLX tennis racquet. This improved version of the flagship Wilson Tour 90 includes the addition of Wilson's new BLX treatment, which involves weaving Basalt fibers into the composition for improved vibration resistance. Wilson claims its BLX technology allows a smoother signal to reach the player after impact for cleaner feedback and the 'perfect feel.'[5]

Any sports team or individual that improves during the off-season can be considered a product improvement. Sometimes this improvement takes place because of trades or purchasing new players, and other times an enhanced product is the result of a new coach or players who are maturing and finally performing to their potential. In either case, product improvements represent an opportunity for sports marketers to promote the improvements (either real or perceived) in product quality.

A final example of a product improvement comes from the Chicago Cubs and their rearranging of a few group areas at Wrigley Field to free up more room in the 97-year-old ballpark to allow more room for fans to mingle. The organization's proposed $500 million ballpark renovations to be completed by 2015, include: a 57,000 square foot Jumbotron, larger home clubhouse equipped with a new weight room, medical area, player's lounge, batting cages, and media center, wider concourse, new restaurants club, improved concessions, more restrooms, enlarged and renovated skyboxes, new plaza area for pre- and post-game festivities, new office building to house team, stadium, and concession personnel, and lastly, a seven-story hotel with a connected walkway.[6]

SPOTLIGHT ON SPORTS MARKETING ETHICS

College sports have become too commercialized

I'd like to use this post to discuss my views on college sports, specifically that college sports have become too commercialized. Not only do I feel that college sports have become too commercialized, I feel this phenomenon has corrupted the academic integrity of colleges. Our nation values college athletics far more than any other nation. Other nations don't even have athletics affiliated with their schools; these athletes simply compete for local clubs.

Who is to blame for the over-commercialization of college sports? In my opinion, several parties are at fault. While the media has definitely had a major effect on how important college athletics have become, society has become infatuated with cheering for these teams. One attractive aspect of college sports is the number of different teams to cheer for, as well as the frequency of competition. Colleges have also fallen victim to the sports culture, especially favoring their successful or revenue-producing sports. College athletics today seem almost like a business, and college coaches will do everything in their power to create a prized program that the university can flaunt to the world.

Colleges, after all, were created for the purpose of educating and preparing students for the future. The NCAA (National Collegiate Athletic Association) will tell you that college athletics builds character and teamwork, but do you really think those factors are of primary concern to college coaches? Schools hire coaches to build successful programs, more or less so schools can have the "bragging rights" of successful teams. Coaches usually feel pressured to attract the highest-quality athletes and neglect their academic qualifications (or lack thereof). This pressure for successful teams can lead to recruiting violations or even academic violations for cheating to keep academically incapable athletes eligible to compete.

What annoys me (and probably many others) is that athletic scholarships praise people for their accomplishments outside the classroom, whereas colleges should retain their focus on what occurs inside classrooms. Another way in which athletes receive special treatment occurs when some are accepted into selective colleges for being an athlete. If an athlete has the coach put in a word with the admissions officers that a certain student needs to be accepted, you can guarantee that student will be accepted, even if that means rejecting a few others who might be more academically-qualified.

Of course, not every student-athlete fits the mold of "dumb jock." Some athletes are very capable students and will do well in their careers after graduation. However, I'm definitely not a fan of the special treatment athletes receive. If they are going to be considered "student athletes," then they should be treated as such, rather than giving athletes the privilege to do whatever they want simply because they are a university's prized tokens.

Source: http://sites.psu.edu/swk5473sec9engl137h/2013/04/03/college-sports-have-become-too-commercialized/.

Repositioning

As defined in Chapter 6, repositioning is changing the image or perception of the sports entity in the minds of consumers in the target market. Sports products such as bowling and billiards are trying to reposition themselves as "yuppie sports activities" by creating trendy and upscale environments in sports facilities that are stereotypically grungy and old-fashioned.[7]

Another repositioning example comes from the city of Moscow, the largest city in Europe with no modern arena to serve the sports and entertainment community. The city of Moscow, partnering with VTB Bank and AEG, are building a massive $1.5 billion sport and entertainment complex to serve Europe's largest market. The arena/stadium project will include the VTB Bank stadium with 6,750 club seats, 98 suites and an expandable seating capacity that serves populations from 33,000–45,000. The VTB Bank Arena will house 1,632 club seats, 82 suites and have a seating capacity of 12,000 expandable to 15,000. These sports venues are targeted to open in 2016 and hope to be an integral part of the 2018 FIFA World Cup competition.[8]

The most common examples of new products are repositioning and product improvements because of the limited risk involved from the organization's perspective. The rearrangement of existing sports products also has its advantages. For example, this type of new product can be developed more quickly than new-to-the-world or new product category entrants, and it already has an established track record with consumers.

However, new-to-the-world products must undergo enhanced research and development because they are new to the organization and to consumers. Moreover, more money must be invested because heavy levels of promotion are necessary to make potential consumers aware of the product. In addition, consumers must learn about the benefits of the new product and how it can help satisfy their needs.

Newness from the consumer's perspective

Another way to describe new products is from the perspective of consumers. New products are categorized as discontinuous innovations, dynamically continuous innovations, or continuous innovations.[9] The new products are categorized on the basis of the degree of behavioral change required by consumers. Behavioral changes refer to differences in the way we use a new product, think about a new product, or the degree of learning required to use a new product. For instance, a new extra-long tennis racquet does not require us to change the way we play tennis or to relearn the sport. However, extensive learning took place for many Americans exposed to soccer for the first time in the 1994 World Cup match and the learning process continues. Similarly, learning will have to occur for the many Americans who will watch cricket or experience the growing sport of lacrosse for the first time. Let us look at the three categories of new products from the consumer's perspective in greater detail.

Discontinuous innovations are somewhat similar to new-to-the-world products in that they represent the most innovative products. In fact, discontinuous innovations are so new and original that they require major learning from the consumer's viewpoint and new consumption and usage patterns. Some of the "extreme sports," such as sky surfing, bungee jumping, and ice climbing, represented discontinuous innovations, but are now becoming more mainstream. New "extremes" such as free diving, hang gliding, cave diving, base jumping, wakeskiing, and kite-surfing are also becoming popular.

Many Southerners who have had limited access to ice hockey may view this sport as a discontinuous innovation. Interestingly, a study found that spectator knowledge of hockey was found to be a significant predictor of game attendance and intention to attend hockey games in the future. An equally important finding in the study was that knowledge of hockey may vary based on sociodemographic variables. In other words, the fan's age, gender, educational level, income, and marital status influence the degree of hockey knowledge.[10]

Even distribution patterns for sport have required new consumption and usage patterns and therefore represent discontinuous innovation. For example, *Sports Business Journal* noted that programs such as Twitter via smartphones could serve sports properties and brands and offer a real time perspective of how people react to a game, a deal, or a critical decision. These instantaneous feed mechanisms provide information and even gratification for consumers searching and desiring up-to-date news.

Dynamically continuous innovations are new products that represent changes and improvements but do not strikingly change buying and usage patterns. For instance, the titanium head and bubble shaft on a golf club or the liquid metal technology aluminum bat are innovations that do not change our swing, but do represent significant improvements in equipment (and hopefully our game). When the shot-clock and three-point field goal were added to basketball, changes took place in how the game was played. Coaches, players, and fans were forced to understand and adopt new strategies for basketball. Most basketball enthusiasts believe these dynamically continuous innovations improved the sport.

The latest dynamically continuous innovations from the golf industry, which thrives on new product development, are the mainstream acceptance of the hybrid club and new surface geometrics of the golf ball. Many low- and high-handicap golfers are replacing their long irons with hybrids – a half iron, half wood alternative to the difficult to hit long irons. The innovative designs of the golf ball which include use of swirls or grooves rather than circular dimples allow balls to fly like rockets in breezy conditions.

Software giant, SAP, has entered the next phase of its sponsorship strategy. They are now using sponsorship and a new strategy of consumerism to put a personal touch on their brand by using new information technology. This technology is adopted by consumers and then spreads to business and government applications. SAP paired up with three professional sports properties: The NBA, the NFL San Francisco 49ers, and, more recently, MetLife Stadium, home of the NFL New York Giants and New York Jets. SAP plans to use this technology in order to enhance the fan experience. Examples of this include offering real-time statistics through NBA.com. This information was not available to the public until now. This is one way SAP is using sponsorship to introduce its brand to new customers.

EA Sports utilize dynamically continuous innovations that enhance the XOS PlayAction Simulator platform, EA's engine used to drive EA's top-selling Madden NFL 13 and NCAA Football 13. Back in 2011, EA Sports added online scouting, online team play and online attribute boost for co-op play to enhance functionality. Previous dynamically continuous innovations include customizable playbooks, diagrams, and testing sequences to better prepare athletes for specific opponents. Additionally, the software includes built-in teaching and reporting tools so coaches can analyze and track the tactical-skill development of their athletes. Instead of simply playing a video game for enjoyment, an athlete can play a game to test and train for upcoming on-field action. For example, a quarterback using the new tool can practice reading a defense, picking up blitzes, and making quick decisions on where to throw the ball, all based on the tendencies of the team he is going to play the upcoming weekend.

A final example of a dynamically continuous innovation comes from the world of trading cards and technology. Upper Deck, not just a sports trading card company, but a world-wide sport and entertainment company, has developed the Shadow Box slot cards. For the first time ever, these interchangeable acetate cards allow collectors the opportunity to customize their own unique trading cards. Certainly, this change represents a new buying behavior for a product (trading cards) that has been on the market for decades.

Continuous innovations represent an ongoing, commonplace change such as the minor alteration of a product or the introduction of an imitation product. A continuous innovation has the least disruptive influence on patterns of usage and consumer behavior. In other words, consumers use the product in the same manner that they have always used the product. Examples of continuous innovations include the addition of expansion teams for leagues such as NBA D-League, MLB, the WNBA, or MLS or even expanding the number of games in the season. Another example of a continuous innovation comes to us from the world of sports video game technology. Continuous innovations include slight improvements over time. Very little usually changes from year-to-year in video games, e.g. Madden 2014 vs. Madden 2015. In fact, many of these games are played much the same way that games were played in editions released decades before.

We often could debate which new product category best represents a team that has built a new arena and changed its venue or any new sports product, but few new products fall neatly into the three categories. Rather, there is a continuum ranging from minor innovation to major innovation, based on how consumers perceive the new product. Knowing how consumers think and feel about a new product is critical information in developing the most effective marketing strategy. Before we talk more about the factors that make new products successful and spread through the marketplace, let us look at how new products are conceived.

The new product development process

Increased competition for sports and entertainment dollars, emergence of new technologies, and ever-changing consumer preferences are just a few of the reasons sports marketers are constantly developing new sports products. As Higgins and Martin point out in their research on managing sport innovations, "Clearly, the list of innovations in sports is extensive and appears to be increasing at a rapid rate. This would suggest that spectators are seeking new and better entertainment and participants are seeking new and better challenges.[11]

Many new sports products are conceived without much planning, or happen as a result of chance. For instance, the modern sport of polo was created by British cavalry officers in India who wanted to show off their horsemanship in a more creative way than the parade ground allowed. Although polo represents a sport that was developed by chance, this is more the exception than the rule. More often than not, sports organizations develop new products by using a systematic approach called the **new product development process**. The phases in the new product development process include idea generation, idea screening, and analysis of the concept, developing the sports product, test marketing, and commercialization. Let us briefly explore each phase in the new product development process.

Idea generation

The first phase of the new product development process is **idea generation**. At this initial phase, any and all ideas for new products are considered. Ideas for new products are generated from many different sources. Employees who work in product development teams, salespeople close to the consumers, consumers of sport, and competitive organizations are just a few of the potential sources of ideas for new sports products.

Naturally, a marketing-oriented sports organization will attempt to communicate with their consumers as much as possible to determine emerging needs. As we discussed in Chapter 3, marketing research plays a valuable role in anticipating the needs of consumers. Moreover, environmental scanning helps sports organizations keep in touch with changes in the marketing environment that might present opportunities for new product development. For instance, in our opening scenario, the entrepreneurs who established Ultimate Fighting understood that the environmental conditions would be conducive to success.

Idea screening

Once the ideas are generated, the next step of the product development process, **idea screening**, begins. During the idea screening phase, all the new product ideas are evaluated and the poor ones are weeded out. An important consideration in the idea screening process is to examine the "fit" of the product with the organization's goals and consumer demand. The concept of new product fit is consistent with the contingency framework, which states that product decisions should consider the external contingencies, the internal contingencies, and the strategic sports marketing process. One formal idea screening tool for analyzing the "fit" of potential products is the new product screening checklist (see Table 8.1).

Sports marketers using some variant of this new product screening checklist would rate potential new product ideas on each item. As Table 8.1 indicates, a score of less than 30 would eliminate the new product from further consideration, whereas a score of 70 or more means the product would be further developed. Obviously, each sports organization must design its own new product screening checklist to meet the demands of its unique marketing environment and organization.

Analysis of the sports product concept or potential

By the third phase of the new product development process, poor ideas have been eliminated. Now, the process continues as the firm begins to analyze potential new products in terms of how they fit with existing products and how consumers respond

Table 8.1 New product screening checklist

Rate the new-product concept using a 10-point scale. Score a "1" if the concept fails the question and a "10" if it meets the criterion perfectly.
Relative advantage
Does the new product offer a cost advantage compared with substitutes?
Does the new product have a value-added feature?
Is your innovation directed at neglected segments of the marketplace?
Compatibility
Is the product compatible with corporate practices, culture, and value systems (i.e., the internal contingencies)?
Is the new product compatible with the market's environment (i.e., the external contingencies)?
Is the new product compatible with current products and services being offered (i.e., product mix)?
Perceived risk
Note: On the following questions absence of risk should receive a higher score.
Does the consumer perceive an economic risk if they try the new product?
Does the consumer perceive a physical risk in adopting the new product?
Does the consumer fear the new technology will not perform properly?
Does the product offer a social risk to consumers?
A bottom-line score of 100 (10 points for each question) suggests a new product winner. For most companies, a score of 70 or better signals a "go" decision on the new product concept. A risk-oriented company would probably consider anything that scores 50 or higher. A score of 30 or less signifies a concept that faces many consumer obstacles.

to these new products. As new product ideas begin to take shape, marketing research is necessary to understand consumers' perceptions of the new product concepts. One type of marketing research that is commonly conducted during the new product development process is referred to as concept testing.

During concept testing, consumers representative of the target market evaluate written, verbal, and pictorial descriptions of potential products. The objectives of concept testing are to understand the target market's reaction to the proposed product, determine how interested the target market is in the product, and explore the strengths and weaknesses of the proposed product. In some cases, consumers are asked to evaluate slightly different versions of the product so that sports organizations can design the product to meet the needs of consumers.

The most important reason for conducting a concept test is to estimate the sales potential of the new product. Often, this is done by measuring "intent to buy" responses from tested consumers. Using the results of concept testing, along with secondary data such as demographic trends, sports marketers can decide whether to proceed to the next step of the new product development process, drop the idea, or revise the product concept and reevaluate. Table 8.2 shows a hypothetical concept test for the Beach Soccer World Wide Tour, a new sports product that has been growing around the globe.

Developing the sports product

Based on the results of the concept test, design of the product begins in order to conduct further testing. Ideally, if the sports organization is employing a marketing orientation, then the product design and development stem from the consumer's perspective. For instance, Nike began its product design efforts for a new baseball glove by asking 200 college and minor league baseball players what they disliked about their current gloves. Eighteen months and $500,000 later, researchers designed a prototype

Photo 8.1 Concept testing is used to understand consumer reactions to sports such as white water rafting.

Source: Shutterstock.com

Table 8.2 Concept test for the Beach Soccer World Wide Tour

The sport of beach soccer is played on a 30-by-40-yard soft sand surface with five players on each team, including the goalie. There are three periods of 12 minutes each with unlimited player substitutions (as in hockey). In the event of a tie, the game goes into a 3-minute overtime period, followed by sudden-death penalty kicks. Beach Soccer World Wide would feature nation against nation (e.g., United States vs. Italy).

What is your general reaction to beach soccer?

How likely would you be to attend an event if the tour stopped in your city?

- Would definitely attend
- Probably would attend
- Might or might not attend
- Probably would not attend
- Would definitely not attend

What do you like most about this concept of BSWW?

What could be done to improve the concept of BSWW?

glove that is lightweight, held together with plastic clips and wire straps, and resembles a white foam rubber clamshell. Nike was hoping this space-age design would not be perceived by baseball purists to be too far afield from traditional models.[12] However, consumers didn't respond favorably and Nike was forced to discontinue the glove line.

In the case of a sporting good, a prototype usually is developed so consumers can get an even better idea of how the product will function and look. Today's superior engineering technology allows manufacturers to develop more realistic prototypes in a shorter period of time. It is common for prototypes to then be sent to select individuals for further testing and refinement. For instance, new golf, tennis, and ski products are routinely sent to club professionals for testing.

Another consideration in **developing the sports product** is making preliminary decisions with respect to the planning phase of the strategic sports marketing process. Potential market selection decisions (segmentation, target markets, and positioning) are considered. Furthermore, packaging, pricing, and distribution decisions are also deliberated. These basic marketing decisions are necessary to begin the next phase of new product development – test marketing.

Test marketing

In the concept stage of new product development, consumers indicate they would be likely to purchase the new product or service. Now that the product has been designed and developed, it can be offered to consumers on a limited basis to determine actual sales. Test marketing is the final gauge of the new product's success or failure.

Test marketing allows the sports organization to determine consumer response to the product and also provides information that may direct the entire marketing strategy. For instance, test markets can provide valuable information on the most effective packaging, pricing, and other forms of promotion.

The three types of test markets that may be conducted include standardized test markets, controlled test markets, and simulated test markets.[13]

In standardized test markets, the product is sold through normal channels of distribution. A controlled test market, also known as a forced-distribution test market, uses an outside agency to secure distribution. As such, the manufacturer of a new product does not have to worry about the acceptance and level of market support from retailers or those carrying the product because the outside agency pays the retailer for the test. A simulated test market uses a tightly controlled simulated retailing environment or purchasing laboratory to determine consumer preferences for new sports products. This type of test market may be especially important in the future as more and more sporting goods and services are being marketed through the Internet.

Whatever type of test market is chosen, it is important to keep several things in mind. First, test marketing delays the introduction of a new sports product and may allow time for the competition to produce a "me-too" or imitation product, thereby negating the test marketer's investment in research and development. Second, costs of test marketing must be considered. It is common for the cost of test marketing to range from $30,000 to $300,000. Third, the results of test marketing may be misleading. Consumers may be anxious to try new sports products and competition may try to influence the sales figures of the tested product by offering heavy discounting and promotion of their own product. Finally, test marketing presents a special challenge for sports marketers because of the intangible nature of many sports services.

Commercialization

The final stage of new product development is **commercialization**, or introduction. The decision has been made at this point to launch full-scale production (for goods) and distribution. If care has been taken at the previous stages of new product development, the new product will successfully meet its objectives. However, even if a systematic approach to new product development is followed, more often than not sports products fail. Just what is it that makes a small portion of new sports products successful while the large majority fails? Let us look at some of the factors that increase the chances of new product success.

New product success factors

The success of any new sports product, such as the NASCAR SpeedParks, depends on a variety of **new product success factors**. First and foremost, successful products

Table 8.3 Critical success factors for new products

Product considerations

- **Trialability** – Can consumers try the product before they make a purchase to reduce the risk?
- **Observability** – Can consumers see the benefits of the product or watch others use the product prior to the purchase?
- **Perceived complexity** – Does the new product appear to be difficult to understand or use?
- **Relative advantage** – Does the new product seem better than existing alternatives?
- **Compatibility** – Is the new product consistent with consumers' values and beliefs?

Other marketing mix considerations

- **Pricing** – Do consumers perceive the price to be consistent with the quality of the new product?
- **Promotion** – Are consumers in the target market aware of the product and do they understand the benefits of the product?
- **Distribution** – Is the product being sold in the "right" places and in enough places?

Marketing environment considerations

- **Competition** – Are there a large number of competitors in the market?
- **Consumer Tastes** – Does the new product reflect a trend in society?
- **Demographics** – Is the new product being marketed to a segment of the population that is growing?

Source: Courtland L. Bovee and John Thill, *Marketing* (New York: McGraw-Hill, 1992), 307–309.

must be high quality, create and maintain a positive and distinct brand image, and be designed to consumer specifications. In addition to the characteristics of the product itself, the other marketing mix elements (pricing, distribution, and promotion) play a major role in the success of a new product. Finally, the marketing environment also contributes to the success of a new product. A brief description of these critical success factors is presented in Table 8.3. Let us evaluate how well the new NASCAR SpeedParks perform on each of the critical success factors.

Based on the critical success factors in Table 8.3, would you predict that the NASCAR SpeedParks will be profitable? The NASCAR SpeedParks would seem to perform well on each of the product characteristics. Families can observe others enjoying the SpeedParks and try the sports product once with limited perceived risk. The NASCAR Go-Karts are safe and built for kids, so product complexity is low. With the NASCAR branding, the sophisticated engineering, and the authenticity, the perceived advantage of these replica cars should be far greater than for "just another Go-Kart." Finally, the SpeedParks are consistent with core values, such as safe and fun entertainment for the entire family.

In addition to the product considerations, other marketing mix considerations have also been well thought out for the NASCAR SpeedParks. Initially, the SpeedParks will be placed in parts of the country known for entertainment (e.g., Myrtle Beach) and the love of NASCAR racing (e.g., Tennessee). Given the signing of Kasey Kahne, Kevin Harvick, Bobby Labonte, and Elliot Sadler, promotion of the SpeedParks should be solid.

The marketing environment also appears to be ready for the growth of the NASCAR SpeedParks. NASCAR is one of the fastest-growing spectator sports in the country and has a huge and loyal fan base. Moreover, there are other Go-Kart tracks, but none with the backing of NASCAR, so competition is limited. In summary, the NASCAR SpeedParks seem to perform well on all the critical success factors, but only time will tell whether this new sports product will run the victory lap.

Product life cycle

From the time a sports product begins the new product development process to the time it is taken off the market, it passes through a series of stages known as the **product life cycle** (PLC). The product life cycle was first introduced by Theodore Levitt in 1965 in a *Harvard Business Review* article, titled "Exploit the Product Life Cycle."[14] The four distinct stages of the PLC are called introduction, growth, maturity, and decline. As shown in Figure 8.1, the traditional PLC was originally developed by marketers to illustrate how the sales and profits of goods vary over time. However, other sports products, such as athletes, teams, leagues, and events, pass through four distinct phases over time. The sport product life cycle often differs from the traditional because it affords sport organizations the opportunity for off-season enhancement. Companies like Dell Computer do not have an off-season to further enhance or develop their product. This unique time lapse provides sport marketers the opportunity to modify strategies to enhance the life cycle of the product. Regardless of the nature of the sports product, the PLC is a useful tool for developing marketing strategy and then revising this strategy as a product moves through its own unique life cycle. Authors Rick Burton and Dennis Howard used the product life cycle as a tool to assess the current state of big league sports. Their conclusion was that all four big league sports (baseball, hockey, basketball, and football) have reached either late maturity or decline. The authors speculate that part of the reason for this decline is that professional sports leagues have experienced "player strikes (MLB, August 1994; NHL, October 1994, September 2004 and 2012), player lockout (NBA, July 1994, 1998, 2011; NFL, March 2011), player free agency and salary demands (all leagues, all the time), various player arrests, rising ticket prices (an annual custom), stadium referendums, franchise movement, and constant legal wrangling." The authors also point out that each league should examine its current position in the marketplace and be prepared to adjust its marketing strategy based on the phase of the product

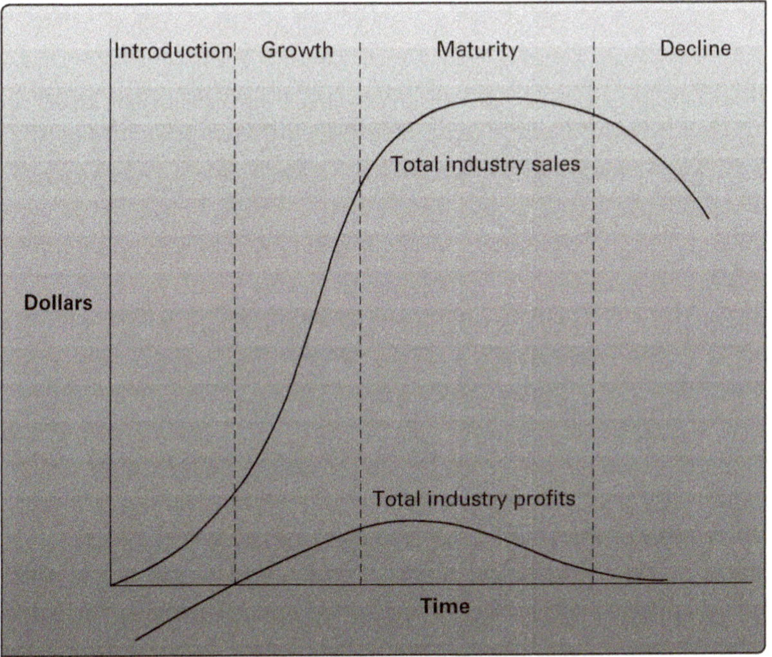

Figure 8.1 Product life cycle

life cycle. As expressed in the article, "despite all the hype and rhetoric, a case can be made that professional sports leagues are marketable brands that require sophisticated marketing plans and an understanding of how the product is perceived, received, and purchased. If a brand is in late maturity or the earliest phases of decline, then new uses, new product features, or new markets must be developed."[15]

The water bike is an excellent example of a sports product whose life cycle mirrors the shape of the conventional PLC. The water bike, or personal watercraft, had its first commercially successful introduction in the early 1970s. It had tremendous growth in the early 1990s. Sales of water bikes reached their peak in 1995 with 200,000 units sold. However, since then unit sales have been steadily decreasing. It was not until 2012 that personal watercraft sales had a significant year-over-year increase, with growth of 10 percent. This was after plateauing at a 10 percent year-over-year decline in the 2011 season.[16] Industry insiders want to believe the water bike is in the maturity phase of the PLC and sales have merely reached their plateau. Others, however, contend the industry has developed an image problem because of the safety and pollution issues associated with the activity. In this case, water bike brands such as Jet Ski and Sea-Doo may need to find ways to extend the life of their products. Makers of personal watercraft have long been committed to changing the product to be more environmentally friendly, quieter, and safer.

Before we explore the four phases of the PLC, keep several important factors in mind. First, the PLC originally was developed to describe product categories, such as water bikes or baseball gloves, rather than specific brands, such as Sea-Doo or Mizuno. Second, the product life cycle was designed to monitor the industry sales and profitability of goods rather than services. Third, the traditional shape and length of the product life cycle is generalized. In other words, it is assumed to look the same

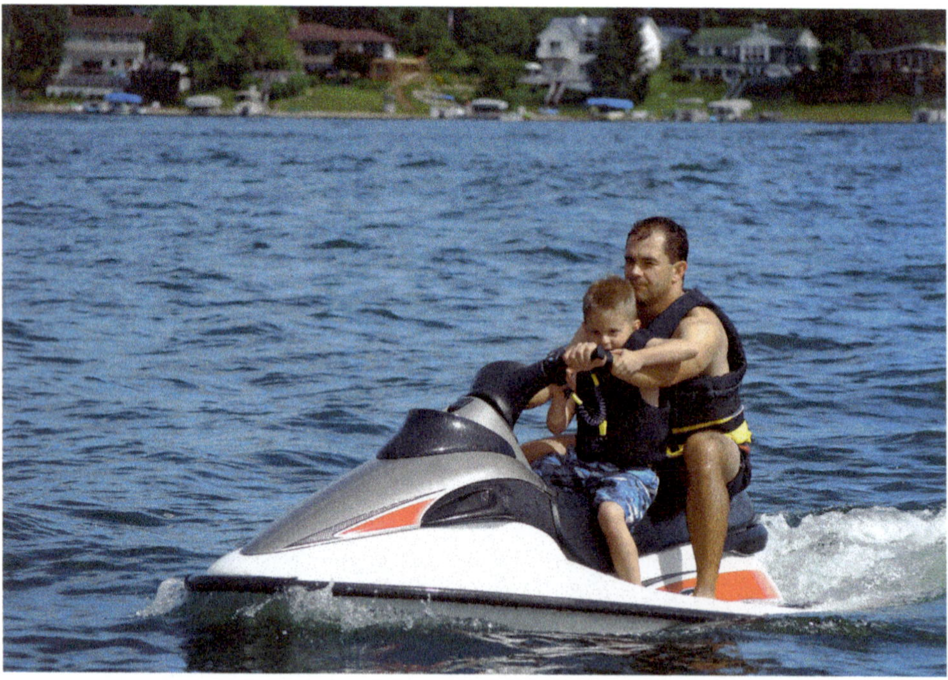

Photo 8.2 Extending the product life cycle of the waterbike

Source: Shutterstock.com

for all products. In reality, the length of the PLC varies for each sports product. Some products die quickly, some seem to last forever, and others die and are then reborn. Collectively, these items as well as the opportunity for off-season enhancement require sport marketers to carefully consider the unique PLC of each of their products on the market. Let us now explore how the PLC can be used for decision making in the strategic sports marketing process.

Introduction

When a new sports productt first enters the marketplace, the introduction phase of the PLC is initiated. New leagues such as the Women's Football Alliance and the National Women's Hockey League are excellent examples of sports products being introduced. Another sport product in the introductory phase is Zoombang protective gear.[17] It fits like a compression shirt and incorporates shock-absorbing padding that minimizes the harshest hits, yet does not in the least diminish flexibility and reach. The padding uses the most advanced material available which dissipates more energy than foams and gels by up to 80 percent while being 40 percent lighter. Zoombang is also available in a variety of sports, including skateboarding and snowboarding and makes products for industrial and military applications too. Already worn by NFL and NHL players, Zoombang is available in the form of padded shirts and girdles, knee and elbow pads, and hand and foot protection.

The broad marketing goal of the first phase of the PLC for any sport product is to generate awareness and stimulate trial among those consumers who are willing to try new products. Typically, profits are low because of the high start-up costs associated with getting the product ready to market.

During the introduction phase, pricing of the sports product is determined largely by the type of image that has been determined in the positioning strategy. Generally, one of two broad pricing alternatives is usually chosen during the **introduction** of the product. If the product strategy is to gain widespread consumer trial and market share, a lower price is set. This low pricing strategy is termed penetration pricing. However, a higher priced skimming strategy is sometimes preferred. The advantages of skimming include recouping the early marketing investment and production costs, as well as reinforcing the superior quality usually associated with higher prices.

Distribution of the new product is also highly dependent on the nature of the product. Usually, however, distribution is limited to fewer outlets. That is, there are a small number of places to purchase the product. Incentives are necessary to push the product from the manufacturer to the consumer. Promotion activity is high during the product's introduction to encourage consumers to try the new product. In addition, promotion is designed to provide the consumers with information about the new product and to provide a purchase incentive.

Growth

Sales are usually slow as the new product is introduced. With the onset of the **growth** stage, sales of the product increase. In fact, a rapid increase in sales is the primary characteristic of the growth stage of the PLC. Because industry sales are growing, the broad marketing goal is to build consumer preference for your product and continue to extend the product line. Although competition is usually nonexistent or very weak at introduction, more competitors emerge during the growth phase. Promotion must stress the benefits of your brand over competitive brands.

For example, the sport of lacrosse is currently in the growth stage in the U.S. market. Ten years ago lacrosse was played only in select East Coast cities and considered a sport for prep schools only. For the last decade, according to the SFIA and the U.S. Lacrosse Participation Survey, lacrosse has been one of the fastest-growing team sports in the country. U.S. Lacrosse chapters have been established in 42 states and nearly 819,000 people played on organized teams in 2013 compared to just over 250,000 in 2001. Overall lacrosse achieved a total 7.1 percent year-over-year (YOY) increase and a 12.4 percent YOY increase in casual participation. Youth lacrosse is the fastest-growing segment of the sport with nearly 30,000 additional players picking up the sport last year. Over 54 percent of all lacrosse participants are under 18 years of age.[18]

Another sport product in the growth phase is the Fatheads wall graphics. Fatheads are "sport posters," approximately 6 feet tall by 3 feet wide, printed on thick, high-grade vinyl with a low-tack adhesive that sticks to almost any wall. Additionally, unlike posters of old, Fatheads can be moved from place to place with no loss of adhesion or damage to the wall. These big, bold, colorful graphics illustrate a 3-D look and appear as if the image is jumping off the wall. A variety of sport and entertainment options, e.g., NFL, NBA, NASCAR, and Disney, are available for purchase. For example, a LeBron James REAL BIG FATHEAD has dimensions of 3'11"W × 6'5"H.

Another example of a sport product in the growth phase, where more and more competitors are starting to enter the market, is distance measurement devices in golf. The external, environmental factors are ripe for this product's continued growth as the technology develops and golf's governing bodies recognize distance measurement devices as part of the game. "With the recent USGA and R&A rulings that have made GPS distance measurement devices allowable for the game of golf, handheld GPS currently represents one of the fastest growing product sales segments in the golf business," said Scott Lambrecht, CEO of GolfLogix, Inc.[19]

During the growth stage, product differentiation occurs by making minor changes or modifications in the product or service. A premium is placed on gaining more widespread distribution of the product. Manufacturers must secure outlets and distributors at this early phase of the PLC so the product is readily available. Finally, the prices during the growth phase are sometimes reduced in response to a growing number of competitors or held artificially high to enhance perceived quality. Let us look at some of the strategic decisions discussed thus far in the context of the growth of the fantasy sports industry.

FANTASY SPORTS BECOMING BIG BUSINESS AS POPULARITY CONTINUES TO RISE

Former poker pro Taylor Caby knows when to place a bet.

Seeing an opportunity to invest in an industry generating close to a billion dollars annually, the 28-year-old online entrepreneur pushed a bulky stack of chips toward the center of the table and created DraftDay.com, an alternative to traditional season-long fantasy sports competition that allows users to wager up to $200 on daily drafts and leagues.

"The casual sports fans who maybe don't want to watch a game every single night or [aren't] interested in managing a team for an entire season, fantasy sports really aren't for them at this point," Caby says.

DraftDay is just one of hundreds of online startups trying to bring more consumers to the fantasy sports conversation and, ultimately, the marketplace. The Chicago-based gaming website, launched last September three weeks into the National Football League season, now hosts more than 10,000 users.

Fantasy sports participation surged more than 60 percent since 2007, and more than 32 million people aged 12 and older play in the United States and Canada, research conducted by Ipsos Public Affairs for the Fantasy Sports Trade Association in the past year showed.

The pastime has become a lucrative pop-culture preoccupation since an estimated 2 million people competed before the Internet went mainstream, says Paul Charcian, who has served as FSTA president for three years.

"A lot of the growth has been driven by the Internet and the simplification that the Internet offers to fantasy play," he says.

Online revolution

A worldwide network of computers made it possible to automatically aggregate sports statistics and instantaneously distribute them around the globe. The Internet had finally eliminated the frustration players such as Michael Grages encountered on a regular basis. Michael and some of his Londonderry, N.H., high school buddies began running a fantasy hockey league in 1997.

"We would have to get together every Sunday night and spend hours pouring over all the box scores and everything in USA TODAY from the whole week, so that we could update every team's stats and try to keep up with it," says Michael, 32, who works in financial services in Manchester, N.H., and avidly follows the Boston Bruins. "Looking back at that it seems ridiculous that we went through all that, because now all you need to do is just go online and [set] your roster and everything's done for you."

The convenience of an online platform finally helped Michael convince his wife and high school sweetheart, Kristin, a technology publicist and fellow Bruins enthusiast, to join one of his 10-team fantasy hockey leagues two years ago. "For me, it was a way to deal with the fact that hockey is always on my TV. My husband will literally watch any game that's on TV," says Kristin, 30, who was surprised by the intuitiveness of the fantasy sports tools on Yahoo.com, the host for their league. "If I was going to be forced to watch hockey almost everyday during the hockey season, I wanted to at least have some fake vested interest in the game," she says.

After becoming so frustrated with her fantasy team's lackluster production she gave up about halfway through the season last year, Kristin was holding down the sixth and final playoff spot this season while Michael, who says he usually finishes in the top four, was in third place.

Yahoo is one of three fantasy sports hosts that dominate the industry in terms of number of users; and although hosts do not disclose the number of people who play on their websites, Yahoo is widely believed to have the most traffic, more than CBSSports.com and ESPN.com.

With so few operators carrying such a disproportionately large share of users, gaining access to meaningful audiences can be challenging for online software developers such as Ziguana.com. The website tailors automated analyses of online rosters to each fantasy league's custom settings, saving time spent creating spreadsheets and browsing third-party player rankings.

"I think that's the hardest part of any young company or developer, is trying to get noticed and trying to reach the market," says Cassidy Morris, who created the company in 2006 with the help of his brother and two college friends. The team has redesigned its product in the last few years to try to take advantage of more business opportunities with league operators, Morris says.

Fantasy sports hosts must decide whether to share data about their operating environments and expose their application program interfaces, or APIs, to outside software developers such as Ziguana. Program designers who have access to a website's API can create apps compatible with the host's operating environment, ensuring optimal performance.

"[League operators] can either close it off and try to do all the development themselves, which puts a lot of pressure on their internal development teams to continue to advance the ball, or they can open it up and try to foster innovation and then leverage their position as kind of the gate keeper, so to speak, of the audience and take a toll or collect a fee," says Scott Frederick, COO of StatSheet.com, an automated online fantasy sports publishing network. "People realize if they expose their data via APIs that they can help foster innovation, and that helps their own ecosystem," he says.

Yahoo opened its domain to external app developers in 2008 as part of its Yahoo Open Strategy. But it's free to manage fantasy sports leagues on Yahoo and use many of the website's features, meaning developers don't profit much from sharing their tools and games on the company's fantasy platform.

Monetizing content

"The Internet has helped everyone get more information. It's also made it tough for people to build applications because there's an expectation for them to be free," says Bo Moon, who in 2010 co-founded Bloomberg Sports, a division of financial-information giant Bloomberg LP, and now serves as head of the group's product sales and business.

Moon had been creating programs to help customers make informed financial decisions when he realized an opportunity for Bloomberg to leverage its analytics in sports as he languished in the cellar of his fantasy basketball league. "I was the commissioner of the league and being in last place for two years in a row was becoming too embarrassing. I was bemoaning the fact that we didn't have tools to help me play better, and yet everyday I was working on tools to help people trade better," he says.

Bloomberg Sports now assists 24 of 30 Major League Baseball clubs with personnel evaluation and game preparation, Moon says. The same technology the company uses to serve MLB clubs also powers Bloomberg Sports Front Office 2012, a comprehensive fantasy baseball app that advises players as they draft and manage their teams.

"Our understanding of the market is that people do have an expectation for free [content]," Moon says, "but if they see value in the tool, they definitely will pay for a more complete experience." The software sells for $19.99 in App Central on the CBS online fantasy games platform, which CBS opened to third-party developers in January and which is being heralded as a "brilliant" way to serve the interests of fantasy games operators, their users and outside developers in a rapidly evolving business.

"What it's going to do is offer ample opportunity for people to be able to change the industry and create a lot of innovation that ultimately will benefit the users of fantasy games and products," says Danielle MacLean, CBSSports.com director of fantasy products. "We've created a full, robust ecosystem."

External software developers can create league-specific apps and market them to the company's relatively affluent audience. Sixty percent of fantasy users pay to play on its website, CBS says. "We really offer customization options that go well beyond some of the standard items that are available from the free providers," MacLean says.

The open CBS online fantasy platform gives everyone who has an original idea the means to access millions of users and the potential to profit from it along with CBS, says FSTA's Charcian. "It's brilliant for CBS because they'll monetize the apps and start building a very strong fantasy platform," he says. "I think CBS is extremely shrewd to do this first, and if I were running Yahoo or ESPN, I would be working very hard on developing a similar platform."

Outside program developers share revenues made from their apps' sales with CBS on a 70/30 split, the same divvies carved out for Apple and its partners in the iTunes store.

CBS launched its online fantasy platform with six companies – Advanced Sports Media, Bloomberg Sports, MLB.com, RotoWire.com, StatSheet and Ziguana. The league operator now has more than 500 developers signed up, which is as easy as registering for the website, MacLean says. "We purposely made that a really low barrier to entry because we want everyone to have an opportunity to get in and bring all of their innovative ideas and products to bear," she says.

Baseball Boyfriend, a fantasy baseball app CBS has offered on its fantasy sports website for $2.99 since early February, is an apt illustration. Created by the husband and wife team of Frank and Missy Panko, the game allows users to draft an MLB player as their "boyfriend" and "date" him for as long as they wish during the season. The "girlfriend" who has the most total points at the end wins.

The product inspired online scrutiny. Henry Schulman of the San Francisco Chronicle wrote a blog post titled, "A fantasy baseball game for girls who happen to live in the 1950s." But the quirky yet creative app gained popularity quickly, a testament to the power of an open API policy.

Each initial partner with CBS developed fantasy baseball products for its new platform.

Ziguana Auto-Pilot ($9.99) automatically manages daily fantasy baseball lineups based on a detailed statistical analysis of the day's matchups; ensuring savvy rosters are set everyday. The company's Forecaster app ($9.99) projects a fantasy baseball team's stats for the entire season based on its current roster, and recommends players who improve the team's odds of winning. "I think we were a good fit [with CBS] because we have a product that we've proven has a dedicated fan base and offers something I think a lot of people find valuable," co-founder Morris says.

StatSmack by Statsheet ($1.99) makes "trash talk quantitative" by providing "the numbers to back it up" in a "fun, snarky, interactive way," says COO Frederick. "It's a great application because most fantasy players are playing against people they know very well. They love to trash talk and they love to have statistics to back it up," he says.

RotoWire.com Fantasy Player News ($9.99) offers the website's award-winning fantasy baseball news to CBS players. RotoWire Player Outlooks ($1.99) provides in-depth analysis on more than 1,800 baseball players with details about skills, injury history and expected team roles. The company benefits from having been around years before many of its peers and, as a result, already partners with the three big hosts as well as NFL.com, says Peter Schoenke, RotoWire president.

"One of the hardest parts of the business, especially for new companies, is getting access to customers and marketing, and [the CBS open fantasy platform] is a great way to do it. You can build an app from day one and get exposure to millions of customers," he says.

Schoenke launched the company as RotoNews.com in 1997 but sold it in 1999 to a dot-com darling, Broadband Sports, who promised riches once the company went public. After that bubble burst when Broadband Sports declared bankruptcy in 2001, Schoenke reacquired the company and changed the name to RotoWire.com, where success allowed him to quit his "day job" as a commodities reporter for Dow Jones.

"Most of the people got into the industry because they like playing fantasy sports as opposed to trying to make money--although people want to make money," Schoenke says. "That usually makes it easier to do deals. The best products usually win out, and the bigger companies are happy to figure out ways to do business with them," he says.

Legal challenges

The industry beloved by its entrepreneurs as much as the fans who spend countless hours playing its games and using its tools was nearly crippled before it could stand. Major professional sports leagues weren't sure what to make of fantasy sports 15 years ago and, as a result, belittled or condemned the pastime.

"Then about 10 years ago the NFL did some studies and figured out that fantasy fans were actually their best consumers," Schoenke says. The league's research revealed fantasy participants attended more games, watched more television and purchased more merchandise, he says.

FSTA research has reached similar conclusions, says Charcian, the group's president. "Fantasy players are generally open to spending money. The vast majority of them don't play in just free-only leagues," he says. "We've done a number of studies that show fantasy players are big spenders."

The industry's use of free player profiles and statistics for profit was examined in federal court when St. Louis-based CBC Distribution and Marketing Inc. filed a lawsuit against MLB Advanced Media, the league's Internet wing, after the MLB Players Association denied CBC a new licensing agreement.

CBC, like many other online fantasy sports leagues, had a licensing deal with the MLBPA from 1995 through the 2004 season and paid 9 percent gross royalties to the association. But when MLB began making exclusive licensing agreements on player profiles and statistics in the fantasy sports marketplace after its own $50 million with the MLBPA, CBC and other smaller online fantasy sports businesses were cut out of the deals.

The ruling by the U.S. District Court in St. Louis gave fantasy leagues and app developers the right to use player names and statistics without licensing agreements because the information can be found in everyday news media and, thus, is not the intellectual property of MLB. "Once that cleared out, that really opened up the flood gates for people and companies to get involved," RotoWire's Schoenke says.

Had the ruling gone in favor of the MLBPA, people who wanted to play fantasy sports online would have had their options limited to the major sports leagues' websites, FSTA's Charcian says.

"It would've completely destroyed innovation in our industry and it would've monopolized our entire industry around the leagues," he says. "The entire way that we enjoy fantasy sports now could have very likely been undermined almost entirely, had the rulings in that case not at least gone in favor of the fantasy sports industry."

Charcian and his colleagues didn't have much time to celebrate, though. Another legal hurdle sprung up during the summer of 2006, when a New Jersey plaintiff claimed online league registration fees paid by some fantasy sports participants constituted wagers or bets, and should be reimbursed pursuant to the state's gambling loss-recovery statutes.

The U.S. District Court in Newark ruled pay-to-play fantasy sports leagues are not illegal, confirming the activity's exemption in the Unlawful Internet Gambling Enforcement Act, which regulates online gambling and became law in 2006.

The distinction between placing wagers in online games such as Texas Hold 'em poker, for example, and paying entry fees for fantasy sports leagues remains contentious. The UIGEA says fantasy sports are different because they have outcomes that reflect the relative knowledge of participants, not chance. But any prizes won from fantasy games must be determined in advance of competition and can't be influenced by fees or the number of players; otherwise, they're considered gambling and illegal.

"Fantasy is clearly a game of skill," Charcian says. "It would be virtually impossible to win a fantasy league if you didn't watch the games, [and] you didn't pay attention and you just randomly set your lineup."

DraftDay's Caby, who started playing online poker in his early 20s, isn't so sure about the boundaries lawmakers regulating gambling have made among online gaming operations. "I've made a living for years playing poker, and it wasn't by accident--it was because I was good at it," he says. "It's really the same in poker that it is in fantasy sports, it's just that the laws at this point are favorable to fantasy sports."

Some states, however, still don't allow their residents to collect cash and other prizes won from participating in online fantasy sports despite federal impunity granted by the UIGEA.

In 2010, Louisiana State Rep. Thomas Carmody pushed a bill to exempt certain fantasy games from the state's anti-gambling laws, but the measure failed, 73–16, in a vote in the state's House of Representatives. Maryland delegate John Olszewski Jr. introduced legislation in January for a third time to try to exempt fantasy sports from the state's gambling regulations.

"A lot of legislators, a lot of people at the state level, just don't even really know what fantasy sports are. Every study shows it's different from gambling," says RotoWire's Schoenke, who is chairman of the FSTA legal committee.

The FSTA launched a political action committee and hired a lobbyist in October to protect the financial interests of fantasy sports companies and to advocate on behalf of the industry in nine U.S. states that still haven't differentiated the activity from gambling, he says.

"Our goal there is to make sure the same victories we've had showing that fantasy sports are legal apply to the state level because some states have murky laws about the legality of fantasy sports," says Schoenke, who lauded the leadership of the FSTA in organizing a winning case in CBC Distribution v. MLB (2006), an effort that saved a thriving industry just now starting to tap the unlimited possibilities of technological innovation.

The future is mobile

"We're at this point in time where the technology really hasn't evolved much since it first became really popular on the Internet," says Caby, who sees opportunities for DraftDay to address the industry's shortcomings as the popularity of smartphones and tablets rises. "Most of the fantasy sites out there have either nonexistent or pretty weak mobile platforms, ourselves included at this point," he says.

Fantasy sports websites have tried to take their traditional content and "cram" it down to a smaller screen instead of tailoring their products to each device, StatSheet's Frederick says. "[People] inherently interact with those devices differently, so the experience should be different [on each one]," he says.

The mobile space isn't "quite there" because even fantasy sports hosts don't have worthwhile apps to change lineups let alone draft teams, says RotoWire's Schoenke, who thinks the industry will "get there pretty quickly, though," with the opening of the CBS online fantasy games platform. "We're trying to be the company that's the leader in the mobile space for fantasy sports information," he says. RotoWire's fantasy baseball draft kit for the iPhone and iPad platforms is one of the top-selling sports apps, he says.

The same factors driving consumer appetite for smartphones and tablets could transform the fantasy sports business.

"With mobile technology, there's a transition toward shorter-form games. The whole nature of mobile is limited or short-term engagement," says Bloomberg's Moon, who thinks traditional season-long competition might be reaching a plateau. "I think people will transition to playing more short-term games, and when that happens, you will see growth," he says.

Caby aims to cultivate the potentially strong demand for "niche" games and help DraftDay "bring fantasy sports into the more modern era of the Internet" by valuing player feedback and continually improving the company's product.

"What I think you're going to see over the next few years is sites that really focus on user experience and providing a great modernized platform will do well," he says.

Source: Article author: Kyle Clapham; http://news.medill.northwestern.edu/chicago/news.aspx?id=205473. Credit: Courtesy Kyle Clapham.

Maturity

Eventually, industry sales begin to stabilize as fewer numbers of new consumers enter the saturated market. As such, the level of competition increases as a greater number of organizations compete for a limited or stable number of consumers. The primary marketing objective at **maturity** is to maintain whatever advantages were captured in growth and offer a greater number of promotions to encourage repeat purchases. Brand strategy shifts from "try me" to "buy one more than you used to." Unfortunately, profitability is also lessened because of the need to reduce prices and offer incentives.

If attempts to maintain sales and market share are unsuccessful in the maturity stage, an organization may try several alternative strategies to extend the PLC before the product begins to decline and eventually die.

One household sport product in the maturity to decline phase of the product life cycle is AstroTurf. In order to extend this dying brand GeneralSports Venue, which recently acquired the rights to the AstroTurf brand, will announce its "re-launch" with a new celebrity spokesman, former pro football quarterback Archie Manning. AstroTurf was the first synthetic turf used on a sports field when it was installed in the Houston Astrodome in 1966. But the product fell on hard times as rivals made technological advances. GeneralSports plans to spend "several million dollars" over the next few years to promote what it boasts is new-and-improved AstroTurf.[20]

Another excellent illustration of a sport that realized it was rapidly moving toward extinction, decided to take corrective action, and developed and implemented new marketing strategies, is badminton. Table 8.4 provides additional suggestions for sports marketers who want to extend the PLC.

Table 8.4 Extending the product life cycle

• Develop new uses for products.
• Develop new product features and refinements (line extensions).
• Increase the existing market.
• Develop new markets.
• Change marketing mix (e.g., new or more promotion, new or more distribution, and increase or decrease price).
• Link product to a trend.

Source: Joel Evans and Barry Berman, *Marketing*, 6th ed. (New York: Macmillan, 1992), 439.

8

JOHN MCENROE'S BOLD MOVE TO REVIVE US TENNIS

Kudos to John McEnroe for taking a very bold step to revive American tennis. He recently opened a $18 million dollar, 20 court tennis facility on Randall's Island in New York.

The most successful player in US Davis Cup history was always ready and willing to represent his country in Davis Cup play. The passion he displayed on the tennis courts is matched by his commitment to bring the US back to its rightful place of prominence in the sport. His passion for this country and tennis is unquestionable.

Unlike many who talk a good game and do nothing, McEnroe has put his money where his mouth is.

I share his long standing frustration to get the USTA, (the governing body of tennis in the US by an act of congress) to construct and put into effect a well thought out and systematic agenda to bring the United States back into the forefront of Tennis and develop the next generation of players to carry on the great tradition of American tennis.

With the exception of Venus and Serena Williams and perhaps Andy Roddick and James Blake the US program has fallen on hard times.

Where are the current counterparts to past top players such as Pete Sampras, Andre Agassi, Jim Courier, Jimmy Connors and Arthur Ashe? There is no question that the USTA has the resources and money for this.

When I last checked Donald Young, a 21 year old African American who had a sensational junior tennis record, has been relegated to playing on the pro satellite tour. What ever happened to Lavar Harper Griffith, another African American player from few years ago who showed promise? When I checked, he was relegated to being a practice player of the US Davis Cup team.

It will be interesting to see if the USTA will find a way to partner with John McEnroe on this project. His younger brother Patrick is the USTA's General Manager of Player Development.

It is a precarious situation, John as the outspoken innovator and Patrick as the company man. In a resent article in Sports Illustrated (May 31, 2010), when asked if he hoped to work with Patrick he said, "He hasn't called to congratulate me. I don't know what that means."

With an annual operating budget exceeding $200 million and top notch training facilities, it should be a no brainer. However, internal politics and unwise financial deals may be a stumbling block. An article in the New York Times (Nov. 24, 2009) revealed that the USTA paid former Chief Executive of Professional Tennis, Arlen Kantarian more that $9 million in 2008.

The USTA Player Development Program has undergone many transformations over the years while having very little to show for players developed and money spent.

A few years ago as National President of the American Tennis Association I had the opportunity to be a member of the USTA Plan for Growth Steering Committee. The organization had committed to spending $35 million to grow the game. I was the only African American on the committee of about 18 that included tennis legend Billie Jean King.

I offered that the growth of the game lies in the urban inner city areas of the country. This is where the majority of the population lives. My comments were ignored. This remains true today. This is not rocket science.

Maybe that is the problem with the USTA hierarchy it makes to much sense. Let's hope that the current situation and John McEnroe's bold initiative move wakes up the establishment.

Let's not forget that the issue of racial diversity is an open sore in the organization that continues to be an issue. Racial exclusion is a well documented fact in the USTA's past.

History was made with the election of the first African American President, but many areas of society still lag behind in leveling the playing field. Shortly after being appointed to his position as General Manager of Men's Tennis for the USTA, Patrick McEnroe fired Rodney Harmon, an

African American and long time employee who held past positions as Director of Men's Tennis, Olympic Men's Tennis Coach, and Director of Minority Participation.

For an organization that is trying live down a past history of racial discrimination the record is not promising.

Zina Garrison was fired as Fed Cup Captain and filed a racial discrimination suit against the USTA that was settled out of court. Cecil Holland and Sande French, two high quality tennis officials, filed a racial discrimination suit and settled out of court. Leslie Allen, a former tour pro player and Magna Cum Laude graduate of USC, was let go as Fed Cup Chair. USTA's first Chief Diversity Officer, Karlyn Lothery left after two years on the job. Not only does the organization have a major problem with player development but racial diversity continues to be a black eye throughout the program.

Source: Article author: Bernard A. Chavis. Rightsholder: Bleacher Report; http://bleacherreport.com/articles/406753-john-mcenroes-bold-move-to-revive-us-tennis.

Decline

The marketing goals for the **decline** stage of the PLC are difficult to pinpoint because decisions must be made regarding what to do with a failing product. These decisions are based largely on the competition and how the sports organization chooses to react to the competition.

The distinctive characteristic of the decline phase of the PLC is that sales are steadily diminishing. Several alternative strategies might be considered during the decline phase. One alternative is referred to as deletion. As the name implies, the product is dropped from the organization's product mix. A second alternative, **harvesting (or milking)**, is when the organization retains the sports product but offers little or no marketing support. A final alternative is simply maintaining the product at its current level of marketing support in the hope that competitors will withdraw from a market that is already in decline.

Other life cycle considerations

The PLC, although an excellent tool for strategic decision making, is not without limitations. These limitations include generalizing the length of the PLC, applying the PLC to broad product categories only, and using the PLC to analyze "pure" sporting goods only. Each of these potential weaknesses of the PLC model is discussed below.

Length and shape of the PLC

Figure 8.1 depicted the traditional length and shape of the PLC. However, each product life cycle has its own unique shape and unique length, depending on the product under consideration and the nature of the marketing environment. Several variants of the typical PLC length, including the fad PLC, the classic PLC, and the seasonal PLC are shown in Figure 8.2.

Fad

The **fad** PLC (Figure 8.2a) is characterized by accelerated sales and accelerated acceptance of the product followed by decline stages. Often, sports marketers

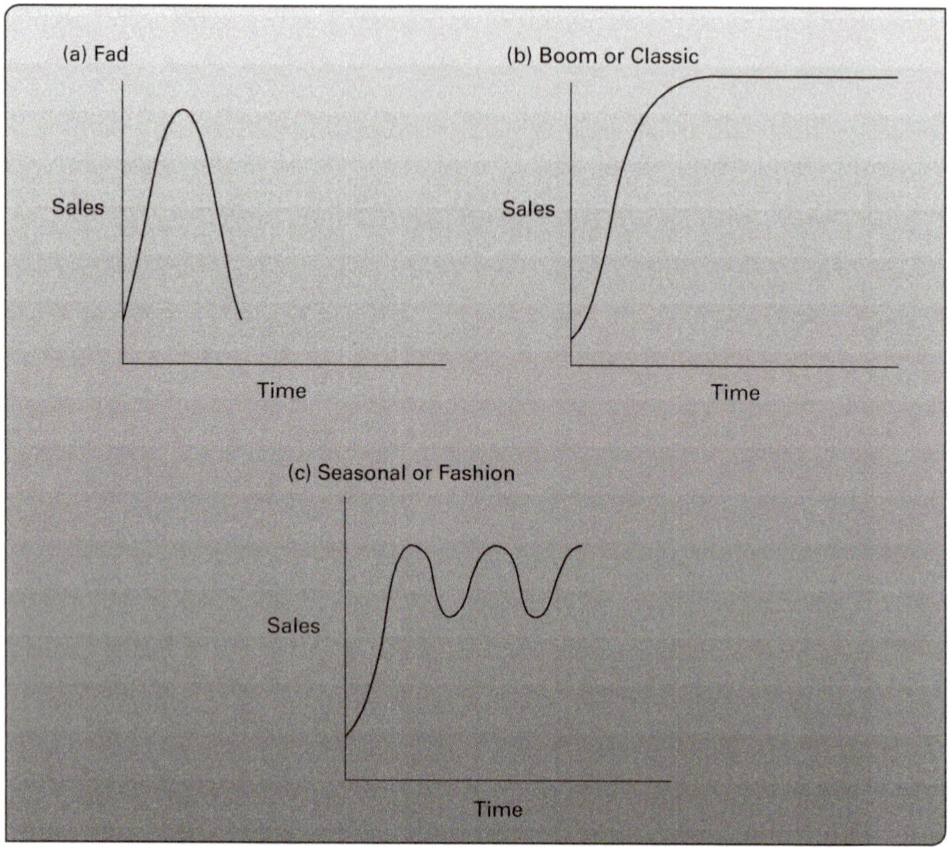

Figure 8.2 Selected product life cycle patterns

realize their products will be novelty items that get into the market, make a profit, and then quickly exit. These one-time, short-term offerings would follow the volatile fad cycle. The ABA red, white, and blue basketball followed the fad cycle, as do many products in the golf equipment industry. Other examples of a fad cycle include the bobblehead doll as a sports promotion and retro look jerseys and sports apparel. Fitness and fads seem to go hand in hand. While some exercise routines and machines have endured the test of time to become classics, others come and go in a flash.

High-impact aerobics might have been the first of the more modern fitness fads in the 1970s, followed by the cardio-fitness movement of the 1980s. Then came the incorporation of strength training into workouts, and more recent fads include the indoor cycling program called "spinning" and cardio-kickboxing. The latest and greatest exercise fad links the mind and body in routines such as P90X, yoga, and tai chi. Who knows what the next fad might bring?

Classic

Another variation of the PLC is characterized by a continuous stage of maturity (Figure 8.2b). Season tickets for the Green Bay Packers, Frisbees, baseball gloves and bats, tennis balls, and hockey sticks all represent other examples of the PLC known as the **classic**.

Seasonal

The **seasonal** life cycle is found in most sports where the sales of sports products rise and fall with the opening and closing day of the season. To combat the seasonal life cycle, some sports have adopted year-round scheduling. Most auto racing series are run on an 8- to 10-month schedule, giving sponsors almost year-round coverage. Professional tennis has also adopted a continual schedule, but this may not be the best thing for the sport.

When asked what he would do to cure the ills of tennis, former star and current TV analyst John McEnroe did not hesitate before responding, "I would cut the amount of events. Now, there are too many tournaments, so people don't have any idea about what's really important. I would make a schedule that would be like the baseball or basketball season, so we wouldn't go 12 months a year."[21]Somewhat surprisingly, the NBA used the "less-is-more" strategy more than 20 years ago, when the league was plummeting in popularity. David Stern, then a rookie commissioner, significantly cut the number of televised games to increase long-term interest in the sport.

The fad, classic, and seasonal life cycles are three common variants of the traditional PLC. Other products, however, seem to defy all life cycle shapes and lengths. Consider skateboarding. Since its inception in the 1950s skateboarding has been a fad in nearly every decade. Now, skateboarding seems to be here to stay, according to the National Sporting Goods Association (NSGA). Skateboarding posted an unbelievable growth rate in participation for youth ages seven to 17 from 1995 to 2010. Over that 15-year period, skateboarding has experienced 160 percent growth in total participation and a 213 percent increase in frequent participation and was second only to snowboarding, in terms of percentage growth, which experienced 160 percent growth in total participation and a 257 percent increase in frequent participation.[22]

The level of product

8

Another consideration for developing marketing strategy based on the PLC is the level of the product. Historically, the PLC was based on total industry sales for an entire product category, such as basketball shoes, bowling balls, mountain bikes, or golf clubs. Although examining the PLC by category is useful, it is also necessary to understand the PLC by product form and product brand.

Product form refers to product variations within the category. For example, titanium woods, metal woods, and "wood" woods represent three variations in product form in the golf club product category. The potential marketing strategies for each of these product forms differ by the stage of the PLC. The titanium woods are in the growth stage, metal woods are in maturity, and traditional woods are near extinction.

In addition to looking at the product category and form, it is also beneficial to examine various brands. Within the titanium wood form, there are a variety of individual brands, such as Titleist 910 D2 and D3, Ping G10, and Nike's SQ MachSpeed Drive. Each of these brands may be in different stages of the PLC. Therefore, sports marketing managers must give full consideration to variations in the PLC, based on the level of the product (category, form, and brand).

Type of product

The PLC originally was designed to guide strategies for goods. However, the notion of the PLC should be extended to other types of sports products. For instance, individual athletes can be thought of as sports products that move through a life cycle just as products do.

The phenomenal rise, success, and fluctuations of stars like Peyton Manning in the NFL, Tiger Woods of the PGA, and Bode Miller from the U.S. Ski Team demonstrate how numerous athletes may waver through the various phases of the product life cycle. Prior to and after sustaining injuries, the number of products that Manning endorsed has rapidly increased because everyone was aware of his star qualities. However, when these athletes become injured, retire, or encounter turmoil, there may be a significant change in their status within the product life cycle. The former Cleveland Cavaliers' star, LeBron James, has gone through an entire life cycle in the Cleveland market; however, overall LeBron continues to have growth and market presence, retaining the best-selling jersey during the 2010–11 and 2013–14 seasons. At the same time, New York Knicks star, Carmelo Anthony, who had the best-selling jersey during the 2012–13 season, is in the growth phase of his PLC, while the former NBA MVP Shaquille O'Neal entered the decline phase of his playing career after being traded to the Cleveland Cavaliers in the 2009–10 season and then with the Boston Celtics in the 2010–11 season before retiring. Although Shaq was entering the decline phase of his playing career, numerous outside endeavors such as endorsements, albums, movie and TV appearances have kept his career outside of basketball in the growth and maturity stages.

Interestingly, some individual athletes have a unique shape to their PLC. Think about the many professional athletes who have come out of retirement to reintroduce themselves. Mark Spitz attempted to come back to Olympic swimming 20 years after winning seven gold medals in Munich and was no longer able to compete. Jim Palmer, Bjorn Borg, Sugar Ray Leonard, Magic Johnson, and Muhammad Ali all tried to come back after years away from their respective sports and failed miserably. Arnold Palmer, with his incredible staying power, will undoubtedly stay in the maturity phase of his PLC and remain a classic even after playing his last competitive golf tournament. Many aging golfers, such as Tom Jenkins, who won $10.5 million since 1998 on the senior circuit, but won only once on the regular PGA Tour, are experiencing tremendous success on the senior circuit. Unfortunately, many athletes experience a life cycle that is best represented by the fad PLC. For instance, Brian Bosworth (Seattle Seahawks linebacker), Mark "The Bird" Fydrich (Detroit Tigers pitcher), and Buster Douglas (boxing) were all athletes who had short-term success, only to quickly fall into decline for a number of reasons.

Sports teams also can pass through the various phases of the PLC. For instance, the National Basketball Development League awarded a franchise to Canton, Ohio in 2011 and it is in the introductory stage of its PLC. In 2012, many considered the Phoenix Coyotes to be in the decline phase as their stay in Phoenix still remains in limbo. Likewise, the Sacramento Kings under previous majority owner the Maloof family were contemplating leaving Sacramento for a new, more appealing market after an impasse in their new arena negotiations. However, the 2013 transaction created an exchange of ownership, offering the organization "an opportunity of adjustment" in the PLC, moving from decline to growth. Under new owner Vivek Ranadivé, the Kings would hope to develop new strategies to enhance the Kings' brand and its offerings to enhance the growth of the organization. Keep in mind that the revitalization of these product examples would each require completely different marketing strategies.

Professional and collegiate sports leagues also pass through the stages of the PLC. Many of the established leagues in the United States are going global and are currently in the introduction phase of their life cycles internationally. Therefore, the leagues have directed their marketing efforts toward making fans aware of them and generating interest. For example, the international markets are attracting a lot of attention by major sports leagues/structures in the United States as the accompanying spotlight illustrates.

SPOTLIGHT ON INTERNATIONAL SPORTS MARKETING

X Games global expansion continues with TV deals in new host markets, syndication deals in multiple other countries

With the 2013 X Games global expansion about to launch in Aspen, the growth of the X Games is taking another step in its own progression, as ESPN and its Local Organizing Committees (LOC) announce agreements with TV partners in each of the four host markets outside of the United States, as well as multiple syndication agreements in other markets. This first group of television partners around the world will be joined by others in the months ahead, as ESPN continues discussions with potential distributors around the world.

In addition to these partners, ESPN and ABC networks in the United States and countries around the world will also televise and stream coverage of the X Games events. Local television coverage varies by country and should check local listings for further details.

As the 2013 X Games schedule launches, television coverage of X Games Aspen will be seen in 184 countries, reaching more than 430 million homes.

X GAMES HOST MARKET TV PARTNERS

ESPN and its LOCs have reached deals with television partners in each of the four non-US event host markets – France (X Games Tignes), Brazil (X Games Foz do Iguaçu), Spain (X Games Barcelona) and Germany (X Games Munich).

- France – Canal+: In France, ESPN partners with Canal+ Events for X Games Tignes, and has reached agreement with Canal+ for a combination of live and delayed coverage for all six global X Games events, including as much as 120 hours of live coverage and up to 50 hours of highlights and packaged programming. The leading pay-TV provider in France, Canal+ is a leader in television and multi-screen technology, and will provide coverage across its Canal+ and Canal+ Sport channels.
- Brazil – Rede TV: In Brazil, where ESPN partners with Brunoro Sport Business for X Games Foz do Iguaçu, ESPN has reached an agreement with Rede TV – one of Brazil's leading television networks – will bring Brazilian fans at least 10 hours of live coverage from X Games Foz do Iguaçu, live or delayed coverage from each of the other five X Games events, as well as highlights, news and information coverage of X Games events.
- Spain – MarcaTV, TV3: In Spain, where ESPN partners with Seven Marketing for X Games Barcelona, ESPN has reached agreements with Marca TV to provide Spanish-language coverage and with TV3 for exclusive coverage in Catalan. Marca TV will also provide a combination of live and delayed

coverage of all six X Games events from around the world. TV3 will provide live, delayed and highlight coverage from all six X Games events across its channels (TV3, Esport3, Super3 and 3/24), with more than 20 hours of live coverage from X Games Barcelona.

- Germany – ProSiebenSat.1 Group: In Germany, where ESPN partners with Munich Olympic Park for X Games Munich, ESPN and ProSiebenSat.1 Group have reached an agreement for a combination of live, delayed and highlights programming on Pro7 free-to-air and pay TV channels, as well as delivering an X Games channel with live streaming and on-demand video on their video portal MyVideo.de. TV and digital coverage will include extensive live, delayed and packaged programming around X Games Munich as well as live and delayed coverage of all five other X Games events.

ADDITIONAL X GAMES TV PARTNERS

In addition to the host markets, ESPN has finalized multiple initial syndication deals in key markets, including:

- Denmark – DR: DR is Denmark's national broadcasting company and the oldest and largest media outlet in the country. DR will deliver live and highlights coverage of all six X Games events to fans throughout Denmark on its newly re-launched channel DR3.
- Italy – Sky Italia: Sky Italia, the leading pay television provider in Italy, will deliver up to 30 hours of delayed and highlights coverage of X Games Aspen, X Games Tignes and X Games Los Angeles to fans in Italy.
- Norway – NRK: The national television and radio broadcaster in Norway, NRK is the country's largest media outlet and will deliver extensive live, delayed and highlights coverage of all six X Games events across its free-to-air channels.
- Sweden – SVT: One of Sweden's leading national media outlets, SVT will deliver up to 40 hours of live and delayed coverage of X Games Aspen and X Games Los Angeles.
- Canada – TSN, RDS: TSN, in which ESPN is a partial owner, will provide live and highlights coverage of X Games throughout the year, beginning with 22 hours of programming around X Games Aspen (including 14 hours of live coverage), at least 20 hours of live, delayed and highlights coverage from X Games Los Angeles and at least 20 hours of coverage across the other four events. Additionally, RDS, the French-language sister-network to TSN, will provide at least 60 hours of coverage across the six events to French-Canadian fans.
- China – Shanghai Media Group, Guangdong TV, POWER Sports, ESPN Star Sports: For Chinese action sports fans, leading Chinese television and media companies, Shanghai Media Group (Great Sports channel), Guangdong TV (Guangdong Sports Channel) and nationwide sports channel POWER Sports will each provide at least 10 hours of highlights programming on their channels from the six X Games events. In hotels and foreign compounds in China, News Corporation-owned broadcaster ESPN Star Sports (in which ESPN was a joint venture partner until Oct. 2012) will deliver

at least 60 hours of highlights and packaged programming coverage from the six events on its networks.

- Hong Kong – TVB: Hong Kong's leading free-to-air channel, TVB will provide at least 12 hours of highlights and packaged programming on its channels from the six X Games events.
- India – ESPN Star Sports: News Corporation-owned broadcaster ESPN Star Sports will bring fans in India at least 60 hours of highlights and packaged programming coverage from the six events on its networks in India.
- Japan – NHK: Japan's national broadcaster will provide at least four hours of highlights coverage from X Games Aspen.
- Southeast Asia – Fox Sports: Fox Sports will bring fans in Southeast Asia at least 60 hours of highlights and packaged programming coverage from the six events on its networks throughout Southeast Asia.
- Europe (pan-Regional) – Extreme Sports Channel: One of the leading action sports media outlets, Extreme Sports Channel and ESPN have reached an agreement for 60 hours of delayed programming and highlights across all six X Games events. The channel, dedicated to delivering top action sports programming 24/7/365, will bring X Games content to more than 30 countries across Europe (some territorial blackouts apply – see local listings for details)
- Worldwide – SNTV: One of the world's leading sports video news agencies, SNTV will feature expanded highlights coverage from each day of all six X Games events across its wire services.
- Worldwide – Laureus: Laureus, comprising the Laureus World Sports Academy, the Sport For Good Foundation and the Laureus World Sports Awards, will feature highlights from X Games Aspen.

ESPN NETWORKS COVERAGE WORLDWIDE

In addition to its third-party television partners, ESPN networks around the world will deliver extensive live, delayed and highlights coverage from all six X Games events in 2013. Among the markets in which ESPN networks will deliver extensive live and/or delayed coverage of X Games events are:

- United States: ABC, ESPN, ESPN2 and ESPN3 will deliver US fans live coverage of all six X Games events, as well as packaged programs, highlights and delayed replay coverage.
- Spanish-speaking Latin America: ESPN's multiple television and broadband networks throughout Spanish-speaking Latin America will deliver extensive live and delayed coverage of X Games events.
- Brazil: ESPN Brazil will provide extensive live, delayed and studio coverage of all six X Games events on television and via broadband streaming.
- Australia, New Zealand, Pacific Islands: ESPN, ESPN2 and ESPN3.com will deliver extensive coverage of the six X games events to fans in Australia, while ESPN will bring live and delayed coverage to New Zealand and the Pacific Islands.
- Europe: ESPN America will deliver a combination of live and delayed replay coverage of all X Games events to more than 20 million

households in more than 40 countries.

- Middle East and Africa: ESPN networks in the Middle East, Israel and Africa will bring fans live, delayed and highlights coverage of all X Games events.

Scheduling details vary by region and by event, and fans should see local listings in the weeks and months ahead for details.

The 2013 X Games season kicks off a new era, with the global expansion's six-event schedule – featuring eight sports, 26 disciplines and new iconic venues – Aspen, Colo., USA; Tignes, France, Foz do Iguaçu, Brazil; Barcelona, Spain; Munich, Germany, Los Angeles, Calif., USA – they will combine to offer the most wide-ranging program of sports and disciplines in X Games history. 2013 will also see the addition of Mountain Bike Slopestyle, Women's Skateboard Park and the return of BMX Freestyle Dirt.

Source: Article author: Grace Coryell. Rightsholder: ESPN; http://espnmediazone.com/us/press-releases/2013/01/x-games-global-expansion-continues-with-tv-deals-in-new-host-markets-syndication-deals-in-multiple-other-countries/.

Each level of sports product must receive careful consideration by sports marketers because of the strategic implications. Sometimes the interaction of athlete, team, and league PLCs can make strategic decisions even more challenging. Take the case of Derrick Rose, point guard for the Chicago Bulls in the NBA. The Bulls and the NBA could be seen in the maturity phase of the PLC, while Rose is in introduction. What about the case of Barry Zito? Zito is a veteran in Major League Baseball, but needed to be marketed as a new product for the Giants. As complex as this seems, sports marketers must remember not to neglect any of these products. Decisions will be made about the perceived relevance of each of these types of products.

Diffusion of innovations

New sports and sports products, or **innovations**, are continually being introduced to consumers and pass through the various stages of the product life cycle as described in the previous section. Initially, the new sport and sports product are purchased or tried by a small number of individuals (roughly 2.5 percent of the marketplace). Then, more and more people begin to try the new product. Consider the "metal wood" in golf. When this innovation was first introduced in the late 1970s, only the boldest "pioneers" of golf were willing to adopt the new technology. Now, only a very small percentage of the golfing population does not carry metal woods in their bags.[23]

The rate at which new sports products spread throughout the marketplace is referred to as the **diffusion of innovation**.[24] The rate of acceptance of a sport innovation is influenced by three factors, which are shown in Figure 8.3. The first factor affecting the rate of diffusion is the characteristics of the new product. These characteristics, such as trialability, observability, perceived complexity, relative advantage, and compatibility, were discussed earlier in the chapter in the context of new product factors. The interaction of these factors can accelerate or slow the rate of diffusion. Perceived newness, the second factor that influences the rate of diffusion, refers to the type of new product from the consumer's perspective (continuous, dynamically

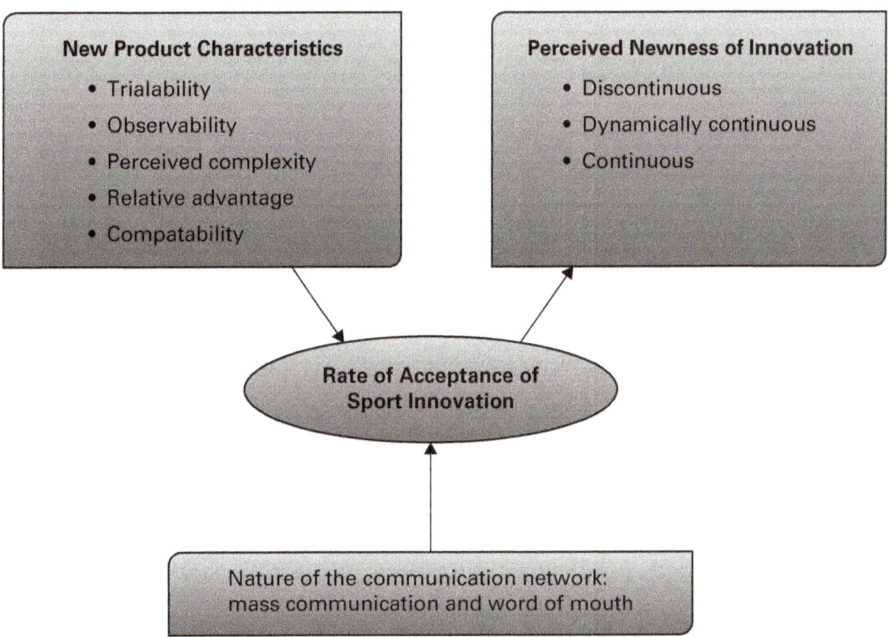

Figure 8.3 Model of the rate of diffusion

continuous, and discontinuous innovations). Typically, continuous innovations have a faster rate of acceptance because they require no behavioral change and little disruption for the adopter. The third factor is the nature of the communication network. The rate and way in which information is shared about a new sports product is critical to its success, as well as the speed of acceptance. Most marketers conceptualize the communications network for innovations as a two-step flow of information. In the first step, the initial consumers try a new product or opinion leaders are influenced by mass communication such as advertising, sales promotions, and the Internet. Then, in the second step, opinion leaders use word-of-mouth communication to provide information about the new product to the rest of the target market. Martin and Higgins believe this two-step flow of information is especially important to sports innovations because, "unlike typical consumer purchase decisions, which involve only the individual, recent studies show that of the consumers who attend sporting events, less than 2 percent attend by themselves."[25]

The diffusion of innovations is an important concept for sports marketers to understand because of its strategic implications. Stated simply, the marketer must know the stage of the life cycle and the characteristics of the consumers likely to try the product at any given stage. Let us examine the characteristics of each group as a product spreads throughout the marketplace.

Types of adopters

There are several **types of adopters. Innovators** represent those consumers who are the first to adopt a new sports product as it enters the marketplace. Because they are the first to adopt, these consumers carry the highest risk associated with the new product. These risks may be social (what will others think of the product?), economic (costs are high and drive up the price), and performance (will the product perform as it was intended?). This younger and usually high-income group of consumers is also known for the high degree of interaction and communication they have with other innovators.

The next group of consumers to adopt a new sports product is the **early adopters**. As with the innovators, this group is also characterized by high social status. It is perhaps the most important group to sports marketers, however, because they carry high degrees of opinion leadership and word-of-mouth influence. As just discussed, these individuals are the key players in communicating the value of new sports products to the majority of consumers.

Once the new sports product has spread past the early stages of the product life cycle, the **early majority** is ready for adoption. This group is above average in social status but more deliberate in their willingness to try new products. In addition, this group is heavily influenced by information provided by the innovators and early adopters.

The **late majority** adopt innovations in the late stages of maturity of the product life cycle. As their name implies, over half (roughly 60 percent) of the market has now purchased or has tried the new product before the late majority decide to do so. These individuals are skeptical and have less exposure to mass media.

The final group of adopters is known as **laggards**. These individuals are oriented toward the past and tend to be very traditional in the sports products they choose. They begin to adopt products in the declining stage of the product life cycle. Clearly, prices must be reduced, and promotions encouraging trial and widespread distribution must all be in place for laggards to adopt new products.

Summary

Few sports products are critical to the success of any organization. Newness, however, can be thought of in any number of ways. The organizational perspective on newness depends on whether the firm has marketed the product in the past. From the organizational perspective, new products are categorized as follows: new-to-the-world products, new product category entries, product line extensions, product improvements, and repositioning.

Conversely, newness from the consumer's perspective is based on the consumer's perception of whether the product represents an innovation. From the consumer's perspective, new products are classified as discontinuous innovations, dynamically continuous innovations, or continuous innovations. Discontinuous innovations represent the most innovative new products, whereas continuous innovations are simply improvements or limitation products.

Regardless of how new products are classified, organizations are constantly searching for the next innovation that will help the firm achieve its financial objectives. Rather than leave this to chance, many organizations use a systematic approach called the new product development process. The new product development process consists of the following phases: idea generation, idea screening, analysis of the concept, developing the sports product, test marketing, and commercialization. Idea generation considers any and all ideas for new products from sources such as employees, competitors, and consumers. During the idea screening phase, these new product ideas are screened and the poorer ones are eliminated. To perform this task, organizations sometime use a new product screening checklist. In the third phase, analysis of the sports product concept, marketing research is used to assess consumer reaction to the proposed product. More specifically, concept tests are used to gauge the product's strengths and weaknesses, as well as the consumer's intent to use the new product. Next, a prototype of the new product is designed so that consumers can get an even better idea about the product. In addition, preliminary decisions regarding marketing strategy are established. In the sixth stage, the new product is test marketed. Depending on the product and the market conditions, sports marketers may use standardized, controlled, or simulated test markets. The final stage of the new product development process is commercialization in which the new product is formally introduced in the marketplace. Whether the product succeeds is a function of a number of factors, such as the product considerations (e.g., trialability and relative advantage), other marketing mix variables (e.g., pricing), and marketing environment considerations (e.g., competition).

As a new product reaches commercialization, it moves through a series of four stages known as the product life cycle (PLC). The PLC is an important marketing concept in that the stage of the life cycle dictates marketing strategy. The four stages of the PLC include introduction, growth, maturity, and decline. At introduction, the marketing goal is to generate awareness of the new sports product. The broad goal of the growth phase is to build consumer preference for the sports product and begin to expand the product line. During maturity, the number of promotions is increased and marketers seek to maintain any competitive advantage they have obtained during growth. Finally, the product goes through decline, where decisions must be made regarding whether to delete the product or extend the life cycle.

Although each product has a life cycle, the length of that life and the speed at which a product progresses through the four stages is unique for each product. Some sports products grow and decline at a rapid pace. These are known as fads. Other products, which seem to last in maturity forever, are called classics. The most common life cycle for sports products is known as seasonal. Other life cycle considerations are the level of product and the type of product. For example, sports marketers might analyze the life cycle of leagues, teams, and individual athletes, as well as other types of sports products.

The rate of diffusion is the speed at which new products spread throughout the marketplace. The rate of diffusion, or speed of acceptance, is based on three broad factors: new product characteristics (e.g., trialability and observability), perceived newness (e.g., discontinuous innovation), and the nature of the communications network. It is critical that sports marketers monitor the rate of diffusion and understand the characteristics of consumers that try new products as they spread throughout the marketplace.

Innovators are the first group of consumers to try a new product. They are generally younger, have higher incomes, and have a strong tolerance for risk. The next group of consumers to try a sports product is the early adopters. This is a larger group than the innovators and, as such, they are key consumers to target. After the product has passed through the initial stages of the product life cycle, the early majority adopt the product. This group is above average in income, but more deliberate in trying new things. The late majority adopts the product during the late stages of maturity and finally the laggards may try new products. Strategically, sports marketers must adopt a different marketing mix when marketing to each new product adopter group.

Key terms

- classic
- commercialization
- continuous innovations
- decline
- developing the sports product
- diffusion of innovation
- discontinuous innovations
- dynamically continuous innovations
- early adopters
- early majority
- fad
- growth
- harvesting (or milking)
- idea generation
- idea screening
- innovations
- innovators
- introduction
- laggards
- late majority
- maturity
- new product category entries
- new product development process
- new product success factors
- new sports products
- new-to-the-world products
- product form
- product life cycle
- seasonal
- test marketing
- types of adopters

Review questions

1. What is meant by a "new sports product"? Describe a "new sports product" from the organization's perspective and from the consumer's perspective.
2. What is the difference between discontinuous, dynamically continuous, and continuous innovations? Provide examples of each to support your answer.
3. Describe, in detail, the new product development process.
4. Why is test marketing so important to sports marketers in the new product development process? What are the three types of test markets? Comment on the advantages and disadvantages of each type of test market.
5. What are the critical success factors for new sports products?
6. Describe the product life cycle concept. Why is the product life cycle so critical to sports marketers? What is it used for? How can the product life cycle be extended?
7. What are some of the variations in the shape of the traditional product life cycle?
8. Define the diffusion of innovations. What are the different types of adopters for innovations? Describe the characteristics of each type of adopter.

Exercises

1. For each of the following sports products, indicate whether you believe they are discontinuous, dynamically continuous, or continuous innovations: WNBA, titanium golf clubs, and skysurfing.
2. Contact the marketing department of three sporting goods manufacturers or sports organizations and conduct a brief interview regarding the new product development process. Does each organization follow the same procedures? Does each organization follow the new product development process discussed in the chapter?
3. In what stage of the product life cycle is Major League Baseball? Support your answer with research.
4. Find an example of a "new sports product." Develop a survey using the critical success factors for new sports products and ask 10 consumers to complete the instrument. Summarize your findings

and indicate whether you think the new product will be successful, based on your research.

5. Some people think boxing may be in the decline phase of the product life cycle. Develop a strategy to extend the product life cycle of boxing.

Internet exercises

1. Search the Internet and find examples of three "new sports products" recently introduced in the marketplace.
2. Find three Internet sites of professional athletes in any sport. In what stage of the product life cycle are these athletes? Support with evidence found on the Internet.
3. Search the Internet for an example of a new sports product that could be classified as a fad. Describe the product and why you think the product is a fad.

Endnotes

1 William Zikmund and Michael d'Amico, *Marketing*, 4th ed. (St. Paul: West, 1993).
2 "Raley Field Pioneers the First Wireless Ballpark; Stadium Launches WiFi – Wireless Technology – Application Throughout Ballpark to Better Serve Fans," *Business Wire* (September 3, 2003).
3 Donna Goodison, "New Balance Adds Brine to Beef Up Sports Shoes," *The Boston Herald* (August 9, 2006).
4 Kurt Badenhausen, "How Michael Jordon Made $90 Million in 2013," *Forbes* (February 27, 2014). Available from: http://www.forbes.com/sites/kurtbadenhausen/2014/02/27/how-michael-jordan-made-90-million-in-2013/, accessed February 25, 2014.
5 "Wilson Seeks 'the Perfect Feel' With New BLX Racquet Technology," *Tennis Industry* (January 2010). Available from: http://www.tennisindustrymag.com/articles/2010/01/wilson_seeks_the_perfect_feel.html, accessed June 19, 2014.
6 Matt Synder, "Chicago Approves $500 Million in Renovations to Wrigley Field," *CBSSports.com* (July 24, 2013). Available from: http://www.cbssports.com/mlb/eye-on-baseball/22873768/chicago-approves-500-million-in-renovations-to-wrigley-field.
7 Mark Glover, "Taking the Cue – New Billiard Parlors Cater to Family Crowds and Aren't Shy About Giving Hustlers the Heave," *The Sacramento Bee* (January 15, 1996).
8 Don Muret and John Lombardo, "AEG Involved in Massive Moscow Sports Complex," *Street & Smith's Sports Business Journal* (March 28–April 3, 2011). Available from: http://www.sportsbusinessdaily.com/Journal/Issues/2011/03/28/Facilities/AEG-Russia.aspx?hl=All%20Sport&sc=0, accessed June 19, 2014.
9 Del Hawkins, Roger Best, and Kenneth Coney, *Consumer Behavior: Building Marketing Strategy*, 7th ed. (New York: McGraw-Hill, 1998), 248–250.
10 James J. Zhang, Dennis W. Smith, Dale G. Pease, and Matthew T. Mahar, "Spectator Knowledge of Hockey as a Significant Predictor of Game Attendance," *Sport Marketing Quarterly*, vol. 5, no. 3 (1996), 41–48.
11 Susan Higgins and James Martin, "Managing Sport Innovations: A Diffusion Theory Perspective," *Sport Marketing Quarterly*, vol. 5, no. 1 (1996), 43–50.
12 Bill Richards, "Nike Plans to Swoosh into Sports Equipment But It's a Tough Game," *The Wall Street Journal* (January 6, 1998), Al.
13 Gilbert Churchill, *Basic Marketing Research*, 3rd ed. (Fort Worth: Dryden Press, 1996).
14 Theodore Levitt, "Exploit the Product Life Cycle," *Harvard Business Review* (November 1965).
15 Rick Burton and Dennis Howard, "Professional Sports Leagues: Marketing Mix Mayhem," *Marketing Management*, vol. 8, no. 1 (1999), 37.
16 "PWC sales improving in 2012," *PowerSportsBusiness* (September 25, 2012). Available from: http://www.powersportsbusiness.com/top-stories/2012/09/25/pwc-sales-improving-in-2012/.
17 http://zoombang.com/, ©2014 Zoombang, Inc., accessed June 19, 2014. ©2014 Zoombang, Inc.
18 SFIA, *SFIA 2013 Participation Topline Report* (2013).
19 "GolfLogix and Garmin Enter Consumer Handheld GPS Golf Market; ForeFront to Exclusively Distribute GolfLogix GPS Devices," *PR Newswire US* (January 25, 2007).
20 David Ranii, "Reclaiming Its Turf; A Raleigh Company That Has the Rights to AstroTurf, the Stuff of Football Legend, Has Big Plans," *The Pantagraph* (April 9, 2007).
21 David Hidgon, "Trim the Season to Grow the Game," *Tennis* (November 1996), 22.

22 "The Action Sports Market," *Active Marketing Group* (2007).
23 James P. Sterba, "Your Golf Shots Fall Short? You Didn't Spend Enough," *The Wall Street Journal* (February 23, 1996), B7.
24 Everett Rogers, *Diffusion of Innovations*, 3rd ed. (New York: Free Press, 1983).
25 Bernard J. Mullin, Stephen Hardy, and William Sutton, *Sports Marketing* (Champaign, IL: Human Kinetics Publishers, 1993).

Promotion concepts

After completing this chapter, you should be able to:

- Identify the promotion mix tools.
- Describe the elements of the communication process.
- Understand the promotion planning model.
- Compare the advantages and disadvantages of the various promotional mix tools.
- Understand the importance of integrated marketing communication to sports marketers.

Just ask anyone the first thing that comes to mind when they think of sports marketing, and they are likely to say advertisements produced by corporations such as Nike, Gatorade, and Anheuser Busch or events such as the Super Bowl, the Masters, Daytona 500, and March Madness. Many of these advertisers utilize star athletes to endorse their products. Sports and sports celebrities have become a major spectacle of today's media culture. Sports celebrities have been looked upon as role models for decades, and with the technological advances in broadcast and interactive media, it appears that the famous and not so famous athletes are everywhere.[1] Some of the most widely utilized advertising spokespersons include famous athletes such as Michael Jordan (Nike, Hanes, Gatorade), Tiger Woods (Nike), LeBron James (Nike, Gatorade) Peyton Manning (ESPN, MasterCard, Direct TV, Sony TV, Gatorade, and newly acquired Papa Johns), and Danica Patrick (GoDaddy.com, Tissot, Hot Wheels). While many of the wealthy athletes make most of their money from endorsements Floyd Mayweather makes 100 percent of his money from salary or winnings. Mayweather makes $85 million on the contracts from his fights and that total does not include any endorsement sums.[2] As we have discussed, sports marketing is much more than advertisements using star athlete endorsers. It involves developing a sound product or service, pricing it correctly, and making sure it is available to consumers when and where they ask for it. However, the necessary element that links the other marketing mix variables together is promotion.

Typically, the terms *promotion* and *advertising* are used synonymously. **Promotion**, however, includes much more than traditional forms of advertising. It involves all forms of communication to consumers. For many organizations, sports are quickly becoming the most effective and efficient way to communicate with current and potential target markets. The combination of tools available to sports marketers to communicate with the public is known as the promotional mix and consists of the following **promotion mix elements:**

- ***Advertising*** – a form of one-way mass communication about a product, service, or idea, paid for by an identified sponsor.
- ***Personal selling*** – an interactive form of interpersonal communication designed to build customer relationships and produce sales or sports products, services, or ideas.
- ***Sales promotion*** – short-term incentives usually designed to stimulate immediate demand for sports products or services.
- ***Public or community relations*** – evaluation of public attitudes, identification of areas within the organization in which the sports population may be interested, and building of a good "image" in the community.
- ***Sponsorship*** – investing in a sports entity (athlete, league, team, event, and so on) to support overall organizational objectives, marketing goals, and more specific promotional objectives.

Within each of the promotion mix elements are more specialized tools to aid in reaching promotional objectives. For example, sales promotions can take the form of sweepstakes, rebates, coupons, or free samples. Advertising can take place on Twitter, Instagram, Facebook, television, in print, or as stadium signage. Sponsors might communicate through an athlete, team, or league. Each of these promotional tools is a viable alternative when considering the most effective promotion mix for a sports organization. Regardless of which tool we choose, the common thread in each element of the promotion mix is communication. Because communication is such an integral part of promotion, let us take a more detailed look at the communications process.

Communications process

The communications process is an essential element for all aspects of sports marketing. **Communication** is the process of establishing a commonness of thought between the sender and the receiver. To establish this "oneness" between the sender and the receiver, the sports marketer's message must be transmitted via the complex communications process.

The interactive nature of the communications process allows messages to be transmitted from sports marketer (source) to consumer (receiver) and from consumer (source) to sports marketer (receiver). Traditionally, sports marketers' primary means of communication to consumers has been through the various promotion mix elements (e.g., advertisements, sponsorships, sales promotions, and salespeople). Sports marketers also communicate with consumers via other elements of the marketing mix.

SPORTS MARKETING HALL OF FAME

Bill Veeck

Known as the Promotion King of Baseball, Bill Veeck single-handedly changed the course of sports marketing. Veeck pioneered promotional events that today have become commonplace. For instance, Veeck initiated Ladies Night and Straight-A Night at the ballpark. One of Veeck's most memorable promotions took place on August 19, 1951, when a pinch-hitter was announced in the bottom half of the first inning in a game between the St. Louis Browns and the Detroit Tigers. Over the furious objections of the Detroit manager, Red Rolfe, the batter was declared a legitimate member of the Browns. Bill Veeck, then owner of the Browns, cautioned his pinch-hitter before he left the dugout that "I've got a man in the stands with a high-powered rifle, and if you swing he'll fire."

What was the fuss? Veeck sent in a 3-foot-7-inch midget named Eddie Gaedel to pinch-hit for the Browns. Gaedel was promptly walked on four straight pitches and removed from the game for a pinch-runner. Gaedel was quoted as saying, "For a minute, I felt like Babe Ruth."

For all his successful promotions, Veeck is also remembered for one that turned sour in the mid-1970s. Called "Disco Demolition Night," the idea of the promotion was for fans to bring their disco albums to the ballpark to be burned in a bonfire. Unfortunately, fans stormed the field, a riot ensued, and the White Sox were forced to forfeit the second game of a doubleheader.

Veeck also instituted a promotion where fans were given signs with "yes" and "no" on them and asked to vote on strategy during a game. The "Grandstand Managers" led the Browns to a 5–3 victory. Promotions such as this led Veeck to be known as a true "fan's fan." He once stated that "every day was Mardi Gras and every fan was king," and "the most beautiful thing in the world is a ballpark filled with people." His marketing and fan orientation forged the way for later marketers of all sports.

Source: Adapted from Bill Veeck, *Veeck as in Wreck: Autobiography of Bill Veeck* (New York: Simon and Schuster, 1962).

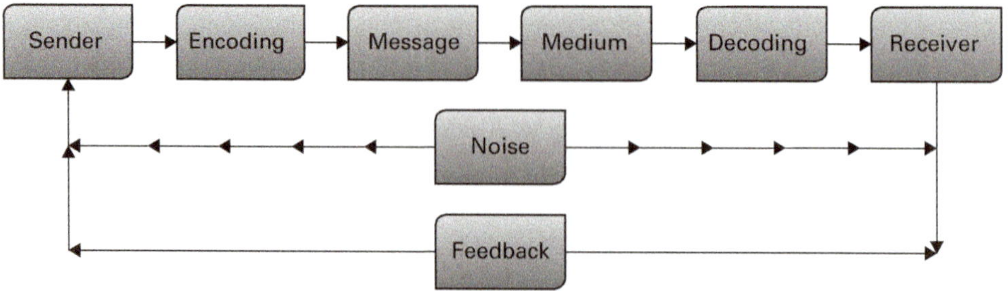

Figure 9.1 Communication process

Source: Solomon, Michael R., *Consumer Behavior*, 3rd Edition, © 1996, p. 194.

For example, the high price of a NASCAR Sprint Cup ticket communicates that it is a higher quality event than the more inexpensive Nationwide Series.

In addition to sports marketers communicating with consumers, consumers communicate back to sports marketers through their behavior. Most notably, consumers communicate whether they are satisfied with the sports product by their purchase behavior. In other words, they attend sporting events and purchase sporting goods.

The communications process begins with the source or the sender of the message. The source encodes the message and sends it through one of many potential communications media. Next, the message is decoded by the receiver of the message, and finally feedback is given to the original source of the message. In the ideal world, messages are sent and interpreted exactly as intended. This, however, rarely occurs because of noise and interference.

Figure 9.1 shows a simplified diagram of the communications process. Each box in the figure represents one of the **elements in the communications process**. These elements include the sender, encoding, message, medium, decoding, receiver, feedback, and noise. To maximize communication effectiveness, it is necessary to have a better understanding of each of these elements in the communications process.

Source

The sender or **source** of the message is where the communication process always originates. In sports marketing, the source of messages is usually a star athlete. For example, you might think of Maria Sharapova shooting pictures with her Canon or Troy Polamalu washing his long hair with Head & Shoulders. Recently, Forbes published the 2013 highest paid athletes.[3]

Interestingly, despite a significant loss of $30 million in revenue, Tiger Woods remained atop the list of athletes to watch as spokespeople in the 21st century. This list also included Roger Federer, Kobe Bryant, LeBron James, Drew Brees and David Beckham. Other notables were Maria Sharapova (22nd), Tom Brady (11th), and Dale Earnhardt Jr (32nd).

Although these sources are all individual athletes, there are many other sources of sports marketing messages. The source of a message might also be a group of athletes, a team, or even the league or sports. Additional sources of sports marketing messages are company spokespeople such as John Solheim, the chairman of Ping Golf, or owners such as Mark Cuban of the Dallas Mavericks.

Sources do not always have to be well recognized and famous individuals to be effective. Sports marketers use actors playing the role of common, everyday sports participants to deliver their message from the perspective of the representative consumer of the sports product or service. Other effective sources are inanimate objects, such as the college mascots like the Big Red mascot from Western Kentucky University featured in the Capital One Mascot Challenge commercials. In addition, sports marketers rely on sales personnel to convey the intended message to consumers. Informal sources, such as friends, family, and coworkers, are also sources of marketing information and messages. As we learned in Chapters 4 and 5, reference groups play an important role in influencing purchase behavior and transmitting the marketing message.

Whatever the source, it is agreed by researchers that to be effective, the source must be credible. **Credibility** is the source's perceived expertise and trustworthiness. A very persuasive message can be created when a combination of these two factors (expertise and trustworthiness) is present in the source. For a source to be trustworthy, that person must be objective and unbiased. Certain athlete endorsers, such as Peyton Manning, former coach Mike Ditka, and Michael Jordan, are known for their perceived trustworthiness. We sometimes look to friends and family as information sources because of their objectivity. In fact, word-of-mouth communication is believed to be extremely persuasive because the source of the message has nothing to gain from delivering the message. Additional unbiased sources are those "man-on-the-street" testimonies given by the common consumer. For example, many of us have seen infomercials that use "regular people" to describe how they lost weight or became physically fit by using the latest and greatest fitness equipment.

Source credibility is also enhanced when the sender of the message has perceived expertise. Naturally, an athlete such as LeBron James is believed to deliver expert messages when the product being promoted is related to athletics, or more specifically, basketball. At least this is what Nike is counting on.

LeBron James, one of NBA's most popular players, came directly out of high school with signing the richest show endorsement deal that any NBA rookie had ever signed. Nike signed James to a $90 million endorsement contract narrowly beating out Adidas, which was the sponsor of James' high school team. James signed endorsement deals with a range of other top companies, including Coca-Cola Corporation. James has endorsed a slew of Coke products, starting with Powerade and eventually moving to Vitamin Water and now Coca Cola. He signed a new shoe contract with Nike in 2010 that pays more than $10 million per year. During the 2012 London Olympics, Nike and McDonald's ran a global advertising campaign that featured James as a champion and rival, respectively.[4]

Ad 9.1 Arnold Palmer: one of the most credible endorsers ever

Source: Lamkin Corporation

Other examples of athletes who endorse products related to their sport include race car drivers such as Dale Earnhardt Jr. promoting Mountain Dew, Chevrolet or Nationwide Insurance and tennis players such as Roger Federer promoting Nike tennis equipment. The general rule of thumb is that the message is more effective if there is a match-up, or congruence, between the qualities of the endorser and the product being endorsed. In fact, the **match-up hypothesis** states that the more congruent the image of the endorser with the image of the product being promoted, the more effective the message.[5]

If the match-up hypothesis holds true, then why do companies pay millions of dollars to star athletes to promote their nonathletic products? For example, Olympic gold medalist snowboarder Shaun White is a pitchman for American Express, hockey star Alex Ovechkin promotes Gillette products, and golfer Phil Mickelson is an endorser for Rolex. First, consumers have an easier time identifying brands associated with celebrity athletes. Second, athletes are used to differentiate competing products that are similar in nature. For instance, most consumers know and associate Derek Jeter with Gatorade. Jeter's association helps to create and then maintain the desired image of Gatorade, which in turn differentiates it from other bottled sports drinks on the market.

Encoding

After the source is chosen, encoding takes place. **Encoding** is translating the sender's thoughts or ideas into a message. To ensure effective encoding, the source of the message must make difficult decisions about the message content. Will the receiver understand and comprehend the message as intended? Will the receiver identify with the message? In 1974, Adidas launched its "Impossible is Nothing" campaign. Originating from a quote taken from the great Muhammad Ali, the notation has been a powerful Adidas slogan for many years and many people will continue to remember the brand with the same philosophy for times to come. However, as of March 2011, Adidas brought together sport, street and style for the very first time collectively highlighting that the company was willing to go "All in" for the consumer.[6] The campaign was the biggest marketing push in the brands history. The premise behind the push was to create intimacy between their assets and the brand fans and consumers. The goal was to help them create and enhance their own style whilst giving them the latest news on hot tendencies.[7] The plan was part of their strategic Business Plan – called Route 2015 – where the company set social and environmental targets that aimed to shape how they would grow and meet their business goals.[8] Adidas wants to close in on the market leader. That is, of course, a name familiar to many: Oregon-based Nike. The company is seeking sales growth of 45 percent to 50 percent by 2015, and "All Adidas" (or "all adidas") is part of that. The idea of the campaign is to show off Adidas' versatility. It won't be just across sports, although those such as the Chicago Bulls' Derrick Rose, soccer stars Lionel Messi and David Beckham, and even the entire Notre Dame Football program is "all in" with the campaign. In addition to sports, the company will highlight its diversity among celebrities, too, with folks like pop star Katy Perry and rapper B.o.B.[9]

Sources have a variety of tools that they use to encode messages. They can use pictures, logos, words, and other symbols. Symbols and pictures are often used in sports marketing to convey the emotional imagery that words cannot capture. The most effective encoding uses multiple media to get the message across (i.e., visually and verbally); presents information in a clear, organized fashion; and always keeps the receiver in mind.[10]

SPOTLIGHT ON SPORTS MARKETING ETHICS

Endorsements remain buyers' market

Twin wrecking balls assaulted sports marketing in 2009. First, the severe recession had the country's biggest brands slashing budgets as never before. Then Tiger Woods, who carried the golf industry on his shoulders, sank into a sex scandal that would end in divorce from his wife and several of his largest corporate sponsors.

So when you ask people across the marketing industry about the state of the individual athlete endorsement market, the best thing they can say is that while those at the top, like Nike's renewal with Maria Sharapova and Puma's renewal with sprinter Usain Bolt, are still getting their deals, it remains a buyers' market. Since marketing can always be done without a celebrity endorser, some brands have always considered endorsements as a luxury. In the worst of times, that's even truer; so the endorsement market has always been erratic.

"The endorsement market has always been tied to the economy, so it took a gigantic and unprecedented nosedive over the past two years that's now flattened out, but I haven't necessarily seen the market go back yet," said John Slusher, vice president of sports marketing at Nike, which has thousands of athletes under contract.

"You still see premium deals for premium assets, like top draft picks, but most NFL and MLB players, we are getting at a fraction of the cost they were before. Most basketball players, we are getting at a fraction of the cost they were two or three years ago. Our strategy hasn't changed. We are buying as many athletes, if not more, but at a better price."

Nike's recent SEC filings show more athletes under contract, but fewer dollars committed.

It's a pretty simple equation," observed Gary Stevenson, the former principal for Wasserman Media Group's corporate consulting practice. "Activation budgets are a lot less, so the endorsement budgets followed suit. You also see a lot of endemic business across sports tanking, and when their business is down it brings marketing around sports down. There used to be 50 guys on the PGA Tour with pretty good equipment deals. Now it's maybe 20 guys." Mike Wiese, director of branded content and entertainment at JWT, said he hadn't detected a slowdown among advertisers using celebrities, but such deals inevitably now take longer to complete. "Especially with procurement departments [at clients] having more influence, there's just more and more people looking at every deal," he said. Still, the top-tier athlete seems to be getting his or her money. "We've seen a lot of companies consolidate at the top," said Sandy Montag, IMG senior corporate vice president. "So that middle tier is having a tough time." Apparently that is even true for Woods, who once set the standard for endorsers. IMG Golf head Mark Steinberg, Woods' longtime agent, said he is still getting calls inquiring about endorsements, even after all the humiliation the golfer has experienced. "There is still demand, for sure," Steinberg said. "I'm not sure we've had the right offers yet. But I'd say the time is right where I'd start to look at expanding his portfolio. . . . There were 18 months when it was really rough sledding. Now what we are seeing is some of the staple industries in golf, like auto and financial, have started to come back strong." There are others who say Woods' follies will harm the golf market for the foreseeable future. Others said they see golf marketing coming back, but believe it will take at least another year to recover. "Tiger's presence in golf over the past decade or more probably prevented a downturn in that market," said Phil de Picciotto, president of athletes and personalities at Octagon, which represents Apolo Anton Ohno, Michael Phelps and Emmitt Smith, among others.

"Tiger and the economy together were a double whammy on golf, and it's going to take a considerable amount of time for that market to return – if it ever does," de Picciotto said. Even if there isn't unanimity of opinion on what effect the fall from grace of golf's top attraction had on the sport, everyone agrees that across marketing a "Tiger effect" chilled – and to some degree is still affecting – brands' willingness to employ athletes as endorsers. The extent to which marketers across sports believe Woods' scandal affected marketing is so varied, it likely depends on how close they were, or indeed, whether they or an associated brand or agency client was tied to Woods. "As much good as Tiger originally did for golf endorsements and golf TV ratings, he may also have done that much harm," said Matt Delzell, group account director at Omnicom's Davie Brown Entertainment marketing agency, which helped pass muster on Woods' endorsements with Gillette and AT&T.

"If you asked me whether the recession or Tiger had more of an impact on endorsements and sports marketing in general, I'd tell you the recession, but not by much. Tiger has that much clout." Added Tony Pace, CMO at Subway, whose endorsers include Philadelphia Phillies first baseman Ryan Howard, Phelps and Fox NFL analyst Michael Strahan: "Because of what happened with Tiger, everyone now gives a third and fourth look at an endorsement prospect, as opposed to just a first and second look before." Frank Mahar at Genesco Sports Enterprises said he's seen no slowdown in demand from clients like Pepsi and Coors, each of which has large league sponsorships they need to complement with player deals. So his version of the Tiger effect is that "we're all a little more aware now – but we already had pretty strong contract language." Still, others insist l'affair d'Tigre has changed endorsement contracts forever. "Breach language and the morals section of contracts are a lot tighter now and you are starting to see some kind of recourse," said Mark Zablow, senior director of marketing at Platinum Rye Entertainment, which secures sports talent for sponsors including Dr Pepper and Procter & Gamble. "In the past, all companies would be able to do is walk away from the deal and stop paying," Zablow said. "Now, we are seeing them ask for money to be paid back. You're also seeing spread-out and back-loaded payments to protect themselves. This is all the Tiger Woods effect. The 'You don't EVER have to worry about him' sell doesn't exist anymore." Davie Brown's Delzell agreed. "Tiger's the example we all reference now," he said. "It's much more difficult to get any program with a celebrity endorser sold in." Jordan Bazant of The Agency, which represents Colt McCoy, Reggie Bush and Troy Aikman, said the industry downturn has had some benefits. "Nothing's being done on pure whim anymore," he said. "The result is a more thorough strategy and a better platform." Steinberg noted that the overall golf market is recovering, and he's back in the market for Woods. "It's clear companies are taking a wait-and-see attitude," he said. "Does that mean there will be bolstered morals clauses? I don't know." Steinberg added that the pinch that Capitol Hill lawmakers put on financial services industry marketing at the height of the recession was equally deleterious as the economy and Woods. Whatever the impact, the situation with Woods accelerated a shift by many marketers from sports to entertainment. "We're all still fighting the Tiger effect, some of which dates back to Kobe," said Doug Shabelman, president of Burns Entertainment & Sports Marketing, in suburban Chicago, an agency that changed its name a few years ago to reflect a broader approach to talent representation. "Five years ago, maybe 35 percent of our business was sports. Now it's 15 percent," said Burns, whose company procures talent for the likes of Unilever and Dannon.

Many of those interviewed said that in addition to price erosion, celebs and athletes are being asked to do more for their fees, whether that's additional appearances, social media or branded content. "The one thing fans all want, it's access, and technology is an accelerant for more access," said John Osborn, president and CEO at BBDO, New York, whose client list includes big sports spenders like FedEx, Gillette and AT&T. "But technology also means their lives are more exposed, whether they like it or not." As an example of effective use of endorsers in new media, Osborn cited campaigns for the launch of Gillette's Fusion ProGlide razor on YouTube and Twitter around the globe resulting in "billions of media exposure, long before the traditional media kicked in."

Gillette has been using sports endorsers for 100 years, and has generally been able to pay less than other categories, due to its heavy media spend, and its penchant for massive retail programs. "Lately that's been true across P&G brands,"' said Greg Via, global director of sports marketing at Gillette, citing Ray Lewis' recent work with Old Spice as an example. "We're looking for 360 branding opportunities for our athletes and so are they." That means you'd better come to brand marketers with more than just a name and a face. "Now you have to package a celebrity with more marketing elements than ever," said Octagon's de Picciotto. So, just as sports properties are becoming media companies, athletes and celebrities are moving in the same direction. Are you ready for the Kobe Network? The Lady Gaga Channel? "Technology has enabled celebrities to become their own media distributors, and our clients want to tap into that passionate fan base," said Greg Luckman, CEO of North America at GroupM ESP, whose clients that use sports marketing include Citi, Xerox and Unilever. "Although it remains a buyer's market, the more forward-thinking and tech-savvy athletes will benefit from this."

Source: Article author: Terry Lefton. Rightsholder: *Sports Business Journal*; http://www.sportsbusinessjournal.com/article/66990.

Message

The next element in the communications process is to develop the **message**, which refers to the exact content of the words and symbols to be transmitted to the receiver. Decisions regarding the characteristics of this message depend on the objective of the promotion, but sports marketers have a wide array of choices. These choices include one- versus two-sided messages, emotional versus rational messages, and comparative versus noncomparative messages.

The **sidedness** of a message is based on the nature of the information presented to the target audience. The messages can be constructed as either one- or two-sided. In a one-sided message, only the positive features of the sports product are described, whereas a two-sided message includes both the benefits and weaknesses of the product.

Another decision regarding the message in the promotion is whether to have an **emotional versus rational appeal**. A rational appeal provides consumers with information about the sports product so they may arrive at a careful, analytical

Table 9.1 Creating a more effective message

• Get the audience aroused.
• Give the audience a reason for listening.
• Use questions to generate involvement.
• Cast the message in terms familiar to your audience and build on points of interest.
• Use thematic organization – tie material together by a theme and present in a logical, irreversible sequence.
• Use subordinate category words – that is, more concrete, specific terms.
• Repeat key points.
• Use rhythm and rhyme.
• Use concrete rather than abstract terms.
• Leave the audience with an incomplete message – something to ponder so they have to make an effort at closure.
• Ask your audience for a conclusion.
• Tell the audience the implications of their conclusion.

Source: James MacLachlan, "Making a Message Memorable and Persuasive," *Journal of Advertising Research*, vol. 23 (December 1983–January 1984), 51–59.

decision, and an emotional appeal attempts to make consumers "feel" a certain way about the sports product. Emotional appeals might include fear, sex, humor, or feelings related to the hard work and competitive nature of sport.

A final message characteristic that may be considered by sports marketers is **comparative messages**. Comparative messages refer to either directly or indirectly comparing your sports product with one or more competitive products in a promotional message. For example, golf ball manufacturers often compare the advantages of their product with competitors' products.

Regardless of the **message characteristics**, the broad objective of promotion is to effectively communicate with consumers. What are some ways to make your sports marketing message more memorable and persuasive? Table 9.1 summarizes a few simple techniques to consider.

Medium

After the message has been formulated, it must be transmitted to receivers through a channel, or communications **medium**. A voice in personal selling, the Internet, television, radio, stadium signage, billboards, blimps, newspapers, magazines, athletes' uniforms, and even athlete's bodies all serve as media for sports marketing communication. In addition to these more traditional media, new communications channels such as social media and the multitude of sports-specific cable programming (e.g., the Golf Channel) are emerging and growing in popularity.

Decisions on which medium or media to choose depend largely on the overall promotional objectives. Also, the media decisions must consider the costs to reach the desired target audience, the medium's flexibility, its ability to reach a highly defined audience, its lifespan, the sports product or service complexity, and the characteristics of the intended target market. These media considerations are summarized in Table 9.2. For example, sports marketers attempting to reach the African American market may choose television as a communications medium

Table 9.2 Making media decisions

- Cost to reach target audience
- Flexibility of media
- Ability to reach highly specialized, defined audience
- Lifespan of the media
- Nature of the sports product being promoted (e.g., complexity of product)
- Characteristics of the intended target market

Table 9.3 Most watched programs in U.S. television history

1. **SuperBowlXLVIII (2014): 111.5 million (Fox)**
2. **Super Bowl XLVI (2012): 111.3 million (NBC)**
3. **Super Bowl XLV (2011): 111 million (Fox)**
4. **Super Bowl XLVII (2013): 108.4 million (CBS)**
5. **Super Bowl XLIV (2010): 106.5 million (CBS)**
6. ***M*A*S*H*** **series finale (1983): 106 million (CBS)**
7. **Super Bowl XLIII (2009): 98.7 million (NBC)**
8. **Super Bowl XLII (2008): 97.5 million (Fox)**
9. **Super Bowl XXX (1996): 94.1 million (NBC)**
10. **Super Bowl XLI (2007): 93.2 million (CBS)**

Source: Nielsen Newswire 2014, "Super Bowl XLVIII Draws 111.5 Million Viewers, 25.3 Million Tweets," http://www.nielsen.com/us/en/newswire/2014/super-bowl-xlviii-draws-111-5-million-viewers-25–3-million-tweets.html, Published February 3, 2014, accessed June 20, 2014.

because this market watches more television than average households. In addition, the African American market watches more WNBA, NBA, and college basketball than the average household. Furthermore, a decision to target women may include advertising specific to the NFL. American women watch the NFL more than MLB and the NBA. In the past decade the NFL has launched several marketing and outreach programs such as coaching clinics, women's apparel, and the donning of pink during Breast Cancer Awareness Month to target the female viewing audience. This audience has grown from 32.6 percent in 2006[11] to over 33 percent in 2013.[12]

As Table 9.3 illustrates there was a record numbers of viewers for Super Bowl XLVIII, XLVI, and XLV. In fact, each of these Super Bowls successfully became the most-watched television program of all time, recording 111.48 million, 111.34, and 111.04 million viewers respectfully.[13] As this number increased the gap between male and female viewers shrank. Forty-six percent of the Super Bowl audience was female; while approximately 54 percent of the U.S. audience was male and about 11 percent of the U.S. audience was African American. For Super Bowl XLVIII there was a continuation of success as it became the most watched program in U.S. history. This is the fourth time in five years that the Super Bowl has set record audiences. The Super Bowl claims the top for the five most watched TV programs, CBS series finale M.A.S.H. claims the sixth spot and the Super Bowl reclaims spots seven through ten.[14]

Decoding

The medium carries the message to the receiver, which is where decoding takes place. **Decoding**, performed by the receiver, is the interpretation of the message sent by the source through the channel. Once again, the goal of communication is to establish a common link between sender and receiver. This can only happen if the message is received and interpreted correctly. Even if the message is received by the desired target audience, it may be interpreted differently because of the receiver's personal characteristics and past experience. In addition, the more complex the original message, the less likely it is to be successfully interpreted or decoded. As the accompanying article illustrates, decoding often varies among consumers and sometimes proper decoding can lead to questionable, and a range of, interpretations of ads.[15]

SPOTLIGHT ON SPORTS MARKETING ETHICS

How impact of "Tiger Recession" changed athlete marketability

Many of us have spent the last 12 months holding our breath, looking for signs that the sports economic landscape is beginning to return to normal. Highest ratings in Super Bowl history? Check. Upfronts went well? Yes. Consumer spending up a little? Perhaps. Things might be looking up. But in the athlete endorsement world, I've noticed signs that things will never be the same.

Rewind to the summer of 2008. Athletes were riding the economic wave that brought deals in multiple categories for even marginal all-star caliber athletes. Any time an athlete got hot, deals followed. And the hotter the athlete, the more leverage the agent had in negotiations with the potential sponsor. But by the next fall, athlete endorsements were dealt a 1–2 blow unlike any punch Mike Tyson ever landed. I refer to that double whammy as the "Tiger Recession." I believe that the Tiger Recession will go down in sports business history as a 12-month span that forever changed the world of athlete endorsements.

The first blow of course was the economic crisis that began in the fall of '08. The meltdown wiped out entire categories such as banking and autos from athlete portfolios. Advertising budgets were slashed. CMOs looking for quick budget cuts found endorsement deals an easy target. Expensive endorsement contracts dried up like Death Valley in August. One example: Two years ago, Vitaminwater boasted more than two dozen athletes on its roster. Today? Just a handful.

The second, and likely more permanent, blow came when the Tiger Woods scandal broke in November of 2009. Prior to that infamous Thanksgiving weekend, Woods sat at the mountaintop of athlete marketability. He was arguably the most marketable athlete of all time. He seemed untouchable. He was the standard bearer: champion, philanthropist, charismatic, family man. When his image came crashing down, and several of his sponsors ran for the hills, sponsors everywhere started to worry about the risk of associating their brands with such potentially high-profile falls from grace. The epilogue to the Woods mess came in December 2009, when TMZ announced plans to launch TMZ Sports. Athletes will be under scrutiny more than ever before. Top that with the LeBronathon, and you get completely new rules for athlete marketing.

As the ice begins to thaw, and sponsors are once again considering aligning with athletes to help increase the strength of their brands, it is

9

foolhardy to assume things in the athlete marketing world will return to normal. Those of us engaged in athlete endorsement deals need to consider two key questions:

1. What will sponsors be looking for from their spokespeople?

2. What can athletes do to increase their marketability in the post-Tiger Recession world?

21st century endorsements

Because deals will remain few and far between as long as the economy sputters, it's a buyer's market. Expectations on spokespeople will increase, and sponsors are likely to expect more for less. During this year's World Congress of Sports, Jackie Woodward of MillerCoors said it best: "Last year we were asking, 'How much?' This year we are asking, 'How much do we get?'"

While Woodward was referring to sponsorships, the same questions are being asked regarding endorsements. During a recent pitch, a potential sponsor asked me to include an activation plan with my athlete proposal. We've always brainstormed activation plans with sponsors, but none has ever asked us to provide a complete activation plan ourselves. I believe this was a sign of things to come, and clearly implies much more onus on the part of the athletes and their agents to deliver more than image/likeness rights and a few appearances.

Athletes looking for deals should expect to deliver beyond a few production days. Here are the key elements of 21st century endorsement deals, and what athletes can do to deliver on those elements:

1. Shorter terms. Sponsors don't want to get stuck with bad contracts any more than teams do. Expect more sponsor renewal options as well. Athletes will have to deliver results during the term to earn renewals.

2. Stronger morals clauses. They'll have real teeth, allowing the sponsor an out any time an athlete is involved in controversy. Athletes interested in endorsements should embrace their role model status and deliver on it.

3. True spokesperson advocacy. Sponsors are looking for athletes who genuinely love their brands. Fit is key. Athletes need to advocate the brands, know their customers and understand their objectives.

4. Increased media obligations. Athletes have microphones in their faces after every game. Sponsors will look for more exposure through traditional media channels.

5. Authentic cause-marketing elements. Athletes need to engage in causes they genuinely feel passionate about.

6. Social media engagement. Facebook fans and Twitter followers are 21st century Q Scores. If athletes don't have loyal, engaged and numerous fans in the social-media world, they're not as valuable to sponsors.

7. Metrics. As marketers continue to receive more pressure to demonstrate ROI, athletes and their representatives will need to do the same. ROI can include Facebook impressions, tweets, clicks and direct sales.

8. Incentives. In addition to minimum guarantees, athletes will be incentivized. Flip is doing this now through their celebrity-branded cameras.

9. Connection with fan base. This may be the biggest lesson from the Le-Bronathon. Who are LeBron James' fans now? Residents of Miami. He won't be much help to sponsors in New York, Chicago, Los

Angeles or Ohio any time soon. An athlete has to have an identifiable and loyal fan base. The broader the market reach and demographic base the better.

Do I believe endorsements are a thing of the past? Absolutely not. There's no one more loyal than the fan of an athlete, and brands will always want to leverage that brand loyalty.

The tenets of athlete marketability remain the same: talent, success, integrity and charisma. To increase their marketability, athletes need to do more than win championships and appear in all-star games. They need to engage in genuine community work, embrace both traditional and digital media, and partner with brands they believe in. And they need to show sponsors with enthusiasm, professionalism and results. Those athletes will earn the lion's share of endorsement opportunities. The rest will be sitting on the bench, wondering where all of the deals went.

Source: Article author: Bill Sanders. Rightsholder: Sports Business Journal; http://www.sportsbusinessdaily.com/Journal/Issues/2010/08/20100802/From-The-Field-Of/How-Impact-Of-Tiger-Recession-Changed-Athlete-Marketability.aspx.

Receiver

The **receiver**, or the audience, is the object of the source's message. Usually, the receiver is the sports marketer's well-defined, target audience. However, and as previously mentioned, the receiver's personal characteristics play an important role in whether the message is correctly decoded. For example, consumers' demographic profile (e.g., age, marital status, and gender), psychographic profile (e.g., personality, lifestyle, and values), and even where they live (geographic region) may all affect the interpretation and comprehension of the sports marketing message.

Feedback

To determine whether the message has been received and comprehended, feedback is necessary. **Feedback** is defined as the response a target audience makes to a message. The importance of feedback as an element of the communication process cannot be overlooked. Without feedback, communication would be a one-way street, and the sender of the message would have no means of determining whether the original message should remain unchanged, be modified, or abandoned altogether. There are several ways for the consumer or target audience to deliver feedback to the source of the message. The target market might provide feedback in the form of a purchase. In other words, if consumers are buying tickets, sporting goods, or other sports products, then the sports marketer's message must be effective. Likewise, if consumers are not willing to purchase the sports product, then feedback is also being provided to the source. Unfortunately, the feedback in this case is that the message is either not being received or being incorrectly interpreted.

When using personal communication media, such as personal selling, feedback is received instantly by verbal and nonverbal means. Consumers will respond favorably by nodding their head in approval, acting interested, or asking intelligent questions. In the case of disinterest or inattention, the source of the message should make adjustments and change the message as it is being delivered to address any perceived problems.

Another common form of feedback comes through changes in attitude about the object of the message. In other words, the consumer's attitude shifts toward a more favorable belief or feeling about the sports product, athlete, team, or sport itself. Generally, the more positive the attitude toward the message, the more positive the consumer's attitude toward the sports product. This should, in turn, lead to increases in future purchases. One of the many uses of marketing research is to gather feedback from consumers and use this feedback to create or redesign the strategic sports marketing process. The control phase of the strategic marketing process is dedicated to evaluating feedback from consumers and making adjustments to achieve marketing objectives.

Thus far, we have only examined feedback in one direction – from consumer of the product to producer of the product. However, feedback is an interactive process. That is, consumers also receive feedback from the sports organization. Organizations let consumers know they are listening to the "voice of the consumer" by reintroducing new and improved versions of sports products, changing the composition of teams and their coaches, adjusting prices, and even varying their promotional messages.

For example, when the Brooklyn Nets season got off to a start fans throughout the tri-state area were not convinced of the hype surrounding the team's much anticipated move from the Prudential Center in Newark, New Jersey. The Brooklyn Nets had yet to sell-out for any of their home games, leaving open seats scattered throughout the $1 billion arena. The closest the Nets had come to a sell-out was for their first home game of the 2012–13 regular season, a 107–100 win against the Toronto Raptors. Attendance for the game was 17,732, according to statistics from The Sports Network, almost 1,000 fewer than the first game of the 2011–12 regular season back in New Jersey. The Nets' second home game, played against the Minnesota Timberwolves, drew only 14,017 fans, the lowest amount for their regular season thus far. Attendance increased for the third and fourth home games, peaking at 17,032 for Brooklyn's win over the Cleveland Cavaliers. Despite not being able to sell-out their new home stadium, the Nets have increased their attendance average by 800 tickets over last year, by listening to consumer feedback.[16]

Noise

The final element in the communication process is noise. Unfortunately, there is no such thing as perfect communication because of **noise**, or interference, in the communications process. Interference may occur at any point along the channel of communication. For example, the source may be ineffective, the message may be sent through the wrong medium, or there may be too many competing messages, each "fighting" for the limited information-processing capacity of consumers.

When communicating through stadium signage, the obvious source of noise is the game itself. Noise can even be present in the form of ambush marketing techniques, where organizations attempt to confuse consumers and make them believe they are officially affiliated with a sporting event when they are not. An excellent example of how noise can affect the communication process is found in ambush marketing, which will be explored in Chapter 11.

Sports marketers must realize that noise will always be present in the communications process. By gaining a better understanding of the communications process, factors contributing to noise can be examined and eliminated to a large extent.

Promotion planning

Armed with a working knowledge of the communications process, the sports marketer is now ready to create an efficient promotion plan. Not unlike the strategic marketing process, promotional plans come in all shapes and sizes but all share several common elements. Our **promotional planning** document consists of four basic phases: (1) identifying target market considerations, (2) setting promotional objectives, (3) determining the promotional budget, and (4) developing the promotional mix.

Target market considerations

Promotional planning is not done in isolation. Instead, plans must rely heavily on the objectives formulated in the strategic sports marketing process. The first step to promotional planning is identifying **target market considerations**. During the planning phase, target markets have been identified, and promotion planning should reflect these previous decisions. Promotional planning depends largely on who is identified as the primary target audience. One promotional strategy is based on reaching the ultimate consumer of the sports product and is known as a pull strategy. The other strategy identifies channel members as the most important target audience. This strategic direction is termed a push strategy. These two basic strategies are dependent on the chosen target of the promotional efforts and guide subsequent planning. Let us explore the push and pull strategies in greater detail.

Push strategy

A push strategy is so named because of the emphasis on having channel intermediaries "push" the sports product through the channel of distribution to the final consumer. If a push strategy is used, intermediaries such as a *manufacturer* might direct initial promotional efforts at a *wholesaler*, who then promotes the sports product to the retailer. In turn, the *retailers* promote the sports product to the final user. When using a push strategy, you are literally loading goods into the distribution pipeline. The objective is to get as much product as possible into the warehouse or store. Push strategies generally ignore the consumer. A variety of promotion mix elements are still used with a push strategy, although personal selling is more prevalent when promoting to channel members closer to the manufacturer (i.e., wholesalers) than the end users.

Pull strategy

The target audience for a **pull strategy** is not channel intermediaries but the ultimate consumer. The broad objective of this type of promotional strategy is to stimulate demand for the sports product, so much demand, in fact, that the channel members, such as retailers, are forced to stock their shelves with the sports product. Because the end user, or ultimate consumer, is the desired target for a pull strategy, the promotion mix tends to emphasize advertising rather than personal selling. It is important to note that because sports marketing is based largely on promoting services rather than goods, pull strategies targeting the end user are more prevalent. In pull strategies, your objective is to get consumers to pull the merchandise off the shelf and out the door. For example, in the past, Sears Craftsman, through its NASCAR relationships, planned to blitz consumers with discount opportunities for a Father's Day sales push. Craftsman was the official tool of NASCAR and the title sponsor of NASCAR's Truck Series dubbed "Craftsman Weekend at the Races."

Coupons good for $10 off a purchase of $50 or more were distributed to fans at 38 races through the NASCAR Whelen All-American Series, a semi-professional and amateur circuit on short tracks throughout the country. It was anticipated that the company would distribute about 75,000 coupons at the events. Coupons had to be used by June 17, Father's Day.

In another example, Burger King signed a six-month, seven-figure agreement to become Major League Soccer's first official quick-service restaurant. Burger King offered in-store and online promotion of a $100,000 sweepstakes, and also gave away Burger King- and MLS-branded soccer balls and "Have It Your Way" gift cards valued at $2.

Although pull strategies are more common in sports marketing, the most effective promotion planning integrates both push and pull components. For example, marketing giant Procter & Gamble's (P&G) objective was to stimulate consumer demand for its Sunny Delight and Hawaiian Punch brands. To do so, P&G designed a promotion featuring the late UCLA basketball coach John Wooden and one of his former star players, Bill Walton. The pull strategy offered consumers a Wooden and Walton autographed picture and coin set for $19.95 and proof-of-purchase. The push promotional strategy was directed at Sunny Delight and Hawaiian Punch distributors and retailers who carried the P&G brands. If the "trade" reached their performance goals during the promotion, they earned a framed picture of Walton and Wooden that was autographed and personalized for the distributor.

Promotional objectives

After target markets have been identified, the next step in the promotion planning process is to define the **promotional objectives**. Broadly, the three goals of promotion are to inform, persuade, and remind target audiences. Consumers must first be made aware of the product and how it might satisfy their needs. The goal of providing information to consumers is usually desired when products are in the introductory phase of the product life cycle (PLC). Once consumers are aware of the sports product, promotional goals then turn to persuasion and convincing the consumer to purchase the product. After initial purchase and satisfaction with a given product, the broad promotional goal is then to remind the consumer of the sports product's availability and perceived benefits.

Informing, persuading, and reminding consumers are the broad objectives of promotion, but the ultimate promotional objective is to induce action. These consumer actions might include volunteering to help with a local 10k race, donating money to the U.S. Olympic Team, purchasing a new pair of in-line skates, or just attending a sporting event they have never seen. Marketers believe promotions guide consumers through a series of steps to reach this ultimate objective – action. This series of steps is known as the hierarchy of effects (also sometimes called the hierarchy of communication effect).

The hierarchy of effects

The **hierarchy of effects** is a seven-step process by which consumers are ultimately led to action.[17]

The seven steps include unawareness, awareness, knowledge, liking, preference, conviction, and action. As shown in Figure 9.2, consumers pass through each of these steps before taking action.

Figure 9.2 Hierarchy of effects

Photo 9.1 Having greater knowledge of sports such as hockey moves consumers through the hierarchy of effects.

Source: Shutterstock

- ***Unawareness*** – During the first step, consumers are not even aware the sports product exists. Obviously, the promotional objective at this stage is to move consumers toward awareness. Awareness may occur in a variety of ways and helps expose a consumer to the products, however, it is important to note that consumption cannot occur if a consumer is unaware of the product.
- ***Awareness*** – The promotional objective at this early stage of the hierarchy is to make consumers in the desired target market aware of the new sports product. To reach this objective, a variety of promotional tools are used.
- ***Knowledge*** – Once consumers are aware of the sports product, they need to gather information about its tangible and intangible benefits. The primary promotional objective at this stage is to provide consumers with the necessary

product information. For instance, the NHL.com Web site has a link called the Learning Center, which is designed to give youth players tips on how to play the game. Similarly, Major League Baseball has a Baseball Basics: On the Field link on its Web page (see: http://mlb.mlb.com/mlb/official_info/baseball_basics/on_the_field.jsp) targeting international fans of the game. Another example of creating and enhancing knowledge is the proliferation of classes called Football 101 targeted toward women and novice fans. Football 101 primers have been held at the Super Bowl Fan Experiences, various NFL and college football game day events, and even been offered in Spanish to accommodate all fans. Teams and organizers hope that once the fans become more knowledgeable, they will then move to the next level of the hierarchy – liking.

- ***Liking*** – Having knowledge and information about a sports product does not necessarily mean the consumer will like it. Generating positive feelings and interest regarding the sports product is the next promotional objective on the hierarchy. The promotion itself cannot cause the consumer to like the product, but research has shown the linkage between attitude toward the promotion (e.g., advertisement) and attitude toward the product.[18] The objective is to create a feeling of goodwill toward the product via the promotion.
- ***Preference*** – After consumers begin to like the sports product, the objective is to develop preferences. As such, sports marketers must differentiate their product from the competition through promotion. The sports product's differential advantage may be found in an enhanced image and tangible product features.
- ***Conviction*** – Moving up the hierarchy of effects, consumers must develop a conviction or intention to take action. Behavioral intention, however, does not guarantee action. Factors such as the consumer's economic condition (i.e., financial situation), changing needs, or availability of new alternatives may inhibit the action from ever taking place. The objective of the conviction step of the hierarchy of effects is to create a desire to act in the mind of the target audience.
- ***Action*** – The final stage of the hierarchy, and the ultimate objective of any promotion, is to have consumers act. As stated previously, actions may come in a variety of forms, but usually include purchase or attendance.

Theoretically, the hierarchy of effects model states that consumers must pass through each stage in the hierarchy before a decision is made regarding purchase (or other behaviors). Some marketers have argued this is not always the case. Consider, for instance, purchasing season tickets to a professional sport for business purposes. The purchaser does not have to like the sport or team to take action and buy the tickets. Regardless of what the hierarchy of effects proposes to do or not do, the fact remains that it is an excellent tool to use when developing promotional objectives. Knowing where the target audience is on the hierarchy is critical to formulating the proper objectives.

Establishing promotional budgets

Global advertising expenditures continue to see steady growth. According to figures provided by ZenithOptimedia, global advertising expenditures were on track to grow 5.5 percent in 2014, to $537 billion.[19] Furthermore, these expenditures are expected to grow by 5.8 percent in 2015 and 6.1 percent in 2016. Total advertising spending in the United States is predicted to reach $191 billion in 2016, accounting for nearly one-third of all global expenditures. China (9.5 percent), Japan (9.4 percent), Germany (4.0 percent), and the UK (3.9 percent) round out the top five countries in global advertising expenditures. Television is predicted to retain the largest share of advertising expenditures accounting for approximately 39.2 percent, followed by the Internet (27.1 percent), newspapers (13.7 percent), magazines (6.4 percent), outdoor (6.8 percent), radio (6.3 percent), and cinema (0.5 percent).[20] As marketers continue to shift budgets towards targeted, digital media, ZenithOptimedia predicts that Internet advertising will increase its share of the advertising market from 20.7 percent in 2013 to 27.1 percent in 2016, while newspapers and magazines will continue to shrink at an average of 1–2 percent per year.[21]

Over the past several years, this growth, in part, has been attributed to a surge in digital spending and continued success across televised platforms, further enhancing opportunities surrounding events such as the Olympic Games. NBC estimated that it would generate billions in revenue for Olympic advertisement spots. In fact, over the past several years TV ad expenditures have increased for most sports with tennis and NASCAR experiencing the greatest percentage increases in spending. The NFL and NCAA football are still king, contributing more than one-half of the dollar volume gain.[22] As shown in Table 9.4, the companies that lead the way in ad spending for sports are makers of beer, telecommunications, and cars with Verizon Wireless, Anheuser-Busch, AT&T Mobility, Ford, Toyota, and Chevrolet at the top of the marketing industry.

In today's environment, digital screens are a critical part of the sport marketing mix and the following landmark figures speak to that irrefutable fact. For example, digital advertising expenditures in the United States are predicted to reach $61 billion by 2017, as ad spending gradually shifts to mobile devices.[23] Today's ads are more complex and engaging, enabling innovative new targeting and rich media strategies that stand poised to offer ever-increasing, targeted value to sports fans, and better returns on investment for marketers. A variety of different industries and organizations are increasingly investing in mobile and Internet ad platforms. Therefore, it's not just sports putting up big numbers. In fact, sports are one of four verticals outside of the overall Top 10 that have experienced triple-digit growth in the past year. However, sports experienced the most dramatic growth, increasing a whopping 489 percent year-over-year compared with 2012 data.[24]

As Frank Weishaupt, SVP of Global Revenue for Millennia Media states, "if the sports vertical were an athlete, we'd accuse him of juicing with that kind of statistical improvement in just one year."[25] While some experts may emphasize that the Olympics and the FIFA World Cup may have fueled much of that bump, the upward trend is projected to continue and it's more likely to be attributed as by-product of the ability to watch almost every pro sport on your mobile device. For example, leading up to the 2014 Super Bowl, the NFL reported seeing a 33 percent increase in the number of fans watching digital video and growth in mobile viewership.[26] Mobile has definitely changed the way we follow our favorite teams. This is not surprising given that the largest viewership times on online videos are tilted towards sports.

Global sporting events such as the Olympics and the FIFA World Cup are big attractions for advertisers and sport appears to be a perfect vehicle to help advertising mediums, especially the digital platforms utilizing Internet and mobile devices, to finally reach their potential. The continued growth in smartphone penetration, faster network speeds, and humanity's love of watching sport have created a perfect melting pot for sport to showcase digital marketing's true potential for marketers. According to Adam French, author of "Sport and the Marketing Revolution" (2013),[27] this melting pot exists for three primary reasons: (1) **Sport = engagement**: Marketers of sports properties are working with a market filled with fans – highly passionate, energized,

Table 9.4 Top 50 sports advertisers (ranked by total sports ad spending in 2011)

2011 rank (2010 rank)	*Company/ brand*	*2011 sports ad spending*	*2011 total ad spending*	*% of ad spending devoted to sports*	*Change in sports spending vs. 2010*	*Change in sports spending vs. 2009*
1 (3)	Verizon	$345,438,719	$1,523,982,375	22.7%	+1.4%	+40.1%
2 (2)	Anheuser-Busch	$299,721,969	$456,239,625	65.7%	−15.9%	−3.8%
3 (1)	AT&T Mobility	$296,940,250	$1,310,781,500	22.7%	−18.9%	+64.4%
4 (4)	Ford	$263,507,645	$1,371,668,594	19.2%	−13.6%	+6.0%
5 (6)	Chevrolet	$249,866,151	$1,029,529,844	24.3%	+4.6%	+49.9%
6 (5)	Toyota	$218,603,617	$1,067,944,875	20.5%	−8.9%	+7.5%
7 (8)	MillerCoors	$203,025,062	$360,294,438	56.3%	−5.3%	−10.4%
8 (10)	Sprint	$171,090,500	$558,439,000	30.6%	−4.5%	−14.6%
9 (15)	Southwest Airlines	$165,499,688	$240,861,062	68.7%	+26.0%	+28.6%
10 (7)	Geico Direct	$163,494,641	$766,306,750	21.3%	−24.6%	−4.1%
11 (12)	Nissan	$153,167,485	$577,850,691	26.5%	−4.9%	+96.9%
12 (11)	DirecTV	$137,980,781	$356,739,531	38.7%	−21.3%	−18.1%
13 (9)	McDonald's	$127,131,258	$996,054,375	12.8%	−37.3%	−18.4%
14 (16)	State Farm	$125,383,266	$523,524,906	23.9%	−3.1%	+7.7%
15 (14)	Warner Bros. Ent.	$123,810,031	$652,460,688	19.0%	−10.7%	+11.9%
16 (19)	Lexus	$120,587,471	$323,716,125	37.3%	−3.5%	NA
17 (25)	Mercedes-Benz	$101,405,853	$287,888,226	35.2%	−6.9%	+56.1%
18 (NR)	Chrysler	$96,888,814	$405,599,655	23.9%	NA	NA
19 (18)	Subway	$96,174,164	$513,575,031	18.7%	−23.3%	−2.8%
20 (23)	Apple	$95,068,961	$338,849,031	28.1%	−14.0%	+0.6%
21 (29)	Honda	$94,147,979	$630,150,868	14.9%	−5.8%	+30.4%
22 (41)	Volkswagen	$93,320,194	$387,565,754	24.1%	+29.5%	+81.9%
23 (28)	Hyundai	$88,229,366	$517,189,031	17.1%	−12.5%	+3.3%
24 (13)	Coca-Cola	$86,550,656	$239,212,750	36.2%	−40.2%	+6.4%
25 (38)	Capital One Bank	$85,617,227	$339,769,281	25.2%	−9.7%	+92.1%
26 (46)	Audi	$85,517,109	$252,945,844	33.8%	+33.0%	+131.1%
27 (34)	T-Mobile	$84,826,672	$454,587,062	18.7%	−2.3%	+53.0%
28 (20)	Taco Bell	$84,553,133	$253,149,594	33.4%	−29.3%	−25.5%
29 (30)	Pfizer	$83,297,672	$628,068,438	13.3%	−14.2%	−35.7%
30 (37)	Universal Pictures	$73,726,648	$406,595,625	18.1%	−8.1%	+18.6%
31 (32)	Lowe's	$73,050,992	$347,208,656	21.0%	−19.1%	−28.9%
32 (36)	Allstate	$71,715,031	$398,728,812	18.0%	−14.7%	+61.5%
33 (17)	NFL	$70,758,070	$90,372,641	78.3%	−43.7%	−9.5%
34 (76)	JPMorgan Chase	$70,541,906	$534,394,750	13.2%	+62.8%	+87.9%
35 (67)	Cadillac	$67,500,812	$269,792,774	25.0%	+41.1%	+25.5%
36 (21)	Microsoft	$67,184,438	$352,056,812	19.1%	−43.5%	−27.9%

Table 9.4 (continued)

2011 rank (2010 rank)	*Company/ brand*	*2011 sports ad spending*	*2011 total ad spending*	*% of ad spending devoted to sports*	*Change in sports spending vs. 2010*	*Change in sports spending vs. 2009*
37 (50)	Paramount Pictures	$64,470,188	$500,229,594	12.9%	+13.0%	+124.8%
38 (97)	Buick	$64,464,672	$214,317,129	30.1%	+104.6%	+306.9%
39 (27)	GMC Trucks	$63,860,890	$193,170,317	33.1%	–39.7%	–28.9%
40 (61)	Jeep	$63,280,872	$328,192,018	19.3%	+25.8%	+125.2%
41 (40)	Home Depot	$63,227,402	$434,258,188	14.6%	–14.8%	–7.2%
42 (24)	Dodge	$61,824,470	$339,502,712	18.2%	–43.3%	–29.3%
43 (72)	Best Buy	$60,000,355	$280,021,406	21.4%	+31.8%	+78.8%
44 (47)	Unilever	$59,547,223	$322,485,812	18.5%	–6.4%	+21.9%
45 (35)	Burger King	$58,906,398	$272,637,781	21.6%	–31.5%	–21.6%
46 (42)	Pizza Hut	$58,641,305	$233,514,531	25.1%	–13.7%	+42.6%
47 (NR)	Ram	$58,501,131	$269,079,493	21.7%	NA	NA
48 (44)	E*Trade Securities	$57,757,773	$128,684,812	44.9%	–14.6%	+47.4%
49 (45)	Acura	$56,203,571	$209,607,530	26.8%	–14.9%	+12.1%
50 (48)	AT&T Inc.	$55,336,977	$437,700,125	12.6%	–12.4%	+4.6%

Source: *Sports Business Journal*

and engaged people rallying around a particular team, individual, or group. French adds that fans are highly passionate and invest their emotions, time, and money into supporting a team, contending that this passion manifests itself in a disproportionate interest in everything connected to that team, including advertising. (2) Sport consists of **easily definable segments**: Leagues and competitions very neatly split markets. Sport segments consist of a group loosely defined as "people with an active interest," and there is a very clear set of large segments within that, split neatly across team loyalty. French noted that the ease of basic segmentation pairs nicely with new digital targeting techniques such as contextual and geographic targeting. (3) Value utilization in **second screening**: In today's environment consumers utilizing a second screen while they watch sport is commonplace and with the onslaught of 4G networks, more fans will be able to watch sport on their mobile, representing another fantastic opportunity. French adds that the statistics, player data, and social banter inherent in most sports make sport a perfect use case for second screening. Collectively, these innovative new targeting and rich media mobile platforms stand poised to offer ever-increasing, targeted value to sports fans, and better returns on investment for marketers, in turn enriching fan experiences.

The NFL generates billions of dollars in revenue yearly and these interests are tied with many other large powerful companies. Companies such as Anheuser-Busch, Sprint, and Barclays, among others, who invested $2.5 billion in ad spending, are concerned what their return on investment will be when leagues are presented with the prospect of cancellation due to a lockout or strike. Though the people who are going to be hurt the most are the fans and the viewers, this interruption of play is a concern for all advertisers.[28]

In addition to companies spending huge dollars on sports advertising, teams and leagues are constantly promoting the sport. For instance, the NHL released the poorly reviewed "Game On" campaign after the strike season, MLB is still trying to capture fans with the "I Live for This" campaign, and the NBA is still using the classic "I Love This Game" promotion. In the case of the NHL, increases in advertising were needed to make potential fans more knowledgeable about and able to appreciate hockey. Major League Baseball wanted to stress the passion that their players have for the game and generate the same passion in their fans. In all cases, teams and leagues are advertising to keep up with the tremendous competitive threat of other entertainment choices for the fans.

In theory, the promotional budget of the NHL or the NBA would be determined based on the many objectives set forth by the leagues' marketing strategy. In practice, **promotional budgeting** is an interactive and unscientific process by which the sports marketer determines the amount spent based on maximizing the monies available. Some of the ways promotional budgets may be established include arbitrary allocation, competitive parity, percentage of sales, and the objective and task method.

Arbitrary allocation

The simplest, yet most unsystematic, approach to determining promotional budgets is called **arbitrary allocation**. Using this method, sports marketers set the budget in isolation of other critical factors. For example, the sports marketer disregards last year's promotional budget and its effectiveness, what competitors are doing, the economy, and current strategic objectives and budgets using some subjective method. The budget is usually determined by allocating all the money the organization can afford. In other words, promotional budgets are established after the organizations' other costs are considered. A sports organization that chooses this approach does not place much emphasis on promotional planning.

Competitive parity

Setting promotional budgets based on what competitors are spending (**competitive parity**) is often used for certain product categories in sports marketing. For example, the athletic shoe industry closely monitors what the competition is doing in the way of advertising efforts. Adidas has an annual budget of roughly $20.09 billion[29] of which approximately 11.6 percent is spent on advertising and marketing. New player to the shoe market Under Armour's annual budget is $2.33 billion which includes footwear revenues of $299 million and a marketing expense of 11.27 percent;[30] Puma's budget is $4.44 billion,[31] with approximately 18.2 percent spent on marketing/retail; and Asics has a budget of $2.5 billion.[32] Other contenders such as Brooks have budgets of less than $500 million.[33] In fact Brooks Sports CEO Jim Weber noted that Nike will spend more by noon today than they will spend on marketing in a whole year.[34]

Competitively, these entities race to keep pace with Nike's promotional spending if they intend to increase market share. Nike, whose annual budget consists of roughly $25.3 billion in revenue, 11 percent ($2.75 billion) of which is spent on "demand creation," a marketing label used to categorize expenditures which consist of advertising, promotion, and the cost of endorsement contracts with athletes, is the current market leader.[35] In fact, according to Matt Powell, Nike spends about $2.8 billion on marketing per year, equating to approximately $8 million a day, some $300,000 per hour or $100 per second.[36]

One athletic shoe company that does not follow its competitors' huge promotional spending is New Balance. New Balance has begun to gear towards a more conventional route for advertising. New Balance is going to begin advertising with TV, print, digital advertising, online communities, and viral video content as well as in-store and event exposure. New Balance had $2.39 billion in sales,[37] spending $14.4 million on marketing and advertising in 2012.[38] Instead of using famous athletes, New Balance has paved its success by understanding its primary consumer, the 35–59-year-old baby boomer. Rather than paying celebrities to endorse its products, they prefer to invest in research, design, and domestic manufacturing. This unique positioning was illustrated in a campaign by New Balance with creative advertisements based on weather conditions and the necessary New Balance gear for each condition, in addition to New Balance's Web page stating "When function, design, and aesthetics unite".[39]

Percentage of sales

The **percentage of sales** method of promotional budget allocation is based on determining some standard percentage of promotional spending and applying this proportion to either past or forecasted sales to arrive at the amount to be spent. It is common for the percentage to be used on promotional spending to be derived from some industry standard. For example, the athletic shoe industry typically allocates 5 percent of sales to promotional spending. Therefore, if a new athletic shoe company enters the market and projects sales of $1 million, then they would allocate $50,000 to the promotional budget. Likewise, if Converse, a subsidiary of Nike Inc. since 2003, totaled $1.45 billion in sales in the previous year, then it might budget $72.5 million to next year's promotional budget.

Although the percentage of sales method of budgeting is simple to use, it has a number of shortcomings. First, if percentage of forecast sales is used to arrive at a promotional budget figure, then the sales projections must be made with a certain degree of precision and confidence. If historical sales figures (e.g., last year's) are used, then promotional spending may be either too high or too low. For example, if New Balance has a poor year in sales, then the absolute promotional spending would be decreased. This, in turn, could cause sales to slide even further. With sales declining, it may be more appropriate to increase (rather than decrease) promotional spending. A second major shortcoming of using this method is the notion that budget is very loosely, if at all, tied to the promotional objectives.

Objective and task method

If arbitrary allocation is the most illogical of the budgeting methods, then objective and task methods could be characterized as the most logical and systematic. The **objective and task method** identifies the promotional objectives, defines the communications tools and tasks needed to meet those objectives, and then adds up the costs of the planned activities.

Although the objective and task method seems the most reasonable, it also assumes the objectives have been determined correctly and the proper promotional mix has been formulated to reach those objectives. For instance, suppose the Vanderbilt University women's basketball team wanted to achieve an attendance increase of 15 percent from the previous season. To this end, the director of marketing for athletics must develop a promotional mix that includes local advertising, related sales promotions, and public relations in an effort to reach all target audiences. Even if the attendance goal is achieved, it is difficult to determine whether the money required to achieve this objective was spent in the most efficient and effective fashion.

Choosing an integrated promotional mix

The final step in building an overall promotional plan is to determine the appropriate promotional mix. As stated earlier, the traditional promotional mix consists of advertising, personal selling, public relations, and sales promotions. The sports marketing manager must determine which aspects of the promotional mix will be best suited to achieve the promotional objectives at the given budget.

In choosing from among the traditional elements, the sports marketer may want to broadly explore the advantages and disadvantages of each promotional tool. For example, personal selling may be the most effective way to promote the sale of personal seat licenses, but it is limited in reaching large audiences. Table 9.5 outlines some of the considerations when deciding on the correct mix of promotional tools.

Although the factors listed in Table 9.5 are important determinants of which promotional tools to use to achieve the desired objectives, there are other considerations. The stage of the life cycle for the sport product, the type of sports product, the characteristics of the target audience, and the current market environment must also be carefully studied. Whatever the promotion mix decision, it is critical that the various elements be integrated carefully.

Promotional planning for sports is becoming increasingly more complex. With the rapid changes in technology, new promotional tools are being used to convey the sports marketer's message. In addition, it is becoming harder and harder to capture the attention of target audiences and move them along the hierarchy of effects. Because of the growing difficulty in reaching diverse target audiences, the clarity and coordination of integrating all marketing communications into a single theme is more important than ever.

The concept under which a sports organization carefully integrates and coordinates its many promotional mix elements to deliver a unified message about the organization and its products is known as **integrated marketing communications**. Think for a moment about the promotional efforts of the WNBA. The promotional goals are to increase awareness and develop excitement about the league. To accomplish this, the WNBA will combine national advertisements, sponsorships, cable and network broadcast schedules, and tie-ins with the NBA. All of these communications media must deliver a consistent message that produces a uniform image for the league to be successful. Not only must the WNBA deliver an integrated promotional mix, but the league's sponsors and the 12 teams must also transmit a unified message.

Table 9.5 Evaluating the promotional mix elements

	Promotional Tools			
	Advertising	**Personal Selling**	**Sales Promotion**	**Public Relations**
Sender's control over the communication	Low	High	Moderate to low	Moderate to low
Amount of feedback	Little	Much	Little to moderate	Little
Speed of feedback	Delayed	Immediate	Varies	Delayed
Direction of message flow	One way	Two way	One way	One way
Speed in reaching large audiences	Fast	Slow	Fast	Typically fast
Message flexibility	None	Customized	None	Some
Mode of communication	Indirect and impersonal	Direct and face to face	Usually indirect and impersonal	Usually indirect and impersonal

The primary advantage of integrating the promotional plan includes more effective and efficient marketing communications. Unfortunately, determining the return on investment (ROI) for an integrated promotion plan is still difficult, if not impossible. Professor Don Schultz has identified four types of information that must be available to begin to measure ROI for integrated communications.[40] These factors include the following:

- ***Identification of specific customers*** – Identification of specific households, including information on the composition of those households to make inferences.
- ***Customer valuation*** – Placing a value on each household based on either annual purchases or lifetime purchases. Without this information on the purchase behavior of the household or individual, the calculation of ROI is of limited value to the marketer.
- ***Track message delivery*** – Understanding what media consumers or households use to make their purchase decisions, and how a household receives information and messages over time. In addition, this involves measuring "brand contacts" or when and where consumers come into contact with the brand.
- ***Consumer response*** – To establish the best ROI, behavioral responses are captured. In other words, consumer responses such as attitudes, feelings, and memory are deemed unimportant and purchases, inquiries, and related behaviors (e.g., coupon redemption) are evaluated.

Summary

Promotional planning is one of the most important elements of the sports marketing mix. Promotion involves communicating to all types of sports consumers via one or more of the promotion mix elements. The promotion mix elements include advertising, personal selling, sales promotions, public relations, and sponsorship. Within each of these promotion mix elements are more specialized tools to communicate with consumers of sport. For example, advertising may be developed for print media (e.g., newspapers and magazines) or broadcasts (e.g., radio and television). However, regardless of the promotion mix element that is used by sports marketers, the fundamental process at work is communication.

Communication is an interactive process established between the sender and the receiver of the marketing message via some medium. The process of communication begins with the source or sender of the message. In sports marketing, the source of the message might be an athlete endorser, team members, a sports organization, or even a coach. Sometimes the source of a marketing message can be friends or family. The effectiveness of the source in influencing consumers is based largely on the concept of source credibility. Credibility is typically defined as the expertise and trustworthiness of the source. Other characteristics of the source, such as gender, attractiveness, familiarity, and likeability may also play important roles in determining the source's effectiveness.

After the source of the message is chosen, message encoding occurs. Encoding is defined as translating the sender's thoughts or ideas into a message. The most effective encoding uses multiple ways of getting the message across and always keeps the receiver of the message in mind. Once encoding takes place, the message is more completely developed. Although there are any number of ways of constructing a message, sports marketers commonly choose between emotion (e.g., humor, sex, or fear) and rational (information-based) appeals.

The message, once constructed, must be transmitted to the target audience through any number of media. The traditional media include television, radio, newspapers, magazines, outdoor billboards, and stadium signage. Nontraditional media, such as the Internet, are also emerging as powerful tools for sports marketers. When making decisions about what medium to use, marketers must consider the promotional objectives, cost, ability to reach the targeted audience, and the nature of the message being communicated.

The medium relays the message to the target audience, which is where decoding occurs. Decoding is the interpretation of the message sent by the source through the medium. It is important to understand the characteristics of the target audience to ensure successful translation of the message will occur. Rarely, if ever, will perfect decoding take place because of the presence of noise.

The final elements in the communications model are the receiver and feedback. The message is directed to the receiver, or target audience. Again, depending on the purpose of the communication, the target audience may be spectators, participants, or corporate sponsors. Regardless of the nature of the audience, the sports marketer must understand as much as possible about the characteristics of the group to ensure an effective message is produced. Sports marketers determine the effectiveness of the message through feedback from the target audience.

Understanding the communications process provides us with the basis for developing a sound promotional plan. The promotional planning process includes identifying target market considerations, setting promotional objectives, determining the promotional budget, and developing the promotional mix.

The first step in the promotional planning process is to consider the target market identified in the previous planning phase of the strategic sports marketing process. The two broad target market considerations are the final consumers of the sports product (either spectator or participants) or intermediaries, such as sponsors or distributors of sports products. When communicating to final consumers, a pull strategy is used. Conversely, push strategies are used to promote through intermediaries. After target markets are considered, promotional objectives are defined. Broadly, objectives may include informing, persuading, or reminding the target market. One model that provides a basis for establishing promotional objectives is known as the hierarchy of effects, which states that consumers must pass through a series of stages before ultimately taking action (usually defined as making a purchase decision). The steps of the hierarchy of effects include unawareness, awareness, knowledge, liking, preference, conviction, and action. Once objectives have been formulated, budgets are considered. In the ideal scenario, budgets are linked with the objectives that have been set in the previous phase of the promotion planning process. However, other common approaches to promotional budgeting include arbitrary allocation, competitive parity, and percentage of sales. Most sports organizations use some combination of these methods to arrive at budgets. The final phase in the promotion planning process is to arrive at the optimal promotion mix. The promotion mix includes advertising, personal selling, public relations, sales promotion, and sponsorship. Decisions about the most effective promotion mix must carefully consider the current marketing environment, the sports product being promoted, and the characteristics of the target audience. Ideally, the sports marketer designs an integrated promotion mix that delivers a consistent message about the organization and its products.

Key terms

- arbitrary allocation
- communication
- comparative messages
- competitive parity
- credibility
- decoding
- easily defined segments
- elements in the communications process
- emotional versus rational appeal
- encoding
- feedback
- hierarchy of effects
- integrated marketing communications
- match-up hypothesis
- medium
- message
- message characteristics
- noise
- objective and task method
- percentage of sales
- promotion
- promotion mix elements
- promotional budgeting
- promotional objectives
- promotional planning
- pull strategy
- push strategy
- receiver
- second screening
- sidedness
- source
- target market considerations

Review questions

1. Define promotion and then discuss each of the promotion mix elements.
2. Describe the elements of the communication process. Why is communication so important for sports marketers? What is the relationship between communication and promotion?
3. Define the source of a sports marketing message and provide some examples of effective sources. What is source credibility? What are the two components of source credibility?
4. What is meant by encoding? Who is responsible for encoding sports marketing messages?
5. Discuss the various message characteristics. What are the simple techniques used to create more effective messages?
6. Why is television considered the most powerful medium for sports marketing messages?
7. Define feedback. How is feedback delivered to the source of the message?
8. Outline the basic steps in promotion planning.
9. What is the fundamental difference between a push and a pull strategy?
10. Describe the three broad objectives of any type of promotion. What is the hierarchy of effect, and how is this concept related to promotional objectives?
11. What are the various ways of setting promotional budgets? Comment on the strengths and weaknesses of each.
12. Comment on how you would choose among the various promotion mix tools. Define integrated marketing communication.

Exercises

1. Evaluate the promotional mix used for the marketing of any intercollegiate women's sport at your university. Do you believe the proper blend of promotional tools are being used? What could be done to make the promotional plan more effective for this sport?
2. Find any advertisement for a sports product. Then describe and explain each of the elements in the communications process for that ad. Do the same (i.e., explain the communications process) for the

following scenario: A salesperson is trying to sell stadium signage to the marketing director of a local hospital.

3. Conduct an interview with the marketing department of a local sports organization and discuss the role of each of the promotional tools in the organization's promotion mix. In addition, ask about their promotional budgeting process.
4. Describe three television advertisements for sports products that are designed to inform, persuade, and remind consumers. Do you believe the advertisements are effective in reaching their promotional objectives?
5. Locate advertisements for three different sports products. Comment on which response in the hierarchy of effects you believe each advertisement is trying to elicit from its target audience.
6. Find an example of a comparative advertisement. What do you believe are the advantages and disadvantages of this type of message?

Internet exercises

1. Using the Internet, find an example of an advertisement for a sports product and a sports-related sales promotion. For each, discuss the targeted audience, the promotional objectives, and the message characteristics.
2. How do organizations get feedback regarding their promotions via the Internet? Find several examples of ways of providing sports marketers with feedback about their promotions.
3. Consider any sports product and find evidence of advertising and sales promotion *not* on the Internet. Then locate the product's promotion on the Internet. Comment on whether or not this organization practices integrated marketing communications.

Endnotes

1 Allen Bush, "Sports Celebrity Influence on the Behavioral Intentions of Generation Y," *Journal of Advertising Research*, vol. 44, no. 1 (2004), 108–118.

2 Kurt Badenhausen, "Mayweather Tops List of The World's 100 Highest-Paid Athletes," *Forbes.com* (June 28, 2012), accessed March 9, 2014.

3 Kurt Badenhausen, "The World's Highest-Paid Athletes 2013: Behind the Numbers," *Forbes.com* (June 5, 2013). Available from: http://www.forbes.com/sites/kurtbadenhausen/2013/06/05/the-worlds-highest-paid-athletes-2013-behind-the-numbers/.

4 "LeBron James Net Worth, Salary, Endorsements," *Celebrity Networth*. Available from: http://celebnetworth.org/lebron-james-net-worth-salary.

5 Michael Kamins, "An Investigation into the Match-Up Hypothesis in Celebrity Advertising: When Beauty May Be Only Skin Deep," *Journal of Advertising*, vol. 19, no. 1 (1990), 4–13.

6 Christy Kilmartin, "Insights into Adidas' New 'All-in' Campaign – 'We Run All'", Adidas Group Blog (March 29, 2012). Available from: http://blog.adidas-group.com/2012/03/insights-into-adidas%E2%80%99-new-all-in-campaign-we-all-run/, accessed March 9, 2014.

7 Ibid.

8 Adidas Group, *Performance Counts Sustainability Progress Report 2011*, Adidas-group.com, accessed March 9, 2014.

9 Michael Santo, "Adidas to Launch Biggest Ever Marketing Campaign With a New Slogan," *Huliq.com* (March 15, 2011). Available from: http:// http://www.huliq.com/3257/adidas-launch-all-adidas-2011-global-marketing-campaign-its-biggest-ever.

10 Martha Irvin, "If Not on Point, Slang Can Make a Tight Campaign Sound Wack," *The Commercial Appeal* (November 29, 2002), C1.

11 Nielsen Newswire, "Football TV Ratings Soar: The NFL's Playbook for Success," *Nielsen Newswire* (January 28, 2011). Available from: http://www.nielsen.com/us/en/newswire/2011/football-tv-ratings-soar-the-nfls-playbook-for-success.html, accessed June 22, 2014.

12 David Broughton, "Report Spotlights Female Fans," *Sports Business Journal* (October 14, 2013), accessed March 9, 2014.

13 Nielsen Newswire, "Super Bowl XLVIII Draws 111.5 Million Viewers, 25.3 Million Tweets," *Nielsen Newswire* (February 3, 2014). Available from: http://www.nielsen.com/us/en/newswire/2014/super-bowl-xlviii-draws-111-5-million-viewers-25-3-million-tweets.html, accessed June 20, 2014.

14 Radio & Television Business Report, "Looking at the Football TV Ratings Explosion," *Radio & Television Business Report* (January 28, 2011). Available from: http://rbr.com/looking-at-the-football-tv-ratings-explosion/.

15 Bill Sanders, "How Impact of 'Tiger Recession' Changed Athlete Marketability," *Sports Business Journal* (August 2, 2010). Available from: http://www.sportsbusinessdaily.com/Journal/Issues/2010/08/20100802/From-The-Field-Of/How-Impact-Of-Tiger-Recession-Changed-Athlete-Marketability.aspx.

16 J. Alan Hayes, "Brooklyn Nets Seek Capacity Crowd," *Ticketnews.com* (November 14, 2012). Available from: http://www.ticketnews.com/news/brooklyn-nets-seek-capacity-crowd-111214732.

17 Robert Lavidge and Gary Steiner, "A Model for Predictive Measurements of Advertising Effectiveness," *Journal of Marketing*, vol. 24 (1961), 59–62.

18 Rajeev Batra and Michael Ray, "Affective Responses Mediating Acceptance of Advertising," *Journal of Consumer Research*, vol. 13 (September 1986), 236–239; Leon Shiffman and Leslie Kanuk, *Consumer Behavior*, 4th ed. (Upper Saddle River, NJ: Prentice Hall, 1996), 237–239.

19 ZenithOptimedia Executive Summary, *Advertising Expenditure Forecasts April 2014*. Available from: http://www.zenithoptimedia.com/wp-content/uploads/2014/04/Adspend-forecasts-April-2014-executive-summary.pdf, accessed June 21, 2014.

20 Ibid.

21 Ingrid Lunden, "Internet Ad Spend to Reach $121B in 2014, 23% of $537B Total Ad Spend, Ad Tech Boosts Display," *Techcrunch.com* (April 7, 2014). Available from: http://techcrunch.com/2014/04/07/internet-ad-spend-to-reach-121b-in-2014-23-of-537b-total-ad-spend-ad-tech-gives-display-a-boost-over-search/, accessed June 21, 2014.

22 Kantar Media, "Kantar Media Reports, U.S. Advertising Expenditures Increased 3 Percent in 2012," Kantar Media (March 11, 2013). Available from: http://kantarmedia.us/press/kantar-media-reports-us-advertising-expenditures-increased-3-percent-2012, accessed March 9, 2014.

23 Felix Richter, "Mobile Share of Digital Ad Spend to Rise Sharply," *statista.com* (August 22, 2013). Available from: http://www.statista.com/chart/1388/digital-ad-spend-in-the-us/, accessed June 21, 2014.

24 Frank Weishaupt, "Mobile ad Spend Increase Across Verticals," *Millennial Media* (March 19, 2014). Available from: http://www.millennialmedia.com/blog/2014/03/mobile-ad-spend-increases-across-verticals-yoy/, accessed June 21, 2014.

25 Ibid.

26 Cynthia Boris, "Sports Goes for the Mobile Ad Gold with Near 500 Percent Growth in Spending," *MarketingPilgrim.com* (March 24, 2014). Available from: http://www.marketingpilgrim.com/2014/03/sports-goes-for-the-mobile-ad-gold-with-near-500-perecent-growth-in-spending.html, accessed June 21, 2014.

27 Adam French, "Sport and the Marketing Revolution," *Mobile Marketer* (October 29, 2013). Available from: http://www.mobilemarketer.com/cms/opinion/columns/16469.html, accessed June 21, 2014.

28 Rich Thomaselli, "Over $12 Billion at Stake if NFL Lockout Prevents 2011 Season," *Advertising Age* (January 10, 2011). Available from: http://adage.com/article/news/12b-stake-nfl-lockout-prevents-2011-season/148093/, accessed March 9, 2014.

29 Adidas AG Delivers Exceptional Fourth Quarter Results," NASDAQ.com, Globalnewswire, Adidas AG (March 5, 2014), accessed March 10, 2014.

30 Jack Lambert, "Tidbits From Under Armour's Annual Report," *Baltimore Business Journal, bizjournals.com* (February 25, 2013), accessed March 10, 2014.

31 Puma.com, *Group Management Report For Financial Year 2012*, accessed March 10, 2014.

32 Kenji Hall, "Asics Wants More Than Runner's High," *Businessweek* (February 26, 2008). Available from: http://www.businessweek.com/stories/2008-02-26/asics-wants-more-than-runners-highbusinessweek-business-news-stock-market-and-financial-advice, accessed June 20, 2014.

33 Kurt Badenhausen, "Brooks Running Shoes Hit Their Stride," *Forbes.com* (May 20, 2013). Available from: http://www.forbes.com/sites/kurtbadenhausen/2013/05/20/brooks-running-shoes-hit-their-stride/, accessed March 10, 2014.

34 Ibid.

35 Matthew Kish, "5 Fun Facts from Nike's Annual Report," *Portland Business Journal, bizjournals.com* (July 23, 2013), accessed March 10, 2014.

36 Matt Powell, "How Much Does Nike Spend on Marketing," *theshoegame.*

com (July 13, 2013). Available from: http://theshoegame.com/articles/how-much-does-nike-spend-on-marketing.html, accessed March 10, 2014.

37 "New Balance Fact Sheet," New Balance (March 2013). Available from: https://www3.newbalance.com/on/demandware.static/Sites-newbalance_us-Site/Sites-newbalance_us-Library/default/v1393572846066/pdf/NB_Factsheet.pdf, accessed June 21, 2014.

38 Andrew Newman, "Campaign Redefines Running as a Social Activity," *New York Times* (July 8, 2013), accessed March 10, 2014.

39 NB News Health & Fitness Report, "Purposeful Design and the Upcoming NB 890," *NB News Health & Fitness Report* (Winter 2011). Available from: http://www.aperfectdealer.com/nbnews/2011/new_balance_nb890_running_shoes.html.

40 Don Schultz, Stanley Tannenbaum, and Robert Lauterborn, *Integrated Marketing Communications: Putting It Together and Making It Work* (Lincolnwood, IL: NTC Publishing Group, 1992); Don Schultz, "Rethinking Marketing and Communications' ROI," *Marketing News* (December 2, 1996), 10; Don Schultz and Paul Wang, "Real World Results," *Marketing Tools* (April–May 1994).

CHAPTER 10

Promotion mix elements

After completing this chapter, you should be able to:

- Describe each element of the promotion mix, in detail.
- Understand the basic process for designing a successful advertising campaign.
- Discuss emerging forms of promotion.
- Outline the strategic selling process and explain why sports marketing should use this process.
- Identify the various forms of promotion.
- Specify the importance of public or community relations to sports marketers.

The CoActive Marketing Group, one of America's leading marketing agencies, has helped design a variety of events, advertising campaigns, and promotions for companies such as Nike and Hiram Walker. CoActive designed a unique sales promotion for Hiram Walker to increase short-term sales of Canadian Club Classic (a 12-year-old whiskey). In this case, the promotion (called a premium) was a baseball card signed by one of four Hall of Fame players, including Willie Stargell, Billy Williams, Ernie Banks, and Brooks Robinson. With each purchase of a 750-ml bottle of Canadian Club Classic, consumers were able to collect one card from the series of cards.

In addition to the end users, Hiram Walker distributors were also involved in the sales promotion. Distributors could win a customized shelf unit to display the set of baseball cards and autographed baseballs. They could win these items for participating in the promotion and selling the idea to their retailers. The prizes motivated distributors to push cases into their retail accounts. By all accounts, the promotion was a huge success. In fact, it was so well received that a second series of cards were issued. To make the sales promotion work, personal selling was needed to secure the baseball legends. Other forms of communication were also necessary to inform the Hiram Walker distributors and consumers about the promotion.

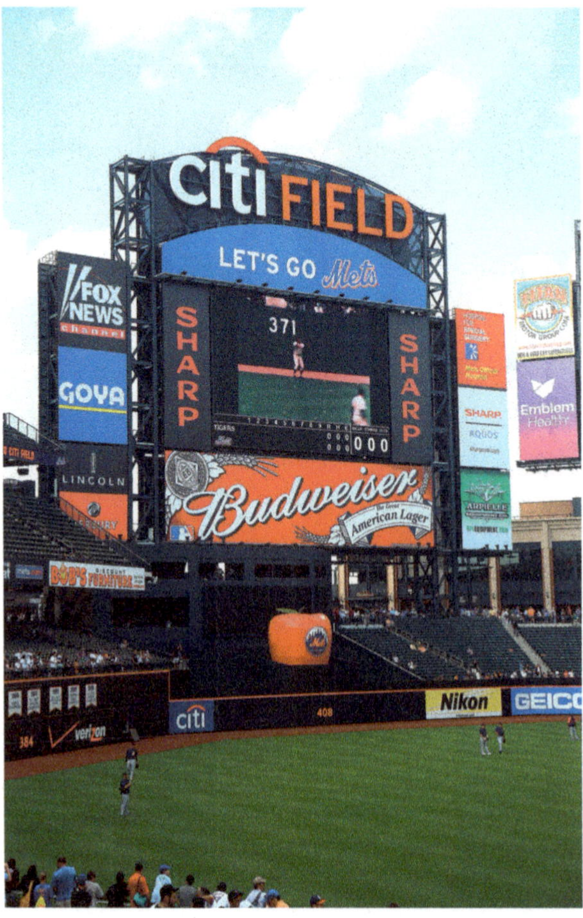

Photo 10.1 Stadium signage – one of the first forms of promotion

Source: Shutterstock.com

CoActive has also been developing strategies for companies like Nike since 2004. For example, CoActive worked with Nike to produce and manage sports events such as the Nike World Basketball Festival as well as the Nike London 10k. For the World Basketball Festival, CoActive transformed the historic Radio City Music Hall Stage into an international exposition of athletes and entertainers.[1] With well over 1,200 teens in attendance, they transformed the stage into a basketball platform, then back into a stage worthy of rap royalty Jay-Z, all within 45 minutes. The event was so successful that they decided to implement an encore performance to send off the USA basketball teams before the London Olympics.

The goal of the Nike 10k was to kick off Nike's Olympic celebration. CoActive set out to create a race as epic as it was personal. Garnering over 27,000 participants through promotional mediums, CoActive enabled the runners the opportunity to run the streets of London and greeted them with an array of personalized interactive experiences.[2] The race exposed runners to enormous technical displays that personalized the feel and environment so that each participant felt like a famous Olympic athlete.

As demonstrated in the Hiram Walker and Nike promotions, sports marketers must carefully integrate the promotion mix elements to establish successful promotions to consumers and trade. In Chapter 9, we explored the importance of communication and the basic concepts of promotional planning. This chapter examines each of the **promotional mix elements** in greater detail. By doing so, sports marketers will be in a better position to choose the most effective promotional elements for the construction of the promotional plan. Let us begin by looking at one of the most widely used forms of promotion – advertising.

Advertising

Advertising remains one of the most visible and important marketing tools available to sports marketers. Although significant changes are taking place in the way sports products and services are advertised, the reasons for advertising remain the same. Advertising creates and maintains brand awareness and brand loyalty. In addition, advertising builds brand image and creates a distinct identity for sports products and services. Most important, advertising directly affects consumer behavior. In other words, it causes us to attend sporting events, buy that new pair of running shoes, or watch the NCAA Women's Basketball tournament on television.

Most of us associate the development of an advertisement with the creative process. As you might imagine, advertising is more than a catchy jingle. To develop an effective advertisement, a systematic process is employed. Some of the steps in this process are very similar to the promotional planning process discussed in Chapter 9. This is not unexpected, as advertising is just another form of communication, or promotional tool, used by sports marketers.

The advertising process is commonly referred to as designing an advertising campaign. An advertising campaign is a series of related advertisements that communicate a common message to the target audience (see Figure 10.1). The

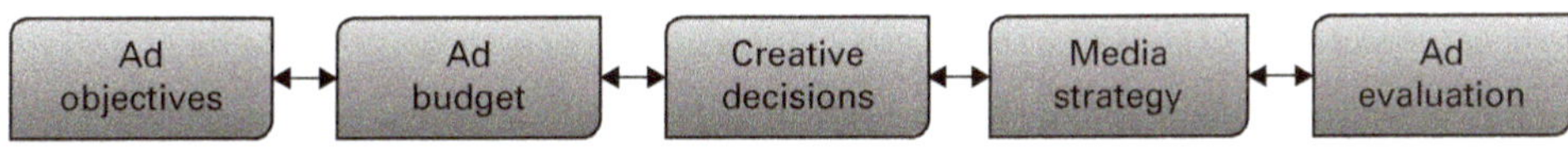

Figure 10.1 Designing an advertising campaign

advertising campaign (similar to the promotional planning process) is initiated with decisions about the objectives and budget. Next, creative decisions, such as the ad appeal and execution, are developed. Following this, the media strategy is planned and, finally, the advertising campaign is evaluated. Let us explore each of the steps in designing an advertising campaign or the ad process in greater detail.

Advertising objectives

The first step in any advertising campaign is to examine the broader promotional objectives and marketing goals. The overall objectives of the advertising campaign should, of course, be consistent with the strategic direction of the sports organization. The specific objectives and budgeting techniques for advertising are much the same as those discussed in Chapter 9. Namely, advertising is designed to inform, persuade, remind, and cause consumers in the target market to take action.[3] In addition to these broad objectives, **advertising objectives** are sometimes categorized as either direct or indirect.

The purpose of **direct objectives** in advertising is to elicit a behavioral response from the target audience. In sports marketing, this behavioral response may be in the form of purchasing tickets to a game, buying sporting goods that were advertised on the Internet, or even volunteering at a local event. Sometimes, an advertisement asks consumers to make multiple behavioral responses – for instance, Danica Patrick is used as a spokesperson to urge people to visit GoDaddy.com and has starred in multiple Super Bowl commercials in which the viewers must visit GoDaddy.com to view the end of the commercials.

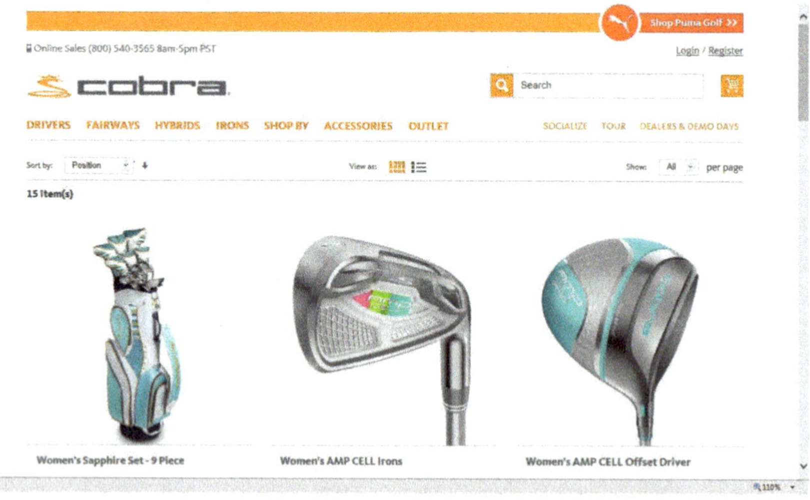

Web 10.1 Cobra Golf using direct objective

Source: COBRA Golf

Direct advertising objectives can be further categorized into two distinct types: advertising to end users and sales promotion advertising. However, both direct response objectives are designed to induce action.

Advertising by sports organizations to end users

In this case, the objectives of advertising are not to enhance the perceived image of the event, the team, or the league, but rather to generate immediate response. With this type of objective, the sports marketer is attempting to build immediate sales. As such, the specific objective of advertising to end users is usually stated in terms of increasing sales volume.

Sales promotion advertising

It is common for contests, sweepstakes, coupons, and other forms of sales promotions to be advertised via any number of media. As such, the objectives of direct response advertisements are to have consumers participate in the contests and sweepstakes or redeem coupons. Objectives, therefore, are measured in terms of the level of participation in the sales promotion.

Web 10.2 Sales promotion advertised on the Web

Source: Upper Deck

Indirect objectives are based on establishing prebehavioral (i.e., prior to action) responses to advertising; that is, accomplishing goals, such as increasing awareness, enhancing image, improving attitudes, or educating consumers. These indirect objectives should, in turn, lead to more direct behavioral responses. Consider the ad for Bank of America promoting the fact that they are the "Official Bank of Major League Baseball." The ad goes on to describe "The story of baseball is an important part of our American culture and our country's passion for it exemplifies our collective and enduring optimistic spirit and sense of community." The objective of this advertisement is solely to enhance the image of Bank of America through its connection with baseball, the American pastime. Ultimately, the advertisement's sponsor hopes these indirect objectives will lead to the behavior response of securing new customers and reminding existing customers to purchase more products and services from Bank of America.

Indirect objectives, such as image enhancement, are always present to some extent in advertising. Sports leagues, such as the NFL, use indirect advertising (Play 60 – national youth health and fitness campaign) to generate awareness of the NFL and its engagement in the community. In addition, these leagues often work with individual teams to further enhance behavioral objectives such as the handful of teams who participated in Major League Baseball's Dog Day Games. At these special events, ticketholders and their best friend sit in a designated section and can take part in activities such as a pregame parade, a costume contest, special treats, and more. Even better, many ballparks donate a portion of these ticket proceeds to local animal charities.

Advertising budgeting

As with advertising objectives, budgeting methods for an ad campaign are largely the same as those for other forms of promotion. For example, techniques such as competitive parity, objective and task, and percentage of sales are again relevant to advertising. Whatever the methods used, it is important to remember that **advertising budgeting** should ideally stem from the objectives the advertising is attempting to achieve. However, other factors, such as monies available, competitive activity, and how the sports organization views the effectiveness of advertising, should be kept in mind.

Creative decisions

After the objectives and the budget have been established, the creative process becomes the focus of the advertising campaign or **creative decisions**. The **creative process** has been defined as generating the ideas and the concept of the advertisement. Advertising and sports marketing agencies hire individuals who possess a great deal of creativity, but even the most innovative people use a systematic process to harness their creativity.

To begin the creative process, most advertising agencies prepare a creative brief. The purpose of any creative brief is to understand clients' communication objectives so the creative process will be maximized. The **creative brief** is a tool used to guide the creative process toward a solution that will serve the interests of the client and their customers. When used properly, the creative brief can be thought of as a marketing-oriented approach to the design of an advertising campaign. Table 10.1 shows a sample of the creative brief.

The three outcomes of the creative process are (1) identifying benefits of the sports product, (2) designing the advertising appeal – what to say, and (3) developing the advertising execution – how to say it. Each of these three elements in the creative decision process is discussed.

Identifying benefits

Designing a distinctive advertising campaign involves identifying the key benefits of the sports product. We have briefly discussed the importance of understanding benefits in the context of segmenting consumer markets. As defined in Chapter 7, benefits describe why consumers purchase a product or service or what problem the product solves for the consumer. For advertising purposes, describing the benefits or reasons why consumers should buy the sports product is a must. Marketing research is used to understand the benefits desired or perceived by consumers who might use or purchase the sports product.

Table 10.1 The creative brief and the client's role in it

"The Creative Brief And The Client's Role In It"
Every advertising agency has its own take on the "creative brief," that most sacred of sacred ad documents. And I've written passionately about how agencies might approach writing an inspiring creative brief in my "Ideas Come From Inspiration, Not Information. Just Ask Lincoln" post on the Ideasicle Blog.
But this isn't an article about *writing* a brief (that's the agency's job). It's about the *client's role* in getting to a great creative brief. Because without your understanding and appreciation of a few important things, the brief has no chance of being brief or inspirational.
The Audience For The Creative Brief Is Not You
This is a critical one. The audience for the creative brief is the creative team. The writer and art director working on coming up with the communications ideas, or in my case the four Ideasicle Experts working on a project virtually. Think of the creative brief as an ad targeted to creative people with the call-to-action being to come up with an idea. As such, there may be some swear words in it, some informal language, and hopefully some passion. While you may see that kind of language as frivolous or even insulting to the seriousness of your business, it's the kind of language creative people pay attention to.
Everything Can't Matter
Philosopher Blaise Pascal once said, "I have made this letter longer, because I have not had the time to make it shorter." He wrote that in 1657 in his "LettresProvinciales." And it's a great lesson in creative brief writing. No creative brief should ever be more than one page. Ever. And if it is, then your agency isn't done yet. Send it back. In fact, I would argue that the creative process begins with the focusing energy inherent in a great creative brief. If the brief is 10 pages long the creative team will hardly be inspired and may not read any of it. A great brief takes time. Time to sort through the input you've carefully provided, time to think through what insights matter most, time to craft the writing of the brief to eliminate all redundancies and be sure that, top to bottom, the brief tells a story. So, if you briefed the agency with a PowerPoint deck, reams of consumer data, and piles of sell-sheets on the product, only to see the agency come back with a one-page brief, don't think they didn't listen. They did. Part of an agency's value is when the account person and brand planner helps you say "no" to what doesn't matter, and "yes" to what does. It's then your job to approve those decisions (or not), move forward as a team, and then for you to sell those decisions into the organization before anyone sees the resulting creative.
The Brief Is A Starting Point, Not The Answer
This notion cuts to the heart of the brief's purpose, which is to inspire a great idea out of the creative team. That resulting creative idea is "the answer." So it's important that we do not ask the brief to be more than what it is. The "single most important thought" (or some such similar phrasing found in most briefs), does not need to be headline quality. It merely needs to be smart, it needs to be the culmination of the rest of the brief, and it needs to be singular. The creative teams will then tell us how to say it, or be it, or whatever. But the brief is a means to an end, not an end. In fact, try this trick. If an agency wants you to approve a creative brief and you're uncomfortable with it, simply ask the account person, "Are you confident that this brief will inspire a solution to our problem?" You will get a beat or two of silence on the other end, but, by putting it back on your account lead, you are sure to get a savage commitment to keep the creatives on track, if the answer is "yes."
Really Want To Inspire Your Agency? Give Them Some Problems
Most agency people are creative. Not just the creative department, but the account people and the brand planners, too. They are all problem solvers and enjoy the challenge of a juicy marketing problem. Input from the client that starts with "How do we. . .?" instead of "Here's what I want" will bring out out the best in your agency team. It's a little further up stream than you might be comfortable with, but try it once in a while. Give your agency a whopper and see what they do for you. Because doing so will prove to them that you trust them, you respect their talent, and you truly consider them partners and not vendors. Too many clients dictate too much to their agencies. It's like going to a Wolfgang Puck restaurant and telling them you want a plain hamburger and fries. If you're unsure about challenging your agency with your problems, you may be with the wrong agency.
In the end, your role is to inform the agency as best you can, and then allow the agency to do its thing. That does not mean you step away and blindly trust them. Quite the contrary. It means you are involved every step of the way, but with a careful eye towards a shared goal: a short, powerful, inspiring creative brief that will yield untold genius for your business.

Source: W. Burns, "The Creative Brief and the Client's Role In It" *Forbes* (2012). Forbes – Reprinted with permission of Forbes Media LLC © 2014.

Advertising appeals

Understanding benefits and developing **advertising appeals** go hand in hand. Once the desired benefits are uncovered, the advertising appeal is developed around these benefits. In short, the advertising appeal recounts *why* the consumer wants to purchase the sports product. The major advertising appeals used in sports marketing include health, emotion, fear, sex, and pleasure.

Health appeals are becoming prevalent in advertising, as the value placed on health continues to increase in the United States. Advertisements and the infomercial craze associated with the fitness industry capitalize on this growing concern of Americans. One important consideration when using health appeals in advertisements is the demographic profile of the target audience. According to IBISWorld, the strongest growth in health club membership is in the 55+ age range. Over the long term, population growth and demographic changes will significantly influence the industry.[4] The mature market (people aged 55 and older) grew nearly 40 percent between 2000 and 2010. This aging population will likely maintain a more active lifestyle that focuses on physical appearance and weight. At year's end, 2013, IBISWorld estimated health club memberships to be in excess of 52 million across the United States. About 25.0 percent of these members will be older than 55, which totals a 562.0 percent increase since 1987.[5]

Rising health care costs will provide added incentives for insurers to promote preventative practices that utilize fitness participation. The aging of the baby boomer generation and the coming of age of their offspring, the echo boomers, have broadened the market for the health industry. The demographics of the audience and the health benefits desired from fitness centers should be carefully studied in the advertising process.[6]

A number of **emotional appeals**, such as fear, humor, sex, pleasure, and the drama associated with athletic competition, are also used in sports marketing promotions. One of the unique aspects of sports marketing is the emotional attachment that consumers develop for the sports product. As discussed in Chapter 5, many fans have high levels of involvement and identification with their favorite athletes and teams.[7] Some fans may even view themselves as part of the team. Recognizing this strong emotional component, many advertisers of sports use emotional appeals. The infamous "Thrill of victory and agony of defeat" message used for decades for ABC's *Wide World of Sports* opening captures the essence of an emotional appeal. Emotional appeals that allow fans to relive the team's greatest moments and performances of past years are often used to encourage future attendance.

One specific type of emotional appeal is a fear appeal. **Fear appeals** are messages designed to communicate what negative consequences may occur if the sports product or service is not used or is used improperly. Scare tactics are usually inappropriate for sports products and services, but in some product categories moderate amounts of fear in a message can be effective. Consider, for example, messages concerning exercise equipment or health club membership. Many promotional campaigns are built around consumers' fears of being physically unfit and aging. Even athletic promoters use moderate fear appeals by telling consumers that tickets will be sold out quickly and that they should not wait to purchase their seats. Effective sports marketers identify their sports products as solutions to the common fears of consumers. For example, manufacturers of bike and skateboard helmets are quick to cite the plethora of head injuries that result without the use of proper headgear.

Another emotional appeal is sex. **Sex appeals** rely on the old adage that "sex sells." Typically, marketers who use sex appeals in their messages are selling products that are sexually related, such as perfumes, jewelry, and clothing. Maria Sharapova is a global icon; she has the beauty and personality to match her talent on the tennis court. Her latest endorsement deal makes her the first athlete to be a spokesperson for legendary jewelry boutique Tiffany & Co.[8] Siberian-born Sharapova moved from Sochi on the Black Sea coast to the U.S. when she was seven years old. In 2004, she achieved global fame by winning Wimbledon at age 17. Major titles followed at the 2006 U.S. Open and the 2008 Australian Open, turning her into one the world's best-paid athletes. Sharapova, who backed Sochi's bid to host the Winter Olympics, earns around $25 million a year, according to *Forbes* magazine. She endorses companies including Nike Inc. (NKE), Swiss luxury watch brand Tag Heuer, jeweler Tiffany & Co. (TIF), and Danone SA (BN)'s Evian water.[9]

In sports marketing, sex appeals are sometimes used, but this is always a delicate and ethical subject. Everywhere we look we find ourselves drawn to images of scantily clad attractive men and women that are supposed to inspire us to purchase products they endorse. Sex appeal can increase the effectiveness of an ad or a commercial because it draws the customer's attention. It's human nature to be curious about sex; however, misuse of connotations in marketing and advertising platforms can be costly.[10] In a recent interview conducted on the Dan Patrick Show, Hope Solo noted that there was no linkage between sex appeal on the field and the quality of the game; however, she did acknowledge that it was an athlete's duty to capitalize on these exploits to bring attention to the game.[11] Further noting that the selling of the sex symbol persona, at the end of the day, does help gain more viewership and more long-term fans.

In another example, an article produced by *Sports Illustrated*'s Alan Shipnuck questioned whether marketing the sex appeal of LPGA golfers was good for the game, it was noted that "exposure" was a key concern. Mikaela Parmlid, a W7 model and LPGA professional, stated that it was okay for women athletes in other sports to be attractive. (The Wilhelmina 7 – or W7 for short – golfers were signed with Wilhelmina Artist Management, a division of the famed Wilhelmina Models agency. Wilhelmina chairman Dieter Esch, quoted in a news release, stated, "We created this initiative to complete a void in the marketplace for beautiful and athletically talented female golfers.")[12] "Women's tennis, beach volleyball, swimming, and track – they're just girls too and it's effortless the way they combine their sexuality with their sports and no one gives them a hard time about it."[13]

10

In other examples of sex and sport, Olympic gold medalist Amanda Beard posed in a 2007 issue of *Playboy*; the ATP Masters tournament held in Madrid has been using female models as ball girls since 2004; and ProBeach Volleyball with its bikini-clad players relies heavily on the sex appeal of its players (both male and female) to attract fans.

SPOTLIGHT ON SPORTS MARKETING ETHICS

Sex sells? Trend may be changing

Sex Sells.

Most of us have heard this phrase so many times, we no longer question its veracity, especially when it comes to sports. As the popular thinking goes, if a female athlete wants to succeed in the endorsement game, she should be willing to trade on her body and her looks first, her athletic talent second.

Just take a glance in the rearview mirror. Over the past 15 years, some of the female athletes who have won biggest in the race for sponsors are Danica Patrick, Maria Sharapova and Anna Kournikova.

In the Nine for IX film "Branded," premiering Tuesday on ESPN (8 p.m. ET), filmmakers Heidi Ewing and Rachel Grady tackle the age-old question in women's sports: Will sex appeal always supersede achievement?

But before we try to answer that, we need to ask ourselves a few more: Does sex really sell now? How do we know for sure? What if I told you it doesn't?

What if I told you there is research to the contrary? As in, research showing that consumers, when deciding whether to buy a sports-related product, respond more to advertisements that portray female athletes as – get this – athletes.

Because that's exactly what grassroots studies have shown, according to Janet Fink, an associate professor in the department of sports management at the University of Massachusetts Amherst. "Another thing we are finding, and this makes sense, is that each time a female athlete is pictured in a sexualized way, it diminishes the perception of her athletic ability," said Fink, who specializes in sports consumer behavior, as well as media and marketing depictions of female athletes.

This perception is true for men, too: When you see a sexualized picture of a male athlete, say David Beckham modeling underwear or Tom Brady wearing Uggs, your subconscious tends to put a little black mark next to his athletic endeavors. Doubt creeps in where none might have existed before, and you begin to question Beckham's soccer skills or Brady's superiority as a quarterback.

Even though this kind of marketing can undercut both genders, the real damage has been done on the women's side, because nearly all of our popular, mainstream representations of female athletes play up their off-the-field appeal, with performance taking a backseat.

In light of the research conducted by Fink and other academics in recent years, just think of the negative effects these marketing images have had on how we, as a society, view women's sports. It goes a long way toward explaining why a highly successful female athlete can often feel like Sisyphus, pushing the rock up the hill only to watch it roll back down – because the sports world is still mostly operating as if bikinis on soccer players and slinky dresses on tennis stars are where the money is.

Changes are coming, though, and some are already upon us, providing a glimpse of how female athletes might be marketed in the future, when we will likely see a wider range of women as endorsers, rather than just a select handful (those traditionally deemed the sexiest and prettiest, within narrow parameters).

Consider WNBA rookie Brittney Griner. In rejecting the age-old marketing model for female athletes – to begin with, she is the first openly gay athlete to sign with Nike – she has made it clear she wants her brand to represent her authentic self, not an ideal that Madison Avenue has created. While Griner and Nike are still determining the exact approach they'll take, both sides have said they want to "break the mold."

Likewise, young girls who are just starting out in sports will take note when they see a fierce competitor like soccer star Abby Wambach pitching Gatorade with a take-no-prisoners attitude on the field. Tough. Sweaty. Strong.

"If girls see more images of female athletes as athletes, then it shifts their thinking," said Nicole Lavoi, a professor at the University of Minnesota and the associate director of the Tucker Center for Research on Girls & Women in Sports. "That's the game-changer. It opens up the idea that we can see and celebrate all female athletes."

Usually a company wants to work with a male athlete if he can check at least one of the following boxes: seems trustworthy, possesses expertise, looks attractive. The more boxes, the higher his worth. But with women, there is typically only one box that marketers care about. "What we seem to do with female athletes is focus on their attractiveness," Fink said. "It's the only thing we sell about them. So if you look at female endorsers, sometimes they are not even the best in their sport."

And then the rock rolls all the way back downhill and we start again.

"The blame isn't on the athlete," Fink continued. "They're playing the only game that exists. I think soon the marketing executives and mainstream media need to realize how the next generation wants to see its female athletes. And that's simply as athletes."

The irony, as both Fink and Lavoi point out, is that some female athletes, and entire leagues, are still glamming themselves up in the name of mainstream appeal, even though several studies have shown (for male and female athletes) there is no correlation between seeing a sexy image and then actually turning on the game to watch the player whose sexy image you have seen.

"Actually, what helps, believe it or not, is to show their true athletic ability," Fink said.

Talent sells.

That might not sound as sexy, but for the next generation of female athletes, it could prove more rewarding.

Source: Kate Fagan, "Sex Sells? Trend May Be Changing," *ESPNW.com* (August 27, 2013). Available from: http://espn.go.com/espnw/w-in-action/nine-for-ix/article/9604247/espnw-nine-ix-sex-sells-female-athletes-trend-changing, accessed June 22, 2014.

Although it may be hard to argue against sex selling sport in today's society, many think enough is enough.[14] In fact, two researchers showed that women's sports gain nothing from marketing the athletes' looks. Mary Jo Kane and Heather Maxwell showed groups of people photos of sportswomen covering the spectrum from highly athletic to highly sexualized. Their initial findings showed that none of those images motivated men to attend games or buy tickets. Kane and Maxwell's research suggests that selling out women to sexist stereotypes does nothing to advance the cause of women's sports, nor does it serve the bottom line.[15]

Pleasure or fun appeals are designed for those target audiences that participate in sports or watch sports for fun, social interaction, or enjoyment. These advertising appeals should stress the positive relationships that can be developed among family members, friends, or business associates by attending games or participating in sports. A recent advertisement by a major credit card company captured the pleasure of a father taking his son to a baseball game. The essence of the appeal was that, although you might not be able to afford it at the time, you will never be able to replace the "priceless" moment of taking your child to his or her first ball game. Another classic example of fun appeals is the Budweiser "Whassup" ads. The campaign, featuring four buddies shouting to each other over the phone, specifically targeted young sports fans.

Advertising execution

The **advertising execution** should answer the appeal that the advertiser is trying to target. In other words, it is not what to say, but how to say it. Let us look at some of the more common executional formats, such as message sidedness, comparative advertisements, slice of life, scientific, and testimonials.

One executional format is whether to construct the message as **one-sided versus two-sided**. A one-sided message conveys only the positive benefits of a sports product or service. Most sports organizations do not want to communicate the negative features of their products or services, but this can have its advantages. Describing the negatives along with the positive can enhance the credibility of the source by making it more trustworthy. In addition, discussing the negative aspects of the sports product can ultimately lower consumers' expectations and lead to more satisfaction. For instance, you rarely hear a coach at any level talk about how unbeatable a team or player is. Rather, the focus is on the weaknesses of the team, which reduces fan (and owner) expectations.

Comparative advertisements, another executional format, contrast one sports product with another. When doing comparative advertisements, sports advertisers stress the advantages of their sports product relative to the competition. For new sports products that possess a significant differential advantage, comparative

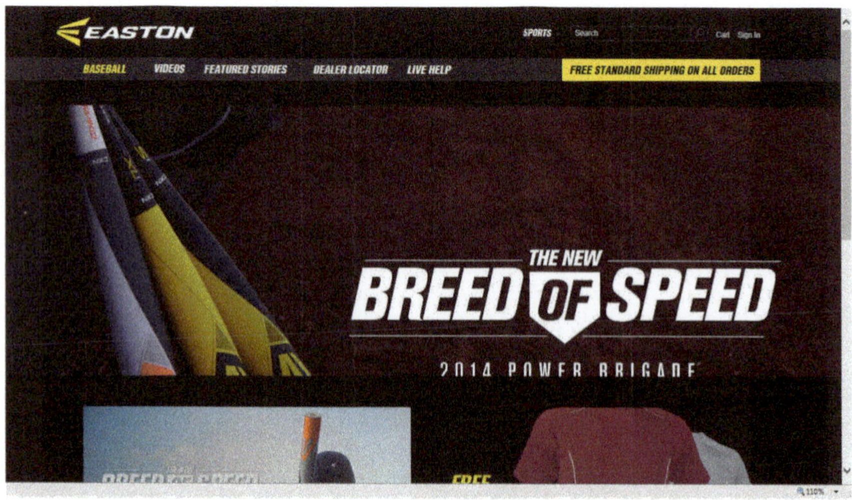

Web 10.3 Easton stresses its competitive advantage

Source: Easton Sports

advertisements can be especially effective. The risk involved with comparative advertisements is that consumers are exposed to your product as well as the competitor's product.

Because of the unique nature of sport, many advertisements are inherently comparative. For example, boxing advertisements touted the "Fight of the Century" between Muhammad Ali and Joe Frazier. In fact, there have been many "Fight of the Century" advertisements that are strikingly similar, comparing two boxers' strengths and weaknesses. Other sporting events, such as the made-for-television Skins Game in golf, use a similar comparative format for promoting the events. Many home teams skillfully use comparative advertisements to attract moderately involved fans interested in the success of the local team. These fans are attracted by the allure of the visiting team or one of its star athletes. For instance, many basketball advertisements promote the big-name athletes of the opposing team, rather than highlight their own stars.

Slice-of-life advertisements show a "common" athlete or consumer in a common, everyday situation in which the consumer might be using the advertised sports or non- sports product. For example, in 2013 Campbell's Chunky Soups teamed up with Clay Matthews and his mother in an effort to promote their new line of pub-inspired soups. The advertisement focuses on promoting unique new flavors further emphasizing the slice-of-life choices between a mother and her child at any age. A slight variation of this style is the **lifestyle advertisements**, wherein the advertisement is intended to portray the lifestyle of the desired target audience. For example, the classic "Just Do It" campaign uses a slice-of-life format that appeals to the participant in each of us. In another slice-of-life example, Zest soap ran a very effective campaign for their product using former football star Craig William "Ironhead" Heyward as their "showering" spokesperson.

Another executional style that is also readily used in sports advertising is called **scientific advertisements**. Advertisers using this style feature the technological superiority of their sports product or use research or scientific studies to support their claims. For instance, many golf ball manufacturers use scientific claims to sell their product. The Srixon UR-X is touted as having the "largest core," which means longer distance. Callaway markets the HX Tour as having "revolutionary hexagonal aerodynamics," and Titleist markets the Titleist Professional ball, which has a core of corn syrup, water, and salts, surrounded by a rubber and plastic like covering. As Bill Morgan, Titleist's senior vice president of golf ball research, admits, "A lot of times, chemical words or technical words are talked about in marketing and nobody really knows what they are talking about. But it sounds high tech. There is a little deception there, really."

One of the most prevalent executional styles for sports advertising is the use of **testimonials**. Testimonials are statements about the sports product given by endorsers. These endorsers may be the "common" athlete, professional athletes, teams, coaches and managers, owners, or even inanimate objects, such as mascots. Table 10.2 highlights the 50 most popular celebrity sport endorsers.

Why are athlete testimonials so popular among sports advertisers? The answer to this question is the ability of sports celebrities to persuade the target audience and move them toward purchase. Athletes' persuasive power stems from their credibility and, in some cases, attractiveness. **Credibility** refers to the expertise and the trustworthiness of the source of the message. **Expertise** is the knowledge, skill, or special experience possessed by the source about the sports product. Of course, successful athletes who promote products needed to participate in their sport

Table 10.2 50 most marketable active athletes

1. Neymar	26. Lindsey Vonn
2. Lionel Messi	27. Alex Morgan
3. Rory McIlroy	28. Mike Trout
4. Robert Griffin III	29. Jack Wilshere
5. Usain Bolt	30. Yani Tseng
6. Novak Djokovic	31. Manny Pacquiao
7. Lewis Hamilton	32. Saul Alvarez
8. Cristiano Ronaldo	33. Lucas Moura
9. Sloane Stephens	34. Bubba Wastson
10. Blake Griffin	35. Shaun White
11. Tiger Woods	36. Ellyse Perry
12. Sebastian Vettel	37. James Harden
13. Virat Kohli	38. Shinji Kagawa
14. LeBron James	39. Seth Jones
15. Viktoria Azarenka	40. Laura Robson
16. Maria Sharapova	41. David Rudisha
17. Alan Oliveria	42. Mark Cavendish
18. Andy Murrary	43. Stacy Lewis
19. Alex Ovechkin	44.Kim Yu-Na
20. Missy Franklin	45. Danica Patrick
21. Vincent Kompany	46. Anderson Silva
22. Carmelo Anthony	47. Dale Earnhardt Jr
23. Caroline Wozniacki	48. Gareth Bale
24. Sergio Perez	49. Robert Kubica
25. Rafael Nadal	50. Katie Walsh

Source: http://www.sportspromedia.com/notes_and_insights/the_worlds_50_most_marketable_2013.

have demonstrable expertise. Examples of the athlete – athletic product match-up include John Wall and Candace Parker – basketball shoe contracts; Tiger Woods and Michelle Wie – golf equipment; Jeff Gordon and Dale Earnhardt Jr. – automotive industry; Albert Pujols and Ryan Howard – baseball gloves; Martina Navratilova and Juan Carlos – tennis racquets; and Sidney Crosby and Alex Ovechkin – hockey equipment. Wall, the first pick in the National Basketball Association 2010 draft, was expected to instantly be one of the top players in the league. Already immensely popular before the draft, Wall signed an endorsement contract with Reebok and while still in college had two popular rap songs written about him. The other dimension of source credibility is **trustworthiness**. This refers to the honesty and believability of the athlete(s) endorser(s). Trustworthiness is an intangible characteristic that is becoming harder and harder for professional athletes to establish. Today's consumers realize athletes with already large salaries are being paid huge sums of money for endorsements. Because of this, the athlete's believability is often suspected. Nevertheless, even some of the highest paid athlete endorsers, such as George Foreman, Arnold Palmer, and Peyton Manning, seem to have established themselves as trustworthy sources of information while others such as Tiger Woods have tarnished their credibility and trustworthiness in the eye of the American public.

In addition to credibility, another factor that makes athletes successful endorsers is **attractiveness**. Although attractiveness is usually associated with physical beauty, it

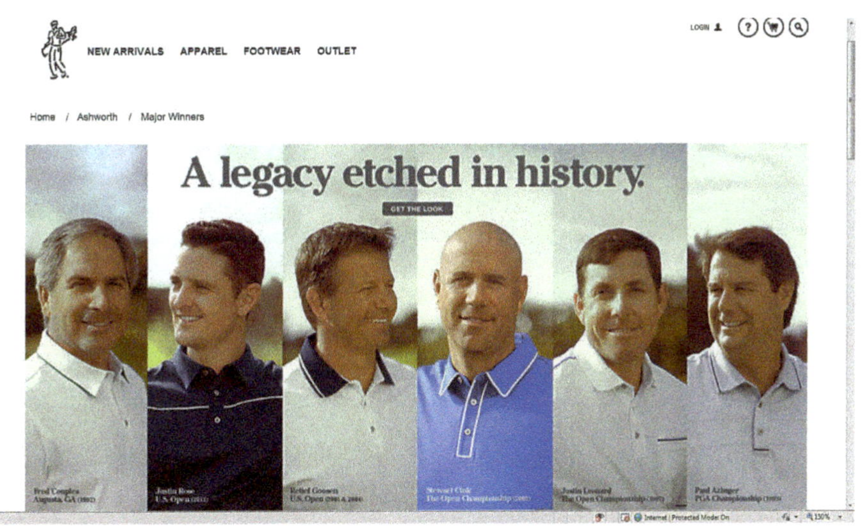

Web 10.4 Ashworth Inc.– Fred Couples creates a powerful message for the Ashworth collection.

Source: ©2014 TaylorMade Golf Company, Inc.

appears to have another, nonphysical dimension based on personality, lifestyle, and intellect. Attractiveness operates using the process of identification, which means that the target audience identifies with the source (athlete) in some fashion. Gatorade's classic "I wanna be like Mike" campaign, featuring Michael Jordan, is a good example of the identification process. Perhaps an even better example is Nike's "I am Tiger Woods" campaign, where kids of all races and ages were found putting themselves in the shoes of Tiger.

Athlete trustworthiness and attractiveness can change in an instance; consider the following opinion of Tiger Woods and how this view is different today. Who will be the most successful and appealing athlete endorsers of the new century? In 2003, a study was conducted by Burns Sports Celebrity Service, Inc. to answer this question. The survey asked more than 2,000 creative directors at national advertising agencies and corporate marketing executives, who hire athletes, to rate the most appealing athlete endorsers. Not surprisingly, the results indicated that the appeal of Tiger Woods continued to grow at an extremely rapid pace. Woods had firmly established himself as one of the top sports celebrity endorsers today, and Burns Sports' president, Bob Williams, believed, "If Tiger Woods takes an aggressive approach accepting endorsements, he could become the first athlete to earn a billion dollars in endorsements. Woods' golf career could last 30 years or more, unlike athletes from other sports whose average career is in the single digits. Hence, the real opportunity to earn a billion dollars from endorsements is within reason for a megastar like Tiger Woods."

Although Williams' comments have merit, the unexpected scandal that developed around Woods' personal life in recent years has potentially tarnished his "megastar" status. American golfer Tiger Woods was once one of the most popular endorsers in the world, and then on November 25, 2009 the *National Enquirer* broke the story of his infidelity to his wife. Tiger's infidelity led him to lose his endorsements with Gatorade, Accenture, AT&T, and others, leading him to lose $22 million in 2010. After Tiger's marital infidelities came to light, Tiger announced an indefinite break from competitive golf at the end of the 2009 season. Tiger's break from golf ended in April of 2010 when he returned for the Masters Tournament; however, Tiger failed to return to top form for the remainder of the golf season.[16] Although his performance has improved since, his identity remains tarnished.

Athlete endorsers can be extremely effective; however, there are risks involved. Athletes are costly, may suffer career-threatening injuries, or just do foolish things. The following article showcases a classic example of how an athlete's choices can have a detrimental impact on endorsers as well as their career.

SPOTLIGHT ON SPORTS MARKETING ETHICS

Lance Armstrong's fall from athletic grace doesn't diminish his greatest triumph

I never thought of Lance Armstrong as a seven-time Tour De France winner – at least not first and foremost. Even now that his athletic record has been permanently – and justifiably – stained, my predominant thought of Armstrong isn't as a cheater.

The most impactful and important label I placed on Armstrong 16 years ago remains the same today.

He is, and will always be a cancer survivor.

Even if at some point down the line, God sees fit to take him from this earth, and cancer be the earthly cause of his passing, that won't change my mind.

I have personally lost so much to that disease. I've seen three grandparents, an aunt, a mother and a sister leave me because of it.

Those are the numbers, but the void it has left is incalculable.

I'm not alone, unfortunately.

According to the Wiley Online Library, almost 600,000 Americans will die in 2012 from cancer; even more will perish worldwide. With numbers like that, it's great to see someone win.

When your life has been touched in such a way, a fighting spirit goes looking for signs of hope.

Armstrong is such a sign for me.

The fact that he went on to compete as a world class athlete after testicular cancer certainly adds to the impact, but it's bigger than that.

I've never been a fan of Armstrong as an athlete or as a personality. I've never been the biggest cycling fan, and his disposition has always been a little off-putting to me.

After all, this is the guy that *ET Magazine* quoted as saying: "If there was a God, I'd still have both my nuts." per Cycling News.

I'm certainly not implying that his recent issues are a derivative of his perceived atheist position, but a guy that makes that type of comment isn't going to be my favorite athlete.

For me, the fact that he lives on is his biggest triumph and purpose. Because of that, these other accomplishments and issues are completely secondary.

I understand the scandal is sexier to discuss – and even to write about – but that PED flavored stain doesn't ruin the image of hope any more than our difference in opinion about faith does.

In the Lance Armstrong situation, the truth has seemingly been proven.

Athletically, the outcome isn't pretty, but I will hold fast to that which is good.

Source: Article author: Brian Mazique; http://bleacherreport.com/articles/1383267-lance-armstrongs-fall-from-athletic-grace-doesnt-diminish-his-greatest-triumph. Rightsholder: Bleacher Report.

In addition, the following narratives illustrate how sport complexities can create adverse situations for endorsers.

- The simplest of things in life can be completed without breaking a sweat, but not a 26.2 mile race. When 23 year old Rosie Ruiz crossed the finish line of the Boston Marathon, she had the third fastest time ever for a female runner while barely glistening, and speculation started to mount. That wariness was justified when onlookers communicated that they saw Ruiz join the race in the final mile. She was stripped of her olive wreath and the rightful winner, Jacqueline Gareau, was crowned.[17]
- In baseball, U.S. prosecutors have begun to pursue new avenues of investigation after a former New York Mets batboy pleaded guilty to selling performance-enhancing drugs to dozens of major-league players. He is cooperating with authorities.
- A special commission set up by Major League Baseball to look into the sport's drug problem asked dozens of players to meet with its investigators and sought medical records from at least two of the game's recent top sluggers, Sammy Sosa and Rafael Palmeiro. The spotlight was not likely to dim as Barry Bonds slugged his way to becoming the all-time home run king, a pursuit that was tarnished as prosecutors investigated whether he lied during grand-jury testimony in a case involving the distribution of steroids to elite athletes. On November 15, 2007, federal prosecutors charged the 43-year-old slugger with perjury and obstruction of justice.[18]
- In a scandal of international proportion, the cricketing world was rocked by acclaimed South Africa captain Hanse Cronje's fall from grace in the biggest match-fixing scandal the sport has seen. In 2000 Cronje confessed to accepting about $130,000 (£68,400) from bookmakers for providing them with match information to fix the results of games. He was banned from the sport for life – a devastating blow to the man who achieved iconic status after leading the Proteas, as the South Africa cricket team is known, to victory in 27 Tests – losing 11 – and 99 one-day internationals out of 138.
- American figure skater Tanya Harding calculated that it would be more difficult for her rival, Nancy Kerrigan, to compete if she had a bad knee. Harding hired Shane Stant to put fellow American figure skater Kerrigan out of commission at the 1994 U.S. Figure Skating Championships, paving the way for Harding's victory. Soon after, her ex-husband cut a plea bargain deal in which he spilled the beans of their scheme implicating Harding. When Harding's time came, she had no choice but to plead guilty and received a $160,000 fine and three years' probation, was banned from U.S. figure skating, and was stripped of her 1994 title.[19]

Although scandals typically involve individual athletes, an entire sport can also be involved in unethical, performance enhancing practices. NASCAR officials have been working to even the playing field for years as teams searched for any edge they could find in a sport in which a tenth of a second of extra speed can determine the outcome of a race. Inspections before and after qualifying for the Daytona 500 in 2006 nabbed no fewer than 5 of the 61 teams trying to make the race. One team's crew chief and another team's director were suspended for four races for failing to cover holes in a wheel well, which was seen as giving the teams an unfair aerodynamic advantage. They were also fined $50,000 and amassed a 50-point penalty for the driver and team owner. In the days before taking part in the Great American Race, six teams were penalized for technical violations. The infractions – which ranged from the unintentional (Jeff Gordon's No. 24 Chevrolet was one inch too low after qualifying because of misaligned bolts in the car's rear shocks) to the blatant (Michael Waltrip's No. 55 Toyota was impounded after inspectors found an illegal substance in the engine manifold) – cast a dark cloud on a sport in which cheating has been omnipresent but never consistently targeted.

NASCAR's president, Mike Helton, said: "There is a need for NASCAR to have that same confidence with the fan, with the TV audience, with the car sponsors, with NASCAR sponsors, with the racetracks and all the constituents of the sport to have confidence in NASCAR's way that it handles its sport."[20] In 2014, NASCAR revamped its "deterrence system" altering the penalty structure and appeals process to further defer infractions from occuring. Steve O'Donnell, NASCAR executive vice president of racing operations, noted that it was not NASCAR's intent to penalize but to implement a policy that is more fair, transparent and easily understood. O'Donnell added that NASCAR officials believe "the system is tailored to fit the needs of the sport, essentially building a firewall between the race teams, their sponsors, and the OEMs (original equipment manufacturers)".[21]

In the past the NFL image was damaged in a series of off-the-field wrongdoings and arrests of some of its athletes. There have been no fewer than 50 player arrests since the start of 2006, and NFL Commissioner Roger Goodell has instituted the toughest code of conduct in professional sports. Despite that, through August of 2013, there were 42 arrests and citations of NFL players. Goodell has shown a willingness to suspend players even before they are convicted in the courts. Goodell stated, "Persons who fail to live up to this standard of conduct are guilty of conduct detrimental and subject to discipline, even where the conduct itself does not result in conviction of a crime." Discipline will include "larger fines and longer suspensions," and for repeat offenders, "the commissioner may impose discipline on an expedited basis for persons who have been assigned a probationary period." The commission also said this about players in trouble, "When that happens, you can be in the wrong place once, twice, maybe three times. But after a certain point, you are reflecting very negatively on the National Football League. It's my job – not law enforcement's job – to protect the National Football League."[22]

Because of the increased risk and incidence of scandal, many sports advertisers are shying away from signing megastar individual athletes to huge contracts and are instead using teams or events as their advertising platform. For instance, Reebok reduced its football endorsement stable from 250 to 150. Baseball endorsers were reduced from 350 to 100, and basketball endorsers were reduced from 100 to 25. Gatorade's vice president of sports marketing, Tom Fox, said it best: "The paradigm in the athlete marketplace has changed. Like a lot of companies, we question the ability of any single athlete to reinforce brand equity to such a huge extent that it would move product off the shelf."[23] Nonetheless, many companies are still using athletes to endorse their products. A recent example of this is Adidas; they signed Derrick Rose to a 14-year $260 million deal. Nike, as always, has had quite a few athletes under their payroll. This includes some large names like LeBron James, Tiger Woods, and Kobe Bryant to name a few.[24] You also have names like Phil Mickelson and David Beckham who are among the leaders of sport endorsement deals. Nike's obligations to pay athletes and teams cumulatively over the lifetime of their contacts had risen in each of the previous three years, dating to fiscal year 2006. The decline in value of those obligations to $3.8 billion in 2010 leaves a total that is more than three times the amount posted in 2002, but it's down $400 million from a record $4.2 billion in 2009. Table 10.3 presents some general guidelines for using sports celebrities in advertising campaigns.

Table 10.3 Guidelines for using sports celebrities as endorsers

• Sports celebrities are more effective for endorsing sports-related products. Match-up hypothesis again holds true – does not matter if consumers recognize the athlete if they cannot remember the product that is being endorsed
• Long-term relationships or associations between the product and the endorser are key – cannot be short-term or one-shot deals to be effective. Examples include Arnold Palmer with Pennzoil and Michael Jordon with Nike
• Advertisements using athlete endorsers who appear during contests or events in which the athlete is participating are less effective
• Athletes who are overexposed may lose their credibility and power to influence consumers. Tiger Woods is planning to limit his association with just five global brands to avoid overexposure

Source: Adapted from Amy Dyson and Douglas Turco, "The State of Celebrity Endorsement in Sport," *Cyber-Journal of Sport Marketing*

ARMSTRONG FACES $200 MILLION SALARY LOSS WITH REPUTATION HIT

Lance Armstrong may lose as much as $200 million in future earning potential, more than the wealth he accumulated in a championship cycling career now gutted by revelations of doping.

Two days after he was officially stripped of a record seven Tour de France titles, Armstrong faces demands that he repay up to $16 million in purses and bonuses from those victories.

Lost earnings potential far outpaces that, said sports marketing analysts. With a net worth estimated by Forbes at $125 million, the 41-year-old American would have had a prosperous future as an endorser and motivational speaker had the evidence gathered by the U.S. Anti-Doping Agency not surfaced, according to Patrick Rishe, an economics professor at Webster University in St. Louis. **Nike Inc. (NKE)** and his other sponsors deserted him after USADA's report.

"To think that he would be able to make $15-$20 million annually over the next 10 years is not out of the question," Rishe said in a telephone interview yesterday. "That puts his loss in potential future earnings at between $150-$200 million."

The French cycling federation, which distributes Tour de France prize money on behalf of the race organizer, the Amaury Sport Organization, said yesterday it plans to cooperate with the family-owned company to reclaim the $3.8 million (2.95 million euros) it estimates Armstrong won during his career. SCA Promotions Inc., which insured bonuses Armstrong received for winning the race from 2002 through 2004, said two days ago it will seek almost $12 million.

Income Increase

Armstrong earned $17.5 million in endorsement and speaking fees in 2005, when he won his last Tour de France, Sports Illustrated reported. That number grew to $21 million in 2010, Forbes said. The revenue gain as his career declined is an indication that Armstrong, who survived cancer and started the Livestrong foundation that has pumped what it says is more than $470 million into helping others with the disease, would have remained a potent corporate spokesman and health advocate.

"But for these doping allegations, which now have been corroborated by USADA's report, he would have always been a cancer survivor and his story would have always been motivational and inspiring," Rishe said. That career is in the past.

"I can't imagine anyone being able to make a positive out of a relationship with him at this point," Jim Andrews, senior vice president of content strategy at IEG, a sponsorship consultant, said in a telephone interview.

First Time

Pauline Juliard, a spokeswoman for the French cycling federation, said in a telephone interview that the group hadn't begun proceedings to try to recoup money paid to Armstrong. It would be the first time they have asked for money back from a rider, she said.

Armstrong sued SCA for failing to pay his $5 million 2004 bonus. The company settled the case, paying Armstrong that money and $2.5 million in interest and court costs. SCA will work quickly to try to regain almost $12 million from Armstrong, said Jeffrey Tillotson, an attorney for the company.

"If you have a claim, you want to pursue it as quickly and vigorously as possible, particularly if there may be other claimants," Tillotson said in a telephone interview.

Lawsuits could arise from either side, though they aren't very likely, analysts said.

Luxottica Group SpA (LUX), whose Oakley brand was the last major sponsor to drop Armstrong, won't try to recoup money paid to the cyclist, said company spokeswoman Cheri Quigley.

'Rebuild Cycling'

"We are deeply saddened by the situation, especially given our longstanding relationship, but we feel it is best for all involved to move on and collectively spend our energy rebuilding the sport of cycling," Quigley, who declined to discuss financial details of Armstrong's contract, said in an e-mail.

That's the approach Armstrong's other former major sponsors probably will take, according to **Paul Swinand**, an equity analyst who covers Nike for Morningstar Inc. in **Chicago**. It's in Nike's best interest to focus on public perception by further distancing itself from the Texan instead of pursuing more action, said Swinand, who also covers Adidas AG, Under Armour Inc. and Luxottica.

"Whether you're Nike, Anheuser-Busch, Oakley, you want to have as little noise about this as possible," Swinand said in a telephone interview. "You don't want more scabs ripped off."

Nike ended contracts with quarterback Michael Vick following his conviction for crimes related to dog fighting and with sprinter Marion Jones after a doping confession. It maintained contracts with basketball player Kobe Bryant and golfer Tiger Woods following acknowledgments of adultery.

Nike Stock

Swinand, 45, was a semiprofessional cyclist in France in 1989-90. He said he owns no Nike shares and currently rates the stock at three-stars, a rough equivalent to a "hold."

An e-mail to Tim Herman, Armstrong's attorney, seeking comment about the French cycling federation's plans, SCA and Armstrong's endorsement deals wasn't immediately returned.

Among Armstrong's other former sponsors, Nike spokeswoman Mary Remuzzi, **RadioShack Corp.**

(RSH) spokesman Eric Bruner, Honey Stinger Marketing Director Len Zanni, and Mark Riedy, a spokesman for Easton Bell Sports which makes Giro helmets and gloves, said their companies had nothing further to add to previous statements ending relationships with Armstrong.

Phillip **Cleveland**, a spokesman for **Anheuser-Busch InBev NV (ABI)**'s Michelob Ultra beer; Eric Bjorling, a spokesman for Trek Bicycle Corp.; Carli LaForgia, a spokeswoman for FRS Co.; and David Zimberoff, a spokesman for Sram International Corp., didn't respond to phone calls and e-mails seeking comment.

USADA Report

USADA released a 202-page summary of its investigation of Armstrong on Oct. 10, saying his cycling career was "fueled from start to finish by doping." Nike became the first sponsor to cut ties with Armstrong on Oct. 17, shortly after he stepped down as Livestrong's chairman, and the International Cycling Union said two days ago that it would not appeal USADA's findings.

Armstrong would have a difficult time seeking payment from the companies because of the breadth of the USADA evidence and because most endorsement deals have moral turpitude clauses that free sponsors if athletes break the law or negatively affect the sponsor's public image, according to Daniel Lazaroff, director of the Sports Law Institute at Loyola Law School in Los Angeles.

"Companies will want to get out of these high-paying contracts if the asset has lost its value," Lazaroff said in a telephone interview.

Lazaroff said he'd be surprised if Nike tried to get its money back from Armstrong "after all, he provided value for them."

Past Strategy

Armstrong has sued those he felt lied or otherwise wronged him in the past, and he'll have to re-examine whether that's a sound strategy now, said **Marc Mukasey**, a partner with Bracewell & Giuliani LLP's White Collar Criminal Defense and Special Investigations practice in New York.

"I imagine that the legal fees are going to cost him a pretty penny," Mukasey said in a telephone interview. "Virtually anybody who ever paid him anything, certainly with some sort of moral turpitude clause in it, is going to try to recoup. I would guess that he will be in contractual litigation for a long time."

Armstrong has denied ever doping and says he's never failed a drug test. Any acknowledgement of drug use now is complicated by the fact that in the original SCA dispute he testified under oath that he had never doped.

Boxed-In

"To say under oath that you never used performance-enhancing drugs, that makes a subsequent admission and apology that much more difficult," said Mukasey, who has no involvement in Armstrong's legal representation. "From a legal perspective, once you box yourself in like that, you better be committed to that story or have a really good excuse as to why you were mistaken or delusional at the time you gave that answer."

While there remain people who believe Armstrong is innocent, it won't mean a return to sponsorships, said Paul Swangard, managing director of the Warsaw Sports Marketing Center at the University of Oregon.

"I see him as tainted goods," Swangard said last week in a telephone interview. "There are plenty of ways to reach your target consumer and Lance just isn't one of them anymore."

Source: Mason Levinson, Eben Novy-Williams, and Alex Duff, "Armstrong Faces $200 Million Salary Loss With Reputation Hit," *Bloomberg.com* (October 21, 2012). Available from: http://www.bloomberg.com/news/2012-10-24/armstrong-faces-200-million-salary-loss-with-reputation-ruined.html. Used with permission of Bloomberg L.P.

One promising alternative that reduces the risk of potential problems is to use athletes who are no longer alive. Nike ran a series of 10 commercials using former Green Bay Packer coach Vince Lombardi. Other corporations that have featured departed stars in their ad campaigns include Citibank (Babe Ruth), Microsoft (Lou Gehrig and Jesse Owens), McDonald's, Coca-Cola, Apple Computer, General Mills (Jackie Robinson), and Miller Brewing (Satchel Paige). Dead athletes are more cost effective, scandal proof, and are icons in the world of sports. Ruth was chosen to represent Citibank in an ad campaign – 49 years after his death and 62 since his last homer – for similar reasons. "Babe's an American sports icon, instantly recognizable," says Ken Gordon, a Citibank vice president, explaining why Ruth got the nod over contemporary ballplayers.[25]

Media strategy

As presented in Chapter 9, a medium or channel is the element in the communications process by which the message is transmitted. Traditional mass media, such as newspapers, television, radio, or magazines, are usually thought of as effective ways of carrying advertising messages to the target audience. However, new technologies are creating alternative media. The Internet, for example, represents an emerging medium that must be considered by sports advertisers. It is important to know the habits and preferences of each market segment and often these behaviors are identified using marketing analytics. Understanding these habits and preferences can enhance communication and marketing efforts for these audiences. For example, teens use a multitude of media each day, and technology is also an integral part of teen life. Technology influences the type of media teens use – from researching potential purchases and schoolwork to maintaining friendships. Teens often actively multi-task or let one medium influence their use on another concurrent behavior. Deciding what medium or media to use is just one aspect in developing a comprehensive media strategy. **Media strategy** addresses two basic questions about the channel of communication. First, what medium or media mix (combination of media) will be most effective in reaching the desired target audience? Second, how should this media be scheduled to meet advertising objectives?

Media decisions or media selection

The far-ranging (and growing) number of media choices makes selecting the right media a difficult task. Choosing the proper media requires the sports advertiser to be mindful of the creative decisions made earlier in the advertising process. For instance, an emotional appeal – best suited to television – would be difficult to convey using print media. It is also critical that the media planner keep the target market in mind. Understanding the profile of the target market and their media habits is essential to developing an effective advertising campaign.

Table 10.4 Profiles of major media types

Medium	Advantages	Limitations
Internet	Allows messages to be customized; reaches specific market; interactive capabilities	Clutter; audience characteristics; hard-to-measure effectiveness
Newspapers	Flexibility; timeliness; good local market coverage; broad acceptability; high believability	Short life; poor reproduction quality; small pass-along audience
Television	Good mass market coverage; low cost per exposure; combines sight, sound, and motion; appealing to the senses	High absolute costs; high clutter; fleeting exposure; less audience selectivity
Direct mail	High audience selectivity; flexibility; no ad competition within the same medium; allows personalization	Relatively high cost per exposure; "junk mail" image
Radio	Good local acceptance; high geographic and demographic selectivity; low cost	Audio only, fleeting exposure; low attention ("the half-heard" medium); fragmented audiences
Magazines	High geographic and demographic selectivity; credibility and prestige; high-quality reproduction; long life and good pass-along readership	Long advertisement purchase lead time; high cost; no guarantee of position
Outdoor	Flexibility; high repeat exposure; low cost; low message competition; good positional selectivity	Little audience selectivity; creative limitations

Source: Adapted from Philip Kotler and Gary Armstrong, *Marketing: An Introduction*, 4th ed. (Upper Saddle River, NJ: Prentice Hall, 1997), 471.

Every type of media has strengths and weaknesses that must be considered when making advertising placement decisions. Table 10.4 demonstrates selected advantages and disadvantages when choosing among advertising media.

Alternative forms of advertising

Because of the advertising clutter present in traditional advertising media, sports marketers are continually evaluating new ways of delivering their message to consumers. Alternative forms of advertising range from the more conventional stadium signage to the most creative media. Consider the following innovative illustrations of alternative forms of advertising: The International Cricket Council has allowed players to sell the top 23 centimeters of their bats for advertising. In Connecticut, 35 public golf courses signed up for a program that put advertisements in the bottom of their holes. Formerly, 7–Eleven entered into a three year $500,000 sponsorship contract with the White Sox, calling for all weekday games to start at 7:11. A company spokesperson called this a "fun way to insert our name into fans' hearts and minds." This sort of creativity could open up other areas where brands can get involved without impacting the field of play, as well as additional inventory for teams to sell.

Stadium signage

Stadium signage or on-site advertising, is back and is an extremely popular form of promotion and sponsorship packages. For some time, nary a sign was found on the outfield wall of an MLB team or on the boards at an NHL game. Now, stadium signage prevails on every inch of available space. Not unlike other forms of advertising, stadium signage is designed to increase brand or corporate awareness, create a favorable image through associations with the team and sport, change attitudes or maintain favorable attitudes, and ultimately increase the sale of product. The Cubs have struck a three-year sponsorship deal with Under Armour to place two 7-by-12-foot signs on the Wrigley Field outfield doors, the first corporate advertising to be placed among the famed brick-and-ivy outfield wall in the stadium's then 93-year history.

Photo 10.2 Coca-Cola creates a positive association with baseball by using stadium signage.

Source: Laura M. Hoffman

Traditionally, stadium sponsors and advertisers have utilized in stadium ads, naming rights and banners visible on TV to capture consumer attention. However, with the advent of digital technology, attention is becoming a scarce resource. Due to consumer behaviors such as multitasking and shorter attention spans, the quality of viewer attention has eroded over the past two-and-a-half decades.[26] Therefore, marketers today must be innovative, integrating more targeted and interactive advertising strategies. Attention economics have been a scarce commodity in the age of information overload. However, in this playing field, aggregating the attention of fans and selling a portion to advertisers and sponsors is where the real riches lie.[27] For example, in the NFL, teams like the Dallas Cowboys earn in excess of $100 million from sponsorships and advertising in a single season, while teams such as the Oakland Raiders and Buffalo Bills earn less than $20 million.[28] Estimated expenditures on stadium signage and sponsorships are expected to continue to increase. Thus, given the advent of new technologies, allowing stadium billboards to be changed and customized for local markets, the use of flat panel displayers for digital out of home advertising will continue to be one of the fastest growing industries and with deployment of stadium signage appear in almost every major world market.

Although stadium signage can be an effective means of advertising, it can also be costly. The new Dallas Cowboys stadium is one of the world's most modern venues, but it came with a significant price tag, $1.2 billion. The stadium features a retractable roof and a signage scheme unlike any other. Cowboys Stadium is home to the world's largest outdoor digital display. The 2,100 inch display weighs in at approximately 600 tons, spans over 25,670 square feet, features back to back high definition LED screens, and has two small screens at each end to accommodate the stadium end zone fans. The cost of this massive display is just a mere $40 million. However, the digital signage does not end there, apart from having the largest outdoor back to back HD screen, they also utilize over 3,000 small displays around the stadium to allow fans to stay abreast of the game and to inform fans of news related to the team. In addition, in other venues across the country items such as rotating/digital scorers and press tables often seen at NBA and collegiate basketball games can cost between $50,000 and $250,000. How is expensive stadium signage sold and justified by sports marketers? First, research has shown that locations considered to be part of the game (e.g., scorer's table or on the ice) are more effective than those locations removed from the action (e.g., scoreboards).[29] Other research found that spectators had improved recognition of and attitudes toward eight courtside advertisers for an NCAA Division I men's basketball team. This finding is, of course, extremely important to sponsors considering the cost and effectiveness of this type of stadium signage.[30]

Other outdoor

A new form of outdoor advertising is also becoming popular at national sporting events. This type of outdoor promotion uses live product demonstrations or characters to attract fans' attention. For example, the 2011 Paribas Showdown became the first professional tennis event in the U.S. to feature digital signage capable of full motion animations. The promoters utilized these digital features to integrate legends like John McEnroe, Ivan Lendl, Pete Sampras, and Andre Agassi thereby enhancing the ESPN broadcast. In addition, the U.S. Army staged a live combat reenactment prior to the start of the Charlotte 500 NASCAR race. In another example, Juan Valdez, the very recognizable brand character for Colombian coffee, showed up in the stands of the U.S. Open tennis tournament. Similarly, Ronald McDonald attended the Kentucky Derby and a Chicago Bulls game to promote new products from McDonald's.

In a related fashion, sports marketers sometimes use variations of product placement techniques. Product placement occurs when manufacturers pay to have their products used in cooperation with sporting events, television shows, movies, and other entertainment media such as music videos. For instance, Gatorade's Jeff Urban teamed up with Major League Baseball's Homerun Derby. Prior to the placement opportunity the brand received little exposure and was confined to the limits of the dugout. The placement initiative afforded Gatorade the opportunity to hand each slugger a bottle of Gatorade and towels with the Gatorade logo near home plate on the sidelines while they conducted their post hitting interviews for television. The Gatorade placement was front and center, in a manner that fans could not help but notice. In other examples, Gordon and Smith surfboards were prominently featured in the movie *Blue Crush*, written about female surfers; and perhaps the earliest sports product placement was when James Bond, 007, used Slazenger golf balls on the links in the classic *Goldfinger*. In the ultimate product tie-in, the Anaheim Mighty Ducks of the NHL were named after the series of movies created by their then parent company, Disney.

Are these product placements effective? Top-rated TV shows aren't necessarily the best places for product placement. That's the conclusion of a new study of television product placement effectiveness conducted by New York-based Intermedia Advertising Group (IAG), a research company whose roots are in measuring the effectiveness and performance of network television commercials.[31] "We both poll viewers and measure the exposure ourselves," IAG co-CEO Alan Gould said. "We code the exposure type; we measure the duration and note factors such as whether the product is embedded into the story line, used as intended, and in the foreground or background."[32] Even though this study seemed to find little support for the effectiveness of product placement, anecdotal evidence shows that product demonstrations seem to work and are certainly popular. Spike TV's and EA Sports' recent product placement recognition involved logo placement in the television series the *Ultimate Fighter*. Others include the likes of Everlast and the former television show *The Contender* as well as recognizable films such as: *Requiem for a Heavyweight, Raging Bull, Ali, Cinderella Man, The Hurricane, Million Dollar Baby*. Other sports product placements in recent movies include the following:

Gridiron Gang – Nike, Puma, Rogers Athletic, Schutt Sports, Spalding; *The Departed* – Adidas; *Invincible* – Adidas; *Talladega Nights* – EA Sports; *Click* – Huffy Bicycle Company; *The Break-Up* – EA Sports, Reebok; and *Failure to Launch* – EA Sports, Nike.

The advantages that have been cited for these alternative forms of advertising include:[33]

- ***Exposure*** – A large number of people go to the movies, rent movies, or could be exposed to a live-product demonstration if they are attending a sporting event or watching television.
- ***Attention*** – Moviegoers are generally an attentive audience. Sports spectators are also a captive audience when they are waiting for the action to begin.
- ***Recall*** – Research has shown that audiences have higher levels of next-day recall for products that are placed in movies than for traditional forms of promotion.
- ***Source association*** – for product placements, the audience may see familiar and likable stars using the sports product. As such, the product's image may be enhanced through association with the celebrity.

Another alternative form of advertising is using the athlete as a "human billboard."[34] The history of athletes wearing an advertisement can be traced back to the 1960s, when organizations began establishing relationships with stock car drivers. Soon, the practice of drivers wearing patches on their clothing spread to other sports, such as tennis and golf. The use of athletes as advertisers is much more common in individual sports because these individuals have the ability to negotiate and wear whatever they want, as opposed to the tight controls imposed on athletes in team sports by their respective leagues.

Today, the use of athletes as human billboards is part of the integrated marketing communications plan rather than a stand-alone promotion. Fred Couples, Rich Beem, Chris DiMarco, Stuart Appleby, and Steve Flesch of the PGA wear sweaters and shirts, in addition to the other advertisements and promotions they perform for

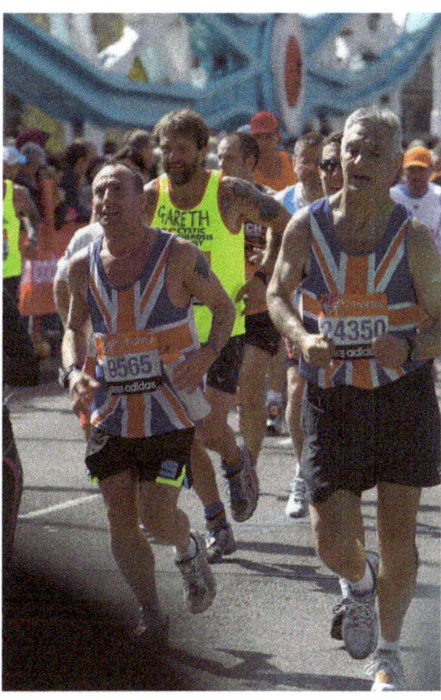

Photo 10.3 These runners all exemplify the human billboard.

Source: Shutterstock.com

Ashworth. The major appeal of this form of advertising is the natural association (classical conditioning) formed in consumers' minds between the athlete and the organization or product.

How much does it cost sponsors to rent advertising space on an athlete's body? An IndyCar driver's helmet might cost between $50,000 and $250,000, depending on the driver. The precious space on a professional golfer's visor would cost between $250,000 and $500,000. Although these prices may seem outrageous, organizations are willing to pay the price for the exposure and enhanced brand equity.

In addition to these more conventional examples, basketball player Rasheed Wallace was asked by a candy company to tattoo his body for the NBA season. This offer was ultimately rejected as it was thought to potentially violate the NBA Uniform Player contract. Additionally, boxers have started to use their bodies as billboards by tattooing corporate logos on their chest and back. The Nevada State Athletic Commission tried to ban body billboards, but ultimately lost to the state court's ruling protecting boxers' right to free speech.

BIG 4 JERSEY RIGHTS VALUE PUT AT $370M

The four big stick-and-ball leagues are leaving a total of more than $370 million on the table annually by not selling jersey advertising, according to new research from Horizon Media.

The NFL, with its unrivaled ratings and concomitantly higher ad rates, topped the list for jersey valuations at nearly $231 million, or 62 percent of all potential big four jersey ad sales. However, the nature of football – with players more crowded together and with less static time facing the camera – means that the NFL offers the least of what the study terms "detections" among the four leagues, with 28,560 calculated over the course of a season. Baseball, meanwhile, with its typical center-field and behind-the-catcher camera angles, scored more than 314,000 detection opportunities.

The total jersey valuation for MLB teams came in at more than $101 million. The NBA total was $31 million, and the NHL at $8 million, according to the report.

Players' amount of static time facing the camera hurt the NFL's value but helped MLB.

While NHL teams posted the lowest monetary value in the survey, the NHL's quality impact score was second only to MLB. Hockey's fast pace of play provides for fewer detection opportunities during game action, but when play is stopped in the NHL, the exposure "duration," or amount of time the jersey is visible on-screen, is higher in hockey than other sports.

Using computerized exposure evaluation techniques and assuming a brand logo across the middle of a team's jersey that would occupy 3.5 percent of the TV screen – comparable to an English Premier League kit – the study formulated media evolutions for the NBA, NFL, NHL and MLB in their top 20 markets over their most recently completed seasons.

The study did not account for logo value in print and digital media, or from being viewed on-site.

Since the study made assumptions on a team's national broadcast appearances, it's not surprising that the top five NFL teams in exposure value are Dallas, New England, the New York Giants, the New York Jets and Philadelphia – all prime targets for the NFL's national broadcast windows.

Likewise, the top three MLB teams in exposure value are the New York Yankees, Boston and the New York Mets. The NBA list is led by the Los Angeles Lakers, New York and Boston, while in the NHL, the top three are Chicago, the New York Rangers and Pittsburgh.

The research noted that the list of teams for potential ad value of jersey sponsorships parallels Forbes' list of the most valuable sports teams.

Jersey ads are a common practice in most of the world, but the big U.S. leagues have thus far resisted selling their jerseys as billboards, except to brands such as Nike, Reebok and Adidas, which hold their apparel rights.

"We don't necessarily see this happening soon in the U.S.," said Michael Neuman, Horizon Media's managing partner for sports, entertainment and events, "but until the revenue potential is clear, it certainly won't go anywhere, and clearly this shows there is significant opportunity at a time when most of the big leagues are looking for new revenue."

Consider, for example, the NHL's exposure value of $8.17 million, compared with its current NBC contract, which is a no-rights-fee, revenue-share deal. Or imagine the incremental value jersey advertising could bring if it were bundled with TV rights for rights holders to sell.

In England, Premiership club deals range in annual price from $32 million for the Aon-Manchester United and Liverpool-Standard Chartered deals to less than $1 million for Blackpool's sponsorship deal with online loan company Wonga.

Of course, the political machinations of jersey ads for the big four leagues are probably greater than what for some is a psychological barrier of swapping an Adidas or Nike logo for Coke or McDonald's. A leading question: Who would sell the uniform ads: networks, leagues or individual teams?

"If I'm an owner, I'm saying that's my real estate. And if I'm a network with league rights and I can't sell it, then I'm paying less for those rights," said Chris Weil, CEO of marketing agency Momentum Worldwide, whose client list includes heavy sports spenders like Coca-Cola and American Express. "You also might run into a problem if you ask a player to take a pay cut, as they are in the current [NFL] labor negotiations, and then sell space on what a player might consider his jersey."

Another constituency that could insist on a piece of the action are the jersey manufacturers, who are accustomed to having their trademarks on pro uniforms. There also likely would be conflicts between individual athlete endorsement deals and the company ad that's on the jersey the player might be wearing.

"My opinion is that it's been a business barrier stopping us from doing this rather than a belief that we would be violating something

POTENTIAL JERSEY SPONSORSHIP VALUES*

LEAGUE	NO.OF DETECTIONS	DURATION (H:MIN:SEC)	DURATION PER DETECTION	QUALITY IMPACT SCORE	MONETARY VALUE
NFL	28,560	18:26:40	2.33	0.209	$230,911,504
MLB	314,280	273:36:00	3.13	0.308	$101,052,782
NBA	127,920	94:11:10	2.65	0.238	$31,186,931
NHL	74,620	60:08:00	2.89	0.248	$8,171,211
TOTAL	545,380	446:21:50	2.94	0.278	$371,322,428

10

sacrosanct," said Phoenix Suns President and CEO Rick Welts, formerly the NBA's chief marketing officer. "I wouldn't say the leadership in our league is against it, but certainly we're not prepared to do it until it comes with a price everybody can be comfortable with. I don't think we're anywhere close to that now."

Source: Article author: Terry Lefton;http://www.sportsbusinessdaily.com/Journal/Issues/2011/02/20110207/Marketing-and-Sponsorship/Jerseys.aspx. Credit: Sports Business Journal.

Regardless of how you slice it, collectively assessing how big the advertising business can be is something that's still being questioned. New methods of advertising are constantly being developed. According to the 2014 Global Games Market Report by Newzoo, the global games market will rocket past the $100 billion market, to reach $102.9 billion by 2017.[35] The Entertainment Software Association estimates that the in-game advertising market for this industry could grow to be $1 billion by 2014, up from $56 million in 2006.[36], [37] "All the forecasts are overstated, but even at the low end, it's a healthy business," said Chip Lange, vice president of online commerce at Electronic Arts, and this "healthy business" contributes further to advertising's bottom line. [38]

Internet

Another major player in the world of advertising media is the Internet. As discussed in Chapter 2, the Internet has already become a valuable source of sports information for participants and fans. In addition, the Internet is fast becoming the favorite promotional medium for sports marketers. A total user base of over 274 million people exists in the United States alone, and Internet usage is growing globally with approximately 2.5 billion users (34 percent of the world population), which is one advantage to promotion via the internet (as seen in Table 10.5).

In addition, according to a BurstMedia report, 35.1 percent of all sports fans – including two-in-three (66.8 percent) devoted fans – go online at least once per day

Table 10.5 World regions by Internet penetration

World Internet usage and population statistics June 30, 2012						
World Regions	**Population (2012 Est.)**	**Internet Users Dec. 31, 2000**	**Internet Users Latest Data**	**Penetration (% Population)**	**Growth 2000–2012**	**Users % of Table**
Africa	1,073,380,925	4,514,400	167,335,676	15.6 %	3,606.7 %	7.0 %
Asia	3,922,066,987	114,304,000	1,076,681,059	27.5 %	841.9 %	44.8 %
Europe	820,918,446	105,096,093	518,512,109	63.2 %	393.4 %	21.5 %
Middle East	223,608,203	3,284,800	90,000,455	40.2 %	2,639.9 %	3.7 %
North America	348,280,154	108,096,800	273,785,413	78.6 %	153.3 %	11.4 %
Latin America / Caribbean	593,688,638	18,068,919	254,915,745	42.9 %	1,310.8 %	10.6 %
Oceania / Australia	35,903,569	7,620,480	24,287,919	67.6 %	218.7 %	1.0 %
World total	7,017,846,922	360,985,492	2,405,518,376	34.3 %	566.4 %	100.0 %

Source: http://www.internetworldstats.com/stats.htm.

for sports-related reasons, e.g., check scores, read sports news, watch sports videos or play fantasy sports games.[39] Nearly one-third (30.4 percent) of all sports fans say most of their time online is spent reading content versus watching online video. "Whether it's consuming original sports content online, sharing likes and tweets with friends, or using a tablet to follow the score, sports enthusiasts have many options to access content," said Mark Kaefer, marketing director, Burst Media, "and with digital media becoming an increasingly significant part of the total sports fan experience, online publishers and advertisers now have access to a much wider set of platforms and tactics to use to engage audiences."[40] Let us take a look at some of the other advantages to promotion via the Internet.

Perhaps the most substantial advantage to using the Internet as a promotional tool is the good fit between the profile of the sports fan and the Internet user. The typical Internet user was described as an entertainment-minded, educated male between 18 and 34 years old. However, today the web is no longer the virtual playground of just well-educated males and technology aficionados. Today the online consumer population is undergoing a major shift. Sixty percent of these new users are women and many earn average or below average incomes. Moreover, 33 percent have had web access for less than a year.[41] These trends require the traditional sport marketers to re-think their communication strategy. For instance, the demographic profile of espn.com users is 94 percent male, 47 percent single, with 66 percent between the ages of 18 and 34.[42] Sound familiar? These characteristics closely match the traditional sports fan.

Digital platforms are fast becoming the choice of media for sports fans and are pushing the boundaries of media convergence across television, Internet, and mobile devices. The television and the Internet now outweigh other media at peak viewing times and twice as many sports fans watch video via mobile devices compared with the average mobile device user. These individuals are also known to multitask, for results indicate that twice as many sports fans use the Internet while watching TV compared with the average user. Ultimately sport users are more engaged and receptive than the average Internet user to online advertising and these users are more likely to increase their sports consumption online due to its ease of use, accessibility, technology, and its real time availability.[43] Finally, the Internet is the ideal medium to target college sports fans due to greater access and usage rates among students. Generally, the Internet allows the sports advertiser to reach an extremely focused targeted market.[44]

Another distinct advantage of promotion via the Internet is the interactive nature of the medium. Promotions attract the attention of the target audience and then create involvement by having consumers point and click on the information they find of interest. For instance, the Major League Soccer site (www.mlssoccer.com) has advertisements asking soccer fans, "are you a true MLS fan?," and then asking fans to go to the Zune store to download MLS screensavers and backgrounds.

A point and click of the mouse will take fans to the Georgia Pacific soccer link, which features the ability to download player screen savers and wallpapers, enter a shootout online contest, and, of course get more information on MardiGras products.

Other advantages of the Internet versus more traditional media include the Internet's ability to be flexible. Web promotions can be updated, and changes can be made almost instantly. This flexibility is a tremendous advantage for sports marketers, who are constantly responding to a changing environment. In fact, the Internet seems to be the perfect tool for sports marketers using the contingency framework for strategic planning. For example, the emergence of social media has supercharged

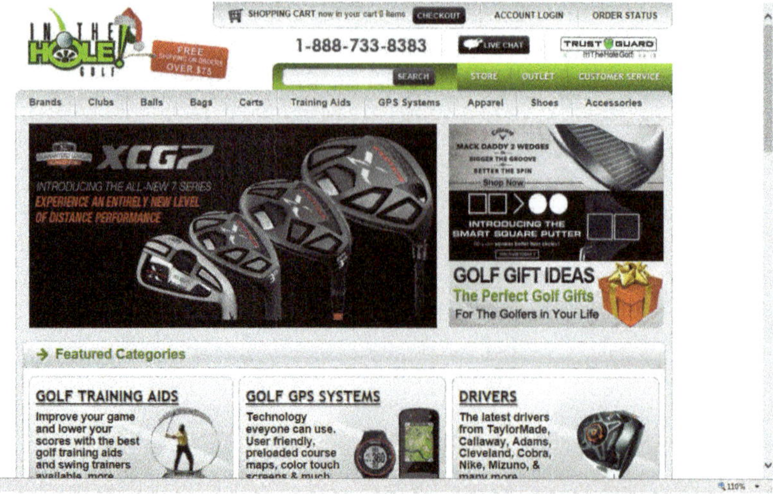

Web 10.5 The Internet has become a popular medium for all forms of online purchasing.

Source: InTheHoleGolf.com

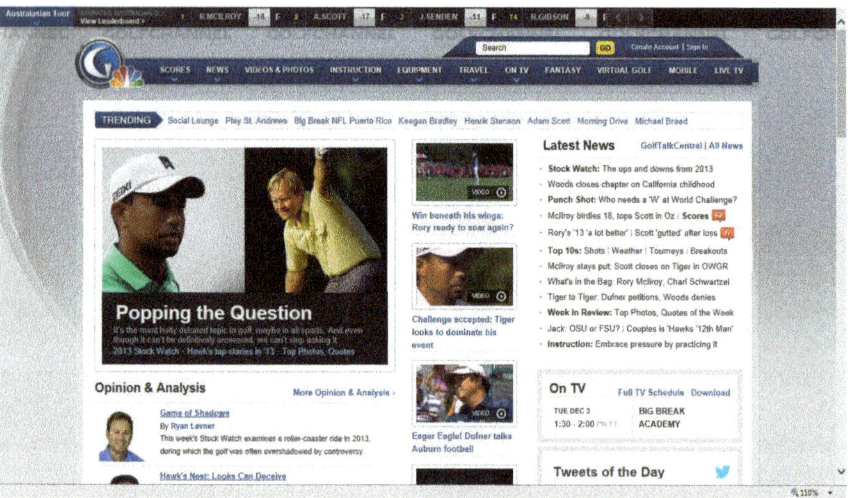

Web 10.6 The Golf Channel, PGA, and LPGA team up for online contests.

Source: GolfChannel.com

an age old consumer activity allowing consumers to chat about things like scores, stats, and other sport interests. This established consumer behavior, now enabled by new technology platforms, is driving a fundamental change in the way sport brand marketing works. Today's relationships are more explicit and must consider the engagement of the message and the consumer; these engagements make platforms much more measurable which constantly inspire new ideas between research, media, and consumer brand perceptions.

A final benefit of promotion via the Internet is its cost effectiveness. The Internet provides organizations with a means of promoting sports to consumers around the world at a low cost. The ability to reach a geographically diverse audience at a low cost is one of the primary advantages of Internet promotion.

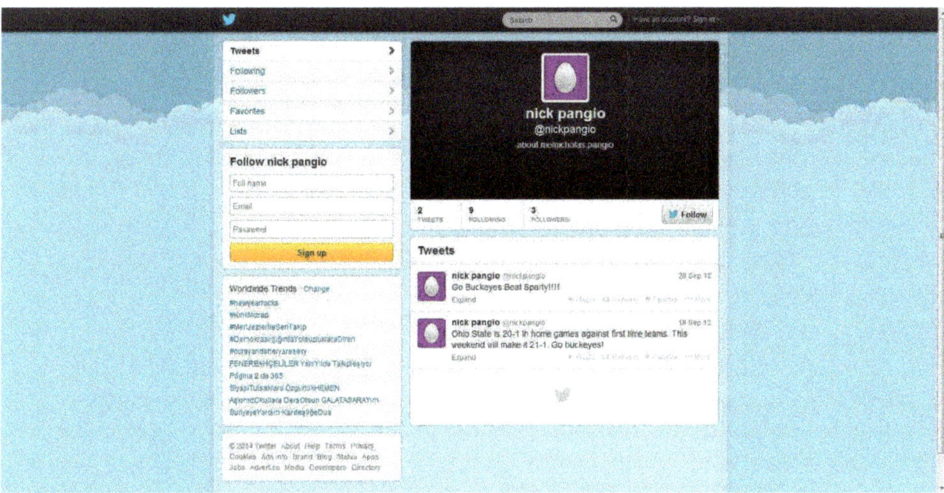

Web 10.7 Social media continue to emerge as an interactive Web strategy.

Source: Twitter; https://twitter.com/nickpangio

Although there are many advantages, promotion via the Internet can also pose potential problems. As with other forms of advertising, it is difficult to measure the effectiveness of sports promotion over the Internet. Often, marketers use the "number of hits" as a proxy for effectiveness, but this cannot be used to determine the interest level of the consumer or purchase intent.

Promotional clutter is another difficulty with Internet promotions. As the Internet becomes a more popular advertising medium, more organizations will compete for the audience and its attention. To break through the clutter, sports marketers must design new Internet promotions. Differentiating among Web promotions will become increasingly important in gaining the attention of consumers and developing a unique position for organizations.

A final disadvantage of promotion on the Internet is its inability to reach certain groups of consumers. Although the Internet is a great medium to reach younger, college-educated, computer-literate consumers, it may be extremely inefficient in trying to promote to the mature market or, perhaps, consumers of lower socioeconomic standing.

Although we have looked at some of the pros and cons of promotion via the Internet, the fact remains that the Internet is here to stay and that the use of personal mobile devices will have a significant marketing presence for years to come. The low costs, ability to target sports fans and participants, and high flexibility far outweigh the disadvantages of this medium. Certainly, sports marketers have accepted the Internet as another important tool in their integrated communications efforts.

Choosing a specific medium

Once the medium or media mix is chosen by the sports organization along with the advertising agency, the specific medium must be addressed. In other words, if the advertisement will appear in a magazine, then we must choose which magazine will be most effective. Do we want our advertisement to promote the NHL to appear in *Sports Illustrated*, *Sporting News Magazine*, the *Hockey News*, or some combination of these specific media? Should we promote Texas Motor Speedway via Internet advertising, text messaging, podcasting, or by more traditional means – television, radio, magazine, and newspaper? To answer this question, we must consider our reach and frequency objectives.

Reach refers to the number of people exposed to an advertisement in a given medium. For the advertiser who wants to generate awareness and reach the largest number of people in the target audience, perhaps *Sports Illustrated*, with a circulation of over 3 million, would be the most effective medium. However, if the target audience is women, then *Sports Illustrated* might be reaching people who are not potential users.

The reach of an advertisement is determined by a number of factors. First, nature of the media mix influences reach. The general rule is that the greater the number of media used, the greater the reach. For example, if the advertising campaign for the NHL were broadcast on television, printed in magazines, and also appeared on the Internet, reach would be increased. Second, if only one medium is to be used, increasing the number and diversity within this medium will increase the reach. For instance, if cable television were chosen as the sole medium for the NHL campaign, reach would be increased if the commercial were aired on ESPN, Lifetime, and Fox Sports versus ESPN alone. Finally, reach can be enhanced by airing the advertisements during different times of the day or day parts. The advertisement might be shown at night after 9:00 P.M. and also in the morning to reach a greater percentage of the target audience.

Along with reach, another consideration in making specific media decisions is frequency. **Frequency** refers to the number of times the individual or household is exposed to the media vehicle. An important point is that frequency is measured by the number of exposures to the media vehicle rather than the advertisement itself. Just because an advertisement is shown on television during the Super Bowl does not mean that the target audience has seen it. Consumers might change channels, leave the room, or simply become involved in conversation. A study examined this issue using Super Bowl viewers in a bar setting.[45] It found that visual attention levels for the game are similar to attention levels for the advertisements, attention to commercials varies by their location in the cluster of advertisements and time of the game, and that Super Bowl commercials may receive more attention than commercials on other programs.

Media scheduling

Four basic **media scheduling** alternatives are considered once the medium (e.g., magazines) and specific publications (e.g., *Sports Illustrated*) are chosen. These schedules are called continuous, flighting, pulsing, and seasonal. A **continuous schedule** recognizes that there are no breaks in the demand for the sports product. This is also called steady, or "drip," scheduling. During the advertising period, advertisements are continually run. Most sporting goods and events are seasonal and, therefore, do not require a continuous schedule. Some sporting goods, such as running shoes, have roughly equivalent demand and advertising spending throughout the year.

A **flighting schedule** is another alternative, where advertising expenditures are varied in some months and zero is spent in other months. Consider the case of the Houston Astros. Heavy advertising expenditures are spent in March, April, and May leading up to the season. Reminder-oriented advertising is placed over the course of the rest of the season, and no advertising dollars are spent in the winter months. This type of scheduling is most prevalent in sports marketing due to the seasonal nature of most sports.

A **pulsing schedule** is a variant of the flighting schedule. Ad expenditures may vary greatly, but some level of advertising is always taking place. Although it sounds similar to a flighting schedule, remember that a flighting schedule has some months where zero is spent on advertising.

Personal selling

Now that we have looked at the advertising process in detail, let us turn to another important element in the promotion mix – personal selling. Personal selling is used in a variety of ways in sports marketing, such as in securing corporate sponsorships, selling luxury suites or boxes in stadiums, and hawking corporate and group ticket sales. In the marketing of sporting goods, the primary applications of personal selling are to get retailers to carry products (push strategy) and consumers to purchase products (pull strategy).

Personal selling represents a unique element in the promotion mix because it involves personal interaction with the target audience rather than mass communication to thousands or millions of consumers. The definition of personal selling reflects this important distinction between personal selling and the other promotion tools. **Personal selling** is a form of person-to-person communication in which a salesperson works with prospective buyers and attempts to influence their purchase needs in the direction of their company's products or services.

All the advantages of personal selling described in Table 10.6 make it an attractive promotional tool, so the ability to use personal selling to develop long-term relationships with consumers is becoming increasingly important to sports marketers. In fact, building long-term relationships with consumers has become one of the critical issues for marketers. More formally, **relationship marketing** is the process of creating, maintaining, and enhancing strong, value-laden relationships with customers and other stakeholders.[46]

As Kotler and Armstrong point out, the key premise of relationship marketing is that building strong economic and social ties with valued customers, distributors, dealers, and suppliers leads to long-term profitable transactions. Many sports organizations are realizing it is cheaper to foster and maintain strong relationships with existing customers rather than find new customers or fight the competition for a stagnant consumer base.

10

Table 10.6 Benefits of personal selling

• Personal selling allows the salesperson to immediately adapt the message they are presenting based on feedback received from the target audience.
• Personal selling allows the salesperson to communicate more information to the target audience than other forms of promotion. Moreover, complex information can be explained by the salesperson.
• Personal selling greatly increases the likelihood of the target audience paying attention to the message. It is difficult for the target audience to escape the message because communication is person to person.
• Personal selling greatly increases the chances of developing a long-term relationship with consumers, due to the frequent person-to-person communication.

Two examples of building relationships with consumers of sport were described in an article entitled "Pursuing Relationships in Professional Sport."[47] In the first example, a promotion was developed by the Pittsburgh Pirates and Giant Eagle Supermarkets. The basic premise of the promotion was that fans could earn discounts and special offers at Pirates games by participating in the Giant Eagle preferred shoppers program. For example, fans with an Advantage Card (given to program participants) were offered discounted ballpark meals for a month, half-price tickets to five games throughout the season, and discounts on Pirates merchandise. The relationship-building program was deemed successful by the Pirates, Giant Eagle, and the fans.

Another relationship-building effort was designed for the fans of the San Diego Padres. The program for season ticket holders, called the Compadres Club, and for single game purchasers called the Frequent Friar Club, rewards fans for attending predetermined numbers of games. Each program is tailored to a specific audience; season ticket holders identified as the lifeblood of the Padres are rewarded for their investment while the Frequent Friar Rewards Club rewards the Friar Faithful for their ticket purchases. Ultimately, fans can redeem their frequency points for Padres merchandise, posters, and dinners. For example, the top earners receive an authentic baseball bat autographed by a Padres player and presented on the field at a special pregame ceremony. Although both the Pirates and the Padres have developed marketing programs to build relationships with fans, the importance of personal selling should not be overlooked. Personal selling was necessary for the Pirates to communicate the benefits of the partnership to Giant Eagle. As a result of selling a successful program to Giant Eagle, the company increased its Pirates-related marketing budget by roughly 25 percent. The Padres, armed with a database of the demographics and buying habits of its most loyal fans, will use personal selling to secure additional sponsorship and advertising dollars.

CAREER SPOTLIGHT

Kevin Rochlitz, Vice President, National Partnerships and Sales, Baltimore Ravens

Career questions

1. **How did you get started in the sports industry? What was your first sports industry job?**

I got my start by working as an intern in the University of Wyoming athletic department in promotions and administration. I knew what I wanted to do from the beginning, so I decided to go ahead and volunteer my time, and I got a lot of work experience from it. My father is a basketball coach and I loved the integration between sports and business. My first sports industry job was the assistant marketing director job at Fresno State University. I learned a lot while I was there and it taught me more about selling and the ability to tie in promotions with partners.

2. **Can you describe the type of work you are doing right now? What are your job responsibilities? What are the greatest challenges?**

Right now, my main goal is to bring in revenue through a number of channels such as signage, television, radio, print, Internet or converged media, trademarks, and promotional opportunities. I work with all of the retail and national accounts as we try to tie them in together. My overall responsibility is to increase revenue for the team and gain market share with our marks. Since we are a young team, the opportunity to have our logo tied in with promotions is a big help. The greatest challenge for us is that we are between two major markets (Philadelphia and Washington) and both have teams, so the ability to use our marks outside our area is difficult. Also, the growing popularity of the Internet and all that it can do and trying to get partners to see this can be challenging.

3. **Do you foresee any changes in demand in this field in the future? If so, what or how?**

Not really. Right now I think it is going to go in the direction of electronic media, and the more people in this industry have the knowledge of this, the better it will help them.

4. **Who or what has influenced you the most in your sports business career?**

I would say my parents as they have taught me to work very hard and things will happen. I love my job and many times I can't believe they pay me to do this. It is a hobby and from the days of working at Wyoming with then Athletic Director Paul Roach, he gave me an opportunity to learn while I was at school, so it was like getting two degrees. Plus one of my old professors at Wyoming, Dr. Brooks Mitchell, who taught me to think outside the box, has been very influential on my career.

5. **What advice would you offer students who are considering a career in sports marketing?**

You are going to have to work hard and get involved in a collegiate marketing department and volunteer your time. The experience at this level can be very beneficial and the folks in the athletic department will help you postgraduation.

The strategic selling process

Now that we have defined personal selling and discussed some of its major advantages, let us examine how the selling process operates in sports marketing. As previously discussed, sports marketers are generally concerned with selling an intangible service versus a tangible good. Most salespeople view the selling of services as a much more difficult process, because the benefits of the sports product are not readily observable or easily communicated to the target audience. It is much easier to sell the new and improved r7 Superquad driver from TaylorMade when the consumer can see the design, feel the weight of the club, and swing the club. In essence, the product sells itself. Contrast this with the sale of a luxury box to a corporation in a stadium that is yet to be built. Selling this sports product is dependent on communicating both the tangible and intangible benefits of the box to the prospective buyer. In addition to the problems associated with selling a service versus a good, the sale of many sports products requires several people to give their approval before the sale is complete. This factor also makes the selling process more complex.

In the ever-changing world of sports marketing, the "good ol' boy" approach to selling is no longer valid. To be more effective and efficient in today's competitive environment, a number of personal selling strategies have been developed. One process, developed by Robert Miller and Stephen Heiman, is called **strategic selling**.[48]

Miller and Heiman suggest the first step in any strategic selling process is performing an analysis of your current position. In this instance, position is described as understanding your personal strengths and weaknesses as well as the opportunities and threats that are present in the selling situation. In essence, the salesperson is constructing a mini-SWOT analysis, analysis of strengths, weaknesses, opportunities and threats. Questions regarding how prospective clients feel about you as a salesperson, how they feel about your products and services, who the competition is, and how they are positioned must all be addressed at the initial stages of the strategic selling process.

Good salespeople realize that they must adapt their current position for every account before they can be successful. To change this position, six elements in the strategic selling process must be considered in a systematic and interactive fashion. These elements, which must be understood for successful sales, include buying influences, red flags, response modes, win-results, the sales funnel, and the ideal customer profile. Let us take a brief look at how these elements work together in the strategic selling process.

Buying influences

A complex sale was earlier defined as one where multiple individuals are involved in the buying process. This is true of large organizations considering a sponsorship proposal or families considering the purchase of exercise equipment for a new workout facility in their home. One of the first steps in the strategic sales process is to identify all the individuals involved in the sale and to determine their buying roles.

Roles are patterns of behavior expected by people in a given position. Miller and Heiman believe there are generally four critical buying roles that must be understood in a complex sale (no matter how many people play these roles). The **economic buying role** is a position that governs final approval to buy and that can say yes to a sale when everyone else says no, and vice versa. The **user buying role** makes judgments about the potential impact of your product or service on their job performance. These individuals will also supervise or use the product, so they want to know "what the product or service will do for them." The **technical buying role** screens out possible suppliers on the basis of meeting a variety of technical specifications that have been determined in advance by the organization. The technical buyers also serve as gatekeepers, who screen out potential suppliers on the basis of failing to meet the stated specifications. Finally, the **coach's role** is to act as a guide for the salesperson making the sale. The coach is a valuable source of information about the organization and can lead you to the other **buying influences**. As Miller and Heiman point out, identifying the individuals playing the various roles is the foundation of the strategic selling process.

Red flags

Once the individuals have been identified, the next step in the strategic selling process is to look for red flags, or things that can threaten a complex sale. Red flags symbolize those strategic areas that can require further attention to avoid mistakes in positioning. In addition, red flags can be used to capitalize on an area of strength. Some of the red flags that can threaten a complex sale include either missing or vague information, buying influences who are not contacted, or reorganization. For example, any buying influences who are not contacted are considered a threat to the sale.

These buying influences who are not contacted are analogous to uncovered bases in baseball. Teams cannot be fielded or successful when there is no shortstop or catcher. Likewise, a sale cannot be successful until all the relevant players have been contacted.

Response modes

After the buyer(s) have been targeted and you have correctly positioned your products or services by identifying red flags, the next step in the strategic selling process is to determine the buyer's reaction to the given sales situation. These varying reactions are categorized in four **response modes**. These modes include the growth mode, trouble mode, even keel mode, and overconfident mode.

The **growth mode** is characterized by organizations who perceive a discrepancy between their current state and their ideal state in terms of some goal (e.g., sales or profits). In other words, the organization needs to produce a higher quality sports product or put more people in the seats in order to grow. In this situation, the probability of a sale is high.

The second response mode is known as the **trouble mode**. When an organization is falling short of expectations, it is in the trouble mode. Here again, there is a discrepancy between the current and ideal states. In the growth mode the organization is going to improve upon an already good situation. However, the trouble mode indicates that the buyer is experiencing difficulties. In either case, the potential for a sale is high.

The **even keel mode** presents a more difficult case for the salesperson. As the name implies, there is no discrepancy between the ideal and current results and, therefore, the likelihood of a sale is low. The probability of a sale can be enhanced if the salesperson can demonstrate that a discrepancy actually exists, the buyer sees growth or trouble coming, or there is pressure from another buying influence.

The final response mode is the **overconfident mode**. Overconfidence is generally the toughest mode to overcome from the salesperson's perspective in that the buyers believe things are too good to be true. Just think about individual athletes or teams who are overconfident. Invariably they lose because of their false sense of superiority. Organizations that are overconfident are resistant to change because they are exceeding their goals (or at least they think so), so sales are difficult. The NFL is one example of a sports league currently at the top in terms of fan popularity, but subject to the overconfident mode. Specifically, off-the-field issues (as noted earlier) may alienate fans and sponsors. Gene Upshaw, the former executive director of the NFL Players Association, commented that "I do not want the fans to turn us off because of off-field behavior. It has happened in other sports, and I would not want that to happen to the NFL."[49] In this stage of the strategic sales process, the response mode of the organization should be analyzed. In addition, each of the buying influences should be examined to determine their perception of the current situation. By analyzing the buying influences and their perceptions, the salesperson is in a position to successfully adapt his or her approach to meet the needs of each buying influence and each customer.

Win-results

Much of sports marketing today is based on the premise of strategic partnerships. The same is true for the strategic sales process. In strategic partnerships, the sales process produces satisfied customers, long-term relationships, repeat business, and good referrals. To achieve these outcomes, the salesperson must look at clients as partners rather than competition that must be beaten.

Miller and Heiman define the **win-results** concept in the strategic selling process as an objective result that gives one or more of the buying influences a personal win. The key to this definition is understanding the importance of both wins and results. A result is the impact of the salesperson's product or service on one or more of the client's business objectives. Results are usually tangible, quantifiable, and affect the entire organization. Wins, however, are the fulfillment of a promise made to oneself. Examples of personal wins for the potential client include gaining recognition within the organization, increasing responsibility and authority, and enhancing self-esteem. It is important to realize that wins are subjective, intangible, and do not benefit all the people in the organization the same way.

The sales funnel

The sales funnel is another key element in the strategic sales process. This is a tool used to organize all potential clients, as opposed to developing a means for understanding an individual client. Basically, the **sales funnel** is a model that is used to organize clients so salespeople might organize their efforts in the most efficient and effective manner. After all, allocating time and setting priorities are two of the most challenging tasks in personal selling.

The sales funnel divides clients into three basic levels – above the funnel, in the funnel, and the best few. Potential clients exist above the funnel if data (e.g., a call from the prospective client wanting information or acquiring information from personal sources) suggest there may be a possible fit between the salesperson's products or services and the needs of the potential client. The salesperson's emphasis at this level is to gather information and then develop and qualify prospects.

Potential clients are then filtered to the next level of the sales funnel. If clients are placed in the funnel (rather than above it), then the possibility of a sale has been verified. Verification occurs once a buying influence has been contacted and indicates that the organization is in either a growth or trouble response mode. Remember that these two response modes represent ideal conditions for a sale to occur.

When all the buying influences have been identified, red flags have been eliminated, and win-results have been addressed, sales prospects can be moved from in the funnel to the "best few." At this final level of the sales funnel, the sale is expected to happen roughly 90 percent of the time.

Ideal customers

The ideal customer concept in strategic selling extends the notion of the sales funnel. In this case, all potential customers outside the funnel are evaluated against the hypothetical "ideal customer." The strategic sales process is based on the belief that every sale is not a good sale. The **ideal customer** profile is constructed to cut down on the unrealistic prospects that should not be in the sales funnel in the first place.

When constructing the ideal customer profile, the salesperson must judge each prospect with respect to organizational demographics, psychographics, and corporate culture. Current prospects can then be evaluated against the ideal customer profile to determine whether additional time and energy should be invested.

Sales promotions

Another promotion infix element that communicates to large audiences is sales promotions. **Sales promotions** are a variety of short-term, promotional activities that are designed to stimulate immediate product demand. A recent Taco Bell sales promotion illustrates how a simple game promotion can affect redemption sales techniques.

Over the years a variety of professional and amateur teams have enticed fans through sales promotions. For example, millions of fans have been part of the Chalupa-hungry crowds that have flooded NBA markets. Markets such as Cleveland, Dallas, and Portland have utilized the 100-point Taco Bell Chalupa promotion for years. In fact, the Mavericks have reached a Chalupa milestone, securing their 100th win in a row when the team has scored 100 points or more; now that is a Chalupa accomplishment. The promotion dates back to the Chalupa's inception in 1999 and is not directly tied to Taco Bell Corporate. The first NBA promotion occurred in Seattle, with the Sonics, when the local Taco Bell owners partnered with the NBA franchise. However, it was not until approximately 10 years later that the promotion became famous. Before a national audience, Cleveland fans booed then team icon LeBron James for selfishly dribbling out the clock at the end of a 99–93 Cavaliers' victory, thereby denying the fans their rightful Chalupas.

Other examples of these redemption strategies include: the NBA Philadelphia 76rs and their 100 point redemption of a Big Mac through McDonald's; The St. Louis Blues of the NHL introduced a Dairy Queen Blizzard coupon giveaway which affords fans the opportunity for a free Blizzard when the Blues score five goals or more. Other NHL teams such as the Columbus Blue Jackets and New York Islanders offer promotions which allow fans to redeem their ticket for a free Wendy's chili when their home teams score three goals or more.

In addition, some teams utilize sales promotions outside the core environment. For example, creativity afforded the Detroit Pistons faithful the opportunity to interact with their players when conducting a promotion for a free gas giveaway. Not only did the fans have the opportunity to win a $200 gas gift card, but the promotion provided the public a chance to chat and secure autographs while the Detroit Pistons players pumped the gas to fill up their tanks. The promotion generated an enormous amount of publicity for the team.

The sales promotions used in sports marketing come in all shapes and sizes. Think about some of the sales promotions with which you may be familiar. Classic examples might include the Bud Bowl; Straight-A Night or all you can eat at the ballpark; coupons for reduced green fees at public golf courses; a sweepstakes to win a free trip to the Super Bowl; seat upgrades to courtside recliners; or Coke's Win-a-Player Promotion.

Minor League Baseball has always been known for its creative sales promotions. For example, the Sacramento River Cats have partnered up with Miller Brewing Company at Raley Field for Miller Lite Thirsty Thursdays where $2 Miller beers and music keep the party going all night long. The River Cats gain the attention of fans on Tuesdays with the introduction of Kraft Singles Tuesday Nights, where tickets are buy one get one free courtesy of Kraft, making the River Cats Tuesday home games a steal for the deal. As stated in the definition, all forms of sales promotions are designed to increase short-term sales. Additional objectives may include increasing brand awareness, broadening distribution channels, reminding consumers about the offering, or inducing a trial to win new customers. To accomplish these objectives, sports marketers use a variety of sales promotion tools.

When the NHL returned to the ice following a lengthy work stoppage, Molson hired Grand Central Marketing to execute a grassroots promotion that would rekindle excitement among fans and position the brand as the beer of choice for hockey fans. The Molson Goalies program took place in seven NHL cities in the weeks leading up to the start of hockey season. In each market, teams of six brand ambassadors wearing Molson-logoed goalie uniforms made unannounced appearances in high traffic locations, outside stadiums and arenas, and in bars. They entertained consumers with goal scoring contests, hockey trivia questions, and games. Wherever the goalies went, they gave away Molson-branded premiums including T-shirts, hats, stress hockey pucks, inflatable goalie sticks, goalie bags, and jerseys.

The promotion succeeded in its "goal" of reaching hockey fans and closely aligning Molson with the sport. Over the course of the promotion, more than 30,000 premiums were distributed. Not only did the goalies cause a stir among consumers, but the local media also took notice. The goalies appeared on television ten times and their photos were in the newspaper seven times.

In a collegiate example, the University of Iowa Hawkeyes promotes men's and women's gymnastics by offering fans a pair of free sunglasses. Along with this giveaway, the Hawkeyes have redemption opportunities for free t-shirts and use other promotions to enhance interaction with the fans.

In 2008 Taco Bell was also involved in a MLB "Steal a Base, Steal a Taco" World Series promotion. If an eligible base was stolen during the World Series games, Taco Bell made an announcement through selected media channels that consumers could obtain their free taco. Everyone in line at participating Taco Bell restaurants before 6 P.M. local time received a free taco. Giving away the free tacos was pretty much a sure thing, but it garnered little attention for the league.

Premiums

Premiums are probably the sales promotion technique most associated with traditional sports marketing. **Premiums** are items given away with the sponsor's product as part of the sales promotion. Baseball cards, NASCAR model car replicas, water bottles, hats, refrigerator magnets, posters, bobbleheads, and almost anything else imaginable have been given away at sporting events. Although premiums are often given away to spectators at events, they can also be associated with other sporting promotions. For example, both *Sports Illustrated* and *ESPN* magazines give away hats, T-shirts, and videos to induce potential consumers to subscribe. In another example, many credit card companies are giving away hats with the logo of the fan's favorite team for applying for a line of credit.

Perhaps the most effective and exciting premium over the past several years has been the bobblehead. The Triple-A Pacific Coast League Portland Beavers, a Padres affiliate, "sent letters to every Bob L. Head they could find" and asked them to submit an essay "explaining why they should be cast as a miniature, head-bobbing figurine." The team narrowed its search to three finalists and the winner had his bobblehead given out to the first 2,000 fans who attended the team's game against the Las Vegas 51s. Who knows what the next premium craze might be in sports?

In 2010 MLB teams dramatically increased their use of premiums to offset the drastically reduced consumer spending and the worst economic conditions since

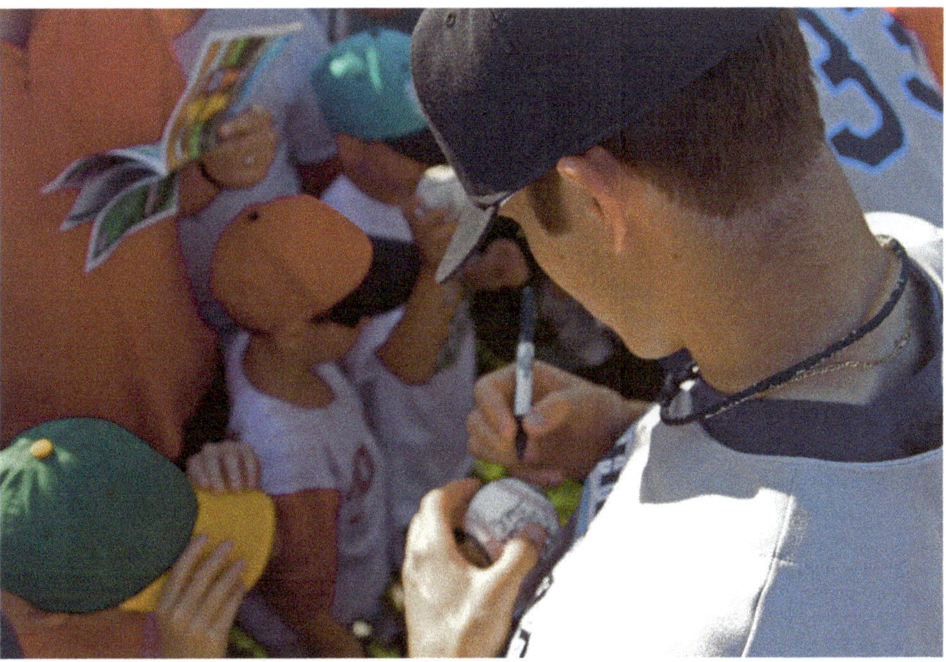

Photo 10.4 Athlete signing autographs

Source: Shutterstock.com

the Great Depression. There was a 16 percent increase over the 2009 expenditures and a 25 percent jump compared to 2008.[50] Sport marketers have traditionally used premiums to increase sales for lower demand games. In the past, popular premiums included items such as hats and bats or low cost items such as pens, pencils, or magnets. Today teams have developed sophisticated models to accurately measure the incremental revenue generated by premiums. They often have to integrate value components while accounting for other variables such as strength of opponent, weather, and the day of the game. Today's consumers demand a higher level of sophistication in the products and although the premium cost is paid for by corporate sponsors, the *Sport Business Journal* reports that professional teams are now including giveaways for weekend and higher demand games even where there are much smaller potential revenue gains from ticket sales.[51]

Although premiums can bring people to games who would not otherwise attend, they can also have negative consequences and must be carefully planned. In the now defunct World Hockey Association (WHA), the Philadelphia Blazers handed out souvenir pucks at the first home game. Unfortunately, the game had to be postponed because the ice was deemed unfit for skating. When the Blazers' Derek Sanderson announced the game cancellation to the crowd at center ice, he was pelted with the pucks.[52] In a similar scenario, the LA Dodgers had to forfeit a game because fans began throwing baseballs (that they had been given) onto the field, endangering players and other fans. The Dodgers can also be used to illustrate the height of premium marketing. In 1984, the Los Angeles Olympic Games created a region-wide craze for pin collecting. Sensing the "legs" of this mania, the Dodgers created six pin-giveaway nights at their stadium. They picked games that would typically have low attendance. The result was that all six of these games sold out on the strength of a $0.60 per unit collector's pin!

Contests and sweepstakes

Sweepstakes and contests are another sales promotional tool used by sports marketers to generate awareness and interest among consumers. Contests are competitions that award prizes on the basis of contestants' skills and ability, whereas sweepstakes are games of chance or luck. As with any sales promotion, the sports marketing manager must attempt to integrate the contest or sweepstakes with the other promotion mix elements and keep the target market in mind.

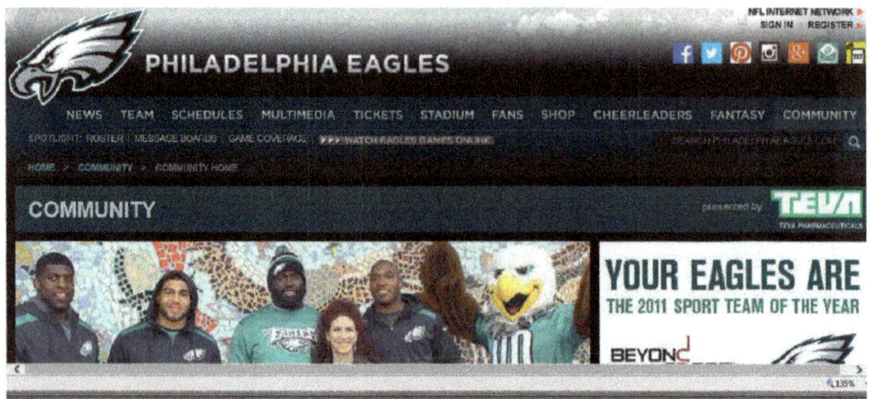

Web 10.8 Philadelphia Eagles reach out to the community

Source: PhiladelphiaEagles.com

One of the classic contests sponsored by the NFL was the punt, pass, and kick competition. In this competition, young athletes competed for a chance to appear on the finals of nationally televised NFL games, making the NFL the winner for promoting youth sports. Other contests have capitalized on the growing popularity of rotisserie sports. Dugout Derby, Pigskin Playoff, and Fairway Golf are all examples of "rotisserie" contests conducted via toll-free numbers where fans could earn prizes for choosing the best fantasy team or athletes. In return, marketers capture a rich database of potential consumers.

As sweepstakes become more and more popular, companies are constantly looking for new ways to break through the clutter. Consider this tremendous opportunity for race fans offered by General Motors. General Motor's Camaro Giveaway Sweepstakes provided an opportunity for loyal fans to win a Chevy Camaro SS vehicle and trip to Daytona Beach, Florida for the Coke Zero 400 NASCAR Race. The winning fan will receive a trip package that includes roundtrip transportation for two, two night's accommodation in a hotel, two tickets to the Coke Zero 400 race, a meet and greet with Jimmie Johnson, and $500 spending money.

In a more recent example, billionaire Warren Buffett, CEO of Berkshire Hathaway, partnered up and insured the Quicken Loans sponsoring of the "Billion Dollar Bracket Challenge". Quicken Loans President and Chief Marketing Office Jay Farner noted that they had seen a lot of contests offering a million dollar prize which got them thinking what was the perfect bracket [correctly predicting the outcome of every game in the NCAA men's basketball tournament] worth?[53] The result's a big "B", a billion dollar sweepstakes with a grand prize that includes a $500 million payout or $25 million a year for the next 40 years. Farner added, their mission is to create amazing experiences for their clients and a billion dollar giveaway definitely fits that bill.[54] Now that's a sweepstakes!

Another recent sweepstakes includes the ESPN Zone Baltimore Ultimate Couch Potato Contest, which is a competition to see who can watch the most continuous television sports coverage among the four chosen finalists. Finalists were chosen based on a required 200 word essay discussing why they should be selected as a finalist. One grand prize winner received a gift certificate to Best Buy in the amount of $1,000, one XZipIt Recliner chair with the logo of the winner's choosing, payment to cover one year of cable bills, a $500 ESPN Zone game card, $500 in food and beverage certificates, and an ESPN Zone Ultimate Couch Potato Trophy.

Other sweepstakes are taking advantage of the Internet as well as the use of mobile devices. Networks such as CBS, ESPN, and Fox offer a variety of opportunities for fantasy football, NASCAR, and baseball enthusiasts through interactive play and chances to compete against analysts. These sweepstakes have grand prizes targeted toward individual players as well as entire leagues. Many of them require the use and exchange of data over the Internet and mobile devices therefore enhancing the opportunity for these networks to secure user profiles. Other sports agencies such as Nike have a multitude of sweepstakes available for the consumer. Niketown.com provides an opportunity for consumers to win gear for a year, which is $1,200 worth of merchandise. Nike promotes to its basketball fans by affording one lucky winner the opportunity for an autographed Kobe Bryant/Aston Martin footwear set. In addition, this sweepstakes provides 220 lucky patrons a place in line at the Staples Center in Los Angeles, California to purchase the collectible packs, which include two pairs of footwear and a Kobe AM leather jacket. Nike provides its golf patrons with opportunities to win three golf vacations as well as provides opportunities through other sweepstakes to exerience Nike's golf and research development facility known as "The Oven." This includes air transportation for the winner and a guest to Fort Worth, lodging and meals, an insider's tour of "The Oven," a round of golf, a chance to demo the latest Nike golf clubs and equipment; entrance into the final round of the Colonial PGA Tournament, and a Nike golf apparel head-to-toe gift pack.

In yet another example, the Miami Dolphins held a sweepstakes giving fans a chance to win tickets to the game against the Giants at London's Wembley Stadium. New season-ticket holders were automatically entered three times, while other fans could enter at miamidolphins.com. The grand prize included round-trip airfare, hotel accommodations, Royal Box tickets to the game, and passes to NFL pre-parties for four fans.

The NBA has put together packages for the NBA 2013 All Star game. Enjoy the ONLY in-arena game hospitality party venue at the Arena! Below are some of the highlighted inclusions in the NBA Events' Exclusive in-arena Hospitality Party Venue:

- **VIP Access for NBA Events Hospitality Venue**
  Saturday: Hospitality is open one and a half hours before events begin.
  Sunday: Pre game hospitality at the NBA All-Star 2013 Game opens when the Arena doors open (approximately 6:30pm). Post game hospitality opens at the end of the NBA All-Star 2013 Game and closes one hour after the end of the game
- **Premium Open Bar**
- **All of the Top-Shelf Food You Can Eat**
- **Meet & Greet with NBA Legends:** Scheduled appearances announced soon!
- **Autographed picture of our Legends**[55]

The Philadelphia Flyers and visitphilly.com granted fans a chance to win a trip for two to Philadelphia for the Ultimate Flyers VIP Experience. The grand prize package included tours of Wells Fargo Center, deluxe hotel accommodations, roundtrip airfare, dinner for two inside Cadillac Grill, a merchandise package, a Love Philadelphia XOXO giftbag, and a pair of premium lower level seats.

For those with a taste for horses, a gourmet luncheon, Kentucky Derby party atmosphere, and ringside seats with spectacular views await a lucky VIP patron at the Fidelity Investments Jumper Classic presented by Porsche. This equestrian event affords fans the opportunity to watch in an elegant setting some of the nation's top riders and horses. Additional amenities include enjoying a sampling of local liquors and wines while the ladies can participate in a hat contest judged by a panel of local magazine editors.

Sampling

One of the most effective ways of inducing customers to try new products that are being introduced is **sampling**. Unfortunately, it is very difficult to give away a small portion of a sporting event. However, sports have been known to put on exhibitions to give consumers a "taste" for the game. Squash demonstration matches have been held in the middle of New York's Grand Central Station, attracting thousands of fans who would have never otherwise been exposed to the sport. The Olympics, of course, have used demonstration sports since 1904, in sports such as roller hockey and bandy (soccer on ice), to provide a "sample" of the action to spectators. If fan interest is high enough (i.e., attendance), the sport can then become a medal sport in the next Olympiad.

In yet another example, the NCAA has often partnered with a variety of companies to provide product samples to consumers to be distributed in conjunction with NCAA March Madness. Examples include the distribution of one million samples of Nivea for Men where employees outfitted as referees, cheerleaders, and basketball players distributed the products both on college campuses and in the streets to prospective consumers. In a more recent example of sampling, Kraft Foods' U.S. Snacks business teamed with the NCAA and CBS Sports to become an Official NCAA Corporate Partner for several of its flagship snack brands, including *Planters, Ritz, Oreo* and *Wheat Thins*. The partnership includes promotional and marketing rights for the NCAA and all 89 of its men's and women's championships. The initial sampling effort during NCAA March Madness featured *Wheat Thins* snacks and two of the company's newest snack products: *Ritz Munchables* pretzel crisps and *Planters Flavor Grove* almonds and cashews. In addition, in people were able to follow Mr. Peanut's Road to the NCAA Final Four in Indianapolis by becoming fans of Mr. Peanut on Facebook.

Point-of-purchase displays

Point-of-purchase or **P-O-P displays** have long been used by marketers to attract consumers' attention to a particular product or retail display area. These displays or materials, such as brochures, cut-outs, and banners, are most commonly used to communicate price reductions or other special offers to consumers. For instance, tennis racquet manufacturers, such as Prince, design huge tennis racquets, which are then displayed in the storefronts of many tennis retail shops to catch the attention of consumers. The Super Bowl, an American classic, provides a forum where many official sponsors and non-sponsors of the game utilize point-of-purchase display tie-ins to interact and attract consumers.

Companies like Heineken have been innovative with their use of point-of-purchase displays with events such as the U.S. Open. Heineken launched an upscale aluminum bottle to U.S. consumers and the bottle when viewed under a black light revealed hidden patterns of stars and trails. In addition to the black light properties, the 16-ounce bottle displayed a progressive European design which further indicated the upscale style and attitude to Heineken's consumers.

Coupons

Another common sales promotion tool is the coupon. **Coupons** are certificates that generally offer reductions in price for sports products. Coupons may appear in print advertisements, as part of the product's package, inserted within the product packaging, be mailed to consumers, printed on or part of an admissions ticket, or be offered as part of a social media strategy. Labeled by many to be a new "social sport" couponing offers an inexpensive way to try something new, often with an emphasis on local business. In fact, the business has its own terminology; for example, "**stacking**" means using both a manufacturer's coupon and store coupon for purchase. Consumer's reasons for utilizing coupons range from critical issues like the economy to simpler reasons such as freeing up more money to spend on fun activities. The idea for many of being able to go out for a meal with friends or family at a discounted price, while also trying out a new sport venue, game or show is a valuable brand asset. Today many organizations utilize social media platforms to gain exposure to key demographics. Surprisingly, the demographic users are wealthier and younger than most people would expect. In many instances, it provides a business a unique opportunity to attract new customers, without spending a fortune on advertising. Couponing is a great way to get people to attend an event, but the task of turning it into repeat purchase or profit lies with the business. For example, utilizing couponing to secure patrons to participate at a fitness center or bowling alley is one thing, getting them to repeat the use or purchase is another. Although coupons have been found to induce short-term sales, there are disadvantages. For instance, some marketers believe continual coupon use can detract from the image of the product in the minds of consumers. It is not a forum that should be utilized with every game or event, but may be utilized several times a year and continue to attract consumers. Another concern is that couponing only affords business an opportunity to make back a portion of the profit. In addition, most coupon redemption is done by consumers who already use the product, therefore limiting the use of coupons to attract new customers.

Public relations

The final element in the promotional mix that we discuss is public relations. Quite often, public relations get confused with other promotional mix elements. Public relations often gets mistaken for publicity. This is an easy mistake to make because the goals of public relations and publicity are to provide communication that will enhance the image of the sports entity (athlete, team, or league). Before we make a distinction between public relations and publicity, let us define public relations. **Public relations** is the element of the promotional mix that identifies, establishes, and maintains mutually beneficial relationships between the sports organizations and the various publics on which its success or failure depends.

Within the definition of public relations, reference is made to the "various publics" with which the sports organization interacts. Brooks divides these publics into the external publics, which are outside the immediate control of sports marketers, and the internal publics, which are more directly controlled by sports marketers. The external publics include the community (e.g., city and state officials, community members, corporations), sanctioning bodies (e.g., NCAA), intermediary publics (e.g., sports marketing agencies), and competition (e.g., other sports or entertainment choices). The internal publics, such as volunteers, employees, suppliers, athletes, and spectators, are associated with manufacturing, distributing, and consuming the sport itself.

Sports marketers have a variety of public relations tools they can use to communicate with the internal and external publics. The choice of tools depends on the public relations objective, the targeted audience, and how public relations are being integrated into the overall promotional plan. These tools and techniques include generating publicity (news releases or press conferences), participating in community events, producing written materials (annual report or press guides), and even lobbying (personal selling necessary for stadium location decisions).

Former Notre Dame's sports information director Roger Valdiserri is regarded by some to be the best ever at his profession. Though maybe best known for the changing of Joe Theismann's name from THEES-man to THEIS-man – which happened to rhyme with Heisman, Valdiserri, in his 30 year tenure, pioneered the use of a variety of publicity concepts that are still in use today. For example, he prerecorded coach Ara Parseghian's answers and presented them to the media, thereby dramatically reducing the time that Parseghian had to spend meeting enormous media demands. He was the king of balancing precious access time. He maximized constituents' effort by affording individuals the opportunity to just do their jobs.

One of the most important and widely used public relations tools is publicity. Publicity is the generation of news in the broadcast or print media about a sports product. The news about a sports product is most commonly disseminated to the various sports publics through news releases and press conferences. Although public relations efforts are managed by the sports organization, publicity can sometimes come from external sources. As such, publicity might not always enhance the image of the sports product. Research by Funk and Pritchard (2005) noted that less committed readers tended to recall more facts from negative articles, while committed fans tended to counter-argue with more favorable thoughts.[56] Because publicity is often outside the control of the sports organization, it is seen as a highly credible source of communication. Information that is coming from "unbiased" sources, such as magazines, newspaper articles, or the televised news, is perceived to be more trustworthy.

In addition to publicity, another powerful public relations tool used to enhance the sports organization's image is **community involvement**. A study was conducted to determine what, if anything, professional sports organizations are doing in the area of community relations. The survey specifically examined the NBA, NHL, NFL, and MLB to determine how they are involved in community relations and how important community relations are to their overall marketing program. All the responding teams indicated they were involved in some sort of community program, with the most common form of community involvement being (1) sponsoring public programs (e.g., food and toy drives, medical programs and services, auctions, and other fund raisers); (2) requiring time commitment from all of the sports organizations' employees; (3) partially funding programs; and (4) providing personnel at no charge. Interestingly, the study found no differences among the importance of community relations by type of league. In other words, the NBA, NHL, NFL, and MLB are all equally involved in community relations.[57]

For example, the Green Bay Packers community outreach program takes many forms. The Packers sponsor special fundraising events, make donations of cash and memorabilia to many charitable organizations, make personal appearances and serve on various community boards and commissions. The Cleveland Browns have many diverse offerings as well. A few highlights include: Annually the Cleveland Browns Foundation positively impacts the lives of more than 10,000 children in NE Ohio; Browns players have participated in the NFL-USO All-Star tour; with the Browns Play 60 Challenge students logged more than 7 million minutes of activity; Browns staff have volunteered to support multiple initiatives offered through the organization, accumulating more than 2000 hours of volunteer service.[58] The NFL and United Way have partnered, e.g., NFL Hometown Huddle program, in an ongoing effort to inspire people to become more engaged in the community. Campaigns such as NFL United Way and NFL Play 60 afford each organization within the league the opportunity to put their added touches to impact the community locally, all the while retaining national identity and publicity. The NFL Play 60 goal is to make the next generation of youth the most active and healthy.

Other examples of the community involvement and outreach component of public relations are shown with the Nashville Predators, Philadelphia Eagles and Pittsburgh Pirates. The Predators players took part in Predators Community Day, a "day of service where nearly every member of the team made an appearance in Middle Tennessee" and interacted with fans at locations including the airport, Supercuts, and Hardee's. The idea was to expand on the normal team participation events by making it a day-long experience."

The Philadelphia Eagles reimburses its employees living in the Philadelphia region and New Jersey who purchase wind energy, making it the first organization to pick up this type of cost for employees. The Eagles presented their Go Green program, which was launched in 2003, during the NFL Business Summit in 2007, as other NFL team representatives shared best practices in the areas of business, marketing, and community relations. Eagles owner Christina Lurie noted that they hope to serve as an example for NFL teams and the corporate sector. "The topic of greening in sports is especially important in cities like Philadelphia with professional teams and sports arenas. Game days have a huge environmental impact considering traffic, trash, energy and material consumption, and water use. They are also opportunities for education and awareness."[59]

The Pittsburgh Pirates continue their community-minded tradition of donating half the ticket sales from a handful of games to such programs as the Boys & Girls Clubs, the United Way of Manatee County, the Manatee Education Foundation, and Wakeland Elementary School, which is located across the street from the Pirate City training complex. Additionally, the organization held a PirateFest street celebration, staged before the game against the Minnesota Twins. The festival featured numerous family activities and free player autographs. Taking another step to cement the bond between team and city, the Pirates increased their charitable efforts. Pitchers Matt Capps and Josh Sharpless and the Pirate Parrot mascot visited children in the pediatric unit of Manatee Memorial Hospital.

The Pirates also held a three-day silent auction inside McKechnie Field that raised almost $8,000 for the Foundation for Dreams Inc., which provides fun, educational, and recreational experiences at Dream Oaks Camp for children with physical and developmental disabilities and serious illnesses. A Sidney Crosby Pittsburgh Penguins hockey jersey drew the top bid of $1,500. "We want to make sure we're always giving back to the community, since the city of Bradenton and Manatee County have been so generous to us," said Trevor Gooby, the Pirates' director of Florida operations. "As part of our efforts, we try to help a lot of (charitable) groups in Manatee County throughout the course of the year that need items for a silent auction or a golf tournament."[60]

Although community involvement benefits any number of stakeholders in the organization, it is typically more than philanthropy alone. As suggested in the accompanying article, sports entities are reaping the rewards of their goodwill.

NBA CARES EVOLVING AFTER 5 YEARS OF SERVICE

NBA Cares surpassed goals of 1 million service hours and $100 million in charitable donations.

The NBA Cares social responsibility program marks its fifth anniversary this week with the effort counting more than $145 million given to charity, far surpassing the $100 million goal set by the league when the initiative launched in 2005.

NBA Cares also has generated 1.4 million hours of hands-on service and has helped complete 527 "live, learn or play" projects, such as the construction of new homes, the creation of reading and learning centers, and the development of new or refurbished basketball courts.

When NBA Commissioner David Stern announced the creation of NBA Cares on Oct. 18, 2005, the five-year plan was to generate 1 million hours of service and build 100 "live, learn or play" projects – a term created by the league for the program – as well as donate $100 million to charity.

"NBA Cares is what we had hoped it would be, not necessarily what we thought it would be," Stern said. "It has become a descriptive phrase for our social programs. Because of what we do and who we are, we are obligated to become leaders in social responsibility, and NBA Cares has become the central focus of our obligation."

Looking ahead, Kathy Behrens, the NBA's executive vice president of social responsibility and player programs, would not disclose specific future spending goals, but said NBA Cares increasingly will focus on the league's NBA Fit program, which targets improving youth health, and addressing environmental issues.

"The [NBA Fit] program is becoming important and so is our green effort," Behrens said. "Five years ago, [green] wasn't on our radar screen."

Before 2005, while the NBA was involved in charitable works such as its Read to Achieve program and its Basketball Without Borders effort, there wasn't a single program that brought all of the league's, the teams' and the players' charitable doings together. NBA Cares became that umbrella operation that also provides flexibility for teams and players to select their own local community partners.

"We obviously have surpassed our goals, but it wasn't as much about the numbers as it was about believing in the importance of getting our teams, players and employees out in the community," Behrens said. "[NBA Cares] has deepened the connection to the community and strengthened the opportunity for our players to give back."

NBA Cares is aligned with a variety of charitable programs, with the league's list of 40 community partners including UNICEF, the Boys and Girls Clubs of America, Habitat for Humanity, and KaBoom! playgrounds.

"The partnerships are on both sides," Behrens said. "We think we partner with the most well-respected organizations in the world. We didn't want to recreate the wheel. We want to find great organizations, shine the light on them, and let them do their work."

While funding outside charitable efforts, the NBA also emphasizes direct team and player involvement in local, national, and international causes as part of NBA Cares, which is led by Behrens and a 12-member staff.

"The NBA above all other leagues has been philanthropic in a strategic way," said Caryl Stern, chief executive officer of the U.S. fund for UNICEF and who is unrelated to the NBA commissioner. "There is a dedicated strategy on how they support us on a number of different levels. It is not just writing a check. They want to see results, and I am in touch with the NBA on almost a weekly basis."

One of the more notable efforts in the five-year history of NBA Cares was the league's Day of Service project centered on the 2008 NBA All-Star Game in hurricane-ravaged New Orleans. The high-profile program included players, league sponsors and league employees participating in a rebuilding effort throughout the city. The project proved so successful that it has become a staple of subsequent All-Star weekends.

"Katrina was impactful, and helping families during [All-Star] weekend resonated with players and staff, and that piece is still important to us," Behrens said.

The NBA's creation of this singular charitable mission has been noticed by other leagues, which have worked to boost their charitable efforts in recent years as well. Major League Baseball, for example, has created its Beyond Baseball charitable program, while the NFL, NHL and MLS have beefed up their own social responsibility efforts in the past few years.

"Whether it is called community relations or social responsibility, leagues around the world are engaged," David Stern said. "World Cup and Olympics bids now talk about social responsibilities and legacies, and we have helped redefine the definition of private participation in social responsibility."

NBA Cares

NBA Cares, the league's global social responsibility program, celebrated its fifth anniversary in October 2010. Since October 2005, NBA Cares has provided more than1.5 million hours of hands-on service, donated more than $150 million to charity and created more than 560 places where children and families can live, learn or play. NBA Cares continues to rely on the expertise of its partners and the dedication of the league and its teams and players to address important social issues around the world.

The NBA is committed to leaving a lasting legacy in communities around the world. As part of that commitment, the NBA has created more than 560 places where children and families can live, learn or play. These new and refurbished basketball courts, libraries, playgrounds, homes and technology rooms are created in partnership with community and marketing partners, and provide

10

key resources that pave the way for communities' future success.

As part of the NBA's commitment to social responsibility, community outreach and volunteer engagement are integral to the NBA's business and its connection with fans and partners. The league coordinates a wide-reaching effort among NBA teams and players, community partners, nonprofit organizations and business partners to benefit communities worldwide. Through campaigns such as NBA Cares Week of Service and NBA Cares Season of Giving, or programs such as Coaches for Kids and Vaccines for Teens, the NBA family works to impact communities year round.

NBA FIT, the league's comprehensive health and wellness program, promotes healthy, active lifestyles for children and adults of all fitness levels. Through programs, grassroots events, products and a nationwide network of community partners, the league, its teams and players are encouraging kids, adults and families to pledge NBA FIT. During the annual NBA FIT Live Healthy Week, the NBA Family joins community members and partners to highlight the importance of a healthy, active lifestyle. Events include hosting fitness clinics, offering healthy living tips from NBA FIT team members, health screenings and inspiring fans to make positive fitness and nutritional choices. NBA Green, created in partnership with the Natural Resources Defense Council (NRDC), is a league wide program that generates awareness and funds for protecting the environment and promoting sustainable practices. Through NBA Green, the league and its teams and players are taking steps to be more environmentally friendly and encouraging fans to take part in local green initiatives. During NBA Green Week each April, the league and teams join together to take part in green efforts, including hands-on community service projects, recycling programs, green giveaways, auctions to support environmental protection organizations and promotions to encourage fans to "go green."

The NBA believes in the power of sport to bring attention to important global issues. Working with internationally recognized organizations, the NBA hosts NBA Cares events alongside its Basketball without Borders, NBA Europe Live, NBA China Games, Jr. NBA/Jr. WNBA programs and at other grassroots events to contribute to communities worldwide. Through these events, the NBA family invests time and money in social issues, including HIV/AIDS awareness, malaria prevention and natural disaster relief efforts. Since October 2005, the NBA has built 93 places in 22 countries and territories where children and families can live, learn or play, demonstrating the NBA's commitment to improving lives around the world.

Through WNBA Cares, WNBA teams and players dedicate their time and efforts to various cause-related campaigns and programs. The WNBA promotes programs that emphasize a healthy lifestyle, positive body image, breast health awareness, youth and family development and education. The WNBA and its teams and players work to make a difference in their communities.

Through NBA D-League Cares, the NBA Development League addresses important social issues with a special emphasis on education, health and wellness and community building. The NBA D-League and its teams host a variety of outreach programs to help improve the lives of the people who live and work in their nearby communities. With these programs, teams establish close connections to their communities, offering unparalleled time and access to the players, coaches and staff.

With the help of these internationally recognized partners, NBA Cares continues to leave a lasting legacy of service and philanthropy in communities worldwide. These partnerships allow the NBA to support a variety of important social issues, and provide community organizations with the unique opportunity to highlight their great work. For more information on these organizations, the NBA's latest community outreach efforts, and how you can join the team, please visit: www.nbacares.com.

Source: Article author: John Lombardo; http://www.sportsbusinessdaily.com/Journal/Issues/2010/10/20101018/Leagues-and-Governing-Bodies/NBA-Cares.aspx. Credit: Sports Business Journal.

Summary

Chapter 10 focuses on gaining a better understanding of the various promotional mix elements. Advertising is one of the most visible and critical promotional mix elements.

Although most of us associate advertising with developing creative slogans and jingles, there is a systematic process for designing effective advertisements. Developing an advertising campaign consists of a series of five interrelated steps, which include formulating objectives, designing an ad budget, making creative decisions, choosing a media strategy, and evaluating the advertisement.

Advertising objectives and budgeting techniques are similar to those discussed in Chapter 9 for the broader promotion planning process. Advertising objectives are sometimes categorized as either direct or indirect. Direct advertising objectives, such as advertising by sports organizations to end users and sales promotion advertising, are designed to stimulate action among consumers of sport. Alternatively, the goal of indirect objectives is to make consumers aware, enhance the image of the sport, or provide information to consumers. After objectives have been determined, budgets for the advertising campaign are considered. Budget techniques, such as competitive parity, objective and task, arbitrary allocation, and percentage of sales, are commonly used by advertisers.

Once the objectives and budget have been established, the creative process is considered. The creative process identifies the ideas and the concept of the advertisement. To develop the concept for the advertisement, benefits of the sports product must be identified; ad appeals (e.g., health, emotional, fear, sex, and pleasure) are designed; and advertising execution decisions (e. g., comparative advertisements, slice of life, and scientific) are made. After creative decisions are crafted, the next phase of the advertising campaign is to design media strategy. Media strategy includes decisions about how the medium (e.g., radio, television, and Internet) will be most effective and how to best schedule the chosen media.

Another communications tool that is part of the promotional mix is personal selling. Personal selling is unique in that person-to-person communication is required rather than mass communication. In other words, a salesperson must deliver the message face to face to the intended target audience rather than through some medium (e.g., a magazine) that is not personal. Although there are many advantages to personal selling, perhaps none is greater than the ability to use personal selling to develop long-term relationships with customers.

In today's competitive sports marketing environment, a number of strategies have been developed to maximize personal selling effectiveness. One process, designed by Miller and Heiman, is called the strategic selling process and consists of six elements. The elements, which must be considered for successful selling, include buying influences, red flags, response modes, win-results, the sales funnel, and the ideal customer profile.

Sales promotions are another element in the promotional mixes that are designed primarily to stimulate consumer demand for products. One of the most widely used forms of sales promotion in sports marketing includes premiums, or items that are given away with the core product being purchased. In addition, contests and sweepstakes, free samples, point- of purchase displays, and coupons are forms of sales promotion that often are integrated into the broader promotional mix.

A final promotional mix element considered in Chapter 10 is public, or community, relations. Public relations is the element of the promotional mix that identifies, establishes, and maintains mutually beneficial relationships between the sports organization and the various publics on which its success or failure depends. These publics include the community, sanctioning bodies, intermediary publics, and competition. Other publics include employees, suppliers, participants, and spectators. The tools with which messages are communicated to the various publics include generating publicity, participating in community events, producing written materials such as annual reports and press releases, and lobbying.

Key terms

- advertising
- advertising appeals
- advertising budgeting
- advertising execution
- advertising objectives
- attractiveness
- buying influences
- coach's role
- community involvement
- comparative advertisements
- continuous schedule
- coupons
- creative brief
- creative decisions
- creative process
- credibility
- direct objectives
- economic buying role
- emotional appeals
- even keel mode
- expertise
- fear appeals
- flighting schedule
- frequency
- growth mode
- health appeals
- ideal customer
- indirect objectives
- lifestyle advertisements
- media scheduling
- media strategy
- one-sided versus two-sided
- overconfident mode
- personal selling
- pleasure or fun appeals
- P-O-P displays
- premiums
- promotional mix elements
- public relations
- pulsing schedule
- reach
- relationship marketing
- response modes
- roles
- sales funnel
- sales promotions
- sampling
- scientific advertisements
- sex appeals
- slice-of-life advertisements
- stacking
- stadium signage
- strategic selling
- sweepstakes and contests
- technical buying role
- testimonials
- trouble mode
- trustworthiness
- user buying role
- win-results

Review questions

1. What are the major steps in developing an advertising campaign?
2. Explain direct advertising objectives versus indirect advertising objectives.
3. Describe the creative decision process. What are the three outcomes of the creative process?
4. Discuss, in detail, the major advertising appeals used by sports marketers. Provide at least one example of each type of advertising appeal.
5. What are the executional formats commonly used in sports marketing advertising?
6. Comment on the advantages and disadvantages of using athlete endorsers in advertising.
7. What two decisions do advertisers make in developing a media strategy? What are the four basic media scheduling alternatives? Provide an example of each type of media scheduling.
8. Discuss the strengths and weaknesses of the alternative forms of advertising available to sports marketers.
9. When is personal selling used by sports marketers? Describe, in detail, the steps in the strategic selling process.
10. Describe the various forms of sales promotion available to sports marketers.

Exercises

1. Design a creative advertising strategy to increase participation in Little League Baseball.
2. Design a survey instrument to assess the source credibility of 10 professional athletes (of your choice) and administer the survey to 10 individuals. Which athletes have the highest levels of credibility, and why?
3. Attend a professional or collegiate sporting event and describe all the forms of advertising you observe. Which forms of advertising do you feel are particularly effective, and why?
4. Visit a sporting goods retailer and describe all the sales promotion tools that you observe. Which forms of sales promotion do you believe are particularly effective, and why?
5. Interview the director or manager of ticket sales for a professional organization or collegiate sports program to determine their sales process. How closely does their sales process follow the strategic selling process outlined in this chapter?
6. Interview the marketing department (or director of community/public relations) from a professional organization or collegiate sports program to determine the extent of their community or public relations efforts. How do sports organizations decide in which community events or activities to participate?

Internet exercises

1. Using the Internet, find two examples of advertisements for sports products that use indirect objectives and two examples of advertisements that use direct objectives.
2. Find 10 advertisements on the Internet for sports products and describe the executional format for each advertisement. Which type of execution format is most commonly used for Internet advertising?

Endnotes

1 MKTGINC, Portfolio, Nike World Basketball Festival. Available from: http://mktg.com/#/project/nike-world-basketball-festival/wbf-page-1, accessed March 17, 2014.

2 Ibid.

3 See, for example, Joel Evans and Barry Berman, *Marketing*, 6th ed. (New York: Macmillan, 1994), 610.

10

4 IBISWorld, "Gym, Health & Fitness Clubs Market Research Report,t | NAICS 71394" (| February 2014). Available from: http://www.ibisworld.com/industry/default.aspx?indid=1655, accessed May 9, 2014.
5 Ibid.
6 "Physical Activity & Older Americans," Agency for Healthcare Research & Quality. U.S. Department of Health & Human Services (June 2010).
7 William A. Sutton, Mark A. McDonald, George R. Milne, and John Cimperman, "Creating and Fostering Fan Identification in Professional Sports," *Sport Marketing Quarterly*, vol. 6, no. 1 (1997), 15–22.
8 "Maria Sharapova Inks Deal with Tiffany & Co." *BrandDunk* (May 22, 2008).
9 "Maria Sharapova Signs Three-Year Sponsorship Deal With Samsung," *www.bloomberg.com* (April 3, 2012).
10 Mark Levit, "Sex in Advertising: Does it Sell?" Partners & Levit Advertising – Alrakboa Sundanese Website. Available from: http://www.alrakoba.net/articles2/showarticle.php?article=2120, accessed June 22, 2014.
11 Dan Patrick, "Hope Solo Talks About Effect of Sex Appeal In Marketing Female Athletes," The Dan Patrick Show (August 22, 2011).
12 Brent Kelley, "Wilhelmina W7 photos," *About.com Sports Golf*. Available from: http://golf.about.com/od/golferswomen/ss/wilhelmina7.htm, accessed June 22, 2014.
13 Alan Shipnuck, "Is Marketing the Sex Appeal of LPGA Golfers Good for the Game?" *Sports Illustrated* (July 2009). Available from: http://www.sportsbusinessdaily.com/Daily/Issues/2011/08/24/Marketing-and-Sponsorship/Hope-Solo.aspx.
14 Kevin Seifert, "Enough Is Enough," *Minneapolis Star Tribune* (April 11, 2007), 3C.
15 Rachel Blount, "Selling Sex and Sports Isn't Working," *Minneapolis Star* Tribune (April 16, 2007).
16 William Wei, "Tiger Woods lost $22 Million in Endorsement in 2010," *BusinessInsider.com* (July 2010).
17 "Rosie Ruiz Tries to Steal the Boston Marathon" *Running Times* (July 1, 1980). Available from: http://www.runnersworld.com/rt-miscellaneous/rosie-ruiz-tries-steal-boston-marathon, accessed March 19, 2014.
18 Christian Red, Teri Thompson, and Michael O'Keeffe, "Feds Unleash a Bonds Blast: Indictment Hits HR King for Lying, Obstruction," *New York Daily News* (November 16, 2007), 90.
19 Craig Christopher, "Top 10 Worst Sporting Cheats from Around the Globe," BleacherReport (April 13, 2010).
20 Viv Bernstein, "No More Cutting Corners as NASCAR Seeks a Clean Start," *The New York Times* (February 18, 2007), 1.
21 "NASCAR Revamps its Penalty Structure, Appeals Process," *Dothanfirst.com* (February 4, 2014). Available from: http://www.dothanfirst.com/story/d/story/nascar-revamps-its-penalty-structure-appeals-proce/22217/tJ2ppMXyC0iwq9KJ2Ok7tA, accessed March 19, 2014.
22 Kevin Seifert, "Enough Is Enough," *Minneapolis Star Tribune* (April 11, 2007), 3C.
23 Terry Lefton, "The Post-Mike Millennium – Gatorade Advertising, *Post*-Michael Jordan," *Brandweek* (January 3, 2000).
24 Rich Thomaselli, "$192 Million: Nike Bets Big on Range of Endorsers," *Advertising Age* (January 5, 2004), 8.
25 Mark Hyman, "Dead Men Don't Screw Up Ad Campaigns," *Business Week* (March 10, 1997), 115.
26 Thales Teixeira, "World Cup Soccer: 770 Billion Minutes Of Attention," *Forbes.com* (June 13, 2014). Available from: http://www.forbes.com/sites/hbsworkingknowledge/2014/06/13/world-cup-soccer-770-billion-minutes-of-attention/, accessed June 22, 2014.
27 Ibid.
28 Kurt Badenhausen, "NFL Stadiums: By the Numbers," *Forbes.com* (August 14, 2013). Available from: http://www.forbes.com/sites/kurtbadenhausen/2013/08/14/nfl-stadiums-by-the-numbers/, accessed June 22, 2104.
29 Jay Gladden, "The Ever Expanding Impact of Technology on Sport Marketing, Part II," *Sport Marketing Quarterly*, vol. 5, no. 4 (1996), 9–10.
30 Douglas Turco, "The Effects of Courtside Advertising on Product Recognition and Attitude Change," *Sport Marketing Quarterly*, vol. 5, no. 4 (1996), 11–15.
31 Wayne Friedman, "Intermedia Measures Product Placements; Study Shows No Correlation Between Ratings, Effectiveness," *Television Week* (December 15, 2003), 4.
32 Marla Matzer Rose, "Firms Gauge Product Placements," *The Hollywood Reporter* (January 20, 2004).
33 George Belch and Michael Belch, *Advertising and Promotion: An Integrated Marketing Communications Perspective*, 4th ed. (New York: Irwin, McGraw-Hill 1998), pp. 431–434.
34 Joe Layden, "Human Billboards," in *Mark McCormack's Guide to Sports Marketing*, International Sports Marketing Group (1996), 129–136.
35 "Global Games Market Report 2014," *Newszoo* (May 15, 2014). Available from: http://www.newzoo.com/insights/global-games-market-will-reach-102-9-billion-2017, accessed June 23, 2014.
36 Entertainment Software Association, "In-Game Advertising." Available from: http://www.theesa.com/games-improving-what-

matters/advertising.asp, accessed June 23, 2014.
37 Terry Lefton, "Will In-Game Advertising Catch Fire?" *Sports Business Journal* (January 15, 2007), 19.
38 Ibid.
39 "Online Insights: Sports Fans and Digital Media A Scorecard on Preferences and Behaviors," *BurstMedia* (September 2012). Available from: http://burstmedia.com/pdf/burst_media_online_insights_2012_09.pdf, accessed June 23, 2014.
40 "Sports Fans Turn to Content Online to Stay Informed," *PR Newswire* (2012). Available from: http://www.prnewswire.com/news-releases/sports-fans-turn-to-content-online-to-stay-informed-174570471.html, accessed June 23. 2014.
41 Nora Macaluso, "One Year Ago: Report: New Profile for 'Typical' Web Surfer," *E-Commerce Times.com* (October 16, 2001). Available from: http://www.ecommercetimes.com/story/14057.html, accessed June 22, 2014.
42 Masha Geller, "Reaching Young Sports Fans Online," *MediaPostNews* (March 12, 2003). Available from: http://www.mediapost.com/publications/article/16862/reaching-young-sports-fans-online.html.
43 "Sports Fans Twice as Likely to Watch Videos on Mobile Phones," European Interactive Advertising Association (June 2008).
44 Raechel Johns, "Sports Promotion & The Internet," *Cyber-Journal of Sport Marketing* vol.1, no. 4 (1997). Available from:, http://fulltext.ausport.gov.au/fulltext/1997/cjsm/v1n4/johns.htm.
45 Fred Beasley, Matthew Shank, and Rebecca Ball, "Do Super Bowl Viewers Watch the Commercials?" *Sport Marketing Quarterly*, vol. 7, no. 3 (1998), 33–40.
46 Philip Kotler and Gary Armstrong, *Marketing: An Introduction*, 4th ed. (Upper Saddle River, NJ: Prentice Hall, 1997).
47 Sean Brenner, "Pursuing Relationships in Professional Sport," *Sport Marketing Quarterly*, vol. 6, no. 2 (1997), 33–34.
48 Robert Miller and Stephen Heiman, *Strategic Selling* (New York: Warner Books, 1985).
49 Mark Maske and Les Carpenter, "Player Arrests Put the NFL in a Defensive Mode," *WashingtonPost.com* (December 16, 2006). Available from: http://www.washingtonpost.com/wp-dyn/content/article/2006/12/15/AR2006121502134.html, accessed June 23, 2014.
50 David Broughton, "Giveaways Grow as the When and Why Evolve," *Street & Smith's Sport Business Daily* (November 1, 2010). Available from: http://www.sportsbusinessdaily.com/Journal/Issues/2010/11/20101101/Marketingsponsorship/Giveaways-grow-as-the-when-and-why-evolve.aspx?hl=Ping&sc=0, accessed June 23, 2014.
51 John Tulchin, "Happy Meals and Ticket Sales," *In Stadium Promotions* (November 9, 2010). Available from: http://www.instadiumpromotions.com/blog/uncategorized/premiums/, accessed June 23, 2014.
52 Ed Willes, "A Legacy of Slapstick and Slap Shots," *New York Times* (November 30, 1997), 33.
53 Rob Dauster, "How a Perfect NCAA Tournament Bracket Will Win You a Billion Dollars," *Collegebasketballtalk.nbcsports.com* (January 21, 2014). Available from: http://collegebasketballtalk.nbcsports.com/2014/01/21/how-a-perfect-ncaa-tournament-bracket-will-win-you-a-billion-dollars/, accessed March 21, 2014.
54 Ibid.
55 "NBA Pick Your Play Sweepstakes." Available from: http://www.nba.com/webAction?actionId=surveyInitialize&target=/analysis/nba_start_of_the_season.jsp&surveyId=1316.
56 Daniel C. Funk and Mark P. Pritchard, "Sports Publicity: Commitment's Moderation of Message Effects," *Journal of Business Research*, vol. 59, no. 5 (2006), 613–621.
57 Denise O'Connell, "Community Relations in Professional Sports Organizations," unpublished master's thesis, The Ohio State University, Columbus, Ohio.
58 *Cleveland Browns 2013 Media Guide*, Cleveland Browns Incorporated (2013). Available from: http://prod.static.browns.clubs.nfl.com/assets/docs/pdf/Cleveland-Browns-Media-Guide.pdf, accessed June 23, 2014.
59 "Philadelphia Eagles to Reimburse Employees for Purchasing Wind Energy; During 2007 NFL Business Summit, Eagles Owner Christina Lurie Hopes to Send a Message," *PR Newswire US* (April 11, 2007).
60 Mike Henry, "Pirates Increase Charitable Work: Team Tries to Give Back to Its Spring Home of 38 Years," *The Bradenton Herald* (March 29, 2007).

Sponsorship programs

After completing this chapter, you should be able to:

- Comment on the growing importance of sports sponsorships as a promotion mix element.
- Design a sponsorship program.
- Understand the major sponsorship objectives.
- Provide examples of the various costs of sponsorship.
- Identify the levels of the sports event pyramid.
- Evaluate the effectiveness of sponsorship programs.

SCHEURING SPEED SPORTS ANNOUNCES PARTNERSHIP WITH FORD MOTOR COMPANY

AURORA, Minn (July 24, 2013) Professional Snocross racing team Scheuring Speed Sports announced today a new partnership with Ford Motor Company to promote the best-selling Ford F-Series Trucks.

"I am extremely proud to partner with Ford," said team owner Steve Scheuring. "With incredible gas mileage, great towing capabilities, and a first class ride, it's obvious why the Ford F-150 is America's best-selling truck. The F-150 is the perfect vehicle to transport our team long distances to races around the country, often through challenging winter conditions"

Scheuring Speed Sports will stop by local Ford dealerships prior to each AMSOIL Championship Snocross Series National races this winter. The team will give away promotional merchandise and race tickets to customers who test drive a new Ford F-150.

Scheuring Speed Sports will also feature their Ford F-150 pickups at numerous off-track promotions throughout the 2013-14 Snocross season.

F-150 is part of the Ford F-Series lineup. Now in its 65th year, F-Series has been the best-selling truck in America for 36 consecutive years, the best-selling vehicle in America for 31 consecutive years, and the brand with the most trucks on the road with more than 250,000 miles, as certified by Polk.

The 2013 Ford F-150 features up to 11,300 pounds of towing capability and best-in-class 3,120 pounds of payload. F-150 is available with four powertrains including a 6.2-liter V8, a 5.0-liter V8, a 3.7-liter V6 and the segment-exclusive 3.5-liter EcoBoost®.

Scheuring speed sports is the original Super Team in the world of Snocross racing and was the first team to bring non-endemic sponsors into the world of snowmobile racing. Scheuring Speed Sports has two of the top drivers in the world, #11 Tim Tremblay, and #4 Robbie Malinoski.

Source: http://www.isocracing.com/2013/09/13/scheuring-speed-sports-announces-partnership-with-ford-motor-company/.Copyright © isoracing.com, Steve Scheuring.

Growth of sponsorship

The opening scenario is just one example of Scheuring Speed Sports and Ford using sponsorship to help achieve their marketing objectives. A wide variety of organizations are realizing that sports sponsorships are a valuable way to reach new markets and retain an existing customer base. Sponsorships can increase sales, change attitudes, heighten awareness, and build and maintain relationships with consumers. It is no wonder that sponsorships became the promotional tool of choice for sport marketers and continue to grow in importance. Before we turn to the growth of sponsorship as a promotional tool, let us define sponsorship.

In Chapter 9, sponsorships were described as one of the elements in the promotional mix. More specifically, **sponsorship** was defined as investing in a sports entity (athlete, league, team, or event) to support overall organizational objectives, marketing goals, and promotional strategies. The sponsorship investment may come in the form of monetary support and trade. For example, nonrevenue sports have been the biggest winners in the University of Kansas Athletics Department's six-year, $26-million sponsorship deal with Adidas.[1] Adidas is sponsoring the university's athletics program to support their marketing objective of increasing awareness of their brand and to associate with a winning NCAA program. Understanding how sponsorship can help achieve marketing goals and organizational objectives is discussed when we look at the construction of a sponsorship plan or program. For now, let us turn our attention to the dramatic growth of sponsorship as a promotional tool.

In our brief discussion of sponsorship, we have alluded to the "dramatic growth" of sponsorship, but just how quickly is sponsorship growing? Review the following facts and figures regarding sponsorship activities:[2]

- North American sponsorship spending is projected to reach $20.6 billion in 2014, a 4.3 percent increase from 2013, according to sponsorship-research company IEG. In contrast, IEG projected in North America for ad spending to rise 2.8 percent while spending on other forms of marketing – including public relations, direct marketing and promotion – would garner a 4.4 percent growth rate in 2014.
- In 2014, global sponsorship spending is projected to reach $55.3 billion with a 4.1 percent growth rate. Comparing global spending forecasts for media and other marketing expenditures, advertising would see the largest growth, 4.6 percent compared with 4.4 percent for marketing/promotions and 4.1 percent for sponsorship.
- According to IEG, of the projected $20.6 billion North American companies would spend on sponsorship in 2014, 70 percent of it would be on sports, 10 percent entertainment, 9 percent causes, 4 percent for arts and festivals, fairs and annual events, and 3 percent for associations and membership organizations.
- IEG noted as it has in most years over the past two-plus decades that sponsorship's growth rate will be ahead of the growth rate experienced by advertising and sales promotion in North America but not globally, for corporate interest in other marketing activities, particularly digital platforms, has dampened enthusiasm of sponsorship spending.[3] Overall, continued interest in major sports properties should make it the fastest growing segment. For example, the NHL is expected to show the largest increase among the big four sports, with spending on the league and its member clubs rising 9.4 percent to $327 million. However, the NFL has the largest sponsorship pot (up 7 percent to $870 million), followed by MLB (up 6.6 percent to $548 million), and the NBA (up 8.5 percent to $536 million).[4] Though Europe will remain the largest source of sponsorship spending ($14.8 billion) apart from North America, growth in Asia ($13.3 billion) and Central/South America ($4.2 billion) are expected to heat up with a forecasted growth of 5.6 percent and 5 percent, respectively.

  Much of the initial impetus behind surging sponsorship growth in Asia was associated with the Beijing Olympics; however, with the advent of the Sochi Winter Games and introduction of programs such as Crickets IPL and Twenty20 (T20) campaigns, sponsorship in the Asian regions continues to grow.

(**Twenty20 cricket**, often abbreviated to **T20**, is a form of cricket originally introduced in England and Wales for professional intercounty competition. A Twenty20 game involves two teams; each has a single innings, batting for a maximum of 20 overs.[5] A Twenty20 game is completed in about three hours, with each innings lasting around 75–90 minutes (with a 10–20-minute interval), thus bringing the game closer to the timespan of other popular team sports. Shortening the game affords matches to be completed in a single evening and the method of play is to score runs quickly rather than eke out a large score over a much larger period of time. The format provides a host of benefits for the game, drawing in broader audiences and securing better and more lucrative TV cricket coverage.)[6] Global cricket sponsorship, which according to a *Sponsorship Today* report is now worth $405 million a year, has come about mainly because of the introduction of these expedited formats.[7] In fact, according to *Sponsorship Today* report editor Simon Rines, the profile of industries sponsoring in developing countries is, in many cases, more healthy for the sport than in developed countries.[8] The report, which analyzed data from 788 deals from all of the major cricket playing nations, found Asia's India account for $165 million of the spending.[9]

Similar to Asia, much of the stimulus for growth in South America may be attributed to the procurement and implementation of the 2014 World Cup and the 2016 Olympic Games. South America provides an opportunity for sponsors, sponsees, and the host country to begin to link and identify long-term benefits. A variety of synergies exist in hosting the two events. These relate to development (i.e., hotels, stadiums and living communities); infrastructure (i.e., telecommunication and transportation), and the use of human resources. Brazil has the world's 6th largest economy; however, growth as of late has been less than 1 percent – a cause for concern. Traditionally, Brazil has not been an everyday stop but an exotic tourism destination. The 2016 Olympics and 2014 World Cup serve as a catalyst to ignite and promote long-term development of sponsorship platforms.[10]

Not unlike other forms of promotion, sponsorship marketing is also reaching its saturation point in the marketplace (see Table 11.1 for the official sponsors of NASCAR). Consumers are paying less attention to sports sponsorships as they become more the rule than the exception and although sponsorship is still seeing steady growth, corporate interest in other marketing alternatives, particularly digital (including social and mobile) media, have altered spending habits. Sponsorship clutter is causing businesses to design more systematic sponsorship programs that stand out in the sea of sponsorships. In addition, businesses are fighting the clutter of sponsoring mainstream sports by exploring new sponsorship opportunities (e.g., X-Games, women's sports, and Paralympics) and by becoming more creative with existing sponsorship opportunities. As IEG noted, instead of viewing "new media" as competition, sponsorship properties would be wise to emphasize their role as catalysts in driving interest, engagement and enthusiasm for these digital, social, and mobile platforms.[11]

One example of a creative sponsorship approach trying to help distinguish their brand in the minds of the consumers and offset the clutter of many traditional sports mediums is shown the accompanying article.

Table 11.1 Official sponsors of NASCAR

3M – Official Partner
Bank of America – Official Bank
Camping World – Official Outdoor and RV Retail Partner
Canadian Tire – Official Automotive Retailer of NASCAR in Canada
Chevrolet – An Official Passenger Car
Coca-Cola – Official Non-Alcoholic Beverage, Official Soft Drink, Official Sport Drink, Official Energy Drink
Coors Light – Official Beer
DRIVE4COPD – Official Health Initiative
Exide – Official Auto Batteries
FDP Friction Science – Official Partner
Featherlite Trailers – Official Trailer
Ford – Official Truck
Freescale – Official Partner
Freightliner Trucks – Official Hauler
Growth Energy – Official Partner
Goodyear – Official Tire
Hellman's – Official Mayonnaise
K&N – Official Partner
Klondike – Official Ice Cream
Mars – Official Chocolate
Mobil 1 – Official Partner
McLaren – Official Partner
Nabisco (Kraft) – Official Cookies and Crackers
National Corn Growers Assoc. – Official Partner
Nationwide Insurance – Official Auto, Home and Life Insurance
New Holland Agriculture – Official Agriculture Equipment
Prevost – Official Partner
Ragu – Official Sauce
Safety- Kleen – Official Supplier
Sherwin Williams – Official Paint
SIRIUS XM Radio – Official Satellite Radio Partner
Sprint – Official Series Sponsor
Sunoco – Official Fuel and Official Convenience Store
Toyota – An Official Passenger Car
Unilever – Official Partner
UPS – Official Delivery Service
UTI – Official Partner
Visa – Official Card
Whelen Engineering Inc. – Official Development Series Partner of NASCAR

Source: http://www.nascar.com/en_us/sponsors.html.

CLEVELAND CAVALIERS 2013–2014 PROMOTIONAL SCHEDULE

Fans Can Lock in Seats for all the Exciting Giveaways and Theme Nights when Single Game Tickets Go On Sale Saturday, October 5th at 10:00 A.M.

Gearing up for an exciting year both on and off the court, the Cleveland Cavaliers *presented by Discount Drug Mart* have announced the promotional schedule for the 2013–14 season! The lineup of premium giveaways and exciting theme nights adds to the anticipated return of Cavaliers basketball and the award-winning fan experience at The Q.

Fans can guarantee a spot in the house for their favorite nights when tickets for the first half of the Cavs 2013–14 regular season (October 30th – January 28th) go on sale Saturday, October 5th at 10:00 a.m. Tickets can be purchased by visiting cavs.com, by calling 1-800-820-2287, at the Quicken Loans Arena Box Office or by visiting any of the 58 Northern Ohio Discount Drug Mart locations, the official drugstore of the Cleveland Cavaliers!

Fan Favorite Giveaways

FIVE Cavs Bobbleheads, T-Shirts, Fatheads and More!

The 2013-14 Cavaliers season presented by Discount Drug Mart tips off on Wednesday, October 30th vs. the Brooklyn Nets with two giveaways to celebrate the home opener presented by Kenda Tires. Fans in attendance will receive a Cavaliers 2013–14 magnet schedule presented by Kenda Tires and a Cavs t-shirt compliments of the Cleveland Clinic. Opening Night will be full of fun surprises to welcome back the home team and, of course, the fans!

This season fans will score with FIVE Cavalier player bobblehead giveaways! The 2013–14 roster of Cavs collectibles will feature #17**Anderson Varejao**, 2013 NBA All-Star **Kyrie Irving**, #13 **Tristan Thompson**, and in their figurine debut, 2012-13 All-Rookie First Team Selection **Dion Waiters** and 2012–13 All-Rookie Second Team Selection **Tyler Zeller**. The Zeller bobblehead was selected exclusively by the Cavs' Wine & Gold United members at their annual meeting.

Fathead Tradeables are the coolest way for kids to show off their Wine & Gold spirit on November 27th vs. Miami AND December 29th vs. Golden State. Children 14 and under will receive these popular surface-friendly decals that will be a slam dunk with them and their friends!

GIVEAWAY	GAME DATE
Opening Night and Magnet Schedule Giveaway presented by Kenda Tires and T-Shirt Giveaway compliments of Cleveland Clinic	Oct. 30 vs. Brooklyn
Cavaliers Player Fathead Tradeable Giveaway (children 14 and under)	Nov. 27 vs. Miami
Cavs Team Poster Giveaway presented by The Jim Giltner Financial Group	Nov. 30 vs. Chicago
Anderson Varejao Bobblehead Giveaway	Dec. 20 vs. Milwaukee
Cavaliers Player Fathead Tradeable Giveaway (children 14 and under)	Dec. 29 vs. Golden State
Dion Waiters Bobblehead Giveaway	Jan. 5 vs. Indiana
Wine & Gold United Select Player Bobblehead Giveaway	Feb. 9 vs. Memphis
Kyrie Irving Bobblehead Giveaway presented by Pepsi MAX	Mar. 4 vs. San Antonio
Fat Dots Giveaway	Mar. 20 vs. Oklahoma City
Fan Appreciation Night T-Shirt and Prize Giveaway	Apr. 14 vs. Brooklyn

Theme Nights

Caped Crusaders, WWE Superstars and More Fun in Store!

This season boasts some of the most exciting Cavs theme nights at The Q to date and many favorites from past seasons! **"Superhero Night"** flies back into action on April 12th vs. Boston to pay homage to the fun and style of classic comic book heroes throughout the night. **"Fan Choice Night"** once again puts power in the hands of the fans as they utilize social and mobile media to create the fan experience – even which night it happens!

New this season, **"WWE Night"** will deliver the fun and excitement of World Wrestling Entertainment to the NBA with activities on the concourse, in-game elements and special guest appearances by current WWE Superstars on January 22 vs. Chicago! Fans can "come on down" to **"Game Show Night** when classic television game shows invade The Q with both memorable and ridiculous antics from fan-favorite programs on December 10 vs. New York. Also, each Sunday game at The Q will feature postgame **"Fan Free Throws"** for fans of all ages with interactive elements and entertainment as they wait to take a shot from the line on the Cavs court.

The annual **Black Heritage Celebration (BHC)** will tip off on January 20th vs. Dallas for Dr. Martin Luther King, Jr. Night with a tribute to the late civil rights leader. The celebration continues throughout the month of February for three signature nights dedicated to celebrating African-American culture, and several community initiatives and activities.

On April 15th, the Cavs face the Brooklyn Nets for the final home game of the regular season and host **Fan Appreciation Night presented by Discount Drug Mart**, the signature celebration of the season-long support from the best fans in the NBA. All fans in attendance will receive a Fan Appreciation Night t-shirt in addition to chances to win one of $1 million in prizes distributed on-and-off the court throughout the night! To top it all off, the players will give fans the actual jerseys and shoes worn in the game as a personal "thank you" for their support.

Special Ticket Packages

Family Fun, All-You-Can-Eat and Super Fun for Super Fans!

New at The Q for a limited time, **ALL-YOU-CAN-EAT SEATS** offer fans an incredible deal that is sure to deliver a fill-up good time. Starting at just $34, fans can chow down on all the hot dogs, potato chips, nachos, popcorn and soft drinks they can handle.* Designated concession stands will offer "speed lines" so fans can make as many trips as they like without missing the action on the court.

GAME DATES	
November 4th vs. Minnesota	December 4th vs. Denver
November 9th vs. Philadelphia	December 10th vs. New York**
November 15th vs. Charlotte	December 17th vs. Portland
November 20th vs. Washington	December 20th vs. Milwaukee
November 30th vs. Chicago**	December 23rd vs. Detroit

****Seating only available in sections 213-215. Maximum of four (4) items per trip to the dedicated concession stand will apply. **Prices for premium games begin at $39.***

Giving families a more affordable way to be part of the Cavaliers excitement this season, the **Family Value Pack** will return to The Q for 25 Cavs home games. The Family Night package includes four Cavs tickets, four hot dogs and four sodas starting at just $59, or $15.75 per person. For a full list of Family Value Pack games, visit **cavs.com/family**.

Access Cavalier & CavFanatic Nights

This year, Access Cavaliers Nights will team up with the CavFanatic Nights to provide exclusive behind-the-scenes experiences for the loudest and proudest fans in the NBA! Each package includes a game ticket, admittance to a pregame all-you-can-eat buffet and a Cavs t-shirt. For more information, visit cavs.com/access or sign up to become a CavFanatic at **www.cavfanatic.com**today!

TICKET PACKAGE	GAME DATE
Access Cavaliers/ CavFanatic Night #1	November 9th vs. Philadelphia
Access Cavaliers/ CavFanatic Night #2	December 20th vs. Milwaukee
Access Cavaliers/ CavFanatic Night #3	January 24th vs. Milwaukee
Access Cavaliers/ CavFanatic Night #4	February 23rd vs. Washington
Access Cavaliers/ CavFanatic Night #5	March 8th vs. New York
Access Cavaliers/ CavFanatic Night #6	April 12th vs. Boston

Additional Cavaliers promotional nights and premium giveaways may be announced throughout the season. For a complete schedule of 2013–14 promotional giveaways and theme nights, and for ticket information, fans can call 216-420-2287 or 800-820-2287 or visit cavs.com.

More Ticket Information

Wine & Gold United Membership

Wine & Gold United memberships and group ticket packages are available NOW! With Wine & Gold United membership, fans can lock in the best all-encompassing experience, with unprecedented members-only access, a voice in the organization, year-round member engagement and enhanced membership privileges and perks. Please visit **united.cavs.com** or call 1-800-820-2287 for more information.

Preseason Games at Quicken Loans Arena presented by Discount Drug Mart

The Cavaliers will host three preseason home games at Quicken Loans Arena on Tuesday, October 8th vs. the Milwaukee Bucks at 7:00 p.m.; Thursday, October 17th vs. the Detroit Pistons at 7:00 p.m.; and Saturday, October 19th vs. the Indiana Pacers at 7:30 p.m. Discount Drug Mart customers using their Courtesy Plus card with the purchase of (2) 8-pack 12 oz. bottles of Pepsi products will receive four (4) free tickets to one of three preseason games hosted at The Q.

Partial Plans

The Cavs are offering two 11-game partial season ticket plans featuring a mix of the hottest games, marquee matchups and weekend and weekday dates. Each 11-game plan starts as low as $264 and offer ticket holders a complimentary home-opener ticket(s), exclusive, added-value benefits and the fun of being a part of the best fan entertainment experience in the NBA.

Group Tickets

Unique Fan Experience packages for group outings (10 or more tickets together) are available for each Cavs home game. Great savings off of single game tickets are available for select games. For more information on how to create a unique group outing, or to place an initial $200 group payment, call 216-420-2153 or visit **cavs.com/groups**.

Ticket Packages are On Sale Now!

For more information or to purchase full or partial season ticket plans, groups, preseason games, or for general ticket information visit cavs.

com or call 1-800-820-2287. Tickets for regular season games go on sale Saturday, October 5th at 10:00 a.m.

Source: http://www.nba.com/cavaliers/releases/promotional-schedule-130927, accessed December 11, 2013. "The NBA and individual member team identifications reproduced herein are used with permission from NBA Properties, Inc. 2014 NBA Properties, Inc. All rights reserved."

ADELAIDE UNITED ENERGISED BY NEW SPONSORSHIP

A-League club Adelaide United has announced green energy company Unleash Solar as its new front-of-shirt sponsor.

In addition to the Unleash Solar logo featuring on the front of Adelaide's shirts throughout the 2012/13 A-League season, the Australian company will also offer the club's fans and members with special offers.

Though financial terms of Unleash Solar's commitment were not released, the Australian press are reporting that the one-year agreement is worth AU$250,000 (US$260,000).

"As a young South Australian company, Unleash Solar is proud to further participate in our local community by becoming the major partner of Adelaide United," said Unleash Solar group general manager Spiro Perdi. "We would like to wish the club all the best for the upcoming season and look forward to working closely with the club as it continues to grow and strive to be national title holders."

"As a company we share many similarities with Adelaide United. We are both focused on growing to build a stronger footprint nationally and internationally, with Unleash having recently expanded to the USA, as in the same way Adelaide United also strives to be a major player in Asia. We encourage all South Australians to get behind these two great teams and make this season a success," Perdi added.

Adelaide United chief executive Glenn Elliott said, "Importantly Unleash Solar is a proud South Australian owned and operated solar business. They have an exceptionally bright future and whilst they are an already successful organisation, they have a desire to grow. Unleash Solar's commitment to the club is a clear indication of its community focus in supporting soccer in this state, and with that being the case, Adelaide United is pleased to recommend Unleash Solar to all of its fans, especially those who may have a shock upon receiving their latest power bill. If our fans are considering investing in solar, they should do it with the company that supports the Reds."

The 2012/13 A-League season will begin 5th October.

Source: Article author: Michael Long; http://www.sportspromedia.com/news/adelaide_united_energised_by_new_sponsorship/. Credit: www.sportspromedia.com.

In essence, a sports sponsorship program is just another promotion mix element to be considered along with advertising, personal selling, sales promotions, and public relations. One difference, however, between sponsorship and the other promotion mix elements is that sports marketing relies heavily on developing successful sponsorship programs. In fact, sponsorship programs are so prevalent in sports marketing that the field is sometimes defined in these terms. Since sponsorship is so critical, let's better understand how to develop the most effective sponsorship program.

Designing a sports sponsorship program

Sports sponsorship programs come in all shapes and sizes. The following are just a few examples:

- High schools are now looking to sponsors to help with funding. For example, Farmers Insurance is in its sixth year of high school sponsorship, and currently has deals with 18 state high school athletic associations, which gives Farmers the rights to activate around state championships. Each of the state deals is worth US$250,000 to US$500,000 annually, while sport-specific partnerships begin around US$20,000. Deals with single schools range from US$2,000 to US$3,500 per athletic season.[12]
- Adidas signed an 11-year, $400 million partnership as the official uniform and apparel supplier of the NBA with 15 team sponsorship deals, some of which will include a new "store-within-a-store" concept that will sell both NBA-licensed merchandise and other company apparel.[13]
- FIFA and Adidas formally announced an extension of their long-term partnership agreement granting Adidas the Official Partner, Supplier and Licensee rights for the FIFA World Cup™ and all FIFA events until 2030. Already one of the longest and most successful partnerships in modern history, the sponsorship will extend their partnership beyond 60 years and provide an estimated $100 million per four year World Cup cycle.[14]
- The Kansas City Chiefs are joining with Hy-Vee, Procter & Gamble and Kansas City Public Schools for the RED Zone Reading Challenge, a collaborative effort designed to encourage the healthy habits of reading and classroom attendance among all elementary school students in Kansas City Public Schools.[15] All elementary school students, kindergarten through sixth grade, in Kansas City Public Schools are eligible to participate. A total of 25 elementary schools will be taking part in the program.[16]
- Weston FC/AYSO 644 soccer club is a 501(C)-(3) non-profit organization located in southern Florida. Weston FC/AYSO 644 is Florida's largest soccer club. Weston FC/AYSO 644 provides both recreational and competitive soccer programs for the Elite, Travel, and Beginner soccer players between the ages of 4 and 19. Weston offers a year-long title sponsorship estimated at $50,000, a Weston Cup, and Showcase Title Sponsorship seeking $15,000 yearly web sponsorships at $350 apiece, Weston Cup & Showcase web sponsorship valued at $150 apiece, practice T-shirt sponsorships at $450, as well as AYSO Team and Team Plus packages.[17]
- The PGA Tour and Tiffany & Co. have a multiyear sponsorship deal. The company will serve as the official awards and gift provider for the PGA Tour and Champions Tour. Tiffany will also "design and craft the FedEx Cup Trophy."[18]
- GE has renewed its sponsorship contract for the Olympic Games until 2020. As for the Rio Olympics in 2016, GE has a large portfolio of solutions that can help build the infrastructure required for the city to be able to host the event, among which: energy generation and distribution systems, image diagnostics, monitoring technology and electronic medical records, lighting systems, aircraft engines, water and sewerage treatment installations and services, equipment and transport management, and others.[19]
- U.S. gold medal-winning skier Lindsey Vonn signed a sponsorship deal in 2009– 2014 to compete with HEAD Ski's boots, bindings, and poles.

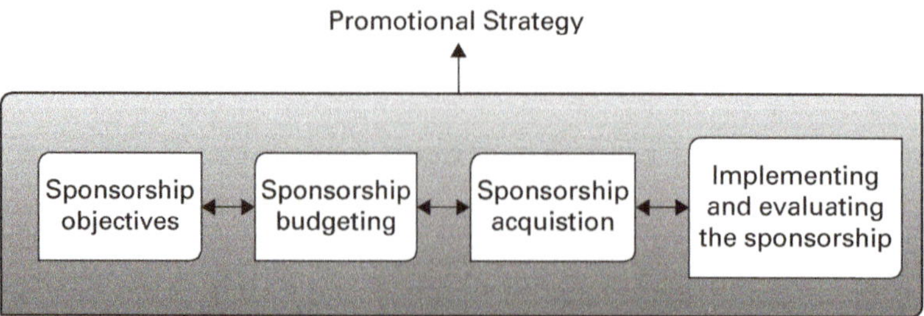

Figure 11.1 The sponsorship process

Source: Hawkins et al., *Consumer Behavior: Implications for Marketing Strategy*, 6/e © 1994 © The McGraw-Hill Companies, Inc.

What do each of these sponsorship examples have in common? First, they were developed as part of an integrated marketing communications approach in which sponsorship is but one element of the promotion mix. In addition, each of the sponsors has carefully chosen the best sponsorship opportunity (with individual athletes, teams, conferences, events, and/or leagues) to meet organizational objectives and marketing goals.

To carefully plan sponsorship programs, a systematic process is being used by an increasing number of organizations. The process for designing a sports sponsorship program is presented in Figure 11.1. Before explaining the process, it is important to remember that sponsorship involves a marketing exchange. The sponsor benefits by receiving the right to associate with the sports entity (e.g., team or event), and the sports entity benefits from either monetary support or product being supplied by the sponsor. Because the marketing exchange involves two parties, the sponsorship process can be explored from the perspective of the sponsor (e.g., Allstate) or the sports entity (e.g., Sugar Bowl). We look at the process from the viewpoint of the sponsor rather than the entity sponsored.

As shown in the model, decisions regarding the sponsorship program are not made in isolation. Rather, the **sponsorship program** is just one element of the broader promotional strategy. It was suggested earlier that all the elements in the promotional mix must be integrated to have the greatest and most effective promotional impact. However, sponsorship decisions influence much more than just promotion. Sponsorship decisions can affect the entire marketing mix, as the accompanying article shows.

UNDERSTANDING WHY SPONSORSHIP CONTINUES TO GROW

"They're like sleeping in a soft bed. Easy to get into and hard to get out of."
– Hall of Fame catcher Johnny Bench, speaking on slumps

As the recent economic fallout settled in globally, but particularly in the United States, cutbacks in consumer and corporate spending were observed in numerous settings. And yet, despite the doubts and concerns of chairmen, CEOs and COOs, and despite bottom-line blame placed on numerous CFOs, researchers, marketers and sales staffs, sponsorship kept growing.

It's been an interesting conundrum (as Newman of TV's "Seinfeld" might say), because as 2011 begins and we watch CEOs (across the U.S. and Canada) increasingly announce improved quarterly results, the marketing budgets of most organizations appear radically different from five years ago. Just look at the reductions in hospitality budgets or companywide moratoriums on travel to corporate-sponsored events.

This has meant that, like crazed, wild-haired scientists, we've been obligated to ask, "Why is it so?"

The two most-read analyses of sponsorship spending in North America – IEG's Sponsorship Report and the Canadian Sponsorship Landscape Study – both noted that although there was reduced growth rate in companies' investment in sponsorship, it continued to grow (or, at least not contract to any great extent) in 2009 and is expected to grow again in 2010 in the U.S., Canada and globally.

Likewise, the PricewaterhouseCoopers' hospitality and leisure sector report for 2010-13 suggested that sponsorship would remain the fastest-growing global sports sector, eclipsing gate revenue, media rights and merchandising by a compounded annual growth rate (CAGR) of 4.6 percent.

All of these studies are supported by happenings in the marketplace. The IOC last year announced two new first-time TOP sponsors (Dow Chemical and Procter & Gamble) to its stable of partners, now at 11, who commit an estimated nine figures each quadrennium for the rights to associate with the Olympic Games. Rumors abound that a 12th TOP sponsor will be added in 2011.

In Russia alone, MegaFon ($260 million), Rostelecom ($260 million), Aeroflot ($180 million), Rosneft ($180 million) and Volkwagen ($100 million) are readying five-year plans to inject nearly $1 billion into the Sochi 2014 Olympic Games. This outpouring of financial support from national partners continues the trend established for the Vancouver 2010 Games, where a reported $750 million was contributed by Canadian sponsors.

How, we ask, is this possible and why is it happening?

First, sponsorship works. There are dozens of academic studies and hundreds of professionally produced evaluations backing this up. Sponsorship is an effective tool to reposition brands, alter consumer perceptions and increase sales. In fact, one of our Ph.D. dissertations found more than 150 objectives that marketers had established as reasons to invest in and embark upon a sponsorship.

Second, sponsorship works efficiently. By this, we mean research has shown the effectiveness of sponsorship to reach specific target markets through association with properties that resonate with those markets. Think Burton Snowboards, Shaun White and snowboarders, or Gillette, baseball and men who shave.

Third, sponsorship works better than advertising. Although debate still exists over the difference between advertising and sponsorship, there is general agreement among many that the two marketing tools are notably different and play different roles.

These three theories support the argument that it is the association differentiating sponsorship from advertising. The old saw has been that advertising is one-dimensional and nonpersonal, whereas consumers who follow sponsorships see the sponsor, the sports property and the linked association between them.

Quite simply, as the consumer is exposed to the association, images are more easily transferred from sponsor to property and vice versa. Conversely, in a (typical) nonintegrated advertisement, the consumer sees the advertisement (often shown during a sports event or on a sports website) but without a compelling association to the property. Each has its advantages and disadvantages, but most will agree that sponsorship is a hybrid form of advertising.

Fourth, sponsorship appears to be more fun, with hospitality, backstage passes and locker room visits, plus it can be staged to incorporate a social responsibility hook to aggressively assuage the guilt that accompanies massive investments in activities that appear (to some) socially trivial. In other words, sponsorship can benefit a charity while executives tour the pits or drop the ceremonial first puck.

But all is not perfect in the sponsorship world, and PwC notes that the mercurial economy "has focused a rising proportion of attention and spending on the biggest sports brands with global reach and pulling-power." This means "mid-level brands [properties] have found it harder to attract major sponsors while sponsorship of the smaller local sports brands has been hit [hard] by potential backers reducing discretionary spend in the economic downturn."

To be sure, it is notable that sponsorship continues to grow and in North America will reach a CAGR of 5 percent in 2012 and 5.6 percent in 2013. The question for many is whether the biggest fish (NFL, IOC, FIFA, EPL, UEFA, etc.) will leave the minnows high and dry.

We'll also have to watch to see if player strikes, owner lockouts or terrorism change sponsorship's trajectory.

Source: Article authors: Rick Burton and Norm O' Reilly; http://www.sportsbusinessdaily.com/Journal/Issues/2011/01/20110124/Opinion/Burton.aspx. Credit: Sports Business Journal.

There are two important things to consider before signing a sponsorship agreement: (1) All your organization is getting is the right to be called a sponsor, not a completed sponsorship plan; and (2) you should spend two to three times your sponsorship fee to leverage your relationship as a sponsor – if you do not have the funds to promote, do not buy the sponsorship.

When designing the sponsorship program, the initial decisions are based on sponsorship objectives and budgets. These two elements go hand in hand. Without the money, the most meaningful objectives will never be reached. Alternatively, appropriate objectives must be considered without total regard to cost. If the objectives are sound, senior-level managers will find a way to allocate the necessary monies to sponsorship.

After the objectives and budget have been agreed upon, the specific sports sponsorship opportunity is chosen from the hundreds available. For example, Pepsi receives approximately 500 sponsorship proposals each year, and Pennzoil reports that they receive 200 proposals annually. Others estimate that several corporations receive over 100 sponsorship proposals each week (for an example of proposal guidelines, see Table 11.2). Regardless of the exact number, there are a wealth of sponsorship opportunities available to potential sponsors. Table 11.3 illustrates how the Wyndham Golf Championship presents various tiers of information to potential sponsors.[20]

Table 11.2 Castrol North America – sponsorship criteria requirements

As you might imagine, we receive a number of requests for a variety of sponsorships from across North America. In order for us to most effectively evaluate each proposal we receive, we have established criteria that will provide us with the pertinent information we need. Including all of the data requested below will improve your chances of a prompt response.	
Timeframe:	
1.	**Submitting a proposal to Castrol North America:** To allow us enough lead-time to line up appropriate resources, your proposal must be submitted at least 6 months prior to the start date of the event/project. We will not consider proposals submitted outside of this timeframe.
2.	**Castrol North America Response:** You should expect a reply within 3 months.
What to send and where to send it:	
1.	**Brief detailed description of sponsorship**
2.	**Contract Information**
3.	**Fees and Payment Terms/Schedule:** All costs Castrol is expected to pay, including sponsorship fee, Value In Kind, promotional fees, signage, literature, printing costs, creative/production costs, equipment, merchandising, etc.
4.	**Direct On-site Sales Opportunities:** Include a three-year history of Castrol or non-Castrol motor oil product sales as well as projected motor oil product sales over the next three years. If this is a new venue with no previous motor oil related sales, please explain why this is an ideal Do-it-Yourself (DIY) automotive demographic.
5.	**Castrol Benefits:** Include items such as TV, radio, and newspaper exposure, Website visits, complimentary tickets, hospitality, and access to special events at the property and quantity as appropriate.
6.	**Product/Category Exclusivity**
7.	**Marketing Opportunities:** On-site and off-site, such as co-sponsor promotional activities, Consumer and Trade promotions available to Castrol, etc.
8.	**List of Other Sponsors:** Indicate whether they are potential or committed. Also please indicate historical sponsors and length of association.
9.	**Term:** (Annual, two-year, three-year, etc.)
10.	**Number of Events per annum**
11.	**Attendance:** Annual ticket sales, paid and unpaid, trend history for the last three years, future projections for three years
12.	**Demographics:** Include where applicable (i.e., if noticeably different), the following demographics for both attendees *and* the media audience.
	a. age;
	b. gender;
	c. % do it yourself (i.e., change their own oil);
	d. ethnic origin;
	e. income profile; and
	f. any other applicable information
13.	**Any Other Pertinent Information**
*Please include as much of this information as possible when sending your proposal to Castrol.*Once your proposal is complete, please forward by mail to the address below:	
Sponsorship Department	
Castrol Consumer North America	
1500 Valley Road	
Wayne, NJ, 07470	
USA	
We appreciate your interest in Castrol North America as a potential sponsor and look forward to receiving your sponsorship proposal.	

Source: www.refresh.castrolusa.com/sponsors. Credit: BP Lubricants USA Inc.

Table 11.3 Sponsorship opportunities for the Wyndham Championship: sponsorship levels

18th Green Luxury Suite
18th Green Luxury Suite – $80,000
Entertain guests in your private Luxury Suite at one of golf's most historic locations – Sedgefield Country Club.
1 Suite on the 18th Green at Sedgefield Country Club
Includes Lunch, Appetizers and Full, Open Bar Thursday–Sunday
70 Luxury Suite Tickets each day Thursday–Sunday
70 Clubhouse Tickets each day Monday–Wednesday
4 VIP Parking Permits & 10 Sponsors Event Invitations
Exclusive opportunity to purchase dual-logoed merchandise bearing your company logo and the Wyndham Championship Logo
17th Green Luxury Suite
17th Green Luxury Suite – $70,000
Entertain guests in your private Luxury Suite at one of golf's most historic locations – Sedgefield Country Club.
1 Suite on the17th Green at Sedgefield Country Club
Includes Lunch, Appetizers and Full, Open Bar Thursday–Sunday
70 Luxury Suite Tickets each day Thursday–Sunday
70 Clubhouse Tickets each day Monday–Wednesday
4 VIP Parking Permits & 10 Sponsors Event Invitations
Exclusive opportunity to purchase dual-logoed merchandise bearing your company logo and the Wyndham Championship Logo
18th Green Skybox
18th Green Skybox – $50,000
Entertain guests in an air-conditioned Skybox with open-air seating at one of golf's most historic locations – Sedgefield Country Club.
1 Skybox on the 18th Green at Sedgefield Country Club
Includes Lunch and Full, Open Bar Thursday–Sunday
40 Skybox Tickets each day Thursday–Sunday
40 Clubhouse Tickets each day Monday–Wednesday
4 VIP Parking Permits & 4 Sponsors Event Invitations
Exclusive opportunity to purchase dual-logoed merchandise bearing your company logo and the Wyndham Championship Logo
16th Green Skybox
16th Green Skybox – $50,000
Entertain guests in an air-conditioned Skybox with open-air seating at one of golf's most historic locations – Sedgefield Country Club.
1 Skybox on the 16th Green at Sedgefield Country Club
Includes Lunch and Full, Open Bar Thursday–Sunday
40 Skybox Tickets each day Thursday–Sunday
40 Clubhouse Tickets each day Monday–Wednesday
4 VIP Parking Permits & 4 Sponsors Event Invitations
Exclusive opportunity to purchase dual-logoed merchandise bearing your company logo and the Wyndham Championship Logo
15th Green Skybox
15th Green Skybox – $50,000
Entertain guests in an air-conditioned Skybox with open-air seating at one of golf's most historic locations – Sedgefield Country Club.

Table 11.3 (continued)

1 Skybox on the 15th Green at Sedgefield Country Club
Includes Lunch and Full, Open Bar Thursday–Sunday
40 Skybox Tickets each day Thursday–Sunday
40 Clubhouse Tickets each day Monday–Wednesday
4 VIP Parking Permits & 4 Sponsors Event Invitations
Exclusive opportunity to purchase dual-logoed merchandise bearing your company logo and the Wyndham Championship Logo
Champions Club
Champions Club – $12,000
Located in the historic Sedgefield Clubhouse overlooking the 9th Green, this package features an upscale buffet lunch, afternoon appetizers, and access to on-course viewing platforms with complimentary beverage service Thursday–Sunday.
15 Champions Club Tickets Each Day Thursday–Sunday
15 Clubhouse Tickets Each Day Monday–Wednesday
2 VIP Parking Permits & 2 Sponsors Event Invitations
Exclusive opportunity to purchase dual-logoed merchandise bearing your company logo and the Wyndham Championship Logo
Viewing Platform Package
Viewing Platform – $400/week or $125/day
Watch all the action from private, greenside elevated platforms around the historic Sedgefield golf course. Complimentary open bar is included.
1 Daily or Weekly Access to Multiple On-Course Viewing Platforms Thursday–Sunday
Open Bar Thursday–Sunday
View as a PDF: Viewing Platform Package

Source: Courtesy of PGA TOUR.

When choosing from among many sponsorship opportunities, three decisions must be addressed. The first decision is whether to sponsor a local, regional, national, or global event. Second, the organization must choose an athletic platform. For instance, will the organization sponsor an individual athlete, team, league, or stadium? Third, once the broad athletic platform is chosen, the organization must decide on a specific sports entity. For example, if a league is selected as the athletic platform, will the organization sponsor the WNBA, MLS, or the NFL?

The final stage of the sports sponsorship process involves implementation and evaluation. Typically, the organization wants to determine whether their desired sponsorship objectives have been achieved. Measuring the impact of sponsorship on awareness levels within a targeted audience is a relatively easy marketing research task. However, as the costs of sponsorships continue to increase, there is a heightened sense of accountability. In other words, organizations want to assess the impact of sponsorship on the bottom line – sales. The shift from philanthropy to evaluating sponsorship return on investment (ROI) is also documented in the academic sport sponsorship literature, and new models are emerging to understand the complexities of sponsorship evaluation.[21] Now that we have a rough idea of how the sponsorship process works, let us explore each stage of the sports sponsorship model in greater detail.

Sponsorship objectives

The first stage in designing a sponsorship program is to carefully consider the sponsorship objectives. Because sponsorship is just one form of promotion, the **sponsorship objectives** should be linked to the broader promotional planning process and its objectives. The promotional objectives will, in turn, help achieve the marketing goals, which should stem from the objectives of the organization. These important linkages were stated in our definition of sponsorship.

Not unlike advertising objectives, sponsorship objectives can be categorized as either direct or indirect. **Direct sponsorship objectives** have a short-term impact on consumption behavior and focus on increasing sales. **Indirect sponsorship objectives** are those that ultimately lead to the desired goal of enhancing sales. In other words, the sponsor has to generate awareness and create the desired image of the product before consumers purchase the product. The indirect sponsorship objectives include generating awareness, meeting and beating competition, reaching new target markets, building relationships, and improving image.[22] One of the reasons that sponsoring sporting events has risen in popularity is that sponsorship provides so many benefits to those involved in the partnership. In other words, both the sponsor and the sports entity (event, athlete, or league) gain from this win–win partnership. Let us look at some of the primary objectives of sponsorship from the sponsor's perspective.

Awareness

One of the most basic objectives of any sponsor is to generate **awareness** or raise levels of awareness of its products and services, product lines, or corporate name. Sponsors must understand which level to target (i.e., individual product versus company name) based on the broader promotional or marketing strategy. For a new company or product, sponsorship is an important way to generate widespread awareness in a short period of time.

From the event or sports entity's perspective, having a large corporate sponsor will certainly heighten the awareness of the event. The corporate sponsor will design a promotional program around the event to make consumers aware of the sponsor's relationship with the event. The corporate sponsor will also want to ensure their promotional mix elements are integrated. In other words, advertising, sponsorship of the event, and sales promotion will all work in concert to achieve the desired promotional objectives. However, a study conducted by Hoek, Gendall, Jeffcoat, and Orsman[23] found that sponsorship generated higher levels of awareness than did advertising. In addition, sponsorship led to the association of a wider range of attributes with the brand being promoted than did advertising.

Competition

Another primary objective of sponsorship is to stamp out or meet any competitive threats or **competition**. Many corporate sponsors claim they are not that interested in sponsorship opportunities, but they cannot afford not to do so. In other words, if they do not make the sponsorship investment, their competitors will. Sponsorship is thought of as a preemptive tactic that will reduce competitive threat. For instance, Texaco sponsors virtually every national governing body of U.S. Olympic sports. They promote only a handful of these sports, but their sponsorship of the others effectively keeps other competitors out of any chance of ambushing their Olympic efforts. Another example of competitive threat comes from the fierce rivalry between Pepsi and Coke, including Pepsi's deal with the NFL, snatching that relationship away from Coke, and Coke's turnabout in securing the NCAA, which had been rival Mountain Dew's domain. More recently, Coke's Sprite renewed its long-term deal with the NBA.

In an attempt to gain a competitive edge in the insurance industry, State Farm Insurance has a multi-year deal as Major League Baseball's official insurer and garner the title sponsorship to the annual Home Run Derby competition on ESPN – one of the highest-rated sports broadcasts of the summer. While State Farm has long had a presence in women's golf and skating, the MLB deal continues an aggressive spend in sports for the company, which is trying to grow in the intensely competitive insurance industry.[24]

Unfortunately, a sponsoring company, such as State Farm Insurance, can still be harmed by competitors who use ambush marketing tactics. **Ambush marketing** is a planned effort (campaign by an organization) to associate themselves indirectly with an event to gain at least some of the recognition and benefits that are associated with being an official sponsor.[25] Ambushing may occur in a variety of ways. Corporations may buy commercial time prior to and during event broadcasts (e.g., Amex '92 and '94 Winter Olympics), sponsor broadcasts of events rather than directly sponsoring the event, (e.g., Wendy's on ABC at '88 Calgary), sponsor individual teams and athletes (e.g., Pepsi and Magic in '92 Barcelona), or use sport event tickets in consumer giveaways, sweepstakes, or contests.[26] One of the earliest examples of ambush marketing at its finest was Nike's 1984 "I Love LA" marketing campaign.[27] Although the company was not an official Olympic sponsor, this campaign inextricably tied Nike to the city and event. Most sports marketers consider this ambush campaign the catalyst for the steady rise in ambush marketing practices and although marketers continue to employ more stringent legislation to combat ambushing tactics, ambushers seem more interested in circumventing the rule.[28]

Today, many examples of ambush marketing exist. However, the Olympic Games seems to be the "sporting event of choice" for ambush marketers. In the 1984 Olympics, Fuji was the official program sponsor of the Games at considerable cost of $40 million. Their competitors, Kodak, became the 'sponsor' of the U.S. track team and of ABC television's broadcast of the Games. Its film thereby became the official film of the U.S. track team, and it also proceeded to use the network's own set of symbols to advertise its merchandise. Arguably one of the greatest ambush moments in the Olympic history occurred in 1992 when Michael Jordan (a Nike icon) covered the Reebok logo with the American flag. Likewise the 1996 Atlanta Games are remembered for Nike's aggressive ambush marketing campaign against Reebok, the official Olympic sportswear partner. Nike bought up advertising billboards throughout the city and established "Nike Town" on the edge of the Olympic park

Other notable Olympic campaigns include American Express's cat-fight of a sort with VISA over two Winter Olympics: "The Olympics only take VISA . . ."(VISA – the official sponsor) vs. "You don't need a visa to travel To Norway . . ." (AMEX). Additionally, the following Olympic ambush moment occurred in Vancouver where the chief executive of the Vancouver Organizing Committee for the 2010 Winter Olympic Games used public pressure in order to get Imperial Oil/Esso, a Canadian petroleum company, to modify a marketing campaign which was accused of constituting ambush marketing.

Imperial Oil/Esso formulated a "Cheer on Canada/Torino, Italy" campaign which involved a competition with prizes of tickets to attend men's and women's Olympic ice hockey games in Turin. Although the competition did not use any Olympic symbols, by referring to the Olympic Games it created an unauthorized association with the Olympic Games in Turin and with the Canadian Olympic team. Although Imperial Oil/Esso is a sponsor of the national governing body (Hockey Canada) and the national team, it is not a sponsor of either the Olympic Games or the Canadian Olympic team. Finally, there is the more recent Nike campaign surrounding the London Games where Nike, not an official sponsor, ran a television advertising campaign "Find your greatness" celebrating athletes of all abilities competing in places called London, but, again, they were "Londons" outside of the UK, so London in Nigeria and London, USA.[29]

Other notable ambushing examples in the realm of sport and entertainment include:[30]

- **Bavaria beer** – Budweiser was the official beer of the 2010 World Cup, but during the Holland vs. Denmark match, 36 attractive women in bright orange mini-skirts descended upon the crowd and stole the show by standing, dancing, and waving their arms in the air. What's the problem you might be asking? Well, they weren't exactly there for the party atmosphere. Allegedly sent by the Dutch beer company, Bavaria, they ambushed the match to subtly promote the Bavaria brand. The dresses only featured a tiny outer label with the Bavaria name but just before the World Cup, the Dutch beer company made sure the dresses had instant brand association by arranging to have one modelled by the well-known wife of Dutch midfielder, Rafael van der Vaart in advertising spots.[31] Budweiser, as official beer sponsor and with tens of millions less in their coffers for the privilege, complained to FIFA and the ladies were swiftly escorted out of the stadium. The two "alleged organizers" were arrested by South African police and football pundit Robbie Earle, to whom the seats were originally allocated, was fired by ITV.
- **Lufthansa** – at the 2006 World Cup, Lufthansa painted a soccer ball on the nose of many of its planes to the annoyance of FIFA and Emirates Air which paid a substantial sum to FIFA to be an official sponsor.
- **Pringles** not only mirrored their product to look like a tennis ball canister but conveniently placed around 24,000 of these cans outside Wimbledon, and the imaginative ambush marketing stunt certainly caught a lot of attention.
- **Vodafone**, noting that the publicity may be utilized to create sales, enlisted a streaker with Vodafone logo printed across their backside to run across the field prior to an All Blacks, (New Zealand Rugby) game. The game was sponsored by Telecome.
- **BMW'**s recent response to an Audi billboard advertisement in Santa Monica, California where Audi noted "your move BMW"; their response Checkmate with a billboard three times the size.

LONDON 2012 SPONSORS AND AMBUSH – AND THE LESSONS FOR RIO 2016

Jason Smith from the sports law division of Brabners Chaffe Street examines some of the ambush marketing that took place around this summer's Olympic Games and the lessons that Rio 2016 must learn if it is to continue to convince domestic sponsors to pay such lucrative rights fees.

It is estimated that the International Olympic Committee's (IOC) TOP sponsorship programme earned approximately US$866 million in the four-year cycle covering the 2006 winter Olympic Games and the 2008 summer Olympic Games, with companies such as Coca-Cola, Visa and McDonald's estimated to have paid up to US$100 million each.

In the midst of a severe global economic downturn, Locog surpassed a sponsorship target of UK£700 million for the London Games. Sochi 2014 and Rio 2016 will vastly exceed this sum, with Rio 2016 estimated to have generated close to US$1 billion from its first three partner deals.

Brabners Chaffe Street advised LloydsTSB, Adidas, Thomas Cook and Nielsen on their deals with Locog and, more recently with Michael Payne, assisted Banco Bradesco on its negotiation with Rio 2016.

London 2012 ambush marketing

Amid much controversy, the UK government introduced one of the most stringent anti-ambush marketing pieces of legislation ever for the Games (the 2006 Act). Essentially, whilst prohibiting the use of certain words, the Act also prohibited any entity from creating any 'association' with the Games unless authorised by Locog (the association right). This gave Locog a massive weapon and the questions were to what extent it would need and choose to use it.

There were many infringements at a lower level where Locog was very quick to act, such as banning a butcher from displaying a sign using sausages to create the Olympic rings and requiring an 81-year-old grandmother to remove a doll's jumper for sale at a charity fair bearing the Olympic rings.

However, at a higher level the much anticipated wave of ambush marketing didn't happen. Whilst the threat of the Act will have been a deterrent, it was also reported that there had been many conversations between Locog and non-Games sponsors at a very senior level in an attempt to persuade such brands not to run ambush campaigns.

Two campaigns though are worth noting in the context of the Rio Games. Nike launched a global ad campaign 'Find Your Greatness' featuring ordinary athletes competing around the world in places outside England that happened to be called London, such as the parish of Little London in Jamaica. A series of Nike press and poster advertisements appeared in many prominent sites in London including Oxford Circus and Piccadilly Circus. Nike then linked the campaign into its Nike+ digital ecosystem, a concept with over 8.5 million worldwide members, aiming to make the day of the Games' closing ceremony the most active day ever recorded with people encouraged to share their experiences through social media, including Nike's own social platforms. It was reported that Locog's legal team examined the campaign but decided that it did not infringe the association right.

The world-famous American rapper Dr Dre also received much publicity for providing Beats by Dre headphones to certain athletes in their national colours, which were used by many immediately pre-competition. With Beats enjoying a 53 per cent share of the US$1 billion headphone market in 2011, the distinctive headphones quickly became the athlete 'must have' item of the Games.

Finally, Rule 40 of the Olympic charter provides that no athlete may allow his/her image to be used

11

for advertising purposes during an Olympic Games, clearly to prevent non-Games sponsors using images of athletes during a Games. Many athletes in London, however, criticised the rule. Defending 100 metre hurdles champion Dawn Harper tweeted a photo with her mouth covered by tape reading 'Rule 40'. A number of athletes, including Usain Bolt, are now preparing to lobby the IOC.

Lessons for Rio

1. Anti-ambush marketing legislation

Even with the 2006 Act in place, some non-Games sponsors engaged in highly successful campaigns. To support its bid to host the 2016 Games, Brazil introduced Law No. 12035. Like the 2006 Act, it forbids the use of many symbols linked to the 2016 Games and the use of terms which have sufficient similarity to those symbols to create association with the 2016 Games. However, it appears that the legislation does not go as far as the 2006 Act in prohibiting activity which would otherwise create an association.

Brazil has a population of almost 200 million and in 2011 the International Monetary Fund (IMF) ranked it seventh in the top ten largest economies in the world. With such a vibrant economy, inevitably non-Games sponsor brands will do all they can to create association with the Rio Games without falling foul of the law. At the same time, with the first three Rio 2016 partners having paid close to US$1 billion, these partners are highly likely to seek the greatest assurances from Rio 2016 that it will have and enforce powers to prevent non-Games sponsors gaining general association with the 2016 Games. Clearly, the current legislation will not enable Rio 2016 to do that.

2. Broadcasting

In the UK over 50 million people watched the Games on television at some point. However, unlike the BBC – a public broadcaster that carries no advertising or broadcast sponsorship – the domestic rights holder for the Rio Games will be a commercial broadcaster, Globo.

Whilst Globo will inevitably have to offer advertising opportunities to IOC and Rio 2016 partners first, in the absence of a law providing the protection of the 2006 Act the likelihood of non-Games sponsors creating an association through this medium will be far greater.

Television advertising will by no means be the only form of media through which such ambusher brands will run their campaigns. As the 'social media Games', London 2012 reportedly saw more tweets posted each day than during the entire duration of Beijing 2008. Over the course of the Games TOP Partner Coca-Cola amassed over 44 million combined Facebook fans, Twitter followers and YouTube subscribers. Brazil has 46 million internet users and is amongst the fastest growing markets for Facebook. Given the fact that there is a further four years until the Rio Games, social media will clearly be a massive platform for both sponsors and non-Games sponsors.

3. Athletes and Rule 40

Rio 2016 will need to keep a close eye for activities such as Dr Dre's in enforcing the IOC's clean venue guidelines but it will also need to keep a close eye on the Rule 40 situation. Combine the current potential for non-Games sponsors to create an association with the likely rollout of such campaigns through Globo and Brazil's social media network and if non- Games sponsors are also able to use the images of competing athletes during the Rio Games, Rio 2016 partners may well be questioning whether they are receiving value for money

Source: http://www.sportspromedia.com/guest_blog/london_2012_sponsors_and_ambush_and_the_lessons_for_rio_2016. Credit: www.sportspromedia.com.

Do most ambush marketing tactics work for organizations that do not want to pay the cost for official Olympic sponsorship? The answer to this question seems to be an overwhelming yes. Studies have shown that most consumers cannot correctly identify the true Olympic sponsors. Research from the Chartered Institute of Marketing (CIM) revealed that brands that adopted ambush marketing strategies enjoyed more public recognition than the official Olympic sponsors.[32] The study, which questioned 1,000 adults regarding brands associated with the Olympics in an official or nonofficial capacity, found that 33 percent of consumers linked either Adidas or Reebok with the Sydney Games despite the fact that neither were official Olympic partners.

On the positive side, Coca-Cola, an official partner of the Games, achieved the most recognition, with 22 percent of respondents associating the soft drinks brand with the Olympics. However, other sponsors fared less well, with Visa International, Samsung, Panasonic, and IBM all scoring less than 5 percent in terms of public recognition. In the case of Visa, this lack of awareness was put into even more perspective by the fact that its main rival, American Express, scored higher recognition despite not being an official sponsor.

BEATS BY DRE GIVES HEADPHONES TO BRITISH ATHLETES, ANGERING IOC

LONDON – Dr. Dre has made his mark on the 2012 Olympics by launching an ambush marketing campaign that has infuriated Olympic chiefs.

The rapper came up with the idea of sending athletes special versions of his Beats headphones, complete with personalization and decked out in national colors.

Rapper Dr. Dre sent Olympic athletes special versions of his Beats headphones. (Getty Images)

Dre and his public relations and marketing teams devised the plan to send batches of the headphones to Great Britain athletes, despite the detailed regulations of the International Olympic Committee that prohibit "advertising" from companies that do not hold official Olympic rights.

Several swimmers and members of the British soccer team have been spotted wearing the headphones. The IOC is considering what action to take. It is unlikely the athletes can be ordered not to wear the items, but they could be prevented from mentioning them in interviews via social media.

"If there is a blatant attempt at ambush marketing or by a group of people with commercial views then of course we will intervene," IOC president Jacques Rogge said.

Tennis players, archers and platform divers, mainly from Britain, were also seen with the flag-emblazoned headphones. There was speculation the success of the project would lead to Beats by Dre offering similar handouts to athletes from other nations.

The popularity of Beats by Dre began to grow during the 2008 Games in Beijing after the company gave headphones to LeBron James and he distributed them to the rest of the NBA players on Team USA. Upon their arrival in Beijing, several of the players were wearing the headphones as the international media greeted them.

The IOC is especially angered as it has an official electronics partner in Panasonic whose interests it is likely to take action to protect.

"We have to be careful because without these measures there could be no sponsorships and without sponsorships there would be no Olympics," Rogge said.

The ambush by Dre has been particularly successful in the Aquatics Centre, with virtually every swimmer at the Games now using headphones to tune out background noise as they walk toward the pool before races.

The situation is the latest in a series of headaches the IOC has suffered in relation to its stringent brand-protection measures. American athletes, including 400-meter sprinter Sanya Richards-Ross, have criticized Rule 40, the IOC code-of-conduct regulation that prevents competitors from using social media to mention their sponsors.

A marketing expert also claimed the rigidity of the regulations has actually allowed some non-sponsors to benefit by positioning themselves as "underdog" brands.

"Everyone has been trying to protect the brands that have invested so much money in the Games," said Gavin Lewis of the Hope and Glory marketing agency. "But in being so strict about what can be done, they have made a rod for their own backs in the sense that they have allowed other brands to get in."

Source: Article author: Martin Rogers. Rightsholder: Yahoo Sports; http://sports.yahoo.com/news/olympics--beats-by-dre-gives-headphones-to-british-athletes--angering-ioc.html. Reprinted with permission from Yahoo. © 2014 Yahoo.

Because ambush marketing tactics are effective and consumers do not really care (only 20 percent of consumers said that they were angered by corporations engaging in ambush marketing), it appears that there is no end in sight for this highly competitive tactic. However, harsh preventive measures are taking place to protect the investments of the actual sponsors of the Olympic Games. As the accompanying article indicates, the IOC continually enacts measures to protect its sponsors.

SPOTLIGHT ON SPORTS MARKETING ETHICS

BRAZIL: Congress adopts legislation to curb ambush marketing during 2016 Summer Olympics

Shortly after Rio de Janeiro was selected to host the 2016 Summer Olympic and Paralympic Games, the Congress passed The Olympic Act (Law 12,035/09 of October 1, 2009). The Act contains a number of special rules required for the carrying out of the Olympic Games, among them specific provisions designed to protect the official symbols and curb ambush marketing during the events.

Under Article 6, federal authorities are responsible for monitoring, investigating and suppressing any unlawful acts that violate the rights in the Olympic symbols in connection with the Rio 2016 Games. The Act broadly defines the symbols as:

- all graphically distinctive signs, flags, mottos, emblems and anthems used by the International Olympic Committee (IOC);
- the names "Olympic Games," "Paralympic Games," "Rio 2016 Olympic Games," "Rio 2016 Paralympic Games," "XXXI Olympic Games," "Rio 2016," "Rio Olympics," "Rio 2016 Olympics," "Rio Paralympics," "Rio 2016 Paralympics" and other abbreviations and variations, and also those equally relevant that may be created for the same purposes, in any language, including those in connection with websites;
- the name, emblem, flag, anthem, motto and trademarks and other symbols of the Rio 2016 Organizing Committee; and
- the mascots, trademarks, torches and other symbols in connection with the XXXI Olympic Games, Rio 2016 Olympic Games and Rio 2016 Paralympic Games.

Further, the Act expressly dictates that unless previously and expressly authorized by the Rio 2016 Games Organizing Committee or the IOC, the use of any symbols in connection with the Rio 2016 Games, whether or not for commercial use, is forbidden.

Also, the Act takes aim at ambush marketing practices in Article 8, where the above prohibition is enlarged to also cover the use of terms and expressions that, albeit outside the list of symbols mentioned in this law, are "sufficiently similar to them to the extent that they are able to invoke an undue association of any products and services whatsoever, or even any company, transaction or event, with the Rio 2016 Games or Olympic Movement."

The Act complements the already-existing rules of other statutes and treaties, which can be used to protect the Olympic symbols and curb ambush marketing. These include the following:

- the Nairobi Treaty for the protection of the Olympic symbol;
- the Brazilian Industrial Property Law (Law 9,279/96), which prohibits the registration as marks of names, prizes or symbols of official sporting events, as well as imitations likely to cause confusion, except when authorized by the competent authority or entity promoting the event;
- the Pelé Law (Law 9,615/98), a provision of which grants the Brazilian Olympic Committee exclusive rights in relation to the flags, mottos, anthems and Olympic symbols, as well as to the names "jogos olímpicos," "olimpíadas," "jogos paraolímpicos" and "paraolimpíadas";
- the copyright protection afforded to symbols, designs and mascots, as well as any other works;
- the protection afforded to the name and image (likeness) of athletes by the Brazilian Civil Code, as well as the Pelé Law;
- rules against unfair competition provided in international agreements such as the Paris Convention and the TRIPS

Agreement and in the Brazilian Industrial Property Law;

- rules against unjust enrichment provided in the Brazilian Civil Code; and
- specific rules against ambush marketing provided by the Code of Ethics of CONAR (Conselho Nacional de Auto-Regulamentação Publicitária, the National Advertising Self-Regulating Council), a private entity created in 1980 by local advertisers, advertising agencies and media companies.

Similar legislation that will apply to the soccer World Cup 2014 in Brazil is under consideration in the Brazilian Senate.

Although every effort has been made to verify the accuracy of items carried in the INTA Bulletin, readers are urged to check independently on matters of specific concern or interest.

Vice Chair of the INTA Bulletin Committee.

Source: Article authors: Rodrigo Borges Carneiro, Dannemann Siemsen Bigler, and Ipanema Moreira. Rightsholder: International Trademark Association; http://www.inta.org/INTABulletin/Pages/BRAZIL CongressAdoptsLegislationto CurbAmbush Marketing During2016SummerOlympics.aspx. Reprinted with permission from INTA Bulletin Vol. 65, No. 2, January 15 2010. Copyright 2010 International Trademark Association, Authors Rodrigo Borges Carneiro, Dannemann Siemsen Bigler, and Ipanema Moreira.

Arguably the most effective means for organizers of sporting events to block out unauthorized advertising is to negotiate deals with stadium owners (which may be, for example, cities, sports clubs, or operating companies), which allow organizers to fully control advertising on the premises. For example, the organizer may demand the stadium to be handed over as a clean site, so that the stadium would have to be cleared of all advertising by unofficial sponsors. The organizer may also require the stadium to be renamed for the time of the event and control access to the stadium grounds, including the airspace above. By cleverly designing the general terms and conditions of ticket sales, organizers can even impose dress codes on the spectators, enabling the exclusion of those wearing shirts or caps which display the logos of nonsponsors.

For example,[33] even though Burger King was an official sponsor of the Olympic Games of London they launched a campaign with focus on the competition. In his official Twitter profile, Brazilian fighter Anderson Silva, who's the poster boy of the fast food chain, anticipated that for each medal that Brazil conquers in London, Burger King will pay double french fries in the company's restaurants the next day. The promotion is available only for the combos.

Reaching target markets

Reaching new target markets is another primary objective of sponsorship programs. One of the unique features and benefits of sponsorship as a promotional medium is its ability to reach people who are attracted to sports entities because they share a common interest. Therefore, sporting events represent a natural forum for psychographic segmentation of consumers, that is, reaching consumers with similar activities, interests, and opinions (AIOs). Stephen Cannon, Vice President of

Marketing for Mercedes-Benz USA sums up their four-year sponsorship deal with the U.S. Open Tennis, replacing Lexus as the Official Vehicle of the U.S. Open by saying, "The partnership with the USTA aligns with our strategy to place Mercedes- Benz at the forefront of marquee events. The Open takes place in one of our most important markets and is an unrivaled opportunity to uniquely connect with fans and attendees."[34] Recognizing the growth of global markets, Mercedes- Benz announced a ten-year agreement for the newly rebranded Mercedes-Benz arena in Shanghai, China. The 18,000 seat arena is the first naming rights deal for Mercedes- Benz outside of Germany and creates a powerful precedent in the global sports marketplace.

Lauded as the world's premier big-wave surf event, the 2010 Mavericks Surf Contest presented by Sony Ericsson was earmarked as the season's most anticipated big-wave surf occurrence. "Sony Ericsson is an incredibly innovative company, and they will capture all of the breathtaking and spectacular action using their mobile devices on Contest Day. And as an environmentally responsible organization, we really appreciate Sony Ericsson's strong efforts toward conservation and recycling," said Mavericks CEO Keir J. Beadling. On Contest Day, spectators are encouraged to bring their old mobile phones to the Sony Ericsson tent to be recycled or take a minute and recharge their current mobile phones. All proceeds from the recycling program will be donated to helping the coastline.[35]

Jetsetter launched a series of NCAA Men's Basketball themed ticket and hotel packages for the 2012 "March Madness" championship series. The flash sale travel site often offered one-of-a-kind ticket and experience packages for events like the Superbowl and Kentucky Derby with deals including but not limited to:

- Packages to each of the Second, Third, Sweet Sixteen and Elite Eight rounds. Each package includes two game tickets and a two-night hotel stay in the city of play. Prices vary by city and date and range from $800–$1,350.
- Four VIP Packs to the Final Four and Championship games, each of which includes two tickets to each of the games in New Orleans (total of three games), a four- night stay at The Ritz Carlton, dinners by acclaimed Chef John Besh and Iron Chef Marc Forgione, drinks from a top mixologist at Club 44, and a meal with a coaching legend. Package is $2,995.
- Two Final Four Ultimate VIP Packs with lower, 100-level seating at the Tournament. Also includes a $100 Jetsetter credit. Package is $3,500.[36]

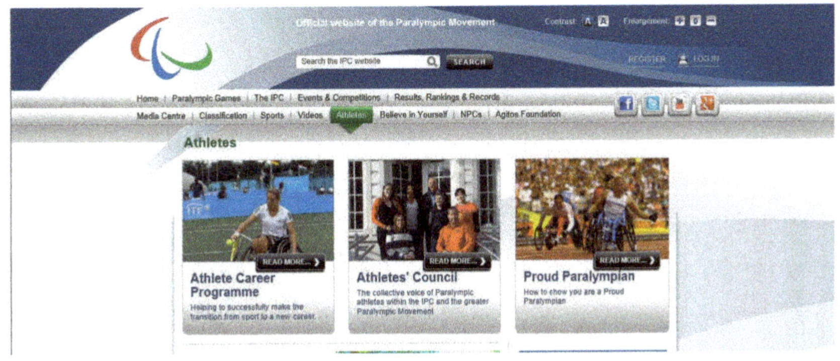

Web 11.1 Disabled athletes compete in Paralympic games

Source: U.S. Paralympics/U.S. Olympic Committee

11

Consider the following examples of how sponsors have attempted to reach new and sometimes difficult-to-capture audiences: The X-Games represent a perfect opportunity to reach Generation Xers, a target market that is "difficult to reach through traditional media." Another target market that has been neglected includes the millions of disabled Americans. With the growth of the Paralympic Games and programs such as A Sporting Chance, which provide opportunities for people with disabilities to participate in sports, marketers are now addressing this market. Begun in 1960 as an event "parallel" to the Olympics, the Paralympics have blossomed into a major competition of their own. The Paralympic Games are a multisport, multidisability competition of elite, world-class athletes held approximately two weeks after the regular Olympics in the same host city. "The Paralympic Games have truly come home and found their pathway to the future here in London," Sir Philip Craven declared to the 80,000 in attendance. Just consider some of the impressive numbers. More than 4,000 athletes from 164 teams competed. The London Paralympics have sold more tickets than any previous Games and been broadcast to more people in more countries. More than 2.7 million tickets were sold for the London Games, which is 900,000 more than in Beijing.[37] Perhaps the fastest growing target market for many marketers interested in sports sponsorship opportunities is women, and the growth of women's sports is taking place at all levels. More and more women are participating in sports and watching sports, which has created opportunities for equipment and apparel manufacturers as well as for broadcast media. In addition, marketing to women through the athletic medium has become an interesting and valuable tool for corporate America. In short, women are becoming the target market of choice for sports marketers.

Although women are growing in importance to sports marketers, relatively little is known about the sponsorship decisions relative to women's sport. What are the women's sports that are experiencing the most sponsorship growth? As seen in Table 11.4, at the collegiate level, soccer, golf, lacrosse, cross country, and softball have all grown in sponsorship spending at a rate of over 100 percent in the last 25 years. Additionally, only two sports (field hockey and gymnastics) have shown a decrease in spending.
A study by Nancy Lough and Richard Irwin was designed to better understand corporate sponsorship of women's sport.[38] The study questioned whether corporate sport sponsorship decision makers differ with respect to why they sponsor women's sport versus more "traditional" sponsorship opportunities. The authors found that

Table 11.4 NCAA women's sports sponsorship growth

Sport	% Growth over 25 years
Soccer	1041%
Golf	286%
Lacrosse	151%
Cross Country	125%
Softball	119%
Outdoor Track	65%
Volleyball	63%
Basketball	45%
Tennis	44%
Swimming	41%
Field Hockey	–4%
Gymnastics	–35%

Table 11.5 Importance of corporate sports sponsorship objectives by sports sponsorship type

Mean ratings (1 – 7) Objective	General	Women's
Increase sales/market share	5.94	5.72
Increase target market awareness	5.88	5.89
Enhance general company image	5.81	5.94
Increase public awareness of company	5.56	5.53
Demonstrate community involvement	4.75	4.88
Build trade relations	4.50	4.29
Build trade goodwill	4.31	4.24
Demonstrate social responsibility	4.19	4.57
Block/preempt the competition	4.19	4.00
Enhance employee relations	3.76	3.78
Demonstrate corporate philanthropy	3.13	3.71

corporate decision makers are more concerned with meeting objectives related to image building and increasing target market awareness, as opposed to building sales and market share. Summarized results of the research are shown in Table 11.5.

Relationship marketing

As discussed in Chapter 10, **relationship marketing**, building long-term relationships with customers, is one of the most important issues for sports marketers in today's competitive marketing environment. Building relationships with clients or putting the principles of relationship marketing to work is another sponsorship objective. Corporate hospitality managers see to it that sponsors are given ample space to "wine and dine" current or perspective clients.

Companies began throwing more lavish sports-related parties at the Super Bowl during the mid-1980s. David M. Carter of The Sports Business Group, a Los Angeles- based sports consulting firm, says the demand for corporate sports hospitality has grown "exponentially" since then. "As sports' fan base has shifted from the everyday fan to the corporate fan, these events have increasingly catered to fans who are there to conduct business-to-business marketing," Carter says. These companies are trying to generate new business and keep current clients as well.

When Bank of America became the sponsor of the BAC Colonial Tournament, the company wanted to create a touring hospitality program that would further enhance the bank's "Higher Standards" brand statement and give them a fitting opportunity to socialize with a large number of current and prospective customers.

"Banking is done at the local level so we use hospitality as a one-to-one relationship building opportunity and a very key part of our marketing mix," said David Jessey, former senior vice president of sponsorship marketing for Bank of America. "Hospitality is more than a sign or a commercial. It is a higher standards experience that the guest actively takes part in."

The result was Hogan's Alley, an environment that resembled more of a leather-clad country club than simply a tent serving hot dogs and cold beverages. The area included a library filled with golf magazines and books on legendary golfer Ben Hogan, a conversation area, a large bar and dining area and cocktail tables.

To measure the business impact of Hogan's Alley and determine the tangible results of its investment from their attendees after their experience, Bank of America established a database for all their guests. The company offered high-end door prizes for guests who completed detailed surveys querying them about the event and their banking activities. According to company research,[39] Bank of America determined that 96 percent of attendees were satisfied with the experience, 73 percent said it was the best corporate hospitality they had ever experienced, and 84 percent said it strengthened their relationship with the bank. More than 88 percent of attendees stated that they were more likely to consider using the bank because of the experience.

Very few academic studies have explored company attitudes toward corporate hospitality or the effectiveness of this activity, but recently Bennett looked at this growing sports marketing function. He found that two-thirds of the companies he surveyed believed that "highly formal" procedures were applied to the management of corporate hospitality and that one-third of the expenses were incorporated into marketing budgets. Additionally, two-thirds of the companies responding to the survey said that the decision on choice of events for corporate hospitality was based on "the in-house assessment of the goodness of the match between corporate hospitality activities and specific clients." Two-thirds of the companies felt that corporate hospitality was a vital element of the marketing mix and even if faced with a recession would not cut their budget in this area. Finally, companies stated that the greatest benefit of corporate hospitality activities was retaining profitable customers.[40]

How much are organizations willing to pay to retain and gain customers? Here's just a glimpse at the prices for hospitality areas at the U.S. Open, hosted at Congressional Golf Course in Bethesda, Maryland. Incidentally, all of these areas sold out:[41]

Where: Founders Pub – located in the Congressional Club House

Highlights: Exclusive use with seating of 120 guests; 200 weekly ticket packages; 8 weekly staff ticket packages; access to a preferred grandstand; 50 preferred parking passes; pre-open golf outing for 8 executives

Cost: $475,000, not including food and beverage

Where: Pro Shop – located in the Congressional Clubhouse

Highlights: Exclusive use of pro shop with seating for 50 guests; 100 weekly ticket packages; 6 weekly staff ticket packages; 40 preferred parking passes; pre-open outing for 4 executives

Cost: $225,000, not including food and beverage

Where: Presidential Village – located on the 1st hole of the Gold course, left of the 18th green of the Championships course

Highlights: Exclusive use of 40 × 40 tent for seating of 80 guests; 100 weekly ticket packages; 6 weekly staff ticket packages; 40 preferred parking passes; pre-open outing for 4 executives

Cost: $195, 000, not including food and beverage

Where: Capitol Club – located in the main ballroom of the Congressional Clubhouse

Highlights: Includes 15 weekly ticket packages; 1 weekly staff ticket package; 5 preferred parking passes; reserve table for the week with seating for 10

Cost: $45,000 ($35,000 – table and admission + $10,000 food and beverage fee)

Although corporate sponsors and their clients live and die by the relationships they forge, the community is another public with which sponsors want to build relationships. Many corporate sponsors believe returning something to the community is an important part of sponsoring a sporting event. With the 2012 Shell Houston Open raising 2.2 million alone, the PGA Tour regular golf tournaments passed $130 million in total charity contributions since 1974. Combined with charitable donations from the Champions and Nationwide events, more than $1.4 billion has been generated for charities over the history of the PGA Tour.[42, 43]

"The outstanding work that is done by our tournaments, players, volunteers and sponsors is an integral part of what the PGA TOUR is all about, and our 'Together, anything's possible' platform will enable us to tell that story in a more compelling way," PGA TOUR Commissioner Tim Finchem said. "Their charitable efforts too often are underappreciated on a national scale, so we want to tell the stories of how they are changing people's lives and provide a means by which individuals can support their favorite causes through 'Together, anything's possible.'"[44]

Image building

Perhaps the most important reason for sponsorship of a sports entity at any level is to maintain or build an image. **Image building** is a two-way street for both the sponsoring organization and the sports entity. The sponsoring organization associates itself and/or its brands with the positive images generated by the unique personality of the sporting event. Ferrand and Pages describe the process of finding a congruence between event and sponsor as "looking for the perfect wedding."[45] The researchers also point out that "any action toward sponsoring an event should begin with an analysis of the common and unique attributes of the event and the brand or product." Waste Management showcased their "green" initiatives through title sponsorship of the Waste Management Phoenix Open. As the following article illustrates, Waste Management utilizes the sponsorship platform to show people ways to better understand and "green up" their businesses.

BEHIND THE SCENES AT THE 2013 WASTE MANAGEMENT OPEN

Waste Management's Zero Waste Challenge returns in 2013 to the Waste Management Phoenix Open. The sustainability program continues to highlight the tournament as the "Greenest Show on Grass".

The 2012 Waste Management Phoenix Open achieved the highest diversion rate of any major sporting event and was the first-ever major sporting event not to use trash receptacles. In the program's inaugural year, more than 97% of tournament waste was diverted from the landfill. The goal this year is 100%!

"Considering the phenomenal attendance at the Waste Management Phoenix Open, the Zero Waste Challenge is a significant achievement led by the Waste Management Sustainability Services team and embraced by tournament organizers, The Thunderbirds, and tournament vendors and patrons," said David Aardsma, Waste Management Chief Sales and Marketing Officer. "In 2013, Waste Management continues the Zero Waste Challenge and will highlight our sustainability and environmental solutions around the course."

Join corporate marketers, Steve Neff of Waste Management and Tom King, Assistant Tournament Chairman and member of The Thunderbirds, talk about the value of this incredible sports marketing sponsorship, as well as take a behind the scenes look at what goes into a sports sponsorship like this one.

Waste Management is the leading provider of comprehensive waste management services in North America. Through its subsidiaries, the company provides collection, transfer, recycling and resource recovery and disposal services. It is one of the largest residential recyclers and also a leading developer, operator and owner of waste-to-energy and landfill gas-to-energy facilities in North America. The company's customers include residential, commercial, industrial and municipal customers throughout North America.

Source: Rightsholder: BMA; http://bmaphoenix.org/events/behind-the-scenes-at-the-2013-waste-management-open/. Credit: Business Marketing Association (BMA), Phoenix Chapter.

Gillette and Major League Baseball have had an historic sponsorship agreement for the past 72 years, extending the longest running sponsorship association of any U.S. sports league into its ninth decade, since 1939. "The MLB relationship serves as a venue for Gillette to reach the oft-elusive male target. Gillette is a sports marketing pioneer that paved the way for modern day sports sponsorship and endorsements," said Tim Brosnan, Executive Vice President, Business, Major League Baseball. "Baseball is a sport steeped in history and tradition, and Gillette's integral role in our game will continue into the next decade." "Major League Baseball has been an important partner for Gillette for more than 80 years," said Gene Barbato, Marketing Director, Gillette. "We look forward to working together as we strengthen the natural link between Gillette, baseball and men."[46]

Consider an event like the Summer Extreme Games (X-Games), which possess a well-defined image that includes characteristics such as aggressiveness, hip, cool, no fear, and no rules. The image of extreme sports such as skysurfing, street luge, or the adventure race will certainly "rub off" or become associated with the sponsoring organization. Taco Bell, Nike, and Mountain Dew will take on the characteristics of the extreme sports, and the image of their products will be maintained or enhanced. "Sponsorship is an opportunity to directly touch consumers and be true to the lifestyle of the brand," explains Chris Fuentes, former VP-marketing at Nautica. "It lets you have a conversation with consumers."

In Chapter 9, the **match-up hypothesis** was described as the more congruent the image of the endorser with the image of the product being promoted, the more effective the message. This simple principle also holds true for sponsorship. However, the image of the sports entity (remember, this may be an event, individual athlete, group of athletes, or team) should be congruent with the actual or desired image of the sponsor's organization or the product being sponsored. In Figure 11.2, we can see how the image of Taco Bell has shifted toward the X-Games and how the image of the X-Games also shifts toward the sponsor.

Sometimes the "match-up" between sponsor and sports entity is not seen as appropriate. Gatorade joined AT&T and Accenture in denouncing its relationship with Tiger Woods following his extra-marital affairs and, as the accompanying article illustrates, Nike broke ties with Lance Armstrong after his recent debacle regarding the use of illegal supplements.

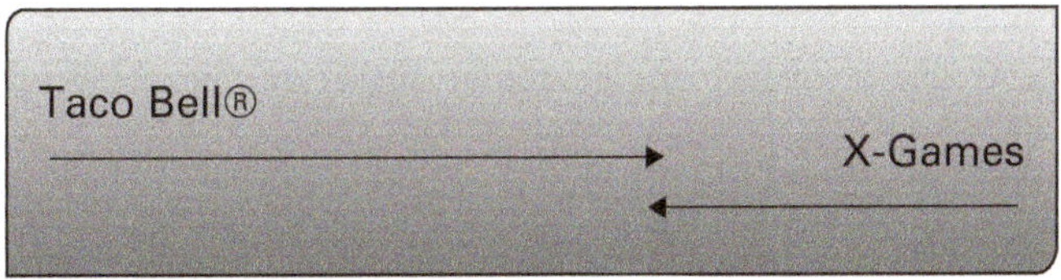

Figure 11.2 Sponsorship match-up

LANCE ARMSTRONG NIKE CONTRACT TERMINATED

Company severs ties with cyclist over doping allegations

NEW YORK – Nike has severed ties with cyclist Lance Armstrong, citing insurmountable evidence that he participated in doping and misled the company about those activities for more than a decade.

The clothing and footwear company said Wednesday that it was terminating Armstrong's contract "with great sadness."

"Nike does not condone the use of illegal performance enhancing drugs in any manner," it said in a statement.

Armstrong said Wednesday, just minutes before the announcement from Nike, that he was stepping down as chairman of his Livestrong cancer-fighting charity so that the organization can steer clear of the whirlwind surrounding its founder.

A representative for Armstrong could not be immediately reached for comment.

Nike Inc., based in Beaverton, Ore., said it plans to continue its support for Livestrong. Anheuser-Busch and the sunglasses company Oakley have already pledged ongoing support for the organization.

The U.S. Anti-Doping Agency released a massive report last week detailing allegations of widespread doping by Armstrong and his teams when he won the Tour de France seven consecutive times from 1999 to 2005.

The 41-year-old Armstrong, who overcame life-threatening testicular cancer, retired from cycling a year ago. He announced in August that he would no longer fight the doping allegations that have dogged him for years.

Nike's courting of top celebrity athletes is well known, as are the inherent risks companies assume when doing so.

After Tiger Woods ran his SUV over a fire hydrant in November 2009, eventually bringing to light his infidelities, Accenture, AT&T Inc. and Gatorade cut ties with him. But EA Sports and Nike stood by the golfer.

Nike signed NFL quarterback Michael Vick to a contract during his rookie year in 2001, but ended that pact in August 2007 after he filed a plea agreement admitting his involvement in a dogfighting ring. Vick spent 21 months in prison.

Nike re-signed Vick, who plays with the Philadelphia Eagles, in July 2011. The company said at that time that it didn't condone Vick's actions, but was supportive of the positive changes he had made to better himself off the field.

Shares of Nike edged slightly higher in early trading.

Source: Article author: Michelle Chapman; http://www.huffingtonpost.com/2012/10/17/lance-armstrong-nike-contract-terminated_n_1973192.html. Used with permission of Bloomberg L.P.

11

In another alcohol-related example, full-page ads in college newspapers called on university leaders, athletic conferences, and the NCAA to "stop the madness" by banning alcohol marketing from college sports. The ads, tied to March Madness and sponsored by the American Medical Association (AMA), ran in college papers in six cities in advance of the NCAA men's basketball tournament: in the *Chronicle of Higher Education* and student newspapers at Georgia Tech, University of Iowa, University of Wisconsin, Indiana University, University of Mississippi, and DePaul University. "The truly insane thing about March basketball is all the money universities get from alcohol advertising," the ads read. An illustration showed cheering sports fans holding signs reading: "Stop the Madness." The ad claimed that the alcohol industry spent more than $52 million to advertise its products during televised college sports in a recent year. Spokesman Bob Williams said the NCAA limits alcohol ads to one minute per hour of broadcast, won't allow ads for hard liquor, and encourages "responsibility themes and messages" in the ads.[47] The AMA has campaigned to the NCAA for years to ban alcohol-related ads.

Philip Morris USA and Philip Morris International (both subsidiaries of Altria) claim they are changed, responsible companies that do not market to kids and are concerned about the health risks of their products. But the companies' actions tell a different story. In the latest example, Philip Morris International is the only tobacco company that continues to sponsor Formula One auto races, which exposes spectators and tens of millions of television viewers worldwide – including millions of children – to the name, logo, and red-and-white colors of the company's best-selling Marlboro cigarettes. Arguably, no responsible company would continue to associate deadly and addictive cigarettes with the excitement and glamour of auto racing, thereby increasing their appeal to children.

Sales increases

The eventual objective for nearly all organizations involved in sponsorship programs is **sales increases**. Although sometimes there is an indirect route to sales (i.e., the hierarchy of effects model of promotional objectives, which states that awareness must come before action or sales), the major objective of sponsorship is to increase the bottom line. Organizations certainly would not spend millions of dollars to lend their names to stadiums or events if they did not feel comfortable about the return on investment. Likewise, the events are developed, in some cases (e.g., the Skins Game and the World's Strongest Man Competition), for the sole purpose of making a profit. Without sponsorship, the event would lose the ability to do so.

It is clear that when organizations are considering a sponsorship program, the first step is to determine the organizational objectives and marketing goals that might be achieved most effectively through sponsorship. However, the primary motivation for organizations participating in sports sponsorships is still unclear. Historically, organizations entered into sponsorships to create awareness and enhance the image of their brands, product lines, or corporations. Numerous studies examining the primary reasons for engaging in sponsorship found increasing awareness and enhancing company image to be the most important objectives.[48] More recently, studies have shown that increasing sales and market share are the primary motives of sponsorship (see Table 11.6).

Regardless of the relative importance of the various sponsorship objectives, organizations must carefully evaluate how the sponsorship will help them achieve their own unique marketing objectives. Along with examining the sponsorship objectives, the organization must find a sponsorship opportunity that fits within the

Table 11.6 Importance of sponsorship objectives

Objectives	Mean Importance Rating
Increase sales and market share	6.14
Increase target market awareness	6.07
Enhance general public awareness	5.88
Enhance general company image	5.47
Enhance trade relations	4.60
Enhance trade goodwill	4.55
Involve community	4.48
Alter public perception	4.15
Enhance employee relations	3.84
Block competition	3.68
Develop social responsibility	3.13
Develop corporate philanthropy	3.12

Source: Doug Morris and Richard L. Irwin, "The Data-Driven Approach to Sponsorship Acquisition," *Sport Marketing Quarterly*, vol. 5, no. 2 (1996), 9.

existing promotion budget. Let us look briefly at the basic budgeting considerations, the next step in the sponsorship model.

Sponsorship budgeting

As with the promotional budget, determining the **sponsorship budgeting methods** includes competitive parity, arbitrary allocation, percentage of sales, and the objective and task method. Because the fundamentals of these budgeting methods have already been discussed, let us examine the sponsorship budgeting process at several organizations.

The only generality to be made about the budgeting process is that decision making varies widely based on the size of the company and its history and commitment to the practice of sponsorship.[49] Larger organizations that have used sponsorship as a form of communication for many years tend to have highly complex structures and those new to sponsorship tend to keep it simpler.

Consider, for example, the budgeting process at Anheuser-Busch. Anheuser-Busch's budgeting process begins with determining the corporate-wide marketing budget. This is usually anywhere from 3 to 5 percent of the previous year's sales (percentage of sales method discussed in Chapter 10). The total budget is then divided among the company's more than 30 brands with Budweiser, the flagship brand, receiving the largest share of the budget. The final decision on budget allocation is made by two high-level management teams, who receive and review potential sponsorships. The first team looks at how the managers plan on supporting their sponsorships with additional promotional mix elements such as point-of-sale merchandising. The second team hears the brand managers present their case and defend their budget.

Although Anheuser-Busch's budgeting process represents a more complex and structured approach, Marriott uses a simpler technique. Marriott, a relative newcomer to sports sponsorship, leaves the whole business to its corporation's hotel and timeshare properties. The same practice holds true for Proctor & Gamble, where managers of individual brands like Tide decide which sponsorship opportunities to pursue and how much money to allocate.

Once specific budgets are allocated, the organization must look for sponsorship opportunities that will meet objectives and still be affordable. To accommodate budgetary constraints, most sports entities offer different levels of sponsorship over a range of sponsorship fees. One example of the cost of sponsorship and the tangible benefits received by the sponsor is the Wegman's title sponsor of the LPGA Championship (see Table 11.7). The professional golf tournament attracts slightly more men (60 percent) than women (40 percent), with more than half of the spectators between 45–64 years old and over half having an average household income of over $100,000. Sponsorship packages are presented in the following areas: hospitality, branding, pro-am, advertising, and tickets. Table 11.7 highlights a few of the sponsorship opportunities within each of these categories.

It is important to note that the sponsorship fee is not the only expense that should be considered. As Brant Wansley of BrandMarketing Services, Ltd., points out, "Buying the rights [to the sponsorship] is one thing, capitalizing on them to get a good return on investment is another . . . . Purchasing a sponsorship is like buying an expensive sports car. In addition to the initial cost, you must invest in the maintenance of the car to ensure its performance."[50] Sponsorship must be integrated with other forms of promotion to maximize its effectiveness. Rod Taylor, senior vice president of the CoActive Marketing Group, adds, "The only thing that you get as a sponsor is a piece of paper saying you've paid to belong. It is up to you as the marketer to convince consumers that you do, in fact, belong!" Bill Chipps, of the IEG Sponsorship Report, says that "the rule of thumb is that for every dollar a company spends on a rights fee, to maximize the sponsorship, they spend another $2 to $3 on leverage."

The average sponsor spends $1.60 to leverage its deals for every $1 it pays in rights fees, according to the IEG/Performance Research Sponsorship Decision-Makers Survey. According to IEG, the survey's high watermark for activation spending was 1.9-to-1. Thirty-five percent of the sponsors said they would increase activation spending over the previous year. Forty-eight percent of these respondents said they would retain the same levels of expenditure, while only 18 percent projected a decrease in their expenditures. Over the past few years, 50 percent of the respondents identified an increase in their return on investment from sponsorship, while only 6 percent identified a decrease on their return on investment.[51]

An excellent example of an organization leveraging its Olympic sponsorship is Coca- Cola. In addition to print and broadcast advertisements, Coca-Cola produced themed collectible Olympic cans and accompanying P-O-P displays to stimulate sales at the retail level. According to Katie Bayne, chief marketing officer of Coca-Cola North America, "The dedication to active living and amazing athletic performances of our Six-Pack of athletes served as an inspiration for these Coca-Cola Olympic Games-themed collectible cans. Our special packaging and overall Coca-Cola Olympic Games program are a great way to celebrate the Games and open a little happiness while enjoying the exciting competition with your friends and family."[52]

Choosing the sponsorship opportunity

Once sponsorship objectives have been carefully studied and financial resources have been allocated, organizations must make decisions regarding the appropriate sponsorship opportunity. Whatever the choices, thoughtful consideration must be given to the potential opportunities.

Choosing the most effective sponsorship opportunity for your organization necessitates a detailed decision-making process. Several researchers have examined

Table 11.7 Wegmans LPGA Championship sponsorship levels

Advertising/Visibility	
Web Site Advertising Banner ad placed on home page of the Wegmans LPGA Championship • www.wegmanslpga.org • Includes banner ad and link • Over 560,000 page views annually • $3,000 Logo placed on the home page of the Wegmans LPGA Championship • www.wegmanslpga.org • Includes logo and link • Over 560,000 page views annually • $1,000	
Electronic Leaderboard Message Package • Your message appears on 6 electronic score boards strategically placed on course • Your message appears for 8 seconds a minimum of 10 times a day • Monday – Sunday • Animated and static graphics • Viewed by 100,000 spectators • $3,000	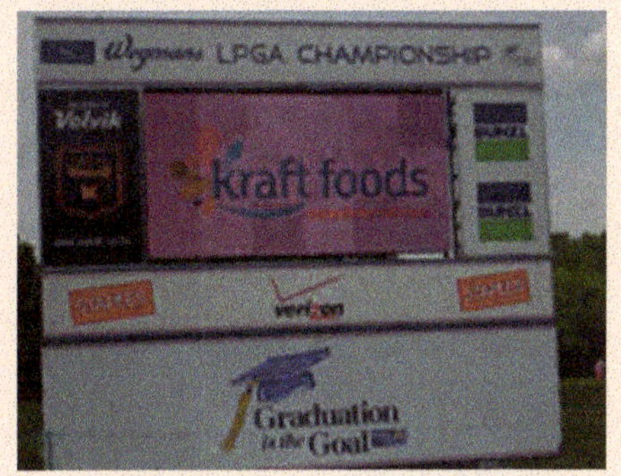
Pairing Sheet Panel Advertising • Full-color panel ad in the daily pairing sheet • Distributed free to all spectators • Monday, Wednesday – Sunday • Ad is 3 (w) x 10 (h) • $5,000	
Tournament Program Advertising 10,000 four-color Tournament Programs distributed at no charge to spectators. Four ad sizes available. **Full page ad** • Full color • 7 ¾ x 10 ¼	

Table 11.7 (continued)

• $2,500 • Includes your choice of one: - 25 good any one day vouchers OR - 6 Clubhouse packages OR - 8 Grounds packages OR - 4 Corporate Suite tickets **Half page ad** • Full color • 3 ⅞ x 10 ¼ • $1,500 • Includes your choice of one: - 12 good any one day vouchers OR - 3 Clubhouse packages OR - 4 Grounds packages OR - 2 Corporate Suite tickets	
Back of Tickets • Your logo is placed on the back of all tournament tickets and passes o Tournament tickets and packages o Clubhouse Tickets o Grounds Tickets o Take away daily ticket • Over 100,000 tickets printed • Tickets are required for all spectators, Monday – Sunday • $15,000 for the entire week • $10,000 for Monday, Tuesday, Wednesday and Thursday OR Friday, Saturday and Sunday	
Branding	
Driving Range Sponsor • Sponsor of the driving range and driving range bleachers • Your logo and signage placed at the driving range for the week • "Seating Courtesy of" signs prominently displayed on the bleacher set • Banner also displayed on the back of bleachers (provided by sponsor, no smaller than 3′ X 6′), • $10,000	

Table 11.7 (continued)

<table>
<tr><td>#1 Bleacher Set
• One bleacher set placed in a high traffic area
• Sponsor Logo and Signage can be placed on the back of bleacher set
• "Seating Courtesy of" signs prominently displayed on bleachers
• $10,000</td><td></td></tr>
<tr><td>9th Green Bleachers Sponsor
• One large set of bleachers located in a high traffic area
• Room for multiple Sponsor Logo and Signage on the back of bleacher set
• "Seating Courtesy of" signs prominently displayed on bleachers
• $10,000</td><td></td></tr>
<tr><td>12th Green Bleacher Set
• One bleacher set on the 12th green
• Your logo and Signage placed on bleacher set
• "Seating Courtesy of" signs prominently displayed on bleachers
• $10,000</td><td></td></tr>
<tr><td>17th Green Bleachers Sponsor
• One large bleacher set on the 17th Green
• Your logo and signage placed on bleacher set
• "Seating Courtesy of" signs prominently displayed on bleachers
• $10,000</td><td></td></tr>
<tr><td>18th Green Bleachers Sponsor
• Corporate logo placed on the front and back of each bleacher set on the 18th green
• "Seating Courtesy of" signs at each stairway
• Viewed by thousands of spectators
• Captured on national television, Thursday – Sunday
• $25,000</td><td></td></tr>
</table>

Table 11.7 (continued)

Caddy Bib Back Sponsor • Your logo prominently displayed on the back of all caddie bibs • Caddies wear the vest on course at all times all during the week (Monday – Sunday) • Viewed by 100,000 spectators • Captured on national television, Thursday – Sunday • $30,000	
Caddy Bib Front Sponsor • Your logo prominently displayed on the front pockets of all caddie bibs • Caddies wear the vest on course at all times all week long (Monday – Sunday) • Viewed by 100,000 spectators • Captured on national television, Thursday – Sunday • $30,000	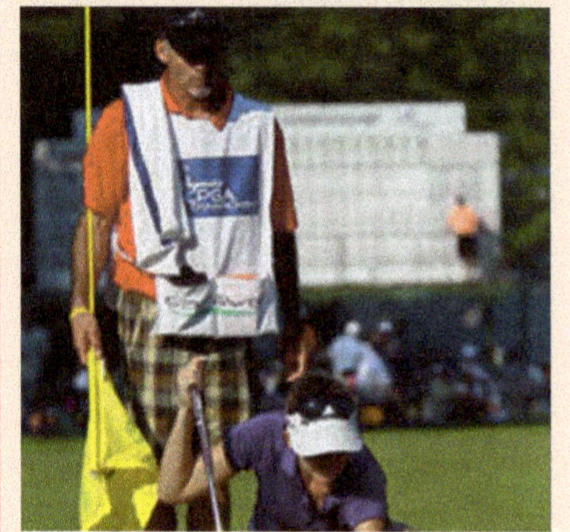
Daily Tournament Sponsor • Your logo will be placed on the front of all tournament tickets • Can distribute literature, coupons, or gift to all spectators at the gate on your designated day • $15,000 for the entire week • $10,000 for Monday, Tuesday, Wednesday and Thursday OR Friday, Saturday and Sunday	
Ecology Box Sponsor • Your one-color logo will appear on one side of the recycle bins and trash boxes • 600 boxes strategically placed on-course • Replaced as needed to keep looking fresh and clean • $15,000	

Table 11.7 (continued)

Electronic Leaderboard Permanent Signage • Permanent signage on 6 electronic score boards strategically placed on course • Also includes your message appearing for 8 seconds a minimum of 10 times a day • Monday – Sunday • Viewed by 100,000 spectators • $15,000	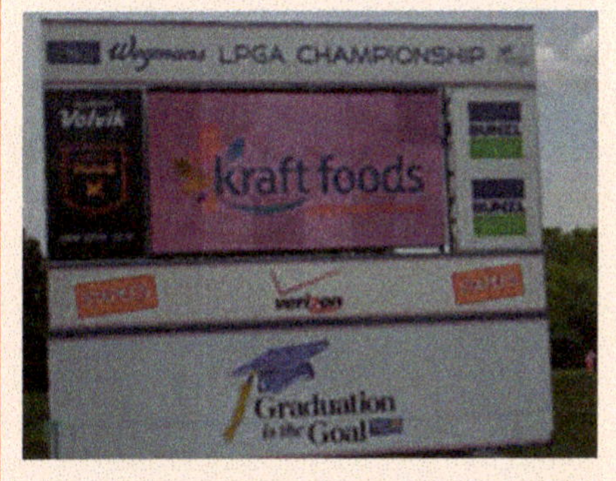
Golf Cart Signage • Sponsorship of the Wegmans LPGA Championship Golf Carts • Logo to be incorporated into the golf cart signage • Approximately 135 golf carts will be on course tournament week • 10 Clubhouse Passes • $11,000	

Media Center Sponsor
Title Sponsor of the Media Center
• Name and logo included on all correspondence with the media
  o Local, regional, national and international
  o Over 233 credentialed media representing 61 national and international media outlets
• Opportunity to build a corporate display inside the Media Center
• Name and logo placed on signage and banners associated with the Media Center
• $30,000

Putting Green Sponsor • Your logo and signage placed at the putting green for the week • Putting green is located by the clubhouse, near the 1st tee in a high traffic area • $15,000	

Table 11.7 (continued)

Quiet Paddles Sponsor • One color logo on 600 Quiet Paddles used on course throughout the week • $15,000	
Premier Community Sponsorship • 10 X 10 sampling space in the Expo Tent - Main entrance to the Wegmans LPGA Championship. Located at the bus loop in a high traffic area - Sampling space includes table, chairs, pipe and drape • Opportunity to interact with 100,000 spectators one-on-one - Sample, demonstrate, distribute literature/coupon, enter to win, etc • 4 Pro-Am playing spots in the Corporate Pro-Am • Full page, four color ad in the Tournament program • Electronic leaderboard message • Recognition on the 18th green during closing ceremony on Sunday • 100 Tournament ticket units • $60,000	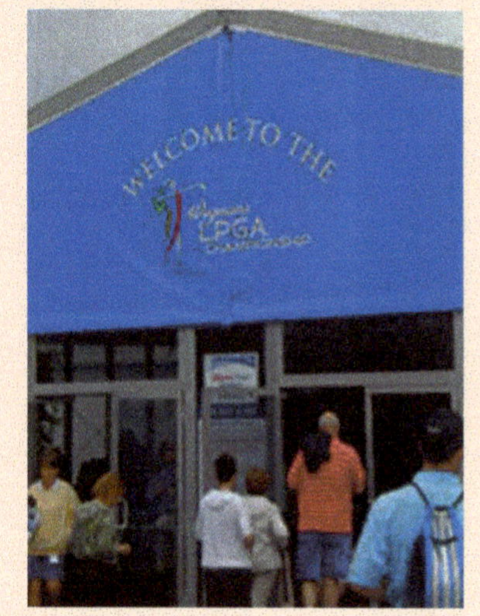
Volunteer Shirt Sponsor Your logo placed on all volunteer uniform shirts • 1,200 volunteer shirts • Volunteers are required to wear their shirts on course, Monday – Sunday • Has shelf life and are worn throughout the community for years • Captured on national TV • 4 Pro-Am playing spots in the Corporate Pro-Am • Full page ad in the Tournament Program • $35,000	
Volunteer Tent Sponsor Naming Rights to the Volunteer Tent • Located near Expo Entrance/Exit, in a high traffic area • Open to all volunteers from 6:00 AM – 5:00 PM, Monday - Sunday • Serves free coffee, breakfast food, water, soda and snacks	

Table 11.7 (continued)

• Air conditioned • Ample seating, a TV and private restroom facilities • Name and logo placed on the gable • $10,000	
Hospitality	
Corporate Suite The Clubhouse Corporate Suite is a private room located within the Monroe Clubhouse. Tables both inside and outside on a beautiful patio overlooking the 18th green provides a relaxing and rejuvenating atmosphere for you and your guests. An array of food and beverages are included. • 8 Corporate Suite Tickets each day (includes all grounds and clubhouse access, as well as all food and beverage) • 4 VIP parking passes each day • Fresh breakfast, gourmet lunch along with afternoon hors d'oeuvres and an open bar • Climate controlled environment with closed circuit TV for enhanced Tournament viewing • $8,000 for the week (includes food and beverage)	 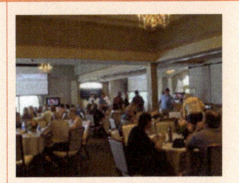
Pro-Ams	

Monday Pro-Am Foursome
• 4 playing spots in the Monday Pro-Am
• Scheduled for Monday, August 11th
• Each Pro-Am playing spot includes
  o 1 round of golf at Monroe Golf Club on Monday with an LPGA Pro
  o 2 Pro-Am Clubhouse badges
  o 2 Pro-Am Meal tickets for Pro-Am Hospitality Suite
  o 1 VIP Parking Pass for Monday, August 11th
  o 10 Grounds Vouchers for any one day admissions Monday, Tuesday, Wednesday
  o LPGA Player assignment based on registration order (First come, first served lottery basis)
  o Pro-Am Gift Package
• $7,000

Table 11.7 (continued)

<table>
<tr><td>Wednesday Corporate Pro-Am Foursome
• 4 playing spots in the Corporate Pro-Am
• Scheduled for Wednesday, August 13th
• Each Pro-Am playing spot includes
o 1 round of golf at Monroe Golf Club on Wednesday with an LPGA Pro
o 2 Pro-Am Clubhouse badges
o 2 Pro-Am Pairings party invitations for Tuesday, August 12th
o 2 Pro-Am Meal Packages for Pro-Am Hospitality Suite
o 1 VIP Parking Pass for Wednesday, August 13th
o 10 Grounds Vouchers for any one day admissions Monday, Tuesday, Wednesday
o Pro-Am Gift package
• $12,500</td><td></td></tr>
<tr><td colspan="2">Tickets</td></tr>
<tr><td>Beer and Food Pairings Party Ticket
• Scheduled for Friday night
• Monroe Golf Club
• Enjoy great beer and food, win fabulous prizes and meet LPGA Players
• Must be 21 or older to attend. Proof of age required at the door
• Limited quantity available and offered while supplies last
$50 thru January 1, 2014
$55 thru June 15, 2014
$60 after June 15, 2014</td><td></td></tr>
<tr><td colspan="2">LPGA Championship Clubhouse Package
Admissions onto the grounds and into the clubhouse. Package includes 3 "good any one day" Practice Round Vouchers and 4 "good any one day" Grounds Vouchers. The clubhouse offers the only enhanced concessions on course.
$99 thru Jan 1, 2014
$135 thru June 15th, 2014
Not available after June 15th, 2014</td></tr>
<tr><td colspan="2">LPGA Championship Grounds Package
Admission onto the grounds only. Package has 3 "good any one day" Practice Round Vouchers and 4 "good any one day" Grounds Vouchers
$75 thru Jan 1, 2014
$95 thru June 15th, 2014
Not available after June 15th, 2014</td></tr>
<tr><td colspan="2">LPGA Championship Clubhouse Voucher
Admission onto the course and into the clubhouse any one day (Thursday – Sunday).
$50 thru Jan 1, 2015
$55 thru June 15th, 2014
$60 after June 15th, 2014</td></tr>
</table>

Table 11.7 (continued)

LPGA Championship Grounds Voucher Admission onto the grounds any one day (Thursday – Sunday). $35 thru Jan 1, 2014 $38 thru June 15th, 2014 $40 after June 15th, 2014
LPGA Championship Practice Round Voucher Admission onto the grounds any one practice day: Monday, Tuesday or Wednesday. $10

Source: http://www.wegmanslpga.org/sponsorship-opps.aspx, accessed December 13, 2013.

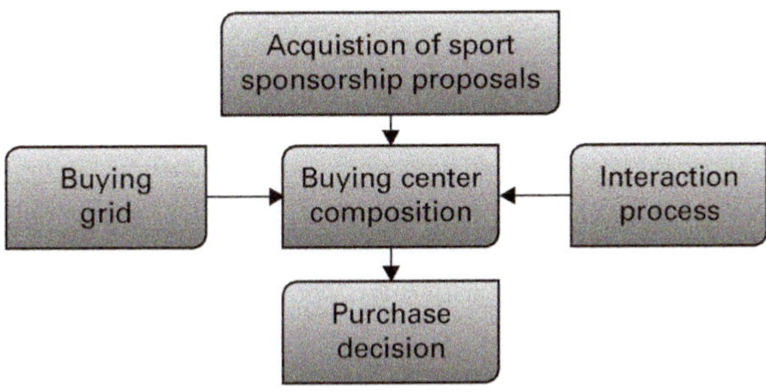

Figure 11.3 Sports sponsorship acquisition model

Source: Reprinted by permission from D. Arthur, D. Scott, and T. Woods. "A Conceptual Model of the Corporate Decision-Making Process of Sport Sponsorship Acquisition, *Journal of Sport Management*, vol. 11, no. 3 (1997), 229.

the organizational decision-making process in attempts to understand the evaluation and selection of sponsorship opportunities. A conceptual model of the corporate decision-making process of **sport sponsorship acquisition** developed by Arthur, Scott, and Woods is shown in Figure 11.3.

The process begins with the acquisition of sponsorship proposals. Generally, this is a reactive process in which organizations receive a multitude of sponsorship possibilities from sports entities wanting to secure sponsors. Within the sponsorship proposal, potential sponsors commonly look for the following information to assist in decision making:

- Fan attendance and demographic profile of fans at the event
- Cost or cost per number of people reached
- Length of contract
- Media coverage
- Value-added promotions
- Sponsorship benefits

After the proposals have been acquired, the next step is to form the buying center. The buying center is the group of individuals within the organization responsible for **sponsorship evaluation** and choice. The buying center usually consists of four to five individuals who each play a unique role in the purchase. Typically, these roles are described as gatekeepers, influencers, decision makers, and purchasers. These roles were previously discussed in the context of personal selling. You will recall that one of the sales activities was to identify the individuals within the organization who performed these roles. Similarly, the sponsorship requester must learn who these individuals are before submitting the proposal. Hopefully, the proposal can then be tailored to meet the unique needs of the individuals who comprise the buying center.

Gatekeepers control the flow of information to the other members of the buying center. They are able to pass on the relevant proposals to other group members and act as an initial filtering device. The **influencers** are individuals who can impact the decision-making process. These individuals often have information regarding the sports entity that is requesting the sponsorship. The influencers have acquired this information through contacts they have in the community or industry. The **decision maker** is the individual within the buying center who has the ultimate responsibility to accept or reject proposals. In our earlier examples, describing the budgeting process for Proctor & Gamble, the brand managers were the ultimate decision makers in the sponsorship acquisition process. Finally, the **purchasers** are responsible for negotiating contracts and formally carrying out the terms of the sponsorship.

The composition of the buying center, in terms of the number of individuals and the interaction between these individuals, is a function of the type of sponsorship decision. The buying grid refers to the organization's previous experience and involvement in sponsorship purchases. If this is the first time the organization has engaged in sport sponsorship, then more information will be needed from the sponsorship requester. In addition, the buying center will have additional members with greater interaction. However, if the sponsorship is simply being renewed (also known as a straight sponsorship rebuy), the buying center will play a less significant role in the decision-making process.

The next step in the sponsorship acquisition model is to make the purchase decision. Typically, it takes an organization three to six weeks to make a final sponsorship decision. While this may seem slow, purchasing a sponsorship is a complex decision that requires the coordination and interaction of all the members in the buying center.

The purchase decision consists of three interrelated steps. In the first step, the organization must consider the desired scope of the sponsorship (e.g., international versus local). To do this, a simple scheme for categorizing sponsorship opportunities has been developed, called the Sport Event Pyramid. The second interrelated step requires the organization to select the appropriate athletic platform for the sponsorship. Does the organization want to sponsor an event, a team, a league, or an individual athlete? Finally, after the organization has chosen the scope of sponsorship and the athletic platform, it specifies the particular sports entity. After the final decision is made, a quick audit can be conducted to determine whether the organization has made the appropriate choice of sponsorship. Let us examine the three steps in the purchase decision-making process in greater detail.

Determining the scope of the sponsorship

The first step in the purchase decision phase of sponsorship acquisition is to determine the desired scope of the sponsorship. David Shani and Dennis Sandler have developed a way to categorize various sponsorship opportunities called the **Sports Event Pyramid**.[53] The Sports Event Pyramid is an excellent first step in reducing the number of sponsorship proposals to a smaller subset.

The Sports Event Pyramid consists of five levels: global events, international events, national events, regional events, and local events. Each level of the Sports Event Pyramid classifies events on the basis of the width and depth of interest in the event. Shani and Sandler describe the width as the geographic reach of the event via the various communications media, and the depth of the event refers to the level of interest among consumers.

Global events are at the apex of the pyramid. As the name implies, global events have the broadest coverage and are covered extensively around the world. In addition to their wide coverage, global events generate a great deal of interest among consumers. Shani and Sandler suggest that the World Cup and the Olympic Games are the only examples of truly global events. Corporations that want to position themselves in the global market should be prepared to pay top dollar for sponsorship of these events due to the tremendous reach and interest in the events.

International events are the next level in the hierarchy. For any event to be considered international in scope, it might (1) have a high level of interest in a broad, but not global, geographic region, or (2) be truly global in scope but have a lower level of interest in some of the countries reached. Examples of international events include Wimbledon, European Cup Soccer, America's Cup (yachting), the Rugby Union World Cup, and the Pan-American Games. Sponsoring these types of events is useful for corporations that have more narrowly targeted global markets.

Extremely high interest levels among consumers in a single country or two countries is categorized in the Sports Event Pyramid as a **national event**. National events, such

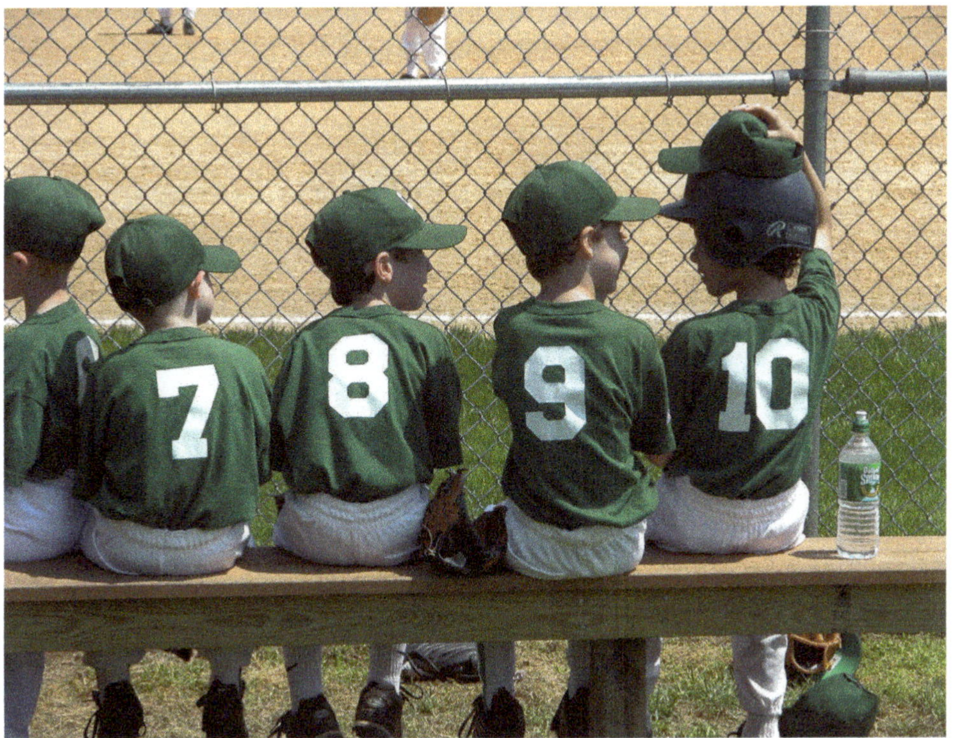

Photo 11.1 Little League (Youth Baseball League)

Source: Shutterstock.com

as the World Series, the NCAA Final Four, and the Super Bowl, attract huge audiences in the United States. Although many of these events attract an international media audience, the focus is still on national consumers.

Regional events have a narrow geographic focus and are also characterized by high interest levels within the region. The Big East conference tournament in basketball and the Boston Marathon are considered good examples of regional events.

In the lowest level of the pyramid are **local events**. Local events have the narrowest geographic focus, such as a city or community, and attract a small segment of consumers that have a high level of interest in the event. High school sports, local races, and golf scrambles are examples of local events.

The primary purpose of the pyramid is to have marketers first develop an understanding of what level of sponsorship is consistent with corporate sponsorship objectives and budgets. Next, the corporation can decide which specific sporting events at the correct level present the best match. The organization may start small and choose to sponsor local events at the beginning. The larger the organization gets, the more likely it will be involved in sponsorship at each of the five levels of the pyramid. For example, Coca-Cola is deeply involved in sponsorships at all five levels.

Although the Sports Event Pyramid is a great tool for marketers developing a sponsorship program, it does have some potential flaws. First, the local events are shown at the base of the pyramid. To some, this may imply the broadest geographic focus whereas, in fact, the local events have the most narrow focus. Second, it may be extremely difficult to categorize certain events. For example, the Super Bowl is cited as a national event that, by definition, has a one- or two-country focus with a high level of interest. The Super Bowl, of course, is broadcast in hundreds of countries, but may have limited interest levels in most. Therefore, it is uncertain as to whether the event should be categorized as a national event, an international event, or both.

Determining the athletic platform

After the general level of sponsorship reach is considered via the sponsorship pyramid, a more specific sponsorship issue must be considered, namely, choosing the appropriate athletic platform. Professor Christine Brooks defines the **athletic platform** for sponsorship as being either the team, the sport, the event, or the athlete.[54] In addition, choice of athletic platform could be further subdivided on the basis of level of competition. For instance, common levels of competition include professional, collegiate, high school, and recreational.

The choice of athletic platform (or, in some instances, platforms) is based on sponsorship objectives, budget, and geographic scope. More specifically, when selecting the athletic platform, several factors should be considered.

- What is the sponsorship budget? What type of athletic platform is feasible given the budget?
- What is the desired geographic scope? How does the athletic platform complement the choice made in the sports sponsorship pyramid?
- How does the athletic platform complement the sponsorship objectives?

Let us take a closer look at each of the broad choices of athletic platform for sponsorship. These include athletes, teams, sports/leagues, and events.

FENTON HIGH SCHOOL LOOKING AT BOOSTING CORPORATE SPONSORSHIP OF ATHLETICS

FENTON, MI – Fans at Fenton school sporting events could be looking at more corporate ads in the future.

Fenton Area Schools is considering a policy that would boost their corporate sponsorship of high school athletics by offering a wider variety of advertising packages.

"In this economic climate, we're struggling to involve more of our local businesses with the corporate sponsorship program we had set up initially," said Mike Bakker, Fenton's athletic director.

For the past three years, the program has had two paying sponsors: Vic Canever Chevrolet and Raymond James and Associates.

A third sponsor – McLaren Health Care – receives advertising in exchange for supplying a portion of Fenton's athletic trainer's salary.

The district currently receives $6,000 a year in advertising but is looking to at least double that with an expanded sponsorship program.

"I would love to see us get to the point where were bring in $12–15,000 over the next few years on a yearly basis," he said. "I don't think that's out of question after talking to other local sports departments, but we have to get the word out there and it takes time to build that."

Money raised from sponsorships goes to the entire athletic department to help fix and replace equipment, lighting and uniforms.

Fenton has offered a sponsorship program for the past four or five years, but it was top-heavy and advertisers felt they weren't getting enough bang for their buck, Bakker said.

The proposed restructuring, based on other successful models in the community, such as Linden, Lake Fenton and Hartland, would offer an array of different sized packages to sponsors.

Utilizing advertising to generate revenue for school districts is a blossoming business.

In the Holly Area School District, sports teams are allowed to gather their own corporate sponsors to raise funds for themselves.

"The reason behind this individual concept is that teams have different perks to offer sponsors," said Deb VanKuiken, Holly's athletic director. "For instance, a baseball team may hang a sign on their field fencing and read announcements at games while the ski team hangs a banner on their warming tent and the soccer team places advertisements in programs."

Three other Genesee Country school districts have signed on with a Troy-based company – Alternative Revenue Development, LLC – that uses advertising to raise money for schools.

"Before it was either go big or not at all," Bakker said. "We're also willing to talk with (advertisers) and negotiate."

Advertisers can display banners in the gym, the football stadium or the fence. They can also display banners in their businesses and receive printed ads in the school's athletic programs.

The booster program is also willing to be flexible in negotiating trades in return for advertising rights, such as donated equipment or lighting.

Another new installment, if the board approves the proposal, would be an advertising position responsible for the management of the sponsors.

Bakker said they are looking at paying the advertising representative 10 percent of all the sales they make, which would be self-sufficient and not draw from the school's budget.

"We have community members who were supportive of athletics in the past with experience in marketing and advertising we'd love to tap into," Bakker said.

Just two people currently run the Fenton athletics department.

"I love the idea of getting somebody who this is their specialty," said board member Nora Kryza. "I think that'll make it much more successful than trying to spread that little bit of peanut butter on the bread."

With the revamped packages, the all-sports booster program would offer color banners for the first time; previously, the banners were black with white writing.

Bakker said the lack of color logos discouraged some advertisers.

Another new sticking point would be scoreboard advertisements.

"I wanted to stay away (from corporate advertising) for as long as possible because I wanted to keep it about the kids, but it's also a revenue that I don't know that we can ignore," Bakker said.

Board member Lynn Hopper questioned whether the advertisements would be sponsorships or endorsements. Bakker assured him they are sponsorships.

"The good news is that corporate sponsorship fees directly impact each program and thereby student athletes," VanKuiken said

Source: Article author: Sarah Wojcik. Rightsholder: Mlive; http://www/mlive/com/news/flint/index.ssf/2012/06/fenton_high_school_proposes_po.html.

Athletes

We have previously examined the opportunities and risks of athletes as endorsers in Chapters 9 and 10. To summarize, athletes can have tremendous credibility with the target audience and can create an immediate association with a product in the consumer's mind. For example, NASCAR fans talk about Danica Patrick driving the "GoDaddy" car or Kasey Kahne driving the "Budweiser" car. Interestingly, when it comes to athletes as sponsors, golfers have always been at the head of the pack. In fact, most believe the entire sports marketing industry was built on the backs of professional golfers, such as Arnold Palmer, Jack Nicholas, and Gary Player. While Tiger Woods' fall from global sports icon to tabloid fodder was stunning, losing Accenture, AT&T, Gatorade, and Pepsi as sponsors, he still carries the flag and remains one of the highest-paid athletes in the world thanks to huge deals with Nike, Electronic Arts and Upper Deck, earning an estimated $105 million.

One athlete that is always surrounded by controversy and seems to exemplify the bad boy image is former Philadelphia Eagles QB and present New York Jets QB Michael Vick. In March 2005 a woman named Sonya Elliot filed a civil lawsuit against Vick alleging that she contracted genital herpes from Vick and that he failed to inform her that he had the disease. Elliot further alleged that Vick had visited clinics under the alias "Ron Mexico" to get treatments and thus he knew of his condition. In another incident with a former team, the Atlanta Falcons, Vick made an obscene gesture at Atlanta fans, holding up two middle fingers during a game against the New Orleans Saints in the Georgia Dome on November 26, 2006. To add further fuel to the fire, Vick surrendered a water bottle to security at Miami International Airport. Due to Vick's reluctance to leave the bottle behind, it was later retrieved from a trash receptacle. The bottle was found to have a hidden compartment that contained a small amount of dark particulate and a pungent aroma closely associated with marijuana. On April 24, 2007, Vick was scheduled to lobby on Capitol Hill, hoping to persuade lawmakers to increase funding for after-school programs. Vick missed a connecting flight in Atlanta and failed to show for his morning appearance.[55] In his most publicized and scandalous act yet, Vick pleaded guilty to a federal dogfighting conspiracy charge on August 27, 2007, in U.S. District Court and served 21 months in prison, followed by two months in home confinement. With the loss of his NFL salary and product endorsement deals, combined with previous financial mismanagement, Vick filed for Chapter 11 bankruptcy in July 2008. Most recently, Vick has been accused of using steroids, but he denies these allegations. Currently, Vick continues to rebuild his broken reputation and regain the trust of the public.

Teams

Teams at any level of competition (Little League, high school, college, and professional) can serve as the athletic platform. Boeing and Starbucks present an excellent example of organizations that have chosen to focus on professional sports teams as their athletic platform.

HOT SEAHAWKS ADD BOEING, STARBUCKS DEALS

Boeing and Starbucks are the newest corporate partners of the Seattle Seahawks as the NFL team looks to lean on its newfound national popularity to stimulate deals.

Locally based Boeing gets branding on the Seahawks' news conference backdrop under the deal, along with permanent signage for all events at CenturyLink Field.

Starbucks, another longtime Seattle corporate stalwart, gets exclusivity in the tea and coffee categories, something not to be undervalued in Seattle. The coffee bean seller and brewer gets exclusive rights to sell coffee within CenturyLink Field, which it will do within all concession stands and in 18 portable "coffee stations" set up on game days. Starbucks is also supporting the "Better Seattle" anti-gang initiative, in which the team and coach Pete Carroll have been involved.

The normally sponsorship-shy Starbucks is also planning to activate with a Seahawks-themed retail promotion at its many local stores, something unheard of for America's top coffee retailer.

"We've been on a push to attract more sponsors looking for national exposure and to take advantage of the growing popularity of our team," Seahawks President Peter McLoughlin said. The Seahawks were one of the league's surprise success stories last year and are scheduled to be on four national TV games this year.

The news conference backdrop exposure for Boeing, which McLoughlin said will generate 250 million annual television impressions, began with the opening of training camp. He said the multiyear deal makes Boeing one of the team's five largest corporate sponsors. While Boeing's support is not a brand play, McLoughlin said that with 80,000 local employees, it is about "employee morale and supporting the overall community, because enthusiasm for this team is at a high, which is saying a lot out here."

He added that after the ascension of quarterback Russell Wilson last season and the team's run in the NFC playoffs, ticket demand is higher than ever in a town that's always Seahawks crazy. Season-ticket renewal, at 98 percent, and the 62,000 season tickets sold both represent franchise highs, McLoughlin said.

An additional allotment of 3,500 single-game tickets, which went on sale Monday, sold out in a day.

Boeing and Starbucks are two of the larger brand names in a sponsorship portfolio that will see revenue increase 15 percent to 18 percent this season, McLoughlin said.

The Seahawks' press backdrop had been sponsored by Oberto Beef Jerky, another Seattle company, which will continue as a Seahawks sponsor.

Source: Author: Terry Lefton; http://www.sportsbusinessdaily.com/Journal/Issues/2013/07/29/Franchises/Seahawks.aspx. Rightsholder: Sports Business Journal.

The accompanying Boeing and Starbucks example illustrates that sponsorship is typically associated with professional teams, but college athletic departments also rely heavily on sponsorship partnerships.

The marketing of collegiate sports has skyrocketed in recent years. For example, advertisers are lining up to take their shots during the National Collegiate Athletic Association's March basketball tournament. According to Kantar Media (2014) over the past decade (2004–2013), the NCAA men's basketball tournament has triggered more than $6.88 billion of national TV ad spending from 269 different marketers.[56] Ad revenue in 2013 was $1.15 billion, up 3.8 percent from the prior year. Since 2011, every tournament game has been aired nationally, producing more advertising inventory for sale – and sharply higher revenue. Over that time, the average cost of an ad during the championship game has been $1.24 million – more than a 30-second spot during the World Series or the NBA finals. The Collegiate Licensing Company, which represents more than 200 colleges, universities, bowl games, athletic conferences, the Heisman Trophy, and the NCAA, including the Men's and Women's Final Four, the College World Series, and all NCAA championships, estimates the licensed collegiate market at around $3 billion in retail sales annually, including both apparel and non-apparel sales.[57] Add to that the multimillion-dollar television contracts and deals that most university coaches have with Nike, Reebok, and Adidas, and college athletics is a huge business (see Table 11.8 for a list of universities with the highest revenues from licensed merchandise sales).

Becoming the official outfitter for a university's athletic teams has become especially lucrative for colleges and has given sponsors great exposure. For instance, the University of North Carolina recently extended a ten-year, $37.7 million contract with Nike to fuel the growth of the university's athletic program.[58] Nike will provide North Carolina's athletic department with the following: (1) Millions in footwear, apparel, and equipment; (2) $2 million to the Chancellor's Academic Enhancement Fund, directed to fund faculty support; (3) $1 million to the athletic department for signing the contract, with those funds being used to overhaul lighting and sound at the Smith Center (http://alumniclefs.alumni.unc.edu/article.aspx?sid=6840).

Table 11.8 University merchandise sales leaders in 2013

Rank	*University*
1	The University of Texas at Austin
2	The University of Alabama
3	University of Michigan
4	The University of Notre Dame
5	Louisiana State University
6	University of Kentucky
7	The University of Georgia
8	University of Florida
9	The University of Arkansas
10	University of North Carolina

Note: Schools not under contract with the CLC (Collegiate Licensing Company) were not included on the list. This includes such as Ohio State, Southern California, and Iowa, many of which handle licensing in-house.

Source: http://www.clc.com/News/Archived-Rankings/Rankings-Q4-2012.aspx.

Sport or league

In addition to sponsoring teams, some companies choose to sponsor sports or leagues. For example, the smoothie retailer Jamba Juice made its first investment in a national sports league by signing a multi-year deal to sponsor the WNBA. The deal will be part of a national marketing campaign promoting health and wellness as well as promotional materials for Jamba Juice stores in WNBA markets. The league will also work with the retailer to promote a program known as Jamba Jump, a fitness routine that uses jump ropes. The goal is to reach 1 million children through the partnership.[59] One advantage to sponsoring women's sports and the WNBA is that there is less sponsorship clutter. Fewer companies are sponsoring women's sports or leagues, and those that do are creating a unique position and differentiating themselves.

For example, cosmetics brand CoverGirl is the presenting sponsor of the WNBA's new marketing campaign WNBA Pride, aimed at the lesbian, gay, bisexual, and transgender community. WNBA Pride is the league's platform celebrating inclusion and equality, while combating anti-LGBT bias. The global consumer products company Procter & Gamble owns CoverGirl. The program would not have seen the light of day without the support and acceptance of other league marketing partners, which include Boost Mobile, Adidas, American Express, BBVA, Anheuser-Busch, Coca-Cola, EA Sports, Gatorade, Nike, Spalding, and State Farm. While the WNBA welcomes all fans, athletes, and partners to our game, the value of marketing partners should not be underestimated in matters where social responsibility conforms or conflicts with business strategies, especially when those conflicts become public knowledge.[60]

Anheuser-Busch is a corporation that has chosen an integrated approach in sponsoring a number of sports or leagues. Anheuser-Busch became the official beer of Major League Baseball in 1996, and became the official beer of the NBA in 1998. Bud Light began its sponsorship of Team Seebold in 1982, sponsors the ChampBoat Racing Series team, and became a founding partner of the Professional Bull Riders in 1993. Anheuser-Busch's sports sponsorship portfolio includes beer sponsorships with the NFL and UFC (Bud Light); MLB and NBA (Budweiser); PGA, LPGA, and Champion's Tours (Michelob ULTRA); and the Kentucky Derby (Stella Artois). The makers of

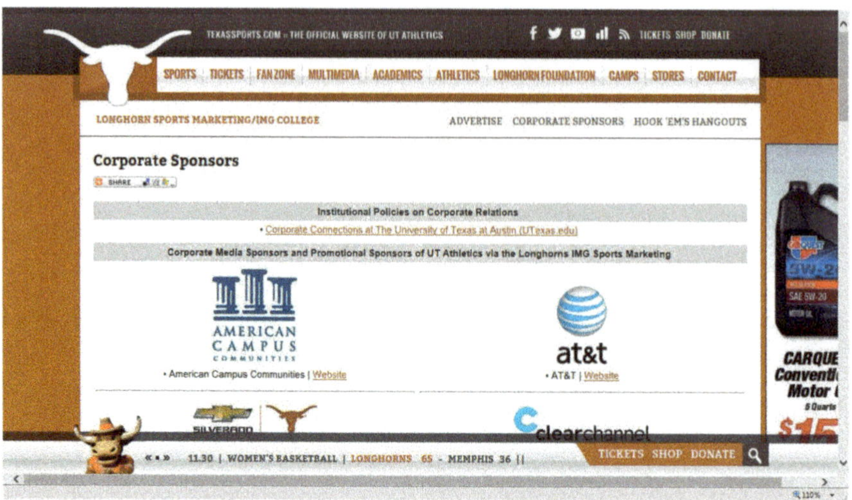

Web 11.2 University of Texas' Corporate partner program

Source: www.texassports.com / UT Athletics

Budweiser and Bud Light are the official beer sponsors of 28 NFL teams; the exclusive alcohol and non-alcohol malt-based beverage sponsor of the Super Bowl, and is the official beer of the entire NFL. In addition, they sponsor 26 MLB teams, 25 NBA teams and Bud Light also signed on as the official beer of the NHL in 1988 and currently sponsors 20 domestic teams.[61] In total, Anheuser-Busch sponsorships include 95 local teams across the four major sports leagues and dozens of local running and cycling events nationwide as well as the No. 29 Budweiser Chevrolet SS driven by Kevin Harvick.[62]

It has been the official alcoholic beverage of Major League Lacrosse since the league started in 2001, and has sponsored the sport since 2004. Current surfer sponsorships include Serena Brooke, Freddy P, Sean Moody, and Benji Weatherly. The AVP Tour named Bud Light its official beer of the tour in 2000. In 2013, Anheuser-Busch was named Sports Sponsor of the Year. Blaise D'Sylva, vice president of media, sports and entertainment marketing for Anheuser-Busch noted "Successful sports marketing execution at Anheuser-Busch is more than purchasing a 30-second spot or signage in a stadium, it is the collective effort of hundreds of people inside the organization, our partners and our wholesalers, working together every day to leverage sports and beer in exciting and innovative ways to connect with our consumers."[63]

The "Ben Hogan Tour" was established in 1990 as a breeding ground for golf professionals who have not cracked the PGA. In 1993, Nike sponsored the tour, followed by Buy.com, which ended its sponsorship in 2002. In 2014, Web.com became the fifth title sponsor in the history of the PGA Tour's developmental circuit, replacing Nationwide. According to the PGA, the 10-year agreement comes four months after the tour also renewed its deal for the FedExCup, a $35 million bonus series.[64] In 2013, the tour negotiated a nine-year television deal with NBC Sports and CBS Sports, establishing television contracts through 2021. The Web.com Tour serves to become the primary path for players to reach the PGA Tour. Starting in September 2013, the top 75 players from the both Web.com and the top 75 PGA Tour players who failed to qualify for the FedExCup playoffs will meet in a three-tournament series that effectively replaces Q-School.[65] A total of fifty PGA Tour cards will be awarded after those three events.

Nike elevated its sponsorship with the addition as a title sponsor of the Winter Dew Tour's season opener, the Nike 6.0 Open. The event hosted at Breckenridge Ski Resort provides a platform for Nike to engage in the growing winter action sports scene. Nike, originally an associate level partner, will receive tour-wide exclusivity in the footwear, athletic and casual apparel, and outerwear categories as well as receive fully integrated marketing benefits that include television ads and online exposure. Nike's linkage with an event such as the Winter Dew Tour illustrates the strength of the property and their brand's commitment to the industry. Lately, a variety of action sports properties have been trying to organize themselves to become more attractive to sponsors. Partnerships across these platforms provide benefits to enhance the involvement and further leverage sponsorship offerings thereby enhancing the procurement of the ultimate dollar.[66]

Action sports were not the first property to think about how best to serve the interests of sponsors. NFL Properties was designed in 1963 primarily to meet and beat the competition posed by Major League Baseball. The league, in attempting to offer a competitive advantage to sponsors, built a system whereby potential sponsors receive collective and individual team rights. That is, sponsors can create opportunities or promotions that feature all NFL teams and local teams in a local market.[67]

Sponsors choose to use the power of the league and its recognizable league logo and, therefore, support all the teams. From the sponsors' perspective, this represents easy and less expensive one-stop shopping. As Burton points out, "If an NFL corporate partner had to design individual local contracts to secure key markets, the collective local team fees would quickly surpass the single sponsorship fee." By allowing sponsors the opportunity to receive collective team rights, the league gains enhanced exposure. As an example, Bose, Inc. (already the official home audio sponsor of the NFL) and the National Football League announced an extension for Bose to replace Motorola to put its corporate logo on the headsets worn by coaches during games. Bose will design, engineer and manufacture new headsets for all NFL coaches to use in-game, enhancing sideline and booth communications in a variety of areas, including play-calling and instant replay. Bose,one of two sponsors to have an on-field presence, will work with the NFL to develop and implement game-changing communication innovations.

Events

An athletic platform that is most commonly associated with sports marketing is the event. Examples of sporting events sponsorship are plentiful, as are the opportunities to sponsor sporting events. In fact, sometimes the number of events far outweighs the number of potential corporate sponsors. For example, the city of Winnipeg staged two national and international sporting events over the space of 16 months. In a city that ranks as the eighth largest in Canada and has a population of only around 680,000, the challenge was to find enough corporate sponsors. In response to this challenge, event organizers were forced to be more creative in designing sponsorship packages that appeal to organizations of all sizes.[68]

The advantages of using an event as an athletic platform are similar to those benefits gained by using other athletic platforms. For instance, the event will hopefully increase awareness and enhance the image of the sponsor. In addition, consumers have a forum in which to use and purchase the sponsor's products. Lexus offered a swing simulator at its vehicle display tent that lets fans take shots on a computer-generated Oakmont course, while AmEx hosted an interactive area open to all ticket holders at the U.S. Open.

In another example, Cincinnati Reds fans received refrigerator and car magnet season schedules courtesy of PNC, who also sponsors many other promotions at the ballpark.

As with the other athletic platforms, one of the primary disadvantages of using events as the athletic platform is sponsorship clutter. In other words, sponsors are competing with other sponsors for the attention of the target audience. One popular way to combat this clutter is to become the title sponsor of an event. Every college football bowl game now has a title sponsor, with the exception of the Rose Bowl – and this too has changed. In 1999 the Rose Bowl added a sponsor's tag line. More formally, this is called a presenting sponsor (i.e., the Rose Bowl presented by VIZIO).

Choosing the specific athletic platform

The choice of a particular athletic platform follows the selection of the general platform. At this stage of the sponsorship process, the organization makes a decision regarding the exact athlete(s), team, event, or sports entity. For instance, if the organization decides to sponsor a professional women's tennis player, who will be chosen – Serena or Venus Williams, or Maria Sharapova? As with the previous decisions regarding sponsorship, the choice of a specific sponsor is based largely on finding the right "fit" for the organization and its products.

A recent trend is for sports marketers to ensure and control the fit by manufacturing their own sporting events. For example, Nike has created a division to create and acquire global sporting events. By creating their own events, Nike will be able to control every aspect of how each event is marketed. Moreover, Nike will be able to develop events that are the perfect fit for their multiple target markets.[69] Other organizations, such as Honda, are pursuing a similar strategy. They have put pressure on their advertising agency to develop sporting events that will be the ideal match for the Honda target market.

Once the decision regarding the general level of sponsorship and the specific athletic platform have been addressed, it may be useful to review carefully the choice(s) of sponsorship before taking the final step. To do so, Brant Wansley of BrandMarketing Services, Ltd. offers the following suggestions for choosing a sponsorship.[70]

- Does the sponsorship offer the right positioning?
- Does the sponsorship provide a link to the brand image?
- Is the sponsorship hard for competitors to copy?
- Does the sponsorship target the right audience?
- Does the sponsorship appeal to the target audiences' lifestyle, personality, and values?
- How does the sponsorship dovetail into current corporate goals and strategies?
- Can the sponsorship be used for hospitality to court important potential and current customers?
- Is there a way to involve employees in the sponsorship?
- How will you measure the impact of the sponsorship?
- Can you afford the sponsorship?
- How easy will it be to plan the sponsorship year after year?
- Does the sponsorship complement your current promotion mix?

SPOTLIGHT ON SPORTS MARKETING ETHICS

Nike won't drop Penn State's Paterno, so we should drop Nike

The Penn State child rape scandal continues to snowball by the day, taking with it advertising and sponsorship dollars, the jobs of those peripherally involved and what's left of Joe Paterno's reputation.

On Monday, Paterno's name was removed from the Big Ten championship trophy. On Sunday, Jack Raykovitz – CEO of Second Mile, the child advocacy group Jerry Sandusky founded then allegedly trawled for victims – resigned from his role. That same day, the Wall Street Journal revealed that at least six advertisers including Cars.com have pulled out of ESPN broadcasts of future Penn State games.

Still, as you'll know if you read my colleague Mike Ozanian's post on Friday, the biggest, most influential sports brand on the planet continues to stick by both PSU and its disgraced former coach Paterno: Nike.

Ozanian's point proved controversial among commenters (myself included): He posited that Nike's decision to stick by troubled stars in the past – Tiger Woods among them – paid off financially once the dust had settled. Their decision to back Paterno will be no different, he said. Fine, maybe so. But this is a different case entirely, one far more serious than dalliances with cocktail waitresses.

It isn't even Nike's continued sponsorship of the Penn State football team that grates. It is Nike's refusal to address the name of a building on its Oregon corporate campus that now seems so oxymoronic it'd be more at home in an Onion.com satire: the Joe Paterno Child Development Center. The Oregonian was the first to report that Nike has no plans to rename this building, where 200 children under age five spend their days.

To spell out why this decision is unacceptable: despite hearing Mike McQueary's eyewitness account of Sandusky raping a small boy in 2002, Paterno did the bare minimum, reporting his one-time assistant coach to the University. He did not alert the police. He did not make any effort to protect the children involved in Sandusky's program from the alleged sexual predator. He did not see fit to stop Sandusky having contact with other kids on his premises, under his own roof, at the very cathedral of football where he presided as Pope. Per the Grand Jury presentment, seven more children were sexually assaulted after that first unreported incident (Sandusky denies all charges). Since this scandal broke, another 10 have come forward, said the New York Times on Monday.

Nike spokeswoman Erin Dobson trotted out a prepared statement when the Oregonian asked about the appropriateness of the Joe Paterno Child Development Center's name. Yesterday, when I approached Dobson to see what Nike meant by "monitoring the situation", she emailed me the same statement, despite my posing specific questions (Who makes these decisions? What sort of allegations would it take for Nike to immediately cut ties with an athlete, coach, or school?)

When I forwarded our correspondence to Nike CEO Mark Parker, he sent it back to Dobson, who responded with the same canned statement:

"Our relationship with Penn State remains unchanged. We are deeply disturbed by the claims brought forth in the indictments. We will continue to monitor the situation closely. We have no current plans to change the name of our child care center."

Prevent Child Abuse America's CEO James Hmurovich said he was disturbed that Nike has thus far decided to maintain the status quo.

"What allegedly happened at Penn State should outrage our nation, and to find that a national brand will not distance itself from Penn State and Joe Paterno in this situation is equally disturbing," he told Forbes. "It begs the question as to what kind of culture exists at Nike to place business issues over the well being of children?"

I emailed or called every member of Nike's board – high-profile appointees like Apple CEO Tim Cook and Eli Lilly CEO John Lechleiter – to see if they agree with the company's position. I have received no responses as yet. I'll be sure to update this post if and when I do.

I'm not naive about the workings of capitalism and understand that global corporations like Nike don't have any real moral obligation. Look at McDonald's: they shill fatty foods to young kids but are still perfectly able to sponsor the Olympics. That's just how it works, and Nike knows that; they'll stick with the Joe Paterno name and Penn State until they believe they are liabilities in the movement of shoes and shirts – the same shoes and shirts Jerry Sandusky gave as gifts to his child rape victims, according to page 15 of the Grand Jury presentment. At that point, Paterno may well be dumped, with much talk of disappointment and a betrayal of the ideals of college sports. Donations to child abuse charities could follow.

But Nike is a company operating a foundation entirely devoted to supporting little girls. It's a company with a smartly designed Code of Ethics available online. On the second page, in stark white letters, is one phrase: Do The Right Thing. The right thing in this situation is to recognize the hypocrisy of claiming to support children, but caring for them in a center named for a man who did not go to the police when he heard his colleague had been seen raping a little boy in a shower.

Source: Article author: Clare O'Connor; http://www.forbes.com/sites/clareoconnor/2011/11/14/nike-wont-drop-penn-states-paterno-so-we-should-drop-nike/. Rightsholder: Forbes. "Reprinted by permission of Forbes Media LLC © 2014".

Sponsorship implementation and evaluation

Once the sponsorship decisions are finalized, plans are put into action and then evaluated to determine their effectiveness. Do sponsorships really work? The findings to this million-dollar question are somewhat mixed. In Chapter 13, we discuss the techniques organizations use to determine whether the sponsorship has met their objectives. For now, let us look at the results of several studies that were conducted to determine consumer response to sponsorship. In a poll conducted by Performance Research, more than half of the respondents indicated they would be "not very likely" or "not at all likely" to purchase a company's products because it was an Olympic sponsor.[71]

Most studies report that sponsorship is having a positive impact on their organizations. For example, Visa reported that since its affiliation with the Olympic Games its market share in the United States increased by one-third, but the number of consumers who considered it the best overall card doubled to 61 percent.[72] Delta Air Lines also increased awareness levels from 38 percent to 70 percent due to its Olympic sponsorship. A recent study by the International Olympic Committee found that 22 percent of respondents would be more likely to buy a product if it were an Olympic sponsor's product.[73] In another study, roughly 60 percent of consumers indicated that they "try to buy a company's product if they support the Olympic Games.[74] In addition, 57 percent of consumers around the world agreed that "they look favorably towards a company if it is associated with the Olympics."

However, some researchers found that the majority of consumers say sponsorship makes no difference to them and their purchase behavior. For example, Quester and Lardinoit conducted a study and found that Olympic sponsors could not expect to find higher levels of brand recognition or loyalty.[75] Additionally, a study by Pitts and Slattery found that over 60 percent of respondents said they would not be more likely to purchase a product just because they knew it was a sponsor's product.[76] One potential reason for these less than encouraging findings is the amount of sponsorship clutter. For example, Ohio-based Wendy's, which had been an OSU sponsor for "more than two decades," decided to drop its sponsorship with the school "under pressure from activist investors to reduce costs and improve its financial performance."[77] The company has also ended its sponsorships of a local LPGA tournament, and the Columbus Blue Jackets in 2011.

Other reasons that sponsorships are dropped or fail are highlighted in Table 11.9.

Table 11.9 Why sponsorships fail

No Budget for Activation – Be prepared to spend several times your rights fees to leverage the property.
Not Long-Term – One-year commitments generally don't work. It takes time to build the association.
No Measurable Objectives – Must have internal agreement on sponsorship goals.
Too Brand-Centric – Sponsorship should be based on the needs of consumers not brands.
Overlook Ambush and Due Diligence – Know what you are not getting is as important is as what you are getting.
Too Much Competition for Trade Participation – When products sold through the same distribution channel sponsor the same property, the impact is diluted.
Failure to Excite the Sales Chain – A sponsorship program will not work unless the concept is sold throughout the entire distribution channel.
Insufficient Staffing – Additional staffing is needed to meet the time demands of sponsoring an event.
Buying at the Wrong Level – Higher sponsorship levels equate to more benefits. Make sure you are reaping all the benefits or buy at a lower level.
No Local Extensions – National brands must create localized execution overlays for a sponsorship to truly reach their audiences.
No Communication of Added Value – For maximum impact, sponsors must be viewed as bringing something to the event. The activity should be "provided by" the brand rather than "sponsored by" it.

CAREER SPOTLIGHT

Lesa Ukman and IEG

Lesa Ukman graduated from Colorado College with a double major in philosophy and political science in 1978. Having worked on the local paper throughout her college years, she initially struggled to find a full-time job in journalism before accepting a job on the Jerusalem post. "It was about six weeks before I was due to go off to Jerusalem to do that," she explains, "and the mayoral race in Chicago was happening. This candidate who I liked needed a press secretary. It was an unpaid job and I volunteered."

With a little help from Ukman, Jane Byrne became the first female mayor of Chicago in April 1979. She took Ukman with her into city hall. "It was such an amazing experience for a political science major to be in Chicago with the mayor," she explains. "But within a week her speeches changed from the campaign and her politics changed pretty much entirely. So I went to resign and the chief of staff said take over special events. I didn't know what that was. But it turned out it's the slush fund from hotel/motel tax revenue that had been used really for whatever the mayor wanted to do personally. So I decided to do something she had promised during the campaign. So I started doing neighborhood festivals; jazz festivals; I had the first ever US picnic for Vietnam veterans – she didn't know who they were! We made the mayor's office open to all the neighborhoods that elected her. She loves the neighborhoods but she also had big business and other interests at heart. I was so idealistic; I didn't realize you compromise in politics. After about eight months I went through the US$3 million, which was a lot of money back then. So I started calling corporations to sponsor our festivals. And they all said yes. I thought, 'oh my God!' I had no idea it was because I was calling from the mayor's office. So after three years of doing this I thought this needs to happen everywhere – cities need to understand this. I thought our audience with IEG would be cities. But it wasn't cities, it was festivals and sports events and marathons. But then it wasn't until 1984 and the LA Olympics that we really started to make money."

Source: http://www.sportspromedia.com/notes_and_insights/lesa_ukman_the_sponsorship_pathfinder/0/. Credit: www.sportspromedia.com.

Summary

The element of the promotional mix that is linked with sports marketing to the highest degree is sponsorship. A sponsorship is an investment in a sports entity (athlete, league, team, or event) to support overall organizational goals, marketing objectives, and/or promotional objectives. Sports sponsorships are growing in popularity as a promotional tool for sports and nonsports products (and organizations). For example, it is projected that $55.3 billion will be spent globally on sports sponsorships in 2014.[78] Because so much emphasis is placed on sponsorship, an organization must understand how to develop the most effective sponsorship program.

The systematic process for designing a sponsorship program consists of four sequential steps, which include setting sponsorship objectives, determining the sponsorship budget, acquiring a sponsorship, and implementing and evaluating the sponsorship. Because sponsorship is one of the promotional mix elements, it is important to remember the relationship it has with the broader promotional strategy. As suggested in Chapters 9 and 10, all the elements of the promotional mix must be integrated to achieve maximum effectiveness.

The sponsorship process begins by setting objectives. These objectives, not unlike advertising objectives, can be categorized as either direct or indirect. Direct sponsorship objectives focus on stimulating consumer demand for the sponsoring organization and its products. The sponsoring company benefits by attaching their product to the sports entity. The sports entity also benefits by increased exposure given by the sponsor. As such, both parties in the sponsorship agreement benefit through the association. Indirect objectives may also be set for the sponsorship program. These objectives include generating awareness, meeting and beating the competition, reaching new target markets (e.g., disabled) or specialized target markets (e.g., mature market), building relationships with customers, and enhancing the company's image.

After objectives have been formulated, the sponsorship budget is considered. The techniques for setting sponsorship budgets are also in accord with the promotional budgeting methods discussed in the previous chapter. Generally, sponsorship of sporting events is not an inexpensive proposition – especially given the threat of ambush marketing. Ambush marketing is the planned effort by an organization to associate themselves indirectly with an event to gain at least some of the recognition and benefits that are associated with being an official sponsor. In past years, the Olympics have been a playground for ambush marketing techniques. For example, Nike, not an official sponsor of the 1996 Summer Olympics, constructed a building overlooking the Olympic Park to associate themselves with the festivities of the Olympic Games. Today, more stringent policing and regulation of ambush marketing is occurring by the sporting event organizers to protect the heavy financial outlay of official sponsors.

The third step of the sponsorship process is to choose the sponsorship opportunity, or acquire the sponsorship. This means making decisions about the scope of the sponsorship, choosing the general athletic platform, and then choosing the specific athletic platform. The scope of the sponsorship refers to the geographic reach of the sports entity, as well as the interest in the entity. Shani and Sandler describe the scope of athletic events using a tool called the Sports Event Pyramid. The Sports Event Pyramid is a hierarchy of events based on geographic scope and level of interest among spectators. The five-tiered hierarchy ranges from international events, such as the Olympic Games, to local events, such as a Little League tournament in your community. Once the scope of the sponsorship has been chosen, the athletic platform must be determined. The athletic platform for a sponsorship is generally a team, sport, event, or athlete. In addition, the athletic platform could be further categorized on the basis of level of competition (i.e., professional, collegiate, high school, or recreational). Decisions regarding the choice of athletic platform should be linked to the objectives set in the previous stages of sponsorship planning. After choosing the general athletic platform, the potential sponsor must select the specific platform. For example, if a collegiate sporting event is to be the general platform, then the specific athletic platform may be the Rose Bowl, the Championship Game of the Final Four, or a regular season baseball game against an in-state rival.

The final phase of the sponsorship process is to implement and evaluate the sponsorship plans. Organizing a sponsorship and integrating a sponsorship program with the other promotional mix elements requires careful coordination. Once the sponsorship plan is put into action, the most critical question for decision makers is, "Did the program deliver or have we met our sponsorship objectives?"

The implementation and evaluation of the strategic sports marketing process and, more specifically, sponsorships are considered in Chapter 13.

Key terms

- ambush marketing
- athletic platform
- awareness
- competition
- decision maker
- direct sponsorship objectives
- gatekeepers
- global events
- image building
- indirect sponsorship objectives
- influencers
- international events
- local events
- national event
- match-up hypothesis
- purchasers
- reaching new target markets
- regional events
- relationship marketing
- sales increases
- sponsorship
- sponsorship budgeting methods
- sponsorship evaluation
- sponsorship objectives
- sponsorship program
- sport sponsorship acquisition
- sports event pyramid

Review questions

1. Define sponsorship and discuss how sponsorship is used as a promotional mix tool by sports marketers. Provide evidence to support the growth of sports sponsorships worldwide.
2. Outline the steps for designing a sports sponsorship program.
3. Discuss, in detail, the major objectives of sports sponsorship from the perspective of the sponsoring organization.
4. What is ambush marketing, and why is it such a threat to legitimate sponsors? What defense would you take against ambush marketing tactics as a sports marketer?
5. In your opinion, why are sports sponsorships so successful in reaching a specific target market?
6. How are sponsorship budgets established within an organization?
7. Describe the various levels of the sponsorship pyramid. What is the Sports Event Pyramid used for, and what are some potential problems with the pyramid?
8. Define an athletic platform. In determining what athletic platform to use for a sponsorship, what factors should be considered?
9. What questions or issues might an organization raise when choosing among sponsorship opportunities?
10. Describe the different ways that sports sponsorships might be evaluated. Which evaluation tool is the most effective?

Exercises

1. Design a proposed sponsorship plan for a local youth athletic association.
2. Provide five examples of extremely good or effective match-ups between sporting events and their sponsors. In addition, suggest five examples of extremely poor or ineffective match-ups between sporting events and their sponsors.
3. Find at least one example of sponsorship for each of the following athletic platforms: individual athlete, team, and league.
4. Contact an organization that sponsors any sport or sporting event and discuss how sponsorship decisions are made and by whom.

Also, ask about how the organization evaluates sponsorship.

5. Design a survey to determine the influence of NASCAR sponsorships on consumers' purchase behaviors. Ask 10 consumers to complete the survey and summarize the findings. Suggest how NASCAR might use these findings.

Internet exercises

1. Search the Internet and find an example of a sponsorship opportunity at each level of the Sports Event Pyramid.

2. Locate at least three sports marketing companies on the Internet that specialize in the marketing of sponsorship opportunities. What products or services are these organizations offering potential clients?

Endnotes

1 "Kansas Athletics renews partnership with Adidas," Kansas University Athletics (June 6, 2013). Available from: http://www.kuathletics.com/news/2013/6/6/060613aab_600.aspx?path=mbball.

2 *IEG Sponsorship Report*, "Sponsorship Spending Growth Slows in North America As Marketers Eye Newer Media and Marketing Options" (January, 7, 2014). Available from: http://www.sponsorship.com/iegsr/2014/01/07/Sponsorship-Spending-Growth-Slows-In-North-America.aspx, accessed May 9, 2014.

3 Ibid.

4 "Report: Pro Sports Sponsorships Are The Real Financial Deal In NFL, MLB, NBA, NHL," *NYSportsJournalism.com* (November 19, 2010). Available from: http://www.nysportsjournalism.com/sports-deals-hit-stride-111810/, accessed June 24, 2014.

5 *Twenty20, 2014, http://en.wikipedia.org/wiki/Twenty20, accessed June 29, 2014.

6 Ibid.

7 "Cricket Sponsorship Passes $400 Million," *IMR Sports Marketing & Sponsorship* (November 21, 2013), accessed June 29, 2014.

8 Ibid.

9 Ibid.

10 Mark Lyberger, "Responses Submitted to Editor John Kiernan, 2014 FIFA World Cup By The Numbers," *Wallethub.com* (June 9, 2014). Available from: http://wallethub.com/blog/world-cup-by-the-numbers/4433/#ask-the-experts, accessed June 29, 2014.

11 *IEG Sponsorship Report*, "Sponsorship Spending Growth Slows in North America As Marketers Eye Newer Media and Marketing Options" (January, 7, 2014). Available from: http://www.sponsorship.com/iegsr/2014/01/07/Sponsorship-Spending-Growth-Slows-In-North-America.aspx, accessed May 9, 2014.

12 Nick Forrester, "High School Sports Look for Outside Revenue," *SportsPro* (August 2010).

13 John Lombardo, "Team Deals Put Adidas Areas in Some NBA Arena Stores," *Street & Smith's Sport Business Journal* (October 16–22, 2006). Available from: http://www.sportsbusinessdaily.com/Journal/Issues/2006/10/20061016/This-Weeks-News/Team-Deals-Put-Adidas-Areas-In-Some-NBA-Arena-Stores.aspx?hl=Arena%20Partnership&sc=0, accessed June 24, 2014.

14 "FIFA and Adidas Extend Partnership Until 2030," *FIFA.com* (January 21, 2013), accessed May 9, 2014.

15 http://www.kcchiefs.com/news/article-2/Chiefs-Encourage-Young-Readers/98aca55d-114b-482f-ae98-d0624ab7a684.

16 Ibid.

17 Weston Fury Soccer Club, http://www.westonsoccer.net/docs/wfscsponsorshipfundraisingdona/sponsorshipopp/Official%20PDF%202012-13%20Weston%20FC:AYSO%20644%20Sponsorship%20Package.pdf.

18 Scott Hamilton, "PGA Tour Adds Tiffany as Sponsor," *Street & Smith's Sport Business Daily* (December 4, 2006). Available from: http://m.sportsbusinessdaily.com/Journal/Issues/2006/12/20061204/This-Weeks-News/PGA-Tour-Adds-Tiffany-As-Sponsor.aspx, accessed June 29, 2014.

19 http://rio2016.com/en/sponsors/ge, accessed May 9, 2014.

20 "Sponsorships – Corporate Hospitality," *Wyndhamchampionship.com* (2014). Available from: http://www.wyndhamchampionship.com/sponsorships/corporate-hospitality/, accessed June 29, 2014.

21 David Stotlar, "Sponsorship Evaluation: Moving from Theory to Practice," *Sport Marketing Quarterly*, vol. 13, no.1 (2004), 61–64.

22 See, for example, Nigel Pope, "Overview of Current Sponsorship Thought," www.cad.gu.edu.au/cjsm/pope21.htm; R. Abratt, B. Clayton, and L. Pitt, "Corporate Objectives in

Sports Sponsorship," *International Journal of Advertising*, vol. 6 (1987), 299–311; Christine Brooks, *Sports Marketing: Competitive Business Strategies for Sports* (Englewood Cliffs, NJ: Prentice Hall, 1994).

23 Janet Hoek, Philip Gendall, Michelle Jeffcoat, and David Orsman, "Sponsorship and Advertising: A Comparison of Their Effects," *Journal of Marketing Communications*, vol. 3, no. 1 (1997), 21–32.

24 "Major League Baseball Properties Announces State Farm as 'Official Insurance Company of major league Baseball,'" *MLB.com* (June 29, 2007). Available from: http://mlb.mlb.com/news/press_releases/press_release.jsp?ymd=20070629&content_id=2055865&vkey=pr_mlb&fext=.jsp&c_id=mlb&partner=rss_mlb.

25 Dennis M. Sandler and David Shani, "Ambush Marketing: Who Gets the Gold?" *Journal of Advertising Research*, vol. 29 (1989), 9–14.

26 A. Choi, "Ambush Marketing – Sport Marketing," USF Sport Management Class Power Point Presentation (2010)

27 Robert Passikoff, "Ambush Marketing: An Olympic Competition. And Nike Goes for Gold," *Forbes* (August 7, 2012).

28 *Atlanta Constitution Journal* (December 29, 1995). Available from: www.atlantagames.com/WEB.oly.getcoke2.html.

29 Robert Passikoff, "Ambush Marketing: An Olympic Competition. And Nike Goes for Gold," *Forbes* (August 7, 2012).

30 Luke Hulse, "Ambush Marketing: The 10 Most Creative Guerrilla Campaigns Ever," *The PrintsomeBlog.com* (February 13, 2014). Available from: http://www.printsome.com/blog/2014/ambush-marketing-10-creative-guerrilla-campaigns/, accessed June 29, 2013.

31 John Kalogiannides, "Ambush Marketing and The World Cup," *The Sponsorship Place* (June 15, 2014). Available from: http://www.thesponsorshipspace.com/#!Ambush-Marketing-and-The-World-Cup-/cb1r/19361BB8-A4B3-4FDE-A79F-F35F25686904, accessed June 29, 2014.

32 "Brands Set Sponsor Ambush," *Sports Marketing* (November 2000), 2.

33 "In a Risky Action Burger King Uses Anderson Silva to Gain Profit with the Olympic Games" (2012). Available from: http://www.carlezzo.com.br/en/ler-noticia.php?id=83.

34 Alina Dumitrache, "Mercedes-Benz to Sponsor US Open, Replaces Lexus," *Autoevolution.com* (October 2009).

35 Keir Beadling, "Mavericks Announce Partnership with Sony Ericsson," *Surfersvillage Global Surf News* (January 2009).

36 "March Madness: Jetsetter Offers Luxury Hotel Packages and Ticket Offerings for NCAA Tournament," (2012). Available from: http://www.gadling.com/2012/03/13/march-madness-jetsetter-offers-luxury-hotel-packages-and-ticket/. Official Press Release – NCAA (February 2008).

37 Paralympic ticket sales smash records (2012). Available from: http://www.aljazeera.com/sport/paralympics/2012/09/201296155157894823.html.

38 Nancy Lough and Richard Irwin, "A Comparative Analysis of Sponsorship Objectives for U.S. Women's Sport and Traditional Sport Sponsorship," *Sport Marketing Quarterly*, vol. 10, no. 4 (2001), 202–211.

39 Dan Migala, "Be a Good Host: How to Increase Revenue Through Non-Traditional Hospitality Outings," *The Migala Report* (June 2, 2004). Available from: http://migalareport.com/node/66, accessed June 24, 2014.

40 Roger Bennett, "Corporate Hospitality: Executive Indulgence or Vital Corporate Communications Weapon," *Corporate Communications: An International Journal*, vol. 8, no. 4 (2003), 229–240.

41 USGA, www.usga.org/championships/U_S_Open_2011_2013_Tickets_Hospitatlity_and_Volunteers/.

42 "$2,145,000 Charitable Donation Announced by Shell Houston Open Officials," Official Press Release – Shell Houston Open (October 2010).

43 http://mavericksinvitational.com/2012/11/gopro-signs-on-as-presenting-sponsor-for-the-mavericks-invitational

44 "PGA Tour's Final Charity Total for 2009 Hits $108 Million," *Pgatour.com* (January 2010).

45 Alain Ferrand and Monique Pages, "Image Sponsoring: A Methodology to Match Event and Sponsor," *Journal of Sport Management*, vol. 10, no. 3 (July 1996), 278–291.

46 "Major League Baseball Announces Extension of Historic Sponsorship with Gillette Dating Back to 1939," Official Press Release – Major League Baseball (April 2009).

47 Jennifer C. Kerr, "Consumer Group Wants College Sports to Nix the Beer Ads," *Associated Press* (November 12, 2003).

48 Robert Copeland, Wendy Frisby, and Ronald McCarville, "Understanding the Sport Sponsorship Process From a Corporate Perspective," *Journal of Sport Management*, vol. 10, no. 1 (1996), 32–48. A. Edwards, "Sports Marketing: How Corporations Select Sports Sponsorships," *The Coaching Director*, vol. 6, no. 3 (1991), 44–47. Jeff

Jensen, "Sports Marketing Links Need Nurturing," *Advertising Age*, vol. 65, no. 13 (1994), 30. Stephen Kindel, "Anatomy of a Sports Promotion," *Financial World*, vol. 162, no. 8 (1993), 48. P. Lucas, "Card Marketers go for the Gold," *Credit Card Management*, vol. 9, no. 2 (1996), 22–26. James H. Martin, "Using a Perceptual Map of the Consumer's Sport Schema to Help Make Sponsorship Decisions," *Sport Marketing Quarterly*, vol. 3, no. 3 (1994), 27–31. Douglas W Nelms, "Going for the Gold," *Air Transport World*, vol. 33, no. 11 (1996), 71–74. Nigel K. Pope, "Sport Sponsorship in the Corporate Plan," *Lecture Notes Week 8* (October 5, 1997). Available from: http://www.cad.gu.edu.au/market/cyber-journal_of_sport_marketing/cjsm.htm. Nigel K. Pope and Kevin E. Voges, "An Exploration of Sponsorship Awareness by Product Category and Message Location in Televised Sporting Events," *Cyber-Journal of Sport Marketing*, vol. 1, no. 1 (1997),16–27. David K. Stotlar and David A. Johnson, "Assessing the Impact and Effectiveness of Stadium Advertising on Sport Spectators at Division I Institutions," *Journal of Sport Management*, vol. 3, no. 2 (1989), 90–102. Douglas M. Turco, "Event Sponsorship: Effects on Consumer Brand Loyalty and Consumption," *Sport Marketing Quarterly*, vol. 3, no. 3 (1994), 35–37.

49 Roger Williams, "Making the Decision and Paying for It," *Mark McCormack's Guide to Sports Marketing*, International Sports Marketing Group (1996), 166–168.

50 Brant Wansley, "Best Practices Will Help Sponsorships Succeed." *Marketing News* (September 1, 1997), 8.

51 "11th Annual IEG/Performance Research: Sponsorship Decision-Makers Survey," *IEG* (March 2011).

52 "Coca-Cola Launches 'Open The Games. Open Happiness' Campaign for the Vancouver 2010 Olympic Winter Games," Official Press Release – The Coca-Cola Company (January 2010).

53 David Shani and Dennis Sandler, "Climbing the Sports Event Pyramid," *Marketing News* (August 26, 1996), 6.

54 Christine Brooks, *Sports Marketing* (Benjamin Cummings, 1994).

55 Jeremy Mullman, "Is Nike Next? ATA Drops Scandal-Prone Vick; Football Pitchman Faces Indictment for His Alleged Role in Dog-Fighting Ring," *Advertising Age* (June 4, 2007), p.6.

56 Kantar Media Press Room, "March Madness Generated $1.15 Billion in Ad Revenue in 2013," Kantar Media (March 10, 2014). Available from: http://kantarmedia.us/press/march-madness-generated-1-billion-ad-revenue-2013, accessed June 29, 2014.

57 Caroline Kennedy, "Selling School Spirit: Say Hurrah for Collegiate Licensed Product, a Growing Category That Taps Team Loyalty and Alumni Pride," *Gifts and Decorative Accessories* (June 1, 2007).

58 "UNC, Nike Sign New 10-Year Contract," UNC General Alumni Association (July 2009).

59 Katie Thomas, "WNBA Signs Jamba Juice as New Sponsor," *Nytimes.com* (August 2010).

60 Barry Janoff, "WNBA Scores Points in Diversity Marketing," *Mediapost.com* (May 27, 2014). Available from: http://www.mediapost.com/publications/article/226619/wnba-scores-points-in-diversity-marketing.html, accessed July 1, 2014.

61 Sammy Said, "The 10 Biggest Event and Sport Sponsorships," *the richest.com* (August 6, 2013). Available from: http://www.therichest.com/sports/the-10-biggest-event-and-sport-sponsorships/, accessed July 1, 2104.

62 Bryan McWilliam, "Anheuser-Busch a Sports Sponsorship Heavyweight," SportsNetworker.com (May 24, 2013). Available from: http://www.sportsnetworker.com/2013/05/24/anheuser-busch-a-sports-sponsorship-heavyweight/, accessed May 9, 2014

63 Ibid.

64 Doug Ferguson, "Web.com Takes over as Title Sponsor of Nationwide Tour, Starting Right Now," *PGA.com* (2014). Available from: http://www.pga.com/news/nationwide-tour/webcom-takes-over-title-sponsor-nationwide-tour-starting-right-now, accessed July 1, 2014.

65 Ibid.

66 "Nike 6.0 Increases Winter Dew Tour Sponsorship with Namesake Breckenridge Stop," *www.theskichannel.com* (September 2010).

67 Rick Burton, "A Case Study on Sports Property Servicing Excellence: National Football League Properties," *Sport Marketing Quarterly*, vol. 5, no. 3 (1996), 23–30.

68 Nancy Boomer, "Winnipeg's Next Flood," www.marketingmag.ca/Content/1.98/special.html.

69 Jeff Jenson, "Nike Creates New Division to Stage Global Events," *Advertising Age* (September 30, 1996), 2.

70 Brant Wansley, "Best Practices Will Help Sponsorships Succeed." *Marketing News* (September 1, 1997), 8.

71 Carol Emert, "Olympic Seal of Approval," *The San Francisco Chronicle* (September 2, 2000), D1.

72 Ibid.

73 Pascale Quester and Thierry Lardinoit, "Sponsors' Impact on Attitude and Purchase Intentions: Longitudinal Study of the 2000

Olympic Games" (December 2001). Available from: http://130.195.95.71:8081/WWW/ANZMAC2001/home.htm, accessed May 7, 2014.

74 Stuart Elliott, "After $5 Billion Is Bet, Marketers Are Racing to Be Noticed Amid the Clutter of the Summer Games," *The New York Times* (July 16, 1996), D6.

75 Pascale Quester and Thierry Lardinoit, "Sponsors' Impact on Attitude and Purchase Intentions: Longitudinal Study of the 2000 Olympic Games" (December 2001). Available from: http://130.195.95.71:8081/WWW/ANZMAC2001/home.htm, accessed May 7, 2014.

76 Brenda Pitts and Jennifer Slattery, "An Examination of the Effects of Time on Sponsorship Awareness Levels," *Sport Marketing Quarterly*, vol. 13, no. 1 (2004), 43–54.

77 "McDonald's to Sponsor Ohio State Athletics" (March 13, 2007). Available from: http://www.bizjournals.com/columbus/stories/2007/03/12/daily9.html?from_msnbc=1, accessed May 8, 2014.

78 *IEG Sponsorship Report*, "Sponsorship Spending Growth Slows in North America As Marketers Eye Newer Media and Marketing Options" (January, 7, 2014). Available from: http://www.sponsorship.com/iegsr/2014/01/07/Sponsorship-Spending-Growth-Slows-In-North-America.aspx, accessed May 9, 2014.

Pricing concepts and strategies

After completing this chapter, you should be able to:

- Explain the relationship among price, value, and benefits.
- Understand the relationship between price and the other marketing mix elements.
- Describe how costs and organizational objectives affect pricing decisions.
- Explain how the competitive environment influences pricing decisions.
- Describe how and when price adjustments should be made in the final stage of pricing.

If you were an executive of a sports franchise, what price would you charge your fans? What factors would you consider when making your pricing decision in a continually changing marketing environment? How would you estimate the demand for tickets? Will the financial benefit of increasing prices offset the negative fan relations?

In this chapter, we explore the subjective nature of pricing sports products. More specifically, we consider how factors such as consumer demand, organizational objectives, competition, and technology impact pricing. Also, we examine how pricing interacts with the other elements of the marketing mix and how effective pricing adjustments are made. Let us begin by developing a basic understanding of pricing.

What is price?

Price is a statement of value for a sports product. For example, the money we pay for being entertained by the Boston Celtics is price. The money that we pay for shorts featuring the Notre Dame logo is price. The money we pay for a personal seat license, which gives us the right to purchase a season ticket, is price. The money we pay to experience the Richard Petty Driving School is price. In all these examples, the price paid is a function of the value placed on the sports product by consumers.

Photo 12.1 To some, golf lessons may be priceless

Source: Shutterstock.com

The essence of pricing is the exchange process discussed in Chapter 1. Price is simply a way to quantify the value of the objects being exchanged. Typically, money is exchanged for the sports product. We pay $26 in exchange for admission to the sporting event. However, the object of value that is being exchanged does not always have to be money. For instance, Play It Again Sports, a new and used sporting goods retailer, allows consumers to trade their previously owned sports equipment for the store's used or new equipment. This form of pricing is more commonly referred to as barter or trade. It is common for kids who exchange baseball cards to use this form of trade. Many golf courses hire retirees and pay them very low wages in exchange for free rounds of golf.

Regardless of how pricing is defined, value is the central tenet of pricing. The value placed on a ticket to a sporting event is based on the relationship of the perceived benefits to the price paid. Stated simply,

$$\text{Values} = \frac{\text{Perceived benefits of sports product}}{\text{Price of sports product}}$$

The perceived benefits of the sports product, or what the product does for the user, are based on its tangible and intangible features. The tangible benefits are important in determining price because these are the features of the product that a consumer can actually see, touch, or feel. For example, the comfort of the seats, the quality of the concessions, and the appearance of the stadium are all tangible aspects of a sporting event. The intangible benefits of going to a sporting event may include spending time with friends and family, feelings of association with the team when they win (e.g., BIRGing), or "being seen" at the game.[1]

The perceived benefit of attending a St. Louis Cardinals game is a subjective experience based on each individual's perception of the event, the sport, and the team. One consumer may pay a huge amount to see the game because of the perceived benefits of the product (mostly intangible), whereas another consumer may attend the game only if given a ticket. In either case, the perceived benefits either meet or exceed the price, resulting in "perceived value."

For the high-involvement sports fan the Cardinals ticket represents a chance to be able to tell his grandchildren that he saw the 2001 Rookie of the Year and 2005, 2008, and 2009 MVP, Albert Pujols. To the no- or low-involvement individual, the same game may appear to be a complete waste of time. Again, it is important to recognize that the value placed on attending the sporting event is unique to each individual, even though they are consuming the same product (in this case, the Cardinals game). As researcher Valerie Zeithaml points out, "What constitutes value – even in a single product category – appears to be highly personal and idiosyncratic."[2]

Using a different example, a Ted Williams rookie baseball card in mint condition may be priced at $1500. A collector or baseball enthusiast may see this as a value because the perceived benefits outweigh the price. However, the noncollector (or the mom or dad who threw our cards away) may perceive the card as having barely more value than the cost of the paper on which it is printed.

In yet another example, professional sports franchises are assigned monetary values based on tangibles such as gate receipts, media revenues, venue revenues (e.g., concessions, stadium advertising, and naming), players' costs, and operating expenses. Further consideration in the value of a professional sports franchise is brand equity, a highly intangible characteristic. Table 12.1 provides a list of the franchises having the highest values in each sport and the respective percentage change from the previous year.

The combination of revenue growth and investments in new, revenue-rich ballparks (for example the New York Yankees and the Dallas Cowboys moved into their new homes in 2010), fueled a 2 percent increase in MLB average team values from 2009, to an average of $491 million. The average NFL team is worth $1.02 billion. The

Table 12.1 Top professional sports franchise values in 2014

Major League Baseball	**Current in millions**	**1-Year Change**
Yankees	$2500	+9%
LA Dodgers	$2000	+24%
Red Sox	$1500	+14%
National Football League	**Current in millions**	**1-Year Change**
Cowboys	$2300	+10%
Patriots	$1800	+10%
Redskins	$1700	+6%
National Basketball Association	**Current in millions**	**1-Year Change**
Knicks	$1400	+27%
Lakers	$1350	+35%
Bulls	$1000	+25%
National Hockey League	**Current in millions**	**2-Year Change**
Maple Leafs	$1150	+15%
Rangers	$850	+13%
Canadians	$775	+35%

average hockey team increased their worth to approximately $228 million, a 2 percent increase from 2009, while NBA teams are worth $367 million.[3]

Two important points emerge from the previous examples of value. First, value varies greatly from consumer to consumer because the perceived benefits of any sports product will depend on personal experience. Second, pricing is based on perceived value and perceived benefits. As such, consumers' subjective perceptions of the sports product's benefits and image are fundamental to setting the right price. In this case, image really is everything.

DEAL TO END LOCKOUT REACHED

The NFL Players Association and the league's owners have reached agreement on the remaining points needed in their 10-year labor deal, sources from both sides said.

Despite the fact the new agreement will require a majority vote from the players, that part of the deal between the two sides is considered a formality, according to sources.

The NFLPA is making plans for a major press conference Monday. But first the player reps' executive committee was scheduled to fly to Washington, D.C., on Sunday so they can vote Monday.

Just as the NFL would not have called a vote Thursday in Atlanta without knowing it would pass in the way it did – 31–0 with one abstention – the NFLPA would also not be going forward without that assurance.

NFLPA executive director DeMaurice Smith knows his executive committee, his players reps and the rest of his constituents well enough to know how they will vote.

Plus, no collective bargaining agreement has ever been turned down by the players when approved by leadership.

The executive committee members and the individual team player reps are perhaps the most informed and involved group that any team sport has seen in recent years.

Many of these players were a part of the CBA process in 2006, providing them the knowledge and experience they used in these talks.

Once the players ratify the deal, training camps and free agency are likely to begin the same day, in what would be the equivalent of merging Thanksgiving and Christmas into one holiday.

By rule, training camps can't start until the new league year does.

Major breakthroughs in Saturday discussions set up the timetable for the resolution to the 130-day lockout.

Owners tentatively agreed to a players-recommended plan for the NFLPA to bring players into team facilities starting as early as Wednesday to physically vote on whether to recertify the current trade association as a union, a source told ESPN.com's John Clayton.

The players' executive committee will meet in Washington on Monday, a move that, according to a high-ranking NFLPA official, was not communicated to the NFLPA executive committee until Saturday morning via phone.

Following that, a recommendation has to be made by the 32 player representatives, likely via conference call. As of late Saturday night, no time had been set for that vote, but it is expected to occur Monday after the executive committee votes to recommend approval, according to the high-ranking official.

The executive committee is also expected to vote to recommend recertifying itself as a union, according to the source. A recommendation also has to be made by the 32 player representatives on that count.

When the executive committee accepts the new CBA, players from certain teams will be granted permission to report to training camps Wednesday and players from other teams will be asked to report to training camps Friday, a source said. The hope from both sides is there are enough votes to recertify the union by as early as Friday.

For that to happen, a 50-percent-plus-one-vote majority of the players have to accept the NFLPA as its union and accept the terms of a CBA.

Much of the confidence in Monday's vote is due in part to the continued working relationship between Smith and NFL commissioner Roger Goodell, a source said. The pair have been working with each other directly as the sides near an agreement and continued to do so through the weekend to ensure the remaining issues were resolved, according to a source.

Smith, a source said, has pledged to Goodell that he will also expedite the remaining issues before the first preseason game is played, creating optimism that those games will not be canceled. In that vein, Smith has personally taken on much of the work on the actual CBA-related documents, with his legal team, including NFLPA lawyer Jeffrey Kessler, assisting.

According to the source, Smith took on this responsibility as a show of good faith, because the NFL's management council executive committee had been skeptical due to its prior experience with Kessler as legal counsel.

The NFL announced Thursday it would open its doors to players under contract two days after the NFLPA executive committee accepts the CBA and settlement terms from existing lawsuits. The league also said that free agency would start the day after the union is recertified.

Therefore, under this tentative schedule for recertification, the pre-league year buffer period could start Wednesday.

Under that scenario, teams could potentially open contract talks with their own unrestricted free agents, restricted free agents and draft choices Wednesday. However, no contracts could be signed until Saturday at the earliest. In that scenario, teams would also be able to renegotiate contracts with players from their own team starting as early as Wednesday.

Upon recertification of the union, free agency could start Saturday at 2 p.m. ET and rosters would be allowed to expand to 90 players.

It is still uncertain when teams would be able to sign undrafted free agents.

It was vital for the NFLPA to have enough time for recertification and have a period of time for the renewed union to work out final details of its benefit plans.

Only a union can negotiate benefits for its members and the NFLPA feared a Tuesday deadline to recertify would not leave enough time to properly negotiate changes in the benefits packages. Under terms of the owners' agreement from Thursday, players would have reverted back to the 2010 benefits plan if they didn't make adjustments within a certain time period.

As talks progressed Saturday, the sides removed one roadblock while moving the dial on another.

A league source said San Diego Chargers receiver Vincent Jackson, one of the 10 named plaintiffs in the players' antitrust lawsuit against the NFL, is now willing to release his claim without compensation, meaning no money or lifting of the franchise tag. Jackson was the last of the 10 named plaintiffs unwilling to drop his claim.

The sides also got closer to settling the $4 billion network television insurance case, according to a source. That case, which is in the court of U.S. District Judge David Doty in Minneapolis, involved damages suffered by the players after Doty ruled against the owners.

Source: Article author: Adam Schefter. Rightsholder: ESPN.com; http://espn.go.com/nfl/story/_/id/6797238/2011-nfl-lockout-owners-players-come-deal-all-points-sources-say.

All too often, price is equated incorrectly with the objective costs of producing the sports product. Because many sports products are intangible services, setting prices based on the costs of producing the product alone becomes problematic. For instance, how do you quantify the cost of spending time with your friends at a sporting event or having the television rights to broadcast NFL games? How do sports organizations provide a quality experience for fans so they feel they are getting their money's worth? Many event promoters believe the solution is to add more value via interactive experiences for the fan. For example:

The Tampa Bay Rays' Tropicana Field is filled with fan interactive zones for fans of all ages to enjoy during the baseball season. Left Field Street consists of a 2k Sports Lounge to play Major League Baseball 2K10, Baseball Trivia Challenge game show, Custom Jersey Shop, Louisville Slugger Wood Shop, Mountain Dew Extreme Zone with batting and Topps Make Your Own Baseball Card. Right Field Street is geared toward the younger fans with the Rays Baseball Carnival, Raymond's Art Studio and

Raymond's Room. Center Field houses the Rays Touch Tank, where fans can touch live cow nose rays for free during home games. In a similar vein, the NCAA created Hoop City for the men's and the women's Final Four. The interactive experience gives basketball fans a chance to participate in a number of hoop skills contests, get autographs, and share the excitement of the national championship.[4]

The stadium experience has also been jazzed up to enhance value. Many professional and collegiate teams are now choosing fans right from the audience to participate in promotions on court or on field during breaks in play. This allows fans to set foot on the playing surface, and provide audience entertainment. Small, in-seat video screens are also becoming popular at stadiums and arenas that want to offer the ultimate balance between watching the action live and on TV. Each seat is equipped with a video monitor that can offer game replays, other cable TV networks, stock market updates, and online service. Furthermore, the use of social media provides teams the opportunities to elevate and enhance the level of interaction with their fans. Utilization of portable smartphones enables teams to provide fans with an interactive experience, thereby enhancing value.

The ultimate question is whether these "extras" create value and add benefits for the fans. Sport Marketing Research Institute (SMRI) research has found that nine out of 10 fans attend sporting events out of a love for the game or team. So are these extras creating real fans or trying to buy their way into fans' hearts? Do stadiums and arenas pay more for the interactive fan elements and end up receiving much less in the end – a fan that attends for the extras, not for the love of sports, the competitive element, the rivalry, the action; in other words – the game?

The determinants of pricing

Now that we have discussed the core concept of price, let us look at some of the factors that affect the pricing decisions of sporting marketers. Pricing decisions can be influenced by internal and external factors, in much the same way that the contingency framework for sports marketing contains both internal and external considerations. **Internal factors**, which are controlled by the organization, include the other marketing mix elements, costs, and organizational objectives. **External (or environmental) factors** that influence pricing are beyond the control of the organization. These include consumer demand, competition, legal issues, the economy, and technology. Figure 12.1 illustrates the influence of the internal and external forces on pricing decisions. Let us look at each of these forces in greater detail.

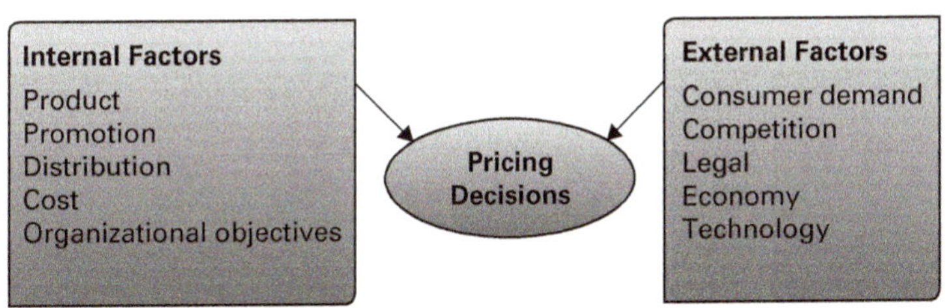

Figure 12.1 Internal and external influences on pricing

Source: Gary Armstrong and Philip Kotler, *Marketing: An Introduction*, 7th ed. 2005. Credit: "Kotler, Philip R; Armstrong, Gary, *Marketing: An Introduction*, 4th Edition, © 1997, pp.471, 312.

12

SPORTS MARKETING HALL OF FAME

Pete Rozelle

Pete Rozelle led the National Football League for nearly three decades, helping it survive bidding wars with three rival leagues and three players' strikes, before retiring unexpectedly in 1989.

Rozelle's pioneering sports marketing accomplishments include Monday Night Football and the Super Bowl, which blossomed into America's most-watched sporting event. The "Father of the Super Bowl" put the NFL on television just about everywhere and transformed the way Americans spend Sunday afternoons.

Rozelle arrived at about the same time as the rival American Football League, a development that created competition for players and television ratings. In 1962, Rozelle negotiated a $9.3 million television contract with CBS, a deal that earned him reelection as commissioner and a $10,000 bonus that pushed his salary to $60,000. By 1966, the two warring leagues, weary of the battle for player talent, merged, creating a single professional football league, with Rozelle as commissioner. The merger also produced a world championship game, which would eventually come to be known as the Super Bowl.

It was Rozelle who brought sports into 10 figures when he negotiated a landmark five-year, $2.1 billion contract with television's three major networks in 1982. Then he expanded to cable, selling a Sunday night series to ESPN in 1986. The current television contract, for which Rozelle set the groundwork, gets $1.93 billion from Fox alone, more than 2,000 times what Rozelle got in his first contract with CBS in 1962.

Along with these accomplishments, Rozelle's biggest contribution may have been introducing revenue sharing in pro football 30 years before it created havoc in other sports. Doing so allowed teams in minor markets like Green Bay to equally share TV revenues – the biggest part of the NFL pie – with teams in New York, Chicago, and Los Angeles.

Rozelle is also credited, along with Roone Arledge, for creating Monday Night Football, now the nation's longest-running sports series. Because the NFL had an agreement not to televise on Friday night or Saturday in competition with high school and college football, he decided Monday night would be the obvious time to showcase a single game nationally. Overall, Rozelle's impact was as much social as it was financial. He changed the nation's leisure habits and lifestyle by making Sunday afternoons and Monday nights sacred during football seasons.

Source: "Innovator Rozelle Dies at 70," *Cincinnati Enquirer* (December 7, 1996), C1, C5. Used with permission of Bloomberg L.P.

Internal factors

Other marketing mix variables

Price is the element of the marketing mix that has been called a "pressure point" for consumers. That is, price can make or break a consumer's decision to purchase a sports product. Although price is critical, the other **marketing mix variables** must be carefully considered when determining the price of a sports product. Pricing must be consistent with product, distribution, and promotional planning. For marketing goals to be reached, all the marketing mix elements must work in concert with one another.

How is price connected to other marketing mix variables? Let us begin by examining the relationship between price and promotional planning. Each of the promotional mix elements discussed in Chapter 9 (advertising, public relations, personal selling, sales promotions, and sponsorships) is related to price. Broadly, the promotion function communicates the price of the sports product to consumers. For example, advertisements often inform consumers about the price of a sports product. In comparative advertisements, the price of a sports product versus its competition may be the central focus of the message.

Many forms of sales promotion are directly related to price. For example, price reductions are price discounts designed to encourage immediate purchase of the sports product. Coupons and rebates are simply another way for consumers to get money back from the original purchase price. Moreover, premiums are sometimes offered for reduced prices (or for free) to build long-term relationships with consumers. For instance, kids can join the Pittsburg Pirates Bucaroos Kids Club for just $15 for the entire season. For this, kids receive the following benefits: ticket vouchers, Web-based newsletters and e-mails about other Pirates/Bucaroos special events, Pirates apparel, invitation to one autograph session, Front-of-the-Line privileges for Kids-Run-the-Bases, and an opportunity to be chosen to participate in select Kids Take the Field events.

The relationship between pricing and promotion also extends to personal selling. Depending on the sports product, sales personnel sometimes negotiate prices. Although not the case for most sports products, some prices are negotiable. The sale of boats, golf clubs, squash lessons, scalped tickets, and luxury boxes each represents an example of a sports product that has the potential for flexible pricing.

The public relations component of the promotional mix is also related to pricing in several ways. First, publicity and public relations (PR) personnel often stress the value of their ticket prices to potential consumers. For example, the Phoenix Coyotes public relations department may provide fans information about how the Coyotes have the lowest cost in the NHL for a family of four to attend a game. The Kansas City Royals may emphasize that they have the lowest average ticket prices in baseball, compared with other major league sports and teams.

Second, public relations are important in the launch of a new sports product. For example, the Dayton Dragons initiated a PR campaign to engage the public prior to naming the team and the onset of their first season. This PR strategy has helped the Dragons achieve record-setting attendance standards that consist of being the first and only team in minor league baseball history to sell out a season before it began. They have sold out every season since their inception in 2000. Media releases that alert the public to the features of the new product, as well as the pricing, are an important aspect of creating awareness. In addition, sources not only inside but also outside of the sports organization play roles in providing information about changes to the product. For instance, when a professional sports team raises its ticket price, you can bet that the story will generate "negative public relations."

A final link between price and promotion is the cost of the promotion itself. The price of running a promotion may influence potential consumers. The price of a Super Bowl advertisement (upward of a record $4 million for a 30-second spot in 2014), upon becoming public knowledge, may shape consumers' expectations and perceptions of not only the advertisement, but also the product and the company. Consumers' expectations for advertisements featured during the Super Bowl are generally higher because of the hype and the advertisement's high price tag. At the same time, the high levels of free publicity generated by Super Bowl advertisements, both prior to and after the event itself, can offset the exorbitant expense and render the advertisements cost effective.

The distribution element of the marketing mix is also related to pricing. The price of a sports product is certainly dictated (in part) by the choice of distribution channel(s). In a traditional channel (manufacturer of the sporting good to wholesaler to retailer to consumer), the costs of covering the various functions of the channel members are reflected in the ultimate price charged to consumers. In a more nontraditional channel, such as purchasing a product over the Internet, prices are generally reduced. For example, the Callaway FT-iz driver may cost $500 in a golf specialty store but is sold for hundreds of dollars less via the Internet.

The retailer is also a common member of the distribution channel that shapes pricing decisions. More specifically, the type of retailer selling the sporting good or facility where the sporting event takes place will affect price perceptions. For instance, consumers expect to pay more for golf equipment in a country club pro shop than they do at a local golf discount outlet. Likewise, consumers who attend a football game at Dallas' new AT&T stadium, formerly Cowboy Stadium, which opened in 2010, paid a record average ticket price of $159.95 last season and would expect to pay higher ticket prices for the state-of-the-art facility than do consumers at an aging facility such as Arrowhead Stadium in Kansas City (built in 1972). A concern facing professional sports is that the new sports palaces being built around the country may drive the common fan out of professional sports markets.

A final element of the marketing mix related to price is the sports product itself. The price of attending a sporting event is related to expectations of service quality. The higher the ticket price being purchased, then the higher fan expectations of customer service. Likewise, the higher the price of the sporting goods, then the higher the consumer's expectations of product quality are. In this way, price is used to signal quality to consumers, especially to those who have little or no previous experience using the sports product.

Pricing is also used to differentiate product lines within the sports organization. An organization will offer product lines with different price ranges to attract different target markets. For example, Converse still offers a canvas basketball shoe at a low price for traditionalists who prefer canvas over the more popular – and more expensive – leather style.

The product life cycle also suggests the strength of the price–product relationship. As illustrated in Chapter 8, pricing strategies vary throughout the stages of the product life cycle. For example, during the introductory phase, products are typically priced either low to gain widespread acceptance or high to appeal to a specific target market and to signal quality. Product prices are slashed during the decline phase of the life cycle to eliminate inventory and related overhead costs.

The design of sports products is the final factor that demonstrates the close relationship between product and price. Product design and pricing are interdependent. Sometimes, product design is altered during the manufacturing process to achieve a target price. For instance, a number of championship teams have dramatically dropped payroll in the year following winning the championship, causing fan dissatisfaction and poor performance on the field or court. In this case, the product design refers to the quality of the team; the manufacturing process is the team's performance on the field. Unfortunately, the team and its fans may suffer from this move to achieve target price. Other times, prices must be adjusted (usually upward) to achieve the desired product design. New York Yankees late owner George Steinbrenner historically spent large sums of money to build a winning team (with a record high payroll of $206 million in 2010), with success as the team has appeared in the World Series Championships seven times between 1996 and 2010.

Research has been conducted to examine the relationship between team payroll and team performance in major league baseball from 1985 to 2002. The results indicated that the relationship has changed over time. Unlike the early years, there is now a much clearer relationship between payroll and performance. Specifically, in the latter part of the 1990s and continuing into the twenty-first century, the greater the team payroll and the more equally this payroll is distributed among team members, the better the on-field performance of the team. This is a problem of particular concern because of the growing disparity in team payrolls, which, in turn, affects the competitive balance of the sport.[5]

Clearly, price is closely associated with the rest of the marketing mix. Usually, there are two ways of coordinating the element of price with the rest of the marketing mix variables: nonprice and price competition. Let us look at these two distinctly different pricing strategies in greater detail.

Nonprice versus price competition

Nonprice competition is defined as creating a unique sports product through the packaging, product design, promotion, distribution, or any marketing variable other than price. This approach permits a firm to charge higher prices than its competitors because its product has achieved a competitive advantage. In turn, consumers are often willing to pay more for these products because the perceived benefits derived from the product are believed to be greater. Nevertheless, an element of risk is attached to using this nonprice competition approach.

Consider a commodity like a golf ball. Bridgestone may adopt a nonprice competition strategy for its brand of golf balls (Precept) by featuring the packaging, the product design, or something other than price. This can be a risky strategy for Bridgestone. What if consumers fail to recognize the superiority of the Precept golf ball? They may instead purchase a competitor's lower-priced golf ball that offers the same benefits.

When adopting the distinctly different **price competition** strategy, sellers primarily stimulate consumer demand by offering consumers lower prices. For example, minor league franchises successfully use price competition to attract dissatisfied fans unable or unwilling to spend large sums of money to attend major league sporting events. In response to a price competition strategy, and to offset its own higher ticket costs, a major league franchise is likely to stress the greater intangible benefits associated with attending its more prestigious events. These benefits include the higher quality of competition, the more exciting atmosphere, and the greater athletic abilities of the stars.

Costs

Costs are those factors associated with producing, promoting, and distributing the sports product. Consider the cost of owning a minor league hockey franchise. To produce the competition or event, players are necessary. These players require salaries and equipment in order to perform. In addition, these players require support personnel such as coaches, trainers, equipment managers, and so on. Also, these players need a place to play, which includes the costs of rent, utilities, cleaning, and maintenance. These represent some of the basic costs for producing a hockey game. However, they do not tell the entire story.

In addition to these core costs, other costs can include advertising, game promotions, and the salaries of front-office personnel (secretaries, general managers, and scouts). Team transportation is another cost. All these costs, or the **total cost** of owning a minor league hockey franchise, can be expressed as the sum of the variable and fixed costs, as shown:

$$TC = FC + VC$$

where TC = total cost
FC = fixed cost
VC = variable costs

Fixed costs are the sum of the producer's expenses that are stable and do not change with the quantity of the product consumed. Almost all costs associated with the minor league hockey team in the preceding example would be considered fixed. For example, rent on the arena, salaries, and transportation are all fixed costs. They do not vary at all with the amount of the product consumed (or in this case the team's attendance). The bulk of the game promotions are determined prior to the season and, as a result, are also considered fixed costs.

Variable costs are the sum of the producer's expenses that vary and change as a result of the quantity of the product being consumed. Advertising may represent a variable cost for the minor league hockey franchise. If advertising expenditures increase from one month to the next because the team is doing poorly at the box office, then the dollar amount spent varies. Similarly, advertising could represent a variable cost if additional advertising or promotions are used because attendance is higher than expected.

Although an athletic team experiences very few variable costs in the total cost equation, a manufacturer of pure sporting goods would encounter a significantly greater number of variable costs. Usually, variable costs for manufacturing a sporting good range between 60 and 90 percent of the total costs. For example, the cost of the packaging and materials for producing the good varies by the number of units sold.

Costs are considered an internal factor that influences the pricing decision because they are largely under the control of the sports organization. The minor league hockey team management makes decisions on player salaries, how much money to spend on advertising and promoting the team, and how the team travels. These costs loom large in the sport franchise because they affect the prices charged to the fans.

Obviously, the most visible and controversial costs incurred by professional sports organizations are player salaries. The Spotlight on Sports Marketing Ethics box discusses whether any athletes are worth the huge payday they are receiving.

SPOTLIGHT ON SPORTS MARKETING ETHICS

Astronomical athlete salaries: Are they worth it?

It is a great day to take in a ball game, do not you think? With our hustling, bustling jaunt through the economy, we probably deserve a relaxing afternoon of hot dogs and peanuts with my favorite baseball team – the Shady Valley Primadonnas. Of course, the hot dogs and peanuts are overpriced, and you might need a second mortgage on your house to buy the ticket, but the expense is worth watching the finest athletes in the world display their world-class athletic abilities. We might even coax an autograph from the Primadonnas' all-star centerfielder – Harold "Hair Doo" Dueterman.

Are these guys worth it?

Although we thoroughly enjoy the game – the Primadonnas come from behind to win in the bottom of the ninth – our favorite player, Hair Doo, strikes out four times and commits an error in center field. This raises a really, really important question in the grand scheme of the universe: Is Hair Doo worth his $10 gadzillion salary? Should Hair Doo get 100 times the salary of an average, overworked, underappreciated member of the third estate?

Hair Doo's salary really raises another more general question: Why does anyone get paid what they get paid? Any questions we ask about Hair Doo Dueterman's salary could also be asked about the wage of any average, overworked underappreciated member of the third estate – Hair Doo's numbers just happen to be bigger. Because wages and salaries are nothing more than prices, the best place to look for answers is the market.

The market says yes!

Let us first ponder the supply side of the market. Hair Doo performs his athletic prowess before thousands of adoring fans – supplies his labor – because he is willing and able to take on his designated duties for a mere $10 gadzillion. If Hair Doo was not willing and able to play baseball for $10 gadzillion, then he would do something else.

Hair Doo's willingness and ability to play our nation's pastime depends on his opportunity cost of other activities, such as deep sea diving, coal mining, ballet dancing, or game show hosting. By selecting baseball, Hair Doo has given up a paycheck plus any other job-related satisfaction that could have been had from those pursuits. He has decided that his $10 gadzillion salary and the nonmonetary enjoyment of playing baseball outweigh his next best alternative. We should have little problem with this decision by Hair Doo, because we all make a similar choice. We pursue a job or career that gives us the most benefits.

But . . . (this is a good place for a dramatic pause) . . . someone also must be willing to pay Hair Doo Dueterman $10 gadzillion to do what he does so well. This is the demand side of the process, which we affectionately call the market. It deserves a little more thought.

The someone who's willing to pay Hair Doo's enormous salary, the guy who signs Hair Doo's paycheck, is the owner of Shady Valley Primadonnas – D. J. Goodluck. You might remember D. J.'s grandfather from Fact 3, "Our Unfair Lives," a wheat farmer on the Kansas plains who had the good fortune of homesteading 160 acres with a BIG pool of crude oil beneath. (The Goodlucks still visit the toilet each morning in a new Cadillac. They did, however, sell their ownership in Houston, Texas, and bought South Carolina.)

Why on earth would D. J. and his Shady Valley Primadonnas baseball organization pay Hair Doo this astronomical $10 gadzillion salary? D. J. must have a pretty good reason. Let us consider D. J.'s position.

Hair Doo's statistics are pretty impressive. In the past five years, he has led the league in umpire arguments, souvenir foul balls for adoring fans, product endorsements for nonbaseball-related items, and instigation of bench-clearing fights. All these have made Hair Doo an all-star, number-one fan attraction.

While Hair Doo may or may not help the Shady Valley Primadonnas win the championship, he does pack fans into the stands. And he has packed fans into the stands for the past five years.

Fans in the stands translate into tickets for the Shady Valley Primadonnas, national television broadcasts, and revenue for D. J. Goodluck. D. J. is willing to pay Hair Doo $10 gadzillion to perform his derring-do, because Hair Doo generates at least $10 gadzillion in revenue for the team. If Hair Doo failed to generate revenue equal to or greater than his $10 gadzillion salary, then D. J. would trade him to the Oak Town Sludge Puppies (the perennial last-place cellar-dwellers in the league), send him to the minor leagues, or just release him from the team.

The bottom line on Hair Doo's salary is the same for any average, overworked, underappreciated member of the third estate – an employer is willing and able to pay a wage up to the employee's contribution to production. If your job is making $20 worth of Hot Mamma Fudge Bananarama Sundaes each day, then your boss – Hot Mamma Fudge – would be willing to pay you $20 per day.

Many are worth even more

As entertainers, athletes are paid for fan satisfaction. The more fans who want to see an athlete perform, the more an athlete is paid. In fact, most athletes – even those who make gadzillions of dollars for each flubbed fly ball, dropped pass, and missed free throw – probably deserve even higher salaries. The reason is competition. The degree of competition on each side of the market can make the price too high or too low. If suppliers have little or no competition, then the price tends to be too high. If buyers have little or no competition, then the price tends to be too low.

In the market for athletes, competition is usually less on the demand side than on the supply side. The supply of athletes tends to be pretty darn competitive. Of course, Hair Doo is an all-star player, but he faces competition from hundreds of others who can argue with umpires and hit foul balls into the stands.

The demand side, however, is less competitive. In most cases, a particular team, like the Shady Valley Primadonnas, has exclusive rights to a player. They can trade those rights to another team, like the Oak Town Sludge Puppies, but the two teams usually do not compete with each other for a player's services. There are a few circumstances – one example is "free agency" – where two or more teams try to hire the same player, but that is the exception rather than the rule.

With little competition among buyers, the price tends to be on the low side. This means that Hair Doo Dueterman's $10 gadzillion salary could be even higher. It means that the Shady Valley Primadonnas probably get more, much more, than $10 gadzillion from ticket sales and television revenue. It means that D. J. Goodluck would probably be willing and able to pay more, much more, than $10 gadzillion for Hair Doo Dueterman's athletic services. The only way to find out how much Hair Doo is worth to the Shady Valley Primadonnas is to force them to compete for Hair Doo's services with other teams.

This is a good place to insert a little note on the three estates. Most owners of professional sports teams, almost by definition if not by heritage, tend to be full-fledged members of the second estate. The players, in contrast, usually spring from the ranks of the third. The idea that one team owns the "rights" of a player stems from the perverse, although changing notion, that the third estate exists for little reason other than to provide second-class servants for the first two estates.

Colleges are worse

If professional athletes who get gadzillions of dollars to play are underpaid, how do college athletes, who get almost nothing, compare? It depends on the sport.

Big-time college sports, especially football and basketball, are highly profitable entertainment industries. Millions of spectators spend tons of money each year for entertainment provided by their favorite college teams. Star college athletes can pack the fans into the stands as well as star professional athletes. With packed stands come overflowing bank accounts for the colleges.

What do the athletes get out of this? What are their "salaries"? Being amateurs, college athletes are not paid an "official" salary. They are, however, compensated for their efforts with a college education, including tuition, books, living accommodations, and a small monthly stipend. Although a college education is not small potatoes – $100,000-plus at many places – this compensation tends to fall far short of the revenue generated for the school. The bottom line is that big-time college athletes, like the pros, are usually underpaid.

The reason is very similar to that of the professional athletes. College athletics have limited competition among the "employers" but a great deal of competition among the "employees." Many more high-school athletes hope to play big-time college ball than ever realize that dream. While different colleges may try to hire – oops, I mean recruit – the same athlete, the collegiate governing bodies, most notably the National Collegiate Athletic Association, limit the degree of competition and fix the "wage" athletes can receive. You often hear about the NCAA penalizing a college because it went "too far" in its recruiting efforts. This translates into the charge that a college paid an athlete "too much" to play, such as new cars, bogus summer jobs with high wages, and cash payments from alumni.

Underpayment is most often a problem for big-time football and basketball revenue-generating sports. Athletes in sports with less spectator interest, such as tennis, gymnastics, or lacrosse, actually may be overpaid based on their contribution to their colleges' entertainment revenue.

Here's a tip to keep in mind in the high-priced world of athletics: Athletes are paid based on their contribution to fan satisfaction. If you think athletes are paid too much, then do not contribute to their salaries by attending games or watching them on television. If, however, you enjoy their performance and are willing to pay the price of admission, then worry not about their pay.

Source: http://cc.kangwon.ac.kr/~kimoon/pr/issues/IS02.html. Credit: Orley Amos.

Whether you agree or disagree with escalating player contracts, there is no dispute that the increasing cost of player salaries has been passed on, in part, to the fans. Table 12.2 shows an example of the Fan Cost Index (FCI) for the MLB. The FCI represents the total dollar amount that a family of four would have to pay to attend a home game. This total cost includes the price of four tickets, two small beers, four sodas, four hot dogs, parking, two game programs, and two twill caps. The other costs indicate the pricing of one unit. In other words, the cost of one beer at the New York Islanders game is $9.50.

Although cost is usually considered to be an internal, controllable factor for organizations, it can have an uncontrollable component. For instance, the league may impose a minimum salary level for a player that is beyond the control of the individual team or owner. The costs of raw materials for producing sporting goods may rise, representing a cost increase that is beyond the control of the manufacturer. Players' unions for professional teams may set minimum standards for travel that are not under the individual team's control. All these examples describe the uncontrollable side of costs that must be continually monitored by the sports marketer.

Organizational objectives

The costs associated with producing a good or service is just one factor in determining the final price. Cost considerations may determine the "price floor" for the sport product. In other words, what will be the minimum price that an organization might charge to cover the cost of producing the sports product? Covering costs, however, may be insufficient from the organization's perspective. This depends largely on the organization's objectives. As we have stressed throughout this text, marketing mix decisions – including pricing – must consider the broader marketing goals. Effective marketing goals should be consistent with the organizational objectives.

There are four categories of **organizational objectives** that influence pricing decisions. These include income, sales, competition, and social concerns. **Income objectives** include achieving maximum profits or simply organizational survival. In the long term, all professional sports organizations are concerned with maximizing their profits and having good returns on investment. Alternatively, amateur athletic events and associations are in sports not necessarily to maximize profits but to "stay afloat." Their organizational objectives center around providing athletes with a place to compete and covering costs.

Sales objectives are concerned with maintaining or enhancing market share and encouraging sales growth. If increasing sales is the basic organizational objective, then a sporting goods manufacturer or team may want to set lower prices to encourage more purchases by existing consumers. In addition, setting lower prices or offering

Table 12.2 An example of the Fan Cost Index (FCI) for the MLB

Team marketing research

Team	Avg. Ticket	Pct. Change	Avg. Premium Ticket	Beer[1]	Soft Drink[1]	Hot Dog	Parking	Program	Cap	FCI	Pct. Change
Boston Red Sox*	$52.32	4.8%	$176.96	$7.75[12]	$4.75[20]	$5.00	$27.00	$5.00	$25.00	$350.78	7.3%
New York Yankees	51.55	0.0%	305.39	6.00[12]	3.00[12]	3.00	35.00	5.00	25.00	337.20	0.0%
Chicago Cubs	44.16	-0.9%	110.49	7.50[16]	4.00[15]	5.50	25.00	4.50	20.00	304.64	2.2%
Philadelphia Phillies	37.42	0.0%	86.25	7.75[21]	4.00[20]	3.75	16.00	5.00	18.00	258.18	0.4%
San Francisco Giants	31.63	5.1%	89.91	7.00[14]	4.50[16]	5.25	20.00	5.00	15.00	239.51	0.7%
St. Louis Cardinals	33.84	2.2%	80.65	6.75[12]	5.25[21]	4.25	10.00	2.50	16.00	233.86	1.3%
New York Mets	25.30	0.0%	83.78	5.75[12]	5.00[16]	6.25	22.00	5.00	19.99	229.68	2.7%
Washington Nationals	35.24	0.0%	187.29	6.50[16]	5.00[24]	5.00	10.00	0.00	12.00	227.96	-3.6%
Miami Marlins*	27.01	-7.7%	116.48	8.00[16]	4.50[24]	6.00	15.00	0.00	19.99	221.02	-3.9%
Detroit Tigers	28.22	7.1%	72.91	5.00[12]	4.25[16]	4.50	20.00	5.00	16.00	219.88	12.5%
Los Angeles Dodgers	25.80	15.3%	254.19	6.75[20]	5.75[24]	5.50	10.00	5.00	18.00	217.69	6.2%
Toronto Blue Jays[2]	22.78	0.0%	53.83	6.82[14]	4.77[24]	5.23	22.74	4.55	20.55	217.69	1.1%
Houston Astros	27.98	-13.6%	69.30	5.00[14]	4.50[21]	4.75	15.00	4.00	16.99	215.90	-3.8%
Minnesota Twins	32.59	0.0%	74.18	7.50[20]	4.50[20]	4.00	6.00	0.00	15.00	215.36	-2.7%
MLB LEAGUE AVERAGE	**27.93**	**2.0%**	**93.41**	**6.09[15]**	**4.02[19]**	**4.32**	**15.09**	**2.84**	**17.23**	**212.46**	**2.3%**
Chicago White Sox	26.05	0.0%	86.94	6.50[16]	4.50[24]	3.75	20.00	4.00	15.99	210.18	0.0%
Seattle Mariners	28.45	0.0%	126.82	6.00[12]	4.50[16]	4.50	20.00	3.00	10.00	207.80	2.0%
Texas Rangers	23.54	4.4%	61.05	5.00[16]	5.25[24]	5.00	12.00	5.00	17.99	203.14	3.6%
Colorado Rockies[4]	23.65	0.0%	47.39	6.00[16]	3.25[18]	4.75	13.00	5.00	20.00	201.60	2.5%
Oakland Athletics*	22.84	3.3%	48.22	5.00[12]	4.50[16]	5.25	20.00	5.00	15.00	200.36	11.0%
Los Angeles Angels	27.40	1.5%	76.74	4.50[16]	2.75[12]	4.50	10.00	3.00	16.00	195.60	0.8%
Kansas City Royals	24.73	24.7%	96.55	6.50[16]	5.00[22]	5.00	10.00	0.00	15.00	191.91	11.4%
Milwaukee Brewers	24.96	0.0%	43.22	6.00[16]	2.50[12]	3.50	9.00	0.00	16.00	176.84	0.0%
Baltimore Orioles	24.97	4.5%	44.93	6.75[16]	1.50[12]	1.50	8.00	5.00	15.00	173.39	2.6%
Atlanta Braves	18.53	3.8%	50.65	7.25[16]	4.75[22]	4.75	15.00	0.00	15.00	171.62	0.5%
Tampa Bay Rays	21.01	3.0%	87.07	5.00[12]	5.00[22]	5.00	0.00	0.00	17.99	170.02	9.3%
Pittsburgh Pirates	18.32	6.5%	61.84	5.50[16]	3.25[16]	3.25	15.00	0.00	22.00	169.28	2.7%
Cincinnati Reds	22.03	3.2%	61.60	5.50[12]	1.00[12]	1.00	17.00	4.00	18.00	168.12	1.7%
Cleveland Indians*	21.31	3.0%	54.33	4.00[12]	3.00[12]	3.00	12.00	0.00	16.50	162.24	0.3%
San Diego Padres	16.37	2.4%	41.18	5.00[14]	4.00[22]	4.00	8.00	0.00	18.99	153.45	1.0%
Arizona Diamondbacks[3]	17.98	6.4%	52.14	4.00[14]	1.50[24]	2.75	10.00	0.00	9.99	126.89	3.6%

Average ticket price represents a weighted average of season ticket prices for general seating categories, determined by factoring the tickets in each price range as a percentage of the total number of seats in each venue. Premium seating (tickets that come with at least one added amenity or is classified by team as premium) are not included in the survey to calculate average ticket price. Luxury suites are also excluded from the survey. Season ticket pricing is used for any team that offers some or all tickets at lower prices for customers who buy season seats. Teams have a say in what seats are considered general or premium.

The Fan Cost Index™ comprises the prices of four (4) adult average-price tickets, two (2) small draft beers, four (4) small soft drinks, four (4) regular-size hot dogs, parking for one (1) car, two (2) game programs and two (2) least-expensive, adult-size adjustable caps. Costs were determined by telephone calls with representatives of the teams, venues and concessionaires. Identical questions were asked in all interviews. Superscript numbers next to Beer and Soft Drink prices denote smallest available size in ounces.

* Boston, Cleveland and Oakland worked with TMR on changes, some retroactive, due to incorrect information provided by the teams. Boston had provide single-game, rather than season ticket prices for years. This corrected for the 2014 report and the percentage change was adjusted accordingly. Cleveland had included tickets and sections not available for season ticket purchases in the past, lowering their average. Oakland had failed to update concession increases, which caused a larger percentage increases in FCI in 2014.

[1] Superscript numbers next to Beer and Soft Drink prices denote smallest available size in ounces.

[2] Prices for the Blue are converted to US dollars and comparison prices were converted using a recent exchange rate provided by the Blue Jays. Last season's prices were converted using the same exchange rate for a valid comparison.

Table 12.2 (continued)

2014 mlb fan cost index

AVER AGE TICKET PRICE UP 2.0 PERCENT AT $27.93; TOTAL FCI UP 2.3 PERCENT TO $212.46

The average Major League Baseball season ticket has increased by 2.0 percent to $27.93 for the 2014 season, according to the Team Marketing Report Fan Cost Index®.

This minor increase is part of a trend; last season, the average MLB ticket increased by 1.8 percent. The year before that, there was no percentage increase. In 2010-11, tickets rose by a com- bined 2.7 percent.

The Fan Cost Index (FCI) total, the average price to take a fam- ily of four to a game, increased by 2.3 percent to $212.46. The FCI is created by combining four non-premium season tickets, two beers, four soft drinks, four hot dogs, parking, two programs or scorecards, and two adult-size hats.

TMR uses season ticket pricing and the lowest full-size prices for the ancillary items, so if a team has an $8 beer and a $6 beer, TMR uses the latter to show how much, or how little, one can spend at a game.

The average "premium" season ticket is $93.41. TMR splits up premium and general seats in its methodology.

The Yankees lead baseball with an average premium price of $305.39, while the Dodgers are second at $254.19.

The "premium" designation is supposed to be used for club seats or any section that has special features. According to TMR research, the MLB average for premium seats is 13.7 percent. The Yankees classify 16.2 percent of season ticket seats as pre- mium, while the Dodgers classify 8.6 percent.

Some teams with newer stadiums have a heavy dose of pre- mium seating. The New York Mets, for example, classify an "amazin'" 59.3 percent of seats as premium. Their premium average ticket is $83.78, compared to a general ticket of $25.30. The Washington Nationals are second-highest in premium per- centage at 26 percent. Their premium average is $187.29, while their general ticket is $35.24.

This season, 17 teams showed increases of more than 1 per- cent in general average tickets, while only two teams lowered their average ticket by more than 1 percent. Eleven teams kept ticket prices essentially flat.

The two teams that dropped prices had the worst records in baseball. After a 111-loss season in its first season in the Ameri- can League, Houston's average ticket price fell 13.6 percent to $27.98. Miami, which lost 100 games, dropped ticket prices by 7.7 percent to $27.01.

Interestingly, many of these increases came from the lower- priced teams. Of the 10 lowest-priced tickets in baseball, nine had percentage increases this season, with only Toronto going down. Just four of the 10 highest-priced tickets increased.

Fresh off an unlikely World Series title, the Boston Red Sox re-main the most expensive average ticket at $52.32, still above the New York Yankees' $51.55, whose season tickets remained flat. The Red Sox's price deserves a minor explanation. We have the Red Sox listed with a 4.9 percent increase. But in the 2013 FCI, we show Boston has an average ticket price of $53.38. As it turns out, the Red Sox had been submitting single-game prices for a few years. We corrected it this season and did a retroactive change to last year's price. So technically, the Yankees had the highest average ticket price last season.

The Chicago Cubs remain baseball's third most-expensive ticket at $44.16, which is down 0.9 percent from last season. Their FCI of $303.64 is third, and includes a $25 parking fee for nearby lots. The Cubs are offering a free lot, with shuttle service, about 2 1/4 miles west of Wrigley this year.

Speaking of the Cubs, after signing a big-money deal with Anheuser-Busch InBev they jettisoned longtime beer partner Old Style from the vendors to stands, while adding Goose Island beers to the vending options. The cheapest beer at Wrigley is $7.50 for a 16-ounce pour at several stands around the park.

The average MLB beer stayed flat, price-wise, at $6.09. The Marlins boast the most expensive, cheapest beer option at $8 for a 16-ounce beer.

The cheapest average ticket this year comes again from the San Diego Padres $16.37, which is a 2.4 percent increase from 2013. The Arizona Diamondbacks, with an average ticket of $17.98 (up 6.4 percent), has the cheapest FCI again at $126.89.

Of course, market size, and fan demographics, often determine prices. Certainly, many fans don't get what they pay for in regard to winning teams.

Of the teams with the top 10 FCIs in 2014, only three - Boston, St, Louis and Detroit -made the playoffs last season.

Compare that to the bottom 10, where five teams - Atlanta, Tampa Bay, Pittsburgh, Cincinnati and Cleveland - made the postseason. Kansas City, fresh off its first winning season since 2003, bumped up prices

Table 12.2 (continued)

2014 mlb fan cost index AVER AGE TICKET PRICE UP 2.0 PERCENT AT $27.93; TOTAL FCI UP 2.3 PERCENT TO $212.46	
by 24.7 percent, the biggest jump in baseball. The Roy- als' average ticket price of $24.73 is still well below the league average. The Dodgers had the second-high percentage increase at 15.3 percent, with an average ticket of $25.80.	**EDITOR'S NOTE:** TMR reserves the right to make retroactive changes to the FCI and could update the official chart after the initial © 2014 Team Marketing Report, Chicago, IL Team Marketing Report • March 2014 The Source For Sports Marketing Ideas

Source: http://www.teammarketing.com/fci.cfm?page=fci_nhi_06_07.cfm/

price discounts may encourage new groups of consumers to try the sports product. By doing so, the team may increase fan identification and, ultimately, fan loyalty. This will, in turn, lead to repeat purchases.

Another broad organizational objective may be to compete in a given sports market. An organization may want to meet competition, avoid competition, or even undercut competitive pricing. These **competitive objectives** are directly linked to final pricing decisions. Traditionally, professional sports franchises are the "only game in town," so competitive threats are less likely to dictate pricing than they would in other industries.

A final organizational objective that influences pricing is referred to as a **social concern**. Many sports organizations, particularly amateur athletic associations, determine the pricing of their sporting events based on social concerns. For example, consider a local road race through downtown St. Louis on St. Patrick's Day. The organizational objective of this race is to encourage as many people as possible to participate in the community and the festivities of the day. As such, the cost to enter the race is minimal and designed only to offset the expense of having the event.

Regardless of which organizational objective is established, each has a large role in setting prices for sports products. In practice, more than one objective is typically set by the sports organization. However, prices can be determined more efficiently and effectively if the organization clearly understands its objectives. Let us look at an example of how the MLS mission statement provides a direction for pricing.

Major League Soccer's mission statement is:

> To create a profitable Division I professional outdoor soccer league with players and teams that are competitive on an international level, and to provide affordable family entertainment. MLS brings the spirit and intensity of the world's most popular sport to the United States. Featuring competitive ticket prices and family oriented promotions such as "Soccer Celebration" at the stadium, MLS appeals to the children who play and the families who support soccer. MLS players are also involved with a variety of community events.

As indicated in the mission statement, MLS is concerned with profitability for its league and teams. Moreover, the pricing of MLS games should be affordable so families who support soccer will be financially able to purchase tickets, reflecting a social concern. Finally, the mission statement reflects the competitive nature of pricing. The interaction of the organizational objectives of the MLS should exert a great influence on the price that fans pay to see U.S. professional soccer.

External factors

Thus far, we have described the internal, or controllable, determinants of pricing and factors believed to be under the control of the sports marketer. The uncontrollable or external factors also play an important role in pricing decisions. The uncontrollable factors that influence pricing include consumer demand, competition, legal issues, the economy, and technology. Let us turn our discussion to each of these major, external factors.

Consumer demand

One of the most critical factors in determining the price of a sports product is **consumer demand**. Demand is the quantity of a sports product that consumers are willing to purchase at a given price. Generally, consumers are more likely to purchase products at a lower price than a higher price. More formally, economists refer to this principle as the law of demand. To better understand the nature of the **law of demand** and its impact on any given sports product, let us examine the price elasticity of demand.

Price elasticity explains consumer reactions to changes in price. **Price elasticity** or **price inelasticity** measures the extent to which consumer purchasing patterns are sensitive to fluctuations in price. For example, if the St. Louis Cardinals raise their bleacher ticket prices from $19.80 to $23.00, will the demand for seats decline? Similarly, if the ticket prices are reduced by a given amount, will the demand increase?

Mathematically, price elasticity is stated as:

$$e = \frac{DQ/Q}{DP/P}$$

where e = price elasticity

DQ/Q = percentage change in the quantity demanded

DP/P = percentage change in the price

Consumer price elasticity may be described in one of three ways: elastic demand, inelastic demand, or unitary demand. **Inelastic demand** states that changes in price have little or no impact on sales. In the previous example, demand probably would have been inelastic, because even relatively large increases in the ticket prices would have had little impact on the number of fans attending each game. If demand is inelastic, then e is less than or equal to 1 (see Figure 12.2a). Because of the great

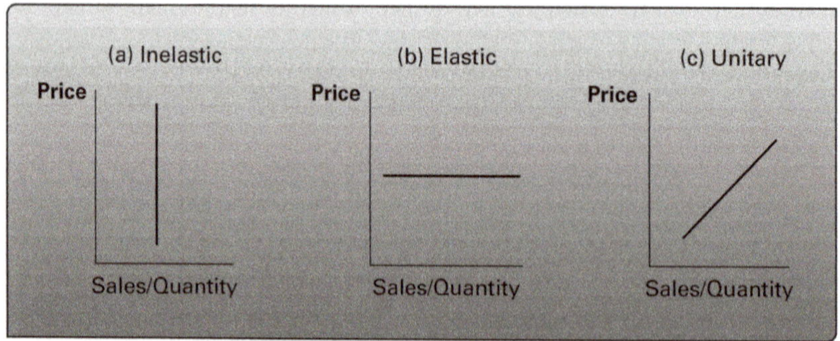

Figure 12.2 Price elasticity of demand

demand for tickets, the Green Bay Packers, who have been sold out on season tickets since 1960, could probably raise their minimum ticket price to $300 and still sell out all their games.

Elastic demand refers to small changes in price producing large changes in quantity demanded. For example, if the average price of a ticket to a Miami Heat game is reduced from $58.55 to $48.00, and if the number of units sold increases dramatically, then demand is considered elastic, because *e* is greater than 1 (see Figure 12.2b).

Finally, **unitary demand** is defined as a situation where price changes are offset exactly by changes in demand. In other words, price and demand are perfectly related. A small change in price produces an equally small change in the number of units sold. Similarly, a large change in price causes an equally large change in the number of units sold. In a situation where demand is unitary, *e* is equal to 1 (see Figure 12.2c).

Estimating demand

The basic notion of demand allows sports marketers to explore the relationship between price and the amount of sports product that is sold. In practice, a sports marketer cannot continually change the price of a product and then determine the impact of this price change. Rather, the sports marketer must develop estimates of demand. The three basic factors that are used in **estimating demand** are consumer trends and tastes, availability of substitute sports products, and the consumer's income. Let us briefly explore the three demand factors.

Consumer tastes

Consumer tastes, both as participants and spectators, play an influential role in estimating demand. For example, consumer demand (as spectators) for football is at an all-time high, which influences ticket prices (and the price of rights to televise football). In addition, as reflected in the 2013 NSGA Sports Participation Report (see Table 12.3), participation trends in flag football (6.8 million) and touch football (8.8 million) are on the rise while participation in tackle football encounter a slight decline 7.9 to 7.5 million, as compared with 2012 participation levels. These participation trends potentially affect the demand for specific "football" consumer products. Similarly, yoga, running/jogging, and archery (target) are the sports reflecting the largest participation rate increases from 2012, so demand for products in these growth categories may be higher than an activity such as camping that encountered a decline of 5.9 million participants. NSGA's Sports Participation in the U.S. report provides participation trends and key demographic/geographic drivers of participation for 51 different sports and recreational activities. The 2013 report identified that participation in sports/recreational activities slowed in 2013, as only one-third of the sports/activities tracked by NSGA experienced participation growth vs. 2012.[6] Fluctuation in participation often affects demand for these "popular" sports which will also affect pricing of equipment to consumers.

With sophisticated statistical techniques, sports marketers can understand what, when, and how factors are influencing consumer tastes and the likelihood of purchasing products. For example, demand for a new design of in-line skates in any given market may be expressed as a function of a number of factors other than price. These factors can include the number of consumers currently participating in this recreational activity, the desire of recreational skaters to have more technologically

Table 12.3 2013 sport/recreational activity participation

Ranking	Sport	2013 Total Participation (in millions)
1	Exercise Walking	96.3
2	Exercising with Equipment	53.1
3	Swimming	45.5
4	Aerobic Exercising	44.1
5	Running/Jogging	42.0
6	Hiking	39.4
7	Camping (Vacation/Overnight)	39.3
8	Bicycle Riding	35.6
9	Bowling	35.2
10	Workout at Club	34.1
11	Weightlifting	31.3
12	Fishing (Fresh Water)	27.0
13	Yoga	25.9
14	Basketball	25.5
15	Billiards/Pool	19.5
16	Target Shooting (Live Ammunition)	19.0
17	Golf	18.9
18	Hunting with Firearms	16.3
19	Boating, Motor/Power	13.1
20	Soccer	12.8
21	Tennis	12.6
22	Backpacking/Wilderness Camping	12.2
23	Baseball	11.7
24	Volleyball	10.1
25	Softball	10.0
26	Table Tennis/Ping Pong	9.8
27	Dart Throwing	9.8
28	Fishing (Salt Water)	9.5
29	Football (Touch)	8.8
30	Archery (Target)	8.3
31	Kayaking	8.1
32	Football (Tackle)	7.5
33	Football (Flag)	6.8
34	Canoeing	6.7
35	Skiing (Alpine)	6.1
36	Roller Skating (In-line)	5.7
37	Hunting with Bow & Arrow	5.7
38	Mountain Biking (off road)	5.2
39	Gymnastics	5.1
40	Skateboarding	5.0
41	Paintball Games	4.8
42	Target Shooting (Airgun)	4.8
43	Snowboarding	4.5
44	Water Skiing	3.6

Table 12.3 (continued)

Ranking	Sport	2013 Total Participation (in millions)
45	Cheerleading	3.5
46	Hockey (Ice)	3.5
47	Muzzleloading	3.2
48	Wrestling	3.1
49	Lacrosse	2.8
50	Scuba Diving (Open Water)	2.7
51	Skiing (Cross Country)	2.5

Source: National Sporting Goods Association.

advanced skates, the amount that the new skates have been advertised or promoted, or the availability of the skates.

Today, successful players in the sport and entertainment industry look to create innovative solutions utilizing marketing research. **Marketing research** as defined by the American Marketing Association is:[7]

> A function that links the consumer, customer and public to its market through the information – information used to identify and define marketing opportunities and problems; generate, refine, and evaluate marketing actions; monitor marketing performance; and improve understanding of marketing as a process. Marketing research specifies the information required to address these issues, designs the method for collecting information, manages and implements the data collection process, analyzes the results, and communicates the findings and their implications. The process allows for the generation, refinement and evaluation of marketing actions. It affords opportunity for the monitoring of performance and adjustment of strategy to improve marketing as a business process.

Plain and simple, marketing research is the process of objectively listening to the voice of the marketplace and then utilizing and conveying the information in an ascertainable manner. In the words of David Ogilvy,[8] "if you're trying to persuade people to do something, or buy something, it seems you should use their language, the language in which they think." Whether it is simple customer comment cards or complex feasibility assessments the research process affords one the opportunity to

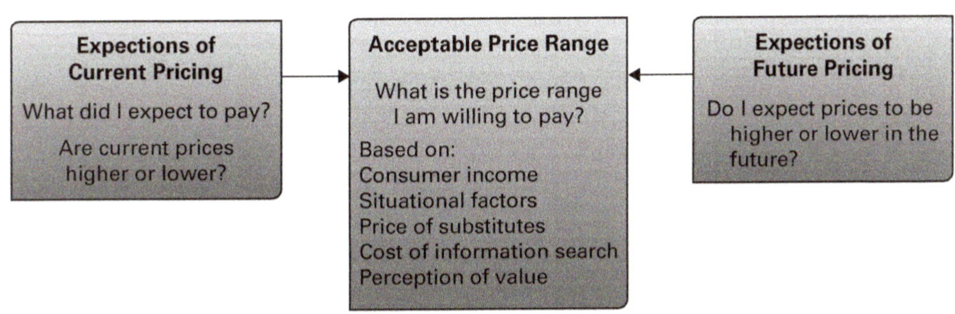

Figure 12.3 Consumer pricing evaluation process

12

enhance the fundamental **marketing** process; the process or function for creating, communicating and delivering value to customers and for managing customer relationships in ways that benefit the organization and its stakeholders.

Marketing research (as discussed in Chapter 3) allows us to estimate demand for new and existing sports products. Firms conduct research to determine consumers' past purchase behavior and the likelihood of their buying a new product. In addition, businesses rely on environmental scanning to monitor changes in the demographic profile of a market, changes in technology, shifts in popular culture, and other issues that may affect the size or tastes of the consumer market.

Environmental scanning and marketing research assist sports marketers in understanding what consumers expect and are willing to pay for sports products. Let us look at how consumers evaluate price (see Figure 12.3).

In the **consumer pricing evaluation process**, acceptable price ranges are determined by consumers' expectations. These expectations are influenced by communicating with other consumers (i.e., word of mouth), promotions or advertising, and, to some extent, past experience in purchasing the products. If the gap between expectations and the actual price is too large, a problem arises for the sports organization. If prices are much higher than expected, the consumer will be much less likely to purchase. However, if prices are much lower, then the quality of the sports product may be called into question.

The sport of professional boxing provides an excellent example of the role past experience plays in determining an acceptable price range for consumers. Fan satisfaction with professional boxing has reached an all-time low because of the short length of heavyweight fights and the heavyweight prices paid by pay-per-view (PPV) customers to watch these fights. To combat this problem of short telecasts, Cablevision introduced a controversial pricing strategy. Consumers who wanted to view the historic title fight between Evander Holyfield and Mike Tyson paid a $10-a-round price with a $50 cap.

This innovative strategy apparently sparked a 200 percent jump in sales in Cablevision's 1.9 million PPV homes (a PPV record). Equally important, the product quality was not called into question. Cablevision paid a flat fee (roughly $4 million) for the rights to the fight, and the boxers did not receive any additional money based on the fight's length.[9]

Along with previous experience with pricing, expectations of future pricing also influence the acceptable range of prices a consumer is willing to pay. For example, when an innovative sports product, such as the Power Block Dumbbell System, is in the introductory phase of the product life cycle, little competition exists and start-up costs are high. Most consumers would expect the price of this product to drop over time, and some may be willing to wait for this to occur. However, sports fans may expect prices to continually rise in the future and purchase the new product immediately rather than waiting for the inevitable higher prices.

Along with expectations of current and future prices, a number of other individual consumer judgments will also play a role in determining the acceptable price range for any given sports product. As shown in Figure 12.3, these variables include consumer income, situational factors, price of substitutes, cost of information search, and perceptions of value.

Consumer income, one of the three demand factors, refers to the consumer's ability to pay the price. Generally, the higher the consumer's income, then the wider the range there is of acceptable prices. For example, a sports fan who has an annual income of $100,000 might perceive a $10 increase in ticket prices as still within his or her price range. However, the same $10 increase in price may be unaffordable to the fan earning $30,000 per year. Significantly, both fans may find the increase in ticket prices unacceptable, but only the latter finds it unaffordable.

The **situational factors** that may affect a consumer's acceptable range of prices include the presence or absence of time, the usage situation, and social factors. Consider the following situations and how each might affect the price you would be willing to pay. First, you are getting ready for a much anticipated round of golf when you discover you only have one ball left in your bag. Typically, you purchase golf balls at your local discount store for roughly $6 a sleeve (package of three). Given the situation (absence of time), you are forced to "cough up" $12 at the pro shop for the three balls needed to get you through the round. This absence of time to shop for less expensive golf balls caused the acceptable price range to double in this situation.

The next scenario illustrates how your usage situation influences the range of acceptable prices. Imagine you are purchasing a new set of golf clubs that will be used only once or twice a month at the local public course. In this situation, the acceptable price range for this set of clubs might be from $250 to $400. It is likely that you may even purchase less expensive, previously owned clubs. However, if you are planning to use the clubs once or twice a week and are more concerned about their quality and your image, the acceptable range of prices would increase.

The final situation places you in the position of purchasing tickets for the Daytona 500. The cost of purchasing one ticket is approximately $105. You are not a huge car racing fan and the thought of spending $105 for a ticket seems disagreeable. However, a group of your best friends are attending the event and encourage you to "go along for the ride." You agree and purchase the ticket because of the social situational influence.

Another interesting social situational influence is referred to as the "mob effect." The **mob effect** (or the crowd effect) describes a situation in which consumers believe it is socially desirable to attend "special" sporting events, such as the NBA Finals, bowl games, or the World Series. Because these events constitute unique situations that can never be duplicated, consumers are willing to pay more than usual for the "right" to be a part of the mob (or crowd).

An additional consumer determinant of acceptable prices is the **expected price range of substitute products**. The prices of competitive products will have a major influence on what you deem acceptable. If a sports organization's pricing becomes out-of-line (higher) versus competition, then consumers will no longer pay the price.

The **cost of information search** also determines what a consumer considers acceptable. A consumer wanting to purchase a series of tennis lessons has a relatively low cost of information search because information is easily obtained from friends or by calling various tennis professionals. In this case, the cost of the search is less than the benefit of finding the best value. Interestingly, in purchasing a sports product, the cost of information search may be negligible because fans may find the search itself to be intriguing.

Finally, as discussed previously, **perception of value** will dictate acceptable price ranges for sports products. Remember, perceptions of value will vary from individual to individual and are based on the perceived benefits. The greater the perceived benefits of the sports product, the higher the range of acceptable prices. Most people would consider $400 an outrageous price to attend a single pro football game. However, that cost might look like the bargain of a lifetime if that single game were the Super Bowl.

Availability of substitute products

Another demand factor, other than price alone, that may affect demand is the **availability of substitute products**. Generally, as the number of substitute products for any given sports product increases, demand for the product will decrease. Consider the case of almost any professional sports franchise and substitute products. Typically, there is no substitute product for the professional sports team. Therefore, demand remains relatively unchanged, even when ticket prices are increased (in other words, demand is highly inelastic). For example, there is no substitute product for the St. Louis Cardinals, although baseball is played in St. Louis at the collegiate, high school, and amateur levels. However, consumers may choose to spend their sports dollars on purchasing televised broadcasts of the Cardinals, rather than pay the price increase.

Consumer's income

The final demand factor that influences the consumer's ability to purchase the sports product is the consumer's income. Simply stated, the more income a consumer realizes, the higher the demand for various sports products. This "income-related" demand factor is related to the cost of the sports product under consideration. That is, the higher the cost of the sports product, the more "consumer income" matters. Consider the case of San Antonio Spurs courtside seats that are priced at $3,400 per seat. For this "paltry" sum, fans get a small TV display and as much food and drink as they can ingest. Exponentially, that would equate to a whopping $139,400 for a 41 home game season, and obviously, these are not seats that most middle-income consumers would be able to afford.[10]

The potential consumer's personal income and ability to purchase products is also highly related to the state of the economy, in general. The economy is one of the "other external factors" that influences pricing, which is discussed in the next section.

Economy

The current economic cycle, or **economy**, also influences pricing decisions. A recessionary period, for instance, is characterized by reduced economic activity. During these times, there is a reduced demand for goods and services. In addition, unemployment rates are typically higher. Although this sounds grim for consumers and sports fans, imaginative sports marketers might be able to take advantage of these slowdowns in the economy by holding or slightly reducing prices, while stressing the continued value of the sports product.

Periods of inflation also require a pricing review. During inflationary periods, the cost of inputs (e.g., supplies or raw materials) necessary to produce the sports product will rise and ultimately increase prices to consumers. Rather than increase prices, sports marketers may adopt a cost reduction strategy during inflation. Such a strategy necessitates reducing or stabilizing costs of producing the product so consumer prices need not be increased.

Whatever the phase of the economic cycle, it is important to understand the direct relationship between pricing and the economy. In the preceding discussion, prices were adjusted due to changes in the economy. The prices set by manufacturers and sports organizations equally have a tremendous impact on the demand for these products and services and, in turn, affect the economy.

Competition

As stated earlier, competition is one of the most critical factors in determining prices. Every sports organization must closely monitor the pricing structure of competing firms to successfully implement prices for its own products. One key to understanding the relationship between price and competition is exploring the sports organization's competitive environment. These four competitive environments include pure monopolies, oligopoly, monopolistic competition, and pure competition.

Most professional sports organizations operate in a **pure monopoly**, which means they are the only seller who sets the price for a unique product. With the exception of New York, Chicago, and California, there are few areas large enough to support two professional sports franchises in the same sport (e.g., the Cubs and White Sox). As such, most professional sports are free to manipulate prices as they want. The same would hold true for many college athletic programs, where college sports may be "the only show in town."

An **oligopoly** is where a small number of firms control a market. Conditions for an oligopoly exist when no one seller controls the market, but each of the few sellers has an impact on the market. In the sports industry, an example of an oligopoly is the sports news networks where ESPN and Fox have dominant control over the market.

In the case of many sporting goods, **monopolistic competition** is the norm. There are dozens of brands with identical products to sell. This competitive environment requires both price competition and nonprice competition. For example, all tennis balls are designed the same, but the many different brands compete based on lower prices and/or other marketing mix elements (promotions, product image, and sponsorships). The same holds true for golf balls, basketballs, and so on.

Pure competition is a market structure that has so many competitors that none can singularly influence the market price. The market conditions that must exist for pure competition include homogeneous products and ease of entry into the market. Although pure competition exists in industries selling uniform commodities such as agricultural products, it does not exist in the sports industry.

Legal issues

In addition to the other external factors, sports marketers must consider **legal issues**, such as constraints imposed on pricing. Several key laws that affect sports marketers were presented in Chapter 2. Table 12.4 presents U.S. legislation that specifically affects the pricing of sports products.

Table 12.4 Laws influencing the price of sports products

• **Sherman Act, 1890** – Establishes legality of restraint/price of trade and fixing. It also restricts the practice of predatory pricing to drive competition from the marketplace through pricing.
• **Clayton Act, 1914** – Restricts price discrimination.
• **Robinson-Patman Act, 1936** – Limits the ability of firms to sell the same product at different prices to different customers.
• **Wheeler-Lea Act, 1938** – Ensures pricing practices are not deceiving to consumers.
• **Consumer Goods Pricing Act, 1975** – Eliminates some control over retail pricing by wholesalers and manufacturers. It allows retailers to establish final retail prices in most instances.

One of the most notable legal issues that the sports industry has been wrestling with for years is the secondary ticket market, or as it is more commonly known, ticket scalping (see the following article).

THE NFL vs. TICKET SCALPERS: SUPER BOWL EDITION

The National Football League announced this week that the most expensive seats for the 2014 Super Bowl at MetLife Stadium in New Jersey would go for $2,600. That's up from $1,250 for the top seats at last February's game in New Orleans. The bump not only reflects the relative size and wealth of the New York market; it also represents an attempt by the league to cut into the profits of ticket scalpers. "We are looking to close the gap between the face value of the ticket and its true value as reflected on the secondary market," league spokesman Brian McCarthy told reporters.

But ticket sellers don't appear to be too worried. "I can't blame them for doing what they did," says Jason Zinna, a partner at Inside Sports & Entertainment Group, an agency that specializes in hard-to-get tickets for rich clients. "Are they closing the gap with the secondary market? Sure. Is there still going to be room for the secondary market to make money? Of course."

Zinna, who says Inside Sports handles about 2,000 Super Bowl tickets every year, expects ticket brokers to follow the NFL's lead in raising prices: "If somebody was going to spend $4,000 for a ticket, will they now spend $4,500 or $5,000? I'm pretty sure they will." The gap between face value and actual price, he says, will probably narrow more at the middle and bottom end of the market.

So what would it take for the NFL to really eat scalpers' lunches? According to secondary market search engine SeatGeek, the top club seats at the Super Bowl in New Orleans went for an average of $5,122. The year before that, in Indianapolis, the best seats went for $7,733. And in 2011 at Cowboys Stadium, for $7,967. Zinna says an open auction for MetLife seats would likely go as high as $8,000 to $12,000. "The anticipation going in from six months ago to now is definitely the greatest that I've seen in recent years," he says.

Source: Article author: Ira Boudway. Rightsholder: Bloomberg Businessweek; http://www.businessweek.com/articles/2013-09-20/the-nfl-vs-dot-ticket-scalpers-super-bowl-edition. Credit: The YGS Group.

Technology

Without a doubt, all sports products are becoming more and more technologically advanced. The trend toward **technology** can have an indirect or direct influence on pricing decisions. Experience tells us that greater technology costs money. The high cost of research and development, as well as the higher costs for production and materials, drive up the price of the sports product. For example, if our stadiums are equipped with mini-screen monitors at every seat, the consumer would be expected to pay the price for this technology in the form of higher ticket prices. In this case, an advance in technology has a direct impact on the pricing.

NEW ERA TICKETS USES IOVATION TO KEEP SCALPERS AND FRAUDSTERS OUT OF THE ARENA

CASE STUDY

"In our business, catching the bad guys can be really difficult. Since there's nothing being shipped, we've got to stop them upfront. Our real challenge is trying to find them fast and reject the order out-right."

Steve Gelb
Vice President of Client Services,
New Era Tickets

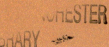

New Era Tickets uses iovation to Keep Scalpers and Fraudsters Out of the Arena

Created by Comcast-Spectacor, New Era Tickets offers highly customized, uniquely branded ticketing options for its customers while keeping fraud rates almost non-existent with iovation ReputationManager 360.

Fraud Challenges

- → Increase in online ticket sales was leading to increasing rates of fraud and higher chargeback rates
- → Fraudsters were using stolen credit and identity information to evade restrictions put in place to prevent scalping and unfair ticket sales
- → Scalpers were working together online to defraud entertainment organizations and their customers

Solution Requirements

- → Identify users independent of credit and identity information
- → Track velocity of purchases coming from individual computers
- → Catch criminals' behavior within a limited window of time

Results using iovation

- → 98% reduction in total fraud losses
- → Fraud losses dropped from triple digits to nearly zero at one site alone
- → Increased operational efficiency prevented the need for as many as 12 additional full-time employees

About New Era Tickets

Created by Comcast-Spectacor in 2004, New Era Tickets brings a new way of doing business to the entertainment industry through its full-service ticketing and database marketing solutions. Making use of the latest technology, New Era Tickets provides a variety of services including internet ticket sales, order fulfillment, customer service, access control and print-at-home technology, up-selling and cross-selling, stored value technology, online ticket exchange, ticket auctions, client training and support team, and database marketing.

In addition to offering a comprehensive list of services, New Era Tickets also makes its solutions highly customizable, offering clients complete control over their ticket prices, branding, and marketing data. By allowing clients to leverage their own brands, and their unique understanding of their customers and markets, New Era Tickets helps its clients realize increased ticket sales and overall revenue growth.

Based out of Exton, Pennsylvania, New Era Tickets serves over 60 clients through the US and Canada, from sports organizations to entertainment companies, including the Philadelphia 76ers, the General Motors Centre, The Rose Quarter, Dover Motorsports and Pocono Raceway. Handling 11–12 million ticket sales annually, New Era Tickets processes $400-450 million in business transactions each year. Additionally, the company manages 30 different customer databases, with each database containing up to 2 million records.

The Fraud Challenge

In the time that New Era Tickets has been in business, the company has seen a significant shift in people's buying habits. "Five years ago, if we could sell 40-50% of the tickets online, that was considered a success. Now, we sell 90% of the tickets online," observes Steve Geib, Vice President of Client Services for New Era Tickets. However, despite the benefit of increased online sales, the down side is that criminals making purchases online can much more easily use stolen or illegitimate credit cards, due to the card-not-present buying environment.

While the challenge of fraudsters using stolen credit cards is common among most online retail sites, the online sale of tickets, as opposed to other "hard goods," presents its own unique challenges. With the advent of new technologies like print-at-home tickets that make the transfer of the good being purchased almost immediate, the review time on transactions is extremely limited. "In our business, catching the bad guys can be really difficult. Since there's nothing being shipped, we've got to stop them upfront. Our real challenge is trying to find them fast and reject the order out-right," says Geib. If the fraudulent behavior isn't caught at the time of purchase, New Era Tickets—who processes the transactions for its clients—faces the potential increase of its chargeback rate at the same time its clients are stuck with the loss of the ticket price.

New Era Tickets Case Study page 2

Another challenge is that online fraud, in all industries, is becoming increasingly dominated by organized individuals with well-planned strategies for taking advantage of the system. With many sporting events and music concerts commanding enormous ticket prices—such as $180 for an NHL ticket, or $750 for an Eagles ticket—fraudsters can make significant profits by fraudulently purchasing multiple tickets online and then quickly reselling them. Obviously, the more demand there is for a ticket, and the closer it is to the time of the event, the easier it will be for a fraudster to turn the tickets around, and thus the more susceptible the event is to fraud.

In one particular case Geib recalls, someone purchased a single ticket to a Rolling Stones concert online, then, using the print-at-home feature, printed the ticket multiple times and sold all of the illegitimate copies for over $1,000 each. The result? Not only did all of the unsuspecting victims who purchased the illegitimate tickets lose their money—as well as their faith in the security of online sales—but since the original ticket was purchased with a stolen credit card, the venue lost as well. In order to combat these kinds of situations and protect both event-goers and the venues, New Era Tickets had to find an effective fraud solution that could catch fraudsters quickly and keep them from coming back.

The iovation Solution

“The reality is that device recognition is one of the only ways to really stop scalping and unfair ticket sales.”

Steve Geib
Vice President of Client Services,
New Era Tickets

When New Era Tickets began looking for fraud solutions, iovation was immediately recommended by multiple merchant services companies in the industry. And, as New Era Tickets began seriously comparing its various options, iovation ReputationManager 360 emerged as the best fit. “Everything iovation does just fit for us. It was quick, it was easy, it was up and running on the first day— and the return was almost immediate,” says Geib.

Part of what makes iovation so effective for New Era Tickets is that it gives the company quick visibility into the activity on its sites by focusing on the computers being used to submit transactions, rather than on the personally identifiable information being submitted. Without this device-based information, organized fraud rings and repeat offenders are extremely hard to identify since they can set up multiple accounts with different information every time. This is partly the reason that government efforts to mitigate scalping and regulate ticket sales have been largely ineffective. “The reality is that device recognition is one of the only ways to really stop scalping and unfair ticket sales,” says Geib. “Every time someone puts in a new address, a new name, etcetera—you can't tell if it's really a different person. But with iovation, I can tell that someone at one machine just bought 80 tickets.”

When New Era Tickets sees fraudulent activity originating from a computer, using iovation ReputationManager, that device can be tagged so that the client site can simply deny any future transactions originating from it. This kind of visibility gives New Era Tickets a powerful advantage. “We know who our scalpers are and where they're coming from,” says Geib. “They think they're fooling us, but we can see them moving around.”

Results

By using iovation ReputationManager 360, New Era Tickets gained the ability to protect its clients from fraud at the same time as regulating ticket sales and keeping the marketplace fair for event-goers. What started out as a significant fraud problem—resulting in nearly six-figure losses from one client alone—turned into an almost non-existent issue, with Geib estimating a 98% reduction on the company's fraud losses, thanks to iovation. The company has been so effective at stopping fraud, in fact, that Geib notices many fraudsters have gotten the hint and simply started avoiding its sites. "There's almost no fraud anymore," says Geib. "Now it's a matter of someone not liking their seat. Can you imagine? Now that's our biggest problem."

Another huge benefit for New Era Tickets has been the savings on operational costs that iovation has made possible. With iovation, the fraud management process is so efficient that New Era Tickets needs only one dedicated full time person. This saved the company from hiring a whole team of people—as many as 12 more full time employees—that would have been required for tracking the fraud without the use of iovation. "When you're talking about manual reviews, the man hours are huge. With iovation, we're so much more efficient. Thanks to this technology, we know exactly who we're dealing with and we can tie it all together quickly. That knowledge is priceless."

For more information about New Era Tickets and their products and services, please contact:

New Era Tickets
930 East Lincoln Highway
Suite 200
Exton, PA 19341
www.neweratickets.com

To learn more about iovation ReputationManager 360 and how it helps organizations fight online fraud and abuse, visit www.iovation.com.

iovation Inc.
111 SW 5th Avenue, Suite 3200, Portland, OR 97204
+1.503.224.6010 tel | +1.503.224.1581 fax
www.iovation.com

Source: Article author: iovation Inc. (2013); https://www.iovation.com/images/uploads/case-studies/PDF/iovation-newera-ticketing-case-study.pdf. Credit: www.iovation.com.

Although technology and higher prices are typically believed to go hand in hand, as illustrated in the following article, technology does not always have to increase pricing. A consumer may be able to buy a King Cobra titanium driver for $299 using electronic commerce (in other words, purchasing it through the Internet). The same driver may cost $125 more if purchased in a traditional retail outlet. In this case, technology is having an indirect influence on pricing, happily reducing the price of goods to consumers.

Price adjustments

As we discussed in the preceding sections, initial prices are determined by a variety of internal and external issues that are continually changing with new market conditions. For instance, more or less competition may provide the impetus for price changes.

ORIOLES RAISE SEASON-TICKET PRICES SLIGHTLY, EXPAND VARIABLE-PRICING SYSTEM

Under dynamic pricing, cost of single-game tickets for higher-profile opponents likely to rise as game nears

When Orioles season-ticket holders receive their renewal packages in the mail over the next few days, they will find slightly higher average ticket prices and an expanded version of the variable-pricing plan the club has used for single-game ticket sales over the past seven years.

The Orioles are raising season-ticket prices on all plans by an average of approximately 5 percent, the first increase in cost since 2008, an Orioles spokeswoman confirmed Friday. Season-ticket packages start at $168 for a 13-game plan; 29-game and full-season packages are also available.

Single-game tickets also will be overhauled, changing the way fans will go to the box office and purchase tickets. There will be no more fixed pricing, as the Orioles are instituting single-game dynamic pricing, in which prices fluctuate from day to day depending on the demand for a specific game. This system is similar to purchasing airline tickets.

Dynamic pricing is becoming a growing trend in professional sports. Since the San Francisco Giants became the first Major League Baseball club to introduce dynamic pricing four years ago, more than a dozen other teams – big and small market alike – have followed suit. Teams that use some type of dynamic pricing include the Arizona Diamondbacks, Atlanta Braves, Chicago Cubs, Chicago White Sox, Colorado Rockies, Milwaukee Brewers, Minnesota Twins, New York Mets, Oakland Athletics, San Diego Padres, St. Louis Cardinals and Toronto Blue Jays.

Under dynamic pricing, prices for single-game tickets against popular teams like the division-rival New York Yankees and Boston Red Sox or the regional-rival Washington Nationals likely will rise as the date approaches. Popular promotions, team success, as well as weekend and holiday dates also could prompt a spike in price as the game nears.

The new system encourages fans to become season-ticket holders, who will save between $2 and $16 per game over initial single-game prices, which likely will go on sale next month. Season-ticket holders also have fewer exchange restrictions and can make additional single-game purchases at the season-ticket rate.

Previously, the Orioles had two price categories for single-game tickets: regular games and more expensive high-profile games, which included games against popular opponents like the Yankees, Red Sox or Nationals.

Now the club's 81 home dates will be divided into five different pricing levels, from six "value" games, including weekday games against the

Tampa Bay Rays and Toronto Blue Jays, to five "elite" games, including Opening Day and Saturday-night games against the Yankees, Red Sox and Cardinals.

The tier below the elite level, the "prime" category, includes all other games against New York, Boston and St. Louis. The majority of the games, 49 total, will fall under the "classic" level.

Source: Rightsholder: December 06, 2013|By Eduardo A. Encina, The Baltimore Sun; http://articles.baltimoresun.com/2013-12-06/sports/bs-sp-orioles-ticket-prices-1207-20131206_1_single-game-tickets-pricing-orioles. Credit: © The Baltimore Sun.

Also, **price adjustments** may be made to stimulate demand for sports products when sales expectations are not currently being met. Finally, prices might be adjusted to help meet the objectives that have been developed. The next section explores some of the ways in which price adjustments are implemented by sports marketers, and as the accompanying article illustrates, there may be new approaches to pricing of traditionally priced products, like season ticket packages.

Price increases and reductions

As with most things in sports marketing, prices are dynamic and decisions are continually being made about whether prices should be increased or decreased based on a number of internal and external facors.

Price increases represent an important adjustment made to established prices. In recent years, many sports organizations have had to increase prices for a variety of reasons, even though consumers, retailers, and employees discourage such actions. One of the primary reasons for increasing prices is to keep up with cost inflation. In other words, as the cost of materials or of running a sports organization increases, prices must be increased to achieve the same profit objectives. Another reason for implementing a price increase is because there is excess demand for the sports product. For example, if thousands of fans join the season-ticket waiting list in the week that a Hall of Fame coach returns to a team, then slight increases to these ticket prices may be acceptable.

A winning season may have a huge impact on the decision to raise prices. For four consecutive years, the Chicago Bears increased their ticket prices after gaining a trip to the Super Bowl in 2007. The 2009 season was the only recent year in which the Bears froze their ticket prices; they resumed increases in 2010.The increase is for all except the most expensive seats in Soldier Field, according to a report in the *Chicago Sun-Times*.[11] Non-club-level seats, which make up about 85 percent of the stadium, will cost $68–125 a game, while club seats will cost $265–365, according to the report.

Because of the negative consequences of raising prices, sports organizations may consider potential alternatives to straight price increases. These alternatives include eliminating any planned price reductions, lessening the number of product features, or unbundling items formerly "bundled" into a low price.

If there are no viable alternatives to increasing prices, it is important to communicate these changes to fans and consumers in a straightforward fashion to avoid potential negative consequences. Remember, much of pricing is based on consumer psychology. If fans or consumers of sporting goods are told why prices are being increased, they may believe price increases are justified. Typically, **price reductions** are efforts to enhance sales and achieve greater market share by directly lowering the original price. In addition to the direct reductions in price, rebates or bundling products are other types of price breaks commonly employed. After a mediocre 2010 season, the New York Mets announced a restructured ticket pricing program for 2011 that includes a reduction of ticket prices by an average of more than 14 percent from the previous season. Mets' Executive Vice President of Business Operations, Dave Howard, is quoted as saying "The Mets are committed to providing quality and value to our fans."[12]

After just their fourth year in the league in 2008, the Charlotte Bobcats reduced their season ticket prices to stimulate demand and attendance. While the Bobcats had been successful by the standards of NBA expansion team, their attendance numbers left them in the bottom of the league, averaging just over 15,000 fans per home game. The concept seemed to work, allowing the Bobcats to raise prices 4 percent to 21 percent on 2,500 seats in the lower level at Time Warner Cable Arena for the 2011–12 season. Regardless, to keep demand high, at the same time, prices for all tickets in the upper bowl – nearly 9,000 seats – were reduced 13 percent to 43 percent for the 2011–12 season. "This was a continuing evolution to get the building priced right for every seat," Bobcats President Fred Whitfield said. "We're trying to make sure we're offering the right value-proposition".[13]

Although teams commonly reduce or increase prices after the season, sports organizations rarely reduce or increase the price charged to consumers during the course of the season to stimulate demand. It is much more common, however, for marketers of sporting goods to reduce and increase prices. Simply said, the Los Angeles Dodgers will probably never have an end-of-the-season sale of tickets. You will, however, be able to find any number of sales of baseball equipment at the end of the summer.

Whatever the form of price reductions, they are frequently risky for sports organizations for a number of reasons. First, consumers may associate multiple price reductions with inferior product quality. Second, consumers may associate price reductions with price gouging (always selling products at a discount so the initial price must be unreasonably high). Third, price reductions may wake a sleeping dog and cause competition to counter with its own price decreases. Finally, frequent price changes make it more difficult for the consumer to establish a frame of reference for the true price of sports products. If tennis balls regularly sell for $4.99 for a package of three, and I conduct three sales over the season that offer the balls for $2.99, then what is the perceived "real" price?

An important concept when making price adjustments (either up or down) is known as the **just noticeable difference (JND)**.[14] The just noticeable difference is the point at which consumers detect a difference between two stimuli. In pricing, the two stimuli are the original price and the adjusted price. In other words, do consumers perceive (notice) a difference when prices are increased or decreased? The following examples illustrate the importance of the just noticeable difference.

Dick's Sporting Goods may sell Wilson softball gloves at a regular price of $49.99 (note the psychological price strategy of odd pricing being used). With softball season right around the corner, Dick's decides to reduce prices and sell the gloves for $44.99. Does this $5 reduction surpass the difference threshold? In other words, does the consumer believe there is a noticeable difference between the regular price and the sale price? If not, then the price reduction will not be successful at stimulating demand.

Suppose that because of the increasing cost of raw materials needed to produce the gloves, the price has to be increased from $49.99 to $54.99. Again, the sports marketer has to determine whether consumers will notice this increase in price. If not, then the price increase may not have negative consequences for the sale of Wilson softball gloves.

Price discounts

Combined with straight price decreases, **price discounts** are other incentives offered to buyers to stimulate demand or reward behaviors that are favorable to the seller. The two major types of price discounts that are common in sports marketing are quantity discounts and seasonal discounts.

Quantity discounts reward buyers for purchasing large quantities of a sports product. This type of discounting may occur at all different levels of the channel of distribution. Using the previous softball glove example, Wilson may offer a quantity discount to Dick's Sporting Goods for sending in a large purchase order. Consumers hope that Dick's Sporting Goods will pass the savings on to them in the form of price reductions. The purchase of group ticket sales is another common example of quantity discounts in sports marketing.

Seasonal discounts are also prevalent in sports marketing because of the nature of sports. Most sports have defined seasons observed by both participants and spectators. Seasonal discounts are intended to stimulate demand in off-peak periods. For example, ski equipment may be discounted in the summer months to encourage consumer demand and increase traffic in skiing specialty stores. Ski resorts also frequently offer seasonal deals. For instance, the Hunter Mountain Ski Resort in New York offers multiple value passes each season. From March 1–May 2 they offer a discount package for $229; full season packages purchased in September providing unlimited skiing and riding on non-holiday midweek days are offered at $349. It also includes a 30 percent discount on weekend and holiday dates during the season.[15]

Web 12.1 Loveland Ski may use seasonal discounting

Source: http://skiloveland.com

In addition to sporting goods, seasonal discounts are often offered for ticket prices to sporting events. The former Kroger Senior Classic (Champions Tour golf) event provided discounts for customers purchasing tickets in advance during the winter months for this summer event. The Holiday Badge promotion allowed consumers to purchase an all-week ground badge for $55 and get the second one free.

Summary

The pricing of sports products is becoming an increasingly important element of the sports marketing mix. Price is a statement of value for a sports product, and understanding consumers' perceptions of value is a critical determinant of pricing. Value is defined as the sum of the perceived benefits of the sports product minus the sum of the perceived costs. The perceived benefits of the sports product, or what the product does for the user, are based on its tangible and intangible features. Each consumer's perception of value is based on his or her own unique set of experiences with the sports product.

A variety of factors influences the pricing decisions for any sports product. Similar to the internal and external contingencies that affect the strategic sports marketing process, pricing influences can be categorized as internal or external factors. Internal factors are those under the control of the sports organization, such as the other marketing mix elements, cost, and organizational objectives. External factors are those factors beyond the control of the sports organization that influence pricing. These include consumer demand, competition, legal issues, the economy, and technology.

Marketing mix elements other than price must be carefully considered when determining the price of the sports product. Promotional mix elements (e.g., advertising and sales promotions) often communicate the price (or price reductions) of the sports product to consumers. The channel of distribution that is selected influences the price of sports products. For instance, consumers expect to pay higher prices (and are charged higher prices) when purchasing tennis equipment from a pro shop versus directly from the manufacturer. Product decisions are also highly related to pricing. Simply, price is used to signal product quality. Generally, the higher the price that is charged, then the greater the perceived quality of the product is.

Two distinct pricing strategies that emerge based on the emphasis of marketing mix elements are price and nonprice competition. As the name suggests, nonprice competition tries to establish demand for the sports product using the marketing mix elements other than price. Price competition, however, attempts to stimulate demand by offering lower prices.

In addition to other marketing mix variables, costs play a major role in pricing decisions. Costs are those factors that are associated with producing, promoting, and distributing the sports product. The total cost of producing and marketing a sports product is equal to the sum of the total fixed costs and the total variable costs. The fixed costs, such as players' salaries, do not change with the quantity of the product consumed, whereas variable costs change as a result of the quantity of the product being consumed. Today, the costs of running a professional sports franchise are skyrocketing because of players' salaries.

A final internal factor that influences pricing is organizational objectives. The four types of pricing objectives include income, sales, competitive, and social objectives. Typically, a combination of these four objectives is used to guide pricing decisions.

External factors, which are beyond the control of the organization, include consumer demand, competition, legal issues, the economy, and technology. Demand is the quantity of a sports product that consumers are willing to purchase at a given price. Price elasticity measures the extent to which consumer purchasing patterns are sensitive to fluctuations in price. For some sports products, such as a ticket to the Super Bowl, demand is relatively inelastic, which means that changes in price have little impact on game attendance. However, when demand is elastic, small changes in price may produce large changes in quantity demanded. Sports marketers try to estimate the demand for products by examining consumer trends and tastes, determining the number of substitute products, and looking at the income of the target market.

One of the most critical factors in determining pricing for sports products is to examine the prices charged for similar products by competing firms. Most professional sports franchises operate in a monopolistic environment in which no direct competitors exist. Because of this market condition, the price of attending professional sporting events is continually increasing. In fact, many "average" fans believe they are being priced out of the market and can no longer afford the cost of admission. In addition to competition, laws influence the pricing structure for sports products. For example, the Sherman Act was designed to protect freedom of competition, thereby freeing prices to fluctuate subject to market forces. The phase of the economic cycle is another important consideration in pricing. During periods of inflation, prices may rise to cover the higher costs, and during periods of recession, prices may be lowered. Finally, advances in technology are related to pricing decisions. Typically, consumers are willing to, and expect to, pay more for "high-tech" sports products. However, this is not always the case, as sometimes technological change can reduce pricing by facilitating marketing of the sports product.

Once the price of the sports product has been determined, adjustments are constantly necessary as market conditions, such as consumer demand, change. Price reductions or increases are used to reach pricing objectives that have been determined. Generally, price reductions are used to help achieve sales and market share objectives, whereas increases are used to keep up with rising costs. Regardless of whether adjustments are made to raise prices or lower prices, an important consideration in pricing is the concept known as the JND, or just noticeable difference. The JND is the point at which consumers can detect a "noticeable" difference between two stimuli – the initial price and the adjusted price. Depending on the rationale for price adjustments, sports marketers sometimes want the change to be above the difference threshold (i.e., consumers will notice the difference) and sometimes it will be below the difference threshold (i.e., consumers will not notice the difference).

Key terms

- availability of substitute products
- competition
- competitive objectives
- consumer demand
- consumer income
- consumer pricing evaluation process
- consumer tastes
- cost of information search
- costs
- economy
- elastic demand
- estimating demand
- expected price range of substitute products
- external (or environmental) factors

- fixed costs
- income objectives
- inelastic demand
- internal factors
- just noticeable difference (JND)
- law of demand
- legal issues
- marketing mix variables
- mob effect
- monopolistic competition
- nonprice competition
- oligopoly
- organizational objectives
- perception of value
- price
- price adjustments
- price competition
- price discounts
- price elasticity
- price increases
- price inelasticity
- price reductions
- pure competition
- pure monopoly
- sales objectives
- situational factors
- social concern
- technology
- total cost
- unitary demand
- variable costs
- quantity discounts
- seasonal discounts

Review questions

1. Define price, perceived value, and perceived benefits. What is the relationship among price, value, and benefits?
2. Discuss the advantages and disadvantages of personal seat licenses from the consumer's perspective and the sports organization's perspective.
3. Outline the internal and external factors that affect pricing decisions. What is the primary difference between the internal and external factors?
4. Provide examples of how the marketing mix variables (other than price) influence pricing decisions.
5. Define fixed costs and variable costs and then provide several examples of each type of cost in operating a sports franchise. Do you believe costs should be considered controllable or uncontrollable factors with respect to pricing?
6. What are the four organizational objectives, and how does each influence pricing? Which organizational objective has the greatest impact on pricing?
7. What is meant by the law of consumer demand? Explain the difference between elastic and inelastic demand.
8. Describe, in detail, how sports marketers estimate the demand for new and existing sports products. What are the three demand factors, and which do you believe is the most critical in estimating demand?
9. What laws have a direct impact on pricing? Briefly describe each law.
10. How do advances in technology influence pricing? How does the economy influence pricing decisions?
11. Describe the different types of competitive environments. Why is competition considered one of the most critical factors influencing pricing?
12. What are the risks associated with reducing the price of sports products? Describe two common types of price discounting.

Exercises

1. Interview five consumers and ask them, "If a new athletic complex was built for your college or university basketball team, would you be willing to pay higher seat prices?" Summarize your results and discuss the findings in terms of perceived value and perceived benefits.
2. Interview five consumers and ask them to describe a sports product

they consider to be of extremely high value and one they consider to be of extremely poor value. Why do they feel this way?

3. Find two examples of sports products you consider to compete solely on the basis of price. Provide support for your answer.
4. For any professional sports franchise, provide examples of how the rest of its marketing mix is consistent with its pricing.
5. Provide two examples of sports organizations that have (either in whole or in part) a social concern pricing objective.
6. Interview five people to determine whether demand could be characterized as elastic or inelastic for the following sports products: season tickets to your favorite basketball team's games, golf lessons from Greg Norman, and Nike Air Jordans.
7. Provide examples of how technology has increased the ticket prices of professional sporting events. Support your examples from a cost perspective.
8. Interview the organizer of a local or neighborhood road race (e.g., 5k or 10k) and determine the costs of staging such an event. Categorize the costs as either fixed or variable. Assess the role of cost in the price of the entry fee for participants.

Internet exercises

1. Using the Internet, find three examples of promotions for sport products that provide consumers with pricing information.
2. Find an example of a sports product that is being sold via the Internet for a lower price than offered via other outlets. How much cheaper is the sports product? What does the consumer have to give up to purchase the product at a lower price over the Internet?
3. Using the Internet, find an example of price bundling sports products.
4. Using the Internet, find an example of product line pricing for the pricing of a sponsorship package (i.e., sponsorship levels at different prices).
5. Searching the Internet, find an example of a sports product that uses prestige pricing. Comment on the construction of the Web site itself. Is it consistent with the prestige pricing?

Endnotes

1 Robert B. Cialdini, Richard J. Borden, Avril Thorne, Marcus R. Walker, Stephen Freeman, and Lloyd R. Sloan, "Basking in Reflected Glory: Three (Football) Field Studies," *Journal of Personality and Social Psychology*, vol. 34, no. 3 (1976), 366–375.

2 Valarie Zeithaml, "Consumer Perceptions of Price, Quality, and Value: A Means-End Chain Model and Synthesis of Evidence," *Journal of Marketing*, vol. 52 (1988), 2–21.

3 http://www.forbes.com/sites/mikeozanian/2013/11/25/the-nhls-most-valuable-teams/; http://www.forbes.com/sites/mikeozanian/2013/08/14/the-most-valuable-nfl-teams/

4 Kurt Foss, "NCAA March Madness 2004: PDF Hoop Dreams." *Planetpdf.com* (April 14, 2004). Available from: http://www.planetpdf.com/enterprise/article.asp?ContentID=596.

5 Frederick Wiseman and Sangit Chatterjee, "Team Payroll and Team Performance in Major League Baseball: 1985–2002," *Economics Bulletin*, vol. 1, no. 2 (2003), 1–10.

6 National Sporting Goods Association (NSGA), "Insights" (June 2014). Available from: http://archive.constantcontact.com/fs119/1101981701899/archive/1117660475100.html, accessed June 24, 2014.

7 http://www.marketingpower.com/AboutAMA/Pages/DefinitionofMarketing.aspx. Credit: American Marketing Association

8 Goodreads Inc. (2014). Available from: https://www.goodreads.com/author/quotes/25181.David_Ogilvy, accessed June 25, 2014.

9 Rudy Martzke, "SET Expects Pay-Per-View Recordbreaker," *USA Today* (1996), 2C.

10 Johnny Ludden, "Spurs Mailbag: For Right Price, Watch Parker Hog Ball up Close," *Spurstalk.com* (April 12, 2006). Available from: http://www.spurstalk.com/forums/showthread.php?t=55121.

11 "Coast to Coast – Chicago," *Street & Smith's Sport Business Journal* (March 12, 2007). Available from: http://www.sportsbusinessdaily.com/Journal/Issues/2007/03/20070312/Coast-To-Coast.aspx, accessed June 25, 2014.

12 "Press Release: Mets Reduce Ticket Prices for 2011," New York Mets (November 3, 2010). Available from: http://newyork.mets.mlb.com/news/press_releases/press_release.jsp?ymd=20101103&content_id=15970796&vkey=pr_nym&fext=.jsp&c_id=nym, accessed June 25, 2014.

13 Erik Spanberg, "Bobcats Raise, Lower Ticket Prices," *Charlotte Business Journal* (January 14, 2011). Available from: http://www.bizjournals.com/charlotte/blog/queen_city_agenda/2011/01/higher-prices-for-some-bobcats-fans.html?page=all.

14 BusinessWire. (2010. "Atlanta Hawks, Atlanta Thrashers, Houston Rockets and Utah Jazz Select Qcue to Power Dynamic Ticket Pricing," *Businesswire.com* (August 16, 2010). Available from: http://www.businesswire.com/news/home/20100816005210/en/Atlanta-Hawks-Atlanta-Thrashers-Houston-Rockets-Utah.

15 Huntermtn.com (2014), http://www.huntermtn.com/huntermtn/tickets-passes/season-passes.aspx, accessed June 25, 2014.

PART IV

Implementing and Controlling the Strategic Sports Marketing Process

CHAPTER 13

Implementing and controlling the strategic sports marketing process

After completing this chapter, you should be able to:

- Describe how the implementation phase of the strategic sports marketing process "fits" with the planning phase.
- Explain the organizational design elements that affect the implementation phase.
- Identify the general competencies and the most important skills that effective sports marketing managers possess.
- Describe the basic characteristics of total quality marketing (TQM) programs and how TQM might be implemented in sports organizations.
- Identify some of the guidelines for designing reward systems.
- Define strategic control and how the control phase of the strategic sports marketing process "fits" with the implementation phase.
- Explain the differences among planning assumption control, process control, and contingency control.

DEW ACTION SPORTS TOUR

Challenge
NBC's Dew Action Sports Tour was a start-up property and didn't have any type of branding or visual identity in place. After a highly competitive agency review, the Dew Action Sports Tour chose Active Imagination to develop the look and feel for the entire property, including logos for the events, sports and the tour itself, as well as marketing collateral, on-site branding at the events and brand usage guidelines.

Solution
Active Imagination performed extensive market research at skate parks, surf shops, concerts and other venues that attract the Dew Action Sports Tour's target market. Using the results of this research, Active Imagination designed the green and black Dew Action Sports Tour logo, as well as alternate logos and individual sports logos, and established guidelines for their use. After creating the Tour's visual brand, Active Imagination developed logos and icons for each individual event that provided recognition and value to the event sponsors, while maintaining the integrity of the overall Dew Action Sports Tour brand.

Results
The Tour has an integrated look that makes any event or sports icon instantly recognizable as belonging to the Dew Action Sports Tour. Fan response to the brand has been positive, and event sponsors and promotional partners are also enthusiastic about the design.

"Active Imagination's team is creative and meets tight deadlines, but more importantly, Active Imagination's team understands that with three different sports, the Dew Action Sports Tour has diverse audiences that must be considered in any element of our creative needs. In other words, Active Imagination can think strategically."
– Ethan Green, Senior Director of Marketing, Dew Action Sports Tour

Source: http://marketingforsports.com/content 393.html.

The opening scenario presents an excellent example of how sports organizations operate in uncertain and changing conditions. Moreover, sports organizations must consider the internal and external environments and formulate a plan that achieves a "fit" with these environments. The strategic sports marketing process is ultimately directed toward the achievement of the organization's mission, goals, and objectives. The contingency theory of sports marketing suggests that there are a variety of marketing plans that can achieve these goals. However, not all these plans are equally effective. Likewise, organizations have a variety of ways to implement and control the strategic sports marketing plan they have developed, all of which are not equally useful for putting the plan into action. Thus, sports marketers should allocate the time and effort necessary to develop a program that will lead to the desired outcomes and most effectively implement and control the planning process.

The remainder of this chapter looks at the last two phases of the strategic marketing process – implementation and control. We begin by examining a model of the implementation process and the organizational design elements that facilitate or impede the execution of the marketing plan. Then, we shift our focus to the control phase and look at some of the common forms of strategic control.

Implementation

Implementation can be described as putting strategy into action or executing the plan. As illustrated in the opening scenario, the Dew Tour's goal of enhancing the brand can be achieved with proper planning. However, none of these plans matters unless the Dew Tour continually monitors the implementation process to make sure plans are being carried out in the correct manner.

To successfully manage the implementation process, the sports marketer must consider a number of organizational design elements. These organizational design elements include communication, staffing, skills, coordination, rewards, information, creativity, and budgeting. Implementation must begin with **communication**. Effective communication requires a leadership style that allows and encourages an understanding of the marketing plan by all members of the sports marketing team. A second critical element involves **staffing** and developing the **skills** in those people who are responsible for carrying out the plan. These people must also be placed within the organization so they can work together to implement the plan, thus a third critical design element is **coordination. Rewards** that are congruent to the plan can provide the motivation and incentives necessary for people to work effectively toward the achievement of the goals and objectives outlined within the plan. **Information** must be available to those people who will carry out the plans so effective decisions can be made throughout the implementation phase. Effective work environments also allow for and encourage **creativity** from individuals who are expected to find ways to carry out the strategic marketing plan. Finally, a supportive **budgeting** system is critical to the successful achievement of strategic goals and objectives. These seven organizational design elements of implementation and their relationship to the strategic sports marketing process are outlined in Figure 13.1.

Each of these seven elements must be carefully considered within the strategic marketing process by the sports marketing manager. The implementation design must be appropriate for the plan. In other words, a "fit" between the planning phase and the implementation phase is required. Thus, a change in the strategic marketing plan of a sports organization could lead to the need to make changes in one or more of these design elements. As you read the accompanying article on the critical issues impacting the Arena Football League,[1] think about what design elements could have been changed to enhance the league endeavors.

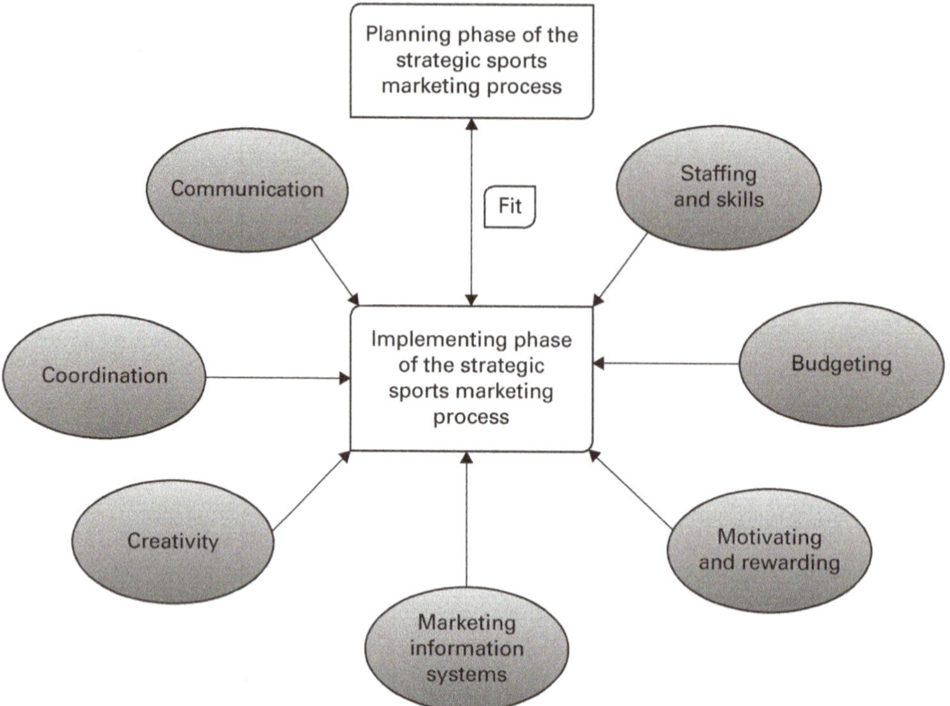

Figure 13.1 Implementation phase of the strategic sports marketing process

BUSY OFFSEASON AHEAD FOR ARENA FOOTBALL LEAGUE: FAN TAKE

With the dust settling on the Silver Anniversary season of the Arena Football League, several challenges lie ahead for the league in the offseason. Near as I can tell, here are the major ones.

Labor issues

The labor issues that wreaked havoc on the 2012 season have been resolved, if Ivan Soto, executive director of the Arena Football League Players Union (AFLPU), is to be believed in his tweet from Aug. 19. "It is official! We have a 5yr deal!" he announced.

Of course, arena football fans have heard this song and dance before, and the league office has yet to announce anything about a deal being reached or what the specific terms are, so I'm not popping the cork on any champagne just yet.

A deal has *got* to get done, though. The already-dwindling fan base can't take another season of uncertainty, replacement players, forfeits, and lost live coverage on the NFL Network.

How many teams return?

The specific terms of any labor deal that's reached are likely to impact how many of the 17 teams return to the Arena Football League in 2013. Already, rumors are swirling among fans as to who will be back and who won't return next season, for a variety of reasons.

AFL commissioner Jerry B. Kurz made indirect reference to the potential that some teams may not return next year in his Aug. 9

letter to fans. An upcoming owners' meeting will likely address this issue, according to Kurz's letter, and when teams can start signing players in September, fans will get a better indication as to who may or may not be part of the league.

My hope is that the league handles things differently than it did when the Dallas Vigilantes vanished without a trace after the 2011 campaign. Silence is not golden in that kind of situation, and if teams are leaving, I'd rather just know upfront.

Developmental league?

Back in May, Kurz announced during Arena Football Friday that the league is bringing back a developmental league, which I found to be a very exciting prospect for a number of reasons. The buzz surrounding that idea kind of died out as the season progressed, however, and I'm left wondering if that's something that the AFL is still going to pursue.

Again, the owners' meeting will probably shed some light on this concept. Perhaps some of the current AFL teams will choose to participate as a developmental team, instead. Perhaps some teams from other indoor leagues would join a developmental league. Perhaps it's too much to expect that a developmental league can get up and running by 2013, and that it's more of a long-term goal.

As with any scenario in which one or more teams leave the AFL next year, it would be nice to hear from the league one way or the other about the plans for the developmental league, even if it's not going to happen in 2013. If it has turned into more of a long-term thing, that's cool. Just let us know, please, as there are some rabid fans in some large metropolitan areas (cough, cough . . . INDIANAPOLIS . . . cough, cough) who would love a developmental team and just want to know where to set expectations.

International play

Replacing the buzz about a developmental league has been the buzz about international play. Openly discussed at the Silver Anniversary Gala Event right before ArenaBowl XXV, the league is quite interested in tapping into the international market – specifically, China and its population of over 1.3 billion.

Given Ron Jaworski's excitement at the gala event about international play and what I heard players and fans discussing while I was in New Orleans for ArenaBowl XXV, my money is on the Philadelphia Soul as one of the teams that is likely to be taking the game to China in the form of an exhibition game or two.

The concept of international play is exciting and scary at the same time. I certainly understand the desire to expose the sport to the most populated country in the world (although road trips from Indianapolis to Beijing to cover games there might be a little lengthy – and wet – but that's my problem, not the league's).

But a part of me also thinks that we're on pretty shaky ground right now in the U.S., so maybe now's not the greatest time to be footing the bill for trips to China. Maybe we should get things squared away stateside before we try expanding to international markets.

Again, though, the owners know their financial situation better than I do, and I'm sure they'll hash this idea out at their meetings. In what is becoming an ongoing theme here, I simply hope that the league keeps us fans informed as things progress.

Schedule

A couple of recent events lead me to believe that the AFL may consider altering the 2013 schedule – perhaps starting the season earlier and/or shortening the season.

The first was the NFL Network's decision to delay broadcast of ArenaBowl XXV until the ridiculous hour of 10:30 p.m. ET so that the Tim Tebow worshippers of the world could watch him play backup quarterback for the New York Jets for the first time (he finished with a dismal 18.2 QB rating, in case you're wondering, and his Jets were stomped by the Cincinnati Bengals).

The second was the news that renovations to New Orleans Arena are going to mess up the 2013 schedule of the New Orleans VooDoo.

Among the options cited by Kurz for working around this hurdle are an earlier start time – Kurz mentioned the possibility of starting the week before the Super Bowl – or front-loading the VooDoo's home schedule. Sources close to the VooDoo have told Paul Murphy of WWLTV.com that the teams is also considering playing home games in alternative sites such as Baton Rouge, Biloxi, Bossier City, and Lafayette.

Given the trouble that the league ran into this year with Tebowmania, it might be prudent to just start the season earlier. The VooDoo wouldn't have to have their home schedule front-loaded – or at least, not much – and they could continue playing at the location with which fans are familiar.

On the back end, the ArenaBowl wouldn't conflict with any NFL preseason games, and we wouldn't be playing our championship game into the wee hours of the morning for much of the country.

Wait and see

I'd love to be a fly on the wall for these owners' meetings, but something tells me that I can wait by my mailbox for an eternity and my invitation will never arrive. Oh well. It's probably not the best place for a fan to be, anyway, if any league business is to be done.

So I'll join the rest of AFL fandom and just wait to see how things shake out. The owners have a lot on their plates this offseason – and probably even more that I'm not aware of – so there's no point in getting antsy in anticipation of how everything will be resolved.

Arena fans know that patience and flexibility are required in buckets in this league. It's just the way things are. I'd much rather wait and hear from the league when something is official than give myself an ulcer anguishing over what may or may not happen regarding any number of things that are important to me.

Please, AFL, just don't leave us fans in the dark.

Source: Article author: Eric R. Ivie. Rightsholder: Yahoo Sports; http://sports.yahoo.com/news/busy-offseason-ahead-arena-football-league-fan-163400668.html. Reprinted with permission from Yahoo.

Communication

Effective communication is critical to the successful implementation of the strategic sports marketing plan. Before we discuss the issues involved in effective communication, we must understand the importance of having a leader who is committed to the strategic sports marketing plan. Without such commitment, the best communication efforts will be ineffective. The values of the marketing leader and the President/CEO of the organization not only affect the strategic sports marketing process, but also the way the plan will be implemented. Strategic leadership requires a "champion," someone who believes so strongly in the strategic marketing plan that he or she can share the "what," "why," and "how" with those who will be responsible for its implementation.

Photo 13.1 Sports organizations often utilize creative marketing strategies to target consumers.

Source: Shutterstock.com

The commitment of the leader to the plan usually dictates the level of commitment among those who will carry it out. In addition, different strategies require different skills, even among leaders. Therefore, when strategy changes, a change in leadership often follows. That relationship may also be reversed. A change in leadership will often lead to a change, or at least an adjustment, to the strategy. As illustrated in the previous article, there is a close relationship between strategy and leadership, and it is sometimes necessary to bring in outside sports marketers to implement a changed or new strategy. Organizations will also often bring in someone new when they believe a new marketing strategy is needed to enhance performance.

Just how important is communication? The results of a recent study indicate that when selecting a new commissioner/CEO to run a major sports property, being able to effectively communicate and manage the media was deemed "extremely important" by 81 percent of the respondents.[2] Certainly, the LPGA had this in mind when they hired their new commissioner, Michael Whan. Unfortunately, the former commissioner who had come to the job after four years as president of a media consulting firm in Los Angeles, got off on the wrong foot with the media at the first tournament of the year, the SBS Open at Turtle Bay. Without warning, media representatives showing up to cover the tournament were told they must agree to restrictive regulations concerning who controlled the images and stories from the tournaments. Rather than sign, the Associated Press walked out, as did two weekly magazines that cover the LPGA, *Golf World* and *Golf Week*.[3] In 2009, Commissioner Bivens was removed from her position, not because of her lack of a golf background or the economic downturn, it was as Alan Shipnuck said, "She stubbornly refused to back down in her demands of so many cash-strapped corporations, clinging to the belief that this was the last best chance to launch the LPGA into the big-time. Instead many companies have simply walked away, resulting in the loss of seven tournaments this year (so far.)" Obviously, all leaders of business today must be willing to adjust their vision. The tool of communication is necessary to have all members of the organization working towards success. Bivens failed early in her attempts at communication and when she needed the support of the LPGA players there was little goodwill.[4] In yet another example, many often question how FIFA, a federation responsible for managing the affairs of the world's most lucrative and popular sport, can be expected to properly organize and run a quadrennial international soccer competition worth billions of dollars in revenue when its own leaders can't even agree in the spotlight?[5] Turmoil among the ranks of FIFA's leaders, prominent as of late, reflects poorly on the interpersonal communication (or lack thereof) within the organization. The conversational "methods of delivery" often prove more damaging than the actual content. The miscommunication might not seem like a big deal upon initial consideration; however, it's an understatement that this is not exactly the professional impression soccer fans might hope to get from the brass of a federation responsible for managing the affairs of the world's most lucrative and popular sport.

As discussed in the FIFA and LPGA examples, organizational leadership sets the tone for communication within the sports organization. Communication may be formal or informal and may use a number of different channels. For example, some organizations may require that all communications be written and meetings be scheduled and documented. Other organizational leaders may have an informal, open-door policy and allow for more "spur of the moment" meetings and "hallway" discussions. Either policy can be effective when it comes to implementing strategy within the sports organization, as long as the necessary information is clearly and accurately communicated.

Strategy was once considered a "top-down" only process where those who had a "big-picture" view of the organization were considered the best candidates for formulating strategy. This often led to huge communication requirements as organizational leaders attempted to inform those who had to carry out the strategy about not only the strategy, but also the rationale for strategic choices made by the top management. Experience and research has shown that the communication process is easier when those who are expected to implement the plan are involved throughout the process. Thus, involving the entire sports marketing team throughout the strategic sports marketing process can usually be more effective than attempting to communicate the plan after it has been developed.

Even when everyone responsible for implementing the plan is involved in its development, strategic sports marketing plans should be communicated often. Due to the contingent nature of the strategic sports marketing process, plans and circumstances can change, and people can forget the original plan and the basic premise on which the plan was formulated. Employees can learn about or be reminded about the content and purpose of the plans in a variety of ways. This information can be communicated in regularly scheduled meetings or at gatherings where the strategic plan is the primary agenda item. Printed material can also be useful. Some sports organizations may give employees desk items, such as calendars or paperweights, with keywords that remind them of the strategy. They may even program screen savers on computers with words that will remind employees of the strategic thrust of the marketing plan. Promotional literature that can be displayed around the office or sent to employees through e-mail is also useful. In essence, sports marketing organizations that can provide daily reminders of the strategy are more likely to keep everyone involved on the same strategic path. Many forms of internal promotion can be used to achieve this goal.

Communication with groups and individuals outside the marketing department is also important. Many such individuals and groups, both within the organization and outside the organization, have a stake in the marketing strategy and can have an impact on the implementation of the plan, and so it is important to inform other departments within the sports organization who affect or are affected by the strategy or the strategic marketing direction. For example, many teams and leagues are in the process of trying to develop long-term relationships with their fans. One of the ways to build these relationships is to allow fans more access and contact with the players. At the collegiate level, many universities have implemented Kid's Clubs offering such benefits as free admission to events, pizza parties, t-shirts, and access to special events and clinics. This creative plan can only be executed by communicating its importance to coaches, members of the teams, and the athletic department as a whole.

On the professional front, many teams hold an annual fan appreciation day and preseason fan fests to enhance fan relations. The Tampa Bay Rays, for example, hold an annual fan fest event prior to the beginning of the baseball season. Highlights of the event include player meet and greets with autographs, clubhouse tours, National Anthem auditions, memorabilia, and interactive play areas. Taking it one step further, the Cleveland Indians have developed a Fan Advisory Council. The council, comprised of groups of 12 to 14 Indians' individual ticket buyers and season ticket holders, meets once per month during the regular season to discuss anything and everything related to Indians baseball and the Progressive Field experience. Of course, the ownership hopes this will help curb a slide in season-ticket sales too. All of these activities contribute to strengthening the team–fan relationship, but as shown in Table 13.1, neither of these teams is among the top fifteen in professional sports.

As with internal promotion, external promotion and communication of the strategic sports marketing plan can take many forms. Some channels for these communications include social media and the utilization of Web sites, annual reports, mailers, marketing specialties such as calendars, or meetings. Again, the key to effectively communicating to outside or inside groups is committed and competent leadership. It is with this leadership and effective communication efforts that the foundation for successful implementation of the strategic sports marketing plan is provided.

Table 13.1 Stadium experience rankings of professional sports teams

1.	Memphis Grizzlies
2.	San Antonio Spurs
3.	Indiana Pacers
4.	Oklahoma City Thunder
5.	Green Bay Packers
6.	Arizona Diamondbacks
7.	Pittsburgh Penguins
8.	Anaheim Ducks
9.	Ottawa Senators
10.	Baltimore Ravens
11.	Cincinnati Reds
12.	St. Louis Cardinals
13.	Detroit Red Wings
14.	Chicago Blackhawks
15.	Denver Broncos
16.	Seattle Seahawks
17.	Tampa Bay Rays
18.	Indianapolis Colts
19.	Texas Rangers
20.	Atlanta Falcons
21.	Houston Texans
22.	Detroit Tigers
23.	Atlanta Braves
24.	Los Angeles Kings
25.	Miami Heat

Source: ESPN.com

SPORTS MARKETING HALL OF FAME

Gary Davidson

Gary Davidson was once called the man who has had the greatest impact on professional sports in America. A former lawyer, Davidson founded and served as president of the American Basketball Association (ABA), the World Hockey Association (WHA), and the World Football League (WFL) in the late 1960s and early 1970s.

These leagues, of course, offered alternatives for professional athletes that would have never existed otherwise. By breaking the virtual monopoly held on talent by the existing NBA, NHL, and NFL franchises, Davidson attracted stars such as Wayne Gretzky, Bobby Hull, "Dr. J." Julius Erving, and Rick Barry to play in his rebel leagues. Davidson and his leagues are also credited with some major rule changes that subsequently were adopted by the existing professional leagues. For instance, the three-point shot was created to add excitement to the ABA and has changed the entire course of modern basketball.

In addition to his ambush marketing tactics, Gary Davidson broadened the scope of professional sports. He placed professional franchises in cities that were previously considered too small to support major league sports. For example, San Antonio and Indianapolis were two of his original ABA teams that are now successful NBA franchises. Davidson's leagues have benefited the fans, the players, and major league sports.

Source: Steve Rushin, "Gary Davidson," *Sports Illustrated* (September 19, 1994), 145. Courtesy of Time, Inc.

Staffing and skills

As we just discussed, it is critical to the success of the strategic sports marketing plan to have a leader who can "champion" and communicate the strategy. As important as the leader is to effective implementation, it is equally important to have a staff that cares about and is capable of implementing the strategy. A group of individuals must be assembled who have the appropriate mix of backgrounds, experiences, know-how, beliefs, values, work and managerial styles, and personalities.

It is important to consider strategy prior to hiring and training new employees and in retraining those who are already with the marketing team. This is especially vital in managerial or other key positions. However, staffing for the implementation of strategic sports marketing plans must go much deeper into the organizational ranks. In fact, putting together an effective marketing team is one of the cornerstones of the implementation process.

A few studies have examined the relationship between types of strategy and staff characteristics. One study of corporate executives and their perceptions regarding the relationship between managerial characteristics and strategy offered two interesting findings.[6] First, experience and exposure to a particular type of strategy has been viewed by corporate executives as being essential for managers. Previous experience and exposure to a strategy can provide an opportunity for these experienced individuals to provide important input into the implementation of the plan. However, the second finding suggests that a "perfect match" between managerial characteristics and strategy is likely to result in an overcommitment to a particular strategy. In other words, managers may not be able to change strategic direction when contingencies change if they are perfectly matched in education, training, experience, and personality to one particular strategy. These findings may be particularly relevant for sports organizations. Because sports organizations operate in changing, uncertain, and unpredictable environments where the internal and external contingencies can change frequently, staffing must consider the capacity for change among employees.

To develop a staff capable of implementing the strategy, three categories of characteristics must be considered: education, training, and ability; experience and previous track record; and personality and temperament. With any team-building activity, it is important to consider the compatibility of the individuals who will work together to implement the strategic sports plan.

Just what skills are necessary to land and keep your dream job in sports marketing? The answer to this question is best addressed in two parts. First, what knowledge

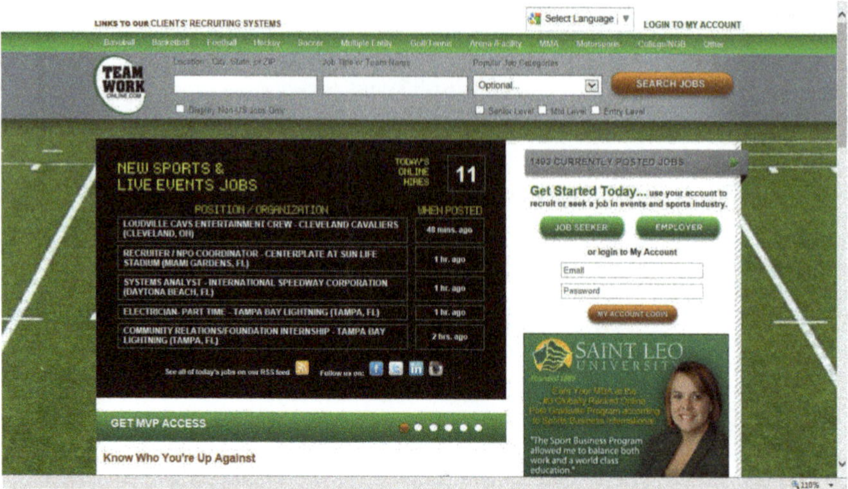

Web 13.1 Sports careers on the Web

Source: http://www.teamworkonline.com

is required for an individual to be successful in all sports management positions? In other words, what are the foundation skills for a successful career? Second, what are the marketing-specific core competencies of the sports marketing manager?

In addressing the first question, the general competencies necessary for all sports marketing management careers include being able to:[7]

- Direct the work effort of people or groups of people.
- Interrelate with the community.
- Negotiate to arrive at a solution to a problem.
- Function within a specified budget.
- Use supervision techniques.
- Evaluate the results of your decisions in light of work objectives.
- Self-evaluate employees' job performance.
- Use problem-solving techniques.
- Interpret basic statistical data.
- Speak before large audiences.
- Apply the knowledge of the history and evolution of sport into the structure of today's society.
- Appreciate the psychological factors that pertain to an athlete's performance and attitude on the playing field.

These general skills are required of all sports marketing managers to some extent, but what about more specific marketing skills? This question was posed to sports marketing professionals employed in sports marketing firms, amateur sports organizations, professional sports organization, and college athletics. The results of this study are presented in Table 13.2.

Remember, changes in strategy may lead to modification of the staff and skill base. Thus, employee training and retraining is often an important part of the implementation process. As strategy is developed and the implementation plan formulated, sports marketers must consider not only new staffing needs, but also new skill needs. Training and retraining programs should be designed and

Table 13.2 Most important skills for sports marketing managers

Presented in rank order where 1 is the most important skill and 20 is the least important skill
1. Establish a positive image for your sporting organization.
2. Achieve sponsors' promotional goals.
3. Stimulate ticket sales.
4. Maximize media exposure for events, athletes, and sponsors.
5. Acquire sponsors through personal contacts.
6. Maintain good relations with community, authorities, and partners.
7. Acquire sponsors by formal presentations.
8. Develop special promotions.
9. Improve budget construction.
10. Negotiate promotion contracts.
11. Evaluate sports marketing opportunities and performance.
12. Design and coordinate content of events.
13. Coordinate press coverage of events.
14. Create contracts.
15. Provide corporate hospitality of events.
16. Build public image and awareness of athletes.
17. Schedule events and facilities.
18. Establish event safety factors.
19. Build rapport with editors, reporters, and other media reps.
20. Buy and resell media rights.

Source: Peter Smolianov and David Shillbury, "An Investigation of Sport Marketing Competencies, *Sport Marketing Quarterly*, vol. 5, no. 4 (1996), 27–36.

included in the implementation plans so the staff is prepared to implement the new or modified strategy. Until all the staff and skills are in place, it is unlikely that the sports organization can proceed with the successful implementation of the marketing plan.

Coordination

Successful implementation of the marketing plan depends not only on capable and committed leadership who can effectively communicate internally and externally and a staff with the necessary skills, but also on the effective organization of those people and their tasks. Structure helps to define the key activities and the manner in which they will be coordinated to achieve the strategy. A fit between strategy and structure has been shown to be critical to the successful achievement of strategy and the performance of organizations. According to one important study of organizations, when a new strategy was chosen, a decline in performance was observed and administrative problems occurred until a new method of organizing people and activities was put into place. Once the new method was implemented, organizational performance began to improve, and the strategy was more likely to be achieved.[8] Thus, the strategic marketing plan must dictate how people and tasks are organized.

One way of coordinating people and tasks in a sports organization is by practicing some form of **Total Quality Management (TQM)**. Quality improvement programs

CAREER SPOTLIGHT

Megan Dotson, Director of Marketing, Greeville Road Warriors (hockey)

The Greenville Road Warriors are a minor league hockey team in the ECHL and are affiliated with Connecticut Whales and the New York Rangers. The Warriors have only one person working the client services and marketing department, Megan Dotson. This differs from major league organizations because their front offers tend to carry a larger amount of staff for individual departments. The Warriors key clients, currently, are New York Life, Bi-Lo and Spinx. It is Dotson's job to keep these clients happy and continue developing relationships with these sponsors in order to keep the organization afloat.

The function of the Warriors marketing department is to promote the Warriors' games, team and management image, and develop the sponsorships needed to run a smaller sporting organization. Fan base is an important part of the marketing done within the Greenville organization because the base is smaller than an NHL team would deal with. Dotson believes that the need for sport marketing is "important simply because sports themselves are such a huge part of American culture that any marketing centered around them is bound to be a very major player in the industry".

Interview with Megan Dotson

1. **What does the word sport mean to you**? Fun, competition, lifelong friends, leadership, character building, and escape.
2. **What is the need for marketing sports from an overall perspective?**
   a. Helps increase funds for the maintenance of the sports teams
   b. Helps make people aware of the various activities of the sports teams
   c. It's the primary way to get sponsorships
   d. Sports marketing is important simply because sports themselves are such a huge part of American culture that any marketing centered around them is bound to be a very major player in the industry.
3. **Can you give me an example of one of the most successful forms of sport marketing?** The new wave of sports marketers are relying on and will continue to rely on social media to help market their clients and their products because of its cost effectiveness and ultimately, its reach. Facebook has over 250 million users, Twitter has over 75 million, Linkedin is at approximately 50 million . . . and you certainly can't forget myriad of other options; blogging, MySpace, YouTube, etc. You can effectively market to all of these groups.
4. **How does marketing sports differ from marketing other things (food, clothes, etc.)?** Sports marketing which focuses on both the promotion of sports events and teams as well as the promotion of other products and services through sports events and sports teams. When it comes to food marketing it brings together the

producer and the consumer. It is the chain of activities that brings food from "farm gate to plate". The marketing of even a single food product can be a complicated process involving many producers and companies.

5. **Who guided you in the direction of a career in sport marketing? In what ways did they do so?** My brother's boss, Sports Information Director at Baldwin Wallace College, introduced me to the field while I was in high school and was really fascinated with it so I pursued it through college and previous and current positions.
6. **Are there risks involved with sport marketing? If yes, what were they?** Yes, an important step in understanding and managing those risks is to take time to identify potential risks that might be encountered.
7. **What was one of the worst marketing experiences you have come across thus far?** Those ideas that are put into the public that are not organized, planned out thoroughly or really thought about. They were advertised because it was crunch time.
8. **What sport do you like to market the most? Does this sport have an advantage in marketing compared to other sports?** I do not have a specific sport that I like to market the most. I have found that I do like to market minor league teams because it allows me to use my creativity more to advertise the team.
9. **What do you hope to achieve in your lifetime from a marketing standpoint?** I want to leave an impression on the sports industry with my innovative and creative ideas. I also would like to educate those who are pursuing the industry and assist them in their success.
10. **If you had one piece of advice to give an aspiring sport marketer what would it be?** It is an area of work that many people would gladly work in for free. Make sure to work hard, put in countless hours of work, and think outside of the box to add value for the people that surround you.
11. **What experiences do you have that qualify you to be a sport marketer?** I have marketing and sales experience along with event planning and excellent communication skills. In addition, I operate successfully in a high-energy environment and have the ability to multitask.
12. **Who are the key clients of the organization?** New York Life, Bi-Lo, Spinx (as of now these are our top clients)
13. **How does the organization utilize sport marketing?** Right now we are using our social media outlets, billboards, print, radio, and grassroots.
14. **What is your specific role within the organization?** My title is Client Services and Marketing Manager. I handle the Website, game operations, game presentation, marketing and fulfillment of sponsorship and contracts.

and practices have become an important and powerful tool for organizations, including sports organizations.[9] Nearly all major corporations and industries in the United States have adopted some type of quality initiative to meet competitive challenges. Traditionally, TQM programs have been focused on manufacturing quality. To manufacturers of sporting goods, quality is likely to mean an excellent consistency of goods and deliveries made by their suppliers. In a manufacturing environment, TQM has been primarily concerned with both the counting and reduction of defects and reducing the cycle time taken to complete any given process.

Even though TQM philosophies originally were used in manufacturing companies, a large number (69 percent) of service organizations are also using the principles of TQM. Although the nature of services is vastly different from those of manufactured products (see Chapter 7), Roberts and Sergesketter argue that the fundamental quality issues are similar.[10] A service organization, like a manufacturing organization, must concentrate on the reduction of defects and cycle times for important processes. As such, the philosophies of TQM are just as applicable for sports services as they are for manufacturing.

Although TQM represents a quality philosophy, there is little agreement as to what TQM (or quality) actually is and how best to manage the TQM process in an organization.[11] Evans and Lindsay define TQM as an integrative management concept for continuously improving the quality of goods and services delivered through the participation of all levels and functions of the organization.[12] In addition, TQM is described as incorporating design, control, and quality improvement, with the customer as the driving force behind the process.

Although the definitions of TQM may vary on the basis of wording and relative emphasis, all quality improvement programs share a common set of features or characteristics.[13] These characteristics include, but are not limited to, the following:

1. ***Customer-driven quality*** **–** Quality is defined by customers, and all TQM practices are implemented to please the customer.
2. ***Visible leadership*** **–** Top management is responsible for leading the quality charge and places quality above all else.
3. ***Data-driven processes*** **–** All TQM processes are driven by data collection, use of measurement, and the scientific method.
4. ***Continuous improvement philosophy*** **–** It is always possible to do a better job, and continual, small changes in improvement are just as critical as an occasional major breakthrough.

Rewards

As we discussed previously, the execution of strategy ultimately depends on individual members of the organization. Effective communication, staffing, skill development and enhancement, and coordination are vital to implementation efforts and should be planned for and considered throughout the strategic sports marketing process. Another critical component in the design of an implementation plan is to provide for motivating and rewarding behavior that is strategy supportive. Thus, a reward system is a key ingredient in effective strategy implementation.

There is no one "correct" reward system. From a strategic perspective, rewards must be aligned with the strategy; therefore, the best reward system is contingent upon the strategic circumstances. These rewards and incentives represent another choice for management. Thus, reward systems will reflect the beliefs and values of the individuals who design them. However, to successfully motivate desired behavior, reward systems must consider the needs, values, and beliefs of those who will be motivated by and receiving the rewards.

Management can choose from several types of motivators, which can be classified on the basis of three types of criteria. Motivators can be positive or negative, monetary or nonmonetary, and long run or short run. Some examples include compensation (salary or commission), bonuses, raises, stock options, benefits, promotions, demotions, recognition, praise, criticism, more (or less) responsibility, performance appraisals, and fear or tension.

Experience has shown that positive rewards tend to motivate best in most circumstances; however, negative motivators are also frequently used by organizations. Many organizations assume that only financial motivators will lead to desired behaviors. However, many organizations have obtained great success with nonfinancial rewards. Typically, a combination of both provides optimal results. Timing is also an important consideration in motivating performance with reward systems. Rewards systems should be based on both short- and long-term achievements so that employees can receive both immediate feedback and yet be motivated to strive for the longer term strategic goals.

In an interesting twist, some sports owners would like to link their teams' on-field performance to salaries. David Gill, former chief executive of Manchester United, English football's biggest brand, said he "would like to see players' salaries more variable, where they win rewards if we are winning." His model is not new to some industry executives, like bankers, but sports is arguably different. Athletes risk injury and the end of their career every time they run out to play, and also have a short career span. Unsurprisingly, the sports stars prefer a guaranteed salary to a performance-related payout.[14]

In summary, reward systems are critical to the successful achievement of the strategic sports marketing plan. To be effective, these systems must motivate behavior that "fits" with and ensures adequate attention to the strategic plan. Although reward systems are contingent upon the internal and external contingencies and the specific circumstances around which a sports marketing group must operate, there are some important general guidelines for developing effective reward systems (see Table 13.3).

Table 13.3 Guidelines for designing reward systems

1.	Rewards must be tightly linked to the strategic plan.
2.	Use variable incentives and make them part of the compensation plan for everyone involved in strategy execution.
3.	Rewards should be linked to outcomes that the individual can personally affect.
4.	Performance and relationship to the success of the strategy should be rewarded rather than the position held by the individual.
5.	Be sensitive to the discrepancies between top and bottom of the organization.
6.	Give everyone the opportunity to be rewarded.
7.	Being fair and open can lead to more effective reward systems.
8.	Reward success generously – make the reward enough to matter and motivate.
9.	Do not underestimate the value of nonfinancial rewards.
10.	Be willing and open to adapting the reward system to people and situation changes.

Source: John Pearce and Richard Robinson, *Formulation, Implementation, and Control of Competitive Strategy*, 5th ed. (Boston: Irwin, 1994).

Information

Accurate information is an essential guide for decision making and action, and necessary for all phases of the strategic sports marketing process. Execution of the sports marketing plan depends on effective information systems. These systems should provide the necessary information but should not offer more than is needed to give a reliable picture of issues critical to the implementation of the strategy.

Reports of information must be timely. The flow of information should be simple, including all the critical data being reported only to the people who need it. In other words, reports do not necessarily need wide distribution.

To aid strategy implementation, information reports should be designed to make it easy to flag variances from the strategic plan. In designing these reports, the critical questions to ask are as follows:

1. Who is going to need this information?
2. For what purpose will they need it?
3. When do they need it?

The NHL provides an example of a sports organization that enhanced their ability to implement marketing strategy through an information system.[15] One of the organizational objectives of the NHL was to make better use of emerging technologies. NHL Commissioner Gary Bettman believes "everything is connected to everything else" and that the league needs to be a leader in the use of technology to achieve its goals. Toward this end, the NHL has implemented a program called NHL-ICE (Interactive Cyber Enterprises), which has developed information systems for the media, fans, coaches, and players. The NHL-ICE program also includes the design and content of the NHL Web site, implementing a real-time scoring system that captures statistics for every hockey game, and integrating network computing solutions into the marketing of the league's products and services.

The WWE and ESPN also present another fine example of information driving strategies. Both have implemented ePrize's Multi-Channel Platform, a proprietary interactive marketing technology that enables seamless consumer interaction via microsite, social networking sites, and mobile devices. The primary feature of the multi-channel platform includes customizing content so that fans can enjoy special offers, coupons, and game experiences based on their registration information and past consumption behaviors. In addition, the platform affords both entities to learn more about their fans by creating a fan profile through an interactive survey.

Professional teams, such as the Portland Trail Blazers, understand the importance of information sharing among their stakeholders. The Trail Blazers were the first NBA franchise to create their own social networking site, marketing to users of blogs, message boards, and other community fan sites. The Blazers launched iamatrailblazersfan.com in February 2007, their first team-run social networking site. The site has assisted in the team's grassroots marketing efforts while increasing fan communication.

"If you are pushing information via e-mail and only 20 percent of fans open up the e-mail, then you want to find a way to spread news about the team in a fast and effective way," said Dan Harbison, Senior Director of Digital Marketing and Media for the Blazers. "Others can leverage sites such as MySpace, Facebook and Twitter, but the Trail Blazers are not able to sell tickets or sponsors through those sites so they are looking at what they see as benefits of their own social network.[16]

Creativity

The design of the strategic sports marketing plan's implementation phase is concerned with putting in place an effective system for executing marketing programs that will lead to the achievement of goals and objectives developed by the organization. The premise of this book is that the changing and uncertain environments in which sports organizations operate often require the need to adjust or change plans based on changing internal and external contingencies. Innovative plans and processes are vital to finding a fit with those contingencies. Thus, innovation, in the context of the strategic sports marketing process, is concerned with converting ideas and opportunities into a more effective or efficient system.

The **creative process** is the source of those ideas and, therefore, becomes an important component in the successful formulation and implementation of strategic sports marketing plans. Without creative endeavors, innovation is unlikely, if not impossible. An increase in creative efforts should likewise lead to an increase in innovative plans and processes.

When we talk about creativity, it is important to consider both the creative process and the people who engage in that process. The creative process can be learned and used by virtually anyone. However, some people have more experience with being creative and more confidence in their ability to be creative than others.

Many organizations can encourage creativity in their employees. This process of creating and innovating within an organization has been referred to as **intrapreneurship**, or corporate entrepreneurship. Intrapreneurial efforts have become popular as organizations have acknowledged the value of innovation in changing and uncertain environments. The watchword of today's businesses, sports organizations included, is change. As we discussed, innovation is vital to an organization's ability to change and adapt to internal and external contingencies. There are two general steps that can lead to an increase in the number of creative efforts and the resulting innovations: education and training regarding the creative process, and establishing an organizational culture and internal environment that encourages creativity.

The creative process

Although creativity is usually associated with promotion, it is important for all elements of the marketing mix. To be competitive, sports organizations must be creative in their pricing, in developing new products and services, and in getting new sports products to the consumer. The first step in increasing creative efforts within a sports organization is educating employees about the creative process. Creativity is a capability that can be learned and practiced. It is a distinctive way of looking at the world and involves seeking relationships between things that others have not seen.

Although they are referred to by different names, there are four commonly agreed-upon steps in the creative process. They are knowledge accumulation, incubation, idea generation, and evaluation and implementation.

The *knowledge accumulation phase* is an often overlooked, but absolutely vital, stage in the process of creating. Extensive exploration and investigation must precede successful creations. Because creations are simply putting together two existing ideas or tangibles in a new way, it is necessary to have an understanding of a variety of related and unrelated topics. This information gathering provides the creator with many different perspectives on the subject under consideration. Information can be gathered through reading, communication with other people, travel, and journal keeping. Simply devoting time to natural curiosities can be useful in this stage. The key is that the more the creator can learn about a broad range of topics, the more there is to choose from as the new creation is being developed.

In phase two, *the incubation period*, the creative individual allows his or her subconscious to mull over the information gathered in the previous stage by engaging in other activities. The creative effort is dropped for other pursuits. Routine activities, play, rest, and relaxation can often induce the incubation process. "Getting away" from the creative endeavor allows the subconscious mind to consider all the information gathered.

Often, when the creator least expects it, solutions will come. The next stage, *idea generation*, is the stage that is often portrayed as the "lightbulb" coming on in one's mind. The opportunity for this has been set, however, in the first two phases. As the body rests from the research and exploration, the subconscious mind sees the creative opportunity or the "light."

The last stage, *evaluation and implementation*, is often the most difficult. It requires a great deal of self-discipline and perseverance to evaluate the idea and determine whether it will lead to a useful innovation. Following through with that implementation is even more challenging. This is especially true because those individuals who are able to generate creative ideas are often not the ones who can turn those ideas into innovations. Creators may fail numerous times as they attempt to implement creative efforts. And as the accompanying article illustrates, sometimes the innovative ideas that do reach the marketplace aren't the most welcomed. [17]

THE 100 WORST THINGS IN SPORTS

While it continues to be the sole reason we get up in the morning, the sports world can annoy and frustrate us to no end. In an effort to embrace everything that is wrong with today's sports, we'll tap into the 100 worst things in sports; an encyclopedia of sports-based mediocrity that will help to put all of the annoying, frustrating and heartbreaking sites and scents into perspective.

Let's go to the mattresses and face all that is wrong with today's athletics.

100. Television Timeouts

If we wanted to listen to Progressive Flo's stale humor or State Farm's magic jingle, we'd chuck the television remote like a normal person. Instead, after every snap, every blown call, every streaking incident, we hear. . ."don't touch that dial, we'll be right back."

Let's keep it to Mike Ditka commercials and call it a day.

99. Length of NBA Playoffs

Four rounds, each one a best-of-7, two months of repetition. The postseason should be short and sweet and doused in glitter. Instead, the NBA playoffs runs nearly a third the time of the regular season. By the third round, we're already pleading for football.

98. Touchdown Celebration Fails

There's an old adage, "act like you've been there before." Unfortunately for many athletes, they've planned their post-score celebration for so long that when it's finally time, they crumble to pieces.

Or worse, they forget to cross the end zone before dropping the ball (see DeSean Jackson).

97. Suzyn Waldman's Voice
Of all the dramatic things we've ever seen, an overweight, overaged pitcher being paid $28 million to pitch whenever he pleases sits right up there with *Requiem for a Dream* and Michael Jordan's game-winning shot in Game 6 of the 1998 NBA Finals.

96. NBA Draft Lottery
A suspenseful showing every year, the NBA draft lottery continues to offer ridiculous opportunities to teams that likely don't deserve them.

With the 14th-worst team in the league able to potentially pick first, the effort to make bad teams better remains inefficient at best.

95. Celebrity Shoutouts at Games
"It's the bottom of the sixth, Game 7 of the World Series and, oh look, there's Larry David, creator of *Seinfeld." (Drop to the floor in awe)*

94. Kickers and Punters
Excluding Jay Feely, who not only tackles like a fearless fourth-string cornerback but also wears sweat bands and gloves to look the part. Otherwise, calling these individuals football players is a stretch.

93. Drunk Fans Who Start Fights
And we're talking buy-a-vowel drunk. These fiery fans don't even know what they're psyched about, but they are super stoked and ready to toss the fisticuffs.

Some fans just can't handle the suds, or society.

92. Two Weeks Between Conference Title and Super Bowl
Why not just cancel the season, or, better yet, save the Super Bowl for the week before next year's preseason? Two weeks between the conference title and big game is just as mind-boggling.

Forget rhythm and bodily routine, what the heck are the fans supposed to do without one full week of football during a postseason run?

91. First Down Celebrations
The only performance more distasteful than a touchdown dance is a first-down pose. And for injured Jets receiver Santonio Holmes, easily the worst of the bunch, first downs happen so rarely that his cocky display builds more criticism than fire in his teammates.

Get up, get back to the huddle and keep your hands to yourself.

90. Losing Four Straight Super Bowls
Although making four consecutive Super Bowls truly was a miraculous achievement for the Bills.

89. Mark Cuban's Arrogance
It was once refreshing, an almost inspirational act of courage for a fiery owner to scream about his team in the stands, toss hateful adjectives at opponents and brag about his club.

But Mark Cuban's rich boy act has gotten stale. It hit rock bottom when the Cubes allegedly bought Nets.com just so that Nets owner Mikhail Prokhorov, who he lost to in the Deron Williams sweepstakes, couldn't. And then fans realized he didn't.

88. Donald Trump Tweeting About Sports
Only the most classless individuals step on a man when he's down, and that's exactly what trolling gillionaire Donald Trump did to Derek Jeter after the latter broke his ankle.

One day after selling his Trump Tower apartment, Jeter found himself injured for the rest of the postseason. Trump, while likely downing his morning eggs Benedict with that day's blotchy bimbo, was quick to comment.

87. Danica Patrick's GoDaddy Commercials

As if there's anything more frustrating than watching the same flirtatious commercials continue to lead to nothing.

Curiosity keeps dragging us down.

86. Annoying People of Fantasy Football

Fantasy football will have you cheering for kickers, missing your childhood and going insane. But heck, it's the only way to fill deprived weekdays.

But sometimes players, often the most enthusiastic, begin neglecting their lineups (gasp), ignoring the league completely (double gasp) and "forgetting" to pay (faint). It's a fast fall for these fantasy phonies.

85. Linsanity Puns

Jeremy Lin's Lin-derella story was only slaughtered by a surfeit of lin-diculous, lin-conceivable puns.

It's become a lin-ddiction.

84. LeBron James' Hairline

Let's be honest, sports fans love to hate on the man dubbed the king of the hardwood. And we're not hating on the hairline as much as the ever-rising headband.

There was a time when James wore it appropriately.

83. The 1919 World Series

Conspired by first baseman Arnold "Chick" Gandil and supplied by New York mobster Arnold Rothstein, the 1919 World Series fix – dubbed the Black Sox Scandal – offered a harsh reality to club owners and the baseball world.

The eight members who were eventually banned from the game for life felt underpaid, and had a patent dislike for penny-pinching owner Charles Comiskey.

**Note: Tossing games is exactly the opposite of what Pete Rose did.*

82. Walt Clyde Frazier's Rhymes

Swishing and dishing, posting and toasting, banking and thanking, all the Knicks with the knack tonight. Walt Clyde Frazier has a legendary aura about him, and once had a historic poof of hair, but try listening to this guy every night and you'll surely be tearing your own poof out.

It don't mean a thing, if you don't have that swing.

81. Random-Lettered Fan Signs

See that sign on the left (ignore the yellow arrow)? "Zeller & Boys Playing For Banners." Not only is it an utter failure grammatically, but it has a lonesome word without a highlighted letter.

Vertical signs only use the first letter, that's an unwritten rule. Get it right.

80. Icing the Kicker

According to ESPN, "Since 2001 (including the playoffs), kickers have hit 81 percent of field goals when no timeout was called (36 yards) before the snap and 76 percent when a timeout was called (39 yards)" (not including overtime).

Let's keep this thing moving, we can't take any more television breaks.

79. Fairweather Fans

Fans who are only seen or heard from during times of success can't be trusted in the world of sports.

The same people who vanish at the first sign of trouble are the loudest during a golden era. Hats, shirts, box seats, a Super Bowl-guarantee tattoo. Oh the humanity.

78. The Heidi Game

Known as the most exciting regular-season game you never saw, the November 17, 1968, game between the AFL rival Raiders and Jets featured a riveting comeback and plenty of angry would-be, viewers.

With only a three-hour time slot for the game seeming adequate, NBC prepared to air the film *Heidi* (girl in the Swiss Alps) at 7 p.m. following the game.

Naturally the game was closing in on three hours when an override of concerned viewers called in to request that the game stay on. As a result, the switchboards burned out and changes couldn't be made.

During that blind minute, in which the switch had already been made with the Jets leading 32–29, Oakland would score two touchdowns and win 43–32.

77. July 11, 2012 (July in General)
The day that sports froze, aside from insignificant soccer and tennis bouts, July 11 taught us a powerful lesson; we need our games.

July is routinely a month that features only baseball, until we're saved by the Olympics.

76. Beach Balls
Not that we don't enjoy a ferocious swat once in a while, but having a random rainbow-colored beach ball hit by a raging soccer mom slam your garlic fries and over-foamed beer is an experience worth forgetting.

On the other hand, when in Rome. . .(Yes? Please continue. . .)

75. Paul Pierce's Style of Play
Watching Paul Pierce slowly deteriorate a defense is a frustrating experience for any fan. Dubbed "The Truth," the longtime Celtic can drain any triple-covered heave from half court and dribble past knowledgeable defenders with just a slight shift of his meaty shoulders.

We're often left wondering, how?

74. Youth League Parent Fights
More frustrated with the lack of hugs they got from *their* parents, little league parents can often become whirling dervishes in times of stress.

But seeing a coach bullrush a referee is like a solar eclipse; we rarely see it, but when we do it's always special.

73. Top 35 Rule
In the Sprint Cup races, the top 35 cars in the standings are automatically excused from qualifying; in other words earning an automatic bid regardless of their qualifying time.

Almost as lame as the BCS polls. And thankfully, that's why it's going to be gone come next year.

72. Lance Armstrong's Legacy
The seven-time Tour de France winner who evidently injected his way to the top, Lance Armstrong has permanently removed himself from Eddy Merckx-Fausto Coppi territory.

His unwillingness to admit his faults leaves us feeling like fools for ever believing that this testicular cancer-defeating inspiration was anything more than a fraudulent phony on the track.

71. Jon Gruden's Syrupy Broadcasts
As a coach and motivator, the man is a legend. As a broadcaster, well let's just say Jon Gruden's syrupy presentations are a better fit on top of a stack of pancakes than in the booth.

Not that we don't love to see big bodies bang as well, Jon.

70. Team Curses
The Cleveland curse of Paul Brown, the Boston curse of the Bambino, the Philly curse of Frank Gifford. Hexes remain iconic excuses for mediocrity. Blame it on talent, not a curse.

And dare we forget the best of all, the Chi-town curse of the Billy

Goat? Although, any team that's titleless since 1908 should probably be studying the art of voodoo.

69. Collusion
Having a salary cap essentially makes the illegal essence of collusion legal. But collusion between owners and commissioners can have players asking questions.

And that's exactly what they did. Last month, a judge considered suing the league for conspiring to hold down salary caps in 2010. There are no conspiracies, or coincidences.

68. Sabermetrics
Coined by baseball writer Bill James, sabermetrics is essentially the overanalyzation of statistics to make accurate predictions. It was a phenomenal process until A's general manager Billy Beane began receiving endless fanfare for using the intriguing approach.

Beane eventually got his own movie, starring Brad Pitt, but he doesn't have a World Series ring to his name.

67. Rush Limbaugh Talking Sports
Having Honey Boo Boo's possible right-wing uncle on the NFL Pregame Show is as irresponsible as eating steak with a spoon. It just doesn't work.

And Rush Limbaugh proved that to us when he sparked nearly political debate surrounding the race issue in the league. Fun experiment while it lasted, fellas.

66. NCAA's Improper Benefits
Athletes from different crevices of the world, some poor, some deprived, some eager for love, flood college athletics every season.

And boosters can't help but tempt potential recruits and star players with gifts. Neither can agents, who toss opportunities and promises at potential draftees in hopes they'll sign with them. But in the end, how can these innocent athletes, still kids, say no?

65. Former Devil Rays Uniforms
Reeking of '90s failure, the former Rays jerseys – back when they were still deviled – were any graphic designer's worst nightmare.

In 2005, several significant green tweaks were made to the uniform. Three years later, the Rays were in the World Series.

64. Anthony Davis' Unibrow
Some might call it the best thing in sports and a potential cash cow, but we see Anthony Davis' epic unibrow as a failed fashion statement.

On the other hand, "The Brow" has a potent ring to it.

63. Nyjer Morgan's Alter Ego
Nyjer Morgan, sometimes known as Tony Plush, other times as Tony Gumble, is one of baseball's strangest personalities.

And he's rarely afraid to educate the public on his Plushdamentals. Even though we rarely have any idea what he's talking about.

62. Tonya Harding's Defining Moment
Oprah Winfrey once said, "This story had it all. . .Drama, scandal, heartbreak, controversy [and] competition." It also had insanity.

Training for the '94 U.S. Figure Skating Championships, figure skater Nancy Kerrigan was attacked by three men who crushed her knee with a metal baton. With Kerrigan out, rival Tonya Harding secured victory.

As it turned out, Harding's ex-husband Jeff Gillooly and his crew were the attackers, and Harding was soon convicted of conspiracy to hinder prosecution and banned from U.S. figure skating for life.

61. The Kermit Washington Incident
During an on-court scuffle between the Rockets and Lakers in December of 1977, Rudy Tomjanovich sprinted toward the fight. Seeing this, Kermit Washington tossed a roundhouse to his opponent's face.

Tomjanovich would drop to the floor with facial fractures and other serious injuries, effectively ending his career and almost ending his life.

60. The New York Jets' Dynamic
Santonio Holmes demanding the ball, Rex Ryan guaranteeing annual Super Bowl victories, cornerback Antonio Cromartie calling himself an elite receiver, Mark Sanchez being coddled. The dynamic of the Jets locker room is not only frustrating for NFL fans, but also covered excessively by every channel known to man.

Take a hike Mike Tannenbaum. Your flashy approach is getting old.

59. Hipster Glasses at Press Conferences
Russell Westbrook often closes in on Steve Urkel territory as the hipster look becomes a trending fad on the professional hardwood. Kevin Durant's backpacks set the tone, and his point guard piled on.

58. Serena Williams' Anger Problems
With the self control of a juiced special teams linebacker, Serena Williams continues to alienate all those who were once inspired by her unique nature.

Keep your comments to dull roars, please.

57. Michael Phelps' Diet
Want to swim like Mike? Start eating like him. . .

Breakfast: Three fried-egg sandwiches loaded with cheese, lettuce, tomatoes, fried onions and mayonnaise. Two cups of coffee. One five-egg omelet. One bowl of grits. Three slices of French toast topped with powdered sugar. Three chocolate-chip pancakes.

Lunch: One pound of enriched pasta. Two large ham and cheese sandwiches with mayo on white bread. Energy drinks packing 1,000 calories.

Dinner: One pound of pasta. An entire pizza. More energy drinks.

56. Super Sports Agents
Ruthless negotiations and money-driven thirsts for power; thus is the life of a sport super agent.

Scott Boras, Drew Rosenhaus, fictional Jerry Maguire. All these guys had one thing in common: Their client was the greatest and deserved the best. . .until a better one came along.

55. Early Running Back Retirements
A bruising position that demands so much from the human body, starting tailback remains the most short-lived role in sports.

Jim Brown, perhaps the greatest ever, dominated for nine years (until he was 29) and Barry Sanders, perhaps the most elusive ankle-breaker in history, retired at 30. In limited time, Brown remains revered as a brutal legend and Sanders remains third on the all-time rushing list with 15,269 yards.

54. The Wave
Better fit for Miley Cyrus concerts and rollercoaster rides, the all-mighty wave has become a mainstay in sports arenas around the world. But while it's a child's activity, it's often the inebriated adults engaging in such affairs. . .and at the *worst* times.

Are we watching a game here or preschool recess? And can we possibly wait until after the final pitch of the bottom of the ninth, when you're back home perhaps?

53. Jay Cutler's Personality
Chicago gunslinger Jay Cutler is despised by most of the football fanbase at this point. Not because of his rocket arm or his inability to win games, but rather because of his apparent disrespect for his teammates and coaches.

Mike Tice was the obvious, heart-crushed victim during this year's game against the Cowboys.

52. Tiger Woods' Self Control
Maybe the greatest ever to swing a golf club, Tiger Woods was once a role model who could do no wrong, an athletic icon hauling in endless cash and endless trophies.

Until it all came crashing down. Perhaps getting married was his greatest mistake.

51. Colin Cowherd's Herd
First off, who calls their audience a herd? The hay-and-straw listeners aren't ready to embrace that label.

Next, as Frank Caliendo properly noted (for the first time we agree with him), all this guy does is reaffirm what he's already said. Cowherd simply clouds us from the awfully boring co-host sitting across the way.

50. Rich Fans Who Show Up Late to Their Great Seats
When you have elitist seats, you better show up on time. End of story.

The only blockage worse than the wave or a beach ball is a wealthy couple with no regard for human life. Enough with the seventh-inning stretch entrances.

49. Jerry Jones
If his yearly proclamations (rather hallucinations) regarding his team's success and his buy-a-championship approach weren't enough to make you despise Cowboys owner Jerry Jones, perhaps a visual of his spectacles being specially cleaned by his son-in-law will.

His glasses aren't always dirty, but when they are he prefers Jerry wipes.

48. Baylor's Neon Green Uniforms
Jamie Squire/Getty Images

In an effort to protect your eyes from the blinding aura, we've provided a small chunk of Baylor's neon catastrophes.

The reflection off the hardwood is nearly as egregious.

47. Tony Romo's Ability in the Clutch
No. 9 just can't catch a break. Surrounded by pressures from fans, his owner and over-analytical pundits around the sports world, Tony Romo continues to crumble under the blinding spotlight.

At least the 32-year-old still throws a mean pickup line (see Candice Crawford).

46. Flopping
The disgraceful act of flopping is also seen on the basketball court, but only in soccer are award-winning performances the norm.

Some actors bide their time by waiting tables, others by dabbling in European football.

45. The Busch Brothers
These trouble-making brothers continue to cause problems in the racing industry.

And at the same time, they dominate.

44. Fur Coats
Some can wear the fur, some can't. Many have tried, few have thrived.

This is just Manny being Manny.

43. Slovenia's Football Uniforms
Tearing a page out of Charlie Brown's playbook, Slovenia football graces the pitch with a sharp stripe and stout smile.

Time for a new look, *Peanuts*.

42. Michael Jordan's Ability to Find Talent

With Kwame Brown and Adam Morrison on his resume, Michael Jordan's reputation as NBA owner can never be revived.

Time will tell whether Kentucky sensation Michael Kidd-Gilchrist can at least save his team's.

41. Dick Vitale-isms

Everything that comes out of Dick Vitale's mouth is questionable, yet always epic. Although like a weekly overdose of bacon, we need to watch our intake if we want to survive.

40. Overhyped Amateurs

On any level it's ridiculous, considering the majority of overhyped – and sometimes over-pressured – young athletes don't make it (see Todd Marinovich).

We had 13-year-old quarterback David Sills committing to USC and now 14-year-old Tate Martell committing to the University of Washington. Mind boggling.

39. Lockouts

Hockey is the essence of all the world's problems, and it's about time we appreciate it.

Unfortunately, Gary Bettman doesn't seem concerned with the growing popularity of the NHL. The short NFL lockout was an emotionally crippling appetizer to the extended hockey lockout.

38. Players Forcing Trades

Dwight Howard was the most serious offender of this harsh crime. A man has to pay his dues and play out his written contract before scratching for a move if he wants to garner respect.

Unfortunately, these owners and general managers have yet to muster up the courage to say no. Change is now.

37. Television Blackouts

The most frustrating television issue known to man, blackouts are the cause of most couch-related disputes and the single-most hated occurrence in American households during sporting events.

36. Barry Bonds Coverage

Despised around the sports world for his chemistry-based destruction of Babe Ruth's home run record, juicer Barry Bonds remains an anomaly in the sports world.

He alienated himself and the game he supposedly loved. Baseball has moved on from the so-called home run king.

35. Malice at the Palace

An on-court scuffle between the Pacers and Pistons in 2004, naturally featuring former bad boy Ron Artest, turned into an arena-wide brawl when Artest (now Metta World Peace) was pegged with an icy drink thrown from the crowd.

It quickly turned into the most heinous disgrace in NBA history.

34. Commissioners

Lockouts, replacement refs, All-Star game ties. It's clear at this point that NHL commissioner Gary Bettman was hired by the fellow three to distract fans from their mistakes by cancelling hockey.

Either that or we just scripted an intriguing thriller.

33. Vancouver Canucks Vintage Uniforms

Whoever made this happen should've been canned on the spot and replaced with a fax machine for the love of comedy.

The Canucks have come a long way.

32. Manny Pacquiao and Floyd Mayweather Not Fighting
Seriously, get it over with already. If Mayweather is ever going to quit with the arrogant shenanigans and Pac-Man is going to establish his greatness, the fight must go on.

But it won't.

31. Michael Jordan Comparisons
Enough with the Michael Jordan comparisons, which we're surrounded by every single season. In no other sport are the comparisons so monstrous, and so constant.

LeBron James: Doesn't have the killer instinct MJ had.

Kobe Bryant: Doesn't have as shiny of a scalp as MJ did.

Kevin Durant: The closest thing.

30. Teams Parodying Gangnam Style
Interesting way for Georgia to open the season.

Is this rhythmic masterpiece slaughtered yet?

29. Replacement Refs
They came from all walks of life and patrolled the gridiron with confidence. Until they had to make a call.

Watching these zebras attempt to control their professional surroundings caused league-wide nausea and worldwide mockery. It was a three-week step back for Goodell & Co.

28. 1988 Olympic Boxing Decision
Dominant pugilist Roy Jones Jr. trampled through the 1988 Olympics, not losing a round en route to a final against South Korea's Park Si-Hun.

A superior performance from Jones in the final turned into superior heartbreak, though, as judges gave the victory to Si-Hun, despite Jones' 86 punches to his opponent's 32. A despicable moment in Olympic boxing.

27. NFL's Addiction to Personal Fouls
In today's game, even the threat of a pinky touching the quarterback seems to garner a yellow flag. A sport that once preached toughness and ruthless bruising is now flooded with unnecessary "roughing the passer" calls and whiny, self-entitled quarterbacks.

Y.A. Tittle's bleeding forehead would agree.

26. ESPN First Take
Loud Skip Bayless vs. louder Stephen A. Smith has become the epitome of a rough wakeup. There's nothing like listening to the *First Take* crew thoroughly discuss everything from Tim Tebow's throwing inadequacies to Tim Tebow's awesome personality.

It might be time to get Jay Pharoah in there.

25. The Decision
Enough judging the decision itself, we're more inclined to rip the approach, although it did generate charitable income for the Boys & Girls Clubs of America.

But live television, millions watching, hairline receding. What a spectacle, and what a pure disappointment.

24. Retaliatory Punches in Hockey
Fighting is allowed for a reason. Retaliatory blind-side sucker punches only taint an already controversial game.

Hockey's raw nature sometimes attracts the worst type of scum, or breeds the worst type of reactions. Face-to-face combat is the only way.

23. Brett Favre's Retirements
Several more retirements and Brett Favre could've produced three separate Iron Man careers. The future Hall of Famer was once a beloved gunslinger from Mississippi.

Unfortunately now his numerous retirements seemingly overshadow his numerous records.

22. No. 1 Pick Quarterback Busts
JaMarcus Russell and his cough syrup in '07, David Carr and his ability to get sacked in '02, Tim Couch and his brutal averageness in '99. The list goes on, but the learning curve stays the same.

Remember "unathletic" pretty boy Tom Brady being taken in the sixth round in '00?

21. Floyd Mayweather Jr.'s Attitude
Everything about undefeated pugilist Floyd "Money" Mayweather reeks of insecure school girl. But the boxer once (still?) backed by 50 Cent remains the most arrogant trash talker in sports.

As Ricky Hatton so eloquently noted; "He's a good fighter, everybody knows he's a good fighter. . .but you don't have to keep telling us." Touche.

20. Anything Swami Sez
If quips like "WHOOOOP" and "Back, Back, Back" weren't enough to make your ears bleed, maybe Chris Berman's heinous rant (NSFW language) can get it done.

Like a toddler attempting to stay inside the lines, Berman's vibrant performance fails mightily.

19. Cost of Tickets
In hopes of attending a three-hour game with the family for a Saturday afternoon, one might consider skipping dinner for a week or two or perhaps selling his '84 Mitsubishi Starion. Although can we blame the industry for giving in to supply and demand? Yes, yes we can.

Save your money, grill some steaks, pop on the Samsung and enjoy the game from the comfort of your own home. To season ticket holders who can barely afford rent, sell the stubs and buy a house.

18. NFL's Lack of Concern for Retired Players
A sport that demands constant physical brutality needs to protect its players, and football certainly hasn't.

Many feel as if the NFL and the league players association, led by Hall of Fame guard Gene Upshaw, don't do enough to help former players who are physically and financially crippled. Gridiron Greats has contrastingly paved the way for improvement.

17. The Designated Hitter
Baseball has always been a game played by baseball players. Running, catching, spitting, grabbing. Not everyone had Ken Griffey Jr. talent, but flaws were embraced as inadequacies paved the way for historic performances.

The designated hitter has allowed clumsy, tip-of-the-iceberg players to concentrate on only one aspect; swinging the pine.

16. Gregg Williams Speech and Bounty Gate
Don't be naive, friendly bounties have certainly been a part of the football world for some time now. But the speech that suspended coordinator Gregg Williams gave to his Saints before last year's divisional game was a shocking reality check for commissioner Roger Goodell.

We don't expect to see Williams back on a professional sideline any time soon.

15. Sports Cliches
They need to generate some offense. We're taking it one game at a time. He gave 110 percent. It's a mental game. At the end of the day. . .

Sick yet?

14. First Pitch Fails
As a blossoming star on the professional hardwood, Wizards point guard John Wall should be able to toss a baseball 60 feet.

He barely scraped 13, though gave cricket scouts a dose of his potential.

13. Bill Belichick
Through bizarre tactics and the luck of the hoodie, Bill Belichick led the Patriots to three Super Bowl wins in four years. Indeed, he remains a respected coach around the league.

But Spygate and constant arrogance make us despise everything he's done.

12. Concussions
A problem without a solution it seems, and only the advancement of technology will guide the way.

They've ruined careers and crippled retirements, but remain unavoidable.

11. BCS Standings and Polls
Voted on by sportswriters and coaches who clearly don't have time to watch every team play, the polls remain a ridiculous aspect of college football.

Didn't realize this was a popularity contest.

10. Alex Rodriguez
With the baseball world at his fingertips, Alex Rodriguez, pulling in over $30 million per season, seemed ready to approach greatness. Now he simply defines everything we despise about sports: wealth, inefficiency and arrogance.

The diamond's highest-paid and once most-gifted talent preaches arrogance over class and continues to flail at pitches like he's a wounded donkey trying to touch his nose with his knee.

Although he took his postseason benching like a pro, mingling with the female fans. . .

9. Sports Bars That Play Loud Music over Games
Most fans prefer the soothing sound of Gus Johnson's colorful annunciations to James Blunt's "You're Beautiful." Unless of course they're frustrated, dragged-to-the-bar girlfriends who are more focused on Philip Rivers' dimples than Peyton Manning's precision.

8. Teams Singing Call Me Maybe
There's nothing like an Ivy League education.

These Harvard ballplayers show us true team spirit with yet another Carly Jae Repsen cover. It's only acceptable at this point when it's weirdly remixed by the Dolphins cheerleaders.

7. Front-runners
The worst brand of fan known to man. Front-runners are self-entitled, often uneducated and clearly insecure with their own choices.

Those bumper stickers may as well be targets.

6. National Anthem Screwups
Nine-time gold medalist track star Carl Lewis was faster than the speed of light. . .in destroying his reputation.

Sports fans are still waiting on that redemption rendition.

5. Racial Profiling
Instead of ethnic breakdowns, it's time scouts blind themselves to skin color.

If he can hit a curve, throw a tight spiral and drain a three, it doesn't matter what he looks like.

4. The Joe Buck and Tim McCarver Tandem
Possibly the most numbingly atrocious broadcasting unit of all time,

Buck-McCarver remain the epitome of mundane. This minute of arbitrary nonsense does, however, distract us from Buck's runway forehead and McCarver's frightening grin.

Mission accomplished; let's just hope extraterrestrials *don't* get this message.

3. Kyle Not Getting More Attention

Depending how you embrace his performance, Kyle the reporter may be sports' greatest gift.

His nonsensical dialogue combines failure with brilliance, perfectly.

2. Ryan Lochte's Interviews

Everyone in this room is now dumber for having listened to this. We award Ryan Lochte no points and may God have mercy on his soul.

Next reality show star? Nope, fashion designer it seems.

1. ESPN's Coverage of Tebow

Whether it's analyzing the length of his nose hairs, detailing his shirtless chest in the rain or interrupting regular Tim Tebow coverage to throw Tim Tebow a birthday (over Magic Johnson might we add), ESPN has made the unique former Gator top priority.

The most scrutinized backup quarterback in history, and a thorough punt protector, Tebow somehow found himself flooded with media members after a climactic Super Bowl. . .which Eli Manning and the big brother Giants won.

Tebowmania remains maniacal.

Source: Article author: Zack Pumerantz. Rightsholder: BleacherReport; http://bleacherreport.com/articles/1375225-the-100-worst-things-in-sports.

Encouraging intrapreneurship

Creative efforts and the innovations within organizations are a function of both individual and organizational factors. Entrepreneurial employees add value to the organization and enhance implementation by finding creative ways to achieve the strategic plan. However, these efforts can flourish only if organizational features foster creativity. To encourage an intrapreneurial environment, staff members must be rewarded for entrepreneurial thinking and must be allowed and even encouraged to take risks. Failure and mistakes must be allowed and even valued as a means to creative and innovative expression.

The key to successfully creating a climate that encourages creativity and innovation is to understand the components of such an atmosphere. Those components include management support, worker autonomy, rewards, time availability, and flexible organizational boundaries. To understand these components, consider the following guidelines used at 3M Company:[18]

- ***Do not kill a project*** – If an idea does not seem to find a home in one of 3M's divisions at first, 3M staff member can devote 15 percent of their time to prove it is workable. In addition, grant money is often provided for these pursuits.
- ***Tolerate failure and encourage risk*** – Divisions at 3M have goals of 25–30 percent of sales from products introduced within the last five years.
- ***Keep divisions small*** – This will encourage teamwork and close relationships.
- ***Motivate champions*** – Financial and nonfinancial rewards are tied to creative output.
- ***Stay close to the customer*** – Frequent contact with the customer can offer opportunities to brainstorm new ideas with them.
- ***Share the wealth*** – Innovations, when developed, belong to everyone.

Sports marketers are always looking for new and innovative approaches to all elements of the marketing mix and technology is transforming the delivery of these marketing experiences. Advances in technology have made information more accessible and put spectators in the heart of the action. Whether the enhancement of promotional delivery systems, broadcast, venue management, sportscape, logistics, or safety and security, people want technology to enhance their sporting lives. Spectators, governing bodies, and event planners are demanding more from their sporting events, therefore, real-time information utilizing multimedia solutions must be integrated into planning and promotion. On the promotion side, for instance, the University of Cincinnati's Department of Athletics introduced *Social Seats*.[19] Social Seats is an exclusive offer to fans of UC Facebook page and followers of the GoBEARCATS twitter account. The program allows fans who purchase tickets for any of the remaining four basketball games as well as those who have already purchased tickets an opportunity to be entered into a random draw. The winners receive upgrades to lower level seats, access to the media room and media hospitality area, as well as the postgame press conference. The Bearcats benefited from the increased exposure on the social network, to fans at the park, and on televised games. On the product side, Sportsline's HydraCoach bills itself as the world's first "intelligent water bottle."[20] You enter your weight and activity level, and then indicators on the side of the unit tell you whether you are meeting your "personal hydration goal." One area of innovation in sports facility design is going green. The Cleveland Indians and Green Energy Ohio installed a new solar electric system at Progressive Field, the first American League ballpark to go solar. The ballpark utilizes recycling containers and biodegradable cornstarch utensils and cups. In addition, the facility composts the garbage, which in turn has reduced the trash pickups by 50 percent since 2007.[21]

National Park, home to the Washington Nationals, is the nation's first major professional stadium to become LEED Silver Certified by the U.S. Green Building Council. LEED is an internationally recognized green building certification system, providing third-party verification that a building or community was designed and built using strategies aimed at improving performance across all the metrics that matter most: energy savings, water efficiency, CO_2 emissions reduction, improved indoor environmental quality, and stewardship of resources and sensitivity to their impacts. The project incorporated a variety of sustainable design elements in regards to its proximity to the Anacostia River. For example, HOK Sport, the ballpark's architect, integrated the first "green roof" at a big league sports facility. The Chesapeake Bay Foundation, an environmental nonprofit, gave a $101,670 grant to the D.C. Sports and Entertainment Commission to cover the cost of planting grass and other plants on top of a 6,300-square-foot waterproof surface above a concession stand in left field.[22]

In other examples, for the first time in the history of any major North American professional sports league, a league-wide uniform innovation had been established. The National Hockey League and Reebok partnered to create a technologically advanced uniform for players called the Rbk EDGE Uniform System.[23] At the time it provided a technology advanced edge for the Reebok brand. However, Adidas, who purchased Reebok in 2005 for $3.8 billion, has recently been contemplating replacing Reebok as the official NHL brand, for the Reebok brand has struggled, continuing to lose ground to Nike for the soles of Americans.[24] In fact according to Sporting Goods Intelligence, from 2005 through 2012, Nike increased its U.S. footwear sales 75 percent, to $6.3 billion, meanwhile Adidas, over the same period, saw its footwear sales rise a more modest 35 percent, to $1 billion.[25] All the while,

Reebok's U.S. footwear sales fell 40 percent, to $597 million, over the same period. Up until 2006, the NBA had Reebok as its official uniform and apparel supplier; however, they decided to move to replace the contract with one that made Adidas the official supplier, a strategy the NHL is now contemplating. In other apparel advances, Under Armour in 2011 unveiled a uniform technology comparable with Nike's Pro Combat used by top football programs across the nation. Branched off its original compression shirts, these Under Armour uniforms were 33 percent lighter, integrated technology that enhanced breathability, afforded heat exchange, and enhanced muscle stability. Under Armour also designed the Mach 39 Speedskating Skin for the 2014 US Olympic Speedskating team. The skin's design was rigorously tested for maximum efficiency. The engineering of the skin focused solely on full-body aerodynamics. Under Armour utilized Lockheed Martin's expertise during a two-year research and testing program. The engineers employed high-speed cameras to help create computational fluid dynamic models that analyzed how air flowed around the skater during key body positions. Coupled with over 300 hours of wind-tunnel testing on reinforced fiberglass mannequins with hundreds of different skins setups and textile configurations, the research allowed designers to zero in – down to the millimeter, actually – on exactly how and where to build the new suit.[26] The goal of the new design was to achieve technological improvements that would be measurable. Unfortunately, during the 2014 Olympic Games, performances were dismal and many experts and athletes readily blamed the suit for these disappointing performances. It was not until the national governing body did a comprehensive review of its preparation heading into the Games that the controversial suits were found not to have anything to do with the sub-par performance; its findings: too much travel, too much training at high altitude, overly optimistic expectations, and not enough time in the new suits.[27]

Budgeting

Budgets are often used as a means of controlling organizational plans. However, the budgeting process can be an important part of the implementation plan if budget development is closely linked to the sports marketing strategy. In fact, the allocation of financial resources can either promote or impede the strategic implementation process.

Marketers within the sports organization must typically deal with two types of budgetary tasks. First, they must obtain the resources necessary for the marketing group to achieve the marketing plan goals. Second, they must make allocation decisions among the marketing activities and functions. These two types of activities require working with individuals and groups internal and external to the sports marketing function.

To develop strategy-supportive budgets, those individuals responsible should have a clear understanding of how to use the financial resources of the organization most effectively to encourage the implementation of the sports marketing strategy. In general, strategy-supportive activities should receive priority budgeting. Depriving strategy-supportive areas of the funds necessary to operate effectively can undermine the implementation process. However, overallocation of funds wastes resources and decreases organizational performance.

In addition, just like the rest of the strategic sports marketing process, the budgeting process is subject to changing and often unpredictable contingencies that may necessitate changes in the marketing budget. A change in strategy nearly always calls for budget reallocation. Thus, those individuals who are responsible for developing budgets must be willing to shift resources when strategy changes.

Control

In the uncertain and changing environments in which sports organizations operate, it is critical to consider four questions throughout the strategic sports marketing process.

1. Are the assumptions on which the strategic marketing plan was developed still true?
2. Are there any unexpected changes in the internal or external environment that will affect our plan?
3. Is the marketing strategy being implemented as planned?
4. Are the results produced by the strategy the ones that were intended?

These questions are considered the basis of strategic control and the fundamental issues to be considered in the **control** phase of the strategic sports planning process model. **Strategic control** is defined as the critical evaluation of plans, activities, and results – thereby providing information for future action. As illustrated in Figure 13.2, the control phase of the model is the third step to be considered. However, it is important to note that the arrows allow for "feedforward." In other words, even though control is the third phase of the model, we consider it as we develop earlier phases of the process. Once the initial plan is developed, the assumptions on which the plan was developed and the internal and external contingencies must be examined and monitored. As the implementation process is set in place and as the plan is executed, strategic control reviews the process as well as the outcomes. Variances

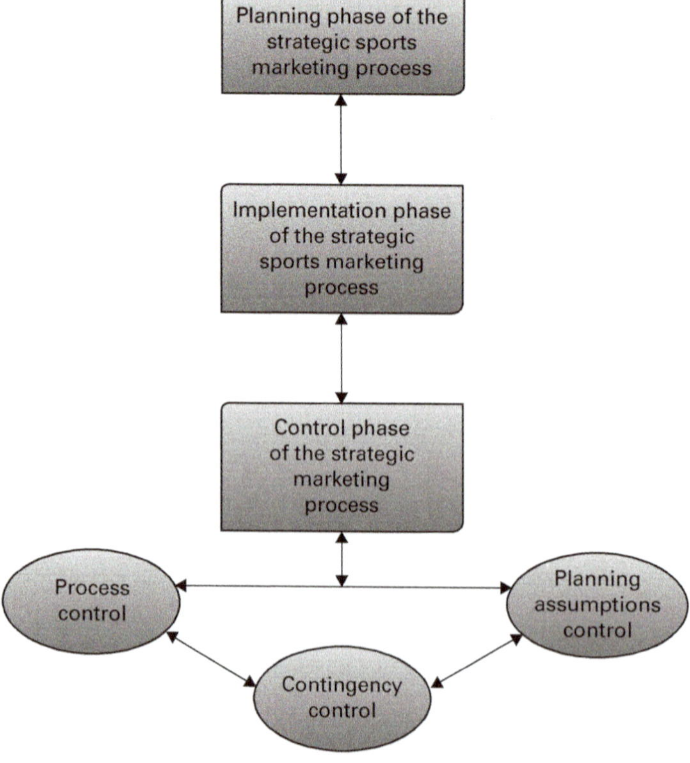

Figure 13.2 Control phase of the strategic sports marketing process

from the original assumptions, plans, and processes are noted and changes are made as needed.

The three types of strategic control that sports marketers must consider are planning assumptions control, process control, and contingency control. The following sections outline each of these three types of control.

Planning assumptions control

As we have discussed throughout this text, it is vital to understand internal and external contingencies and formulate strategic sports marketing plans that establish a fit with those contingencies. During the planning phase, it is often necessary to make assumptions concerning future events or contingencies about which we do not have complete information. In addition, individual planners may perceive and interpret data differently. In other words, the strategic sports marketing plan is based on a number of situation-specific premises and assumptions. This level of control attempts to monitor the continuing validity of these assumptions. Thus, in **planning assumptions control**, the sports marketer asks the question: "Are the premises or assumptions used to develop the marketing plan still valid?" To fully evaluate the responses to this question, the assumptions used during the development of the marketing plan must be listed. This step is vital to the success of this control mechanism so those individuals who are responsible can monitor them throughout the process.

A good example of planning assumptions control at work resides within the realms of the Big East Conference. As the conference struggles to compete with the cash cow, that is college football, now the third most popular sport in America but even more important, a money-making machine, the conference fights to retain a basketball presence. Many feel college basketball has been lost in the shuffle, often being overlooked as far as conference realignment goes and undoubtedly the Big East was the conference that took the biggest hit. Losing major schools like Miami, Syracuse, and Pitt to the ACC, to splitting into two separate conferences altogether, the new Big East offered some great moments on the college basketball landscape, but it definitely was not an improvement on the legacy the previous incarnation developed over the past 35 years. Three new teams – Creighton, Butler, and Xavier – joined the Catholic 7, and although Creighton and Xavier made some noise by making the NCAA Tournament (http://www.sbnation.com/march-madness) the Big East could use some extra firepower in its quest to return to dominance.[28]

Another example of a planning control assumption has been associated with the marketing and endorsement of players and teams. Scandals with teams such as USC, Penn State, Syracuse, the Ohio State University, and Miami and with players the likes of Tiger Woods, extramarital sex scandal, Michael Phelps, marijuana use, Lance Armstrong, doping, and Barry Bonds regarding steroid use, have made corporate partners rethink their plans and uses.

Because of the complexity of the decision-making process, it may be impossible to monitor all the assumptions or premises used to formulate the strategic sports marketing plan. Therefore, it is often practical not only to list the premises, but also to prioritize them based on those that may most likely effect a change in the marketing plan.

Although all assumptions should be considered in this form of control, two categories of premises are most likely to be of concern to the sports marketer: external environmental factors and sports industry factors. As we discussed earlier, strategic sports marketing plans are usually based on key premises about many of these variables. Some examples of external environmental factors include technology, inflation, interest rates, regulation, and demographic and social changes. The relevant sports industry in which a sports organization operates is also usually a key premise aspect in designing a marketing plan. Competitors, suppliers, league regulations, and leadership are among the industry-specific issues that need to be considered when identifying the critical assumptions used to develop the strategic plan.

Monitoring the premises or assumptions used to develop the strategic sports marketing plan is vital to the control phase of the strategic sports marketing process, but it is not sufficient. In other words, this form of control does not measure how well the actual plan is progressing, nor is it able to take into account the aspects of the internal and external environment that could not be detected during the planning phase when the premises were developed. Thus, effective control must consider two additional forms of evaluation: process control and contingency control.

Process control

Process control monitors the process to determine whether it is unfolding as expected and as desired. This type of control measures and evaluates the effects of actions that have already been taken in an effort to execute the plan.

Because of changes in premises and contingencies, the realized strategic marketing plan is often not the intended strategic marketing plan. Changes and modifications to the plan usually occur as a result of the process control activities carried out by marketers. In other words, during this stage of control, sports marketers attempt to review the plan and the implementation process to determine whether both remain appropriate to the contingencies. Either the marketing plan or the implementation process put in place to execute the plan may not proceed as intended. These variances may lead to a need to change the plan or the process or both. Thus, the key question asked by this form of control is: "Should either the strategic plan or the implementation process be changed in light of events and actions that have occurred during the implementation of the plan?" It is important to note that to change or modify the marketing plan or implementation process is not necessarily a decision to avoid. The benefit of this form of control is that sports marketers can minimize the allocation of resources into a strategic plan or implementation process that is not leading to achievement of the objectives and goals they deem important. To answer the preceding question, two measures are typically used: *monitoring strategic thrusts* and *reviewing milestones*. As we discussed earlier, the strategic sports marketing plan is a means of achieving strategic and financial organizational goals and marketing objectives. An important part of evaluating the plan and process is to review the achievement of these objectives and goals during the execution of the plan. Because objectives are not time specific or time bound (as discussed in Chapter 2), strategic thrusts can be examined to evaluate progress in the direction of strategic and financial objectives. On the other hand, reviewing milestones typically examines achievement of marketing objectives. Let us look at each of these two forms of process control more closely.

Monitoring strategic thrusts

Monitoring strategic thrusts attempts to evaluate or monitor the strategic direction of the plan. As a part of the overall strategic plan, smaller projects are usually planned that will lead to the achievement of the planned strategy. Successful pursuit of these smaller projects can provide evidence that the strategic thrust is the intended one. However, if these projects are getting lost to other "nonstrategic" projects, it could mean that the overall strategy is not progressing as planned.

One strategic thrust of special interest to sports organizations and organizations marketing their products through sports is, of course, sponsorship. Determining the effectiveness of a sponsorship program is becoming increasingly more important as the costs of sponsorship continue to rise. A Turnkey Sports Poll was conducted with 400 senior-level sports industry executives to understand just how important measurement can be to the sponsorship package. Half of those surveyed indicated that the fact that "certain sponsors are paying closer attention to measuring return on investment" is "good for sports." Additionally, nearly 60 percent of the executives indicated that in the last three years spending on consumer research was either "up slightly" or "up significantly."[29]

Just how, then, do we measure or determine whether we are seeing a return on our marketing investment? Lesa Ukman, former CEO of IEG, which publishes the IEG Sponsorship Report, believes sponsorship return can be measured. Ukman stresses the following regarding sponsorship measures:[30]

Sponsorship return can be measured. The key lies in defining objectives, establishing a presponsorship benchmark against which to measure, and maintaining consistent levels of advertising and promotion so that it is possible to isolate the effect of sponsorship.

The lack of a universal yardstick for measuring sponsorship is a problem, but it is also an opportunity. The problem is that sponsorships often are dropped, not because they don't have measurement value, but because no one has actually measured the value.

The lack of a single, standardized measurement is also an opportunity because it means sponsors can tailor their measurement systems to gauge their specific objectives.

HOW ATHLETES ARE FIGHTING FOR ENDORSEMENT DOLLARS

Brands are becoming more judicious in the way that they choose who to endorse, according to panelists in a discussion about athlete endorsements. The fallout from the Tiger Woods scandal, for example, has caused sponsors to think longer and harder about who they sign and about the language they include in their contracts.

Celebrities and musicians have started to encroach further into the sponsorship realm, as well, adding to the competition for endorsements. "Ten years ago, the celebrities who were getting the big bucks before were saying, 'Hey, these athletes are encroaching on my space,'" said Unilever's Rob Candelino. "[Now] these guys are starting to treat themselves like brands. It's gone full circle."

U.S Olympic swimmer Cullen Jones said that he thinks of

himself as a brand and believes that is what has to happen for athletes to be recognized. When even relatively unknown reality TV stars are competing for deals, agents and brands are focusing more on an organic, authentic match-up and becoming better storytellers.

Quick hits:

Jim Tanner, on what drives marketing: "One of the things we always tell new clients is don't start with branding. Start with performance. That drives 90 percent of marketing."

Matt Mirchin, on figuring out what reaches your customers: "As a brand you want to associate yourself with something that resonates with your consumer. From our perspective, Under Armour is all about making athletes better. So it's nice when entertainers or celebrities wear our product. But we're going to go right to that sweet spot with the athletes because that's who resonates with us."

Candelino, on Unilever's athletes representing Dove Men: "Every one of them has told a story or a sentimental moment that has shaped them as men. We think that has been a winning formula because it resonates with our brand. If we started trying to be a sports brand, then we've lost the plot. I think far too often nowadays, brands, particularly ones that don't have both feet firmly entrenched in sports, subcontract their responsibility of brand equity to the athlete. If you do that, you're done."

Allan Zucker, on athlete overexposure: "People talk about overexposure all the time. Whether it's Tiger Woods or Peyton Manning or Danica Patrick, [they say] 'I see them everywhere.' Yea, they are everywhere, but people keep calling. So obviously they must be doing something right with their brands or people wouldn't want to work with them anymore."

Jones, on using Twitter: "Granted, I might have thoughts that I might want to instantly put out there, [but] It's not smart to do that. I consider myself a brand."

Source: Rightsholder: Sports Business Journal; http://www.sportsbusinessdaily.com/SB-Blogs/Events/Sports-Marketing-Symposium/2012/10/Athlete-Endorsements.aspx.

Since there are no universal measures, companies struggle with finding the resources and determining what the right things to measure are. In the sporting world, it is not uncommon for companies not to measure return from sponsorship. In fact, in 2012 when IEG asked the question, does your company actively measure return from its sponsorship, a full one-third of the sponsors said no. Companies often choose the easiest method of assessment focusing on awareness of products, attitudes and brands. The more challenging methods that focus on the harder-to-determine effectiveness measures are further down the purchase funnel. Marketers also continue to rely on their property partners for evaluation assistance, with survey respondents ranking their dependence on rightsholders to help them measure return as a 6 on a 10-point scale.[31] Here are a few of the more popular ways of measuring sponsorship effectiveness and brand impact against the objectives of awareness and exposure, sales, attitude change, and enhancing channel-of-distribution relationships:

- N-Score is a new measurement system from Nielsen that rates the brand impact of professional athletes and sports personalities, enabling advertisers to make smart marketing decisions on commercial endorsements. Based on Nielsen's strategic collaboration with E-Poll Market Research, N-Score provides the most comprehensive, in-depth look at a sports figure's overall endorsement potential. A potential endorser's N-Score is the result of a model that factors in awareness, appeal (how strongly one likes or dislikes an individual) and 46 specific personal attributes.

  The N-Score is available for over 1,000 athletes, coaches, broadcasters, and other sports personalities, on both a national basis and in 30 local markets. Advertisers can use N-Score to evaluate how effective a sports figure will be when endorsing their products. N-Score can also measure the positive and negative impact of off-field events on an athlete's effectiveness, including the impact across different demographic groups.[32]
- For the NASCAR Sprint Cup Series, Sprint identified three metrics specific to return on investment. According to Tim Considine, director of sports marketing Sprint Nextel Corp., they generate return by assessing the size of the customer base, average revenue per unit-total revenue divided by the number of customers, and churn. Considine noted that they prefer to achieve low churn, high average revenue per unit, and large customer base.[33]
- Number of stories and mentions in popular media, such as newspapers, televised shows, and magazines, serve as a measure of exposure as well. For example, John Hancock Financial Services measured the impact of its football bowl sponsorship using this method. In one year, approximately 21 binders of newspaper clippings were collected at an estimated advertising equivalency of $1 million.[34]

Awareness is also assessed through "media equivalencies," that is, determining how much "free" time the sponsor has accumulated through television coverage. For example, Joyce Julius & Associates had estimated that Louisville-based Yum Brands earned almost $2.7 million in exposure in its debut as the first presenting sponsor of the Kentucky Derby.[35]

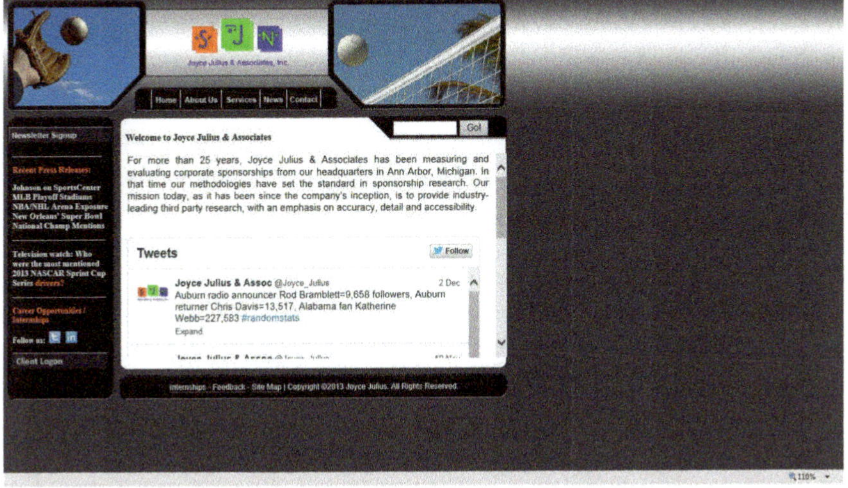

Web 13.2 Sponsorship ROI evaluation

Source: Joyce Julius & Associates, www.joycejulius.com

While the measurement of brand exposure has historically used human observation, companies like Margaux Matrix are testing electronic tools to perform the same operation more accurately.[36] Not all researchers are sold on the notion of media equivalencies. In fact, a study by the former public relations firm Jeffries-Fox's led to the official Institute for Public Relations (IPR) position that "The IPR Commission does not endorse Ad Value Equivalencies as a measurement tool."[37]

- Sales figures for products and services can be examined both prior to (pre) and after (post) the event to estimate the potential impact of the sponsorship. Other methods of tracking sales include looking at sales for the sponsorship period versus the same time period in prior years or measuring sales in the immediate area versus national sales. In addition, sales might be tied directly to the sponsored event. For example, discounts for products might be offered with proof of attending the event (show ticket stub); therefore, the number of redemptions might be tracked. Of course, many other factors, such as competitive reaction and additional sales promotions, will influence the sales figures.

One final variation of measuring the impact of sales is to involve the sales force in tracking the value of leads and contacts generated through sponsorship.

- To assess consumer attitudes toward various products and services, as well as the sponsored event, research is conducted in the form of surveys or in-depth interviews. This primary market research is used to gauge the image of the event and its sponsors, attitudes that consumers have toward the event and its sponsors, and awareness of events and sponsors' products and services.

When determining the impact of sponsorship on channels of distribution, it is common practice to track the number of outlets carrying the given product before and after the sponsored event. In addition, sponsors may want to assess the number of retailers or dealers participating in a program versus previous promotions. Finally, companies may measure incremental display at the point of purchase in retail outlets.

For example, M&M's MARS brand continues to employ the "Race Day is better with M" slogan on a range of confectionary displays offered to meet the snacking needs of NASCAR fans. In fact, M&M's estimates that approximately 83 percent of consumer purchases are unplanned. Therefore, M&M's displays often employ impulse strategies that seek to trigger or solicit immediate consumption (IC) or future consumption (FC) responses. IC responses seek to trigger an "immediate" impulse purchase e.g., items that are often available at checkout lines, while FC displays often focus on enhancing exposure in high traffic areas e.g., a lobby where shoppers are purchasing for others.[38] Overall implications and strategy goals: to interrupt trips with off-shelf displays to keep MARS NASCAR products on the top of mind on fan trips; important to display product for pantry-load trips; and critical to have immediate consumption displays to capture the impulse purchase. The strategic approach highlighted message reach, increased focus on home viewer and consumer engagement with quarterly giveaways. M&M's committed to providing national advertising and PR support integrating television, FSI, in-store, promotional radio, online, PR, social, POP and shopper marketing strategies. The ultimate goal, to utilize displays to tempt the passionate fan and trigger impulsivity by making chocolate more mentally available in-store, sounds delicious.[39]

Milestone review

The second form of process control is **milestone review**. Marketing managers at sports organizations usually establish milestones that will be reached during the

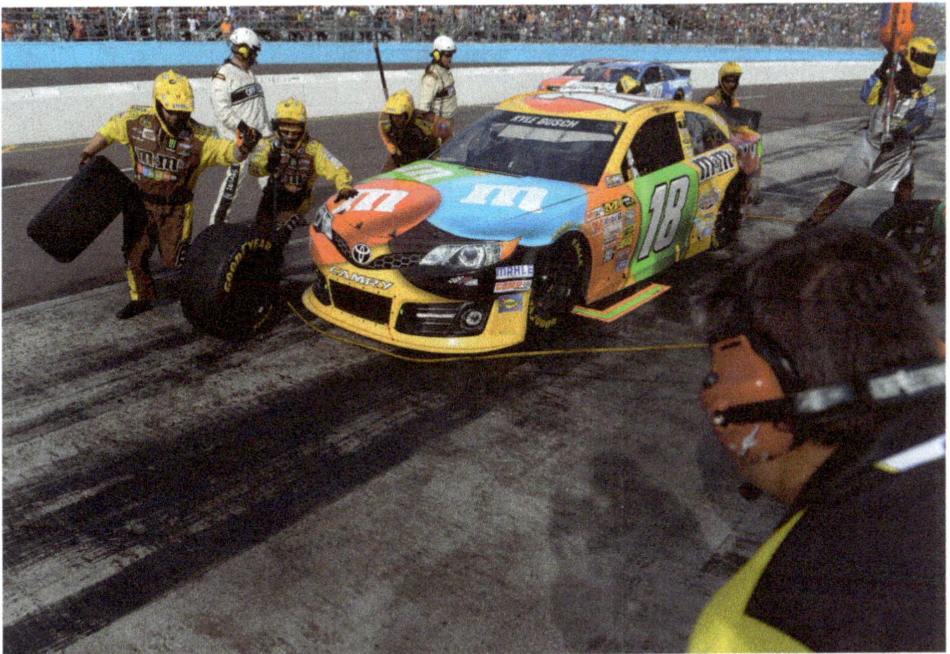

Photo 13.2 Sponsors such as M&M must design controls to evaluate sponsorship effectiveness.

Source: Getty Images

execution of the marketing plan. These milestones may be critical events, major allocations, achievements, or even the passage of a certain amount of time. They are often an integral part of a program evaluation and/or network analysis strategies. Critical path or milestone reviews help market planners to prioritize goals and objectives, define time lines, as well as the sequence, order, and thresholds of market strategies. As these milestones are reviewed on a continuous basis, an evaluation of the advisability of continuing with the plan and the process is afforded.

Financial analysis

Financial information can be used to understand and control the process of strategic marketing plan implementation; that is, to perform **financial analyses**. It is important for any sports organization to have a good accounting system. In terms of process control, the accounting system can provide the following:

- A ready comparison of present financial performance with past performance, industry standards, and budgeted goals.
- Reports and financial statements that can be used to make appropriate strategic decisions.
- A way of collecting and processing information that can be used in the strategic sports marketing process.

Two important components of a good accounting system are the *income statement* and *balance sheet*. The balance sheet and income statement are the traditional financial statements that have been required in annual reports for many years.

Income statements provide a summary of operating performance. These documents summarize both money coming into and going out of the sports organization and the

Table 13.4A Rich Creek Rockers income statement

Income statement for the year ended December 31, 2012		
Revenues:		
Single game admissions	$140,000	
Season ticket holders	275,000	
Concessions	250,000	
Advertising revenue	95,000	760,000
Expenses:		
Cost of concessions sold	100,000	
Salary expense – players	235,000	
Salary and wages – staff	130,000	
Rent	150,000	615,000
Profits before taxes		145,000
Income tax		33,000
Income after taxes		$112,000

Table 13.4B Rich Creek Rockers balance sheet

Balance sheet at December 31, 2012			
Assets		**Liabilities and Owner's Equity**	
Cash	$10,000	Accounts payable	$20,000
Accounts receivables	82,000	Capital stock	50,000
Equipment	40,000	Retained earnings	62,000
Total assets	$132,000	Total liabilities and owner's equity	$132,000

marketing department or division. Because income statements are a good measure of customer satisfaction and operating efficiency, they should be prepared frequently – at least every three months, if not monthly. Balance sheets provide a summary of the financial health of the sports organization at a distinct point in time. The balance sheet provides the sports marketer with a summary of what the organization is worth; what has been invested in assets, such as inventories, land, and equipment; how the assets were financed; and who has claims against the assets. Tables 13.4A and 13.4B provide simple examples of the information typically found on income statements and balance sheets. In contrast, the statement of cash flows, which replaced the statement of changes in the late 1980s, shows the sources and uses of a firm's cash. The statement of cash flows details where resource of cash comes from and how they are used. It provides more valuable information about liquidity than can be obtained from the balance sheet and income statements.

One of the more useful methods of financial analysis for control purposes is known as **ratio analysis**. Financial ratios are computed from income statements and balance sheets. These ratios can tell the sports marketing manager a lot about the progress and success of the strategic sports marketing plan. In other words, using financial ratios can help a sports marketing manager assess whether the marketing strategy continues to provide an appropriate fit with internal and external contingencies. There are several types of financial ratios that can be categorized as follows:

- ***Profitability ratios*** **–** Provide an indication of how profitable the organization or division is during a period of time.
- ***Liquidity ratios*** **–** Indicate the ability of the organization to pay off short-term obligations without selling off assets.

- ***Leverage ratios* –** Measure the extent to which creditors finance the organization.
- ***Activity ratios* –** Measure the sales productivity and utilization of assets.
- ***Other ratios* –** Determine such things as return to owners in dividends, the percentage of profits paid out in dividends, and discretionary funds.

Table 13.5 lists some of the more commonly used ratios, how each is calculated, and what each can tell the sports marketing manager. Examples of how these ratios are applied and interpreted are shown in Table 13.6.

Table 13.5 Summary of selected key financial ratios

Ratio	Calculation	Question(s) Answered
Gross profit margin	Sales – Cost of goods sold / Sales	What is the total margin available to cover operating expenses and provide profit?
Net profit margin	Profit after taxes / Sales	Are profits high enough given the level of sales? Are we operating efficiently?
Return on total assets	Profit after taxes / Total assets	How wisely has management employed assets?
Asset turnover	Sales / Average total assets	How well are assets being used to generate sales revenue?
Current ratio	Current assets / Current liabilities	Does our organization have enough cash or other liquid assets to cover short-term obligations?
Debt-to-assets load	Total Debt / Total assets	Is the organization's debt excessive?
Inventory turnover	Cost of goods sold / Average inventory	Is too much cash tied up in inventories?
Accounts receivables turnover	Annual credit sales / Account receivables	What is the average length of time it takes our firm to collect for sales made on credit?

Table 13.6 Examples of key financial ratios

Net profit margin	$\frac{112,000}{760,000} = 14.7\%$
Interpretation – Approximately 15 percent of sales is yielding profits. This percentage should be compared with industry (similar sports organizations) averages and examined over a period of several years. Declining or subpar percent could mean expenses are too high, prices are too low, or both.	
Return on assets	$\frac{112,000}{132,000} = 84.8\%$
Interpretation – This is a measure of the productivity of the assets in the sports organization. Once again, this number should be compared with similar sports organizations and examined over several years. If this number is declining, it may indicate that assets are not being used as effectively or efficiently as they were in previous years.	
Inventory turnover	$\frac{2,500,000}{100,000} = 25$ times
Interpretation – Inventory turnover is a measure of the number of times inventory is sold during a period of time. Assuming an average inventory of $100,000 (beginning inventory + ending inventory/2) the inventory (in this example – concessions) was sold 25 times. If this number is higher than the average for this type of sports organization, then ordering costs may be too high and stockouts may be occurring. If the number is lower, it may mean too much inventory is being stored, tying up money unnecessarily, and the products (in this case – food) may lack freshness.	

Contingency control

The third form of control, **contingency control**, is based on the assumption that sports marketers operate in an uncertain and unpredictable environment and that the changing nature of the internal and external environments may lead to the need to reassess strategic choices. Although it is included as a part of the control phase, this form of control should be of concern throughout the strategic sports marketing process.

The goal of contingency control is to constantly scan the relevant environments for internal and external contingencies that could affect the marketing planning process. Foreseeability, the ability to anticipate the future events, outcomes or results of an action based on the circumstances, past experiences, apparent riders or reasonable sense expected of a human being, is critical to the success of contingency control. Unlike planning assumptions control, the goal here is to remain unfocused so any unanticipated events will not be missed. In other words, the "big picture" is of most concern in this phase of control. The primary question to be addressed here is: "How can we protect our marketing strategy from unexpected events or crises that could affect our ability to pursue the chosen strategic direction?" Attempts to control without a prestructured list of variables of concern may not seem to make sense at first. However, it is easier to understand this form of control if one thinks in terms of how a crisis usually occurs. The daily events leading up to an unpredicted event lead to a focus in the form of a crisis. Previously unimportant or unnoticed events become more problematic until an actual crisis requires some action. Learning to notice and interpret signals thus becomes an important way to circumvent crises. Thus, the goal of contingency control is to learn to notice these signals and to have a plan of action in place to cope with a crisis if it occurs.

Sports scandals and crises are not infrequent. Anyone who reads a newspaper sports section has observed situations that could lead to a public relations nightmare for a sports organization or individual athlete. More research is now being conducted on better understanding the defining characteristics of scandal and attempting to quantify the magnitude of a specific scandal. Hughes and Shank found that media and corporate sponsors generally identified four consistent characteristics that make an event in athletics scandalous or not.[40] These characteristics included an action that was either illegal or unethical, involved multiple parties over a sustained period of time, and whose impact affected the integrity of the sport with which they are associated.[41]

The top 10 sports scandals of all time are presented in Table 13.7.[42]

Although crises such as these are unpredictable, it is useful to plan so the chosen response can be not only faster, but also more effective. A **crisis plan** should include the following:[43]

- Well-defined organizational response strategies
- Specific procedures that will lead to a more efficient and effective response
- Steps that will deal effectively with potential media impact and will enhance image
- Efficient ways to deal with a variety of problems that could occur

Moreover, sports organizations may benefit from an informal and a formal crisis response plan. The key is that any crisis plan should offer priorities for proactive and reactive response under a variety of circumstances. It should have the capacity to both alert and calm people during an unexpected event that could have the potential for major consequences.

Table 13.7 Top ten sports scandals

1 O.J. Simpson It's not every day that the NBA finals are overshadowed by a Heisman Trophy winner and former NFL star on the run from double murder charges. While acquitted during the most publicized trial of all time, years later OJ now sits in prison convicted of robbery.
2 Pete Rose Baseball's all time hits leader and manager of the Cincinnati Reds gets thrown out of the game for illegally betting on baseball (including games in which the Reds were playing). Years later Pete's banishment still stands and Major League Baseball's Hall of Fame refuses to consider him for induction.
3 Tiger Woods On his way to becoming the greatest golfer of all time, 2009 saw a series of events that included a car accident, more than a dozen mistresses, divorce and therapy derail his career and personal life. Two years later Tiger is still trying to recapture his golf greatness and another Masters title.
4 Barry Bonds and Steroids Baseball's steroid era and the Mitchell Report gave us hulking players (Mark McGwire, Sammy Sosa, Barry Bonds) who easily shattered Roger Maris' and Hank Aaron's home run records. In the wake of player admissions and denials, most have been tried in the court of public opinion and require the use of asterisks when analyzing their baseball accomplishments.
5 Soviet Union Basketball Win over United States in 1972 Olympics The US Men's Basketball team had won every single game between 1936 and the 1972 final. Had it not been for a referee adding three seconds back on the clock, the US would have beaten Russia on this day as well. To date, the US team refuses to accept their Silver Medal from the '72 games and gave rise to the creation of US Olympic Basketball "Dream Teams."
6 Tonya Harding and Nancy Kerrigan Seeking to eliminate her main rival leading up to the 1994 Olympics figure skating competition, Tonya Harding, her husband and others assaulted Nancy Kerrigan by striking her in the leg with a club during a skating practice session. Harding wound up finishing 8th at the Olympics, while Kerrigan took home the silver medal.
7 Penn State Sex Abuse One of college football's most celebrated programs and coaches failed to report and likely covered up when allegations of child molestation against former defensive coordinator Jerry Sandusky surfaced. Fast forward, Coach Paterno has passed, Sandusky convicted and a university and administration still in turmoil and under investigation for a massive cover up.
8 New Orleans Saints Bounty Program "Bountygate" was a fund that rewarded Saints players with financial bonuses for inflicting injuries on opposing players that forced them to leave games. Following an NFL investigation, the Saints will play their 2012 season without their head coach, defensive coordinator and key players who have all been suspended by commissioner Roger Goodell.
9 1918 Chicago Black Sox In response to notoriously cheap team owner, Charles Comiskey, who leveraged loopholes in contracts and MLB laws to prevent playing his star players, eight members of the 1919 Chicago White Sox were banned from baseball for life for taking money from underworld figures to intentionally lose games (including the 1919 World Series). The scandal, which was also immortalized by the film Eight Men Out, remains one of baseball's darkest and enduring moments.
10 SMU Death Penalty To date this remains the most severe penalty handed down to any athletic program. SMU's entire 1987 schedule was cancelled due to massive violations of NCAA rules and regulations including slush funds and illegal payments to athletes for over a decade. Following the death penalty, the SMU Mustangs had only one winning season over the next 20 years.

Source: http://www.mensfitness.com/leisure/sports/11-biggest-sports-scandals-of-all-time?page=2.

Summary

Implementing and controlling the strategic sports marketing process is the emphasis of Chapter 13. After the planning phase of the strategic marketing process is completed, the implementation and control phases are considered. Implementation is described as an action step where strategic marketing plans are executed. Without the proper execution, the best plans in the world would be useless. To facilitate the implementation process, seven organizational design elements must be addressed. The organizational design elements include communication, staffing and skills, coordination, rewards, information, creativity, and budgeting. To begin, the organization must effectively communicate the plan and its rationale to all the members of the sports marketing team who will play a role in executing the plan. In terms of staffing and skills, there must be enough people and they must have the necessary skills and expertise to successfully implement the strategic marketing plan. Research has shown that the skills deemed most important for sports marketing managers include establishing a positive image for your sports organization, achieving sponsors' promotional goals, stimulating ticket sales, maximizing media exposure for events, athletes, and sponsors, and acquiring sponsors through personal contacts.

Coordination is another of the organizational design elements that influences implementation. Coordination involves determining the best structure for the organization to achieve the desired strategy. Research has shown the importance of good fit between structure and successful implementation. One way of coordinating people and tasks that has received considerable attention over the last decade is through total quality management (TQM). TQM philosophies are based on aligning the organizational structure to best meet the needs of the customers.

Another important organizational design element that affects implementation is the rewards structure of the sports organization. With proper pay and incentives, employees may be motivated to carry out the strategic plan. Some guidelines for designing effective rewards systems include linking rewards to the strategic plan, using a variety of incentives: link performance with rewards, give everyone the opportunity to be rewarded, and be willing to adapt the rewards system.

Information is one of the most essential elements of effective implementation. To aid in the gathering and dissemination of information for strategic decision making, organizations must design information systems. Before gathering information, consider who is going to need this information, for what purpose is the information needed, and when do they need it?

Fostering creativity, another organizational design element, is yet another important aspect of implementation. Creativity and innovation within the organization is called intrapreneurship or corporate entrepreneurship and is developed through education and training. To enhance employee creativity the creative process, consisting of four steps, is used by organizations. These steps include knowledge accumulation, idea generation, evaluation, and implementation. Efforts to encourage intrapreneurship are also enhanced by creating an organizational environment that cultivates such thinking.

The final organizational design element that has a direct impact on implementation is budgeting. Without proper monies, the strategic sports marketing plan cannot be properly implemented or carried out. Budgets must be secured for all marketing efforts within the larger organization. Once these monies are obtained, they must then be allocated within marketing to achieve specific marketing goals that have been prioritized.

After plans have been implemented, the control phase of the strategic sports marketing process is considered. Strategic control is defined as the critical evaluation of plans, activities, and results, thereby providing information for future action. In other words, the control phase explores how well the plan is meeting objectives and makes suggestions for adapting the plan to achieve the desired results. Three types of strategic control considered by sports marketers include planning assumptions control, process control, and contingency control.

Planning assumptions control asks whether the premises or assumptions used to develop the marketing plan are still valid. Two categories of assumptions that should receive special consideration from sports marketers are those concerned with the external contingencies and the sports industry. Because plans are typically developed by carefully considering the external environment and the sports industry, assumptions with respect to these two issues are critical.

Process control considers whether the plan and processes used to carry out the plan are being executed as desired. The key issue addressed by process control is whether the planning or implementation processes should be altered in light of events and actions that have occurred during the implementation of the plan. To make decisions about whether plans or the implementation process should be changed, sports organizations review milestones that have been set or monitor strategic thrusts. Milestones such as financial performance are more specific objectives that can be examined, while strategic thrust evaluates whether the organization is moving toward its intended goals.

Key terms

- activity ratios
- budgeting
- communication
- contingency control
- control
- coordination
- creative process
- creativity
- crisis plan
- financial analyses
- implementation
- information
- intrapreneurship
- leverage ratios
- liquidity ratios
- milestone review
- monitoring strategic thrusts
- planning assumptions control
- process control
- profitability ratios
- ratio analysis
- rewards
- staffing and skills
- strategic control
- total quality management (TQM)

Review questions

1. What are the organizational design elements that must be managed for effective implementation?
2. Why must there be a fit between the planning and implementation phases of the strategic sports marketing process?
3. What are some of the common ways of communicating with groups both inside and outside the sports organization?
4. What are the marketing-specific core competencies of the sports marketing manager?
5. Define TQM. What are the common characteristics of any TQM program? Why is it important for sports organizations to practice a TQM philosophy?

6. What are the guidelines for designing rewards systems?
7. What is intrapreneurship? What are the four steps in the creative process? How can sports organizations encourage intrapreneurship?
8. Define strategic control. What are the three types of strategic control that sports marketers must consider?
9. What two measures are typically used during process control?
10. How can we evaluate sponsorship effectiveness?
11. Describe the different financial ratios that can be calculated to assess whether a sports organization's financial objectives are being met.
12. What are the fundamental components of a crisis plan?

Exercises

1. Describe three sports organizations that have a strong leader who communicates well outside the sports organization. What are the common characteristics of these leaders, and why do these leaders communicate effectively?
2. How does the training that you are receiving complement the marketing-specific skills required of sports marketing managers?
3. Locate the organizational charts for the marketing department of two professional sports organizations. How will this structure facilitate or impede the implementation of their strategic marketing effort?
4. Design a rewards system to encourage intrapreneurship.
5. Discuss the last three major "crises" in sport (at any level). How did the organizations or individuals handle these crises?
6. Discuss how being the quarterback of a football team is similar to being a marketer responsible for implementing and controlling the strategic sports marketing process.
7. Interview three marketing managers who are responsible for sponsorship decisions in their organization. Determine how each evaluates the effectiveness of their sponsorship.

Internet exercises

1. Browse the Web site of the **Sports & Fitness Industry Association (SFIA)**, formerly the SGMA (www.sfia.org) and discuss how the information found on this site might be useful for developing a strategic marketing plan for the new IBL.
2. Find two Web sites that would provide sports marketing managers with information about whether their planning assumptions regarding the demographics of the U.S. population remain valid.
3. Find examples of three nonsports organizations that advertise on ESPN's Web site (www.espn.com). How might these companies evaluate the effectiveness of their Web-based advertising?

Endnotes

1 Eric Ivie, "Busy Offseason Ahead for Arena Football League: Fan Take," *Yahoo.com* (August 20, 2012). Available from: http://sports.yahoo.com/news/busy-offseason-ahead-arena-football-league-fan-163400668.html, accessed May 7, 2014.

2 "Turnkey Sports Poll," *Sport Business Journal* (November 13, 2006). Available from: http://www.sportsbusinessdaily.com/Journal/Issues/2006/11/20061113/SBJ-In-Depth/Turnkey-Sports-Poll.aspx, accessed May 7, 2014.

3 Joe Logan, "LPGA's First Female Commissioner Rides Out Bumpy Start," *Buffalo News* (New York) (July 20, 2006), D1.

4 Alan Shipnuck, "LPGA Commissioner Carolyn Bivens was Undone by Unflinching Commitment to her Vision for the Tour," *Sports Illustrated* (July 10, 2009). Available from: http://www.golf.com/tour-and-news/lpga-commissioner-carolyn-bivens-was-

undone-unflinching-commitment-her-vision-tour, accessed May 7, 2014.
5 Andrew Todd-Smith, "Commentary: 2022 Qatar World Cup Decision Raises Questions About FIFA Leadership," *The Lantern.com* (January 9, 2014). Available from: http://thelantern.com/2014/01/commentary-2022-qatar-world-cup-decision-raises-questions-fifa-leadership/, accessed May 6, 2014.
6 Anil K. Gupta and V. Govindarajan, "Build, Hold or Harvest: Converting Strategic Intentions into Reality," *Journal of Business Strategy* (Winter 1984), 41.
7 Peter Smolianov and David Shilbury, "An Investigation of Sport Marketing Competencies," *Sport Marketing Quarterly*, vol. 5, no. 4 (1996), 27–36.
8 Alfred D. Chandler, *Strategy and Structure* (Cambridge, MA: MIT Press, 1963).
9 Marlene L. Mawson, "Total Quality Management: Perspectives for Sport Managers," *Journal of Sport Management*, vol. 7 (1993), 101–106.
10 Harry Roberts and Bernard Sergesketter, *Quality Is Personal* (New York: Free Press, 1993).
11 George Easton and Sherry Jarrell, "The Effects of Total Quality Management on Corporate Performance: An Empirical Investigation," *Journal of Business*, vol. 71, no. 2 (1998), 253–261.
12 James Evans and William Lindsay, *The Management and Control of Quality*, 2nd ed. (St. Paul, MN: West, 1993).
13 Ibid.
14 "Pay for Performances: Why Footballers Are Not Remunerated Like Investment Bankers," *Financial Times*, London, (January 27, 2007), 10.
15 BusinessWire, "NHL Teams with IBM to Promote and Enhance Hockey Through New Alliance, NHL-ICE," *Freelibrary.com* (September 5, 1996). Available from: http://www.thefreelibrary.com/NHL+tea ms+with+IBM+to+promote+and+enhance+hockey+through+new. . .-a018651230.
16 John Lombardo, "Blazers First with Social Networking Site," *Sport Business Journal* (March 5, 2007). Available from: http://www.sportsbusinessdaily.com/Journal/Issues/2007/03/20070305/This-Weeks-News/Blazers-First-With-Social-Networking-Site.aspx, accessed May 8, 2014.
17 Zack Pumerantz, "The 100 Worst Things in Sports." *Bleacherreport.com* (October 22, 2012). Available from: http://bleacherreport.com/articles/1375225-the-100-worst-things-in-sports.
18 R. Mitchell "Masters of Innovation," *Business Week* (April 10, 1989), 58–63.
19 "Bearcats Announce Football Social Seats Promotion," *Bearcats.com* (2014). Available from: http://www.gobearcats.com/sports/m--footbl/spec-rel/091012aaa.html, accessed July 6, 2014.
20 "Sportline Hydracoach User Guide," *Hydracoach.com* (2007). Available from: http://www.hydracoach.com/Techsupport/HydraCoach%20User%20Guide-v.2.pdf, accessed July 5, 2014.
21 "Community – Our Tribe is Green," Cleveland Indians Inc. (2014). Available from: http://cleveland.indians.mlb.com/cle/community/green.jsp, accessed July 6, 2014.
22 "Green Ballpark," Washington Nationals (2010). Available from: http://washington.nationals.mlb.com/was/ballpark/information/index.jsp?content=green_ballpark, accessed May 8, 2014.
23 "Reebok and NHL to Unveil New Technologically Advanced Uniform System," *Marketwired.com* (2007). Available from: http://www.marketwired.com/press-release/reebok-and-nhl-to-unveil-new-technologically-advanced-uniform-system-631899.htm, accessed May 8, 2014.
24 Josh Kosman and Larry Brooks, "Adidas May Distance Reebok from NHL," *New York Post*, (February 1, 2014). Available from: http://nypost.com/2014/02/01/adidas-may-distance-reebock-from-team-sports/, accessed May 8, 2014.
25 Ibid.
26 Tim Newcomb, "U.S. Speedskating Finds Edge with High-Tech Engineered Skins," *Sports Illustrated.com* (January 16, 2014). Available from: http://sportsillustrated.cnn.com/-olympics/news/20140116/sochi-olympics-speed-skating-under-armour-mach-39-skin/#ixzz318YY9EIF, accessed May 6, 2014.
27 Kelly Whiteside, "U.S. Speedskating Says Don't Blame Under Armour Suits," *USA Today* (May 1, 2014). Available from: http://www.usatoday.com/story/sports/olympics/2014/05/01/us-speedskating-under-armour-suits/8589263/, accessed May 6, 2014.
28 "Should the Big East Expand to 12 Schools," *SB Nation* (March 24, 2014). Available from: http://www.bigeastcoastbias.com/2014/3/24/5543726/should-the-big-east-expand-to-12-schools, accessed May 7, 2014.
29 Noah Liberman, "Agencies Roll Out New Measurement Tools as Sponsors Seek to Justify Their Investments," *Sports Business Journal* (September 26, 2005). Available from: http://www.sportsbusinessdaily.com/Journal/Issues/2005/09/20050926/SBJ-In-Depth/Agencies-Roll-Out-New-Measurement-Tools-As-Sponsors-Seek-To-Justify-Their-Investments.aspx?hl=Nokia%20Corp&sc=0, accessed May 8, 2014.

30 Lesa Ukman, "Evaluating ROI of a Sponsorship Program," *Marketing News* (August 26, 1996), 5.

31 "How Athletes are Fighting for Endorsement Dollars," *Sportbusinessdaily.com* (October 4, 2012). Available from: http://www.sportsbusinessdaily.com/SB-Blogs/Events/Sports-Marketing-Symposium/2012/10/Athlete-Endorsements.aspx, accessed May 8, 2014.

32 William Chipps, "Sponsorship Spending: 2010 Proves Better Than Expected; Bigger Gains Set for 2011," *Sponsorship.com* (January 6, 2011). Available from: http://www.sponsorship.com/About-IEG/Press-Room/Sponsorship-Spending–2010-Proves-Better-Than-Expe.aspx. accessed May 8, 2014.

33 "State of the Media: Year in Sports 2010," *Nielsen.com* (2010). Available from: http://www.nielsen.com/us/en/reports/2011/year-in-sports-2010.html, accessed May 8, 2014.

34 "And Now a Word From Our Sponsors," *Marketing Tools* (2005). Available from: www.demographics.com/publications/mt/95_/9506_mt/mt169, accessed June 2, 2009.

35 "Team Sponsorships and Partnerships," Joyce Julius & Associates Inc. (June 2006). Available from: http://www.joycejulius.com/Newsletters/a_second_look__june_2006.htm, accessed July 6, 2014.

36 "Sponsorship: Keeping an Eye on the Ball," *Marketing Week* (October 30, 2003), 43.

37 "Institute for Public Relations Releases First-Ever Guidelines for Measuring Importance of Interest Audience," *US Newswire* (February 17, 2004).

38 M&M MARS, http://mars24seven.com/handler/download.ashx?FileName=2014_NASCAR_Cstore_Selling_Story.pptx, accessed May 7, 2014.

39 Ibid.

40 Stephanie Hughes and Matt D. Shank, "Defining Scandal in Sport: Media and Corporate Sponsor Perspectives," *Sport Marketing Quarterly*, vol. 14, no. 4 (2005), 207–216.

41 Ibid.

42 "Top 10 Sports Scandals," *Topyaps.com* (June 21, 2010). Available from: http://topyaps.com/top-10-sports-scandals/, accessed May 5, 2014.

43 "Defining Crisis and Crisis Planning." Available from: www.sports.mediachallenge.com\crisis\index.html#feature, accessed May 6, 2014.

Appendix A

Career opportunities in sports marketing

Many of us have dreamed of becoming a professional athlete. Unfortunately, reality sets in rather quickly. We discover that we cannot throw a 90-mile-per-hour fastball or even touch the rim – much less slam-dunk. However, here are many other opportunities for careers in sports. In fact, there are a wide variety of sports careers in sports marketing. In this appendix, we will explore some of the career options in sports marketing and present some interview and resumé writing tips for landing that dream job. Finally, we will examine some additional sources of information on careers in sports marketing.

Before we look at some of the career alternatives in sports marketing, it is useful to think about how the concepts discussed in this text can be useful in your job search. As you know, the strategic marketing process begins by conducting a SWOT analysis. You should build a SWOT into your career planning. First, ask questions about your own strengths and weaknesses. You can be sure the organizations you interview with will be asking similar questions. Next, try to identify the opportunities that exist in the marketplace. What sports are hot? Where are the growth areas in sports marketing?

The next step of your strategic career search should be to gather information and conduct research on prospective employers. Research could be conducted by talking to people within the organization to gain a better understanding of the culture. In addition, observation might take place both before and certainly during the interview.

Next, you need to consider your target market. Do not apply for all of the sports marketing jobs in the world. Target the job opportunities based on location, type of position, and how the position or organization fits with your current and potential strengths. You also need to position yourself. Remember, careers in sports marketing are in demand and you need to find a way to market yourself and stand out from the competition.

The marketing mix variables also should be considered in your job search. The product, in this case, is you. You are the bundle of benefits that is being offered to the prospective organization. You should also enter into the strategic career search with some understanding of price. What is the value you attach to the service and expertise that you will provide? Are the salary and benefits package being offered a satisfactory exchange?

Your resumé, cover letter, interviewing skills, and ability to sell you are the elements of the promotion mix. These elements communicate something about you to prospective employers. Finally, the place element of the marketing mix is the location in which you are willing to work.

From this brief discussion, you can begin to understand that finding the right job for yourself in sports marketing can be done in a systematic, organized fashion. By using the basic principles of the strategic marketing process, you will be in a better position to land your dream job. Let us turn our attention to some of the job opportunities that exist in the field of sports marketing.

Job opportunities in sports marketing

There are a wide variety of jobs in sports marketing that may be of interest to you. Here are just a few of the opportunities that exist. As you look through this section, pay attention to the sample advertisements and the qualifications that are stressed for each position. In addition, remember not to suffer from marketing myopia when you look for your first job. Have a broad perspective and think of your first job as an entrée into the sports industry.

Internships

Nearly 70 percent of sports marketing executives began their careers interning for a sports organization, and 90 percent of sports organizations offer some type of internship. Many sports marketing students believe they will secure high-paying, glamorous, executive-level positions upon completion of their degree. The truth is, jobs in sports marketing are so competitive that internships are usually the only route to gaining the experience needed for a permanent position. By working as an intern, you become familiar with the organization and learn about the sports industry. In turn, the organization learns about you and reduces its risk in hiring you for a permanent position.

Sample advertisements

- **Sales and Marketing Manager** – Interns will assist the marketing department in the following areas:
  sponsorship fulfillment, lead qualification, sampling/couponing programs, health and fitness expo at the Los Angeles Convention Center, and race day festival. Must be hardworking, detail oriented, friendly, energetic, computer-literate, and have good communication skills. Hours would be flexible to fit interns' schedule.
- **Marketing Intern** – We have an opening for a sports marketing intern to assist in marketing programs designed to facilitate the growth of our products and services. Ideal person should have a sports marketing or sports management background. Computer, organization, and strong communication skills are essential. Internet experience preferred.

Facilities management

Whatever the sport, there must be a place to play. From brand-new multimillion-dollar sports complexes such as Nationals Stadium in Washington, D.C. to community centers used for recreational sports, facilities management is an important function. Although facilities management positions are more managerial in nature, they do include a strong marketing emphasis. For example, facilities managers are expected to perform public and community relations tasks, as well as have a strong promotion management background. Two of the largest facility management companies in the United States that you may want to explore are Global Spectrum (www.global-spectrum.com) and SMG (www.smgworld.com).

Sample advertisements

- **Advertising and Public Relations Manager** – Opportunity for a creative, energetic, hands-on individual to develop and implement advertising and PR programs for an established golf course facility. Minimum of five years' experience in advertising, esign, broadcast production, and media planning. Desktop experience a must. Internet experience a plus. Must be able to maximize preestablished budgets.
- **Facility Manager** – The Special Events Center is seeking candidates for the position of facility manager. Candidates should be sales and marketing driven with experience in event planning, marketing and promotions, and facility management. Bachelor's degree with three years' related experience required. Primary liaison between users and facility staff. Provide leadership in event planning, onsite event management, and customer service.

Professional services

As the sports industry grows, the need for more and more business professionals in all areas is increasing. Today, sports careers are automatically associated with being a sports agent because of the Jerry McGuire "show me the money" phenomenon. However, professional services are also needed in sports law, advertising, accounting, information systems, marketing research, finance, and sports medicine. Having the appropriate educational background before attempting to secure sports industry experience is a must. Salaries for professional services positions vary greatly depending on the job type and responsibilities.

Sample advertisements

- **Director of Special Olympics** – Seeking persons with excellent communication, fund raising, and management skills. Special Olympics is a year-round program of sports training and competition for children and adults with intellectual disabilities. Responsibilities include planning and organizing competitive events, training programs, public awareness campaigns, and fund-raising activities. Candidates for position must possess excellent communication and fund-raising skills as well as administrative, organizational, and volunteer management experience. Previous Special Olympics experience not required, but helpful.
- **Global Advertising/Merchandising Manager** – Multinational manufacturer of cycling components. Responsible for leading the creation and execution of global advertising; athlete and event sponsorship; media planning and communication; global product merchandising; global cost center management. This position requires an analytical thinker with excellent leadership and execution skills. A successful candidate is an MBA who has in-depth knowledge of ad strategy, planning, and production.

Health and fitness services

As the sports-participant market continues to grow, so will jobs in the health and fitness segment of the sports industry. Numerous jobs are available in management and sales for health clubs. Additionally, health and fitness counseling or instruction (personal trainer or aerobics instruction) represents another viable job market in health and fitness. Careers in sports training and sports medicine are also increasing. In addition to working for sports organizations as a trainer or physical therapist, a number of sports medicine clinics (usually affiliated with hospitals) are targeting the recreational participant and creating a host of new jobs in the prevention or rehabilitation of sports injuries.

Sample advertisements

- **Director of Campus Recreation** – Major responsibilities: provide opportunities to enhance participant fitness, personal skills, and enjoyment for a variety of student recreational activities; supervise, coordinate, and evaluate the activities of the department; prepare operating and capital expenditure budgets; develop goals, objectives, policies, and procedures; and perform personnel administration within the department. Qualifications: Master's degree and three years' experience in recreation or a similar field, two years' experience in administrative position, and current CPR and first aid certification required.
- **Fitness Club Operations Director** – Oversee all pool and tennis associates. Duties include hiring, training, supervising, and reviewing the performance of staff; administering weekly payroll; designing employees work schedules; and overseeing maintenance/cleanliness of facilities and inventory. Bachelor's degree; minimum two years' experience in athletic club/resort and one year in club management; basic knowledge of tennis, fitness and aquatics; excellent communication skills. Sales and marketing experience, with a strong member services background and experience developing/implementing member retention programs preferred.

Sports associations

Nearly every sport has a governing body or association that is responsible for maintaining the integrity and furthering the efforts of the sport and its constituents. Examples of sports associations include the Fédération Internationale de Football Association (FIFA), National Sporting Goods Association (NSGA), United States Tennis Association (USTA), and the National Thoroughbred Racing Association (NTRA). Each sports association has executive directors, membership coordinators, and other jobs to help satisfy the members' needs.

Sample advertisements

- **U.S. Tennis Association** – Assist director of marketing in sponsorship, donations, and ad sales. Professional tournament operations for one tournament and booth promotions at all Northern California tournaments.
- **Research Associate** – A nonprofit golf association. Duties include survey research, statistical analysis, report writing, and database management. Knowledge of SAS and related bachelor's degree a must. Proficiency required in mapping, spreadsheet, and word processing software. Position requires demonstrated experience in technical writing and good verbal communication skills. Knowledge of the golf industry a plus. Entry-level position.

Professional teams and leagues

Along with being a sports agent, the types of jobs most commonly associated with sports marketing are in the professional sports industry segment. Working as the director of marketing for one of the "big four" sports leagues (NBA, MLB,

NHL, or NFL) or one of the major league teams requires extensive experience with a minor league franchise or college athletic program and a master's degree. Job responsibilities include sales, designing advertising campaigns to generate interest in the team, and supervision of game promotions and public relations.

Sample advertisements

- **Assistant Marketing Director** – Develops season ticket campaign strategies, negotiates advertising and media tradeouts, directs promotion coordinator, sales representative. Master's degree preferred; bachelor's degree required, preferably in marketing. Excellent communication skills a must. Should have extensive experience in working with corporate sponsors and developing a client base to support athletic sales.
- **Advertising Sales** – Major sports league seeks account executive to sell print advertising for event publications. The ideal candidate will possess two to four years' consumer or trade publication sales experience; excellent written and verbal communication skills; a proven track record of increasing sales volume; the ability to work in a fast-paced environment; and the flexibility to travel.

College athletic programs

If your ultimate career objective is to secure a position with a professional team or league, college athletic departments are a great place to start. Nearly all Division I and Division II athletic programs have marketing, sales, and public relations functions. In fact, most of the larger Division I programs have an entire marketing department that is larger than most minor league franchises.

Sample advertisements

- **Coordinator of the Goal Club** – Responsibilities include identifying, cultivating, soliciting, and stewarding donors together with managing special events and direct mail programs. Candidates must possess a bachelor's degree and two or three years of fund-raising experience.
- **Athletic Recruiting Coordinator** – Responsibilities include developing and organizing a vigorous recruiting program for eight sports within the guidelines of NCAA III, represent the athletics department at college fairs, and coordinate all recruiting activities with the admissions department.

Sporting goods industry

Sporting goods is a $60+ billion industry that is growing and presents career choices in all of the more traditional marketing or retailing functions. Opportunities include working for sporting goods manufacturers' (e.g., Nike, Adidas, Callaway, or Wilson) or retailers such as Dick's Sports Authority, or Foot Locker.

Sample advertisements

- **Associate Buyer** – Lady Foot Locker is looking for a professional. To qualify you will need chain store buying experience. Sporting goods exposure a plus.
- **General Manager/Catalog Division** – An outdoor recreation equipment retailer in the burgeoning backpacking/mountaineering/climbing industry is looking for a hands-on GM with full responsibility for its fast-growing catalog division.

Responsibilities include bottom-line profitability, strategic planning/execution, financial planning, marketing, prospecting, circulation and database management, catalog development and production, purchasing and inventory control, and systems coordination. Qualifications include five-plus years' management in a mail-order operation.

Event planning and marketing

Rather than work for a specific team or league, some sports marketers pursue a career in events marketing. Major sporting events such as the World Series, All-Star games, or the Olympics do not happen without the careful planning of an events management organization. The largest and most well-known events management company is the International Management Group (IMG) (www.imgworld.com) with offices worldwide. Event marketers are responsible for promoting the event and selling and marketing sponsorships for the event.

Sample advertisements

- **Event Management Leader** – A service management association serving the bowling industry. Candidates will have a bachelor's degree in business or hotel management along with a proven track record of professional event production.
- **Event Planner** – National sports marketing firm organizing sports leagues and special events for young professionals is seeking an entry-level candidate to assist with operations and promotions of sports leagues, parties, and special events. Should be sports minded, extremely outgoing, and organized for this very hands-on position.

Researching companies

The previous section gives you a good idea of the types of job opportunities in sports marketing. Having considered your options, it is now time to get serious about finding that first job that will launch an exciting career. You will soon send out cover letters and resumés tailored to each position and organization. If they are not, the prospective employer will sense you have not done your homework. Your research efforts should include the following types of information: age of the organization, services or product lines, competitors within the industry, growth patterns of the organization and of the industry, reputation and corporate culture, number of employees, and financial situation.

Today, most of the organizational information can be obtained quickly and easily via the Internet. Other popular sources of industry and company information include the following: Team Marketing Report's Inside the Ownership of Professional Sports Teams, Million Dollar Directory (Dun & Bradstreet), Standard and Poor's Register, and Ward's Business Directory of U.S. Private and Public Companies.

Cover letters and resumés

Once you have researched prospective employers, you are ready to communicate with the organizations that you wish to pursue. Let us look at how to construct simple, yet persuasive, cover letters and resumés. Remember, these documents are within your complete control (think of this as an internal contingency); use this to your advantage and present yourself in the best possible light. Let us begin with the fundamentals of cover letter preparation.

Cover letters

The major objective of any cover letter is to pique the interest of the prospective employer. First impressions are everything and the cover letter is the employer's first glimpse of you. A cover letter is a vital tool in marketing yourself to prospective employers for several reasons: An effective cover letter will draw attention to your qualifications and experiences that are most relevant to the position for which you are applying. Employers often use letters to assess the written communication skills that you will need for any position. A letter provides you the opportunity to convey to a potential employer your interest, enthusiasm, and other personal attributes that are not easily expressed in a resumé alone. There are a few basic guidelines that you can follow to make your cover letters more effective.

In the first paragraph, state the letter's purpose and how you found out about the position. Follow this with an overview of your most impressive job-related attributes such as skills, knowledge, and expertise. Obviously, the attributes you choose should relate to the position in mind. The third part of the cover letter should stem from all the research previously gathered on the organization. Show off your knowledge of the company and their current needs. Finally, let the organization know how you can help solve their current needs. Stress the fit between your background and values and the organization's culture.

Resumés

Now that your cover letter has been constructed, you are ready to begin work on an effective resumé. Here are seven tips for writing a resumé that are guaranteed to tell your story.

1. **Be thorough** – A good resumé should give the employer an indication of your potential based on your previous accomplishments. Include things such as job-related skills, previous work experience, educational background, volunteer experiences, special achievements, and personal data.
   Activities that you might deem to be unimportant could provide a great deal of insight into your ability to succeed on the job. For example, how about the student that has coached a Little League team throughout his or her collegiate career? Some candidates might view this as totally unrelated to the job. However, wise candidates will see how this activity could be used to demonstrate unique aspects of their personality such as patience, leadership, and good organizational skills.
2. **Be creative** – Most students are under the false impression that there is a right way and a wrong way to organize their resumé. In fact, most career development centers use a boilerplate format making every student's resumé standard and neglecting the job and the industry.
   All resumés should include topical areas such as job objectives, skills, knowledge, accomplishments, personal data, education, employment history, observations of superiors, and awards. Organizing and writing these sections is limited only by your imagination. The most important thing to remember is that the format should reflect both you and the job you are seeking.
3. **Use quotations** – A powerful tool that is not widely used in resumé preparation is the use of quotations. These quotes can be found in old performance evaluations or letters of recommendation. Here is an example of a quote that was used to reinforce the strength of an application.

"Mr. Gamble has contributed in a positive manner to the success of the athletic department at WPU by organizing and implementing an effective game day promotional plan."

– Melissa Luekke, promotions manager, athletic department, WPU.

Quotes like this can provide further evidence of your abilities while relieving you of having to toot your own horn.

4. **Make the resumé visually appealing** – Looks are everything. In one study, 60 percent of employers indicated that they formed an opinion about the candidate on the basis of the resumé's appearance. The resumé that looks good will be given more consideration than one that does not. The resumé that is badly written and produced will be tossed, regardless of the applicant's qualifications. A few things to think about when designing your resumé include length (keep it to one page), paper (high-quality stock in white or off-white), spelling, grammar, and neatness (any error is unacceptable).
5. **Include a career objective** – Most employers consider the career objective to be the most important part of the resumé. Why? A specific career objective indicates that you know what you want in a job. This type of goal-directed behavior is what employers want to see in a candidate. Narrate to demonstrate to the reader what you have helped the organizations accomplish.
   On the other hand, some resumé preparation experts strongly disagree with this line of reasoning. They argue that by placing an objective on your resumé, you are limiting the potential position. In other words, if you leave your options open, the employer will direct your resumé to the job that best suits your qualifications.
   The best advice is to have multiple resumés prepared and ready to go with multiple career objectives. Most people have multiple career interests and do not have to settle for just one job. If you are truly practicing target marketing, you should have several different resumés ready. You should try to make the career objective sound like the description of the job you are targeting. Here is a sample career objective for a student who wishes to pursue a public/community relations position at a major university or professional sports franchise:
   Public Relations Assistant – Interested in copywriting, editing, writing speeches and news releases, photography, graphics, etc. Desire experience on organization's internal and external publications. Good writing and speaking skills with communications background should assist in advancement to a management position within the athletic department of a major university or professional sports organization.
6. **Honesty is the best policy** – Employers are checking prospective candidates' qualifications more than ever before, due to a wave of people falsifying their credentials. Obviously, deceiving the employer about what you have done, or what you are able to do, is no way to start a positive relationship.
7. **Spread the word** – You should seek feedback and constructive criticism about your resumé by showing it to everyone you know. Ask for comments from other students, your professors, and career development specialists at school. In addition, you should circulate it among people in the sports industry. Resumé writing is a dynamic process that requires constant changes and improvement.

Interviewing

Most jobs in sports marketing require a high degree of interpersonal communication; therefore, the interview becomes a place to showcase your talents. Each person should have his or her own interview style, but here are some tips that should assist all job candidates with their interviewing skills.

1. **Be mentally prepared** – As with athletes, mental preparation is the name of the game for job seekers. Most job candidates do not come to the interview fully prepared. To get ready, you should have thoroughly researched the sports organization. Next, you need to learn as much as possible about the person or people who will be conducting the interview. Being mentally prepared means being able to ask intelligent questions. Naturally, the types of questions you ask will vary by the position of the interviewer. Here are just a few of the potential questions that you might ask of the personnel manager or human resource representative:

- What do employees like best about the company? What do employees like least about the company?
- How large is the department in which the opening exists? How is it organized?
- Why is this position open?
- How much travel would normally be expected?
- What type of training program does a new employee receive? What type of professional development programs are offered? Who conducts them?
- How often are performance reviews given and how are they conducted?
- How are raises and promotions determined? What is the salary range of the position?
- What are the employee benefits offered by the company?

Possible questions for your potential supervisor include:

- What are the major responsibilities of the department?
- What are the major responsibilities of the job?
- What would the new employee be expected to accomplish in the first six months or year of the job?
- What are the special projects now ongoing in the department? What are some that are coming in the future?
- How much contact with management is there? How much exposure?
- What is the path to management in this department? How long does it typically take to get there, and how long do people typically stay there?

Here are some questions that might be asked of would-be colleagues:

- What do you like most or least about working in this company? What do you like most or least about working in this department?
- Describe a typical workday.
- Do you feel free to express your ideas and concerns? Does everyone in this department?
- What are the possibilities here for professional growth and promotion?
- How much interaction is there with supervisors, colleagues, external customers? How much independent work is there?
- How long have you been with the company? How does it compare with other companies where you have worked?

2. **Be physically prepared** – Image is important to all organizations, and a large part of the image that you project is largely a function of your physical appearance. In other words, if you look the part, the chances of getting the job increase exponentially. The key to dressing for an interview is not only to be professionally dressed, but to convey an image that is consistent with the company and the position. An interview is not the time to redefine the meaning of professional dress. Make sure you feel comfortable in the clothes that you choose to wear to

the interview. If you look good and feel good, you will undoubtedly convey these positive feelings throughout the interview.

3. **Practice makes perfect** – Many marketing experts have discussed the similarities between finding a job and personal selling. When you are job hunting, you are, in essence, marketing or selling yourself. If you were selling a product, you would strive to become as familiar as possible with that product. You would not only learn the positive features and benefits of the product, but understand the limitations of the product. In this case, you have to know everything the interviewer could conceivably ask about you. This should not be difficult, but you have to be prepared. The best way to prepare is through practice and repetition, so that you feel confident answering questions about yourself.
   The following is a list of questions regarding school, work, and personal experiences that are often asked during the interview. The more you have thought about these questions prior to the interview, the better your responses.
   Questions pertaining to school experiences might include:

- Which courses did you like most? Why?
- Which courses did you like least? Why?
- Why did you choose your particular major?
- Why did you choose to go to the school you attended? What did you like most or least about this school?
- If you could start college again, what would you do differently?

Questions pertaining to work experiences might include:

- What did you like most or least about the job?
- What did you like most or least about your immediate supervisor?
- Why did you leave the job?
- What were your major accomplishments during this job?
- Of all the jobs you have had, which did you like the most and why? Of all the supervisors you have had, which did you like the most and why?

Questions pertaining to personal experiences might include:

- Of all the things that you have done, what would you consider to be your greatest accomplishment and why?
- What do you consider to be your major strengths? What do you consider to be your major weaknesses?
- What kind of person do you have the most difficulty dealing with? Assuming that you had to work with such a person, how would you do it?
- What do you think are the most valuable skills you would bring to the position for which you are applying?
- What are your short-term goals (within the next five years), and what are your long-term goals?

4. **Maintaining a proper balance** – A good interviewee will know when to talk and when to listen. Your job is to present a complete picture of yourself without dominating the conversation. The best strategy for success is adapting to the interviewer and following his or her lead. When you are answering questions, do not let your mouth get ahead of your mind. Take a moment to think and construct your answers before rushing into a vague and senseless reply.

5. **The interview process does not end with the interview** – After the interview be sure to write a letter expressing your thanks and desire for future consideration. It is a good idea to mention something in the body of the letter that will trigger the memory of the interviewer. Look for unique things that happened or were said during the interview and write about these. Too often, students neglect writing this simple letter and lose the opportunity to present their professionalism one more time.

Where to look for additional information

Sports career books

Aspatore Books. *Career Insights: Presidents/GMs from the NFL,MLB, NHL and MLS on Achieving Personal and Professional Success: Landing a Job with a Sports Team* (Boston: Aspatore Books, 2004).

Field, Shelly. *Career Opportunities in the Sports Industry* (NY, NY: Checkmark Books, 2004).

Fischer, David. *The 50 Coolest Jobs in Sports: Who Got Them, What They Do, and How Can You Get One!* (New York: Arco, 1997).

Floyd, Patricia A., and Allen, Beverly. *Careers in Health, Physical Education, and Sports* (Ohio: Brooks/Cole, 2003).

Heitzmann,William Ray. *Opportunities in Sports and Fitness Careers* (NY, NY: McGraw-Hill/Contemporary Books, 2003).

Holzhauer,Tom. *Sports Career Tips for Teens* (Bloomington, IN: AuthorHouse, 2006).

Menard,Valerie. *Careers in Sport* (Hockessin, DE: Mitchell Lane Publishers, 2001).

Stein, Mel. *How to Be a Sports Agent* (Harpenden, England: Oldcastle Publishing, 2006).

Sports career Web sites

careerplanning.about.com/od/occupations/a/sports_industry.htm

www.jobsinsports.com/

www.jobs4sports.com/

www.onlinesports.com/pages/jobs.html

www.scottishsport.co.uk/business/jobs.htm

www.sgma.com/jobbankdisplaylistings.cfm

www.sportscareers.com

www.sportscareerfinder.com/

www.sportsdiversityrecruiting.com/

www.sportsmanagementworldwide.com/courses

www.teamworkonline.com/

www.usgolfjobs.com/

www.wiscfoundation.org/

www.womensportsjobs.com/

www.workinsports.com/

General career preparation books

Bennett, Scott. *The Elements of Resume Style: Essential Rules and Eye-Opening Advice for Writing Resumes and Cover Letters That Work* (AMACOM/American Management Association, 2005).

Hansen, Katherine, and Hansen, Randall. *Dynamic Cover Letters Revised* (Berkely, CA: Ten Speed Press, 2001).

Kador, John. *201 Best Questions to Ask on Your Interview* (NY, NY: McGraw-Hill, 2002).

Rosenberg, Arthur, and Hizer, David. *The Resume Handbook: How to Write Outstanding Resumes & Cover Letters for Every Situation* (NY, NY: Adams Media Corporation, 2003).

Whitcomb, Susan Britton. *Resume Magic: Trade Secrets of a Professional Resume Writer*, 3rd ed. (St. Paul, MN: JIST Publishing, 2006).

Appendix B

Some sports marketing sites of interest on the Internet

Category	URL	Annotation
Professional Sports	www.nba.com	Official site of the NBA
	www.nhl.com	Official site of the NHL
	www.nfl.com	Official site of the NFL
	www.mlb.com	Official site of MLB
	www.fifal.com	Official site of FIFA
	www.mlssoccer.com.	Official site of MLS
	www.wnba.com	Official site of the WNBA
	www.pga.com	Official site of PGA
	www.pgatour.com	Official site of PGA Tour
	www.lpga.com	Official site of the LPGA
	www.nascar.com	Official site of NASCAR
	www.indycar.com	Official site of Indy Car
	www.pba.com	Official site of PBA
	www.atpworldtour.com	Official site of ATP
	www.milb.com	Official site of Minor League Baseball
	www.formula1.com	Formula One Racing
	www.theahl.com	Official site of the AHL
	www.avp.com	US Pro Beach Volleyball
International Sports	www.sportcal.com	Database of International Sports
	www.ausport.gov.au	Australian Sports Directory
	www.ismhome.com	Institute of Sport Management
	www.olympic.org	International Olympics Committee
	www.sportaccord.com	Umbrella organization of all Olympic & non-Olympic international sport feds

	www.nbcolymics.com	NBC Olympic coverage
	www.paralympic.org	Paralympic information
	www.ontariohockeyleague.com	Official site of the OHL
	www.cfl.ca	Official site of the CFL
	www.uefa.com	Official site of UEFA
	www.irb.com	International Rugby Board
	www.rugbyworldcup.com	Rugby World Cup
Sports Media	www.espn.go.com	ESPN
	www.foxsports.com	Fox
	www.cbssports.com	CBS
	www.cbssportsnetwork.com	CBS Sports Network
	www.nbcsports.com	NBC
	www.cnsi.com	CNN and Sports Illustrated
	www.sportingnews.com	The Sporting News
	www.sportsnetwork.com	Sportsnetwork sports
	www.sportsmediajournal.com	Sports Media Journal
	www.sports-media.org	Video/Education
	www.sportsmedianews.com	Sports Media Press Releases
Women in Sports	www.womenssportsfoundation.org	Women's Sports Foundation
	www.womenssportsnet.com	Women's Sports
	www.womenssportscareers.com	Women's Sports Careers
	www.shapeamercica.org formerly	
	www.aahperd.org/nagws	National Assoc. of Women in Sports
Careers in Sports	careerplanning.about.com/od/ occupations/a/sports_industry.htm	Job opportunities
	www.sportsmanagementworld wide.com	Job opportunities
	www.scottishsport.co.uk	Job opportunities
	www.workinsports.com/	Job opportunities
	www.teamworkonline.com/	Job opportunities
	www.wiscfoundation.org/	Job opportunities
	www.sportscareers.com	Job opportunities
	www.sportsdiversityrecruiting.com/	Job opportunities
	www.womensportsjobs.com/	Job opportunities
	www.sportscareerfinder.com/	Job opportunities
	www.jobsinsports.com/	Job opportunities

	www.usgolfjobs.com/	Job opportunities
	www.sfia.org formerly www.sgma.com/jobbankdisplay listings.cfm	Job opportunities
	www.onlinesports.com/pages/jobs.html	Job opportunities
	www.teammarketing.com/jobs.cfm	Job opportunities
Sporting Goods & industry info	www.sfia.org	Sport & Fitness Industry Association formerly Sporting Goods Manufacturers Association
	www.americansportsdata.com	Sporting Goods Research
	www.sportinggoodsresearch.com	Sporting Goods Research
	www.nsga.org	National Sporting Goods Assoc.
	www.esports-report.com	E-Commerce in Sports
College Sports	www.ncaa.com	Official site of NCAA Sports Marketing Industry
	www.teammarketing.com	General Sports Marketing Info and Research
	www.sportbusinessdaily.com	General Sports Marketing Info
	www.sportmarketingassociation.net	Sport Marketing Association
	www.nasss.org North American	Society for Sociology of Sport
	www.sportseconomics.com	Sports Economics Info
	www.sportsbusinessjournal.com	The Sports Business Journal
	www.sportsbusinessnews.com	Sports Business News
	www.nassm.org	North American Society of Sport Management
	www.joycejulius.com	Joyce Julius Sponsorship
	www.sbrnet.com	Sport Business Research
	www.sportsbusiness.com	Sports Business
	www.bleacherreport.com	Sports Highlights
	www.scarborough.com	Scarborough Research
	www.nielsen.com	Nielsen Research
	www.kantarmedia.com	Media Research
	www.kff.org	Henry J. Kaiser Foundation
	www.sponsorship.com	IEG

Other Sports	www.soccerlinks.net	Soccer links
	www.uslacrosse.org	US Lacrosse
	www.usa-gymnastics.org/links	Gymnastics
	www.churchilldowns.com	Horse racing
	www.ntra.com	Horse racing
	www.baseball-links.com	Baseball links
	www.baseballprospectus.com	Baseball
	www.tennis.com	Tennis links
	www.golflink.com	Golf links
	www.tenpin.org	Bowling links
	www.hockeyzoneplus.com	Hockey news and information
Indices	www.el.com/elinks/sports	Index for general sports links
	www.sports.yahoo.com	Index for general sports
	www.refdesk.com/sports.html	Index for general sports
	www.anythingresearch.com	Research Index
Educational Opportunities	www.nassm.com/InfoAbout/Sport	Colleges offering sports business
	MgmtPrograms	
	http://whatcanidowiththismajor.com/major/sport-management	

Glossary

activity ratios measure the sales productivity and utilization of assets.

advertising creating and maintaining brand awareness and brand loyalty.

advertising appeals telling why the consumer wants to purchase the sports product.

advertising budgeting budgeting methods stemming from the objectives the advertising is attempting to achieve.

advertising execution the format of the advertising.

advertising objectives direct or indirect actions designed to inform, persuade, remind, and cause consumers in the target market to take action.

aesthetic value one of Wann's 8 basic motives for watching sport: to appreciate the beauty of the performance and the pleasure of the art form.

affective component the part of attitude based on feelings or emotional reactions.

agent intermediary whose primary responsibility is leveraging athletes' worth or determining their bargaining power.

AIO dimensions statements describing consumers' activities, interests, and opinions.

amateur sporting event sporting competition for athletes who do not receive compensation for playing the sport.

ambush marketing a planned effort by an organization to associate itself indirectly with an event to gain some of the recognition and benefits associated with being an official sponsor.

antecedent states temporary physiological and mood states that a sports consumer brings to the participant situation.

arbitrary allocation setting a promotional budget without regard to other critical factors; allocating all the money the organization can afford.

assurance the knowledge and courtesy of employees and their ability to convey trust and confidence.

athletic platform for sponsorship, the choice of team, sport, event, athlete, or level of competition.

attitudes learned thoughts, feelings, and behaviors toward a given object.

attractiveness characteristics of personality, lifestyle, and intellect of the source (athlete) that lead the target audience to identify with him or her in some fashion.

availability of substitute products as the number of substitute products increases, demand for the product will decrease.

awareness consumers' knowledge of a company's product and services, product lines, or corporate name.

behavioral component the part of attitude based on actions.

behavioural leaning concerned with how various stimuli (information about sports) elicit certain responses (feelings or behaviours) within an individual.

behavioral segmentation grouping consumers based on how much they purchase, how often they purchase, and how loyal they are to a product or service.

benefits the goods or services consumers derive from a product.

benefits segmentation describing why consumers purchase a product or service or what problem the product or service solves for consumers.

brand awareness making consumers in the target market recognize and remember the brand name.

brand equity the value that the brand contributes to a product in the marketplace.

brand image consumers' set of beliefs about a brand, which shape attitudes

brand loyalty a consistent preference or repeat purchase of one brand over all others in a product category.

brand mark the element of a brand that cannot be spoken.

brand name the element of the brand that can be vocalized.

branding a name, design, symbol, or any combination that a sports organization on individual athlete uses to help differentiate its products from the competition.

branding process establishing brand awareness; developing and managing brand image; developing brand equity; and sustaining brand loyalty.

budgeting obtaining the resources necessary to achieve the marketing plan goals, and making allocation decisions among the marketing activities and functions.

buying influences the various roles of individuals involved in the buying process.

classic type of product life cycle characterized by continuous stage of maturity.

coach's role acting as a guide for the salesperson making the sale.

cognitive component the part of attitude concerned with beliefs.

cognitive dissonance experiencing doubts or anxiety about the wisdom of a decision.

cognitive learning concerned with the ability to solve problems and use observation as a form of learning.

commercialization final phase of the new product development process in which full-scale production and distribution of the product begins.

communication allowing and encouraging an understanding of the marketing plan by all members of the marketing plan by all members of the marketing team; also, the process of establishing a commonness of thought between the sender and the receiver.

community involvement community activities in which the sports organization sponsors public programs, requires time commitments from its employees, partially funds programs, provides personnel at no charge, and so on.

comparative advertisements contrasting one sports product with another.

comparative messages directly or indirectly comparing a sports product with one or more competing products in the promotional message.

competition the attempt all organizations make to serve similar customers; also, a threat that is thought to be reduced by sponsorship.

competitive objectives those that are directly linked to final pricing decisions.

competitive parity setting a promotional budget based on what competitors are spending.

concomitant variation the extent to which a cause and an effect vary together.

consumer demand the quantity of a sports product that consumers are willing to purchase at a given price.

consumer income consumers' ability to pay the price of the product.

consumer pricing evaluation process using consumers' expectations to determine acceptable price ranges.

consumer socialization learning the skills, knowledge, and attitudes necessary to be a consumer.

consumer tastes trends and desires of consumers.

contingency control scanning the relevant environments for internal and external contingencies that could affect the marketing plan.

contingency framework for strategic sports marketing a model for predicting and strategically aligning the marketing process with internal and external contingencies.

continuous innovations ongoing, commonplace changes such as minor alterations of a product or introduction of an imitation product.

continuous schedule continually running the advertisement during the advertising period without any breaks.

control phase of the strategic sports planning process model

control phase the phase of the strategic sports marketing process of evaluating the response to plans to determine their effectiveness.

convenience sampling techniques choosing sample data collection units that are easy to reach but may not be representative of the population of interest.

coordination the effective organization of people and their tasks to implement the marketing plan.

cost of information search affects a consumer's determination of the acceptable price of a product.

costs factors associated with producing, promoting, and distributing the sports product.

coupons certificates that offer reductions in price to induce sales.

creative brief tool used to guide the creative process toward a solution to serve the interests of the client and the customers.

creative decisions the advertising campaign.

creative process the source of innovative ideas; knowledge accumulation, incubation, idea generation, and evaluation and implementation; also; generating the ideas and concepts of the advertising.

creativity a distinctive way of looking at the world, seeking relationships between things that others have not seen.

credibility a source's perceived expertise and trustworthiness.

crisis plan well-defined organizational procedures and strategies to deal with problems that could occur.

cross-sectional studies surveys that describe the characteristics of a sample at one point in time.

cultural values widely held beliefs that affirm what is desirable by members of society.

culture the set of learned values, beliefs, language, traditions, and symbols shared by members of a society and passed down from generation to generation.

data collection techniques methods of collecting information about a population of interest.

decision maker in the buying center, the person with the ultimate responsibility to accept or reject proposals.

decision-making process problem recognition; information search; evaluation of alternatives; participation; and post-participation evaluation.

decline stage of product life cycle when sales are diminishing.

decoding the interpretation by the receiver of the message sent by the source.

demographic environment population trends such as total number of consumers, age, ethnic background, geographic dispersion, and so on.

demographic factors variables such as population, age, gender, education, occupation, ethnic background.

demographic segmentation grouping consumers on the basis of demographic variables such as age, gender, ethnic background, or family life cycle.

dependent variable the variable to be explained, predicted, or measured.

developing the sports product phase of the new product development process in which basic marketing decisions are made.

diffusion of innovation the rate at which new sports products spread throughout the marketplace.

dimensions of service quality reliability, assurance, empathy, responsiveness, and tangibles.

direct competition competition between sellers producing similar products and services.

direct objectives designed to elicit a behavioral response from the target audience.

direct sponsorship objectives objectives that have a short-term impact on consumption behavior and focus on increasing sales.

discontinuous innovations products that are so new and original that they require major learning by consumers and new consumption and usage patterns.

diversion from everyday life one of Wann's 8 basic motives for watching sport: to "get away from it all."

dynamically continuous innovations new products that represent changes and improvements but do not strikingly change buying and usage patterns.

early adopters consumers who adopt a new sports product after innovators and communicate its value to others.

early majority consumers who adopt a sports product after being influenced by innovators and early adopters.

easily defined segments grouping people with active interest across neatly split markets.

economic activity the flow of goods and services between producers and consumers.

economic buying role a position that governs final approval to buy and that can approve a sale even when others say no, and vice versa.

economic factors controllable (such as the price of tickets) and uncontrollable (such as average income) factors that affect game attendance.

economic value one of Wann's 8 basic motives for watching sport: the potential for economic gains from gambling on sporting events.

economy the current economic cycle, which influences pricing decisions.

elastic demand the principle that small changes in price will produce large changes in quantity sold.

elements in the communications process sender, encoding, message, medium, decoding, receiver, feedback, and noise.

emotional appeals using such emotions as fear, humor, pleasure, or identification with a team or athlete in advertising.

emotional versus rational appeal attempting to make consumers feel a certain way about a product, or providing information so consumers can make an analytical decision.

empathy the caring, individualized attention a firm provides to its customers.

encoding translating the sender's thoughts or ideas into a message.

entertainment value one of Wann's 8 basic motives for watching sport: sports as a form of entertainment.

environmental scanning a firm's attempt to continually acquire information on events occurring outside the organization so it can identify and interpret potential trends.

esteem according to Maslow, the need for recognition and status.

estimating demand studying consumer tastes, availability of substitute products, and consumers' income to determine the relationship between price and the amount of product sold.

ethnic background a type of market segmentation that groups consumers on the basis of having a common race, religion, or nationality.

eustress one of Wann's 8 basic motives for watching sport: because it is enjoyable and exciting to the senses.

evaluation of alternatives considering and judging the acceptability of a range of criteria.

evaluative criteria the features and characteristics that a decision maker looks for.

even keel mode characterized by a buyer that is experiencing no discrepancy between the current and ideal states.

evoked set alternatives given the greatest consideration by a decision maker.

exchange a marketing transaction in which the buyer gives something of value to the seller in return for goods and services.

expected price range of substitute products the prices of competitive products have a major influence on what consumers deem an acceptable price.

experiential source an external information source.

experimentation research in which one or more variables are manipulated while others are held constant: the results are then measured.

expertise the knowledge, skill, or special experience possessed by the source of a message.

extensive problem solving (or extended problem solving) comprehensive information search and evaluation of many alternatives on many attributes.

external contingencies all influences outside the organization that can affect its strategic marketing process.

external (or environmental) factors factors beyond the control of the organization that influence pricing decisions, such as consumer demand, competition, legal issues, the economy, and technology.

external source a personal, marketing, or experiential source of information.

facility aesthetics the exterior and interior appearance of a stadium, which can play a role in fan satisfaction and attendance.

fad type of product life cycle characterized by accelerated sales and acceptance of the product by consumers followed by decline.

family influence the influence of family members on decisions.

family life cycle the concept describing how individuals progress through various life stages.

family ties one of Wann's 8 basic motives for watching sport: to foster family togetherness.

fan identification the personal commitment and emotional involvement customers have with a sports organization.

fan motivation factors reasons why individuals are sports fans or sports consumers.

fear appeals telling what negative consequences man occur if the sports product or service is not used or is used improperly.

feedback the response of a target audience to a message.

financial analysis comparing present with past financial performance, and collecting and processing financial information that can be used to make strategic decisions.

fixed costs the sum of the producer's expenses that are stable and do not change with the quantity of the product consumed.

flighting schedule advertising expenditures vary in some months and zero is spent in other months.

focus group a moderately structured discussion session with 8 to 10 people.

frequency the number of times an individual or household is exposed to the media vehicle.

game attractiveness a situational factor that varies from game to game; its perceived quality based on the skill level of participants.

gatekeepers in the buying center, those who control the flow of information to other members.

geodemographic segmentation grouping consumers by combining geographic and demographic characteristics.

geographic segmentation grouping consumers on the basis of local, regional, national, or international characteristics.

global events at the top of the Sports Event Pyramid; events that have the broadest international coverage and generate a great deal of interest among consumers.

goal a short-term purpose that is measurable and challenging, yet attainable and time specific.

goods tangible, physical products that offer benefits to consumers

growth stage of product life cycle when sales increase.

growth mode characterized by a buyer wanting to improve an already good situation.

habitual problem solving (or routinized problem solving) limited information search and evaluation of alternatives; a decision becomes a habit or routine.

harvesting (or milking) when an organization retains the product but offers little or no marketing support.

health appeals telling why purchasing the product will be beneficial to consumers' health.

hierarchy of effects seven steps of leading consumers to purchase the product: unawareness, awareness, knowledge, liking, preference, conviction, action.

idea generation initial phase of the new product development process; consideration of any and all ideas.

idea screening phase of the new product development process in which ideas are evaluated on how well they fit the organization's goals and consumer demand.

ideal customer a hypothetical customer model against which all potential customers can be evaluated to determine where salespeople should invest time and energy.

idle product capacity "down time" in which a service provider is available but there is no demand.

image building a sponsoring organization associates itself and/or its brands with the positive images generated by the unique personality of the sporting event.

implementation putting strategy into action; executing the plan.

implementation phase phase of the strategic sports marketing process of deciding who will carry out the plans, when the plans will be executed, and how the plans will be executed.

income objectives concerned with achieving maximum profits or simply organizational survival.

independent variable the variable that can be manipulated or altered in some way.

indirect competition sports marketers' competition with all other forms of entertainment for the consumers' dollar.

indirect objectives establishing pre behavioral responses to advertising that should lead to direct behavioral responses.

indirect sponsorship objectives objectives that ultimately lead to the desired goal of enhancing sales; generating awareness, beating competition, reaching new target markets, building relationships, and improving image.

inelastic demand the principle that changes in price will have little or no impact on sales.

influencers in the buying center, those who can affect the decision-making process.

information accurate information is essential for decision making and necessary in all phases of the strategic sports marketing process.

information search seeking relevant information to resolve a problem.

innovations new sports or sports products.

innovators consumers who are the first to adopt a new sports product as it enters the marketplace.

integrated marketing communications how a sports organization integrates and coordinates its promotional mix elements to deliver a unified message.

internal contingencies all influences within the organization that can affect its strategic marketing process.

internal factors factors controlled by the organization, including other marketing mix elements, costs, and organizational objectives, which influence pricing decisions.

internal source information recalled from memory, based on previous experience.

international events the second level of the Sports Event Pyramid; events that have a high level of interest in a broad but not global geographic region, or that are global in scope but have a lower level of interest in some of the countries reached.

intrapreneurship the process of creating and innovating within an organization, or corporate entrepreneurship.

introduction initial stage of product life cycle when the product is introduced in the marketplace.

judgment sample study participants chosen subjectively based on the researcher's judgment that they will best fit the purpose of the study.

just noticeable difference (JND) the point at which consumers detect a difference between the original price and the adjusted price.

laggards consumers who adopt a sports product in its declining stage.

late majority consumers who adopt a sports product in its late stages of maturity.

law of demand the principle that consumers are more likely to purchase products at a lower price than a higher price.

layout accessibility referring to whether spectators can move freely about a stadium.

learning a relatively permanent change in response tendency due to the effects of experience.

legal issues factors such as legislation that affect pricing.

leverage ratios measure the extent to which creditors finance the organization.

licensing a contractual agreement whereby a company may use another company's trademark in exchange for a royalty or fee; also, a practice whereby a sports marketer contracts with other companies to use a brand name, logo, symbol, or characters.

lifestyle advertisements portraying the lifestyle of the desired target audience.

limited problem solving internal and sometimes limited external information search and evaluation of a small number of alternatives on few criteria.

liquidity ratios indicate the organization's ability to pay short-term obligations without selling assets.

local events the lowest level of the Sports Event Pyramid: events that have the narrowest geographic focus and attract a small segment of consumers who have a high level of interest.

logo see brand mark.

logotype see brand mark.

longitudinal study a study conducted over time in which several measurements are made.

love and belonging according to Maslow, the social need to be a respected part of a group.

macroeconomic elements the big picture, such as the national income.

majority fallacy assuming that the largest group of consumers should always be selected as the target market.

market niche a very homogenous group of consumers as reflected by their unique need.

market segmentation identifying groups of consumers based on their common needs.

market selection decisions decisions made to segment markets, choose targeted consumers, and position the sports product against the competition. These decisions that dictate the direction of the marketing mix.

marketing environment the competitive forces to be assessed in the strategic sports marketing process.

marketing mix integrating sports products, pricing, promotion, and place to meet identified sports consumer needs.

marketing mix variables factors that must be considered when determining the price of a sports product.

marketing myopia the practice of defining a business in terms of goods and services rather than in terms of the benefits sought by customers.

marketing orientation concentration on understanding the consumer and providing a sports product that meets consumers' needs, while achieving the organization's objectives.

marketing research the systematic process of collecting, analyzing and reporting information to enhance decision making throughout the strategic sports marketing process

marketing sources information from advertisements, sales personnel, brochures, Web sites, and so on.

Maslow's hierarchy of needs a theory of human motivation based on classification of needs.

match-up hypothesis Belief that states the more congruent the image of the endorser with the image of the product being promoted, the more effective the message

mature market adults, age 55-plus, about 21 percent of the U.S. population.

maturity stage of product life cycle when sales stabilize.

media scheduling continuous, flighting, pulsing, or seasonal types of advertising schedules.

media strategy determining what medium or media mix will be most effective in reaching the desired target audience, and how this media should be schedules to meet advertising objectives.

medium a communications channel, such as television, radio, newspapers, signage, billboards, Web sites, and so on.

message the exact content of the words and symbols to be transmitted to the receiver.

message characteristics the attributes of the promotional message.

methodology description of how a study is conducted.

microeconomic elements smaller elements of the big picture, such as consumer income level.

milestone review evaluation of critical events, major allocations, achievements, or the passage of a certain amount of time as part of process control.

mob effect a situation in which consumers feel it is socially desirable to attend "special" sporting events

model of participant consumption behavior model that tries to understand how consumers arrive at their decisions.

monitoring strategic thrusts evaluating the strategic direction of the marketing plan.

monopolistic competition an environment where numerous brands with identical products are sold requiring both price competition and non-price competition.

monopoly when one seller sets the price for a unique product.

motivation an internal force that directs behavior towards the fulfillment of needs.

national events in the Sports Event Pyramid, events that have an extremely high level of interest among consumers in a single country or two countries.

need for affiliation fans' need to feel connected to the community and to identify with the team.

new product category entries sports products that are new to the organization, but not to consumers. The sample units are chosen subjectively by the researcher

new product development process idea generation, idea screening, analysis of the concept, development of the product, test marketing, and commercialization.

new-to-the-world products brand new sports innovations such as the first in-line skates, the first sailboard, or the advent of arena football.

niche marketing the process of carving out a relatively tiny part of a market that has a very special need that is not currently being filled

noise interference in the communications process.

nonprice competition the creation of a unique sports product through the packaging, product design, promotion, distribution or any marketing variable other than price

nonprobability sampling the researcher chooses sample units subjectively so there is no way of ensuring that the sample represents the population of interest.

objective and task method identifying promotional objectives, defining the communications tools and tasks needed to meet those objectives, and then adding up the costs of the planned activities.

objectives the long-range purposes of the organization that are not quantified or limited to a time period.

oligopoly a small number of firms controlling a market.

one-sided versus two-sided messages that convey either just the positive or both the positive and negative features of the product.

organizational culture the shared values and assumptions of organizational members that shape an identity and establish preferred behaviors in an organization.

organizational objectives Signposts along the road which help an organization focus on its purpose as stated in the mission statement.

organizational strategies the means by which the organization achieves its objectives and marketing goals.

organized sporting events Sporting competitions that are sanctioned and controlled by a controlling authority such as a league, association or sanctioning body.

overconfident mode characterized by a buyer that believes it is already exceeding its goals.

participant consumption behavior actions performed when searching for, participating in, and evaluating the sports activities that consumers feel will satisfy their needs

participants those who take part in a sport.

perceived risk the uncertainty associated with decision making and the concern for the potential threats of making the wrong decision

percentage of sales determining a standard percentage of promotional spending and applying this proportion to past or forecasted sales to arrive at the amount to be spent.

perception the complex process of selecting, organizing and interpreting sports-related stimuli.

perception of value the acceptable price ranges for sports products, which varies from person to person and is based on perceived benefits.

perceptual maps created through advanced marketing research techniques to examine product positioning.

perishability the ability to store or inventory "pure goods," whereby services are lost if not consumed.

personal selling a form of person-to-person communication in which a salesperson works with prospective buyers and attempts to influence their purchase needs in the direction of his or her company's products or services

personal source information from friends and family.

personal training products designed to benefit participants in sports at all levels of competition (e.g., fitness centers, health services, sports camps, and instruction).

personality a set of consistent responses an individual makes to the environment

physical environment natural resources and other characteristics of the natural world that have an impact on sports marketing.

physical surroundings the location, weather, and physical aspects of the participation environment.

physiological needs according to Maslow, the biological needs to eat, drink, and meet other physiological needs, such as have some level of physical activity.

planning assumptions control monitoring the validity of the assumptions used to develop the marketing plan.

planning phase phase of the strategic sports marketing process of understanding sports consumers through marketing research and identifying their wants and needs.

pleasure or fun appeals directed at target audiences that participate in or watch sports for fun, social interaction, or enjoyment.

political, legal, and regulatory environment legal and political issues that affect sports and sports marketing.

point-of-purchase or P-O-P displays a promotional display designed to attract consumers' attention to a particular product or retail display area

positioning fixing the sports product in the minds of the target market by manipulating the marketing mix

postparticipation evaluation evaluation of a decision after making it and participation has begun.

premiums items given away with the sponsors product as part of the sales promotion.

pretest a "trial run" for a questionnaire to determine if there are any problems in interpreting the questions.

price a statement of value for a sports product

price adjustments changing the price of a product to stimulate demand.

price competition stimulating consumer demand primarily by offering consumers lower prices

price discounts incentives offered to buyers to stimulate demand or reward behaviors that are favorable to the seller

price elasticity the extent to which consumer purchasing patterns are sensitive to fluctuations in price

price increases raising established prices to keep up with inflation or if there is excess demand for the product.

price inelasticity see price elasticity.

price reductions efforts to enhance sales and achieve greater market share by directly lowering the original price

primary data data gathered for the specific research question at hand

primary reference group those people, such as friends and coworkers, who have frequent contact with us and have the power to influence our decisions

probability sampling objective procedures in which sample units have a known and nonzero chance of being selected for study and the accuracy of the results can be estimated.

problem definition specifying what information is needed to assist either in solving problems or identifying opportunities

problem recognition the result of a discrepancy between a desired state and an actual state large enough and important enough to activate the entire decision-making process

process control measuring and evaluating the effects of actions that have already been taken to execute the marketing plan.

producers and intermediaries the manufacturers of sports products or the organizations that perform some function in the marketing of sports products.

product characteristics the important attributes or characteristics that, when taken together, create the total product.

product design the aesthetics, style and function of the sports product

product form product variations within a category.

product life cycle a useful tool for developing marketing strategy and then revising this strategy as a product moves through the stages of introduction, growth, maturity and decline

product line a group of products that are closely related because they satisfy a class of needs, are used together, are sold to the same customer groups, are distributed through the same type of outlets or fall within a given price range

product mix the total assortment of product lines the sports organization sells

product quality consumers' perception of the performance, features, reliability, conformance, durability, serviceability, aesthetics, and perceived quality of a product.

product warranties statements indicating the liability of the manufacturer for problems with the product.

professional sports sporting competitions in which athletes receive compensation, commonly classified as major or minor league status.

profitability ratios indicate how profitable the organization is during a period of time.

projective techniques methods that allow respondents to project their feelings, beliefs, or motivations onto a relatively neutral stimulus.

promotion all forms of communication to consumers.

promotional budgeting determining the amount to spend on promotion based on maximizing the monies available.

promotion mix elements the combination of elements, including advertising, personal selling, sponsorship, public relations and sales promotion designed to communicate with sports consumers.

promotional objectives informing, persuading, and reminding the target audience.

promotional planning identifying target market considerations; setting promotional objectives; determining the promotional budget; and developing the promotional mix.

psychographic segmentation grouping consumers on the basis of a common lifestyle preference and personality.

public relations the element of the promotion mix that identifies, establishes and maintains mutually beneficial relationships between the sports organizations and the various publics on which its success or failure depends

pull strategy any method a company uses to generate demand for a product. A pull marketing campaign is customer-focused, but should still start with the analysis of the product the company wants to sell. The company needs to determine what the product's key features are and who is most likely to demand it through extensive market research. Often used to stimulate demand for the sports product so that retailers are forced to stock the sports product, target audience is the ultimate consumer.

pulsing schedule ad expenditures may vary greatly, but some level of advertising is always taking place.

purchasers responsible for negotiating and formally carrying out the terms of the sponsorship.

pure competition a market structure that has so many competitors that none can singularly influence the market price. It does not exist in the sports industry.

pure monopoly one seller who sets the price for unique product.

push strategy focuses on taking the product through the channel of distribution to the customer, and putting the product in front of the customer at the point of purchase. This type of marketing strategy hopes to minimize the amount of time between a customer discovering a product and buying that product. To accomplish this, companies use aggressive and wide-reaching ads to make the biggest and most immediate impact they can on customers.

quality dimension of goods how well a product conforms to specifications related to design and function.

quantity discounts rewarding buyers for purchasing large quantities of a sports product by lower prices.

quota sampling sample elements chosen on the basis of some control characteristic or characteristics of interest to the researcher

ratio analysis quantitative analysis of information based on line items in financial statements like the balance sheet, income statement and cash flow statement; the ratios of one item – or a combination of items – to another item or combination are then calculated. Ratio analysis is used to evaluate various aspects of a company's operating and financial performance such as its efficiency, liquidity, profitability and solvency.

reach the number of people exposed to an advertisement in a given medium

receiver the audience or the object of the source's message.

regional events in the Sports Event Pyramid, events that have a narrow geographic focus but high interest levels in the region.

reference groups individuals who influence the information, attitudes, and behaviors of other group members

relationship marketing the process of creating, maintaining, and enhancing strong, value-laden relationships with customers and other stakeholders.

reliability the ability to perform promised service dependably and accurately.

reposition to change the image or perception of the sports entity in the minds of consumers in the target market.

research design the framework or plan for a study that guides the collection and analysis of data.

research objectives the various types of information needed to address a problem or opportunity.

research problem statement definition of the problem to be solved or opportunity to be identified.

research proposal a written blueprint that describes all the information necessary to conduct and control the study.

response modes the various reactions of buyers in a sales situation.

responsiveness the willingness to help customers and provide prompt service

rewards as part of an implementation plan, used to motivate behavior that supports the strategy.

roles patterns of behavior expected by people in a given position.

safety needs according to Maslow, the need to feel physically safe and to remain healthy.

sales funnel a model of organizing clients so that sales people can allocate their efforts in the most efficient and effective manner.

sales objectives concerned with maintaining or enhancing market share and encouraging sales growth.

sales promotions a variety of short term, promotional activities that are designed to stimulate immediate product demand.

sample a subset of the population of interest from which data is gathered to estimate some characteristic of the population.

sampling inducing customers to try new products by giving away a product or putting on an exhibition game.

sanctioning authoritative permission or approval that makes a course of action valid, often surrounding a consideration, influence, or principal that dictates an ethical choice.

scientific advertisements featuring the technological superiority of the advertised product or using research or scientific studies to support these claims.

scoreboard quality a dimension of the stadium that is sometimes seen as the focal point of the interior.

seasonal type of product life cycle characterized by rise and fall of sales according to opening and closing dates of the sports season.

seasonal discounts reduction in prices to stimulate demand in off-peak periods

seating comfort perceived comfort of the seating and the spacing of the seats relative to each other in a stadium.

secondary data data that has already been collected, but is still relevant to the research question.

second screening a supplementary social, and synchronized experience that delivers enhanced content to a tablet or smartphone, engaging a consumer through a second screen (Second Screen Society, 2014).

selective attention a consumer's focus on a specific marketing stimulus based on personal needs and attitudes.

selective interpretation consumers perceive things in ways that are consistent with their existing attitudes and values.

selective retention the tendency to remember only certain information.

self-actualization according to Maslow, the individual's need to fulfill personal life goals.

self-esteem enhancement one of Wann's 8 basic motives for watching sport; to enhance or maintain self-esteem through associating with a winning team.

separability the ability to separate the quality of a good from the quality of a service.

service quality the physical, interactive, and corporate dimensions of a product.

services intangible, non-physical products.

sex appeals type of emotional appeal used in advertising.

sidedness based on the nature of the information presented to the target audience; only positive features of the product, or both benefits and weaknesses.

signage a factor of the sportscape that affects spectators' enjoyment of the game experience.

simplified model of the consumer-supplier relationship Framework for describing the consumers of sport, the sports products that they consume, and the suppliers of the sport product.

simulated test market nontraditional test market approach in which respondents participate in a series of activities in a laboratory environment.

situational factors factors that may affect a consumer's acceptable range of prices; presence or absence of time, usage situation, and social factors.

situational factors temporary factors within a particular time or place that influence the participation decision-making process

slice-of-life advertisements showing an athlete or consumer in an everyday situation in which the consumer might be using the advertised product.

social class the homogeneous division of people in a society sharing similar values, lifestyles, and behaviors that can be hierarchically categorized.

social concerns a type of organizational objective that influences pricing.

social learning watching others and learning from their actions.

social surroundings the effect of others on a participant during participation in an event.

socialization learning the skills, knowledge, and attitudes necessary for participation.

socializing agents direct and indirect influences on children.

socioeconomic segmentation grouping consumers on the basis of social class and income.

sociological or external factors influences outside an individual that affect the decision-making process.

source sender of a message; beginning of the communication process.

space allocation a factor of the sportscape that affects spectators' enjoyment of the game experience.

spectators consumers who derive their benefit from the observation of the event.

sponsor the individual or group that provides the support, similar to a benefactor.

sponsorship investing in a sports entity (athlete, league, team, event, etc.) to support overall organizational objectives, marketing goals, and/or more specific promotional objectives

sponsorship budgeting methods determining competitive parity, arbitrary allocation, percentage of sales, and the objective and task method.

sponsorship evaluation process of determining the sponsorship decision by the buying center in the organization.

sponsorship objectives direct or indirect objectives.

sponsorship program one element of the promotional strategy.

sport a source of diversion or a physical activity engaged in for pleasure.

sport sponsorship acquisition model of the corporate sponsorship decision-making process by Arthur, Scott, and Woods.

sporting event the primary product of the sports industry – the competition.

sporting goods tangible products that are manufactured, distributed, and marketed within the sports industry.

sports equipment manufacturers responsible for producing and sometimes marketing the sports equipment used by consumers.

Sports Event Pyramid Shani and Sandler's model of categorizing various sponsorship opportunities.

sports information news, statistics, schedules, and stories about sports.

sports involvement the perceived interest in and personal importance of sports to an individual participating in a sport.

sports marketing applying marketing principles and processes to sports products and nonsports products associated with sports.

sports marketing mix the coordinated set of product and service strategies, pricing decisions, and distribution issues that sports organizations use to meet marketing objectives and satisfy consumers' needs.

sports product a good, a service, or any combination of the two designed to provide benefits to a sports spectator, participant, or sponsor.

sports product map the intersection of the dimensions of goods–services and body—mind.

sports sponsorship exchanging money or product for the right to associate a name or product with a sporting event.

sportscape the physical surroundings of the stadium that impact spectators desire to stay at the stadium and ultimately return to the stadium.

stacking using both a manufacturer's coupon and a store coupon for purchase.

stadium access issues such as availability of parking, ease of entering and exiting the parking areas, and location of parking relative to the stadium.

stadium factors variables such as newness of the stadium, stadium access, aesthetics of the stadium, seat comfort, and cleanliness of the stadium, which are all positively related to game attendance.

stadium signage on-site advertising.

staffing and skills having a leader who can champion and communicate the marketing strategy and a staff that cares about and can implement the strategy.

standardization receiving the same level of quality over repeat purchase.

strategic control the critical evaluation of plans, activities, and results, thereby providing information for future strategic action

stategic selling a personal selling strategy that takes into account buying influences, red flags, response modes, win results, the sales funnel, and the ideal customer profile.

strategic sports marketing process the process of planning, implementing, and controlling marketing efforts to meet organizational goals and satisfy consumers' needs.

strategic windows a limited period of time during which the characteristics of a market and the distinctive competencies of a firm fit together well.

sweepstakes and contests sales promotional tools; games of chance or luck and competitions that award prizes on the basis of contestants' skills and ability.

tangibility the ability to see, feel, and touch the product.

tangibles the physical facilities, equipment, and the appearance of the service personnel

target market considerations identifying the target market and planning promotions to reach that specific market.

target marketing choosing the segment(s) that will allow an organization to most efficiently and effectively attain its marketing objectives

task definition the reasons that occasion the need to participate in a sport, which affect the decision-making process.

TEAMQUAL a survey instrument used to evaluate spectators' perceptions of service quality for an NBA team.

technical buying role screening potential suppliers on the basis of meeting or failing to meet a variety of technical specifications that have been determined in advance.

technology a rapidly changing environmental influence on sports marketing; it can have an indirect or direct influence on pricing decisions.

test marketing introducing a new product or service in one or more geographic areas on a limited basis.

testimonials statements about the sports product given by endorsers.

time a situational influence on the decision-making process.

total cost sum of the variables and fixed costs.

Total Quality Management (TQM) an integrative management concept for continuously improving the quality of goods and services at all levels of the organization.

trademark identifies that a sports organization has legally registered its brand name or brand mark and thus prevents others from using it.

trouble mode characterized by a buyer experiencing difficulties.

trustworthiness the honesty and believability of the athlete endorser.

types of adopters various groups of consumers likely to try a product at any given stage.

unitary demand the situation when price changes are offset exactly by changes in demand; price and demand are perfectly related.

unorganized sports the sporting activities people engage in that are not sanctioned or controlled by some external authority.

user buying role making judgments about the potential impact of the product on job performance.

values widely held beliefs that affirm what is desirable in a culture.

variable costs the sum of the producer's expenses that vary and change as a result of the quantity of the product being consumed

vision a long-term roadmap for where the organization is headed.

win-results in the strategic selling process, an objective result that gives one or more of the buying influences a personal win.

Illustration credits

Chapter 1

Ads

Ad 1.1 – Concept of sports marketing

Credit: Reprinted with permission. www.cartoonstock.com Ref. aton1188

Ad 1.2 – Become a Fantasy Football God Ad: Fantasy sports blurring the line between spectator and participant

Source: Sporting News

Articles

Sports Marketing Hall of Fame: Mark McCormack

Source: Susan Vinella, "Sports Marketing Pioneer Dead at 72"; "IMG's McCormack Hailed as Visionary," *Plain Dealer*, May 17, 2003, a1; Eric Fisher, "IMG Founder McCormack Spiced Up the Sports World," *The Washington Times*, May 18, 2003, c3.

Credit: The Washington Times

URL: http://www.washingtontimes.com/news/2003/may/18/20030518-120347-6818r/?page=all

Girls get their game on – with great gear: Sports teams cater to women fans with new lines of feminine fashion

Article Author: Ellen Warren

Rightsholder: Courtesy of Chicago Tribune

URL: http://articles.chicagotribune.com/2011-01-28/lifestyle/sc-cons-0127-warren-shopping-super-bo20110127_1_women-fans-sports-leagues-team-colors

Figures

Figure 1.3 – Top 10 Sports Websites (March 2011; Total U.S. Home, Work, and University Internet Users

Source: Created by Author, adapted from: http://www.ebizmba.com/articles/sports-websites

Photos

Photo 1.1 – Fans in grandstand

Source: Shutterstock.com – ID # 1855093

Credit: © aceshot1/Shutterstock.com

Photo 1.2 – The sports collectors dream – the Baseball Hall of Fame. The Baseball Hall of Fame's plaque gallery, housing plaques for all Hall of Famers, November 26, 2011 in Cooperstown, NY.

Source: Shutterstock.com # 90134158

Credit: © Aspen Photo/Shutterstock.com

Tables

Table 1.1 – 25 Coolest Minor League Stadiums

Source: Author Generated Table

Article Author: Doug Mead

Rightsholder: BleacherReport

URL: http://bleacherreport.com/articles/842135-power-ranking-the-25-coolest-minor league-stadiums

Table 1.2 – NFL Media Rights

URL: http://espn.go.com/nfl/story/_/id/7353238/ nfl-re-ups-tv-pacts-expand-thursday-schedule

Table 1.3 – Most Popular Sports and Fitness Activities Based on Core Participation (age 6 and above; U.S. residents)

Credit: Reproduced with kind permission of Sports & Fitness Industry Association, www.sfia.org

Webcaptures

Webcapture 1.1 – ESPN: The growth of sports information on the Web

URL: www.espn.go.com

Webcapture 1.2 – Ski.com: Ski.com provides information for ski enthusiasts

Courtesy ski.com

URL: www.Ski.com

Webcapture 1.3 – NCAA: One of the most powerful sanctioning bodies

Copyright: © National Collegiate Athletic Association, 2012. All rights reserved.

URL: http://www.ncaa.com/

Chapter 2

Ads

Ad 2.1 – Cobra stresses an improved performance based on their technological product improvements

Source: Cobra Golf

Ad 2.2 – NCAA capitalizes on the new opportunities based on the growth in women's sports.

Source: NCAA © National Collegiate Athletic Association, 2012. All rights reserved.

Articles

NBA Releases 2011-2012 Regular Season Schedule

Source: Slamonline.com

Credit: The NBA and individual member team identifications reproduced herein are used with permission from NBA Properties, Inc. © 2014 NBA Properties, Inc. All rights reserved.

URL: http://www.slamonline.com/online/nba/2011/12/nba-releases-2011-2012-regular-season-schedule/

On the Industry's Radar

Article Author: Dan Muret

Rightsholder: *Sports Business Journal*

URL: http://m.sportsbusinessdaily.com/Journal/Issues/2012/01/16/In-Depth/Trends.aspx

Big-Time College Sports is an Out-of-Control Monster

Article Author: Ken Reed

Credit: Courtesy of Ken Reed

URL: http://leagueoffans.org/2013/06/11/big-time-college-sports-is-an-out-of-control-monster/

MLB Forms Diversity Committee

Article Author: Associated Press

Credit: Used with permission of Bloomberg L.P. Copyright© 2014. All rights reserved.

URL: http://espn.go.com/mlb/story/_/id/9158114/mlb-forms-task-force-study-how-increase-diversity

Photos

Photo 2.1 – After the Lockout, the NBA is Still Thriving: Chris Bosh #4 participates in an NBA basketball game at the Air Canada Centre on January 24, 2010 in Toronto, Canada. The Toronto Raptors beat the Los Angeles Lakers 106-105.

Source: Shutterstock.com – ID # 49724977

Credit: Domenic Gareri/Shutterstock.com

Photo 2.2 – The mature market: staying young and having fun in record numbers

Source: Shutterstock.com – ID # 3105993

Credit: Lisa F. Young/Shutterstock.com

Tables

Table 2.1 – College Sports TV: The Main Players

URL: http://www.broadcastingcable.com/news/news-articles/battle-college-sports-fans/106216

Table 2.2 – Top 10 Sports Video Games (Ranked by total U.S. units sold)

URL: www.complex.com/video-games/2012/12/the-10-best-sports-video-games-of-2012/fifa-13

Webcaptures

Webcapture 2.1 – Myrtle Beach Pelicans using a low-cost market niche strategy

Source: BB&T Coastal Field

Credit: Reproduced courtesy of Myrtle Beach Pelicans

Webcapture 2.2 – ESPN Fantasy Sports: ESPN.com providing sports information via the Internet

Source: ESPN.com

Webcapture 2.3 – C-12 Lacrosse showing its latest advances in Lacrosse Technology

Source: C-12 Lacrosse

Reproduced with permission of Entrotech.com

Chapter 3

Articles

Marketing Research in Action: the Gary Southshore RailCats

Source: Center for Sport Recreation and Tourism Development, KSU / Gary Southshore RailCats Feasability Study

Hitting a Home Run with the Digital Generation

Rightsholder: Scarborough USA 2012

URL: http://www.prnewswire.com/news-releases/hitting-a-home-run-with-the-digital-generation-145950285.html

Case Study: A Sponsorship Measurement Solution

Source: A Sponsorship Measurement Solution, IEG October, 2011. Ukman, L & Krasts, M

Credit: IEG

URL: http://www.sponsorship.com/ieg/files/07/07903e35-98d1-4f1c-b318-7524b3104222.pdf

Drivers should take a spin online, study shows

Article Author: Tripp Mickle

Rightsholder: Sports Business Journal

URL: http://www.sportsbusinessdaily.com/Journal/Issues/2012/11/05/Research-and-Ratings/NASCAR-study.aspx

Case Study: Survey Shows Split on Racial Opportunity

Article Author: Mark Fainaru-Wada

Rightsholder: ESPN – Originally published in The Good Men Project

URL: http://sports.espn.go.com/espn/otl/news/story?id=6006813

Figures

Figure 3.4 – Designing a questionnaire

Source: Churchill. *IM/TM - Basic Marketing Research, 3/E*, 3E. © 1996 South-Western, a part of Cengage Learning, Inc. Reproduced with permission.

URL: www.cengage.com/permissions

Photos

Photo 3.1 – Field Hockey: The growing number of women's sport participants is being monitored through secondary marketing research.

Credit: Elissa Unger

Photo 3.2 – Focus groups

Source: Shutterstock.com – ID #55855492

Credit: Franz Pfluegl/Shutterstock.com

Tables

Table 3.3 – North American Golf Report Table of Contents

Credit: Golf Research Group

URL: http://www.golf-research-group.cpm/reports/22/content.html

Webcaptures

Webcapture 3.1 – SBRNET: Sport Business Research is an excellent source of primary and secondary data

Credit: Courtesy www.SBRNET.com.

Chapter 4

Ads

Ad 4.1 – Wrangler® & Brett Farve

Source: Wrangler®

Credit: Courtesy Wrangler®

Articles

Spotlight on International Sports Marketing

Article author: Richard Lewis

Credit: Courtesy of Sport England

URL: http://sportengland.org/about-us/what-we-do/annual-report/

Sports Marketing Hall of Fame: Babe Didrikson Zaharias

Credit: Elizabeth Lynn, *Babe Didrikson Zaharias: Champion Athlete* (New York, Chelsea House, 1989). 1-55546-684-2 © 1989 by Chelsea House Publishers an imprint of Infobase Learning.

High School Sports Participation Tops 7.6 Million, Sets Record

Article Author: Lauren Fellmeth

Source: "High School Sports Participation Tops 7.6 Million, Sets Record"

Credit: NFHS: National Federation of State High School Associations.

URL: http://www.nfhs.org/content.aspx?id=3282.

P90X vs. Insanity: Which is the best for you?

Article Author: Rebecca Anderson

Source: Sports & Fitness

URL: http://weekly.blog.gustavus.edu/2013/02/22/p90x-vs-insanity-which-is-the-best-for-you/

Figures

Figure 4.2 – Maslow's Hierarchy of Needs

Source: A.H. Maslow, *Motivation and Personality,* 2nd ed. (New York: Harper and Row, 1970).

Credit: Maslow, Abraham H.; Frager, Robert D.; Fadiman, James, Motivation and Personality, 3rd Edition, © 1987.

Reprinted by permission of Pearson Education, Inc., Upper Saddle River, NJ.

Figure 4.5 – Model of Attitude Formation

Source: Adapted from Del Hawkins, Roger Best, and Kenneth Coney. Consumer Behavior: Building Marketing Strategy, 7/e © 1998 The McGraw-Hill Companies, Inc.

ISBN 0256218951

Rightsholder: McGraw-Hill Companies

Credit: © The McGraw-Hill Companies, Inc.

Figure 4.6 – Model of Consumer Socialization

Source: John Mowen, *Consumer Behavior* 3rd ed. (New York: Macmillan, 1993)

Rightsholder: Macmillan

Figure 4.7 – The Structure of Social Class

Source: Richard P. Coleman, "The Continuing Significance of Social Class to Marketing," *Journal of Consumer Research*, vol. 10 (December 1983), 265-280.

Rightsholder: *Journal of Consumer Research*

Credit: Reprinted by permission of the University of Chicago Press.

Photos

Photo 4.1 – Father and son fishing together by the ocean

Source: Shutterstock.com – ID # 57789094

Credit: BlueOrange Studio/Shutterstock.com

Photo 4.2 – Many consumers see a discrepancy between the "ideal" and "actual" body.

Source: Shutterstock.com – ID # 106274624

Credit: Diego Cervo/Shutterstock.com

Photo 4.3 – A growing number of consumers participate in high-risk sports.

Source: Shutterstock.com – ID # 107616701

Credit: Vitalii Nesterchuk/Shutterstock.com

Photo 4.4 – Sports participants fulfilling the need for self-actualization.

Source: Shutterstock.com – ID # 97358237

Credit: Dudarev Mikhail/Shutterstock.com

Photo 4.5 – The high involvement cyclist

Source: Shutterstock.com – ID # 107083253

Credit: Ljupco Smokovski/Shutterstock.com

Photo 4.6 - Karate: Girls' sport participation is eroding traditional gender roles

Source: Shutterstock.com – ID # 59662453

Credit: Lipik/Shutterstock.com

Photo 4.7 – Marathon

Source: Shutterstock.com – ID # 162584165

Credit: Suzanne Tucker/Shutterstock.com

Tables

Table 4.1 – Sport Participation Changes from 2013 (Participants ages six and up)

Credit: Courtesy The Sporting Goods Marketing Association

Table 4.2 – Golfer's Self-Reported Traits and Personality Characteristics

Source: Yankelovich Partners, "How Golfers Are Likely to Describe Themselves." Rightsholder: Yankelovich Partners

Credit: The Futures Company Worldwide

Table 4.3 – Why People Participate in Sports

Source: George Milne, William Sutton, and Mark McDonald, "Niche Analysis: A Strategic Measurement Tool for Managers," *Sport Marketing Quarterly*, vol. 5, no. 3 (1996), 17–21.

Rightsholder: Sports Marketing Quarterly

Credit: Courtesy of Fitness Information Technology, Morgantown, WV.

Table 4.4 – Segmentation of Runners by Motives

Source: Andrew J. Rohm, George R, Milne, and Mark McDonald, "A Mixed-Method Approach for Developing Market Segmentation Typologies in the Sports Industry," *Sport Marketing Quarterly*, 2006, 15, 29-39, © 2006 West Virginia University

Rightsholder: Sports Marketing Quarterly

Credit: Courtesy of Fitness Information Technology, Morgantown, WV.

Table 4.5 – Core American Values

Source: Leom Shiffman and Leslie Kanuk. *Consumer Behavior*, 5th ed. (Upper Saddle River, NJ: Prentice Hall, 1994).

Credit: Courtesy The Sporting Goods Marketing Association

Table 4.6 – Household Income for Select Sports and Activities

Credit: reproduced with kind permission of Sports & Fitness Industry Association, www.sfia.org

Webcaptures

Webcapture 4.1 – Kayak Online: Online information source

Source: Kayak Online

URL: http://www.kayakonline.com

Chapter 5

Articles

Baseball Suffers Drop in Attendance

Article Author: Ken Rosenthal

Rightsholder: Foxsports

URL: http://msn.foxsports.com/mlb/story/attendance-down-not-just-at-miami-marlins-games-060513

Sports Marketing Hall of Fame: David Stern

Source: Adapted from E.M. Swift, "Corned Beef to Caviar." *Sports Illustrated* (June 3, 1991), 74-87.

Credit: Time, Inc.

Sports Wagering

Rightsholder: American Gaming Association

Credit: American Gaming Association

URL: http://www.americangaming.org/industry-resources/research/fact-sheets/sports-wagering

Figures

Figure 5.2 – Model of Sportscape

Source: K.L. Wakefield, J.G. Blodgett, and H.J. Sloan, "Measurement and Management of the Sportscape," *Journal of Sport Management*, vol. 10, no. 1 (1996), 16.

Credit: Courtesy of Human Kinetics, Inc.

Figure 5.3 – Model for Fan Identification

Source: William A. Sutton. *Sports Marketing Quarterly*.

Rightsholder: *Sports Marketing Quarterly*

Credit: Courtesy of Fitness Information Technology, Morgantown, WV.

Photos

Photo 5.1 – Group of happy Brazilian soccer fans commemorating victory, with the flag of Brazil swinging in the air.

Source: Shutterstock.com – ID # 160923683

Credit: mangostock/Shutterstock.com

Photo 5.2 – Traditional corrida - bullfighting in Spain. Bullfighting has been prohibited in Catalunia since 2011 for animal torturing.

Shutterstock.com – ID # 155340746

Credit: Matej Kastelic/Shutterstock.com

Tables

Table 5.1 – Differences between Spectators and Participants

Source: Adapted from John Burnett, Anil Menon, and Denise T. Smart, "Sports Marketing: A New Ball Game with New Rules," *Journal of Advertising Research* (September-October 1993), 21-33.

Rightsholder: *Journal of Advertising Research*

Credit: Courtesy www.warc.com

Table 5.2 – Who's a Sports Fan?

Source: "Americans to Rest of World: Soccer Not Really Our Thing," page 8

Credit: Courtesy of the Pew Research Center

URL: http://www.pewsocialtrends.org/2006/06/14/americans-to-rest-of-world-soccer-not-really-our-thing/

Table 5.3 – Eight Value Dimensions of Sport to the Community

Source: James J. Zhang, Dale G. Pease, and Sai C. Hui, "Value Dimensions of Professional Sport as Viewed by Spectators," *Sports and Social Isssues* (February 21, 1996), 78–94. Copyright © 1996, SAGE Publications.

Credit: Reprinted by Permission of SAGE Publications.

Table 5.4: What's Your Favorite Sport? Favorite sport to watch by interest in sports news.

Source: "Americans to Rest of World: Soccer Not Really Our Thing," page 9

Credit: Courtesy of the Pew Research Center

URL: http://www.pewsocialtrends.org/2006/06/14/americans-to-rest-of-world-soccer-not-really-our-thing/

Webcaptures

Webcapture 5.1 – Richard Petty Driving Experience: Allowing NASCAR fans to feel racing thrills

Source: Richard Petty Driving Experience

Credit: Richard Petty Driving Experience / DrivePetty.com

URL: http://www.drivepetty.com/

Webcapture 5.2 – New sports facilities such as the Cowboy Stadium in Dallas influence attendance.

Source: dallascowboys.com

Chapter 6

Ads

Ad 6.1 – Hodgman is capitalizing on the growing mature market.

Credit: Pure Fishing – Columbia

Ad 6.2 – Pygmy is segmentation on the basis of the family life cycle.

Credit: www.pygmyboats.com

Ad 6.3 – 47 Brand positions itself as the official licensee of the National Basketball Association.

Credit: Forty Seven Brand

Articles

Technical Report: Sport England Market Segmentation

Source: Sport England

Credit: Courtesy Sport England

URL: http://www.sportengland.org/research/about-our-research/market-segmentation/

Generation M2: Media in the Life of 8 to 18 Year Olds, The Henry J. Kaiser Family Foundation, 2013.

Credit: Courtesy The Henry J. Kaiser Family Foundation

URL: http://kff.org/other/poll-finding/report-generation-m2-media-in-the-lives/

ESPN W Brand

URL: http://blogswithballs.com/2010/10/espnw-a-brand-for-female-athletes/

The IWFL and the History of Women's Tackle Football

Credit: Reprinted with permission from Yahoo. © 2014 Yahoo.

URL: http://voices.yahoo.com/the-iwfl-history-womens-tackle-football-4268395.html

NFL May be Hitting Stride with Female Fans

Rightsholder: ESPN, published 2/3/12

URL: http://espn.go.com/espnw/news-commentary/article/7536295/nfl-finding-success-targeting-women-fans-merchandise-fashion [accessed 1/2/14]

Move over Fútbol. The NFL Scores Big With Latinos

Rightsholder: Dialogo Public Relations (http://Dialogo.us/), published 1/3/12

Credit: Diálogo Public Relations

URL: http://www.dialogo.us/move-over-futbol-the-nfl-scores-big-with-latinos/ [accessed 1/2/14]

Spotlight on International Sports Marketing – NBA continues to grow internationally

Source: http://www.nba.com/2012/news/10/26/nba-international-growth.ap/index.html

Rightsholder: NBA.com

Credit: The NBA and individual member team identifications reproduced herein are used with permission from NBA Properties, Inc. © 2014 NBA Properties, Inc. All rights reserved.

Baseball Continues to Assist Storm Relief Efforts

Article Author: John Schlegel and Mark Newman

Rightsholder: MLB.com

URL: http://washington.nationals.mlb.com/news/article.jsp?ymd=20121102&content_id=40155972&vkey=news_chc&c_id=chc

Figures

Figure 6.1 – Pro-Sports that Appeal to Teenagers: Youth who say they are very or somewhat interested in the sport.

Credit: With permission of The Futures Company

Photos

Photo 6.1 – Young boy watching a baseball game: Professional sports are realizing the importance of the kid's market to their long-term success.

Source: Shutterstock.com – ID # 1240253

Credit: Christopher Penler/Shutterstock.com

Photo 6.2 – Polo European Championship match Switzerland against Germany on September 10, 2010 in Ebreichsdorf, Austria: Polo is a sport that has typically appealed to the upper class

Source: Shutterstock.com – ID # 63037606

Credit: fritz16/Shutterstock.com

Tables

Table 6.2 – Most Popular Sports/Athletic/Fitness Activities U.S. Population, Age 55+, Based on Total Participation

Credit: reproduced with kind permission of Sports & Fitness Industry Association, www.sfia.org

Table 6.3 – AIO Dimensions

Source: Journal of Advertising Research

Credit: courtesy www.warc.com

Table 6.4 – Lifestyle Analysis Report: Lifestyle Ranking Index

Source: PRIZM 2010, Experian Marketing Solutions, Inc, 2010. Nielson 2010

Table 6.5 – Five Market Segments for Golf Participants

Source: Sam Fullerton and H. Robert Dodge, "An Application of Market Segmentation in a Sports Marketing Arena: We All Can't Be Greg Norman," *Sport Marketing Quarterly*, vol. 4, no. 3 (1995), 43–47.

Rightsholder: *Sports Marketing Quarterly*

Credit: Courtesy of Fitness Information Technology, Morgantown, WV.

Table 6.6 – PRIZM Cluster Categories and Descriptions

Source: *How to Use PRIZM* (Alexandria, VA: Claritas, 1996). Courtesy of Claritas, Inc., of Arlington, VA.

Rightsholder: Neilsen

Table 6.8 – Six Dimensions or Attributes of Sports

Source: James H. Martin, "Using a Perceptual Map of the Consumer's Sport Schema to Help Make Sponsorship Decisions," *Sport Marketing Quarterly*, vol. 3, no. 3 (1994), 27–33.

Rightsholder: *Sports Marketing Quarterly*

Credit: Courtesy of Fitness Information Technology, Morgantown, WV.

Webcaptures

Webcapture 6.1 – Cleveland Browns Youth Football: A wide array of youth football programs exist that target participation in youth football and cheerleading.

Credit: Reprinted with permission Cleveland Browns Inc. (2014).

Webcapture 6.2 – ESPN W: Reaching women's soccer fans on the web

Source: ESPN.com

Chapter 7

Articles

Spotlight on International Sports Marketing - 5 Worst Athlete-Endorsed Products of All Time

Article Author: Adam Dietz

Rightsholder: Bleacher Report

URL: http://bleacherreport.com/articles/1165407-the-worst-athlete-endorsed-products-of-all-time?search_query=athlete endorsements#/articles/1434868-the-50-biggest-sports-fails-of-2012

Spotlight on Sports Marketing Ethics – NCAA Native American Mascot Controversy

URL: http://www.bernardgoldberg.com/ncaa-native-american-mascot-controversy/

Miami Marlins attendance reverts to old Sun Life Stadium levels

Article Author: Douglas Hanks

URL: http://www.miamiherald.com/2013/08/01/3537432/marlins-attendance-reverts-to.html

Sports Marketing Hall of Fame – Phil Knight

Source: http://www.biogs.com/famous/knightphilip.html

Credit: © 2002-2014 Danny Rosenbaum All Rights Reserved

Photos

Photo 7.1 – This baseball, glove, and bat represent pure goods.

Source: Shutterstock.com – ID # 62893237

Credit: David Lee/Shutterstock.com

Photo 7.2 – This competition represents a pure service.

Credit: Courtesy Cory Hindel

Photo 7.3 – Future Redbirds in their St. Louis Cardinals licensed baby gear

Source: Courtesy Matthew Shank

Photo 7.4 – Bike manufactures must stress the importance of product design and technology.

Source: Shutterstock.com – ID # 81690598

Credit: Dudarev Mikhail/Shutterstock.com

Tables

Table 7.1 – Wilson Sporting Goods Product Mix

Source: Paraphrased by Author – Wilson Sporting Goods, www.wilsonsports.com

Credit: Courtesy Wilson Sporting Goods

Table 7.3 – Importance Weights Allocated to the Five TEAMQUAL Dimensions

Source: Mark A. McDonald, William A. Sutton, & George R. Milne, "TEAMQUAL: Measuring Service Quality in Professional Team Sports," *Sport Marketing Quarterly*, vol. 4, no. 2 (1995).

Rightsholder: *Sport Marketing Quarterly*

Credit: Courtesy of Fitness Information Technology, Morgantown, WV.

Table 7.4 – Quality Dimensions of Goods

Source: Adapted from D.A. Garvin, "Competing on the Eight Dimensions of Quality," *Harvard Business Review* (November-December 1987). 101-109. Copyrighted ©1987 by the President and Fellows of Harvard College; all rights reserved.

Credit: Reprinted by permission of Harvard Business School Press.

Webcaptures

Webcapture 7.1 – TaylorMade-Adidas Golf Extends Their Product Line with Adidas Golf Footwear and Apparel

Credit: © 2014 Taylor Made Golf Company, Inc.

Webcapture 7.2 – Sports logos gallery on the web

Rightsholder: Baseball Almanac, Inc

URL: http://www.baseball-almanac.com/

Webcapture 7.3 – Licensed merchandise on the Web

Credit: Reproduced with kind permission of FansEdge™, Incorporated

Chapter 8

Articles

Nike + FuelBand Makes Life a Sport

Article Author: Nike, Inc.

Credit: Courtesy of Nike, Inc.

URL: http://nikeinc.com/news/nike-fuelband-makes-life-a-sport#/inline/6742

Sports Marketing Hall of Fame – Bill Rasmussen

Source: Richard Hoffer, "Bill Rasmussen," *Sports Illustrated* (September 19, 1994), 121

Credit: Courtesy of Time, Inc

Spotlight on Sports Marketing Ethics – College Sports Have Become Too Commercialized

URL: http://sites.psu.edu/swk5473sec9engl137h/2013/04/03/college-sports-have-become-too-commercialized/

Credit: Reprinted with permission of Samuel Kantner

Fantasy Sports Becoming Big Business as Popularity Continues to Rise

Article Author: Kyle Clapman

Credit: Courtesy Kyle Clapham

URL: http://news.medill.northwestern.edu/chicago/news.aspx?id=205473

John McEnroe's Bold Move To Revive US Tennis

Article Author: Bernard A. Chavis

Rightsholder: BleacherReport

URL: http://bleacherreport.com/articles/406753-john-mcenroes-bold-move-to-revive-us-tennis

Spotlight on International Sports Marketing – X Games Global Expansion Continues With TV Deals in New Host Markets, Syndication Deals in Multiple Other Countries

Article Author: Grace Coryell

Rightsholder: ESPN

URL: http://espnmediazone.com/us/press-releases/2013/01/x-games-global-expansion-continues-with-tv-deals-in-new-host-markets-syndication-deals-in-multiple-other-countries/

Photos

Photo 8.1 – Concept testing is used to understand consumer reactions to sports such as white water rafting.

Source: Shutterstock.com – ID # 102918779

Credit: Ammit Jack/Shutterstock.com

Photo 8.2 – Extending the product life cycle of the waterbike.

Source: Shutterstock.com – ID # 26118115

Credit: Heather Renee

Tables

Table 8.3 – Critical Success Factors for New Products

Source: Courtland L. Bovee and John Thill, *Marketing* (New York: McGraw-Hill, 1992), 307-309. 9780070067349

Table 8.4 – Extending the Product Life Cycle

Source: Joel Evans and Barry Berman, *Marketing*, 6th ed. (New York: Macmillan, 1992), 439.

Webcaptures

Webcapture 8.1 – The new sport of Bossaball combines volleyball, football, gymnastics, and capoeira.

Credit: www.Bossaballsports.com

Chapter 9

Ads

Ad 9.1 – Arnold Palmer: one of the most credible endorsers ever.

Source: Lamkin Corporation

Articles

Sports Marketing Hall of Fame – Bill Veeck

Source: Adapted from Bill Veeck, *Veeck as in Wreck: Autobiography of Bill Veeck* (New York: Simon and Schuster, 1962).

Spotlight on Sports Marketing Ethics – Endorsements Remain Buyers' Market

Article Author: Terry Lifton

Rightsholder: *Sports Business Journal*

URL: http://www.sportsbusinessjournal.com/article/66990

Spotlight on Sports Marketing Ethics – How impact of "Tiger Recession" changed athlete marketability

Article Author: Bill Sanders

Rightsholder: *Sports Business Journal*

URL: http://www.sportsbusinessdaily.com/Journal/Issues/2010/08/20100802/From-The-Field-Of/How-Impact-Of-Tiger-Recession-Changed-Athlete-Marketability.aspx

Illustration credits

Figures

Figure 9.1 – Communication Process

Credit: Solomon, Michael R., *Consumer Behavior*, 3rd Edition, © 1996, p. 194. Reprinted by permission of Pearson Education, Inc., Upper Saddle River, NJ.

Photos

Photo 9.1 – Having greater knowledge of sports such as hockey moves consumers through the hierarchy of effects

Source: Shutterstock # 109773617

Credit: muzsy/Shutterstock.com

Copyright: Michael Pettigrew/Shutterstock.com

Tables

Table 9.1 – Creating a More Effective Message

Source: James MacLachlan, "Making a Message Memorable and Persuasive," Journal of Advertising Research, vol. 23 (December 1983-January 1984), 51-59.

Rightsholder: *Journal of Advertising Research*

Credit: courtesy www.warc.com

Table 9.3 – Most watched programs in U.S. television history

Source: Nielsen Newswire 2014, "Super Bowl XLVIII Draws 111.5 Million Viewers, 25.3 Million Tweets," published 2/3/14

URL: http://www.nielsen.com/us/en/newswire/2014/super-bowl-xlviii-draws-111-5-million-viewers-25–3-million-tweets.html [accessed June 20, 2014]

Table 9.4 – Top 50 Sports Advertisers

Source: *Sports Business Journal*

Chapter 10

Articles

Spotlight on Sports Marketing Ethics – Sex Sells? Trend May be Changing

Article Author: Kate Fagan

Source: ESPNW

URL: http://espn.go.com/espnw/w-in-action/nine-for-ix/article/9604247/espnw-nine-ix-sex-sells-female-ahtletes-trend-changing

Spotlight on Sports Marketing Ethics – Lance Armstrong's Fall from Athletic Grace Doesn't Diminish His Greatest Triumph

Article Author: Brian Mazique

Rightsholder: Bleacher Report

URL: http://bleacherreport.com/articles/1383267-lance-armstrongs-fall-from-athletic-grace-doesnt-diminish-his-greatest-triumph

Armstrong faces $200 million salary loss with reputation hit

Credit: Used with permission of Bloomberg L.P. Copyright© 2014. All rights reserved.

URL: http://www.bloomberg.com/news/2012-10-24/armstrong-faces-200-million-salary-loss-with-reputation-ruined.html

Case Study – Impact of Facebook Advertisments

Rightsholder: Neilson

Big 4 jersey rights value put at $370m

Article Author: Terry Lefton

Rightsholder: *Sports Business Journal*

URL: http://www.sportsbusinessdaily.com/Journal/Issues/2011/02/20110207/Marketing-and-Sponsorship/Jerseys.aspx.

NBA Cares evolving after 5 years of Service

Article Author: John Lombardo

Rightsholder: *Sports Business Journal*

URL: http://www.sportsbusinessdaily.com/Journal/Issues/2010/10/20101018/Leagues-and-Governing-Bodies/NBA-Cares.aspx.

Photos

Photo 10.1 – Stadium signage – one of the first forms of promotion

Source: Shutterstock.com – ID # 63289540

Credit: Eric Broder Van Dyke/Shutterstock.com

Photo 10.2 – Coca-Cola creates a positive association with baseball by using stadium signage.

Rightsholder: lauramontrose@gmail.com, Laura M. Hoffman

Photo 10.3 – These runners all exemplify the human billboard

Source: Shutterstock.com – ID # 100671805

Credit: Mr Pics/Shutterstock.com

Photo 10.4 – Athlete signing autographs

Shutterstock.com – ID # 3638294

Credit: Chad McDermott/Shutterstock.com

Tables

Table 10.1 – The Creative Brief & The Client's Role

Source: Forbes

Credit: Reprinted by permission of Forbes Media LLC © 2014

Table 10.2 – 50 Most Marketable Active Athletes

Authors: David Cushnan, James Emmett, Eoin Connolly, Ian McPherson and Michael Long

Credit: www.sportspromedia.com

URL: http://www.sportspromedia.com/notes_and_insights/the_worlds_50_most_marketable_2013

Table 10.3 – Guidelines for Using Sports Celebrities as Endorsers

Source: Adapted from Amy Dyson and Douglas Turco, "The State of Celebrity Endorsement in Sport," Cyber-Journal of Sport Marketing

URL: www.cad.gu.edu.au//cjsm.dyson.htm.

Table 10.4 – Profiles of Major Media Types

Source: Adapted from Philip Kotler and Gary Armstrong, *Marketing: An Introduction*, 4th ed. (Upper Saddle River, NJ: Prentice Hall), 471. *Kotler, Philip R; Armstrong, Gary, Marketing: An Introduction*, 4th Edition, © 1997, pp. 471, 312. Credit: Reprinted by permission of Pearson Education, IIIC., Upper Saddle River, NJ.

Table 10.5 – Top 5 Countries by Internet Penetration

Source: http://www.internetworldstats.com/stats.htm

Credit: © 2000 - 2014, Miniwatts Marketing Group. All rights reserved.

Webcaptures

Webcapture 10.1 – Cobra Golf using direct objective

Source: Cobra Golf

Webcapture 10.2 – Upper Deck: Sales promotion advertised on the Web

Source: Upper Deck

Webcapture 10.3 – Easton Sports: Easton stresses its competitive advantage

Source: Easton Sports

Webcapture 10.4 – Ashworth Inc – Fred Couples creates a powerful image for the Ashworth Collection

Credit: © 2014 Taylor Made Golf Company, Inc.

Webcapture 10.5 – In the Hole Golf – The Internet has become a popular medium for all forms of online purchasing.

Source: InTheHoleGolf.com

Webcapture 10.6 – Golf Channel – The Golf Channel, PGA, and LPGA team up for online contests.

Credit: Golf Channel.com

Webcapture 10.7 – Twitter – Social-media continue to emerge as an interactive web strategy

Source: Twitter

Credit: Nick Pangio

URL: https://twitter.com/nickpangio

Webcapture 10.8 – Philadelphia Eagles reach out to the community

Source: Philadelphia Eagles.com

Credit line: Courtesy of the Philadelphia Eagles

Chapter 11

Articles

Scheuring Speed Sports Announces Partnership With Ford Motor Company

URL: http://www.isocracing.com/2013/09/13/scheuring-speed-sports-announces-partnership-with-ford-motor-company/

Cleveland Cavaliers 2012-13 Promotional Schedule: Fans Will Wig Out, Fly High and Get a "Kick" Out Of This Season's Premium Giveaways, Theme Nights and More!

Credit: The NBA and individual member team identifications reproduced herein are used with permission from NBA Properties, Inc. 2014 NBA Properties, Inc. All rights reserved.

URL: http://www.nba.com/cavaliers/releases/promotional-schedule-130927 , accessed 12-11-2013.

Adelaide United Energised by New Sponsorship

Article Author: Michael Long

Credit: www.sportspromedia.com

URL: http://www.sportspromedia.com/news/adelaide_united_energised_by_new_sponsorship/

Understanding Why Sponsorship Continues to Grow

Article Authors: Rick Burton and Norm O'Reilly

Rightsholder: *Sports Business Journal*

URL: http://www.sportsbusinessdaily.com/Journal/Issues/2011/01/20110124/Opinion/Burton.aspx

London 2012 Sponsors and Ambush – and the Lessons for Rio 2016

Credit: www.sportspromedia.com

URL: http://www.sportspromedia.com/guest_blog/london_2012_sponsors_and_ambush_and_the_lessons_for_rio_2016.

Beats by Dre Gives Headphones to British Athletes, Angering IOC

Article Author: Martin Rogers

Rightsholder: Yahoo Sports

Credit: Reprinted with permission from Yahoo. © 2014 Yahoo URL: http://sports.yahoo.com/news/olympics--beats-by-dre-gives-headphones-to-british-athletes--angering-ioc.html

Illustration credits

Spotlight on Sports Marketing Ethics – Congress Adopts Legislation to Curb Ambush Marketing During 2016 Summer Olympics

Article Authors: Rodrigo Borges Carneiro, Dannemann Siemsen Bilger, & Ipanema Moreira

Rightsholder: International Trademark Association

Credit: Reprinted with permission from INTA Bulletin Vol. 65 No. 2January 15 2010 copyright 2010 International Trademark Association, Authors Rodrigo Borge" Carneiro, Dannemann Siemsen Dilge', & Ipanema Moreira.

URL: http://www.inta.org/INTABulletin/Pages/BRAZILCongressAdoptsLegislationtoCurbAmbushMarketingDuring2016SummerOlympics.aspx

Behind the Scenes at the 2013 Waste Management Open

Rightsholder: BMA

Credit: Business Marketing Association (BMA), Phoenix Chapter

URL: http://bmaphoenix.org/events/behind-the-scenes-at-the-2013-waste-management-open/

Lance Armstrong Nike Contract Terminated

Article Author: Michelle Chapman

Credit: Used with permission of Bloomberg L.P. Copyright© 2014. All rights reserved.

URL: http://www.huffingtonpost.com/2012/10/17/lance-armstrong-nike-contract-terminated_n_1973192.html

Fenton High School looking at boosting corporate sponsorships of athletics

Article Author: Sarah Wojcik

Rightsholder: Mlive

URL: http://www/mlive/com/news/flint/index.ssf/2012/06/fenton_high_school_proposes_po.html

Hot Seahawks add Boeing, Starbucks Deals

Article Author: Terry Lefton

Rightsholder: *Sports Business Journal*

URL: http://www.sportsbusinessdaily.com/Journal/Issues/2013/07/29/Franchises/Seahawks.aspx.

Spotlight on Sports Marketing Ethics – Nike Won't Drop Penn State's Paterno, So We Should Drop Nike

Article Author: Clare O'Connor

Rightsholder: Forbes

Credit: Reprinted by permission of Forbes Media LLC © 2014

URL: http://www.forbes.com/sites/clareoconnor/2011/11/14/nike-wont-drop-penn-states-paterno-so-we-should-drop-nike/

Career Spotlight – Lesa Ukman and IEG

Credit: www.sportspromedia.com

URL: http://www.sportspromedia.com/notes_and_insights/lesa_ukman_the_sponsorship_pathfinder/0/

Figures

Figure 11.1 – The Sponsorship Process

Source: Hawkins et al., *Consumer Behavior: Implications for Marketing Strategy, 6/e* © 1994 © The McGraw-Hill Companies, Inc. ISBN: 0256139725

Credit: © The McGraw-Hill Companies, Inc.

Figure 11.3 – Sports Sponsorship Acquisition Model

Source: Reprinted by permission from D. Arthur, D. Scott, and T. Woods. "A Conceptual Model of the Corporate Decision-Making Process of Sport Sponsorship Acquisition" *Journal of Sport Management*, vol. 11, no. 3 (1997), 229.

Credit: Courtesy of Human Kinetics, Inc.

Photos

Photo 11.1 – Little League (Youth Baseball League)

Source: Shutterstock.com – ID # 503982

Credit: Timothy Kosheba/Shutterstock.com

Tables

Table 11.1 – Official sponsors of NASCAR

Source: Adapted from http://www.nascar.com/en_us/sponsors.html

Table 11.2 – Castrol North America – Sponsorship Criteria Requirements

Credit: BP Lubricants USA Inc.

URL: www.refresh.castrolusa.com/sponsors

Table 11.3 – Sponsorship Opportunities for the Wyndam Championship Sponsorship levels

Credit: Courtesy PGA TOUR

Table 11.6 – Importance of Sponsorship Objectives

Rightsholder: *Sport Marketing Quarterly*

Source: Doug Morris and Richard L. Irwin, "The Data-Driven Approach to Sponsorship Acquisition," *Sport Marketing Quarterly*, vol. 5, no. 2 (1996), 9.

Credit: Courtesy of Fitness Information Technology, Morgantown, WV.

Table 11.7 – Wegmans LPGA Championship Sponsorship Levels

Credit: Children's Success Fund Special Events, LLC / Wegmans LPGA Championship

URL: http://www.wegmanslpga.org/sponsorship-opps.aspx, accessed 12-13-2013.

Table 11.8 – University Merchandise Sales Leaders in 2013

Credit: Collegiate Licensing Company - an IMG Company

URL: http://www.clc.com/News/Archived-Rankings/Rankings-Q4-2012.aspx

Webcaptures

Webcapture 11.1 – Disabled athletes compete in Paralympic games

Source: U.S. Paralympics/U.S. Olympic Committee

Credit: © International Paralympic Committee

Webcapture 11.2 – University of Texas' Corporate partner program

Credit: www.texassports.com / UT Athletics.

Chapter 12

Articles

Deal to end lockout reached

Article Author: Adam Schefter

Rightsholder: ESPN.com

URL: http://espn.go.com/nfl/story/_/id/6797238/2011-nfl-lockout-owners-players-come-deal-all-points-sources-say

Sports Marketing Hall of Fame – Pete Rozelle

Source: "Innovator Rozelle Dies at 70." *Cincinnati Enquirer* (December 7, 1996), C1, C5. Credit: Used with permission of Bloomberg L.P. Copyright© 2014. All rights reserved.

Spotlight on Sports Marketing Ethics – Astronomical Athlete Salaries: Are They Worth It?

Credit: Orley Amos

URL: http://cc.kangwon.ac.kr/~kimoon/pr/issues/IS02.html

The NFL vs. Ticket Scalpers: Super Bowl Edition

Article Author: Ira Boudway

Rightsholder: Bloomberg Businessweek

Credit: The YGS Group

URL: http://www.businessweek.com/articles/2013-09-20/the-nfl-vs-dot-ticket-scalpers-super-bowl-edition

New Era Tickets uses iovation to Keep Scalpers and Fraudsters Out of the Arena

Article Author: iovation Inc. (2013)

Credit: www.iovation.com

URL: https://www.iovation.com/images/uploads/case-studies/PDF/iovation-newera-ticketing-case-study.pdf

Orioles raise season-ticket prices slightly, expand variable-pricing system

Article Author: Eduardo A. Encina

Credit: © The Baltimore Sun

URL: http://articles.baltimoresun.com/2013-12-06/sports/bs-sp-orioles-ticket-prices-1207-20131206_1_single-game-tickets-pricing-orioles

Figures

Figure 12.1 – Internal and External Influences on Pricing

Source: Gary Armstrong & Philip Kotler; *Marketing: An Introduction*, 7th ed. 2005.

Credit: Kotler, Philip R; Armstrong, Gary, *Marketing: An Introduction*, 4th Edition, © 1997, pp. 471, 312. Reprinted by permission of Pearson Education, IIIC., Upper Saddle River, NJ.

Photos

Photo 12.1 – Golf Lessons: To some, golf lessons may be priceless

Source: Shutterstock.com – ID # 812018

Credit: Cindy Hughes/Shutterstock.com

Tables

Table 12.2 – An Example of the Fan Cost Index® (FCI) for the NBA

Credit: Fan Cost Index® / Team Marketing Report.

URL: http://www.teammarketing.com/fci.cfm?page=fci_nhl_06-07.cfm

Table 12.3 – 2013 Sport/Recreational Activity Participation

Source: Courtesy National Sporting Goods Association

Webcaptures

Webcapture 12.1 – Loveland Ski may use seasonal discounting

Credit: Loveland Ski Area

URL: http://skiloveland.com

Chapter 13

Articles

Dew Action Sports Tour

Credit: Active Imagination Inc. Sports Marketing

URL:http://www.marketingforsports.com/content393.html

Busy Offseason Ahead for Arena Football League: Fan Take

Article Author: Eric R. Ivie

Rightsholder: Yahoo Sports

Credit: Reprinted with permission from Yahoo. © 2014 Yahoo.

URL: http://sports.yahoo.com/news/busy-offseason-ahead-arena-football-league-fan-163400668.html.

Sports Marketing Hall of Fame – Gary Davidson

Source: Steve Rushin, "Gary Davidson," *Sports Illustrated* (September 19, 1994), 145.

Credit: Courtesy of Time, Inc.

Illustration credits

The 100 Worst Things in Sports

Article Author: Zack Pumerantz

Rightsholder: BleacherReport

URL: http://bleacherreport.com/articles/1375225-the-100-worst-things-in-sports

How Athletes are fighting for Endorsement Dollars

Rightsholder: *Sports Business Journal*

URL: http://www.sportsbusinessdaily.com/SB-Blogs/Events/Sports-Marketing-Symposium/2012/10/Athlete-Endorsements.aspx.

Photos

Photo 13.1 – Sports organizations often utilize creative marketing strategies to target consumers

Shutterstock.com – ID # 143657812

Credit: RTimages/Shutterstock.com

Photo 13.2 – Racing & Sponsorship: Sponsors such as M&M must design controls to evaluate sponsorship effectiveness.

Disclaimer: M&M'S, M, M in a Circle and the M&M'S Characters are registered trademarks of Mars, Incorporated and its affiliates. These trademarks are used with permission. Mars, Incorporated is not associated with Routledge.

Credit: Getty Images

Tables

Table 13.1 – Experience Rankings of Professional Sports Teams

Source: ESPN.com

Table 13.2 – Most Important Skills for Sports Marketing Managers

Source: Peter Smolianov and David Shillbury, "An Investigation of Sport Marketing Competencies, *Sport Marketing Quarterly*, vol. 5, no. 4 (1996), 27-36.

Rightsholder: *Sport Marketing Quarterly*

Credit: Courtesy of Fitness Information Technology, Morgantown, WV.

Table 13.3 – Guidelines for Designing Reward Systems

Source: John Pearce and Richard Robinson, *Formulation, Implementation, and Control of Competitive Strategy*, 5th ed. (Boston: Irwin, 1994). 0-256-12634-8. 11th edition published by McGraw Hill, 2008

Credit: Reproduced with permission of McGraw-Hill Education, LLC

Table 13.7 – Top Ten Sports Scandals

Authors: Michael Dub and Patty Hodapp

Credit: MensFitness.com

URL: http://www.mensfitness.com/leisure/sports/11-biggest-sports-scandals-of-all-time?page=2

Webcaptures

Webcapture 13.1 – Teamwork Online – Sports careers on the Web.
Source: http://www.teamworkonline.com

Webcapture 13.2 – Sponsorship ROI Evaluation
Source: Joyce Julius & Associates, www.joycejulius.com

Disclaimer

The publishers have made every effort to contact authors/copyright holders of works reprinted in *Sports Marketing 5th Edition* and to obtain permission to publish extracts. This has not been possible in every case, however, and we would welcome correspondence from those individuals/companies whom we have been unable to trace. Any omissions brought to our attention will be remedied in future editions.

Index

Please note that references to non-textual material such as Figures, Photographs or Tables will be in *italics*, while references to Notes will be followed by the letter 'n'.